Dear Reader,

The Great Healing is an engaging introduction to all of the complicated issues around building healthy soil, growing nutritious food, protecting communities and the planet, and, yes, eating animals.

The author's focus on Five Compassions to Save the World will be familiar to Natural Grocers customers, since they often dovetail with our own Five Founding Principles: nutrition education, high quality healthy products, affordable prices, successful employees and thriving communities. The Great Healing reminds us again and again that there is one system, Earth, which needs to be cared for at every level.

As you read these compelling stories about the communities, families, animals, and insects affected by industrial agricultural practices, we think you will appreciate why our high standards and hard science matter more than ever. Our food choices are the one small way we can all be part of positive change.

Yours,
Heather Isely, EVP
Natural Grocers by Vitamin Cottage

"Erickson's ability to connect climate science, copious data, and public policies with the lived experiences of people and other creatures sets this book apart. His emphasis on humane and caring methods reminds readers that winning hearts and minds is a prerequisite to capturing carbon. An inspired synthesis of environmental, cultural, economic, and political calls to action."

— **Kirkus Reviews**

"The ambitious book's five chapters highlight compassionate approaches toward animals, self, the land, community, and democracy. Erickson's writing displays passion, clarity, and a grasp of every topic he tackles."

— **Kirkus Reviews**

"A comprehensive entreaty to save a rapidly dying Earth with compassionate activism... Emotional descriptions (often illustrated by vivid photos) of animal cruelty, oceanic dead zones, and Farm Bill subsidies for 'Big Ag' elicit compassion, outrage, and shame. Erickson takes care to balance his concerns with suggestions for solutions... This alarming but not alarmist work provides purposeful, accessible, and concrete ways to counter and prevent ecological damage."

— **Book Life Review by Publishers Weekly**

"An exceptionally well and persuasively written clarion call to personal and collective action. Unreservedly and urgently recommended."

— **Midwest Book Review**

"Big job, great contribution."

— **Timothy LaSalle (CEO, The Rodale Institute, 2007-2010)**

"All so important to cultural transformations we need to embrace in our common future."

"This is critical for humanity."

"This is so good! You captured perfectly the majesty of Green Leaf - the farm, the neighborhood, the people. So evocative! I was magically transported to a place I frequent in my real life."

"I am happy and honored at the way you used my work here."

"I've been aware for some time of what the world has in store if we don't band together and give to our earth and animals the nutrients and care they deserve. However, *The Great Healing* prompted me into action in a way I never expected. It has truly changed my life. I'm a chef and how I eat, what I buy to prepare for my family and others, and how I even look at my backyard with visions of ways to rejuvenate my own soil and create a small farm, fills my mind daily. This is a life-altering read. I'm not one to proselytize, but after reading *The Great Healing* I'll take to the streets and spread the word. Believe."

STEPHEN ERICKSON BIO

Our meerkat lookout, who appears in this book's introduction and keeps popping up throughout, is an exquisite creature. In German, he is called Erdmännchen which means "Little Earth Man." He is one reason I was compelled to write this book. Hazel, our photogenic triplewart sea devil is another. As are Sherneka Johnson and Sky Smith, Thomas Quicksilver, Brady Kluge, Lucinda Monarch, Earl "the Worm," Marlon Foster, and Wendell Berry. As are you.

I've been fortunate enough to make a living with my writing for my entire career, yet *The Great Healing* is my first manuscript. I have B.A. degrees from the University of California San Diego in both Visual Arts and Economics, along with a minor in Psychology to help me figure out why I did both. I received a M.F.A. in Film and Television from the graduate film school at the University of California Los Angeles. As an entertainment executive, I originated and established one Home Entertainment label and then ran another, overseeing the licensing, development, marketing and worldwide release of nearly 400 programs onto broadcast, DVD and digital delivery platforms.

I did that while starting a family and fathering my children. I helped raise them on this fascinating planet during a short window of time that may prove to have been the most magnificent years for human beings ever to be alive.

Global warming now, *during our lifetime*, threatens to bring about the end of our Anthropocene Epoch — and us along with it. Over one million species of plants and animals at this very moment are facing extinction. Things are going to get worse, much worse, and there's no way we can avoid that. I wrote this book for all of us, but particularly for my children, for millennials, and for Generation Z — because you need to mobilize in a big way *immediately*, to protect what remains of your opportunity to one day raise your families in a stable society and an environment fairly similar to the one we now enjoy, as opposed to being trapped in a sweltering, ugly, calamity — humanity's increasingly chaotic, stricken, and panicked exit from the global stage.

We are, each one of us, more than exquisite creatures — we are a special generation. This book will explain why. You have a choice. Compassionate awareness and activism — or not. Saving a habitable Earth — or not. The Great Healing cannot manifest without you, without impactful numbers of inspired compassionate activists of all ages.

Join us in what will become the most important cause of all of humanity's endeavors to date.

THE
GREAT
HEALING

THE
GREAT
HEALING

Five Compassions That Can Save Our World

STEPHEN ERICKSON

PRESS

For information about permission to reproduce selections from this book, write to: Permissions, TGH Press, 10736 Jefferson Blvd. #224, Culver City, CA 90230

First Edition
Second printing, January 2020

The author is grateful for permission to include the following previously copyrighted material: Excerpts from *World as Lover, World as Self* (1991, 2007) by Joanna Macy. Reprinted with permission of the author and Parallax Press, Berkeley, California, www.parallax.org; Excerpts from *Fast Food Genocide* (2017) by Joel Fuhrman, M.D. Reprinted by permission of the author; Excerpts from *Eat Fat, Get Thin* (2016) by Mark Hyman, M.D. Reprinted by permission of the author; Excerpts from interviews on *iThrive! Rising from the Depths of Diabetes & Obesity* (2017) by Jonathan Hunsaker, Jonathan McMahon, Michael Skye. Reprinted with permission of the authors and iThrive Publishing LLC; Excerpts from *Growing A Revolution* (2017) by David R. Montgomery. Reprinted by permission of the author; Excerpts from interviews on *Symphony of the Soil* (2012) by Deborah Koons Garcia. Reprinted with permission of the author and Lily Films; Excerpts from *The Monarch* (2017) by Kylee Baumle. Reprinted by permission of the author; Excerpts from *The Soil Will Save Us* (2014) by Kristin Ohlson. Reprinted by permission of the author; Excerpts from *Who Really Feeds the World?: The Failures of Agribusiness and the Promise of Agroecology* by Vandana Shiva, U.S. edition published by North Atlantic Books, copyright © 2016 by Vandana Shiva. Reprinted by permission of North Atlantic Books; Excerpts from *It Starts with The Soil and Organic Agriculture Can Help* (2008) by Dr. Frederick Kirschenmann. Reprinted by permission of the author; Excerpts from *Daring Democracy* (2017) by Frances Moore Lappé and Adam Eichen. Reprinted by permission of the authors.

Internet addresses in this book were accurate at time of publishing.
www.thegreathealing.org

Library of Congress Cataloging-in-Publication Data is available upon request.
ISBN 978-1-7332027-0-1 (1st ed pbk)
ISBN 978-1-7332027-1-8 (ebook)

Cover designed by Gregg Nakawatase
Cover concept by Caroline Placensia

Printed in the United States of America

Visit our website for updates, events and other resources: www.thegreathealing.org
Follow our blog and be a part of our growing community. Join us!

Follow us on Twitter @TheGreatHealing

To the compassionate activists of our special generation.
Time now to awaken, rise, and save our world.

We are now at a point unlike any other in our story. Perhaps we have, in some way, chosen to be here at this culminating chapter or turning point. We have opted to be alive when the stakes are high to test everything we have ever learned about interconnectedness and courage — to test it now when it could be the end of conscious life on this beautiful water planet hanging like a jewel in space.

In primal societies rites of passage are held for adolescents, because it is then that the fact of personal death or mortality is integrated into the personality. The individual goes through the prescribed ordeal of the initiation rite in order to integrate that knowledge, so that he or she can assume the rights and responsibilities of adulthood. That is what we are doing right now on the collective level in this planet-time. We are confronting and integrating into our awareness our mortality as a species. We must do that so that we can wake up and assume the rights and responsibilities of planetary adulthood.

– Joanna Macy, *World as Lover, World as Self*

CONTENTS

INTRODUCTION

want to introduce you to exquisite creatures. Sherneka Johnson and Sky Smith, Thomas Quicksilver, Brady Kluge, Lucinda Monarch, Earl 'the Worm', Marlon Foster, and Wendell Berry. The challenges each one of them faces are very different. But it turns out, their challenges are interrelated. The day I realized that I had to stop, recover my breath, and keep my balance. Because the severity of what is confronting each one of them reveals the immensity of the threat facing each one of us.

We are entering the fight of our lives — a fight *for* our lives. World War II was a biggie. This one is bigger.

And we may not prevail.

The challenge each of these exquisite creatures faces reveals something else as well. Maybe, just maybe... a solution.

Five Compassions.

Acting with inspired compassion, you can help enable all of us to achieve The Great Healing.

"All of us?" Who is this "all of us?"

Everyone. Every living creature on this planet.

The Great "what?" What needs to be healed? Life is good.

And in so many ways, when you think about it, it really is.

Each of us has been born into a moment in time that affords us unprecedented access to, understanding of and possibility in, a world of wondrous beauty and complexity. This is an amazing moment in the history of human evolution.

With your computer or your cellphone, and Internet access, you can quickly, with remarkable efficiency, find out just about everything — past or present — on any subject, any science, anyone, any *thing* about any aspect of life just about anywhere on this planet.

For example... Meerkats.

These little guys weigh about two pounds each. In German, their name — Erdmännchen — means "Little Earth Man." Are these little earth men smart? Do they have social skills? What's up with them?

Meerkats are not soloists. They are intensely social animals that live together in groups in bolt-holes, which are burrows with long tunnels and usually several entry points, in the desert grasslands of South Africa.

They peek out of their bolt-holes at dawn, emerging to forage together in packs called "mobs." One meerkat is selected to remain on high ground or in a tree as lookout to keep watch for predators. If an eagle, a hawk or a jackal nears, he'll signal everyone.

Imagine that's me. That guy is a lot cuter than I am, but for a stretch imagine that's me. I'm the lookout at the moment and I've just spotted a threat. I'm about to alert you. But bad timing — you're busy in the middle of your morning mob scene. Using your keen sense of smell, you've just located and dug up a plump, juicy scorpion, a tasty delectable, and you're all set to dig in.

The threat is a venomous Cape cobra. The hungry snake has locked its gaze on its prey and is close enough — the targeted meerkat faces near certain death. The Cape cobra's lunging strike will be lightening quick and the venom from its bite is poisonous enough to kill an animal the size of six adult humans.

The other meerkats don't stand around watching.

Nor do they run away.

They encircle the cobra and, the instant before it strikes, another meerkat lunges at it from the side, its sharp claws slicing the ground right by the cobra's exposed flank. The snake has to turn protectively and face this meerkat, then turn to fend off another, then another. Collectively, the meerkats — lunging one at a time — control the snake's attention and then... a couple of them shift aside, creating an opening. An opening which the snake realizes is an escape path. Its *only* escape path. The meerkats have decided in which direction they will allow the cobra to retreat and they keep clawing at it until the snake backs down from a fight where it most certainly would have been badly wounded, undulating away from the meerkat mob, away from their foraging area, and away from the bolt-holes where their young are nestled.

The little earth men have learned the advantages and power of collective action. Their survival depends on it.

Any living creature's day-to-day most fundamental goal is survival.

Given our preoccupations — striving to achieve our goals and our desires, utilizing all of our devices and skillsets, secure amidst our comforts and a standard of living within the civilization we have created — it can easily be taken for granted, that survival for each of us is job number one as well.

Say someone showed you a photo of this fish and you wanted to find out where she lives, what she does for fun, and what that weird thing is sticking out of her head:

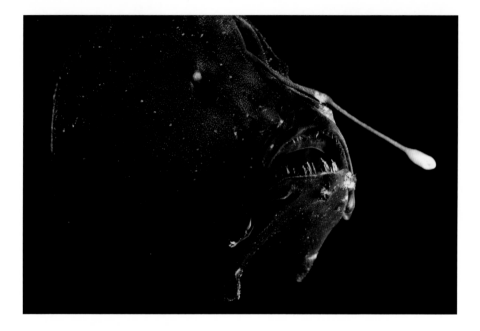

You can easily find out.

She's a triplewart sea devil who swims around in the deep ocean. By deep, I mean at depths down to 15,000 feet. In a swimming pool, the water pressure at a depth of 10 feet is .3 atmospheres (atm), which is about 4 pounds of force per square inch on your body. When you swim underwater along the bottom in the deep end you may feel a little pressure, especially in your ears. Oceanic water pressure at 15,000 feet is around 459 atm or 6,749 *pounds of force per square inch.*[1] How is a creature built to withstand that kind of pressure? We have to submerge in a mini-submarine protected by a specially designed shell to visit her in order to avoid being instantly pancaked by the water pressure — and here she is looking at us.

With *eyes.* How do those eyes withstand this tremendous pressure? How are they made? Blue eyes straight from *Game of Thrones...*

Sunlight fades as you descend in the ocean. Aqua-blue water darkens as more and more water separates you from sunlight until, at around 650 feet down you leave the photic zone and descend into a depth where sunlight no longer penetrates.[2] You find yourself immersed in ocean darkness. Complete wet blackness.

This triplewart sea devil — let's call her Hazel — lives here. She will never see sunlight. She navigates in perennial darkness. So, she has a light sticking out of her head.

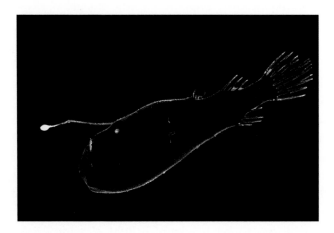

Is that to avoid bumping into rocks? Hazel's face looks like she's run into more than a few. Is it to illuminate her features to attract a potential mate? She's swimming solo. Should she consider suspending it a bit further back to cast a more diffuse light on her facial features, perhaps creating a more sex-appealing allure for that chance encounter?

How did that light get there? Did it start as a growth that somehow lit up and elongated over several thousand generations until at last, arriving at the optimal hanging lantern position? Is it a tactile appendage, like *ET*'s finger?

It turns out that this light's appendage is an evolution of the triplewart sea devil anglerfish's dorsal fin. And Hazel keeps it suspended right where it is with good reason. Right in front of her mouth.

We've got the technology and we've got the skills. Whatever I want to know about triplewart sea devils like Hazel, if someone knows it, it's not difficult to find out.

Hazel is indeed a female. Her 'light' is actually an aggregation of glowing bioluminescent bacteria that attracts other fish who mistake it for prey.[3] They swim in to eat it, only to become Hazel's meal in short order.

Now that I know a little bit about Hazel, I'm concerned about her and this is why.

It turns out that we humans can and do extend our reach, sinking into Hazel's depths without a submersible. Plastic bags, as well as some of the other countless varieties of discarded plastic that we're filling the oceans with, drift current-carried into her depths.[4][5] Non-biodegradable translucent phantoms appear like jellyfish, a food staple of many fish. Other small, often brightly colored, plastic objects descend like food remnants, appearing like torn bits of fish that have fallen prey to and been partially devoured by surface dwellers above. These objects are consumed by fish like tuna and whales in the surface depths, and by the denizens of the lower depths, like Hazel.[6][7]

If during her wandering, a bit of baggie appears before Hazel's glow and she eats it, it'll coat her stomach like some horrible wallpaper or laminate that she can't redecorate away. It'll adhere, indigestible, covering her stomach lining or clogging her intestine like those of so many of the whales beaching themselves[8][9] or the fish fishermen are catching, or sea birds like these on Midway atoll: youtube.com/watch?v=ozBE-ZPw18c [10]

Hazel's at risk because she's not aware of this new threat. It took her countless generations to get her lantern light glowing bright and well. She's eaten very little that was not food to sustain her. Will she and her fellow triplewart sea devils learn to distinguish prey from plastic? Or will they perish in silent agony having failed to figure it out?

For every species — even us humans — awareness of new threats entering our environment is essential. Understanding those threats and then adapting by finding and implementing solutions, enables us to survive.

It's easy for us to become complacent as it appears we've done a thorough job taking control of our planet. There are over 7 billion humans alive today. We've done a pretty good job adapting.

Or so it would seem.

. . .

Animals. Why is it, then, that right now, *tens of thousands* of species are in critical decline, either going extinct or facing extinction? The *Living Planet Report 2018* from the World Wildlife Fund reveals "an astonishing

60% decline in the size of populations of mammals, birds, fish, reptiles, and amphibians in just over 40 years."[11] *60%...* We have the technology, a tremendous toolset the likes of which this world has never before seen. We can learn about — even visit and experience first-hand — fascinating creatures. So how is it we can't seem to do something to stop their demise? Why is this happening?

Moreover, how is it that *billions* of other creatures — animals in human care — are enduring lives of incessant cruelty and suffering on factory farms? How have we come to this?

Self. Why is it that so many of our teenagers have grown so overweight that they are unable to run at a moderate pace for six minutes on a treadmill, or do a single push up, their bodies so bloated they hesitate to take their t-shirts off when swimming at a beach or public pool? Obesity, diabetes, heart disease, cancer and dementia, even adjusted per capita, are at record highs. Seventeen million people die *each year* from heart attack, stroke, or other cardiovascular diseases. Over 35% of adults in West Virginia, Alabama, Arkansas, Mississippi and Louisiana are obese, and the rate is now 30% or higher in 25 states according to a 2017 State of Obesity report.[12]

In an era of unprecedented health awareness and nutritional understanding, why are so many of us in poor health? If you are a patient diagnosed with one or more of these conditions, why is it your doctor will treat your symptoms but probably not adequately inform you about the *causes*? And what are the causes? What's really going on?

Land. When you fly over or drive across our country, you may notice the big farms that cover the prairie, and how vast their crop acreage is. Corn and soybeans as far as the eye can see. When the crops have been harvested, all you witness is brown, exposed soil baking in the sun. Topsoil, the soil that every plant grows from, takes millions of years to accumulate — *millions* of years. The most productive soil in the world is prairie soil. While 7% of the world's land is prairie soil, when the United States looked at the cards it was dealt in the game of Soil Poker, we drew a winning hand — 22.5% of our landscape is prairie soil.[13] Yet in just the last 100 years, we've managed to lose most of it. Soil degradation has intensified to the point where, over just the last 40 years, 30% of the world's cropland — over one billion acres — has been abandoned as unusable.[14]

The Deputy Director General of the Food and Agriculture Organization are bringing about our epoch end.

Over just the next few decades, life on this planet for your children, born and unborn, for you and everyone you know, is going to change profoundly. Why?

Because of global warming.[20] Things are heating up. Each passing year becomes one of the hottest ever measured. Weather patterns and events are getting more and more extreme. And we are the cause. This is humankind-created global warming. The evidence, the scientific studies and the broad consensus of the world's scientific community are overwhelming. This is indisputable. Steven Pinker writes in *Enlightenment Now*, "One response to the prospect of climate change is to deny that it is occurring or that human activity is the cause... Anthropogenic climate change is the most vigorously challenged scientific hypothesis in history. By now, all the major challenges... have been refuted, and even many skeptics have been convinced."[21] An analysis of nearly 12,000 peer-reviewed scientific literature abstracts found that 97% of those expressing a position on global warming determined that humans are causing it.[22]

Former Vice President Al Gore observes that, "We are now trapping as much extra heat energy in the atmosphere as would be released by 400,000 Hiroshima-class atomic bombs exploding on the Earth's surface every day. We live on a big planet, but that is an unimaginable amount of heat energy."[23]

Our situation, it turns out, is even worse than anticipated. The United Nations Intergovernmental Science-Policy Platform on Biodiversity and Ecosystem Services (IPBES) report, a three-year assessment prepared by 150 experts from 50 countries released May 6, 2019, confirms that species are dying off at a rate "tens to hundreds times higher than the average across the past ten million years."[24] *One million* plant and animal species are now threatened with extinction due to human activities.[25] A 2017 study published in the Proceedings of the National Academy of Sciences of the U.S.A., *Biological Annihilation Via the Ongoing Sixth Mass Extinction Signaled by Vertebrate Population Losses and Declines*, concludes that "Dwindling population sizes and range shrinkages amount to massive anthropogenic erosion of biodiversity and of the ecosystem services essential to civilization. This 'biological annihilation' underlies the seriousness for humanity of Earth's ongoing sixth mass extinction event."[26] Invertebrate populations, such as bees and beetles, have decreased 45% in 35 years.[27] 7% of the planet's invertebrate species have now been lost[28] and a January 2019 study determined that the world's total mass of insects is decreasing 2.5% a year.[29] In 2018, 40% of the world's bird species are in decline with 1,469 species (1 in 8) facing extinction.[30]

Biodiversity loss and global warming are interrelated. The planet's ability to sustain its biosphere is deteriorating even more rapidly than projected because those entities that are warming are interacting in unexpected ways, further accelerating the world's rising temperatures.

The earth's warming forests, which are increasingly populated at higher and higher altitudes by dead and beetle stricken trees, are now ravaged by extreme forest fires (megafires) sweeping through them. They blaze with such intensity that they create their own weather patterns and are virtually unstoppable, each one burning hundreds of thousands of acres and releasing additional billions of tons of carbon into the atmosphere.[31] [32] In 2018, wildfires ravaged not only the far northern hemisphere in Greenland, Alaska, and Canada — but the forests *above* the Arctic Circle in Sweden, Norway, Finland, and Russia.[33]

Snow and ice surfaces reflect the sun's heat away from the earth. As these melt away, those surface areas become heat-absorbing water and land, warming the oceans and the planet. As ice and permafrost melts away across Alaska, Greenland and Arctic regions, the newly exposed tundra contains large amounts of stored up carbon dioxide and methane that it then releases into the air, further accelerating global warming.[34] [35] More than twice as much carbon is stored in this permafrost than is currently in our atmosphere.[36] A study published in April 2019 revealed that melting permafrost is releasing significantly more methane than previously realized. Methane is nearly 300 times more potent a greenhouse gas than carbon dioxide.[37] [38]

These are just several of hundreds of examples leading scientists to the conclusion that the *More-severe Climate Model Predictions Could be the Most Accurate* — that there is a 93% chance of a global temperature increase exceeding 4 degrees Celsius (4°) by the end of this century.[39] (BTW: America is the only major country that does not use the Celsius scale. 1° equals 1.79° Fahrenheit.)

This photograph by Paul Nicklen[40] is one of the most beautiful photos I've ever seen. It is also one of the scariest.

This is the ice cap at Nordaustlandet, Norway on August 7, 2014. These amazing waterfalls cascading 700 feet into the Atlantic Ocean are Arctic ice meltwater.

In an annotation to his stunning 2017 article *The Uninhabitable Earth*, David Wallace-Wells quotes Joseph Romm's writing in *Climate Change – What Everyone Needs to Know*: "Many cornerstone elements of our climate began changing far faster than most scientists had projected. The Arctic began losing sea ice several decades ahead of every single climate model used by the IPCC, which in turn means the Arctic region warmed up even faster than scientists expected. At the same time, the great ice sheets of Greenland and Antarctica, which contain enough water to raise sea levels ultimately 25–80 meters (80–260 feet), have begun disintegrating 'a century ahead of schedule.'"[41]

The Arctic — the northernmost part of our planet — has lost nearly 620,000 square miles of winter sea ice cover since 1979.[42] Our southernmost continent, Antarctica, has lost *3 trillion tons* of ice — trillion, not billion, not million — since 1992.[43] And the rate of ice loss in the Antarctic, home to penguins, leopard and elephant seals, the wandering albatross and blue whales, has tripled over the past five years.[44] The March 2019 report

2018 Continues Record Global Ocean Warming concludes, "2018 has set a new record for ocean heating, surpassing 2017, which was the previous warmest year ever recorded."[45]

More and more people are becoming aware of the truth about the dire situation we find ourselves in and resolving to do something about it. But what? What can each of us do? The train has left the station — and it is a huge locomotive.

NASA released satellite data confirming that the carbon dioxide level in the atmosphere has risen over the dreaded 400 ppm (Parts Per Million) level.[46] [47] Scientific consensus is that 350 ppm is a level which protects stability for human life. We raced past that about 50 years ago.

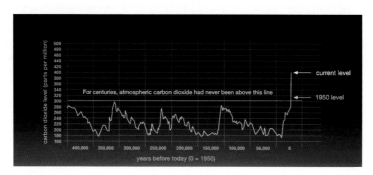

This graph from NASA's Jet Propulsion Laboratory, which plots the carbon dioxide increase over the last *400,000 years*, shows the line is now heading virtually straight up. The planet's global average temperature has risen .8° since the industrial revolution. If it rises just another 2°, life as we know it will change profoundly. If it goes up 4 degrees Celsius (7.1 degrees Fahrenheit), according to Kevin Anderson, professor of energy and climate change at the University of Manchester in the U.K., and one of the world's leading climate scientists and an authority on carbon budgets, that increase is "incompatible with any reasonable characterization of an organized, equitable and civilized global community."[48] Elevate beyond that threshold and soon after, the Anthropocene Epoch will end, as will we.

The World Meteorological Organization reported that, in 2016 alone, atmospheric carbon dioxide concentrations rose rapidly from 400 ppm to a record 403.3 ppm and that the "abrupt changes in the atmosphere witnessed in the past 70 years are without precedent."[49]

Raising the carbon dioxide level in the atmosphere by 1 ppm means adding 7,800,000,000 tons of carbon dioxide. In 2017, global human activity added *41.6 billion* total tons of it into the atmosphere[50] [51] [52] raising the level by another 5.1 ppm.

On May 14, 2018 the level recorded at the Mauna Loa Observatory in Hawaii was 412.45 ppm.[53] [54] On May 12, 2019 the level reached 415.39.[55] The carbon dioxide concentration in our atmosphere is now the highest it has been in 15 million years.[56]

Daniel Rothman, a geophysics professor at the Massachusetts Institute of Technology, notes that when certain climate thresholds are reached, "it will kickstart changes that will 'amplify' everything that has come before. These same changes... have been associated with all previous mass extinctions on Earth."[57] The reality is that even with best efforts at immediately combating climate change, an additional global temperature rise of a minimum of 1.5° by 2100 may be already baked in.[58] And we are not making "best efforts."

Over 20,000 scientists from around the world have now signed onto the report published on November 13, 2017, *World Scientists' Warning to Humanity: A Second Notice*, urging world leaders to take action to avoid planetary catastrophe.[59] [60]

The environment our next generation inherits is not going to be a better place.

Professor Anderson believes we only have a 5% chance at best of keeping global warming below a 2 degree increase. "All I can say is, my deepest apologies and sympathy. The West should have done much more... But that 5% is a choice. Realistically, unless emissions start coming down very rapidly in the next three or four years — I mean very rapidly indeed — then I think we will fail on 2°C of warming. We have a handful of years to make some very rapid and radical changes. We know what we need to do. We know it's all our responsibility to engage with this. We have everything at our fingertips to solve this problem. We have chosen to fail so far but we could choose to succeed."[61]

We humans do have the science, tools and technology to limit our emissions, but at present, no technology exists capable of drawing this enormous amount of carbon out of our atmosphere.

However, there *is* a solution. And it is here, at our fingertips — *right now*. We are failing to take action to implement the solution because what we lack is awareness. Awareness will lead to broad unified understanding and the focused willpower necessary to take decisive action.

One immediate goal then, as an essential step toward the solution, is widespread awareness of two seemingly disparate things.

First, most of us don't even realize who, exactly, the villain, our *Arch-Villain* — the *main cause* at the heart of the problem — is, let alone how the Arch-Villain operates. (And BTW, the *main* culprit is *not* the fossil fuel / dirty energy industry. Exxon and the corporations leading that industry, because of their abject failure to develop and shift to clean energy, are certainly a major, essential culprit to be addressed, and addressed promptly, but they are a secondary villain — not our principal adversary.)

It will not be possible to win this fight without a clear, widely acknowledged understanding of who our main opponent is.

Each one of the questions raised earlier — about animals, our health, the soil, community, and democracy — calls out a significant problem, one connected directly to global warming and to the situation we find ourselves in today. They are all interrelated. And they are related — well related — to our Arch-Villain.

Second, we need to understand the power each of us has as individuals living compassionately.

Each chapter of this book focuses on one of five Compassions. Compassion for Animals, for Self, for the Land, for Community, and for Democracy. Why? Compassion — true consideration for others — inspires action.

And inspired compassion can create The Great Healing: the healing of our planet, the prevention of the sixth great extinction, and the preservation of as many species and as many living creatures in our biosphere as possible.

Life on Earth in some form will survive with or without us. Each of Earth's prior mass extinction events was followed with a period of time, ranging from tens of thousands to millions of years, when remaining life forms — mostly bacteria and microbes — survived and the evolutionary process gradually got rolling again. I think the dinosaurs were fascinating creatures, and who knows what they would be like today if they'd had another 60 million years or so to evolve. Maybe they'd be lying out in these huge lawn chairs serving one another coconuts. Who's to say? I may be biased, but I think human beings are even more interesting. With our devices and skillsets, our intelligence and our potential, we may even be more interesting than whatever life form might next evolve on this planet in our absence a few million years or so from now. So, I for one, would prefer life on earth to continue with us, and for us to continue living on a life-sustaining planet bearing some resemblance to the environment we currently share.

Most of us do not realize how dire our situation is. All of us need to. If the time were 1941, an analogous situation would be that many of us are sleeping peacefully in Pearl Harbor, not even realizing we're entering World War II, that unseen, unanticipated attack aircraft are en route and just moments away.

This generation's World War is not going to be a conflict between countries. It's bigger than that. It is a fight where all of us must be allied against a global threat. It is a fight for humankind on this planet.

And we may not prevail.

Our Arch-Villain may very well become our nemesis. Recent research confirms Professor Anderson's assessment that we have less than a 5% chance of preventing Earth from warming more than the 2 degrees and averting catastrophe.[62]

. . .

The chapters that follow will reveal exactly who our Arch-Villain is. We are going to have to rally and defeat our Arch-Villain. And quickly. Very quickly. There are no two ways about this.

And Chapter 3 will show you our singular solution.

I like the word *humankind*, because in it resides the path to our solution: human kind. "Kind" referring not to species, but to our character.

Embracing the five Compassions even carries bonus ride-alongs. I love discovering "added value" and "bonus features." In acting compassionately to heal our planet, one bonus ride-along is that we can also heal ourselves.

Sherneka Johnson and Sky Smith, Thomas Quicksilver, Brady Kluge, Lucinda Monarch, Earl 'the Worm,' Marlon Foster, and Wendell Berry appear in the pages that follow. Collectively, they hold a secret — the answers to all these questions.

And they are an inspiration to me.

Inspiration like this:

When you are afraid, of anyone, of anything you hear or see, of anything in this book, do not let your fear paralyze you. Let it inspire you.

You matter. You. There is a reason you were born here in human form at this very special time. You have the power to help create the future you want to see. Your voice matters. You must find your voice and use it. This is a call out to you — to act. Find your courage, take a stand.

Join with us in what will become the most important cause of all of humanity's endeavors to date.

We do not want to arrive at "end time." Or anywhere nearby. And when you clearly understand who our Arch-Villain is, remember the meerkat's strategy against the Cape cobra, and the power of collective action.

Be open-minded. Always be learning. Most of us have been enabling the Arch-Villain without even realizing it. Like Hazel, shine your light into the darkness.

Live fully, compassionately, gratefully and well. Help others, heal our planet. You have the power. More than you realize. You'll see.

And for now — just for now — we have the time.

1

Compassion for Animals

I

Sherneka Johnson drives through the North Carolina countryside just east of the town of Warsaw. Her life is the road appearing before her, her family, the neighborhood known as Yellow Cut, which she holds dear, and most importantly, the package in the back seat she happens to be delivering. The smoothly paved road is a single lane in each direction. It's fall and the cottonwoods and oak trees, intermingled through the woods amidst the loblolly and evergreen pines, still have their leaves. The trees are close now, right along the roadside. They could almost envelope you with their beauty, catching and holding the sunlight while suggesting mysteries in the darker places deeper in the woods. Creeks meander through this rich verdant land before swelling into rivulets and entering the rivers or swamping parts of the flood plain.

The package in the back is Sky, Sherneka's five-year-old daughter, securely fastened into a booster seat. A backpack containing her school books lays on the seat beside her. As Sky tells her mom she's enjoying school, she watches the side of her mother's face, the edges of her mouth, watches for her smile... and it appears. And it's true — she is enjoying her kindergarten teacher and is making friends with other students.

Sherneka glances back. When Sky's happy, her feet sometimes waggle, dangling in the air as they haven't yet grown to reach the floor. Sky's wearing her favorite jeans, and under her jean jacket, a top featuring her favorite colors, pink and purple. When they were getting ready this morning, after her bath, Sherneka tied pink and purple ribbons in Sky's hair. Some days it's pearl earrings, other days hair bows, on special days combinations. Sky's looking forward to the picture book they will be reading in kindergarten later this morning. The classroom has different activity stations and today she gets to spend time in one of her favorites, Blocks, which has Legos.

Around a bend, the woods are now cut back from the road making room for crop fields, each spanning several acres. Crops harvested, grass fields hayed, most are now tilled leaving turned soil naked and exposed to the sky. A large John Deere tractor rests in one of them, the shiny red metal arms of its plow left with its steel discs angling diagonally up, shining, looking like an insect's jagged antennae. Wide driveways become dirt roads leading a hundred yards or more back to livestock farms containing pigs, chickens, or turkeys — partially or completely hidden by the surrounding woods from which their land has been cut. Puffy, low-hanging clouds drift across a heavy sky, wearing traces of pinks and oranges, gifts from the rising sun.

They drive now past people's homes — modest brick houses, small clapboard ones little more than shacks, rectangular immobile mobile homes with built-on front porches. Some dwellings are well maintained, others are run down with front porches and siding in need of painting. These homes spread along the roadway have been here a long time. Those that have been abandoned remain, broken down, collapsing and decomposing, left to the elements and surrendered back into the earth. All along Sherneka and Sky's morning drive to school, there is not a single new home being built, nor mobile home being set in place.

On these country roads, most often there are no fences separating neighbors. Sometimes a strand of trees or an occasional hedge defines a border, but green lawns flow between homes, and property lines are surmised rather than rigidly defined. To the folks living here, this area is affectionately known as Yellow Cut.

Sherneka is 27 and has a pretty, gentle face. She's lived in Duplin County her entire life. This is the only area she has ever known. Growing up, even when her family took a modest vacation, they usually didn't travel far. They'd go on day trips to nearby towns to shop. Their most common expedition for a long weekend or a holiday vacation with the extended family was to Myrtle Beach, South Carolina, just a two-and-a-half-hour drive away. On school days like today, Sherneka is driving Sky to kindergarten at Rose Hills - Magnolia Elementary School.

The cars ahead of her slow and start to bunch up behind an 18-wheeler whose flat-colored steel surfaces dull the morning sun. Rows of oval holes are cut top to bottom along its sides. This is an animal transport truck and judging by how it glides smoothly along the roadway without bouncing, Sherneka knows it is full.

As traffic slows, her mind drifts and Sherneka remembers when she was young, living along a nearby road much like the one she is traveling now…

She's hurriedly packing her books and homework into her schoolbag, grabbing her inhaler for her asthma, saying goodbye to her mom and rushing out the door.

From her front porch, Young Sherneka spots the neighborhood kids gathered just down the road awaiting the middle school bus. The smell hits her and this morning, it's bad again. The pig farm behind them sprays pig waste on its corn field most mornings around six. With cloud cover low and close, humidity high, and the day's seasonal heat already rising, it's particularly objectionable. She knows from experience to adjust, slowing her pace as she walks over to join the other students.

Loud metal banging jars Sherneka's attention back to the present as an empty animal transport hastens past in the opposite direction, bouncing over road bumps. This country road used to be quiet, mainly neighbors driving to work or on errands, but as the large pig farms and chicken farms expanded and multiplied, the trucks servicing them became more and more prevalent. This has become the preferred route for delivering pigs to a slaughterhouse, the largest pork-processing plant on the planet,[1] and chickens to the House of Raeford, another rendering facility over in nearby Rose Hill. Here the transport trucks are less visible than they would be over on the interstate. "Less visible" is better.

The smell of the animals ahead reaches Sherneka, intensifying as cars turn off, leaving her and her daughter closer behind the laden transport.

Her turnoff for the school is in about 300 yards, so she and Sky begin reciting a prayer out loud. It's the same one every morning, a prayer of traveling mercy to protect Sky throughout her school day. "Dear Heavenly Father, thank you for waking us up this morning and for giving us life, health and script, and we ask that you lead Sky throughout her day, protect her, lead her down the right path, open her ears so she may be able to listen, and open her mind so she may be able to comprehend. We ask these things in your name. In the name of the Father, the Son and the blessed Holy Ghost. Amen."

Today the animal transport in front of them is not a pretty sight. Through its oval holes two levels of pigs are visible, crammed inside, jostled around.

Manure and piss drips and spews from the back of the truck, catching the air, bits spraying onto the grills, hoods and windshields of cars following too closely. Pig vomit streaks down the side.

Sherneka remembers moments like this growing up as well. Awaiting the morning middle school bus along with other neighborhood kids, students dressed nicely, standing proudly in their fresh clean clothes a few feet back from the road. Some days a livestock transport truck would fly past, animal waste blowing off of it. The students step further away from the road, enduring it — it's the way things are. The approaching school bus is spotted and spirits rise for the shelter it offers.

When she was in elementary school, Sherneka's bus would stop right in front of her home to collect her. She remembers the hug her mom would give her while standing on their porch, her words of encouragement, and how her mother would often remain outside, watching. Sherneka would hurry onto the bus and find a window seat. When she'd look out, her mother's eyes would meet hers, and stay focused on her, regarding her, creased at the corners, squinting into sunlight. As Sherneka waved goodbye, she saw a softening of her mom's resolute face, her features filling with love and pride for her school-bound daughter. She recalls her mother's sensitive strength, a silent resolve in her direct glance, "We've provided this for you, my lovely daughter, your father and I — your life, a home we can call our own in this beautiful countryside, our loving family, the support that is your foundation, the opportunity for you to go to school to be educated, and all of that is something these big farms and these trucks and these smells, all these changes for the worse that are beyond our control, cannot take away." The school bus pulls out, and her mother glides away.

This morning, as Sherneka pulls up with Sky at the elementary school, and a traffic monitor opens the rear door and helps the little girl out, Sherneka glances over at her five-year-old, not fully realizing that she's regarding her daughter the very same way.

On this same morning, J'vion and Jemarion are riding together on a school bus. J'vion is thirteen and in the 7th grade. He likes playing football and this year he's old enough to play on the middle school team, which means he gets to wear a helmet and full pads. He's not huge but he is solidly built. Like his mother, Jennifer Dudley says, "He's got some meat on his bones." He is the fullback. When the offense ends their drive and possession of the football goes over to the other team, he stays on the field because he is also the starting middle linebacker on the defense. His favorite sport is basketball, and his dream is to play pro hoops. He's already handsome, and when he decides he's ready to pay a certain kind of attention to them, it's a given that the girls are going to direct a lot of interest his way. He has also shown a proclivity for math. His mom laughs, "I don't know where J'vion got that from because neither me nor his dad are good at math. But he is excellent at math."

J'vion is Snapchatting, his attention locked into the phone that is his lifeline. Jemarion glances at his big brother's screen. Jemarion is not just a good looking eight-year-old, but really good looking, with deep sensitive eyes and a face the shape you might choose if you could make a choice before your life began. He is in 3rd grade. He idolizes his big brother. Kenansville Elementary School is both elementary and middle school, so they get to ride in together. Although small for his age, Jemarion plays flag football in an afterschool recreational league in the town of Warsaw. He's the quarterback, but he'd rather run with the ball than pass it. This can't please the wide receivers on the team. His mom worries about him running the football because, "He is really, really little." It's true — he is.

On the bus some of the girls talk and boys joke around. Jemarion's thoughts are elsewhere. He doesn't focus on the passing homes with their front lawns or the intermittent driveways that lead past them to access the pig farms cut out of the woods further back. No one pays any attention as up ahead, a garbage truck coming from one of the pig farms takes advantage of a gap in the traffic and turns onto the road ahead of the bus.

Moments later, everyone notices. The students react to an overpowering acrid smell that can only be one thing — the smell of rotting carcasses coming from that oversized garbage truck. Windows are quickly closed but nothing can keep the stench out. Quickly, every child on the bus has their t-shirt or top up covering their noses. Several audibly react. A few younger children rub tearing eyes with free hands.

These garbage trucks are known as "Dead Trucks" because they travel pig farm to pig farm emptying out the metal dumpsters called "Dead Bins" containing dead pigs. Dead Trucks usually begin their rounds in the pre-dawn hours, but there's a lot to do. Extra pick-ups become necessary when the dumpsters fill up faster than usual. Decaying, pestilent carcasses piling up in open-top dumpsters in the humid heat and searing sun emit an increasingly powerful request to be emptied.

The pig factory farmers place their Dead Bins closer to the road and away from their barns because carrion is often diseased. They don't want viral contagions incubating in sweltering open-air dumpsters adjacent to or even near barns containing thousands of live animals.

Most of the students are accustomed to this and don't even look up. They know what the source of this smell is. Several who do look ahead aren't pleased they did as their curiosity is rewarded with the unsettling view of the head and upper torso of a mature pig hanging out over the edge of the overfilled Dead Truck.

When these children were younger, this putrid concentrated smell of decomposing animals would cause them to vomit. It's an instinctive response. Your body finds disease, death and decay repellant. It sends you the strong urge to heave as a signal to keep away. Today, these school-bound children recoil but each one of them is sufficiently accustomed to keep things together.

Not a moment too soon, their bus turns off in another direction. Some days the weather is cool, so the pestilent smell of carrion is less pungent, but on a humid morning like this with the sun's heat rising, the smell of the Dead Truck lingers inside their bus. They open their windows, but it takes the breeze blowing in a while — they've traveled half-a-mile, before the smell is dissipated and gone.

No one pays any attention as the bus passes another long driveway. It's really an unpaved road, which cuts back through forest trees and leads to another pig factory farming operation and its adjacent spray field...

. . .

Thomas Q. Piglet lives down this road. He's a little guy with short white hair that doesn't quite cover all of his soft pink skin. He's got a really big head. And a long nose and pointy extendo ears. When he looks at you what may first strike you is his sharp, perceptive awareness, but right now his eyes are on the one who is most important in his young life — his mother.

She's not sleeping, she's not hurt, just confined inside the metal bars of a farrowing crate. She can stand up, but the dimensions of the crate are so narrow, the metal bars barely wider than the width of her body, that she can only step a foot or so forwards or back. She is unable to turn around. Thomas looks at his mother, nudges her snout and she looks back recognizing her piglet. She is having some difficulty breathing and looks tired — she isn't well. She was brought here nearly three weeks ago when she was about to give birth. Thomas Q. is one of her ten babies in this cement and steel farrowing pen. She lies on her side to nurse them. Thomas and his brothers and sisters are confined in the narrow space beside her where you see him now.

Pigs like to bask and play in the sunlight as it warms their soft sensitive skin. When cool, scent-filled breezes blow across their farm-yard enveloping their faces and bodies, there's nothing better. They quickly learn an array of sounds and gestures to communicate with each other. They form social groups. Pigs wag their tails when they are happy, and they learn to respond to their own names.[2] They develop a strong memory for faces and will immediately recognize ones they like and others they'd prefer not to be around. Most of all, they love to root in muddy ground, to forage with their snouts in the wet fields amidst grass and bugs and all kinds of scents and mysteries in the wet soil. Mud keeps them cool as they don't have many sweat glands. Pigs need to ingest the microbes and 'dirt stuff' to maintain their health.[3] However, despite their penchant for rooting in the soil and running around in the fields, pigs are clean animals. They prefer to go to the bathroom well away from the areas where they eat, rest or anywhere near their farrowing pens.

Thomas hasn't experienced any of that yet. He's naturally curious but there's nothing stimulating or interesting for him in this claustrophobic, fetid space. He and his mother, brothers and sisters live on this cold metal floor in this darkened room. The floor is grated, with lines of rectangular openings narrow enough so their feet don't fall in, while wide enough for their urine and their poop to drop down into a collection space underneath before draining through pipes that lead outside into a vast adjacent cesspool called a lagoon.

As Thomas glances at his mom, she is not covered with dirt and bits of field grass and straw from a welcome journey outside — she hasn't left this crate. Instead, she is covered in her own waste. His mother hasn't stood up since yesterday. This concerns him but she's alive and nurses him - so it must be okay. This is all he's ever experienced, all he knows. This is how it's supposed to be, right?

A human is approaching. Thomas is wary. When the humans appear, nothing good ever happens. Already in their young lives, Thomas and each of his brothers and sisters have been hurt by humans, receiving pain for reasons beyond their understanding. It's best when the humans pass by leaving them alone. Pigs not only have very good memories, but they are really smart. They are most likely smarter than your dog, and maybe even as smart as cats although a cat would never admit that.

Thomas Q. would respond to human affection. Only he has never had that kind of experience. Fearful, he backs away from the workers as they approach. A week ago, a worker came into his pen, grabbed him by his hind legs and lifted him into the air. He squealed loudly, terrified and twisted his body but could not escape. The worker held a very sharp scalpel in one hand and cut off his tail, which really hurt as he was given no anesthetic to kill the pain, then made two cuts in his backside, squeezed, drawing his young testicles out from inside his body and tore them off.[4] As Thomas squealed loudly, writhing in searing pain, his mother went berserk. Roaring at the intruder, she pressed hard against the metal bars. Thomas was cast aside on the filthy floor. He watched helplessly as, one by one, each of his scurrying bothers were caught, raised and their squeals of terror turned into high pitched shrieks from the pain of tail docking and castration.

Today the human pays no attention to Thomas or his brothers and sisters, focusing instead on his mom. It matters to this worker that she's not standing. It's a nuisance. He carries a long metal rod, called a 'poop stick,' with which he prods her to get her to stand. The sows must stand at least once every day. Thomas watches as his mom is poked harder, harder still, again — until she rises. The worker then uses the stick to slide the masses of feces that have accumulated around her body into and through the openings in the floor. A mature sow, she weighs well over 400 pounds and produces around 16 pounds of excrement a day. The omnipresent, concentrated and highly toxic ammonia and hydrogen sulfide fumes from pig waste creates breathing problems for the pigs as well as a hazardous environment for the workers. Once the worker has finished, he moves along the row to the sow in the next gestation crate. Thomas hears the cries of other sows and piglets, their neighbors off in the darkened space of this vast room.

Later, in another building, Thomas will be assigned a number, which will be inked into his skin by half-inch long spikes mounted on a big hammer-like tool. He will be stuck with it and tattooed four times around his forward haunches. Sows are given a bright earring, more specifically an ear tag — like the yellow one you see his mother wearing — applied with a riveter. These pigs are not afforded even an instant of compassion; they're barely considered animals. They are just production units on an assembly line. Thomas won't be cared for, or even cared about. He is just kept alive and fed to maintain his value.

Thomas Q. isn't even his name. He doesn't have one. I named him. No one on this farm cares enough about him to give him one — nor ever will.

100 million pigs are raised for food each year in the United States. Today, 99% of these pigs spend their entire lives on factory farms in conditions similar to Thomas and his mother.[5] The pork industry and its trade organizations like the American Association of Meat Processors and the North American Meat Institute promote the appearance of happy pigs living natural lives in idyllic pastures on small family farms to consumers, often using idealized images of these homesteads in their advertising and food packaging. They evoke a nostalgia for rural life, for this is what American family farms were like in the 1940s, 1950s and to a diminishing extent, the 1960s and 1970s. But for 99% of pigs today, this image couldn't be further from their reality.

The industry refers to this as a farm, but it isn't one in the traditional sense — it's a factory. This is a factory farm, also referred to as a CAFO, which is an acronym for Concentrated Animal Feeding Operation. The tiny space Thomas, his mother, brothers and sisters occupy is just one in a long row of identical spaces extending over 200 feet, the entire length of this cavernous barn. Numerous identical rows of these gestation crates span the width of this farrowing outbuilding. 2,000 sows and piglets fill this darkened space.

On a traditional farm each animal is cared for, its needs are met, and it is afforded enough space to live according to its animal nature. The farmer's living depends on raising thriving, healthy animals to full market weight and price. The pigs enjoy a good, fit, natural life. By contrast, raising livestock on a factory farm is just a numbers game. Thomas and all the pigs and sows here are considered a commodity, and the fact that they are living creatures rather than production units on an assembly line, is an inconvenience. If, during the manufacturing process as Thomas Q. is grown to market size and weight, he is badly hurt or becomes diseased, then Thomas-Q. — the "production unit" — will be deemed broken, of no value, and will be cast aside. There's a Dead Bin waiting for him if that's how it goes. Any care or attention paid to any of these production units beyond the barest minimum necessary to get them through the assembly process is an unnecessary expense to be avoided.

Today, noise and commotion command the pig's attention. Something's going on. Humans appear. *Eight* of them. The entirety of this huge factory farm and all of its barns is staffed by just ten workers. Thomas rarely sees

more than one or two at any time, yet on this Friday, *eight* of them are entering. Suddenly, the back of Thomas's pen opens, and a worker enters. He's got the red paddle — the scariest color. It's a wide, flat barrier Thomas Q. and his siblings can't get around. The worker yells at them, shakes a plastic jug with frightening noisy things rattling in it. Thomas cowers beside his mother, tries to nudge himself under her for protection but to no avail. His mother has no energy to rise. She can't shelter him.

The other door opens — the one on the other end of the pen. Mysteriously. No human blocks this path, this way out.

The Q in Thomas's name stands for Quicksilver. He's a fast little guy and he quickly realizes: this is his chance. Escape! This is the way!

Thomas Quicksilver is the first to dash out, leading his brothers and sisters into the middle aisle. Surprise! They are joined by piglets rushing out of the other pens on both sides, fleeing rattles and red paddles. Jailbreak! Piglets flood in. Thomas notices that the big doors at the far end are open. It's darkness beyond — maybe a path out of this barn. The piglets herd together, head in that direction. Is it time now to see the sun? Is this the way to the grass and the rooting soil? The piglets are finally leaving this dark, scary, hurtful place, all they have ever known.

Thomas and hundreds of piglets move through the open doors and find themselves in another dark hallway. It leads to another. Leaders are cautious, wary, but have no choice but to keep advancing, pressed forward by those behind them. Another dark corridor, but this time, at its end... an open door with slices of brightness along its edges — the promise of sunlight beyond. Thomas and the other piglets head instinctively to the sunlight, which none of them have ever before experienced.

As they herd through this narrower door they emerge onto a metal ramp that leads them up into a transport truck. The sliver of sky above, vivid and warm is eclipsed as the piglets behind Thomas force him forward into the truck.

Thomas is leaving the farrowing barn and will be driven to a grow-out barn where he will be housed in a small pen along with several other pigs. He will spend his remaining days there, until he approaches full size and market weight, at which time he will be transported to the rendering plant and to slaughter. Thomas will never set foot in a meadow or grassy farmland, never bask in the sun. He will never be able to root in wet mud or straw, never have space to run around and play with his friends. Or develop any of the complex social relationships pigs have the natural capacity for.

Back at the farrowing barn, it's his mom's turn. She, and all the sows have watched as their babies have been driven away. Now, it's their turn to vacate this barn. The workers prepare a path to a different destination and they spread out, each manning turning points to direct traffic along the route. Just one sow is released at a time. The workers are prepared. They know from experience that sows will react in different ways.

The first sow released is one who has just delivered her first litter. First timers are excited to get out of their cramped crates. They haven't been able to walk or even turn around for over three weeks. Now, the metal bars they have been pressing futilely against shift aside! These sows erupt into the middle aisle, discovering some space to move around. They follow the scent of the piglets, hoping to reunite with their own.

Once one sow hastens through the big doorway, and turns along the second section of the path, a worker lets out the next sow.

This sow is one who has been through this before. She leaves her crate stepping into the middle aisle but is more reluctant, lethargic. This is the second common reaction. Pigs, like dogs, can remember faces, bodies, and smells. They can quickly identify animals or people that they have encountered, even years before, remembering whether these experiences were good or bad. This sow has delivered several litters in this barn, she remembers this experience. She knows where she's going, how it has ended before.

These sows are being transferred to the gestation barn, which is nearly as large as the farrowing barn, and where they will be forced into gestation crates barely wider than their bodies. These new crates are even smaller than the ones they are now leaving, as there is no additional space necessary for the nursing of piglets. They will each spend the next three months, three weeks and three days in those narrow confines, unable to walk, back up or turn around. 3 months, 3 weeks and 3 days... Two thousand seven hundred and sixty-six hours. After about two weeks there, they are forcibly artificially inseminated and the whole cycle begins again.

For the first timers being moved, the end of this journey is an emotionally wrenching and often violent one. The workers know from experience that the very instant a first timer sow, so excited to be out of the torturous confines of a farrowing crate, turns the corner and faces the end of the path — not an open field, not an expansive enclosure, not even a modest size pen, or anything natural, of nature or even close — but a dark, tiny metal cage, smaller even than the one she just came from, that surprise, the total shock of this realization, quickly becomes angry rebellion. These large animals often turn and struggle to avoid going into this kind of space again — and must be forced. Two workers stand poised to use tools of personal preference — electric shockers, metal pipes, a length of rebar, whatever works best for them to gain compliance — to get each sow into the open gestation crate awaiting her.

Many experienced sows, those that have borne numerous litters, take this walk but must be prodded by the worker manning each new section of the route, in addition to being motivated at trail's end to enter one of these narrow confinement cells.

For the workers, there are so few of them and so many animals. They are overworked, underpaid, and vastly overtasked. The hours are long, the job is dangerous, injuries are common. The workplace air they breathe is rife with dirt, fecal and other particulate matter, and disease. A quarter of them will develop respiratory problems such as asthma, bronchitis and organic toxic dust syndrome.[6] Working at this factory farm, each one of them is now six times more likely to catch and carry the antibiotic-resistant MSRA (Methicillin-resistant Staphylococcus aureus) bacteria which can cause deadly skin, blood and lung infections and is highly contagious.[7] Their labor is considered unskilled so most are paid minimum wage, if that. Having to put up with, be complicit with and manage so much animal suffering, the job is soul deadening — a job very few people would want, one you take to survive, as an immigrant in a new land, as an unskilled, under-educated or underachieving person who's strong of body, who has applied for work at manufacturing plants or businesses in town, and can find no other employment. The attitude requires a detached resignation to get the assigned tasks done each day while protecting what remains of your energy so that by shift's end, you can clean up and head out into your private life, to the family you are providing for, to whatever pleasures or routine satisfaction you have some control over for the remainder of your living day.

Workers tend to get frustrated with the animals. Each day, there is only enough time to complete their assigned tasks if everything goes smoothly. To stay on schedule, they must get the animals to comply, even those incapable of it. When there's a moment of brightness, when an animal's sensitivity, feeling or intelligence shines through, it must be paid no attention to. Compassion does not exist here. Nothing can interfere with the factory farming process.

There was one morning when two workers entered the barn to discover two sows, along with their piglets, wandering loose along the middle aisle. The workers stopped and watched to try and figure out what exactly was happening. And what they saw amazed even them. One of the sows had figured out how to loosen her crate door hinges with her tongue, work a pin up, back and forth — again and again — until it fell open. She escaped with her babies. A second crate door, the one adjacent, lay on the ground as well. Rather than flee with her piglets through the far door and a chance at freedom, the sow had chosen to stay and free her neighbor. The workers watched in disbelief as she was now at a third gestation crate and, angling her snout from the outside in, was managing to lift and rock that door open as well. She succeeded, and the workers witnessed this third sow and her piglets emerge. The workers regarded one another, impressed with this animal's intelligence, feeling an affinity with her selflessness in delaying her cherished escape to freedom to help others find theirs. They watched as she moved down the line and stopped at the next farrowing crate. At this point the workers stopped her as they had no time to spare in their schedule for *these* escapees, let alone more. They remounted the crate doors, then returned the piglets to their pens, and the sows to their crates. All except one. The ringleader. Who now knew how to open a gestation crate door. She would not forget that, and she won't stop doing it. So, she must be put down. And right there, right then, in front of her piglets, in front of all of them, she was.

The third most common type of animal reaction on this Friday is displayed by the sows that are absolutely unwilling, or due to injury, unable to be moved. Today, Thomas's mother is one of them.

Thomas's mother is four years old. Worn down and depleted from delivering and suckling three litters of piglets every year, living completely without exercise in this intensive confinement on cement and metal flooring, her leg muscles are weak and wasted away from lack of use, her swollen leg joints — increasingly painful even to put weight on — are now crippled. She finds herself unable to stand in her opened crate. She has an increasingly hard time breathing, having developed respiratory problems over years of inhaling the dust, dander and the poisonous gases released from the buildup of her urine and feces as well as what rises up from the accumulation space below from the waste of her 2,000 neighbors. Watching her babies taken from her, knowing from past experience that she will never see them again, companionless, comfortless, never once having succeeded in chewing through the bars of her crate despite having broken several of her teeth trying, prone now to dementia from the omnipresent stress and depression, she has withdrawn from this life as well.

A worker looks at her chart. She hasn't eaten for three days.

Each hog's food trough and water dispenser are checked daily. In yet another way the factory farming system cuts down on labor costs, the pig feed — stored in silos elevated outside each barn — is dispensed automatically through feeding pipes into individual rations into each sow's trough. Due to the high risk of infectious disease in this exceedingly pestilent environment, the food delivered to the farm arrives laced with antibiotics. When a sow stops eating, it is recorded. On the third consecutive day a worker typically will then go to the refrigerator, get a syringe of tetracycline antibiotic, and inject the pig to knock back any infection she may have.

North Carolina hog farms are still reeling from the highly contagious PED (Porcine Epidemic Diarrhea) virus that appeared in the United States in May 2013, which spread rapidly throughout most of the country, killing or prompting the killing of over seven million pigs in the first year alone.

Thomas's mother was given the shot yesterday. Today she is still not eating. And now she refuses all efforts to move her. She may have an infection. Or she may not. Terminally ill sows often are left to suffer for a week, even two, on the chance they might rebound. But Thomas's mom is older and has had a productive life. The decision is made. She won't be allowed back with the other hogs in the super-confined quarters of the gestation barn.

When a sow or a piglet must be terminated, workers have two options — the gas cart or "bolting." The standard factory farm industry practice used for decades to kill injured pigs is "thumping." You pick up a young pig by its hind legs, whip it high around and over your rotating body, and rocket it down, slamming its head with as much force as possible onto the concrete floor. You "thump" it off the floor. This practice may need to be repeated but when you get adept at it, the odds are good that you end the pig's life on the first thump. "Thumping" is less common nowadays if the barn has a "death cart."

One worker is wheeling this along the middle aisle now. Piglets that did not survive the move are tossed into its plastic tub, some alive, others dead. When the tub is full it is sealed and CO_2 gas is pumped into it, which, over ten slow minutes, should succeed in suffocating all the animals.

Grown sows like Thomas Quicksilver's mother don't fit into the tub.

A worker approaches her. He stands in front of her.

She looks up and regards him. He has a bolt gun in hand — it's time for "bolting." He raises it and presses it to her forehead. Her eyes watch him and, with a sudden excruciating shock, a steel bolt crushes through her skull and drives two inches into her brain. Senses, then consciousness leave her, and her suffering, miserable life finally, mercifully, ends.

. . .

In his article, *Hog Hell — The CAFO Industry's Impact on the Environment and Public Health*, Adam Skolnick writes, "Thirty years ago, there were 22,000 farmers in North Carolina raising 2 million pigs. Most of those were pasture-raised... An industrial takeover took root in the 1970s and '80s."[8] By 2018, there were 2,300 pig factory farms in North Carolina containing approximately eight million nine hundred thousand pigs, the second highest number of any state.[9] [10] Duplin County, with 2.3 million pigs in that county alone, is now the top hog producer not only in the state but in the country. Adjacent Sampson County ranks second.[11]

The nearer people live to these farms, the more likely they have asthma.[12] A 2018 research study found that residents living within 1.2 miles of a hog factory farm are 4.5 times more likely to die from kidney disease, and over 3 times more likely to die from bacterial blood infections than residents living at a safe distance (6.2 miles away or further).[13][14] Hospital admissions and emergency department visits are 5 times higher. The animal agriculture industry does everything it can to deny responsibility for this correlation.

Pigs in North Carolina generate 2.8 *billion* gallons of feces and urine each year, which is collected in huge open-air cesspools. There are over 15,000 of these "lagoons."[15] Based on a conservative estimate that pigs, on average, produce seven pounds of waste each day,[16] North Carolina's pigs produce 62,300,000 pounds of waste daily. Converting pounds to gallons based on a similarity in consistency with yogurt weight (one gallon of yogurt weighs eight pounds), North Carolina's pigs produce 7,787,500 gallons of waste each day.

When the lagoons fill — and they fill quickly — that amount of fecal matter must be disposed of *each and every day*. Irrigation systems like center pivot and boom-type sprayers are used to spread aerosolized pig waste on adjacent crop fields and grass fields — in far greater amounts than the soil can absorb. These fields are often in low-lying areas with a high groundwater table and are intentionally graded to facilitate drainage into the aquifer and nearby streams and waterways. Since the water table can be less than just under a few feet under the soil, Dr. Michael Mallin, a biologist and research professor at UNC Wilmington, notes that when swine waste is sprayed onto these fields, "Within a few hours what passes through the soil can be in the water table."[17] Because of the number of pig factory farms in these river floodplains, "The water pollution in the state has reached such an extreme level that American Rivers listed the Neuse and Cape Fear rivers (which are the source of drinking water for 40% of North Carolinians) among their list of America's Most Endangered Rivers."[18] 40% of North Carolinians now drink water contaminated by pig fecal matter and bacteria. (The situation in Iowa, which hosts the largest number of factory-farmed pigs of any state is similarly grave.)[19] Many local residents living near pig farms have discovered that their well water is also polluted.

Aerosolized particulate waste drifts in the air onto surrounding residences and roads up to several miles away. In *How Drug-Resistant Bacteria Travel from the Farm to Your Table*, published in Scientific

American, Melinda Wenner Moyer quotes Tara Smith, an epidemiologist studying emerging infections at the University of Iowa who tested pigs for MRSA at Iowa farms, who says, "We ended up sampling 270 pigs in the first round — we just went out and swabbed a lot of pig noses and had no idea what we'd find. About 70 percent of them were positive for MRSA."[20] Smith and her colleagues have published a series of studies showing the prevalence of MRSA on American hog farms. They found MRSA growing in the nostrils of 64 percent of workers at one large farm and found that feed on another farm harbored MRSA even before it got unloaded from the delivery truck. 235 yards downwind of another farm, Smith found MRSA floating in the air. "In a study conducted in Pennsylvania, people who were the most heavily exposed to crop fields treated with pig manure — for instance, because they lived near to them — had more than 30 percent increased odds of developing MRSA infections compared with people who were the least exposed."[21]

Other drug-resistant bacteria have been found around poultry farms: after researchers at the Johns Hopkins Bloomberg School of Public Health drove cars with windows down, behind trucks that were transporting chickens in Maryland and Virginia along the Delmarva Peninsula, they found antibiotic-resistant enterococci — a group of bacteria that causes 20,000 infections in the U.S. every year — in the air inside their cars, as well as resting on the top of soda cans in the cup holder.

Devon Hall, cofounder and project manager at the Rural Empowerment Association for Community Help (REACH),[22] an organization that strives to improve the quality of life for people of color in the area, told me, "You can't imagine what it's like to live next to one of these hog operations. On days like this people don't sit on their porches and enjoy the view. They close their windows, they can't hang their laundry out on a clothesline to dry or it will become embedded with the smell. It's hard to enjoy the outdoors and it's embarrassing to invite company over. The flies and the smells make life miserable."

The air for those who live near factory farms contains increased amounts of ammonia, hydrogen sulfide, and methane as well as residues of veterinary antibiotics and bacteria.[23] The Environmental Working Group identified over 60,000 residential parcels occupied by an estimated 160,000 people within 1/2 mile of either a pig or poultry factory farm or one of its cesspools.[24] Adam Skolnick notes that, "Peer-reviewed scientific studies in North Carolina and other states have documented health problems, reduced air quality and noxious odors three miles or farther from CAFOs... 960,000 or more residents could fall within a three-mile nuisance zone."[25]

Sherneka and her family have lived in this area for generations. They love this lush verdant countryside, the woods, warm sunlight, the promise of a new day, of being able to call what once was a healthy clean rural environment, home. Now they are trapped here. Homeowners wanting to move find prospective buyers are scarce, even scarcer still is a buyer who will offer them anything close to what their property once was worth.[26]

Growing up, Sherneka had a lot of trouble breathing. "I went out a couple of times, so it was bad. It's real scary because you can feel it coming on." 'Went out' is her way of saying she lost consciousness. "Your chest gets tight, it gets hard for you to breathe. Sometimes you had to vomit to get air. It was worst when I was eleven and twelve. I was in middle school when I passed out the first time." She had inhalers and a nebulizer. Asthma kept her from physical activity. "You can't get too hot, you can't get too cold. If you overdress certain things trigger your asthma. And certain foods. Certain smells. The pig farms, when the smell was worse, it triggered the asthma."

Sherneka picks up Sky on her lunch hour and drives her home to leave with her mom — whom Sky affectionately calls Granma Louise. As she drives away from Rose Hills — Magnolia Elementary School, past the adjacent crop field, the cow farms and the chicken hatchery complex, Sky tells her about the fire drill.

About ten o'clock, the alarms resounded and the entire school assembled out in the courtyard and playground. It took forever for everyone to line up. Woods border one side of the school grounds, a cow farm and crop field the other. This morning the center pivot reel field irrigation system was on, dispersing animal waste across the crop field. There was an incoming breeze and particulate matter was drifting over onto Sky and the dutifully assembled student body who had to endure it until the teachers signaled that the buildings were free of fire.

The moment Sherneka picks Sky up at school and hugs her, she smells the pig smell on her daughter's clothes and in her hair. But she doesn't say a word. She'll have her mother give Sky a bath when they get there. Sherneka glances at her lovely daughter. Sky loves to play outside and swing on her swing set in the yard. She loves the digital tablet that she carries everywhere, the games she plays on it — *Uno* and *Dress Up Barbie* — and the You Tube videos she watches, especially *Sis vs. Bro*. Sky has had asthma as long as her mom can remember. Nights when she's deeply congested, Sherneka raises Sky's head and chest on her pillow and holds her close.

Sky's baby teeth have been badly weakened by the asthma medication she has been prescribed. She's had to have dental work done, including silver caps in the back of her mouth to strengthen them enough so she can keep them. She must take allergy medicine every day. The last time Sky had an upper respiratory infection, her antibiotics made her have a seizure and she had to spend three days in the hospital. Sherneka has had to take Sky to the emergency room four times. Sky is five years old.

Something has happened; traffic is stopped ahead. Fire trucks are on scene, emergency lights flashing. Sherneka brakes, the incident comes into view.

A Dead Truck is stuck. It was making the turn onto Yellowcut Road toward Valley Proteins, the plant at the end of the street where all the dead animals are processed. The driver turned too fast causing its load to overturn and spill across Highway 117. This load isn't fresh carcasses. It's liquidy, goopy animal remains.

Sherneka shudders. She and Sky quickly close their windows and she turns off the fan circulating air, but the smell hits them anyway, and it's overpowering. Traffic backs up behind them. Highway 117 is just single lane each way. They can't turn around.

A brown chemical has been sprayed over the animal remains covering the roadway. A fire crew and a team from the processing plant are working the edges of the spill with shovels, corralling and collecting it. Sky, covering her nose, asks her mom what's happening. She tells Sky not to worry.

The recent PED epidemic that caused millions of pigs to have to be euthanized and buried in mass graves crosses Sherneka's mind. Some farms in the area continue to have the yellow PED warning signs posted — they still haven't been certified as PED free. Body fluids ooze out from the Dead Trucks regularly as they make their rounds, blowing into the air on pedestrians, onto the windows of passing and trailing vehicles. No one seems to voice concern about this. But the moment one of these trucks has a spill like this, the fire department and clean up teams are out in full force... Sky watches her mother's expression, her pursed lips, emulates her mother's calm. "This isn't right, Mama." Sherneka can't disagree.

Jemarion rides the school bus home on his own as J'vion has stayed for football practice. When he gets home, he'll be on his own for a while as both his mother and father work until early evening.

His mother, Jennifer, is a Certified Nursing Assistant, providing patient care at the local hospital. She's nearly completed a two-year course to receive her Medical Assistant certificate. Once she has that credential, she plans to shift from the hospital to work at a clinic or for a private company doing front office work like scheduling appointments or filing medical records in addition to working directly with the patients drawing blood, giving injections and prepping and caring for them like she does now.

Jennifer's also lived in this area her whole life and she's also well acquainted with asthma. Her husband Corey is a logger who operates the machinery loading logs onto transport trucks. To try and distance themselves from the pig farms, they decided to move down the road into a double-wide mobile home set back in the pine trees. I had to drive along a bumpy windy path threading back through mature pine trees to reach them.

Moving into this home in the woods seems to have worked. No pig manure scent was in the air that day. Just the smell of the pine trees. When they're back out driving on the roads however, they can't avoid it. Jennifer doesn't like seeing the Dead Man's Trucks, "We always call them the Dead Man's Trucks — when they're picking up, when they're dumping the dumpsters of dead hogs into the truck. And I have to drive by that all the time with my kids. Or I'll be riding behind a transport truck and the hogs are pooping and that stuff is flying back on my windshield. That's nasty as well and it has a smell. But there's no getting used to the smell from the Dead Man's Trucks. No matter how many times you smell that smell you never get used to it."

After we'd been together for a time, Jennifer and Corey told me about what happened to Jemarion...

They realized early on that both of their sons had asthma. As babies they'd always be congested. Jennifer and Corey could tell that, whenever their breathing started changing in their sleep, there was an attack coming on. But under the age of two, doctors won't diagnose asthma. As their sons got older and were diagnosed, Jennifer and Corey sent a nebulizer to day care and school with each of them.

Jemarion, the little one, had it worse. "His first year on this earth was rough for him. He was really sick. He was put in the hospital, into the ICU.

They had to tube him." Jennifer pauses for a moment. "His tonsils was too large so when he'd lay his head back they'd flop back and he'd stop breathing." They'd bring Jemarion to sleep in their bed in-between them. "The first time he done it I actually picked him up and started shaking him because he wasn't breathing. So, I sat him up and he started breathing I guess because they flopped back down."

Jennifer remembers J'vion wheezing and gasping for air. "'Momma,'" he'd say, "'I need a breathing treatment,' and he go in and get the nebulizer." Corey adds, "He didn't have it as bad as the little knuckle. You might as well say it in so many words — Jemarion like... checked out of here."

"When I first took my baby boy to the doctor, they could never tell me what was wrong with him." Jennifer continues, "They kept saying 'common cold, common cold' and I'm, like, 'There's no way a common cold is stopping him from breathing like that.' Finally, he was referred to an ear, nose and throat doctor and they said his tonsils needed to come out. But when they put him under, they almost lost him then and the doctor came out and said they weren't equipped there for what he needs."

So Jemarion was sent to a city hospital for the operation. Jennifer's voice goes quiet. "The doctor, she said, 'You go with him straight to the hospital. He needs to go into surgery right now. And you're going to have to stay with him.' So, I went with Jemarion and she was right — I didn't come back. The doctor took one look at him and immediately realized what it was. They operated on Jemarion right away, but he wasn't that strong. We stayed in Greenville a long time. But we came back with our living son... The doctors around here kept saying 'Common cold, common cold.'"

As Jemarion travels on the school bus it pulls up to a stop sign and waits to turn out onto the main road. An animal transport truck slows to a stop beside it. Normally Jemarion and the others don't pay much attention. The trucks are a common sight carrying animals every day, seven days a week, two levels of hogs heading for slaughter. There's nothing rewarding about looking. The animals crammed inside are dirty and they're not happy. So, the students are versed in looking at one another, at the backs of the seats, at their smartphones — looking away.

But this time some of the girls started to coo, "oouughhh" and "aughh" and "Look how cute they are." As the bus begins a slow tight turn, the girls press against their windows. Jemarion looks out his window as well. The eighteen-wheeler transport truck is right by them and through the metal holes along its side, there are piglets. This transport is carrying several hundred piglets.

And the piglets are really cute. Jemarion smiles. He's young, his brother isn't there, so he can be a sensitive boy.

Thomas Quicksilver is on this truck. He looks out one of the metal openings at the wide-open countryside, at sunlight, at trees and bushes, flowers and grass. As his truck slows to a stop, the children on the school bus glide beside him, slowing, stopping as well. He regards them.

A girl's eyes are on him. Another. And a boy whose name is Jemarion.

They smile at Thomas Q. — more than just how cute he is, they perceive his gentleness, his sensitivity, the intelligent curiosity in his gaze.

Thomas has never before seen a human looking at him this way. He has never seen a human smile.

"So, it can't be all bad, can it? Surely my life holds promise. There is sunshine — I see it. And these fields... There will be space to run around in and play, breathe fresh air at last, get out into this warm day, finally some wet dirt to wallow and snoggle in. Happiness. I know it... My mom's not feeling well but she's going to get better. We'll be together soon."

The Golden Rule is part of our journey. You know the one — "Do unto others as you would have them do unto you." More than how we treat other human beings, it applies to how we treat animals, and our entire world.

For Jemarion, for Thomas Quicksilver, for each one of us...

It's all about the Golden Rule...

II

At Cottonwood Creek Farms[27] on the high plains west of the Rocky Mountains, the pigs wake up when the sun is high enough to warm them. They rise from deep straw beds and emerge out from under the canvas tarped roofs of their hoop structures into the open fresh air of the new morning. As many as 75 pigs live together in one covered structure set in the middle of an 8,000 square foot pen where they can wander around and eat, where they herd together and where they have access to mud holes big enough for 30 of them to wallow in.

Matt Kautz and his wife Alyssa raise and care for 300 pigs and several thousand chickens on their sixty-acre farm in Merino, Colorado. Their pastured pigs and chickens enjoy a quality of life a world removed from factory farmed animals.

The hoop structures are tarp-shaded 30 by 30-foot open-air houses. Along the inside they are walled with deep bed straw, and the floor is layered with one to three feet of composting straw. The deep bedding generates good heat from slow decay, providing warm and comfy nests for the cold and snowy winter days. The pigs have full-time access to the outdoors. Water misters are in place to provide cool relief on hot summer days. The pigs choose areas in the back to manure in, leaving lots of clean soil for resting, wallowing, and rooting — plenty of space to wander around and be pigs.

Matt told me that there's no point in time when these pigs go inside any kind of four walled building or live under artificial light. "We give them shelter and everything they need to be happy and just let them be."

Matt keeps eight boars in individual pens, introducing sows to them two at a time. When it is time for a sow to have her babies, she is moved over to a 7 by 8-foot open farrowing hut.

Piglets are born and suckle in these farrowing huts, which, like the hoop buildings, allow sunlight and breezes in, yet are padded with deep straw which shelters them from the harsher elements. Each mom has ample room within to farrow and raise her babies, to move around and to settle in any position she wants. She can come and go whenever she chooses into the wide outside area, which is about 8 by 40 feet and gives her access to sunlight or shade, sand, mud, water, and cooling misters.[28] At about two weeks of age, groups of the babies and their mothers are shifted to a nursing area, which is covered "group housing." Here the sows can remain together with their piglets as they further develop. Matt's not boasting when he says, "We don't ever run into an animal on our farm that's in distress because of its environment. Unless we accidentally let the feed run out — and then they'll holler at you." It's just the way life is for the livestock in Matt and Alyssa's care on their farm.

The pigs eat non-GMO corn and soy which Matt's family grows on their farm. They also enjoy eating the weeds and wild bits of grass that Matt and Alyssa's four sons, Luke, Hank, Jack and Buck pull up and toss their way. In contrast, factory farmers feed their pigs GMO (Genetically Modified Organism) corn or soy. GMO crops contain glyphosate residues, the pesticide routinely sprayed on them, which is cited by the state of California as a known possible carcinogen,[29] and which is banned in many countries throughout the world.[30] Feed used in factory farms is commonly laced with antibiotics and other additives to enable factory farmed pigs to survive in their pestilent environment and grow more rapidly to optimal weight. It is delivered by truck, which pollutes the environment and carries the additional transportation cost. Matt and Alyssa just transport their pig's food from his brother's nearby field. And their healthy pigs have no need for any pharmaceuticals or growth promoters. They get a vitamin and mineral supplement, and a pair of vaccinations.[31] That's all.

On Cottonwood Creek Farms, pig waste isn't collected in virulent lagoons. It's put to use enriching their pasture soil as nutrient dense fertilizer. When the pigs are shifted from one hoop building to another, their deep bedding is replaced with fresh straw. The used bedding is composted on the farm. Matt and his brother are committed to maintaining, if not improving the richness and quality of their soil. They have no need to purchase costly, synthetic industrial fertilizer, or to pay to have it trucked in.

Matt and Alyssa watch as Luke and Hank finish their chores. Jack and Buck are playing around. Berkshires approach them, healthy pigs hoping for a pulled weed treat, living naturally, contentedly and well.

Matt takes Alyssa's hand, smiles. It's a beautiful life they've created for themselves and their family. Pigs and piglets regard them, looking up from the mud they've been rooting in, eyes squinting in the morning sun.

III

Here then is the call. Calling out to you. An essential component of **The Great Healing** is **compassion for animals**. The compassionate treatment of *all* animals. The Great Healing will not be possible without this.

The Great Healing will not be possible without fully realizing and regaining our humanity. Mahatma Gandhi said, "The greatness of a nation and its moral progress can be judged by the way its animals are treated."

The intelligence, social skills, the core emotions and sensitivities of Thomas Quicksilver and his mother, of Matt and Alyssa's pigs, of each farmed animal, are no less developed than your dog or cat, and fundamentally not much different than your own. Pigs wag their tails when they are happy and they can recognize their own names.[34] They can be fearful, joyful, sorrowful. They feel happiness, excitement, contentment, as well as loneliness, misery and despair. They grieve and mourn their dead.[35] They empathize, form social groups, play games, recognize and remember animals they want to be around, and ones they don't. They are creatures of exquisite beauty.

On your life's path, I hope you haven't drifted away from a sense of wonder. Of fascination; of amazement with the exquisite beauty and diversity of life on this planet. Of life itself. Compassion for other living creatures is an essential part of that tapestry. Living a compassionate life must include standing up for and protecting any animals that are not treated kindly, ethically or humanely. It must include extending your circle of compassion to embrace factory farmed animals.

Here is what you can do.

Make these three adjustments and stick with them:

- Eat less meat and dairy.
- Stop buying meat or dairy products that come from factory farms. Full stop.
- Advocate. When you adjust your path and realize that this is in line with your values, it feels good and it's the right thing to do, share your feelings and your thoughts with your friends and family and those in your social network. Increase their awareness. Your story, your insight, becomes your gift to them.

Find a place to start. In your heart, what feels right for you?
Resolve not to try, but do.
And begin.

There is something else you should be aware of. Factory farming operations exist on a massive scale not just for Thomas Quicksilver and other pigs but for cows, chickens, ducks and geese, fish, and animals raised for their fur.

There are nine million **dairy cows** producing milk in the United States.

These Holstein cows have just ambled in for a drink of fresh water as the sun sets on a day spent grazing in the grassy field you see behind them. They have a barn they can head to but, since this night will be warm, after they are milked, they'll probably choose to stay outside.

In her article *10 Things to Love About Cows*, Rhea Parsons writes, "Like humans, cows seek pleasure and love to play. When let outside after being cooped up for too long, cows run, prance and jump with joy... Cows form strong bonds and friendships, choosing to spend much of their time with just a few preferred individuals. They even have best friends. Cows help each other, learn from each other and make decisions based on compassion and altruism."[36] One study suggests cows have "eureka moments" — that they react emotionally to learning new things.[37] Cows are intelligent, inquisitive animals.[38]

Rhea Parsons observes that, "Cows have a social hierarchy... There is often one cow in the herd who is seen as the boss and who dictates behavior to the rest of the cows. Any cows that don't follow the leader will become isolated from the herd. When a new cow is introduced to a well-established herd, she will have to network and build relationships until she is accepted into the pack... Cows have great memories and are very good at remembering and recognizing faces even after long periods of time. Cows also have good spatial memory. They can remember where things are located such as food, water, shelter, and best grazing spots."[39]

These cows deliver, on average, 5 gallons (45 pounds) of milk a day. This is the milk you want to drink if you are a cow milk drinker. Any cheese or yogurt that you consume should also originate from milk from pastured, grass-fed dairy cows.

The richer the soil, the more nutritious the grasses that grow from it will be, and in turn the milk from these pastured cows will contain an optimal nutrient balance. Matthew Kadey, R.D., writes in *4 Things You Need to Know About Grass-Fed Milk*, "Organic whole milk from grass-fed cows contained 62% more omega-3 fats and 25% fewer omega-6 ones than the conventional kind in a 2013 study. This ratio is key, since a bigger proportion of omega-3s to omega-6s is linked to lower risk of chronic disease. Grass-fed milk also provides more iron and vitamin E." Dairy researcher Charles Benbrook, Ph.D., explains in the same article, "When cows are fed grass and legume-based forages as they were evolved to do, they'll produce milk with a healthier mix of fats and other nutrients."[40]

Omega-3 and omega-6 are the only two known essential fatty acids. They are called "essential" because you need them for good health. Your body does not naturally synthesize them. They are necessary for normal tissue function. Omega-3, as best-selling author, Joel Fuhrman, M.D., explains in his book, *Fast Food Genocide*, is the "Building block for the body to make EPA and DHA... that have anti-inflammatory effects and are necessary for brain growth and repair. Optimal brain function requires adequate DHA, which makes up 8% of the total volume of a healthy brain."[41] Omega-3s are found in green leafy vegetables, nuts and seeds, seafood, and in pastured grass-fed cows. Your body needs the correct balance of omega-6s and omega-3s. Dr. Fuhrman continues, "Excess omega-6 fat (in relation to omega-3 fat) is pro-inflammatory and accelerates common diseases, such as heart disease and cancer." Fast foods, processed foods and factory farmed animals contain excess omega-6 fat. The Bulletproof Staff notes in their guide to omega fats that "the average American eats a ratio of anywhere from 12:1 to 25:1 omega 6 to omega 3... For most people, a ratio of 4:1 is ideal... Anti-aging experts suggest going even further, maintaining a 1:1 ratio." The ratio of omega-6s to omega-3s in organic milk is 1 to 1, a ratio in your body for optimal health and to minimize the risk of heart attack.[42]

The vast majority of dairy cows in the United States are not fed grass. They've never even set foot in a pasture. These cows are factory farmed. The health benefits that Matthew Kadey and Dr. Fuhrman write about are not present in the milk of factory farmed dairy cows. Because life is very different for them.

Dairy cows value access to pasture as highly as they do fresh feed.[43] This dairy cow has never once been allowed to graze in a grass pasture. Fewer than 5% of dairy cows in the United States have access to pasture during grazing season. She is not even fed grass, the food her digestive tract has evolved to process. She has spent nearly every day of her life confined on the manure covered cement floor of this stanchion barn in this filthy industrial dairy farm.

She hasn't slipped in this photo. She can no longer stand.

No one at this factory farm has named her or ever will. So, we will.

Her name is Ruth.

Ruth's suffering on this industrial dairy factory farm is something the industry doesn't want you to see. This image is a frame grab from a video shot by an undercover investigator and provided to Mercy For Animals.[44] This is a dairy factory farm. 90% of American cow's milk originates in dairy factory farms like this.

Since a dairy cow, like most mammals, only produces milk after giving birth, Ruth has been artificially inseminated and given birth yearly for her entire life. Dairy cows have been selectively bred favoring increased milk production and, in addition, the unnatural diet of soy and corn she is fed can be laced with bovine growth hormone which further increases her lactation.[45] Ruth is a modern girl and, after calving, she produces one hundred pounds of milk daily. *One hundred pounds each day.*

The excessive milk production she has been designed for and endures leads to mastitis, an excruciatingly painful bacterial infection of her udders. Remember how it felt when you really had to go to the bathroom to urinate after having had to put it off for a while? The milk that collects in her udder must be passed *daily*, through swollen, bleeding, pus-oozing udders. The standard half-gallon carton of whole milk that you might buy at the market weighs 4.3 pounds. The volume of milk Ruth produces each day will fill nearly *23* of these. Mastitis is the most commonly reported health problem in the dairy industry. Nearly 25% of dairy cows in the United States get mastitis, one in twenty die from it.[46][47] Ruth, mother cow, one of the most sensitive, benevolent animals on this planet, endures a life of suffering and cruelty, and she's just one dairy cow out of millions confined in factory farm dairies.

And what about Ruth, the mother? She's carried each of her calves, felt and experienced life arriving, each one of them growing inside her over nine months to term. Each time Ruth gives birth she licks her beautiful calf clean, beholds it, admires it, smells it and checks it intimately, lovingly and guardedly — and it rises and stands up beside her. When she nurses it, its bond with its mother, and her powerful bond with it, is fully established.

Rhea Parsons continues, "Cows have strong maternal bonds and are attentive, protective and loving parents. When allowed, a mother cow may nurse her calf for as long as three years. The mother-child bond continues after weaning; mothers and their children remain close to each other for life."[48]

A calf craves its mother's milk, but that milk is destined instead for human consumption, so at an industrial dairy farm, Ruth's calf is separated from her and taken away, usually within just an hour or two after it is born. The experience is traumatic for each of these deeply feeling animals. The helpless newborn realizes it is being taken away from its mother, the one who is essential for its survival in this world. Ruth cries out because she knows her calf can't survive without her. Dairy cows will cry out for hours for their calves, until despondency becomes overwhelming, and resignation sets in. Since this is not her first calf and cows have very good memories, Ruth knows something that her newborn doesn't yet realize: they will never see each other again.

Imagine for a moment. Imagine you are a woman on the verge of giving birth, ready to become a mother, so ready, your breasts enlarged with the milk you will soon be nursing your baby with. Like Ruth, you have felt and experienced life arriving over nine months, growing inside you to term. You endure childbirth, releasing this life into this world. You hold your newborn, peer into its eyes as it finds focus, draw it to your chest, bonding in those precious moments.

Suddenly, you have your baby taken from you. You won't be able to nurse it from your aching breasts, providing it with your milk which is loaded with the vital and unique nutrients it needs right away to optimally develop its body, brain and immune system. Imagine realizing you will never see this baby — your child — ever again.

Ruth's calf, if female, may be given the opportunity to live a life similar to its mother's. If male, a small number will become bulls or veal calves, but most offspring will end up in industrial feedlots before going to slaughter.

Ruth's body and spirit have been stressed since day one and she is worn down. In a pastoral setting she could live for 20 years. But an industrial dairy farm is a far cry from a natural setting. Ruth is only four years old and her body is crippled — she is unable to stand, unable to carry on. Her milk production is waning. Yesterday she collapsed but workers were able to make her stand and milk her. Today, she will be kicked, beaten with a pipe or cane, or prodded and stabbed with pitchfork or penknife, or electrically shocked, or have a raging torrent of firehose water sprayed directly from just a few feet away into her face, nose and eyes — until workers are convinced that, on this day, she really can no longer rise. She will then be moved, which most often means chained to a fork lift and dragged across the cement floor and out into the yard.

A farm animal no longer able to get up and walk on their own is called a "downer." In most countries, "downed" animals are not allowed to be slaughtered for food, and Ruth would be killed to spare her this final agony, but as I write this, in the United States it remains common practice on factory farms to make every last cent of profit, and thus, to send downer cows to slaughter. So there in the yard she will remain, without being given a painkiller, scraped, bleeding, agonizing, possibly with a dislocated or broken leg from being dragged, often for hours, even overnight. Until a truck arrives onto which she will be hoisted, usually by forklift, for her final ride. At the slaughterhouse she will endure more of the same as they remove her from the truck and take her inside.

75% of downed animals in this country are factory farmed dairy cows.[49] A 2007 review revealed the number of downer cattle in the United States is close to 500,000 each year.[50] Ruth was just one of them. In 2006, milk producers "self-reported" that 14% of their dairy cows — one out of every seven — suffered lameness. Studies done in Wisconsin and Minnesota revealed it may be as high as 24.6%.[51] The incidence of lameness is much higher with factory farmed dairy cows than with pastured ones.

Factory farm dairies force these docile, sensitive animals to produce until the day they collapse and can no longer stand. They ruthlessly ring out every last cent of their value. They are used and abused until they are used up.[52]

Beef cattle tend to have a more natural life. Almost all beef cattle are pastured or "grass-fed" until around age two, when they become full-grown.

Will Harris owns and runs White Oak Pastures, a 3200-acre farm in Bluffton, Georgia.[53] His family has owned this farm for 152 years; his daughter manages it and his grandchildren will be the 6th generation on the land. When ownership was passed down to him, he continued to raise cattle but decided to do things differently. He told me, "I was a very Western alpha linear industrial farmer, a monoculture cattleman, and the first shiny object that came my way towards change was animal welfare, and that was what I focused on." He pastured his cattle applying Alan Savory's holistic planned grazing techniques, rotating them in a concentrated herd daily through newly paddocked field sections. Will also stopped using industrial

agriculture's synthetic nitrogen fertilizers on his fields because it was killing the microbial health of his soil. "The regenerative land management was a function of the animal welfare. Our pastures are better than they've ever been because we don't till them up, we don't use chemical fertilizer, we don't use pesticides. They're more teeming with life, more nutrient dense. The organic matter in our pastures has gone from less than a half of a percent to over five percent in fifteen years."[54]

Will notices that his cattle are healthier and happier than they've ever been. He raises his cattle without using hormones or other drugs. Antibiotics are used only to treat the occasional sick animal. His beef is superior and he gets a higher price for it. "You have to get a higher price for your meat because the cost of raising the animal is higher than in the industrial model. It is essential that you get a premium to recover the additional costs of production." Significantly, his input costs have been cut way down. He feels that the 26 bald eagles that now choose to reside on his property are testament to the ecological health of his farm.

Will is expanding his acreage, buying adjacent land from his neighbors who operate in the conventional industrial agriculture monocrop manner and are not doing nearly so well. Like Matt and Alyssa Kautz at Cottonwood Creek Farms, Will believes proper animal stewardship is when an animal is given the freedom and allowed to behave in its instinctive natural manner. "We don't just think animal welfare is not inflicting pain and discomfort," he says, "We think animal welfare is creating an environment in which they can express instinctive behavior. And it's a good life."[55]

Industrial animal agriculture's consolidation and control over slaughterhouses has put the 500,000 American livestock producers in a bind. There used to be thousands of regional slaughterhouses across the United States, but with the consolidation of the industry in recent decades, there are now just 13. Owned by four major operators, Tyson, Cargill, JBS, and National Beef, they process 80% of the animals.[56] These companies restrict the access of small and mid-size producers to processing, making it harder for them to compete.[57] Will Harris took a huge risk and built an abattoir on his farm. When it comes time to select his cattle for market, a few of the sturdiest are selected as breeding bulls, while the others are processed there. If unlike Will Harris, ranchers do not have access to a local small-scale slaughterhouse, no matter how well their grass-fed animals are raised, they must be sold at auction where there are only 4 major buyers.

97% of U.S. cattle are sold at these auctions and transported to factory farm feedlots where they will live out the final months of their lives crowded together side by side with thousands of other cows.[58]

You don't see any grass under-hoof in the feedlot pictured below. Here, cows —regardless of where they came from — are grain fed (also termed "conventionally fed") an unnatural diet of GMO soybeans or corn.

Cows are called ruminants because they have 4 chambered stomachs including a rumen that break down grass and absorb nutrients from it. There is nothing "conventional" about feeding a grass-eating animal something unsuitable for its digestive system. Grass doesn't have a chance to grow in feedlots and it is seldom trucked in. The system of factory farming is predicated on feeding animals industrial-agriculture-grown commodity crops. Growth hormones are added which help fatten them up to "optimal" market weight.

Dr. Fuhrman notes that corn-fed "cattle grow significantly faster compared with grass-fed cattle, but they are also profoundly unhealthy. A corn-fed cow loses its natural immune function, so to reduce its risk of developing bacterial infections, ranchers mix high doses of antibiotics into its food."[59] They stand day after day on the feedlot ground covered with four or more inches of their own waste, breathing in the acrid, ammonia fouled air. Previously healthy cattle can become ill and diseased in this environment, so the antibiotics are also necessary to keep them well.

Like the milk from factory farmed dairy cows, raising cattle on grain rather than grass changes the chemistry of their beef significantly, increasing the omega-6 inflammatory fats while decreasing levels of super-beneficial omega-3s. The ratio of omega-6s to omega-3s in grain-fed beef is about 7.5 to 1. In grass-fed beef it is a much healthier and desirable balance, almost a perfect balance for human consumption − around 1.5 to 1. Grass-fed beef also contains much higher levels of many important vitamins.

Feedlot operations are conduits to the high-speed slaughterhouses. Animals are slaughtered on the killing floor at increasing rates of speed.[60] Worker injuries are common and pre-slaughter stunning often inadequate. Animals at slaughter are exposed to the bacterial contaminants and pathogens carried in by other animals and shared with all passing through.[61] The majority of meat emerging from Big Ag slaughterhouses and packaged for distribution and sale contains measurable amounts of fecal matter, E. coli bacteria, and/or other pathogenic microbes.[62]

This is why, in many states, when you look at a restaurant menu, it is very likely that it will have a disclaimer on it like this: "Eating raw or undercooked fish, shellfish, eggs or meat increases the risk of foodborne illnesses, especially if you have certain medical conditions." That's good health advice, but it also protects the restaurant. If you order your meat rare or medium rare, i.e. "undercooked," and you get sick, even seriously ill from it, and take issue, the restaurant has a legal defense stating in effect, "We warned you."

A small percentage of pasture-raised grass-fed cattle, like Will Harris's, are not sent to these feedlots. They remain on pasture most of the year, foraging for healthy natural wild grasses and baled hay. They are sent to be processed at smaller regional slaughterhouses, which are far less virulent places. They will be slaughtered more humanely. This is 100% grass-fed pastured beef. Another term is "Grass-fed, grass-finished" beef. This is the beef you should ask for when you eat out or shop for home. Sales of grass-fed beef are increasing significantly as more and more people become aware of the health drawbacks of factory farmed meat and dairy. Certification by the *American Grassfed Association* assures you that pastured and grass-fed livestock is the highest standard for dairy, beef, pork, sheep, goats and chickens. Their website enables you to find certified producers whose livestock is American pasture raised, never confined to a feedlot or treated with hormones or antibiotics.[63]

Ranchers want to deliver their grass-fed livestock for processing in this manner. Its health value and the price they can get for it is much higher. However, the Big Ag stranglehold on slaughterhouses and meatpacking leaves many with no choice but to deliver their livestock to auction where it will be purchased at the lowest possible price and delivered to the feedlots. Currently, the American demand for grass-fed grass-finished beef so outweighs the marketed supply that most of the grass-fed beef sold in the United States is imported from Australia, New Zealand, Argentina, Brazil and other countries. Here is a handy guide, the *Meat, Eggs and Dairy Label Guide*,[64] to help you recognize meat labels and know what they mean. The website *Eatwild.com* lists the numerous health benefits of grass-fed grass-finished meat and dairy, and has a state-by-state directory of local farmers who sell directly to consumers.[65] Mark's Daily Apple site — *marksdailyapple.com* — is another.

Broiler chickens are chickens raised for their meat and **egg laying hen**s, called "layers," are valued for their eggs.

These egg layers living at the Stone Barns Center for Food & Agriculture in New York are heritage breeds. They move about confidently and well, and their body proportions are what you'd expect to see.

Their foraging is not limited to just this large enclosure. There is an open door on one side through which they can go outside to pasture or to an adjacent hen house lined with nesting areas where they can lay their eggs. When outside, these chickens will roam around, eating insects and scratching the soil with their claws, traversing several miles of distance

each day while fertilizing the soil with their droppings.

Chickens have distinct, individual personalities. Their self-awareness is akin to primates and other developed species. Their communication is complex. They have the self-control to hold out for greater rewards. Lori Marino, a senior scientist for The Someone Project, reports, "Chickens perceive time intervals and can anticipate future events. Like many other animals, they demonstrate their cognitive complexity when placed in social situations requiring them to solve problems... The birds are able to experience a range of complex negative and positive emotions, including fear, anticipation and anxiety."[66] They form friendships.

Wait a minute... *That one's* not a chicken... Stone Barns has Maremma sheepdogs who live with the chickens and the pigs to protect them at night from roaming coyotes, foxes and other skillful predators. At Stone Barns, all wildlife is revered and respected. Nothing is done to harm predators who are recognized as a natural part of the ecosystem. It may seem like the Maremmas are dozing most of the day, but they'll spring into action in a heartbeat. They remain on guard all night long making sure that nocturnal predators steer clear of the Stone Barns animals.

8.5 billion **broiler chickens** are raised in the United States each year. 99% of broiler chickens in America do not live like this.[67] And they don't look this way either.

On factory farms, broiler hens grow unnaturally large and shockingly misshapen. In 1965 a broiler chicken grew to an average weight of 3.48 pounds over 63 days, gaining a pound of weight every 18 days. In 2016, broiler chickens average a weight of 6.16 pounds at just 47 days, gaining a pound of body mass every 7.7 days.[68]

For the 99%, this is how it begins.

Genetically altered and selectively bred for extreme, rapid growth, their breasts grow vastly oversized while their skeletons, joints, muscles, heart, lungs, and internal organs can't keep up. The lower legs of these "Franken-chickens" are garishly huge — yet most can't support the weight of the rapidly bloating bodies above them. Most chickens endure chronic pain and crippling leg problems.

And this is how it ends:

Broiler chickens can be male or female. This one is Rebecca. She can no longer stand. Her hip joints can no longer support her body weight. The oversized chicken breasts you may see at a grocery store? That's what's weighing Rebecca down here.

John Webster, Professor Emeritus at the University of Bristol, says, "Broilers are the only livestock that are in chronic pain for the last 20% of their lives. They don't move around much... because it hurts their joints so much." For Professor Webster, the broiler industry is "the single greatest example of human inhumanity toward another animal."[69]

Factory farmed broiler chickens live crammed together on the floor of barns containing 20,000 to 100,000 or more. Barn lights are kept on which prohibits sleep and encourages excessive eating. This is where Rebecca has lived her entire life since arriving here as a chick.

These chickens spend their entire lives walking around on their own droppings. The concentrated ammonia sears their lungs causing respiratory ailments and corroding and burning their skin, causing painful abrasions and lesions. When they break down, no longer able to support their weight, they languish helplessly in their own waste, unable to move to get to food and water.[70] And no help will be coming. Rebecca will starve to death right in that spot you see her now. Daily, factory farm workers will walk through this barn picking up dead chickens and casting them into trashcans or the scoop of a trailing tractor.

When the barn is cleared and the chickens sent to slaughter, often the factory farmer doesn't even take the time, effort and modest expense to refresh the ground, and a whole new generation of chicks is introduced onto this searing, waste covered, abrasive, pestilent surface. Millions of American chickens suffer and die each year in these conditions never even making it to slaughter.[71]

Sara Shields of Humane Society International observes that, at six weeks old, these Franken-birds "still peep like baby chicks when they're slaughtered."[72]

The European Union has banned the import of American chicken since 1997. Factory farms and poultry processing facilities stateside are so virulent, that *after* poultry is processed, it is washed in chlorine or other chemical disinfectants. In her article, *No 'Dirty' American Chickens, Say British Food Safety Experts*, Eileen Guo writes that this practice is "banned under European food safety standards. In Europe, chicken is typically washed in cold water. According to standards set forth in a World Health Organization and UN Food and Agricultural report, disinfectants 'must not be used to mask poor hygiene conditions...' In the U.S., poultry is mostly raised in factory farms with birds crammed into small areas. This reduces cost for farmers but increases the likelihood of disease. The UK briefing paper cites that 97% of American chicken breast is contaminated with salmonella and E. Coli. In comparison, the European Union has higher standards for raising poultry, with legally mandated minimums for space, light, and ventilation provided to the birds. This is more expensive, but poultry that are raised in more space are less likely to fall sick and spread disease."[73]

This free-range, **egg-laying hen** is enjoying a sunny day, foraging about, pecking and scraping into the dirt and field grass, eating the insects it finds, enriching the soil with its droppings.

Because these hens are heritage breeds, their bodies have naturally evolved over centuries and are perfectly proportioned to survive in nature. They can roam for miles each day but will return to their coops when it is time to lay an egg. They are clean, adept at grooming their feathers, keeping them dry and well arranged. When establishing a pecking order and dominance hierarchy, a hen can stand up for herself or back down and retreat from conflict when she chooses to. So, when hens establish their groupings they rarely seriously injure one another.

Like Will Harris, Lou Preston also rotates his animals through his fields. In his case, it's sheep and then chickens. Here's what Lou Preston's mobile chicken coops look like at Preston Vineyards in the Russian River Valley of Sonoma, California.[74]

Lou Preston is best known for his wines. Mature vines like these produce lush grapes that, once harvested, blended and bottled become wines of heralded taste and complexity. These hens forage after bugs while fertilizing his fields and play a valuable role in enriching his soil. They produce flavorful, nutrient rich eggs coveted by restaurant chefs and popular at local outdoor farmer's markets and his farm store. They always sell out.

However, 97% of the 300 million layer hens in the United States have a far different existence. To begin with, these 300 million layer hens are the *survivors* who lived to see day two.

Industrial agriculture has no place for an additional 260 million chicks that are hatched each year in the United States. Chicks like these…

When these newborns are given a little squeeze on day one of their lives and found to be male, they are killed that day by being poured into garbage bags then suffocated, or electrocuted, or placed on a conveyor belt that deposits them into a grinder to be macerated while still alive.[75] These newborns in this photo along with 260 million others die in the United States each year.

When the hen survivors are delivered to factory farms, they are inserted in groups of around 10 into battery cages so small, that once they are grown, they can never fully extend their wings. They have little more room to move around on than the space inside a shoebox.[76]

These cages are stacked high in long rows, tens of thousands of birds filling long windowless barns where the light and temperature are controlled to maximize laying cycles.

In nature, chickens are tree-dwelling foragers who spend their time digging in the ground with their claws and beaks for insects and things of interest. They do not attack and obsessively peck at one another. Trapped in these cages hens often develop behaviors such as pecking at each other. If you look closely, you see what's left of their feathers, this after incessant conflict with one another, exacerbated by the frustrating lack of space and

because they are unable to ever retreat or flee to safety. Their beaks are often trimmed so that they won't peck each other to death. Hens also peck at themselves because mites are prevalent and cover them. The cages they are confined in are stacked atop one another in rows five to eight high. The urine and excrement from chickens above rain down incessantly on the ones below, irritating and scalding their skin. Their lungs fare no better as they breathe constant dust and dander mixed with the acrid piercing ammonia wafting up from their accumulating waste.

When a hen dies, its rotting corpse is often just left in with the other birds. This is how little care and compassion these birds receive.

Imagine for a moment. Imagine you are confined in a two-person jail cell, only there are six of you. You never leave the cell, you are unsupervised; you are bullied. You are repeatedly physically attacked, and you and your cellmates soon realize that no one on the outside will pay any attention, let alone come to help you. If you are injured, you will not receive medical attention. You can even be killed and there will be no recourse, no consequences for your attacker(s), except that they'll have to share the bloodied cell with your decaying corpse.

That is the horror, the situation those chickens in the photo above — that *tens of millions* of chickens — are experiencing right now as you read this. This very second. This one too.

It's all about the Golden Rule.

On Cottonwood Creek Farms chickens don't seriously injure one another. When there is conflict, when they are establishing a pecking order, the loser has space enough to withdraw and be left alone. The same holds true for the chickens at Stone Barns or at Preston Winery.

With regard to **ducks or geese** farmed to make foie gras, there are no humane examples to cite.

Ducks are water birds, spending their lives paddling in lakes, wading along waterways, foraging for food on river banks and in the water. They are generally monogamous, selecting mating partners in the fall whom they stay together with throughout the winter and spring mating season. They can swim away or take flight from a threat. When migrating, they can travel hundreds of miles a day.

The lives of well over 50 million ducks and geese end each year in foie gras factory-farms.[77][78] "Foie gras" is a French term and translated, means "fat liver." Paté de foie gras is basically the fattened liver of a duck or goose made into a paste. So how does one's liver get "fat?"

Factory farmed ducks and geese spend a large portion of their lives confined in large barns, prevented from going into the water which their bodies need and were born for, prevented from accessing sunlight, the wind, or any of their natural habitat. These birds won't fly through the open sky or migrate anywhere except perhaps to the opposite side of their barn enclosure, from one squalid patch of dirt to another.

Then, one day, things get even worse. They are taken to a special barn where each of them will be confined in small group or in individual cages for the final stage, the "completion of fattening." There, two or three times a day, a worker will grab their heads and force a tube down their soft, sensitive extended throats to force-feed them. To prevent them from vomiting, the tube is inserted down the length of their long throats to their stomach. The volume of mushy food forced into them is a much larger quantity than they'd ever ingest themselves. It is food their body has a very difficult time digesting, and, in attempting to cleanse their insides, their livers become distressed, dis-eased and swollen. Each duck will be force-fed this way every day for 12 to 15 days during which time their livers will swell *6 to 10 times* normal size. It enlarges to reach 8–9% of the duck's body weight, taking up nearly half of their abdominal and chest cavity. It is estimated that 1,250,000 foie gras ducks die before this process ends.[79]

When something is wrong in your digestive tract your body makes you aware of it. It's discomforting, and when something is acutely wrong, it's agonizing. Imagine your liver working so hard that it starts to swell. Like an inflating football, it swells to a size where it takes over most of the space your stomach and digestive tract occupy. You have difficulty breathing because it is expanding against your lungs. Meanwhile, your stomach presses back as it is stuffed with a mass of mush multiple times a day. The final weeks of each foie gras duck or goose's life is spent living in abject misery, a hell on earth.

• • •

With regard to **animals farmed and raised for their fur** there are also no humane examples to cite. 85% of those raised for their fur are bred on fur factory farms, the other 15% are trapped in the wild.

Jo-Anne McArthur is a masterful investigative photographer. Some of her photographs are published in her two books, Captive *and* We Animals.[80] *Her images are as heart wrenching as they are engaging, beautiful in spite of the horror they often reveal.*

FUR FARM
by Jo-Anne McArthur

Getting to our destination is a trek. We can't rock up to the front door and park. The security team and I stash our cars along rarely used country roads. If we are numerous enough, we can spare a driver, who stays in the car and picks us up when signaled. Tonight though, we'll walk several kilometers through forests and brush and crop fields. We're obliged to take circuitous routes so we're out of sight of car headlights and human eyes, hidden by the trees and long grass. In the fall, towering corn stalks block our line of sight entirely and we rely, as we so often do, on our GPSs to get to our destination. The farms are often in out-of-the-way places because the industry doesn't want you to see, hear or smell what's happening in their facilities.

The moon is my constant companion during those walks. Even on a cloudy night, she peeks momentarily from between clouds, reassuring me that this is but a moment in time and that for most of history, we have not incarcerated others in this way or in such numbers. And that this too shall pass.

Typically, we work at a farm from midnight or later — until 5am.

My adrenaline keeps me focused on safety and the task soon at hand, but under the big sky I also remember that this moment is a blip in time and a blight on the history of humanity, and that our current practices towards animals will end. My job in this place, at this time, is to help speed the end of fur farming.

Being immersed in the quiet of night and the murmurings of nature is the "best" part of investigative work. There is no other good part, except perhaps for leaving successfully, images tucked safely away in my camera.

I'm an investigator of animal industries. This work has taken me around the world now to almost sixty countries. I enter these places of exploitation and document what I see with my camera, and I show those photos to the world. I try to get those photos as far as they can reach because they're important. They're historical. They expose the egregious and wholly unnecessary cruelty to the billions of animals we eat, wear, experiment on, and use for entertainment, work, and religious practice. I say the photos are important but what I mean is that the individuals in the images are important. Their suffering is unimaginable, as real as the suffering you or I might experience in a similar state of deprivation and control. My hope is that the pictures will illuminate how we treat these billions of animals, and why it has to change.

My investigative work has included fur farms across North America and Europe. This is an industry that, simply put, must die. I have spent months of my life at these places. Though I am not religious, I would still describe them as godforsaken. They are devoid of anything good, or natural, or kind. They are built to wring maximum profit from as many suffering individuals within as little space and with as little effort as possible.

I visit these hideous places at night because my camera and I are simply not welcome during the day. If I were to be invited, the farm would likely be cleaned of excrement and bodies ahead of time; half-cannibalized animals would be removed from cages and killed or separated into a shed into which I would not be allowed. They would tell me there's nothing to see in there or perhaps that the shed is empty. Unsuspected and uninvited, one can see what fur farms look and smell like when farmers don't have to make a good impression for the media.

There are so many smells to take in during those walks. Once it was a field alternating between lavender and nettle. Ouch. Most times, our noses are overcome with the dankness of a forest floor in spring, the ripeness of fertile soil in summer and all that grows from it — fields of potatoes, peas, pumpkin, and that musty smell unique to tomato plants.

The sensory sweetness comes to an end before we reach our destination, however. Fur farms announce themselves before we see them. The odour of this mink farm is so strong that our eyes immediately begin to water. Mink farms smell of excrement, and fox farms smell of excrement and a bright skunk-like scent (their marking scent). The smell is like a slap, and it makes us slow our pace.

With all the investigations I've taken part in, it's endlessly disturbing how close these fur farms are to the wild and rightful habitats of the animals. Beyond the putrefaction of their own waste below them, these animals can smell and see the forest just beyond their reach. That proximity feels particularly perverse and cruel.

It's time for additional caution, and all of our faculties are focused on potential danger. For us, dangers are not the forest animals or the night. Dangers, for us, are people.

Countless times, we have had to leave before we began. Barking dogs. Damn barking dogs! Don't they realize we are there to help their kin? Motion lights. Alarms. Cameras. And so, we take our time. Multiple nights worth of time, in fact. For safety. So that we can enter and exit

without leaving a trace. People sometimes call what I do "breaking and entering," but I have never broken anything. I have climbed walls, scaled fences, and walked through open and unlocked doors.

This family of mink kits is clustered around the body of their dead mother.

Individuals kept in cages, including human beings, will eventually fight one another — for food, space or dominance. The confinement that mink endure is especially difficult because in the wild they are solitary creatures, spending most of their time in or near water. At farms, up to ten of them live in extremely small cages with no access to water apart from small nozzles for drinking.

Each of these white mink has an injury due to fighting and we see only the remains of another. Mink fight and cannibalize one another in closed quarters.

I do this work in part because I am compassionate and sensitive. I navigate the world in an empathetic way and I want to alleviate the harm that is caused and suffered in the world. For that reason, it's probably particularly hard for someone like me to enter a fur farm. To get face to face with the suffering we cause feels like I am confronting the depths of our depravity. The instinct is to run away from it instead of looking at it. Tolstoy famously advised to get closer to suffering, to see it, and to alleviate it. I am there. Close. Close enough to document twitching whiskers, torn ears, cannibalized kits, wide-eyed fear. But I can't alleviate it. That is the most painful part of my work. I do this work in the hopes of ending this cruelty, to reduce the number of animals in farms from millions to zero. But I can't help the animals I photograph from one cage to the next. It's this reality that causes post-traumatic stress in so many front-line photographers. We are trying to help, but we can't help *them*.

From cage to cage, I photograph. I try to stay calm so as not to additionally rouse the animals, who are already feeling panicked by this unusual event of lights shining on them in the middle of the night, and the smell of strangers. I work quietly and quickly. With the habit of using words, I utter apologies under my breath, a useless attempt at alleviating their pain and my own.

A tiny cage is crammed with a mother and nine rapidly growing kits. Mink are wide-ranging, semi-aquatic solitary animals. We could hardly have devised a more effective way to remove them so fully from anything natural. A fox has chewed off her tail. These families of raccoon dogs cower. This fierce mama mink shrieks at us, covering her kits with her body, circling and watching and circling and standing and circling and screeching. I move from one cage to the next, and to the next, and there are so many — too many.

These mink huddle under the mash of food that is placed atop their cage once-a-day. There are a lot of deaths at this farm because they've not yet separated the grown kits, so they're all cramped and fighting. This family of ten are now eight.

All I want to do is leave, but I employ my willpower with each step forward and continue documenting until I have seen the entire farm.

If there is any doubt about the death rates at this place, the "dead pile" outside the front proves the misery here. The sick consolation is that these young didn't live a year in a cage only to be gassed and skinned. Fuck all of this and anyone who can be so blatantly, inexcusably cruel by making a living off the misery of others.

I took photos of the skinning machine. It's in the barn and I took the photo through the window. Next to the machine the walls are covered in soft porn; women posing half naked with what appears to be fur.

There's a lot I don't understand.

We leave when the work is done, having documented as much as we possibly can. Sometimes we have to make a quick departure; a security team member has given us a code yellow through our walkie-talkie earbuds, or worse, a code red, which means, "Get the hell out, we're in trouble."

On our walk back to the car, the early morning dew begins its slow but inevitable soak through our clothes, and though it makes me cold, I don't mind so much. We're a bit numb anyway from the experience, and we know that we'll have the car heaters on soon enough. Most of us don't wear waterproof pants because they make such loud, swishy noises when we walk, and we try to keep the clothing we wear during investigations as noise-free as possible — not only so that we can be audibly attuned to our surroundings, but it would be horrible to rouse a nearby light sleeper due to the swishing of five pairs of waterproof pants, thus ruining an entire investigation and endangering us to physical or legal retributions. No swishy pants!

The fur industry *is* dying. Norway, a huge fur-producing nation, is the most recent European country to ban production by 2025. Bans continue worldwide, slowly but surely, and the practice is dwindling. Unfortunately, some countries such as my own, Canada, continue to subsidize this unnecessary industry. People are becoming aware of the cruelties and the green washing, however, and successful corporate pressure campaigns have meant that hundreds of fashion brands are now fur-free.

I have hope that I will see the end to fur farming in my lifetime. Alongside so many others who believe in justice, compassion, and respect for all animals, it's a goal I'll work towards.

People inevitably ask me how I do what I do. How I continue to endure the sights, smells, and crushing realities of these industries. It's because I hope — stubborn, enthusiastic hope. And when you have your eye on the prize, you need endurance as well, and I have that in abundance. Animal suffering is an emergency — yes — but emancipation is a marathon, not a sprint. Hope paces me. Good people, community and solidarity pace me. And my memories of all the animals I have met pace me.

I also think that people are fundamentally good. That, given the opportunity to care — and to be empowered to care — they will.

• • •

Animals at factory fur farms are not given names. I named this one. This mink's name is Roger.

The other 15% of fur-bearing animals including coyotes, bobcats, foxes and beavers are trapped in the wild. They are strangled by snares, drowned in Conibear traps, or have a limb crushed in a vicious steel-jaw leghold trap.

In *Animal Cruelty and the Importance of Ending the Commercial Fur Trade*, Rhiann Moore writes, "Trapping is a deeply violent act... the animals suffer absolute horrors while in these traps. While waiting for a hunter to come and kill them the animals will struggle with everything they have to get out of the traps. Often the captured animals break their teeth, chew off their paws or break bones to try and break free. They also suffer from dehydration, blood loss, hypothermia and more. Trapping is entirely unselective, often capturing animals who are companions or endangered creatures... The practice causes terrible suffering for any animal trapped."[81] Over 100 countries have banned steel-jaw leghold traps. In the United States, not only are these traps still legal, but they remain a trapper's preferred tool for capturing and killing millions of creatures each year for the fur market.[82]

Veal calves[83] and farm-raised fish,[84] in the Notes section, fare no better.

IV

So. Why should we care? For the most part, these are not animals living in the wild and they are not pets. They are brought into the world and raised to maturity for a specific purpose — either to produce something we consume such as pork, foie gras, milk and eggs, or wear.

I, for one, care deeply. Subjecting another living creature to willful, deliberate sustained cruelty is never okay. Not one animal and certainly not hundreds of millions.

Awareness can be troubling, even painful. It can be excruciating to witness willful cruelty and suffering, let alone begin to realize how widespread it is. Awareness however, is a package deal. One which includes experiencing the beauty and interrelatedness of everything in this exquisite world — a world that each one of us has the unique and extraordinary opportunity to experience — during this lifetime in human form.

For the philosopher Joanna Macy, our ability to witness, to "suffer with," lives at the very heart of compassion. As she writes so beautifully in *World as Lover, World as Self*, "In owning this pain, and daring to experience it, we learn that our capacity to 'suffer with' is the true meaning of compassion. We begin to know the immensity of our heart-mind, and how it helps us to move beyond fear. What had isolated us in private anguish now opens outward and delivers us into wider reaches of our world as lover, world as self.

"The truth of our inter-existence, made real to us by our pain for the world, helps us see with new eyes. It brings fresh understanding of who we are and how we are related to each other and the universe. We begin to comprehend our own power to change and heal. We strengthen by growing living connections with past and future generations, and our brother and sister species."[85]

We can bring an end to factory farming.

You can make a significant impact. How is that possible? Here's how.

. . .

Realize what factory farming is and how widespread it has become.

Most of us aren't aware of the appalling conditions these animals are raised in, the lifetimes of pain and suffering they endure.

Factory farms are also known as CAFOs, Concentrated Animal Feeding Operations. This name says it all. It doesn't contain the word "farm" because these are not farms. They are concentration camps for animals, a living testament to our inhumanity. Nothing less.

By the 1970s, large corporations like Tyson, Smithfield and Cargill, encouraged and incentivized the growth of factory farms nationwide. They were able to produce more meat and dairy products for less money. Corporate executives were unconcerned with animal welfare, and they were equally unconcerned with the hundreds of thousands of small family farmers they were forcing out of business, a necessary step as these corporations took control of American meat and dairy production. Livestock farmers wanting to remain in business had to sign a contract with them and operate under their control, reducing them to little more than tenant farmers. Working every day, deeply in debt from the half-million and million dollar loans they've been required to take out to build the factory farm confinement facilities, contractually obligated to upgrade them when required by their corporate overseer, and with little or no control over either their operating costs or the market price of their "product," they net a yearly pittance for all their work.[86] The few immensely powerful corporations controlling and profiting from factory-farmed animal agriculture in the U.S. have even managed to shift responsibility for the enormous environmental pollution and degradation these factory farms are causing, away from themselves and onto the contract farmers. The corporations know that at a future point in time should government demands for environmental clean-up manifest and have to be acted upon, these farmers will not be financially able to undertake these remediation costs — but ultimately, they won't have to. Those costs, akin to Superfund clean-up sites, will be passed on to taxpayers.

Meanwhile, Big Ag has expanded swiftly, gaining control of domestic meat and dairy processing and distribution as well. And they are introducing and expanding factory farming worldwide.

Big Ag has implemented a long-term campaign of confusion. It takes great care and spends hundreds of millions of dollars designing and mounting huge marketing, public relations, and advertising campaigns in an effort to hide all of this from you. And successfully. A 224-page report published in April, 2017, *Animal Welfare: Issues and Opportunities in the Meat, Poultry and Egg Markets in the U.S.*, reveals that 58% of U.S. consumers "are more concerned about animal welfare than they were just a few years ago," however only one out of three consider themselves well-informed about the treatment of animals.[87]

The industry, when doing damage control in responding to the latest damning undercover video or investigative report, suggests that the undeniable cruelty and suffering revealed is an aberrant situation from a particularly onerous farm, an industry outlier. Wrong. That videotape, almost invariably, documents routine conditions commonplace on factory farms. The treatment of animals revealed is not that of rogue, sadistic workers. Excessively brutal? Certainly, some are. But the factory farming system itself is designed to optimize profit, every last penny, so these workers — underpaid, overworked and laboring in dangerous, physically demanding, pestilent workplaces — are tasked to deal with an overwhelming number of animals. This is institutional. This is the way factory farming operations are *designed*, and the manner in which they are run.

A 2017 poll revealed that 70% of respondents now "have some discomfort with the way animals are used in the food industry" and 69% feel that "factory farming of animals is one of the most important social issues in the world today."[88]

Now you know.

So...

For Joseph Mercola, D.O., an osteopathic physician and best-selling author, the choice is clear: "While CAFOs promote antibiotic-resistant disease, traditional farming practices combat it. At small, regenerative and diversified farms, where pigs, hens and cattle are raised together in a sustainable way, there are many reasons why disease is kept to a minimum, even without the use of antibiotics in animal feed." Farms like Cottonwood Creek. When animals have more space to move around they are heartier, when they are weaned at a later age they have more fully developed immune systems. Exposure to the sun is a natural sanitizer, and the mud pigs wallow in is a natural anti-parasitic.[96]

Purchase only meat and dairy products from animals that have *never* been treated with antibiotics or hormones, animals that are humanely raised, pastured or free range, and grass-fed. Grass-fed grass-finished is optimal. A FoodPrint infographic, *A Tale of Two Cows* — well worth viewing — is linked to this endnote.[97] These animals are much safer to eat.

They are far more nutritious as well. Pasture-raised animals contain more vitamins and enzymes and higher fatty acids. They contain 50% more vitamin A; they are significantly richer in omega-3 fats, which are vitally important for your health and longevity; and they are produced in an environmentally friendly manner as opposed to factory farms whose pollution is devastating the environment. Eggs from pastured chickens contain three times more vitamin E, twice the omega-3, seven times more beta-carotene, and 1/3 less cholesterol.[98] And as Matt and Alyssa Kautz will tell you, the meat of pasture-raised animals is more tender and tastes much better as well.

Find healthy food.

Source healthy, sustainably and ethically raised meat and dairy products from small local family farms, regenerative farmers and other suppliers. Over 90% of the chicken or pork available in restaurants and markets is from factory farms, so you need to learn where to shop.

Here are links to resources that will help you locate healthy organic or regenerative produce and humanely raised pastured meat and dairy, as well as compare products in your supermarket.

- localharvest.org can help you source organic and sustainably grown foods including farmers' markets and family farms in your area.[99]

- The Cornucopia Institute's homepage has a Scorecards tab which provides health scorecards on cereals, dairy, eggs, grains, pet foods and a variety of products and brands: cornucopia.org [100]
- The Environmental Working Group's (EWG) Food Scores site rates over 80,000 foods found on supermarket shelves based on 3 criteria: nutritional value, concerns about ingredients and contaminants, and the degree and type of processing. There is also a home furnishings guide and a tap water database. A free phone app enables you to scan bar codes while shopping to check a product's rating and compare it with dozens of similar products. Ewg.org/foodscores [101]
- A Greener World's search tool enables you to find stores in your area that sell grass-fed high-welfare-managed meat, dairy, and other products. [102]
- The Center For Food Safety has a free phone app, the True Food Shoppers Guide, that lets you immediately identify whether or not a food product contains GMO (also referred to as GE, "genetically engineered") ingredients. The site also has a guide to avoiding GMO food, and information on the dangers of GMO / GE foods. [103]
- The American Society for the Prevention of Cruelty to Animals' (ASPCA) Meat, Eggs and Dairy Label Guide lists certification labels and defines what they mean. [104]
- This endnote is a contact list of other groups and organizations to help you identify and locate healthy delicious food. [105]

These sites and apps will inform you of how to read product labels carefully as manufacturers often make them deliberately misleading. The Food Label Guide is also a quick easy reference to find out what a food label means. [106]

Let your store manager know what you are looking for and cannot find. If the store is part of a larger supermarket or discount chain, the manager will pass customer comments up the line. I have worked with supermarket chains and mass merchants, and I can attest that they take customer feedback seriously because they realize you have shopping choices and, in a competitive marketplace, they value and want to keep your business.

Shop around. Once you have found where you can buy humanely raised, antibiotic and hormone free meat and dairy, and organic fruits and vegetables, shop there.

Natural Grocers is a great example of a grocery chain that is focused on natural and organic products. Their 154 stores in 19 states (all west of the Mississippi River) are among the healthiest you can shop. None of the meat, dairy or eggs they sell is factory farmed. All meat is pasture raised, and hormone and antibiotic free. They emphasize 100% grass-fed beef. As stated on their website, "Cattle must have access to pasture, and poultry are required to have access to the outdoors and ample space to express natural behaviors while they are inside."[107] The same high standards apply to dairy products. Natural Grocers customers get all the benefits from animals raised "as nature intended — dairy that is better for you, the animals, the farmer and the environment." In addition, grocery products they stock do not contain artificial colors, flavors, preservatives or sweeteners. All of their produce is USDA certified organic. "Our customers and employees do not have to worry about commingling, cross-contamination, or figuring out which variety of produce is organic and which is conventional. It is all organic."[108]

Whole Foods, PCC Community Markets, The Good Earth, Erewhon Natural Foods Markets, MOM's Organic Markets, many co-ops and independent health food stores such as the 225 in the Independent Natural Food Retailers Association[109] also stock whole healthy food items. There are many more.

What about if you live in a "food desert?"

A food desert is typically a low-income, urban area or a less population-dense rural region characterized by a near complete lack of available healthy food options. You can find out if you live in one by visiting the interactive map on the USDA.gov site.[110] The *Food Insecure Children* section of the *The State of Obesity* site states, "More than 29 million Americans live in 'food deserts,' meaning they do not have a supermarket or supercenter within a mile of their home if they live in an urban area, or within 10 miles of their home if they live in a rural area, making it challenging to access healthy, affordable food."[111] 55% of the zip codes in America are food deserts. For Dr. Fuhrman, "When grocery stores, farmers' markets, and other healthy food providers aren't available, the corner store or fast food restaurant becomes the primary source of nutrition, particularly for people who don't own a car... They sell commercial foods that create health problems. Imagine going into your local corner store and finding that every item on the shelf is unsafe for prolonged human consumption. That is the stark reality for more than 29 million Americans and 8 million children."[112]

If you live in a food desert, a starting point is to:

- Use the site resources above to find out where the closest healthy food is.
- Eat more vegetables and fruits. Make vegetables (cooked or raw) a greater portion of your meals. Beans, peas, lentils, seeds and nuts are all good.
- Prepare your meals using whole food ingredients.
- Reduce the portions of meat you eat when you eat meat and design one meal each day that skips it entirely.
- Reduce your dairy consumption.
- Significantly reduce consumption of processed foods and oils, desserts, sugary sweets, soft drinks and fast food.

These online resources, in addition to helping you source healthy food, can be your connection to others who are improving their well-being by taking the same journey. It is easier when making changes to achieve a healthier lifestyle if you have the support of friends, family, or others heading in the same direction. You can find this kind of advice and support online on these sites.

When enjoying casual fast dining, eat at restaurant chains like Chipotle and Panera that make every effort to purchase humanely raised animal products. Patronize eateries that do the same and feature locally sourced, farm to table food.

When you order a meal out and aren't sure, ask whether their meat and dairy are organic and free range or factory-farmed. Is their fish wild caught or farm-raised? Do not order farm-raised fish. If your server cannot say that the meat or diary ingredients are from humanely raised animal sources, order something else that is.

For decades, the large chain fast food drive-thru restaurants have been factory farm's most loyal and steadfast customers, a virtual pipeline from the factory farm to you and from industrial agriculture to you. And far too often for regular fast food customers, the connection extends one link further — from you to illness, disease then your doctor. Reverend Michael Bernard Beckwith, founder of the Agape International Spiritual Center, has a name for this. When you are driving along a road where numerous fast food restaurants are clustered, you are driving down "Death Row."

This is what makes Chipotle so unique and special.

Steve Ells once had a food-sourcing problem. In 2015, Chipotle found out that one of its pork suppliers was not raising pork in compliance with Chipotle's required animal care standards, so Chipotle dropped them. Steve Ells then discovered that the factory-farmed dominance of the American pork industry was so near complete, that it was now impossible for Chipotle to source the quantity of humanely raised pork it needed. Rather than compromise its core values, Chipotle removed pork from its menus at more than 1500 restaurants — and for a prolonged period of time — despite the fact that carnitas was one of their popular menu items.

Imagine Steve Ells' strength of character and his core resolve. In the ultra-competitive fast food arena, he risked a mass exodus of customers to Taco Bell, Del Taco, El Pollo Loco or other chain restaurants operating without comparable concern at their executive level regarding the humane treatment of the animals they source for food. In a hyper-competitive industry where "food fashion" can shift quickly, Steve Ells had Chipotle steadfastly adhere to its values.

Chipotle customers, like myself, tend to be loyal and aware, informed and issue-oriented. And we remained Chipotle customers. And DuBreton, North America's largest pork producer, agreed to raise 300,000 pigs in a humane manner.[113] DuBreton changed a significant part of its operation to supply changing customer demand for healthier, antibiotic free, humanely raised pork — thanks to a company like Chipotle who gets it, whose mandate, whose corporate DNA insists on it.[114] This is not just a reflection of the compassion and caring of Steve Ells. This is also a demonstration of his courage.

If Chipotle can source healthy, ethically raised food for its 1,900 restaurants, it reveals that other national chains operating on that scale are not unable, but rather unwilling and uninterested in changing. When you learn that the food being offered to you at a drive-thru or sit-down restaurant comes from a factory farm, make that meal there your last one.

. . .

Another compassionate action you can take is: Eat less meat.

If you want to find out in less than a minute or two how many animals' lives you will be saving by reducing your meat consumption, visit the Meat-Calculator, a quick and easy way to learn how it all adds up for you based on your personal diet: blitzresults.com/en/meat/ [115]

There are so many easy adjustments to make to eat less meat: Make some meals meat-free. For example, just going Meat-free on Mondays cuts your meat consumption by nearly 15%. Meatless Monday is a global campaign.[116] Another increasingly popular idea is VB6, "Vegan Before 6."

Reduce the serving sizes of meat and dairy that you eat at each meal, use less sausage or meat balls in your spaghetti, less cheese or meat on your pizza, or select vegetable centered dishes like veggie stir-fries, substituting in more of the healthy food your body needs: delicious vegetables, fruits, nuts and whole grains.

More and more of us are doing just that — a lot more of us. By mid-2018, over 530,000 people signed this pledge posted by the global activism group, Avaaz: "As a citizen concerned about animal welfare, climate change, and biodiversity, I pledge to eat less meat (or no meat at all!), and encourage workplaces, schools, supermarkets, and restaurants to join in helping spread this critical culture change more widely. This will help animals, the planet, and my health, and contribute to keeping our planet safe for future generations."[117]

Consumers in Great Britain are increasingly choosing to eat meat-free dinners. In January 2018, 29% of British evening meals contained no meat or fish.[118] 57% of consumers in Germany as well as 55% in Poland and 45% in both France and Italy now regularly choose to have meat-free days.[119] Nearly 30% of Brazilians polled in 2018 said that they were either reducing or eliminating meat consumption.[120]

Processed meats tend to be the least healthy for you. The World Health Organization confirmed that eating bacon, hot dogs, sausage and other meats processed with nitrates and nitrites increases your risk of cancer.[121] In terms of cancer risk, processed meats are now ranked in the same category as cigarettes and asbestos.

In the Physicians Committee for Responsible Medicine blog, Neal Barnard, M.D., writes, "In the United States, researchers studied Seventh-day Adventists, a religious group that is remarkable because, although nearly all members avoid tobacco and alcohol and follow generally healthful lifestyles, about half of the Adventist population is vegetarian, while the other half consumes modest amounts of meat. This fact allowed scientists to separate the effects of eating meat from other factors. Overall, these studies showed significant reductions in cancer risk among those who avoided meat."[122] [123]

countries that consume the highest levels of dairy products have among the highest rates of osteoporosis.[137] Doctors David S. Ludwig and Walter C. Willett concluded after an extensive research study, published in 2013 in the Pediatrics Journal of the American Medical Association, "Throughout the world, bone fracture rates tend to be lower in countries that do not consume milk compared with those that do. Moreover, milk consumption does not protect against fracture in adults, according to a recent meta-analysis."[138] Another study, the Harvard Nurses' Health Study involving 72,000 women over 18 years, arrived at a similar conclusion.[139] A British study of over 100,000 people spanning 20 years determined that high milk intake "was linked to higher mortality in some men and women."[140]

Fortunately, we now have an expanding array of alternatives to dairy. One third of consumers now state a preference for plant-based milks such as almond, soy, oat, and coconut milks, and sales have grown dramatically. From 2011 to 2015, while the total milk market shrank by more than $1 billion, almond milk sales grew 250%.[141] From 2000 to 2016, American milk consumption decreased nearly 22% as consumption of non-dairy plant-based milk alternatives increased by triple digits.[142] According to 2018 mid-year data, sales of non-dairy milk the previous 12 months increased 9% to $1.6 billion.[143] Milk sales dropped 6% in the same timeframe.[144]

The global plant-based milk market will exceed $16 *billion* in sales in 2018, up from $7.4 billion in 2010[145] and is projected to increase to $34 billion by 2024[146] — an extraordinary shift based on consumer purchasing choices.

However, *at the same time*, retail sales of organic grass-fed milk and dairy products continue to increase, from $1.2 billion in 2002 to $5.5 billion in 2014. Consumer demand for grass-fed organic milk has increased to the point that, according to a USDA Market News report, despite the increase in certified organic cows in the United States from 2000 to 2008, "milk processors have informed customers that they can't meet demands for organic milk a number of times since the organic dairy sector gained traction with consumers."[147]

In a time of lax USDA oversight, larger industrial dairies are trying to game the system by labeling their milk "organic." Before buying milk make sure it is grass-fed organic and check a brand's health rating on the Cornucopia Institute's Organic Dairy Scorecard.[148]

Compassionate informed consumers are changing this industry. Join us. If you drink cow's milk, consume organic milk from humanely raised pastured grass-fed cows.

Commit to yourself, right now, that you will no longer condone or support animal cruelty.

Tell yourself that animal cruelty and suffering does not align with your values, what you believe in, or what you stand for.

When you stop supporting factory farms, you are no longer enabling the horrendous animal cruelty and suffering on them. You are also no longer supporting one of the most environmentally polluting and toxic industries on the planet. And you are no longer supporting one of the world's biggest bullies — an industry that condones, even incentivizes, factory farm development in some of the poorest communities around this country such as Duplin, North Carolina, creating and exacerbating serious health issues for large numbers of the people living there. People like Sherneka Johnson and Sky Smith, and J'vion, Jemarion, Jennifer and Corey Dudley.

The industry would like you to believe that factory farming is necessary to "feed the world," to supply an increasing global demand for animal products, while the reality is: it is *not necessary*.

All of the horrendous suffering inflicted upon billions of factory-farmed animals in the United States each year can be ended *if Americans cut their meat demand by half*. Paleoclimatologist, Maureen Raymo and her colleagues at Columbia University's Earth Institute, published a study on December 5, 2017, revealing "that switching from today's factory farm model to pasture-raised cows could support nearly half of America's current beef consumption." And that, "This changeover would reduce the nation's water use by 24% and slash fertilizer use by 28%. It would cut carbon emissions by two-thirds, saving approximately 590 million tons of carbon dioxide equivalent from entering earth's atmosphere each year."[149]

In a thorough analysis, *Eating Meat: Constants and Changes*, based on his book, Vaclav Smil finds that factory farming will no longer be necessary *if Americans cut their meat demand by 30%*. He projects that shifting to entirely pastured meat production based on truly sustainable grazing — on existing pastures, with forages augmented by food crop and highly nutritious crop processing residues — could supply close to 70% of today's meat consumption. Because "innovations and productivity improvements alone cannot prevent further increases in already significant environmental burden of meat production," the 30% shortfall will require us to moderate our meat consumption.[150]

And the welcome news is that we are already moving in that direction.

Americans consume on average about 209 pounds of meat per year, while a "wealth of evidence confirms" that less than 100 pounds is "compatible with good health and high longevity." Vaclav Smil notes that, "In the U.S., where beef consumption has been already in long-term decline, extraordinarily high rates of overweight and obesity, accompanied by enormous waste of food, offer a perfect combination of reasons for greatly reduced meat consumption."[151]

We must move faster because the global warming time clock is ticking. We can do this. If, like meerkats, each one of us does our part.

If some of the meerkats ran away from the Cape Cobra, leaving fewer of them to challenge it, the snake, insufficiently distracted or threatened, would strike and kill a meerkat and devour it. Days later, it would return to strike another, or enter a bolt hole for its fill of the young. Before long that meerkat colony would cease to exist.

Each meerkat knows what needs to be done and does its part. If you travel to South Africa, you'll see — meerkats are still around.

. . .

Purchasing healthy nutritious organic or regenerative produce and pastured meat and dairy products will save you money.

Time out. Hold on a minute. How is this claim possible?

As you explore this you may wonder, "How can I budget organic fruit and vegetables or humanely raised meat and dairy since they are more expensive?"

The answer is: In several ways.

Meat is one of the most expensive food items. Processed foods tend to be costly as well. By eating smaller portions of both, or eating them less frequently, you can balance out the higher cost of buying healthier grass-fed and pastured meat and organic produce.

Protein sources like organic vegetables, nuts, legumes and grains are less expensive than meat so making them a greater portion of your diet will also save you money. Dr. Fuhrman cites from his family's experience that, "Frequently, the healthiest foods in the world, such as thick green leaves

— kale, collards, mustard greens and different varieties of cabbages — are affordable and also keep for weeks if they are refrigerated or kept in a cool place."[152]

A recent French study compared the cost of a "standard" weekly shopping basket for a family of 4 to a "flexitarian" basket, which consisted of 2/3 vegetable proteins and 1/3 animal proteins. Compared to the "standard" basket, the flexitarian option included 31% less meat, 40% less fish, 69% less high fat, salt or sugar processed foods, and 46% less volume of products based on refined flours. It included 95% more vegetables, cereals and legumes. The vegetables in the flexitarian basket included nearly 50% organic or regeneratively grown produce. *The cost of the flexitarian basket was 21% less.*[153]

More and more of us understand this.

Build some meals around vegetables, not around meat. Shift gradually. Americans consume, on average, 3600 calories a day, which is far more than the USDA recommendation of 1,600 to 2,000 for a sedentary adult female and 2,000 to 2,600 for a sedentary adult male. Eating the right types of calories and fewer of them will improve your health and save you money.[154]

You can get all the protein your body needs from non-meat and dairy foods.

While per item, regenerative or organic produce is more expensive, as is grass-fed meat and free-range eggs, the French study reveals that, in the context of your overall food spending, it can be cheaper.

For Ocean Robbins of the Food Revolution, the *10 Secrets for Eating Healthy on a Budget (Yes, It Is Possible!)*[155] include creating a weekly meal plan and making a grocery list before you shop, buying locally grown and in season as much as possible, and choosing the healthiest inexpensive foods.

Traditionally, consumer food purchase decisions have been motivated by three drivers: price, taste and convenience. However, in 2015, a study by Deloitte and the Grocery Manufacturer's Association found that for over *half* of consumers, four new "evolving drivers" are influencing their product purchasing: health and wellness, safety, social impact, and experience. The report states, "It's important to know that the shift towards evolving drivers and a broader purchase consideration set is not driven by certain region, age or income groups. It is pervasive across region, age and income. This means that each and every consumer targeted by food manufacturers and retailers has changed in a fundamental and impactful way."[156]

Please also take into consideration your *overall* family budget. Someone once advised me (and if I remembered who I would attribute this to them) to "Add your food bills and future health bills in the same bucket and then tell me what your food costs are."

One of the most important, if not *the* most important aspect to factor into your overall budget are your health care costs. Protecting your family's well-being through healthy eating has considerable long-term savings when you factor in the health benefits. In Chapter 2, we will explore the biggest financial savings of all — the benefits to you and your loved ones of living a healthy lifespan while minimizing the costs and hardships of illness and disease, if not avoiding them entirely. Honor your body by eating healthful, truly nutritious foods.

You can factor in one other saving as well. This one is of highest value, priceless in fact: Time.

Your life's time span. The amount of time you get in your body, in this life, to enjoy and experience this exquisite earth, this beautiful place during these unique and very special moments in time, along with everyone and everything in it.

Finally, you are also supporting small family farmers and their employees. They are entrepreneurs overseeing small businesses, gamed out of the generous government subsidies factory farmers and the larger industrial farmers get to take full advantage of, and vulnerable to the price fluctuations of the marketplace. They labor to provide you with healthy, nutrient-superior, better tasting food options. They honor labor — their own and their employees. Support them by purchasing their products.

Be like Hazel.

Like our triplewart sea devil, I'm now turning my lantern light in a slightly different direction. Here are two things a fully aware compassionate person cannot support in any way, shape or form:

When you encounter foie gras in a restaurant or on a store shelf, or clothing made with fur, these are the products of horrendous animal cruelty. Don't order it. Don't buy it. Don't wear it. Not even a little taste, not even a garment border trim.

Never buy or eat foie gras, or foie gras paté, or anything with foie gras in it. Consider voicing your objection to it when you see it on a restaurant menu. I've left my table and my dining party to have a private word with a restaurant manager to make sure he or she is aware of the suffering those animals are subjected to so that bits of their appallingly swollen livers can end up offered on their menu. You can choose to let them know that you won't be returning to their restaurant, that you'll be telling your friends why, and that you'll be posting on social media restaurant review sites like Yelp.

Nineteen countries now have bans in place on forced feeding, foie gras production and/or foie gras products.[157] On January 7, 2019, the U.S. Supreme Court rejected the latest industry challenge to California's 2004 ban on foie gras, enabling it to go back into effect statewide.[158]

And don't even think about wearing fur. Ever. Yes, the characters in *Game of Thrones* and *Vikings* look incredibly good wearing fur as part of their costumes. Stunning actually. And fur feels incredible. In centuries past, wearing fur to keep warm for protection from the cold winds and snow drifts was optimal, even a survival necessity. No longer. There is such a wide range of insulating clothing options, even living in snow country fur is no longer a practical necessity.

Wearing fur today is still a fashion statement. But not the one the industry wants you to think you are making. When you wear fur, while you think you may be attesting to your affluence and social status or your elegance and taste, the statement you are really making is this: that you are either unaware of the immense suffering and cruelty each and every one of the animals whose skins you are wearing endured — entire wretched lifetimes — or worse, that you *are* aware of that and it doesn't matter to you, that your compassion for other living creatures is severely limited or nonexistent. Wearing fur and thereby announcing either your lack of awareness, or lack of compassion, is not flattering — it's not a good look. Lack of compassion for animals may also suggest that your empathy for others outside your family or tribe might be somewhat narrow as well.

In January 2018, Norway's newly elected governing body announced a total ban on all fur farming by 2025. Currently nearly 1 million foxes and minks are raised and killed on 340 fur farms in Norway each year. So, this is a big deal. Norway becomes the 14th European country to enact a fur ban.[159]

Germany passed legislation in 2017 banning fur farms by 2022. Germany

The school district, inspired in part by an eighth grader, Lila Copeland, who founded the nonprofit Earth Peace Foundation, began a pilot program offering a vegan school lunch option. It was immediately successful, with 13% of the students, including many non-vegan students, choosing the option. The Food Services Division expanded the vegan option into 35 schools and plans to offer a vegan lunch option at all schools. "We are thrilled with the reaction to the pilot and that most of the kids trying the new lunches were not vegan or vegetarian," says Copeland. "We think more kids will now choose a healthy lunch option."[169]

On April 18, 2017, the LAUSD Board of Education, now attuned to this issue, passed a resolution ending McDonald's McTeacher's Nights. Hannah Freedberg of Corporate Accountability describes what a "McTeacher's Night" is: "McDonald's has teachers work behind the counter of a local McDonald's, serving burgers, fries, and soda to their students and students' families. While McDonald's gets the kind of marketing money cannot buy, schools are left with a paltry percentage of the proceeds from the night (sometimes as little as 10 percent) — and impressionable children come away with the idea that their trusted teachers endorse McDonald's food."[170] While the teachers volunteer working behind the counter, McDonalds can cut employee hours saving that coin as well. No longer. Not at L.A. Unified.

And better: In 2018, the California Federation of Teachers, representing over 120,000 education professionals, passed a resolution to "oppose and reject" McTeacher's Nights.[171] McTeacher's Nights will be history in California. And other school districts around the country are taking note.

And even better: On February 7, 2019, the American Federation of Teachers passed a resolution directing more than 1.7 million educators nationwide to reject junk food fundraisers including McTeacher's Nights.[172] 50 teachers unions representing 3 million teachers have now taken a stand against McTeacher's nights.[173]

The Los Angeles Unified School District now provides healthy lunch options to 700,000 children — meals that improve their health and their academic performance.

You want that for your child.

The story gets better still. Mercy For Animals has a food policy program, working with schools and other institutions, which is succeeding in switching 26 *million* meals a year to plant-based.[174]

For Dr. Fuhrman, "It's crazy that almost half of all entrees served in elementary schools include processed meats (such as hot dogs, ham, sausage, luncheon meats, corned beef, and canned meats), yet World Health Organization has declared that processed meats are a class 1 carcinogen in humans, placing them in the same category as asbestos and cigarette smoking."[175] Citing numerous research studies, including one that concluded that based on data from 12,000 students in the 5th to 8th grades, students who ate processed and fast-foods performed worse in math, reading and science, Dr. Fuhrman writes, "The junk food diets that our children regularly eat directly affect their academic performance. And yet, fast food is being served to kids at breakfast, lunch, and dinner all around the country. It is high time that this information becomes public knowledge so that we can change these accepted 'normal' patterns."[176]

Beginning in September 2018, all schools in California's Santa Barbara Unified School District stopped serving processed meats, including bacon, deli meat, pepperoni and hot dogs. A popular plant-based option is already available at each meal. Of the two million meals the district serves its students each year, half of all meals are now entirely plant based. For Nancy Weiss, the district's Food Service Director, "It's the right thing to do to ensure that our students are getting the highest-quality food. There's no room for carcinogens on the lunch line."[177]

On March 11, 2019, Mayor Bill de Blasio announced that all New York City public schools will have Meatless Mondays beginning with the 2019-2020 school year.[178]

An insightful article revealing successful initiatives in school districts nationwide and how important this is for children is, *10 Revolutionary Ways School Lunch in America is Improving (Plus Healthy School Lunch Ideas)*.[179]

When people communicate with one another and voice their concern shifts like this happen.

When an outcry against veal in the 1980's led by the Humane Farming Association's National Veal Boycott raised public awareness nationwide of exactly what a veal calf is, and how it is raised, the demand for veal plummeted from 3.4 million calves a year to 500,000 in 2017.[180] Italian restaurants that cater to an older or traditionally cultured clientele can find themselves trapped. Many of these customers expect, order and enjoy veal dishes on their menus. You can support these businesses while helping them become more compassionate. If you enjoy eating at one of these restaurants continue to do so — just no longer order veal anything.

In making even gradual modest shifts in what you eat, you are now living more compassionately.

Celebrate what you've achieved.

By choosing this compassionate path and adding to the demand for healthy, tastier, higher quality organic produce and humanely raised animals and animal products, you are enabling farms like Cottonwood Creek Farms to sell every egg, every animal they raise, and they are at their capacity. You enable farmers like Lou Preston to sit down at the end of a long work day and savor a glass of his wine while reflecting on the demand for all the healthy, exquisitely tasteful products of his land, the eggs, vegetables, his breads and olive oils. This opens the door for new entrepreneurs to engage in this style of farming. Imagine tens of thousands of new vibrant small family farms appearing to meet the rising demand for humanely raised meat and dairy.

When this modern version of traditional farming is scaled, by multiplying the number of farms, not the density of animals, it will grow to meet the substantial but decreasing consumer demand for meat and dairy products.

You are bringing an end to factory farming.

You are helping the return of small farms, of a modern day Grange, of the local foods movement, of food-to-table, and the creation of 500,000+ new farmers and farming jobs over the next decade, all of which will result in the rebirth and revitalization of rural towns and communities.

The Voiceless Animal Cruelty Index ranks the animal welfare performance of the 50 largest livestock producing countries in the world. The United States ranks second highest in animal cruelty.[181] We, as a country, should be ashamed of that. You are helping to change that.

As Susan Sontag observed in *Regarding the Pain of Others*, "Compassion is an unstable emotion. It needs to be translated into action, or it withers."[182] Compassionate activism is compassion flourishing. It is compassion realized. Get active. Engage your compassionate activism.

You are now part of what will become one of the essential social justice movements in our nation's history.

You are now a seminal participant speeding our country's evolution into a more compassionate nation.

Consumer demand for organic produce has now grown to a 15 billion dollar a year business. Many farmers are adjusting their crops and practices to accommodate this demand. Consumer awareness and preference will shift animal production away from huge factory farming operations, which will not be able to adapt and change. Factory farm operations will become untenable.

Realizing that your reach and influence now extends beyond your community and out into the world can be invigorating. There is new-found power with this as one purpose in your purposeful life.

You are helping to manifest the Great Healing.

Jane Goodall has famously said, "You cannot get through a single day without having an impact on the world around you. What you do makes a difference, and you have to decide what kind of difference you want to make."

Cynthia Millburn, in her article *How Showing Compassion for Animals Can Improve Your Health*,[183] writes that, "Compassion can help broaden our perspective and redirect our focus away from ourselves. Compassion might boost our sense of well-being by increasing a feeling of connection to others. Social connection helps us recover from illness more quickly, strengthens our immune system and even increases our lifespan."

I love bonus benefits and added value. Demonstrating compassion for animals has *yet another* nice ride-along: We can find ourselves living with even greater compassion toward, patience with, and understanding of, one another.

Here is one more benefit, perhaps the most important of all, and one Joanna Macy describes beautifully in *World as Lover, World as Self*:

"Not only seers and shamans, but scientists also, have revealed the capacity of the human spirit to know and be informed by its connectedness with other life forms. The will to do this is a gift and saving grace. For human mentality presents a distinctive feature: the capacity for choice. To be human, to win a human birth, brings the option of changing one's karma. That is why, in Buddhist teachings a human life is considered so rare and priceless a privilege. And that is why Buddhist practice, in venerable traditions, begins with meditation on the precious opportunity that a human experience provides: the opportunity to wake up for the sake of all beings."[184]

Compassion for animals is one compassion we need to embrace and live to have a chance of achieving The Great Healing.

There are four more.

V

It's night-time in Duplin County, North Carolina. The inviting smells of cooked foods linger on the cool air of a pleasant fall evening. Neighbors have kept their windows open having enjoyed their dinners. The air is fresh tonight, crisp and fragrant carrying the scents of the woods and the trees, the soil and the plants. The stars are bright in the sky.

Sherneka lives in her mother's home. She looks in on Sky, who is sleeping peacefully. Sherneka smiles, silently thanks the Lord that her daughter hasn't had to suffer to breathe as badly as she did.

Sherneka loves this area, the only place she has ever lived. The only place she has ever known. It's home for her and on nights like this it can still be a beautiful place. She has a soft and sweet voice and she hasn't lost her optimism or a sensitive joyfulness, even humor. She hopes the pig factory farms will go away. "This cannot change fast enough for me."

Later this same evening, in the middle of the night, tucked in their home under a pine tree canopy and a full moon, Jennifer moves quietly along her hallway. She nears J'vion's room, stops and listens. Then she steps over beside Jemarion's door. And listens. She does this every night — listens to their breathing. This night, all's well. They're breathing fine.

2

Compassion for Self

I

Brady Kluge was crossing the patio area of Hunt Meadows Elementary School at recess, when he realized she was talking to him. She was a 4th grade classmate, someone he knew but not all that well. One of her friends was with her, a classmate who Brady thought was really cute. In fact, he had a crush on her.

Brady is a soft-spoken, sensitive nine-year-old. He's a good student who communicates well in class. Other students are pleased when they learn they are teamed with him on a class project because they know they'll get a good grade — but outside of the classroom, no one pays much attention to him. So, when this girl tells him she and her friend are interested in seeing how fast he can run, Brady hides his surprise. Can he run over to the playground area and back? Would he do that for them?

It's a sunny, warm spring day in Easley, South Carolina. Flattered to be spoken to — almost polite to a fault — he glances at the friend, making the briefest of eye contact, trying not to blush as she smiles at him. She *smiles* at him. He isn't used to this. So, he agrees. He runs, as fast as he can, over towards the playground. Arriving there, he steps demonstrably onto its surface edge marking his turn so they can see he didn't cheat, that he is running the whole way.

Breathing hard, Brady runs back toward them. They are still watching him and they're *smiling* — their attention stays on him the whole time. Inspired, he surmounts his fatigue, keeps running. Nearing, he can hear them — they are cheering, clapping — *for him!* He finishes strong, pulls up before them. "Good job, Brady! That was a really good job." He thanks them, basks in their smiles. He says an awkward sheepish goodbye, their pretty faces, their eyes still focused on him, especially the friend. She is one of the most beautiful girls he has ever seen. As if he was a camera, he tries to freeze-frame her smiling face and store that image forever in his mind. Brady turns and heads away, not wanting to get all sweaty in front of them, aglow in the remnants of their attention.

About a week later another classmate, a girl who is a family friend, asks Brady about those girls and the day he ran for them. His spine tingles, nervous concern rising. His running for them wasn't that big a deal, so why would she even be bringing it up? It turns out she's friends with both girls and when they told her the story they were laughing. They asked Brady to run because he is overweight, and they wanted to watch his belly fat wobble as he ran. They didn't seem to be laughing at him — not that Brady could tell — so he had no idea. Apparently, however, they found the story enormously entertaining recounting it afterwards to different groups of friends.

Brady Kluge has a gentle voice, "I felt ashamed learning that. And it certainly didn't help my self-confidence." Like most children, he is acutely self-aware. In the maelstrom most of us get to experience known as elementary school, middle school and high school, we yearn for inclusion, making friends. We also learn to mask that while trying to be cool, to fit in, to be interesting and to be accepted. To come across as too needy — let alone desperate — for friendly attention is a surefire way to attract the wrong kind or none at all.

When Brady had an experience that was a blow to an already fragile self-esteem, he would take stock, analyzing the situation in his characteristic way: He was polite and had good manners. He was well regarded in classes because he was smart and he knew the material. He even had a sense of humor, so his peers didn't categorize him as a nerd. And he wasn't immodest about his academics — he didn't brag or exude any air of superiority. He offered to help others. He wasn't bad looking. But he didn't have any school friends. Not one. At home, he had his three brothers and his parents but every year on his birthday, his party turned out to be a family affair — no classmates ever came. The reason he was ostracized could only be one thing: his weight.

Brady was 5 feet 3 inches tall. He weighed 190 pounds and had a 36" waist. He had a face widened by fatty tissue, a small double chin and he had a bit of fatty skin across the back of his neck that made him appear slightly hunched over. He conceded to himself that his belly fat would wobble up and down — as it must have done while he was running as fast as he could for the girls.

Five years later, Brady is now age 14 as his mother drives him to Easley Pediatrics for his annual physical with Dr. Gary Goudelock. In an examination room wallpapered with pleasantly illustrated kid-friendly elephants, giraffes and other animals — one that Brady has been returning to for as long as he can remember — his pediatrician enters and performs his exam. Brady's mom, Tinna, sits patiently as always.

Brady's weight is now 215 pounds, his waist 38 inches around. Scanning Brady's health history, Dr. Goudelock notes Brady's inability to stop gaining weight. He has counseled Brady about this during previous physical exams. "I know it's hard. I understand. I'm fighting this battle with you." His doctor is empathetic. He struggles with his own weight.

Body Mass Index (BMI) is your weight divided by height squared. The Centers for Disease Control and Prevention (CDC) have defined "obese" as a BMI of 30 or higher. Based on this definition, 36% of adults in the United States — over 94 *million* Americans — are obese.[1] Approaching middle age, your BMI to body fat closely correlates: a BMI of 30 means that approximately 30% of your body mass is fat. The percentage is lower earlier in life and increases in your later years. A formula developed by Deurenberg, Weststrate and Seidell in the Netherlands precisely calculates body fat at every age level based on your BMI and taking your age and sex into account.[2]

The CDC defines "overweight" as a BMI of 25 to 30. Based on that definition, *181 million* Americans are overweight or obese.[3] 33.4% of children ages 2 to 19 — one in three — in the United States are now either overweight (16.2%) or obese (17.2%). In Brady's age group, children ages 12 to 19, obesity has increased from around 5% in 1976 to 20.6% today — one out of every five is obese.[4] One of them is Brady.

There have never been, in all of human history, more obese and overweight people alive.

Obesity is the pathway to diabetes.

Dr. Goudelock regards mother and son, meets their eyes. Before this medical professional even speaks a word, a concern in his lingering gaze spreads out creasing his face, and Brady and his mother silently realize... there is a problem, something is wrong.

Based on Brady's vital signs, his blood sugar level, and his BMI, Brady is pre-hypertensive. Hypertension is abnormally high blood pressure.

He is on the path to becoming pre-diabetic. As his pediatrician explains his increasing risk of medical problems should he become diabetic as he approaches his twenties, the 14-year-old fidgets, avoids eye contact with Dr. Goudelock, wanting this visit to end. The slights at school, the glances-at shifting quickly into looks-away, the ridicule whispered sideways between amused confidants — almost privately — Brady's radar field of nervousness is acutely attuned. Now, in this moment, he is again caught in the headlights, unworthy, weak, a glutton, a failure, the subject of condescending disdain, and all he wants is to mute it out, to flee, and get away to solitude and safety.

Hearing the word "diabetic" applied to her son actually doesn't cause his mother immediate or inordinate concern. Tinna is overweight, as is Brady's father, John. A number of people she knows, including her mother-in-law, are diabetic and the medications they take seem to be handling their situations just fine. Besides, Dr. Goudelock's prefix "pre" and even better, the "becoming" before that offer the comforts of distance and time.

But as Dr. Goudelock provides more detail, growing apprehension slows and draws her breathing, the tiny muscles underneath the skin of her face release and her expression falls until she becomes aware of that, and of needing to mask any concern in front of her son.

A program, New Impact, has just opened at the children's hospital nearby. Dr. Goudelock feels intervention at this stage is the best plan of action, and he wants to refer Brady there.

Brady and Tinna are quiet as she drives them home. As a mother, she's usually savvy enough to think of something to say, to lighten things when moods dampen or topics become dour, but right now her mind is working, she's thinking things through. She has an action plan in mind before they even set foot on their driveway.

Tinna and John love their children and are succeeding in providing a nice home for them, the best they can given their steady modest income. Evidence of that love is, in part, the food they serve at their dining table. Their food culture living in South Carolina consists mainly of the rich, fatty, sugary traditional dishes, the comfort food of the American south, combined with today's national brands of appealing calorie-rich processed foods, snacks and beverages. Her husband, John, and Brady's three brothers don't know it yet, but Tinna is now resolved. It's been torture for her, feeling helpless watching her son get bigger and bigger.

She and John have been struggling with weight issues of their own. The entire family will now begin eating a healthier diet and exercising more. Done deal. Junk food and processed foods are going to become scarcer in her kitchen. Even though she doesn't yet know what that "healthier diet" will consist of, she will be going with Brady to New Impact where they will learn more about it together. The family Kluge is going to be on board, this will be a team effort. Done. "Pre"-done. Even though neither Brady's older brother, Joseph, or either of his younger brothers, Chandler and Nicholas, are overweight, Brady's mom knows they'll rally, that the family will circle the wagons around him. Done. Chandler is strident in his opinions — Tinna knows he'll put up a fight and will still refuse to eat vegetables — but that can be tolerated. Double done.

Going forward, Tinna will be driving Brady weekly to New Impact. There, he will be provided with four specialists. Dr. Sease will be his medical doctor — she's the clinic's director so that sounds like a good thing — and Brady will also be assigned a nutritionist, a psychologist and an exercise advisor.

Brady and Tinna have just learned from Dr. Goudelock that Brady is on the path to becoming pre-diabetic. And what that means.

What that means is this...

* * *

If Pre-Diabetic is the name of the road you are on, then the city you are heading to is named Type 2 Diabetes. It's a big city — 95% of diabetics live there. When Brady arrives in that city, his neighborhood — given his young age — has a special name: Early-onset Type 2 Diabetes. Once he moves into Type 2 Diabetes, if he remains a resident there, his life expectancy will be reduced by 15 years.[5] Brady will likely not live beyond his mid-60s.

All those wonderful years of your life's full span spent living with the knowledge you've gained, the experiences and adventures you've had, the family and friends you have created, the joys and the sorrows enabling you to arrive at an understanding of life, a perspective unique to who you are, infusing a sharp brain riding high on a healthy savvy body, sensually attuned and more than adequately ambulatory, ready now for new adventures and experiences captained by a discerning mind, clever now, learned, influential, perhaps even wise. These are years young Brady can barely even conceive of, let alone envision — his mid-60's, the 70's and 80's, stages of life that Tinna is looking forward to enjoying and living through for herself, and that she now realizes, if her son becomes diabetic, he will likely never experience.

Even worse, Brady's diabetic trajectory into his 30's, 40's and 50's will be years lived while enduring increasingly limited physical stamina and ability. He'll experience low energy and diminished brain function, years spent in an expanding body at high and ever-increasing risk of heart attack, stroke, cancer, liver and kidney failure, of neuropathy worsening over time into limb amputations, declining vision leading to blindness, erectile dysfunction, brain fog, anxiety, depression and dementia.

Eventually diabetes reduces kidney function to the point where dialysis becomes imperative for survival, but surprisingly few diabetics need that treatment — just those who actually live that long.

In the 1960s, type 2 diabetes was rare, effecting 1 out of 100 people. The American Heart Association's (AHA) 2019 update of its *Heart Disease and Stroke Statistics* reports 26 million American adults have been diagnosed with diabetes. 26 million is 9.8% of the population — nearly one in ten adult Americans.[6]

The AHA estimates that an additional 9.4 million, or 3.7%, of American adults have diabetes that has yet to be diagnosed.[7] Diabetes then, whether diagnosed or undiagnosed, affects 13.1% of American adults. 1 out of every 8 of us has it. As of 2015, 1.5 million Americans are being diagnosed with diabetes *every year*.[8]

These are the numbers of an epidemic.

Our situation is actually even more dire. The same report notes that *in addition*, "about 91.8 million, or 37.6% of American adults have pre-diabetes."[9] That means *half* of all Americans — of all ages — have been diagnosed with diabetes, have diabetes and don't realize it, or are pre-diabetic.

Up until fairly recently, the medical term was "adult-onset diabetes." This condition has now been renamed "type 2 diabetes" because it is affecting so many children, and at younger and younger ages.

Obesity leads to diabetes.

Childhood obesity rates have tripled in the U.S. since 1980. As of October 2017, the childhood obesity rate nationwide was 18.5%. The rate rises as children get older: 13.9% of 2 to 5-year-olds are obese as are 18.4% of all 6 to 11-year-olds. For 12 to 19-year-olds, 20.6% are obese.[10] Obesity rates are rising faster in children than adults.

Obesity in adolescence is significantly associated with severe obesity in adulthood along with the increased likelihood of life-threatening maladies.[11] If you are obese as a child it is five times more likely you will be obese as an adult.[12] 70% of Americans are now overweight or obese.[13]

Over 25% of our *children* have some kind of chronic health problem. Over 50% of all Americans do. Four million deaths are attributed solely to obesity each year.

Tinna and John love their four sons. They have parented Brady; taken care of him, raised him and are so proud of the outstanding young man he is becoming. He's a straight-A, honor roll student. He's the one who makes sure everyone else is okay. He is more than they ever hoped for. And now the family pediatrician tells her that the food they have been providing for their children is harming them?! Tinna's mad at herself and questions rush to her mind. Questions like, "How is this happening to our son?" "*Why* is this happening to our son?" "Why didn't I think to ask more about that while I was right there?" And as she and her son pull into their driveway, "What the heck?!"

Doctors are delivering diagnoses like Brady's to increasing numbers of children and their parents. Millions of us aren't doing so well — despite our education, our medical and technological advances, all the skillsets and tools at our disposal...

We have the knowledge. We lack the understanding.

Diabetes is a gateway.

Diabetes is *the* gateway to heart disease.

Heart disease is the number one cause of death in the United States. And the biggest risk factor for heart disease aside from smoking is pre-diabetes or type 2 diabetes.[14] Should Brady become diabetic, the odds that he will have a heart attack become much greater. According to the American Heart Association (AHA), "adults with diabetes are 2 to 4 times more likely to die from heart disease than adults without diabetes."[15] In fact, heart disease is the number one cause of death for diabetics.

AHA 2019 statistics show that 800,000 Americans die each year from heart disease, stroke and other cardiovascular illnesses. That's 1 out of every 3 deaths. 48% of American adults — 121.5 million people — are living with coronary heart disease, heart failure, high blood pressure or the after-effects of stroke.[16] On average, one American has a heart attack

earlier still as a baby, even earlier in the womb... "It's not just children that are becoming obese, it's that the American diet reduces intelligence in your child, it interferes with your child's ability to concentrate in school. We're not just talking about Attention Deficit Hyperactivity Disorder [ADHD], which is linked to that. Even the diet a mother eats in her pregnancy affects whether her child gets autism or not, whether her child gets childhood cancer. Eating luncheon meats and high-nitrated foods, and a lot of processed foods and a low level of phytochemicals in her diet are linked to having a child with an autoimmune condition or childhood cancer. And then your child doesn't do well in school. Their intelligence is based on how properly they are fed and how properly the mother ate.

"Parents should be wary because even before your kids become overweight, even before they become diabetic, feeding them these high glycemic, greasy, fried fast foods and processed foods is destructive to their potential, to their brain function, to their being able to realize the American Dream, and be economically and emotionally successful in life."[29]

Diabetes is also a gateway to liver disease, kidney and renal failure.

Your blood circulation is impaired when high levels of sugars in your bloodstream react with and damage molecules of the cells lining your blood vessels. Diabetes encourages inflammation and weakens your body's immune system. As your blood circulation is impaired, so is your body's ability to cleanse and heal itself. This impacts not just a specific organ such as your heart, liver, or your brain, but the *entirety* of your circulatory system leading to a myriad of complications. These include erectile dysfunction, retinopathy, which is impaired vision including glaucoma that can progress to blindness, and neuropathy which is damage to your nerves, a condition that often begins as a loss of sensation or a tingling in your fingers and toes and worsens over time until amputations become necessary.

Over the entire span of human evolution, today is a tremendous time to be alive, to enjoy life, to take in every wonderful moment of an elongated optimized lifespan.

Our science and technology have broadened our knowledge and understanding of this world and everything in it, and we are especially well equipped in the field of medicine with our tools and skillsets. In just the past two centuries, humankind has experienced the virtual eradication of polio, smallpox and tuberculosis. Malaria may soon join that list. As a civilization, we invest significant resources, energy and effort into scientific research and discovery resulting in innumerable medical advances, including antibiotics, vaccines, and surgical procedures that have demonstrably increased our quality of life, our potential and our longevity.

Until now.

Our next generation's life expectancy will decline. Our children, on average, will not live as long as we do.

American life expectancy began to decline in 2015 and 2016. Mike Stobbes' 2018 Associated Press report, *U.S. Life Expectancy Will Likely Decline for Third Straight Year* notes that the last time a three-year decline occurred was "in 1916, 1917 and 1918, a period that included the worst flu pandemic in modern history."[30]

Almost all of us have relatives, friends, colleagues or others we know who are overweight, or diabetic, and have had their lives cut short or their quality of life severely diminished as a result.

It is hard to comprehend, but the numbers of us at risk are even higher. Many of us who appear thin, fit and healthy externally, are also at risk of diabetes. Our blood work can reveal fat accumulation inside our vascular systems and organs (visceral fat) at levels similar to those of us who are overweight. This fat is much more hazardous than the fat accumulating under our skin (subcutaneous fat). Dr. Hyman writes that "23% of adults look skinny but are what doctors term *metabolically obese normal weight*, or TOFI (Thin on the Outside, Fat on the Inside)." The vast majority are undiagnosed. Dr. Hyman continues, "So there's a good chance that you have it and don't even know it. And it's the very thing standing in your way of losing weight and living a long, healthy life."[31]

I take it back. This is more than an epidemic. These are the numbers of a pandemic.

. . .

Doctors are very well trained to treat the symptoms of disease — but not the cause.

Diabetes is preventable. It is also reversible.

Doctors are taught to *manage* diabetes. Insulin is a hormone and as I've mentioned, insulin resistance is the base cause of type 2 diabetes. All of its symptoms are related to elevated blood sugar. Using insulin and other drugs, doctors can manage patient's blood sugar levels, yet these drugs do not eliminate the sugar, they just shift it into the organs and muscles of the body. Therefore, while their patient's blood sugar levels seem to be under control, their diabetes is actually progressing.

Jason Fung, M.D., is a nephrologist who specializes in kidney disease. He has witnessed the tragic failure of this standard approach of managing diabetes. In his book, *The Obesity Code*, he is candid, and he is certain: "I can make you fat. Actually, I can make anybody fat. How? By prescribing insulin. It won't matter that you have willpower or that you exercise. It won't matter what you choose to eat. You will get fat. It's simply a matter of enough insulin and enough time... At the very beginning of obesity, a person will manifest little insulin resistance, but it develops over time... Persistent high insulin levels lead gradually and eventually to insulin resistance... Excessively high insulin resistance is the disease known as type 2 diabetes... That high insulin levels cause both obesity and type 2 diabetes has profound implications. The treatment for both is to lower insulin levels, yet current treatments focus on increasing insulin levels, which is exactly wrong."[32] In the compelling 9-part documentary series, *iThrive! Rising From the Depths of Diabetes & Obesity*, Joseph M. Mercola, D.O., concurs, stating with regard to people in the early stages of type 2 diabetes, "If you are a type 2 diabetic, and 95% of diabetics are, and you are prescribed insulin, you are absolutely, unequivocally accelerating your path to death... When you give someone insulin you only make insulin resistance worse. It's the worst thing you can do."[33]

This epidemic of premature death, disease, and misery — all of this loss of life expectancy, of human potential, of quality of life while suffering through and enduring worsening diabetes — is avoidable. 80% of our health care spending goes toward chronic diseases that are not only reversible but preventable.[34]

But doctors are inadequately taught how to cure diabetes by addressing its cause, and no less importantly, how to advise patients, including children and their parents, on how best to avoid becoming diabetic when, like Brady, their physicals and blood panels indicate they are heading in that direction.

Doctors do not receive proper nutrition training. 105 medical schools were surveyed across the United States in 2010 to quantify the number of required hours of nutrition education for each medical student. It found that only 25% of the institutions even had a required nutrition course. Medical students received, overall, just 19.6 hours of nutrition instruction *during the entire multi-year span* of their medical school careers. The report came to this obvious conclusion: "The amount of nutrition education that medical students receive continues to be inadequate."[35]

Dr. Hyman has an apt analogy for this: "Disregarding the underlying causes and treating only risk factors is somewhat like mopping up the floor around an overflowing sink instead of turning off the faucet."[36]

Dr. Fuhrman is candid in his assessment: "A serious problem in our country — and in the modern world generally — is the lack of acceptance that chronic, dietary-induced diseases such as diabetes, obesity, heart disease, stroke, and dementia are almost totally preventable through proper nutrition. Our economy is being weighed down by an expensive and largely ineffective medical system — a system that relies on expensive tests, treatments, and last-minute heroics to combat the effects of a nation poisoning itself with a rich, disease-causing diet."[37]

Once Brady is residing in the city named Type 2 Diabetes, and has a doctor who is convinced that managing his blood sugar levels is the best way to mitigate his dis-ease, Brady will embark on a lifelong, very costly path of increasing drug use which will succeed, not in healing him, but in undermining his quality of life as it reduces his life expectancy.

I sense a villain afoot.

Dr. Fuhrman does as well.

• • •

Excellent health and ideal weight are not the results of genetics or luck. The reality is that our dietary choices directly affect our health.

Joel Fuhrman, M.D.,[38] is a board-certified family physician with over 25 years of experience practicing nutritional medicine. Five of his books are New York Times bestsellers. His eating plan incorporates the latest advances in nutritional science. It is designed to empower you to reach your ideal weight and best enable you to avoid or reverse chronic conditions such as heart disease, diabetes, auto-immune diseases, migraines and even some early-stage cancers.

Dr. Fuhrman coined the term "Nutritarian" to describe an eating plan that is nutrient-dense, plant-rich, and includes anti-cancer superfoods, which also facilitate weight loss. These foods supply both the right amounts of macronutrients (protein, fat, and carbohydrates) and the vital micronutrients (vitamins, phytochemicals, and minerals) that unleash the body's incredible power to heal itself and slow the aging process, giving the body renewed vitality.

ADVANCES IN NUTRITIONAL SCIENCE SAVE LIVES
by Joel Fuhrman, M.D.

In spite of lip-service to eating and living healthfully, the facts are that physicians in America today are part of the problem, not the solution. We are a nation eating ourselves to a premature death with lots of needless suffering before we die. Headaches, body aches, mood disorders, fatigue, asthma, hundreds of different autoimmune diseases, diabetes, high blood pressure, high cholesterol and atherosclerosis plague our modern population; and the answer of the medical profession is more prescription drugs. Our population is ubiquitously deficient in antioxidants and phytonutrients from the lack of vegetables in their diet and they continue eating foods with sweetening agents, white flour, oil, salt and way too many animal products.

We are a green vegetable dependent primate whose immune system is dependent on green and other colored vegetables for normalcy.

While the public clamors for better and less expensive access to medical care and drugs, we must be aware that medications are synthetic chemicals that increase cancer rates and do not and cannot remove the cause of the problem; they just cover up the symptoms while the underlying disease process from eating the wrong foods continues to fester and advance. The public is still not aware that proper nutrition does not just prevent disease; it is therapeutically more effective to reverse disease, because it addresses causation — that is why the problem developed in the first place. If you are overweight or have a medical problem, you should consider eating sufficiently healthfully to get rid of it and not take drugs to control it while you stay sick the rest of your life. Prescription drugs can confound and magnify the problem and themselves be a leading cause of cancer and premature death.

Every person should be aware that advances in nutritional science presently enable over 90 percent of our population to avoid cancer and heart disease. We can age slower, live longer, and live healthier if we adopt a Nutritarian diet-style — a diet style with a robust exposure to high nutrient plants with documented efficacy to prevent cancer. And, when you regularly consume these nutrient-rich, anti-cancer foods, you lose weight easily, drop to a favorable weight, and your heart disease and type 2 diabetes resolve. In other words, food is your best medicine, and the same foods — **G-BOMBS** — are the foods most protective against all common diseases.

G   cruciferous greens
B   beans or legumes
O   onions and scallions
M   mushrooms
B   berries
S   seeds

Each one of these foods is dramatically protective against cancer by itself, but when you put them together in a dietary portfolio that includes them all — the magic happens. In other words, our body does not create disease when we feed it optimally. Our genetic and epigenetic weaknesses become suppressed, repaired, or controlled by optimal nutrition. For example, we may have a genetic weakness to get lung cancer — but that will not matter if you don't smoke cigarettes. You may have a higher genetic risk of developing high blood pressure or diabetes, but they will not happen if you eat right, avoid salt, and stay slim.

The thousands of people who have reversed their serious chronic illnesses and the medical research published to support this eating style are overwhelming. These people found as their health improved, their mood improved, and even their ability to be creative and think clearly was heightened, and their taste and smell also improved so the food actually tastes better. They learned to really enjoy the recipes and flavors of this new style of eating. The Nutritarian Eating Plan[39] uses no gimmicks or fads. There's no yo-yo dieting. You'll achieve your ideal weight while maintaining excellent muscle and bone mass for the rest of your life. Following it will pay incredible dividends in your life and in the lives of those you love. In short, the Nutritarian Eating Plan can help you achieve optimal health and longevity.

I hope you learn about and embrace a new way of eating with more high nutrient plant foods and you avoid the commercialized, disease-causing "Frankenfoods" that most of our population eats so much of. Your health is truly in your hands as nutritional excellence can give you the power to control your health destiny and live disease-free and robust to approximately 100 years old.

* * *

In 2018, my health insurance provider was Health Net. An article in their newsletter, *Keep Diabetes in Check*,[40] suggested things to have checked with regard to diabetes when you next visit your physician. There is a photo of a father seated at a dining table with his daughter, his arm wrapping around her as he checks her blood sugar level by holding a lancing device and pricking the tip of her thumb. The father looks pleased, perhaps because he has this technology easily available, or because his daughter cooperates and she appears relieved that it didn't hurt. This tool enables them to check her blood sugar level on this day and on others to come. There must be relief, even contentment knowing that, as her blood sugar rises, as she becomes pre-diabetic, and then diabetic, there are a suite of existing and ever-improving medicines and treatments awaiting her to manage her symptoms. A lifetime full of them. And their Health Net health insurance is in place to protect their family by paying a large percentage of their medical expenses that, if this young girl becomes pre-diabetic and then diabetic, will be vastly more expensive than most American families have the means to pay.

In 2014, the American Diabetes Association estimated that the cost of treating diabetes over the course of the remaining lifetime of someone diagnosed at age 40, is $211,400.[41] This figure will prove to be low. In recent years, as Elisabeth Rosenthal notes in her powerful book, *An American Sickness*, "The cost of insulin and other products used to manage diabetes skyrocketed... The monthly wholesale price of Humulin, the most popular insulin, has risen to nearly $1,000, up from $258 for the average patient between 2012 and 2015."[42] In addition, the $211,400 estimate does not include treatment of the many other diseases that a diabetic person will be at increasingly higher risk. On top of that, this man's young daughter, already diagnosed by her doctor and prescribed a lancing device to monitor her blood sugar level, is not age 40 — she's not yet even a teenager.

People wonder how their insurance company can stay in business. How can it meet its obligation to cover the lion's share of these exorbitant medical bills? Not just for this girl but for the thousands and thousands of people it insures. It turns out that insurance companies don't mind. As an insurance company covers the medical expenses of its policyholders, it will raise its premiums to continue to operate as a profitable business. Maintaining proportionate profit margins means that the more health care costs an insurance company covers, the more premium revenue it will generate and the more profitable the insurance company becomes.

The smiles of the professional models in this photograph, this sweet daughter and loving father, are convincing and may evoke an emotion in the reader almost every parent can relate to: The satisfaction of protecting your child's health and wellbeing.

But what will her path forward be? This sweet girl. And her doting father as well? Or the similar path millions of pre-diabetics are on? Will it be a healthy plant-based diet reversing the blood sugar warning markers her tests have revealed, enabling her to avoid diabetes and embrace an optimal, full life? Or will her future be a managed-care descent into pre-diabetes, diabetes, and an exponentially increasing risk of life-threatening disease?

The best way to get his daughter to the point where she will no longer need any more lancing devices and finger pricks is through a healthy diet — the foods this family eats. The same holds true for the father as well. If he was aware of this, he'd guide his daughter on that path. But he might not be. Most of us aren't. Brady wasn't.

"The body is a miraculous, self-healing machine when fed properly," writes Dr. Fuhrman. "Through dietary excellence, high blood pressure, high cholesterol, and diabetes melt away, and even advanced cases of atherosclerosis (coronary heart disease) resolve, removing the need for expensive, invasive, and usually futile medical care.[43]

"This sensible approach, with doctor as teacher and motivator for healthier habits rather than merely prescriber of medication and doer of procedures, is not 'alternative medicine' or 'holistic medicine;' rather, it is *progressive medicine*. It is where medicine should have gone — and would have gone — if the financial incentives and political and economic power of the pharmaceutical industry were not so massive and influential."[44]

For decades we have been told that the solution is calorie intake and exercise. Dr. Fung realizes that exercise is not the solution. You can't exercise your diabetes away because exercise does not address the cause. You can't exercise your fatty liver. Counting calories is not a solution either: "The caloric-reduction model was just wrong. It didn't work... 'A calorie is a calorie' implies that the only important variable in weight gain is the total caloric intake, and thus all foods can be reduced to their caloric energy. But does a calorie of olive oil cause the same metabolic response as a calorie of sugar? The answer is, obviously, no. These two foods have many easily measurable differences. Sugar will increase the blood glucose level and provoke an insulin response from the pancreas. Olive oil will not. When olive oil is absorbed by the small intestine and transported to the liver, there is no significant increase in blood glucose or insulin. The two different foods evoke vastly different metabolic and hormonal responses... The entire caloric obsession was a fifty-year dead end."[45]

The cause and the cure reside in a whole foods plant-based diet. No junk foods, minimal processed foods, no sugary sodas or drinks, limited meat.

The American Heart Association has identified seven key health factors — "Life's Simple 7" — that determine cardiovascular health. They are: "not smoking, physical activity, healthy diet, body weight, and control of cholesterol, blood pressure, and blood sugar."[46] Of the seven, the final five are all determined primarily by the food you eat.

David Katz, M.D., the founding director of Yale University's Yale-Griffin Prevention Research Center, stated in 2018, "Whole foods, close to nature, mostly plants, are good for people. That never changes... you'll find that most experts agree on a few fundamentals of nutrition: that vegetables, fruits, whole grains, beans, lentils, nuts, seeds and plain water should make up the majority of what people eat and drink. If there is such a thing as a 'best' diet, that's it."[47]

"Dr. Kim Williams, former president of the American College of Cardiology, has called heart disease 'a 99% food-borne illness.' With the accumulated evidence available today, it is clear that heart disease, the leading cause of death in the United States, is the result of nutritional folly.

This fact makes almost every cardiac-related hospitalization, every death, every stroke victim's injuries the more tragic. We know this is all needless suffering and needless premature death," states Dr. Fuhrman, "because these people could have learned to eat differently."[48] Other studies have demonstrated conclusively that meat contributes to obesity to the same extent as sugar,[49] that a diet heavy in animal proteins increases stroke risk by 47%,[50] and significantly increases the risk factors for both diabetes[51] and type 3 diabetes (Alzheimer's).[52]

The same holds true for cancer. A Harvard School of Public Health study involving 89,000 women over a 20 year period found that, "Compared with women who had one serving of red meat a week, those who ate 1.5 servings a day appeared to have a 22% higher risk of breast cancer. And each additional daily serving of red meat seemed to increase the risk of breast cancer by another 13%."[53] [54] In addition, researchers at Yale linked high meat intake to increased risk of cancer of the stomach and esophagus.[55]

An eight year study involving over 100,000 French adults published in 2018 in The BMJ (formerly the British Medical Journal), revealed a 10% increase in cancer risk among those whose diet included a 10% increase in consumption of ultra-processed foods which were defined as "foods that undergo multiple physical, biological and mechanical processes to be highly palatable, affordable and shelf stable." These included sodas, sugary snacks and desserts, mass-produced breads, processed meats, frozen or shelf stable ready meals, and breakfast cereals.[56]

Regarding the risk of developing Alzheimer's and other dementias, Neal Barnard, M.D., founder of the Physicians Committee For Responsible Medicine, cites several studies that show that people whose diets are lower in saturated fats (milk and dairy products, meat) have less than one-third of a chance of developing Alzheimer's than those whose diets are higher in saturated fats. One study confirmed that people eating a primarily plant-based diet have a significantly lower risk of developing memory problems (Mild Cognitive Impairment) as they age. Another study discovered similar results with people whose diets were lower in trans fats and processed foods.[57]

Regarding depression, a 2018 meta-analysis published in *Molecular Psychiatry*, which reviewed 41 studies on diet and depression, found that people whose eating regimens included high amounts of processed meats and the trans fats found in junk foods had increased rates of clinical depression.[58] [59]

Dr. Goudelock understood the path that Brady was on and that, over several years, the teenager was unable to correct it. This pediatrician was highly skilled and trained as a doctor but not as a nutritionist — so he made Brady and his mother aware of the hazard, and he provided a resource. He referred Brady to New Impact and a path to healing.

Brady and his mother would soon come to understand the benefits of preparing their own meals, eating whole foods and a plant-based diet.

This is the cure, and the solution. Poor nutrition is the fundamental, overriding reason for our current disease pandemic.

It's not a secret virus from Russia or some weird gas secreting up from middle earth. Aliens are not weakening us and thinning us out prior to landing.

It's all about the food...

II

Brady tried the plan. It was 2013 when he first visited New Impact. He would participate in their program for three years. He was selected to appear in Laurie David and Katie Couric's feature documentary, *Fed Up*, about the food industry and the health consequences of the food we eat.[60] Dr. Mark Hyman, who was an adviser on the project, provided nutritional guidance and recipes for the Kluge family.

Tinna mobilized everyone and the family started preparing and eating healthier meals together. Whole foods, fruits and vegetables increased their presence in the Kluge kitchen. Brady began taking regular long walks through his neighborhood with his father. After a short period of time, it was heartening for him to step onto a scale and find that he was 25 pounds lighter.

However, healthy food options in the area where they lived were limited. Brady's middle school and high school cafeterias offered an increasing predominance of sugar and processed-carbohydrate rich, nutrient deficient food selections. The same could be said just down the road at Canes Corner, the convenience store, pizza place and gas station where students congregated after school. It's best known for its Hurricane Fries, which are French fries covered with bacon, then a generous amount of melted cheese, topped with Ranch dressing and served in a large to-go box. At the closest grocery store, healthy whole food choices were also in limited supply. The television programs Brady would watch were bracketed by and impaled with commercials parading a dizzying array of the latest versions of soft drinks, children's cereals, sweets, pizzas and fast foods, all high energy and fun, zestfully enjoyed — even devoured — by the hip and culturally attuned actors portraying socially accepted peers. Advertisements pervasive in print, on billboards, and online, were everywhere he'd turn; soundbites and jingles filled his head.

There was one place that should have become unwelcome terrain, the Kluge kitchen, but even there, in the refrigerator and neighboring cabinet shelves, processed food products just metamorphosed into "low fat" or "low calorie" versions of their prior selves, as sugar rich and nutritionally barren as they used to be re-packaged proclaiming change for the better. Complicating matters was the fact that their household wasn't just Tinna, John and Brady. Each one of Brady's three brothers had favorite foods and beverages to eat and drink and snack on, and none of them shared Brady's problem of excess weight. In fact, his older brother Joseph had always had a bigger appetite than Brady and he was never even overweight, let alone obese.

Brady tried to create healthy eating habits, but for a behavior to become habitual, like brushing your teeth, it requires sustained successful repetition without distraction — and strong willpower. One of the hardest things for Brady was to resist the cravings, the temptation, the simple easy walk to the kitchen for something satisfying, especially in moments of unhappiness, frustration, loneliness, or fatigue.

Arriving earlier than most of the other students in the school gym locker room before gym class, Brady takes off his clothes. As soon as he takes something off, he puts something on, changing quickly and efficiently, masking his nervousness, his self-consciousness about his body, spending as little time in the locker room as possible. He doesn't mind the exercise aspect of gym class. He just prefers to dress for it as inconspicuously as possible. Invisibly would be ideal.

The mile run is a run-walk for him, but he tries his best and even though he's among the last to finish, he always completes it. He tries to hide his embarrassment and his frustration with the exercises he is increasingly unable to do physically. He cannot do a bar pull-up, not a single one, as he can't even come close to lifting his body weight. He cannot do a push up. In the time it takes him to do a few sit-ups or crunches, other kids do fifty. Through all of this his coach, Mr. Brown, encourages him, telling him in earshot of other students that he is proud of him. One day Brady's mother asks Mr. Brown why, given that her son's results are less than the other students. The coach tells her, "Your son is one of my favorite students because he tries the hardest. He does his best."

Brady does not stick with the new food regimen.

Research studies spanning 68 years have found that 85% of people who diet to lose weight gain it all back.[61]

Brady is one of them. He gains all the weight back, and then begins gaining more. He falls short not from lack of effort. Not from lack of desire, of wanting it badly enough. He falls short for the same reason that so many people watching their weight or trying to lose weight do. Dr. Mark Hyman explains why: "The idea that willpower is the key to weight loss, that all one needs to do is limit calories and increase exercise. The logical conclusion about this distorted thinking is this: If you are overweight, it must be because you are a lazy glutton who shuns exercise and loves to eat. The subtle message here is that the overweight person wants to be fat. It is their fault that they are fat. Yet, in treating more than 20,000 patients, I have never met a person who wakes up and says, 'Hey, today I am going to see how much weight I can gain.' On the contrary, most wake up with every intention of losing weight but can't, not because of a character defect, but because of bad advice based on incorrect medical assumptions."[62]

Brady's world is filled with the temptations of addictive, calorie saturated and nutrient depleted, but really good-tasting fast foods, junk foods and processed foods. Dr. Furhman observes that, "The desire for fast food actually becomes more intense the more often it is eaten, because it excites impulse pathways in the brain. This drives the deadly cycle of overeating, weight gain, and more overeating."[63]

One research study, *Food Addiction in the Light of DSM-5*, compared food addiction to drug addiction. It discovered significant similarities when analyzing diagnostic criteria for substance dependence including tolerance — defined as "consuming increasing amounts of a substance to achieve the same effects or experiencing diminished effects with continued use of the same amounts" — withdrawal, habitual use, and a "reduction of social, occupational, or recreational activities because of substance use."[64]

Other research studies confirm a correlation with depression.[65] The Whitehall II study in 2017 presented strong evidence linking sugar intake from sweet food, beverages, and added sugars to depressive symptoms in several populations. It confirmed an adverse effect of sugar on long-term psychological health and concluded that the reduction of sugar intake can lessen and even prevent depression.[66]

Brady wants friends. Like almost every teenager, he has to deal with peer pressure as he tries to be socially accepted in school. And that includes the culture of food. His environment features an overriding scarcity of good whole healthy food. The pervasive social culture embraces and endorses the comfort and satisfaction these unhealthy foods provide and lacking a better understanding of what healthy whole food actually is, he lapses. And he knows it, and convinced he has failed, he grows frustrated, angry and ashamed.

Brady's weight is now taking a toll on him emotionally as well as physically. He told me, "In middle school bullying kids just kinda said what they wanted to. In high school, they wouldn't really talk to you, they'd just ignore you."

"Every guy wants guy friends to go hang out with or go to the football games or what not. And I just didn't have that. People want to say, 'Oh, I don't judge anybody by their looks or what not,' but why would you not want to be friends with them if they're friendly and they have nothing wrong with them except for the fact that they're overweight? It just doesn't make sense."

Every moment of every day Brady lives within an oversized body, and he peers out at the world and watches everyone looking back. Robert L. Reece identifies "fat stigma" as "driven by a society that conflates size and health and uses size to define individual self-control and worth." It is especially acute during adolescence and in school, and he warns that, "From destructive behaviors to low self-esteem to discrimination, the known negative effects of fat stigma should cause significant concern."[67]

Brady's social awareness is acute. Moving around school through bustling corridors in-between classes, he is observant, trying not to get in anyone's way, on guard for inbound signals that he's somehow inconvenienced someone, anyone, of hostility or slight or — God forbid — a threat directed his way. Peering ahead with a roving subtle glancing eye, he casts a kind of visual net out in front of him in the faint hope of catching a friendly glance, a hint of a smile, an amicable something directed his way.

For years, Brady would eat his school lunch by himself. Food was certainly a comfort for him, he enjoyed food, but he didn't enjoy eating much in large public places. Students would look at him and who knows what, if anything, was on their minds, but behind the glances there just might be, "There's the fat kid eating" or "There's the refrigerator — he's always full of food." One time there was another student, who was eating alone, so Brady sat down next to him. The boy gave him an uncomfortable look, stood up with his tray and resettled further down the table. Brady wondered if the boy had friends about to join him, if maybe Brady had encroached on the space they would need, but none appeared.

Brady would like to eat lunch with someone, to eat comfortably in shared company. He is open, he is outgoing, and he is ready to welcome someone to join him should that ever happen.

One day it did.

Caitlin was a 10th grader as well — a slender, short brunette — and when they first sat down and ate lunch together neither said hardly a word. But they accepted each other's company and that was more than enough. For the rest of 10th grade and throughout junior year, whenever they had the same lunch period they would find each other. When they emerged from the cafeteria line with lunch trays in hand, they wouldn't enter the large dining hall with its teeming mass of students, its noise and energy, preferring instead to eat together over at one of a few tables by the cafeteria entrance. Once they'd finished eating and deposited their trays, they walked into the commons — the large wide corridor that a visitor would enter upon arriving at the school. Opposite the glass cases displaying trophies and photographs of the school's champion football teams and triumphant student athletes from years gone by, there's an alcove a few feet deep with sets of double doors that open into the school auditorium. Brady and Caitlin would spend the remainder of the lunch period seated on the alcove floor facing one another, each with their back to the wall.

During all of these lunch periods together spanning nearly two years of high school, they spoke very little. They never saw each other in class or elsewhere in or outside of school. But having each other's acceptance and company meant a lot to both of them. All Brady knew about Caitlin was that early in high school, or it might have been in middle school, she was put into a special needs class. She felt she didn't need to be in a class with the developmentally disabled and she tried to get out of it but was not allowed to. Caitlin was soon regarded almost like a den mother by these students. Brady remembers, "She was the first to speak up if anyone tried to bully them and the kids looked up to her because she was above their level intellect-wise."

When the semester ended, and that class was over, she found that she was branded — she was held back academically. And other students knew. Students always know. It affected her social status, her social life. And while Caitlin never talked much about her personal life, Brady sensed that she might have been dealing with family issues as well. He knew that she was really intelligent, but was never able to rise out of the academic track or escape the social stigma she was mired in. Caitlin was not allowed to graduate high school on stage or with a diploma.

Brady's peers judged him from the outside — based on his weight. Caitlin was judged from the inside — her peer status was based on her academic track. They both based their own self-worth on what their peers perceived them to be, not on who they really were. Caitlin would return to school in a later year to get her GED. They reconnected after a few years. Brady told her that he "was thankful for her during that time for just being someone to talk to and sit with and because she always accepted me for who I was." And she told him, "No — thank *you*. I was in a position where everyone I thought were my friends left me. You still spoke to me and made me feel like a regular person and that I could still do what I wanted no matter what... You inspire me to do what I do now. I often think, 'What would Brady have me do?'" Brady showed me two photographs of her that she gave to him. Caitlin is beautiful.

At home, Tinna continued her best efforts to keep Brady on track.

"He was my little chatterbox. And he's always been driven. When he was little, I used to tell my sisters, 'He's every mom's dream.' He was the perfect kid. He did not have the terrible twos. Usually I could just look at him mean and he'd stop what he was doing. He was just easy, the most compliant kid you ever met. He would get his homework done, he'd get straight A's, he'd remind me of stuff when I was overwhelmed, he was like my little sidekick. He'd get in and cook with me, he'd clean the house on his own. So, it was a bummer, it was real hard for me when he hit teenage years because things changed so much." Tinna tried to understand and to help but felt increasingly helpless. He was eating too much, he was eating in-between meals, he was snacking before bed. "I didn't really know what to do." She can't go without food in the house because she's feeding four boys. They argue — increasingly — and Brady withdraws, retreating more and more, deeper and deeper, into his room, his sanctuary.

Brady knows he has a problem, but he doesn't fully understand it. "It wasn't a specific incident. I don't know why I went through that period. I don't know why I felt so withdrawn. It wasn't just a mental health issue. It was a physical problem, like I would be tired all the time. I felt awful and sick all the time and didn't want to get out of bed."

He surrenders to the satisfaction of something in life he can control, the pleasures of food. Somehow, and he doesn't understand why, he can no longer feel it when he is full.

Dr. Mark Hyman explains that. "When you eat carbs and sugar, insulin spikes and your blood sugar drops. The insulin drives most of the available fuel in your bloodstream into fat cells, especially the fat cells around your middle, otherwise known as belly fat. So, your body is starved of fuel, and this stimulates your brain to make you eat more. You could have a year's worth of stored energy in your fat tissue and yet feel like you are starving."[68]

Sleep apnea sets in and deeply restive full-night sleep eludes Brady. A recent study found that overweight patients who ate a diet high in fat and ate processed meats often, as Brady did, had twice the severity of obstructive sleep apnea compared to patients who ate processed meats rarely or never.[69]

In senior year, working part time as a supermarket cashier, he begins to experience acute pain, like needles, in his feet. The strain of the body weight he is carrying on a job where he's always standing has given him plantar fasciitis, an increasingly painful foot condition resulting from the inflammation of the thick band of tissue connecting his heel bone and his toes.

At 16, he now has high blood pressure and based on his blood sugar level and BMI he is now officially pre-diabetic. His doctor determines it has not yet reached the point where medication is recommended. He weighs 250 pounds and has a 42-inch waist. If the doctor had recommended at that moment that he begin medication, Brady would've gone down that road.

Brady's self-esteem, low ever since elementary school, bottoms senior year. He sees guys dating, pretty girls giving him no attention. He lacks the friends everyone else seems to have and it's depressing. A numbness — a resignation — threatens to become overwhelming and he often awakens now to find himself not wanting to get out of bed.

Dean Ornish, M.D., best-selling author and president/founder of the Preventive Medicine Research Institute, emphasizes a compassionate approach to those suffering from depression and loneliness. "One of the worst things about depression is that you feel like you're seeing things clearly for the first time. That all the times you ever thought you'd be happy or healthy or things would go well you were just fooling yourself and now you're really seeing things clearly. That's why one of the hallmarks of depression is a sense of helplessness and hopelessness... Part of the power of darkness is to obscure the fact that you really do have a choice... While I've found that fear of dying is not a very sustainable motivator, joy of living is and a sense of meaning is... What is sustainable is joy and pleasure and freedom and love. And if you feel like you're freely choosing to do this, if you feel like this is going to really improve the quality of your life, not just prevent something bad from happening down the road, 'Oh, I think more clearly, I have energy, I look better, I look younger, I lose weight, I sleep better at night, I can think more multi-dimensionally,' these are the things that really make a difference... And you don't have to wait long to see the benefit."[70]

Brady wasn't seeing that benefit.

Happiness directly influences your health and visa-versa. Numerous research studies have confirmed that happiness and a positive state of mind have beneficial effects on heart health,[71] stress levels, and susceptibility to illness and disease. Brady was not healthy — and he was profoundly unhappy.

But his situation has a silver lining — something his parents cannot be prouder of. Brady was always an outstanding student. He told me that upon entering 8th grade, "They put me in Honors because I was really good at math. And I really loved science, even at that age. I had a great science teacher, Mrs. Crenshaw who even to this day I really respect, and who helped me develop my liking for science." Spanning his scholastic career, and throughout junior year, Brady maintained his straight-A grades. He passed an Advanced Placement (AP) test in U.S. History and applied for early acceptance into North Greenville University, a small college nearby with an esteemed Pre-Med undergrad program whose graduates have a high acceptance rate into medical school. Brady was offered admission.

That gave Tinna and John great comfort because senior year, Brady lost the desire and will to attend school. And no one could persuade him or motivate him to go. They all tried. He stopped attending classes and his grades plummeted. In the spring semester Brady needed to be homeschooled in order to pass the class units he needed to graduate.

. . .

Brady and his mother realized how calorie rich, refined carbohydrate loaded, and sugar amped their accustomed diet was. They learned the benefits of eating whole foods and a plant-based diet. So, they made healthy adjustments.

What they didn't realize is that something insidiously perverse has happened to the food we eat. The core ingredients in the vast majority of products on supermarket shelves, as well as in the meals you order in restaurants, have changed.

They are now significantly different in these ways:

- New sugars and a vast array of synthetic ingredients have been created in recent decades and, along with refined carbohydrates, are now contained in hundreds of thousands of processed food products that the food industry creates and markets. These have become leading drivers in our growing diabetes and disease epidemic.[72]
- Corn, wheat and other grains, vegetables, as well as meat and dairy products no longer contain the vitamin and mineral quantities, and consequently the nutritional value, they once did. Frequently, not even close.
- GMO (Genetically Modified Organism) crops — also known as GE (Genetically Engineered) crops — now dominate American agriculture and bring with them two other unique hazards.

Sugar has changed.

Sugars are a major cause of diabetes. Americans eat — on average — 152 pounds of sugar per person per year. In and of itself, that's way too much sugar, but on top of that, *sugar* has changed.

Natural sugar, which is found in cane or beets, is sucrose, which when broken down yields a 50/50 mixture of glucose and fructose.

Mr. Beet and Ms. Cane have found that their family of sugars has grown. Rather than spawning genetically related sweet little offspring, they now have sugary siblings showing up at the door — hundreds of them — who bear little genetic or chemical resemblance to them but have been cast into their "adoptive" family. And these new sugars don't affect your body in the same way.

High-fructose corn syrup is a sweetener that arrived at the door in the late 1960s. Glucose and fructose are digested, absorbed and metabolized differently in the body. "Whereas almost every cell in the body can use glucose for energy, no cell has the ability to use fructose... Once inside the body, only the liver can metabolize fructose." Dr. Fung continues, "Excess fructose is changed into fat in the liver. High levels of fructose will cause fatty liver. Fatty liver is absolutely crucial to the development of insulin resistance."[73]

High-fructose corn syrup tastes even sweeter than sugar. Food manufacturers also like it because it extends shelf life, keeps breads softer, and also important from their perspective, it is a less expensive ingredient. Your body doesn't like it because it breaks down more rapidly, spiking your blood sugar level and forcing your liver to work harder to metabolize it — all before it gets stored as fat.

Data from the American Society for Clinical Nutrition links the increase in high-fructose corn syrup consumption to the obesity epidemic.[74] High-fructose corn syrup is found, in large amounts, in soft drinks and juices, sauces like spaghetti and barbeque sauce, commercial salad dressings and condiments like ketchup, and is common in significant quantities in processed foods.

Consumption of high-fructose corn syrup in the United States increased 1,000% between 1970 and 1990.[75] It has now become the biggest source of calories in our diet with Americans consuming more than 50 pounds a year on average.[76]

High-fructose corn syrup is especially dangerous as a driver of obesity, diabetes, cancer, liver and heart disease.

Dr. Hyman writes, "In the late 1970s, in concert with Big Ag (the likes of Cargill and Monsanto) and fueled by new agricultural subsidies that promoted massive increases in the production of corn and soy, Big Food poured high-fructose corn syrup and hydrogenated fats into 600,000 industrial processed foods, 80% of which contained added sugar. These high-sugar, high-glycemic foods are highly addictive and spike insulin, which in turn leads to fat storage, hunger, a slow metabolism, and the cholesterol profile most linked to heart disease."[77]

Dr. Robert Lustig, Professor of Pediatrics in the Division of Endocrinology at U.C. San Francisco, is a leading expert on childhood obesity. In his lecture, Sugar: The Bitter Truth, he states, "Fructose is a carbohydrate but fructose is metabolized as a fat... A low-fat diet isn't really a low-fat diet. Because the fructose or sucrose doubles as fat, it's really a high-fat diet. That's why our diets don't work... Fructose is also a toxin... Glucose is good carbohydrate. Glucose is the energy of life. Fructose is poison."[78]

A research team at Princeton University demonstrated that rats drinking high-fructose corn syrup, at levels well below those in soft drinks, gained significantly more weight than rats drinking sugar water, even when calories consumed were the same. The rats drinking the high-fructose corn syrup exhibited signs of metabolic syndrome, a dangerous condition in humans, including abnormal weight gain, especially visceral belly fat.[79] Bruce Blumberg, Professor of Developmental and Cell Biology and Pharmaceutical Sciences at the University of California, Irvine, says, "Crystalline fructose doesn't exist in nature, we're making that. Fructose is not a food. People think fructose comes from fruit, but it doesn't. The fructose that we eat is synthesized. Yes, it's derived from food. But cyanide is derived from food, too. Would you call it a food?"[80]

The documentary feature Fed Up reveals the power of the food industry with its dominant corporations (Big Food) leading the charge. In the 1980s when a Congressional panel examined the dangerous health risks to Americans from consuming increasing amounts of sugar, the sugar industry moved decisively to attack their report. U. S. Congressman Tim Ryan, in The Real Food Revolution, writes, "In 2003, when the World Health Organization (WHO) published dietary guidelines suggesting that no more than 10% of an adult's daily calories should come from 'free' sugars (those added to food, as well as natural sugars in honey, syrup, and fruit juice), the U.S. Sugar Association pressed the federal government to withdraw funding for the WHO if the organization did not modify its recommendations."[81] The WHO withdrew them.

Eleven years later in 2014 the WHO finally overcame industry pressure and published an updated report — one that, based on new health data, went even further and recommended cutting the sugar percentage of an adult's daily calories to 5%.

Congressman Ryan cites, "One example of the strength of the corporate lobbying dollar is the Corn Refiners Association (CRA), a trade association that is made up of six giant corporations including Cargill and Archer Daniels Midland. In recent years the CRA has been spending tons of money to promote the positive image for high-fructose corn syrup. Between 2000 and 2013, the CRA spent approximately $5.2 million in federal lobbying. It was also revealed that the CRA spent more than $30 million on a private PR campaign, including $10 million to fund a four-year research project by a cardiologist that disputed the contention that there are any negative health consequences from corn-based sweeteners!"[82]

In your supermarket, you may notice that, on the Nutrition Facts labels appearing on food product packaging, on the line for the ingredient Sugar, there is no percentage listed. The percentages of daily value based on a standard calorie-a-day diet appear beside the other itemized ingredients, but not next to Sugar. Food manufacturers are not required to list the sugar percentage. If it had to be revealed, it would most likely be scary-high. The sugar industry has fought very aggressively, and successfully, to be exempted from having to reveal that information to you.

A modeling study, *Cost-Effectiveness of the US Food and Drug Administration Added Sugar Labeling Policy for Improving Diet and Health*, published April 15, 2019, projected that adding a sugar label can, "Prevent or postpone nearly 1 million cases of cardiovascular disease and diabetes," and "Save $31 billion in net healthcare costs and $61.9 billion in societal costs over 20 years."[83] [84]

At long last, this sugar labelling exemption is scheduled to end in 2020.

There is another reason why the food industry prefers synthetic sugars and has developed so many of them. This is another way to hide how much sugar is in any given food or beverage. Processed and packaged foods like yogurt, spaghetti sauce, ketchup, and salad dressings often contain large amounts of *multiple* sugars.

If sugar is one of the main ingredients by volume in a food product and you want to mask that, one way is to mix in several different types of

46%, iron by 27%, magnesium by 24%, and potassium by 16%.[92]

In her article, *The Great Nutrient Collapse*, Helena Bottemiller Evich writes about Irakli Loladze. Irakli is a mathematician, and like many mathematicians, he wanted to solve a mystery. The mystery perplexing him was this: Why, over the past 70 years, has the vitamin, mineral and protein content of our most important grains, fruits and vegetables been declining? He had a theory as to why, and in 2002 he set about to test and prove it. He suspected that the rising level of carbon dioxide in the atmosphere due to global warming was the cause. And he was right.

Helena Bottemiller Evich writes, "As best scientists can tell, this is what happens: Rising CO2 revs up photosynthesis, the process that helps plants transform sunlight to food. This makes plants grow, but it also leads them to pack in more carbohydrates like glucose at the expense of other nutrients that we depend on, like protein, iron and zinc... Across nearly 130 varieties of plants and more than 15,000 samples collected from experiments over the past three decades, the overall concentration of minerals like calcium, magnesium, potassium, zinc and iron had dropped by 8 percent on average."[93]

There is a correlation between the increase in chronic diseases and the diminished nutritional value in the foods we are consuming.

Meat, milk, cheese, yogurt, and other dairy products that come from factory farms have changed.

The meat and dairy products of factory farmed animals that are fed an unnatural diet of vitamin and mineral deficient soy and corn commodity crops, contain lower vitamin and mineral levels than pastured animals feeding off of the diverse, minerally robust grasses growing in healthy soil these creatures evolved to eat.

David Thomas turned his attention to the mineral content in ten kinds of meat, and found that copper has declined by 24%, calcium by 41%, iron by 54%, magnesium by 10% and potassium by 16%.[94]

As mentioned in Chapter 1, it's important that you consume only the meat and dairy products of pasture raised, grass fed non-factory farmed animals. While in that chapter, it is presented to spark compassion for animals, here it is to focus on health and the self — you. And with that in mind, there are two other significant differences as well:

In order to function properly, our bodies need the omega-6 and omega-3 fatty acids pastured animals provide *in proper balance*. Omega-3s enable the body to produce EPA and DHA. Dr. Fuhrman observes that these have "anti-inflammatory effects and are necessary for brain growth and repair. Optimal brain function requires adequate DHA, which makes up 8% of the total volume of a healthy brain."[95] Research studies have associated brain deficiencies in omega-3 with lower intelligence, poor school performance, aggression and hostility, depression and suicide, memory loss and cognitive decline, and dementia.[96] Foods rich in omega-3s include, what? Green vegetables, nuts and seeds, seafood and... *pasture raised, grass fed* meat and dairy products.

Remember that the food products of factory farmed animals — like Thomas Q. Piglet and Ruth the Cow — which dominate the American marketplace and are core ingredients in fast foods, junk foods and the majority of processed foods, are significantly lower in omega-3s.

Finally, factory farmed animals are routinely fed antibiotics, in part to keep them alive in the virulent environments they are forced to endure, and traces of those antibiotics as well as toxins prevalent in those environments stay with the meat and dairy product as it is processed and delivered.

In addition to the reasons detailed in Chapter 1, limit your food intake of meat and dairy products and confine it to grass-fed, grass-finished, free range and organic for the nutritional health imperative here. And yes, I'll keep coming back to this as we take this journey together. Why? Because what is happening — or not happening — in the food industry and how it is affecting our entire internal and external eco-system is the key to just about everything in our world. It is central to our lives.

Just ask Brady.

The GMO horror show.

GMO wheat, corn, and soy crops grown in the industrial agriculture system (which we will visit in Chapter 3) are nutritionally deficient of essential vitamins and minerals by a significant margin when compared to today's non-GMO versions of these crops.

They stand up even more poorly when compared to traditional non-GMO crops grown just several decades ago.

That's problem number one. There is *yet another* significant hazard associated with GMOs.

GMO Roundup Ready seed crops are designed to be routinely sprayed with Bayer's potent poison Roundup. Roundup contains the herbicide glyphosate, which kills weeds, insects, and the living microorganisms essential to soil health. Over 2.6 billion pounds of glyphosate herbicide have been sprayed on GMO crops on U.S. farmland between 1992 and 2012 — crops that become our food or the food for factory farmed animals.

The International Agency for Research on Cancer (IARC), the specialized cancer agency of the World Health Organization, determined in 2015 that glyphosate is "probably carcinogenic to humans."[97] [98] The State of California and the Center for Food Safety determined that glyphosate is a known carcinogen and sought to label products containing it as such per California law. Glyphosate's manufacturer, Monsanto (acquired by Bayer in 2018), challenged this decision in court. In April 2018, the court sided with the State of California.[99]

A research study released in February 2019, found a "compelling link" between exposure to glyphosate and a 41% increased risk of non-Hodgkin lymphoma cancer in humans.[100] [101]

38 countries have bans in place on GMO crops including almost the entirety of the European Union.[102] 64 countries around the world including the European Union, Japan, Australia, Brazil, Russia and China require the package labeling of genetically modified foods. The U.S. *does not*.[103]

The manufacturer of glyphosate has it registered as an antibiotic. "Biotic" is a word of Greek origin meaning "pertaining to life" or "of life." *Anti*-biotic is something that, by definition, kills life. When you take an antibiotic to rid your body of an infection, you take it for just enough time to do its job because antibiotics also kill your vital gut bacteria — your microbiome.

A healthy gut microbiome is essential to your wellbeing. David Montgomery and Anne Biklé make the connection between the microbiome in the soil and the one inside our bodies, "Many practices at the heart of modern agriculture and medicine — two arenas of applied science critical to human health and wellbeing — are simply on the wrong path. We need to learn how to work with rather than against the microbial communities that underpin the health of plants and people."[104]

Glyphosate is a powerful poison. Since its manufacturer classifies glyphosate as an antibiotic, it is not something you want introduced into your healthy stomach and gut microbiome. Is there a correlation between the rising number of people with "leaky gut" and other stomach and intestinal disorders and ingestion of GMO foods and the antibiotic glyphosate?

In 2018, the Environmental Working Group tested glyphosate levels in 45 samples from more than a dozen popular oat cereals, oatmeal and granola snack bars. Government regulators at the Food and Drug Administration have been testing dietary exposures for glyphosate for two years and have kept their results secret. So, the EWG scientists tested independently to provide Americans with this vital information.

Nature's Path Organic Honey Almond Granola. Quaker Steel Cut Oats. Lucky Charms. Kashi Heart to Heart Organic Honey Toasted Cereal. Cheerios. Bob's Red Mill Steel Cut Oats. Nature Valley Crunchy Granola Bars. Kellogg's Cracklin' Oat Bran. 43 of the 45 product samples tested contained glyphosate. Nearly *three-fourths* of them had levels higher than the benchmark EWG scientists consider protective of children's health with an adequate margin of safety.[105]

Notice the words "organic" and "nature" in the names of some of the products listed here. Using the resources annotated in Chapter 1, you will soon learn that words like "Natural" and "Healthy," while attractive for consumers, are hollow in terms of factual nutritional promise. "Organic" is meaningful but read the packaging to make sure the product is made from non-GMO ingredients.

Testing products that schools typically serve on their breakfast menus, the Center for Environmental Health (CEH) reported in December 2018, that, "Nearly 70% of the oat-based breakfast foods tested contain concerning levels of glyphosate."[106] Two Quaker products, Old Fashioned Oats and Instant Oatmeal, contained, "Glyphosate contamination more than six times the safety threshold developed by the EWG." The glyphosate contamination in Cheerios exceeded five times that level.[107]

In February 2019, the United States Public Interest Research Group (PIRG) revealed that 19 of 20 beers and wines it tested contained glyphosate. The beer brands included Budweiser, Coors, Miller Lite, Sam Adams, Samuel Smith Organic and New Belgium. Wines included Beringer, Barefoot and Sutter Home.[108]

In her comprehensive and compelling book, *Whitewash - The Story of a Weed Killer, Cancer, and the Corruption of Science*, Carey Gillam concludes, "There is simply too much evidence that pesticides contribute to elevated rates of chronic diseases such as different cancers, diabetes, neurodegenerative disorders that include Parkinson's disease and

Alzheimer's disease, and reproductive disorders... Everyone who eats foods produced with these pesticides is also at risk. And though the chemical agribusiness industry has long contended that low-level exposures pose no risk to human health, numerous scientists and medical professionals no longer are willing to accept that false assurance."[109]

And jurists aren't either.

Kara Cook of PIRG writes, "In 2018, a jury in California found that Roundup was a major cause of a man's cancer, and awarded him $78 million in damages. Thousands of other people, mostly farmers, are now alleging that their incurable cancers may have been caused by Roundup."[110] On March 19, 2019, a separate jury determined that glyphosate was the cause of another California man's non-Hodgkin lymphoma cancer. Eight days later they awarded plaintiff Edward Hardeman $80 million in damages.[111] On May 13, 2019 a third jury agreed with couple who claimed their cancers resulted from using Roundup awarding them just over $2 billion.[112] Bayer AG faces 13,400 other lawsuits in the U.S. alleging that glyphosate causes cancer.[113]

"In January 2019, France banned the use of Roundup, citing it as a 'serious risk' to human health. Other countries in the EU are considering similar bans," notes Kara Cook.[114] The U.S. at this time, is not.

The majority of processed foods, fast foods, and food products on your supermarket shelves contain GMO ingredients. The Center for Food Safety provides a free app that you can easily download to your phone to help you find and avoid GMO or GE ingredients wherever you shop.[115]

In a peer-reviewed 2018 study, *Survey Reports Improved Health After Avoiding Genetically Modified Foods*, 3,250 participants reported health improvements in 17 areas after reducing the amount of GMO foods they ate including: Digestive: 85.2%, Fatigue, low energy: 60.4%, Overweight or obesity: 54.6%, Clouding of consciousness or "brain fog": 51.7%, Food allergies or sensitivities: 50.2%, Mood problems, such as anxiety or depression: 51.1%, and Joint pain: 47.5%. The study noted that these individuals' health improvements "are consistent with reports by physicians and others about the improvements accompanying a switch to largely non-GMO and organic diets."[116]

In her book, *Who Really Feeds The World?*, Dr. Vandana Shiva writes, "Food, whose primary purpose is to provide nourishment and health, is today the single biggest health problem in the world: nearly one billion people suffer from hunger and malnutrition, two billion suffer from diseases like obesity and diabetes, and countless others suffer from diseases including cancer, caused by poisons in our food."[117]

Purchase organic and pesticide free fruits, vegetables and grains, or ones produced to an even higher standard that is regenerative agriculture. If a food label says "Non-GMO" that's important. Purchase Non-GMO.

III

Brady and the others look on as Tracy writes out the transition state of an organic chemical reaction on the whiteboard. The whiteboard dominates the wall and her neat writing soon sprawls, taking over its surface. At last, she figures out the mechanism and arrives at the end product of this complex chemical reaction. Then she walks everyone through it. She actually *walks*, walking everyone through it as her writing spans more than 10 feet. Brady smiles as Tracy explains this chemical reaction, undecipherable to the uninitiated, and it soon makes complete sense to each one of them. She's the smart one, the "go to" for the answers to the toughest problems. Brady says Tracy knew everything, "We'd always roll our eyes, 'But *of course* you got a good grade on that.'"

Actually, these third-year college students are *all* smart ones. They take most of their classes together because they are all on the same track at North Greenville University and it's a smaller school than most colleges. Brady is the funny one in this study group, the one cracking jokes. He and Aleena brought everyone together. They've been friends since college sophomore year when they met in Anatomy class. Aleena was the first friend Brady ever succeeded in making and she his closest friend.

Tracy sees that everyone now understands this chemical reaction and smiles sweetly, easily.

Brady told me, "In college when we were taking organic chemistry, which is one of the hardest classes I've ever had to take, we'd get together on test nights and carpool over to nearby Furman University. We'd go there because they had a section of their library which stayed open all the time, 24-7, and rooms like this one with long whiteboards."

These are all, each one of them, Brady's friends — something new for him, something different. They enjoy one another and are comfortable together.

Haley is the serious one with a sometime sense of humor. Josh has seemingly no work ethic and never appears to be making an effort. This evening like most, he'll spend time playing on his phone, the lazy-seeming guy in the corner whom they all enjoy being with but makes them so jealous because he's a natural — despite his aloof appearance, Josh is taking it all in and he always gets really good grades. Then there's Caleb — quiet, supremely competent, easy going, amusing. And Bailey, who masks any sense of humor because humor often comes at someone else's expense. Brady describes her as "the one who would never say anything negative about anybody."

Each one of them is an exceptional student.

Brady's period of withdrawal and his academic tumble throughout the spring of his high school senior year carried over into college. His grades in his first semester at North Greenville University were poor. After finishing fall semester, he met with his course advisor, Dr. Nathaniel, about choosing classes for the second semester of his freshman year. She made it clear to him that he would not be accepted into medical school if his poor performance continued. She suggested that Brady consider relinquishing his dream of medical school; that there were other less difficult majors, each leading to an undergraduate degree that can pave the way to an interesting and rewarding career. If he stays on the pre-med track, another semester of grades like these and not only can he forget medical school, but he may no longer remain in good academic standing at North Greenville University...

With his back to the wall, Brady again made a very good choice. Right then and there, sitting across from his advisor, his sense of purpose and his resolve came back alive for him, his passion for learning and for medicine.

That was two years ago. From that meeting on, Brady is back getting straight A's. His junior year, when the classes became exceedingly difficult like this one, O-Chem, he continued to get all A's. He was even asked by the faculty to tutor students the following semester in classes he had just passed with flying colors.

These university students, gathered together at two in the morning facing a fully subscribed whiteboard, are close. They have a group Snapchat. They are bonded as friends, ones that also share a higher aspiration: they are teammates, helping one another on a journey with a difficult objective: they are pre-meds aspiring to be accepted into med school to become doctors.

Tonight, most of them will stay the night to cover all the material while others will leave before long to get a few hours of sleep. Their organic-chemistry midterm is tomorrow.

"A lot of people this age would think 'boyfriend, girlfriend.' But to me, Friends! To me, this was great because I've never had that before." In this regard, Brady couldn't be happier. He has developed meaningful friendships with follow students — friends who are inclined to stay in touch once they get into their medical schools or beyond, wherever their careers take them.

Aleena, Tracy, Haley, Josh, Caleb and Bailey enjoy Brady, his intellect, his sense of humor, and the kind person he is. His weight never mattered to them. Brady now weighs 338 pounds. That's a lot of mass on his 5'9" frame.

At Wren High School during the spring semester of his senior year, Brady could not lose weight so he stopped trying. He didn't fully realize even then that most "low calorie" foods and the "diet" soft drinks on supermarket shelves are little better than the original versions: they are loaded with hidden sugars and other highly processed ingredients of little nutritional value. Lacking the fiber density of whole natural fruits, grains and vegetables, they are not filling or satiating. They are designed to create cravings for more. They gave him pleasure, they tasted good, and they were always available — something in Brady's life that he could control. He still didn't realize how addictive they were.

That last year of high school he wasn't attending classes any longer, there would be no senior prom in Brady's plans, and when he walked the stage on graduation day to receive his diploma, students asked him where he'd been. That summer, Brady moved in with his mother's sister, whose family lived just around the corner, to get some distance from conflict and old patterns at home. It turned out to be a good decision. "If you have someone in a certain situation who is not doing well and you keep them in that situation then they're not going to be able to heal," Brady shared. "I needed somewhere that I was not used to, that I was not comfortable with, to force me to adapt. Before I could try to heal my relationship with my family, I needed to heal myself." In hindsight, Brady would have been best served taking a "gap" semester before attending university, as his social withdrawal carried over into his first semester at North Greenville.

At university that first year, Brady made a courageous decision. He was taking prescribed medication. He decided he could cure himself, so he went off his meds, taking his bottle of Zoloft pills and flushing them down the toilet. He waited for several days to see what was going to happen as the drug waned in his body and his mind. And he discovered that he was okay, he was fine on his own. Another good decision.

Brady, content in the company of his friends as he studies for his O-chem midterm, has kept something to himself: the problems with his body are getting worse. His sleep apnea is in full force. His blood sugar level is way too high. To have a little spending money he works part time in a grocery store. He has to stand his entire shift and the strain of his body weight has exacerbated his painful plantar fasciitis. His lower back is often sore; his core strained from his distended body mass.

He came through academically again, though, acing his Organic Chemistry final as well as the other fall semester classes of his junior year of college.

Brady then makes another important decision.

He considers fasting. Doctors confirm the effectiveness of intermittent fasting for weight loss. It slows the progression of, or reverses type 2 diabetes, while reducing risk of heart disease and cancer. It improves immune and cognitive function, and increases longevity.[118] Intermediate fasting is just not eating for 14 to 16 consecutive hours a couple of times a week — basically skipping breakfast. You eat lunch and dinner, no snacks in-between, making sure to finish eating 3 hours before going to bed. Adding a monthly 4-day water-only fast can provide additional benefit.

Brady also researches bariatric surgery, which is essentially forced fasting. He and his mother go together for the consult.

He has a new SECA examination and his results are not good. His BMI is now 55.1. Obesity is defined as having a BMI of 30 or higher, and extremely obese is 40 or more. Brady has now entered the category of *morbidly obese*. His waist circumference is measured and if it is greater than 40" it means he is at high risk of heart disease, arteriosclerosis, and type 2 diabetes. And at just 20 years old, Brady's is 55". It is clear that not just his heart, but all of the organs in his young body are under tremendous strain. Heart attacks and strokes are becoming increasingly common at younger and younger ages.

In a vertical sleeve gastrectomy — also called the gastric sleeve procedure — a surgeon laparoscopically removes around 85% of your stomach. This is less invasive than the Roux-en-Y Gastric Bypass, which, in addition, alters the intestinal path limiting the digestion of the food that does get through.

Dr. Fung's experience is that either of these surgeries can be "very successful at reversing type 2 diabetes, proving that type 2 diabetes is a reversible condition... and can reverse type 2 diabetes very quickly. The reason people get better is because it is essentially forced fasting and the body is now forced to burn off its own sugar and fat." When this happens "your blood glucose goes down and when your blood glucose goes down, you don't need to take insulin anymore." For Dr. Fung, "It's not the total fat in your body that causes diabetes. It's the fat in your organs that causes that problem."[119]

Tinna told me, "I'm torn. I do not want Brady to do the surgery. It's risky. Things could go wrong. I want him to try and get healthy a different way. But I know he's miserable. I know that if he stays at the weight he is, he probably will not continue. I don't think he'll have the chance to go to med school. I think his weight will completely hold him back in his life. I don't want him to waste his years."

Brady is trapped. He can't exercise in the body he currently has and diet — even if successful — will only reduce his mass slowly. Despite his excellent grades and even with a solid medical school entrance exam score, he foresees that following his med school in-person interviews they might decline him for one of the coveted spaces, privately rationalizing, "Is an obese doctor really setting a good example for his patients?" or "Will his health going forward allow him to endure the physical rigors of internship and medical practice, or to complete a full career arc down the road?"

Brady decides to undergo surgery.

. . .

Over the past few centuries life expectancy worldwide has increased steadily. Max Roser has the statistics. "Since 1900 the global average life expectancy has more than doubled and is now approaching 70 years. No country in the world has a lower life expectancy than the countries with the highest life expectancy in 1800."[120] How much longer is the average lifespan for those of us who lived from age 5 onwards? Max Roser has that answer as well: "To see how life expectancy has improved without taking child mortality into account we therefore have to look at the prospects of a child who just survived their 5th birthday: in 1841 a 5-year old could expect to live 55 years. Today a 5-year old can expect to live 82 years. An increase of 27 years."[121]

Imagine you were approaching age 60 a century ago. You were aged. Life was more brutal, more physically demanding, modern medicine — such as you then perceived it — was crude, inept, inadequate, even barbaric by today's standards. You were a smaller person — a foot shorter on average. Weather, illness, and disease hit you with more severity. You were approaching the ceiling of the average lifespan for that time. Many of your contemporaries would have already passed, perhaps even one or more of your children.

Approaching age 60 today should not mean entering the twilight of your life — or anywhere near it. Our 50's, our 60's, and our 70's can be the most creative, fertile, enjoyable of times.

Life expectancy has decreased in the United States each of the past three years. For our next generation, if we don't change things decisively, it will be lower still — much lower.

IV

Here then is the call. Calling out to you. The second Compassion essential for **The Great Healing** is **compassion for self**. Fundamental to living a compassionate life is taking compassionate, loving care of your health and your self.

It all starts with you. It has to. Just as when you are flying and you are instructed that should the plane have a problem and the oxygen masks drop down, you must secure your own mask first before reaching to help your children or any others you are traveling with.

Karen Bluth, a self-compassion and mindfulness researcher and teacher with a Ph.D. in Child and Family Studies, writes, "Almost 80% of us treat others with more compassion and kindness than we offer to ourselves. When our friends have a bad day, we support them in every way we know how; when we're having a bad day or fail at something, we generally beat ourselves up with self-criticism."

She notes, "Research has shown that teens and adults can benefit from self-compassion in a variety of ways. For teens self-compassion appears to have a protective effect against trauma, peer victimization, depression and self-harm, and low self-esteem. Contrary to what some believe, studies suggest that self-compassionate people have greater motivation to improve, not less: They don't let themselves off the hook for bad behavior but confront their shortcomings head-on. Self-compassionate people don't get mired in selfishness or self-pity," and here it comes, the ride-along, the bonus value... "but actually have greater compassion toward others."[122]

The Golden Rule. Time honored advice to behave admirably, honorably and well toward others. Consider the Golden Rule in terms of nourishing and taking care of your body temple by reversing its order: Do unto yourself as you would do unto others. The Golden Rule is one of compassion.

You were born into this world with a purpose.

That may be a plan in mind for you from a higher power, whatever you believe that source to be. It may come from within, a soul-deep sense of destiny. Or you may feel you are here to discover your purpose on your life's journey. You *are* here to learn from and overcome challenges and adversity, to evolve and to fulfill that purpose. And you will need your toolkit with all the means you have at your disposal, the array of skills you have learned and developed — your gifts and the talent and the perspective that are uniquely yours and yours alone.

You can't realize your fullest potential if you are not as physically healthy as you can be — and if the majority of us no longer are then we need to recognize that, understand why, and take action to regain full health and vitality.

You are being victimized. Your health may have been, is being, or is in danger of being taken away from you. But you need not be a victim.

Dr. Hyman writes, "I never tell my patients to lose weight. I only tell them how to get healthy. When you get rid of the bad stuff and put in the good stuff, your body can heal and repair quickly. It doesn't take months or years. It takes days."[123]

It is very important what you eat, every time you eat. "Food is not just a source of energy or calories. *Food is information*. It contains instructions that affect every biological function of your body. It is the stuff that controls everything. Food affects the expression of your genes (determining which ones get triggered to cause or prevent disease) and influences your hormones, brain chemistry, immune system, gut flora, and metabolism at every level," observes Dr. Hyman. "It works fast, in real time with every bite."

Numerous studies prove how important and effective a healthy diet and lifestyle is in reducing diabetes and the risk factors for all of these diseases. One study, *Healthy Living is the Best Revenge* looked at 23,153 Germans who were among 500,000 participants from ten countries in the European Prospective Investigation into Cancer and Nutrition. The study identified lifestyle adherence to four factors in that group: they had never smoked, they had a BMI of 30 or lower (i.e. they were not obese), they engaged in 3.5 hours per week of physical activity, and they ate a healthy diet defined as a "high intake of fruits, vegetables, and whole-grain bread and low meat consumption." The data was studied with a follow up of 7.8 years.

Take a moment to consider that before you read the results that follow. This was a *huge* recent study, involving a half a million people — *a fully realized study spanning nearly 8 years*.

Compared to the participants in the study who did not adhere to those four healthy diet and lifestyle factors, the group that did had 93% less diabetes and 81% fewer heart attacks. They suffered 50% fewer strokes and had 36% less cancer.[124]

Those are large, significant numbers. Be one of them. Embrace this lifestyle.

Nourish your body with healthy food.

Each year, *U.S. News & World Report* ranks 40 leading diets after they are evaluated by a panel of health experts based on these criteria: easy to follow, nutritious, safe, effective for both short- and long-term weight loss, and protective against diabetes and heart disease. In 2019, the top three — the Mediterranean Diet, the DASH (Dietary Approaches to Stop Hypertension) Diet, and the Flexitarian Diet — each emphasize predominantly plant protein. They recommend fruits, vegetables, whole grains, healthy fats (such as olive oil) and lean proteins. They limit red meat, processed foods and refined sugars. These diets are linked in the Notes section here.[125] [126]

A study published in the Proceedings of the National Academy of Sciences, *Analysis and Valuation of the Health and Climate Change Co-benefits of Dietary Change*, revealed that changing to diets consuming fewer animal-sourced foods has major health benefits resulting in 5.1 million avoided deaths worldwide each year: "45-47% of all avoided deaths were from reduced coronary heart disease, 26% from stroke, 16-18% from cancer, and 10-12% from type 2 diabetes."[127] A separate study involving over 500,000 people confirmed that a diet low in red and processed meat intake is associated with increased longevity.[128]

The Global Burden of Disease, published by The Institute for Health Metrics and Evaluation at the University of Washington, is an in-depth global evaluation of health risks in 188 counties. It identified 14 avoidable dietary risk factors that combine to contribute to the highest number of deaths worldwide. In 2013, 21% of total deaths in the U.S. were attributed to these, "including diets low in fruit, whole grains, and vegetables, and diets high in red meat and sugar-sweetened beverages." Dr. Ali Mokdad, an author in this study, said, "Many of the leading causes of death in the U.S. are preventable. It is important to remember that we need to focus on preventing these risk factors such as smoking, obesity, and poor diet."[129]

Regarding diabetes, in *Too Much Animal Protein Tied to Higher Diabetes Risk*, Frank Hu, M.D., of the Harvard School of Public Health is quoted, "Several previous studies have found that higher intake of total protein, especially animal protein, are associated with long-term risk of developing diabetes... In other studies, plant protein sources such as nuts, legumes and whole grains have been associated with lower risk of diabetes, therefore, replacing red meat and processed meat with plant sources of protein is important for diabetes prevention."[130]

Regarding heart attack and cardiovascular risk, the benefits of a healthy diet happen right away. A plant-based diet is shown to reduce blood pressure and other risk factors in cardiovascular patients within four weeks.[131]

In 2017, insights firm GlobalData found that 70% of consumers worldwide are now moderating their meat intake or avoiding meat altogether. "Consumer perceptions around protein and the role of

Expect that healthy, whole nutritious food products be made available by the food industry.

Force this change with your food purchasing decisions.

"The food companies profit from producing low-cost, low-nutrition Frankenfoods designed to be addictive." Dr. Fuhrman continues, "The medical establishment profits from treating disease on a cause-by-cause basis, refusing to acknowledge, prescribe, or enforce effective lifestyle changes that actually prevent and reverse symptoms and diseases. And last, as a culture we continue to embrace unhealthy foods as if the data on how these foods are destroying lives do not exist or do not apply to us."[146]

Force food companies to provide healthy food by your food purchasing decisions. Do not buy unhealthy or deceptively labeled food.

Expect to receive sound nutritional advice as well as illness prevention counseling from your physician.

Americans spend more on health care than any other country in the world. In 2016, health care spending *per person* was $10,348, which is 31% higher than Switzerland, the next highest spender. Other wealthy countries — on average — spend half as much as the United States. 18% of our Gross National Product goes to health care costs, yet we have the highest rates of obesity, hypertension, and chronic illness worldwide. And our health care spending continues to rise at an average exceeding 4% per year.[147]

This is the direct consequence of a health care approach based on diagnosing and treating disease — on disease management. $10,348 spent *on average* each year for *every* American age zero on up signifies a vastly unhealthy population.

For Dr. Hyman, "Functional medicine is the best model we have for addressing our chronic illness epidemic. It is the medicine of *why*, not the medicine of *what*. It is about why you have the disease, not just naming what disease you have. It strives to treat the underlying cause of the disease, rather than merely suppressing the symptoms."[148]

This is the awareness your doctor should have. Your life depends on it.

"Physicians should consider recommending a plant-based diet to all their patients, especially those with high blood pressure, diabetes, cardiovascular disease, or obesity." That is the determination doctors made in *Nutritional Update for Physicians: Plant-Based Diets*,[149] but in that same report they noted, "Despite the strong body of evidence favoring plant-based diets, including studies showing a willingness of the general public to embrace them, many physicians are not stressing the importance of plant-based diets as a first-line treatment for chronic illnesses... Physicians should be informed about these concepts so they can teach them to staff and patients... Too often, physicians ignore the potential benefits of good nutrition and quickly prescribe medications instead of giving patients a chance to correct their disease through healthy eating and active living. If we are to slow down the obesity epidemic and reduce the complications of chronic disease, we must consider changing our culture's mind-set from 'live to eat' to 'eat to live.' The future of health care will involve an evolution toward a paradigm where the prevention and treatment of disease is centered, not on a pill or surgical procedure, but on another serving of fruits and vegetables."

Honor your body temple by making every bite of food healthy, whole and predominantly plant-based. Choose a physician who understands this and gives you sound nutritional, diet and disease prevention advice as part of your health evaluation.

You should be able to expect — and count on — this kind of counseling from your doctor.

You have a right to expect Big Pharma and Big Med, the corporations that control the medical industry, to shift away from a business model incentivizing relentless profit maximization to one that is more compassionate and prioritizes healthy living and disease prevention.

How can you help move a massive industry away from a profit driven imperative that is now the pervasive objective throughout each of its sectors including the managing of illness and disease, filling hospital beds and operating tables, and the marketing and distribution of medical supplies and drugs?

The first step is the most important step you can take.

Do your very best to avoid being a customer.

86% of healthcare costs in the United States go toward the treatment of entirely preventable diseases and illnesses that are the result of eating unhealthy food.[150] Secure and protect your good health and that of your loved ones and friends. Communicate your choices and inspire others to follow suit.

Originally, the goal of Health Care was health care. The stated purpose of the American Medical Association (AMA) when it was founded in 1847 in Philadelphia by 250 doctors, included "scientific advancement, standards for medical education, launching a program of medical ethics, improved public health."[151] To this day it publishes the most widely circulated medicine journal in the world, the *Journal of the American Medical Association* (JAMA).

But times have changed. Elisabeth Rosenthal writes, "Our healthcare system today treats illness and wellness as just another object of commerce: Revenue generation. Supply chain optimization. Minimization of tax liability. Innovative business modeling. Things sold. Services rendered. Bills to be paid... The AMA is a multiheaded hydra that is, in many respects, as much a diversified corporation as a nonprofit professional group... The AMA Foundation is today supported by a Corporate Roundtable, 'a group of key stakeholders,' who meet with the AMA to discuss their shared 'commitment to public health in America.' Its platinum, gold, and silver members are all from the pharmaceutical and healthcare industry."[152] Is it any wonder the AMA does little to control health care costs? In fact, the AMA operates very aggressively to protect its business interests and presumably those of the corporate members of its Roundtable, as it spends over $20 million on lobbying yearly, making it one of the top handful of spenders on lobbying in the United States. Its political action committee — AMPAC — contributes millions to political campaigns.

The goal in each sector of the U.S. healthcare system is now to maximize profit. "From 1997 to 2012, the cost of hospital services grew 149%, while the cost of physician services grew 55%. The average hospital cost per day in the United States was $4,300 in 2013, more than three times the cost in Australia and about ten times the cost in Spain," according to Elisabeth Rosenthal.[153]

The pharmaceutical industry, Big Pharma, has also experienced exponential growth. In 2012, it spent $27 *billion* on drug promotion, $24 billion of which was allocated to marketing its drugs to physicians. That is a huge sum of money spent informing and influencing physicians. The remaining $3 billion was spent on advertising campaigns to influence you, the consumer.[154] This level of spending proved successful in increasing prescriptions written because in 2014, Big Pharma increased its drug advertising spend to $4.5 billion. $3.4 billion of this was allocated to promoting just the top ten drugs.[155] Drug company direct-to-consumer advertising has grown so massive that annual ad spends on just a single new drug frequently exceed annual spends for Pepsi, Budweiser, or Nike.[156]

The United States and New Zealand are the only two countries in the world that allow direct-to-consumer advertising for prescription drugs. Truth-in-advertising laws, however, require any television commercial that indicates the uses of a prescription drug must give full disclosure of side effects.

One typical example is Intermezzo. If you have problems sleeping, there can be many reasons. For Brady and others battling diabetes, obesity is a direct risk factor for obstructive sleep apnea. To begin to get a good night's sleep, you can shift to a plant-based diet and nutritious foods. Or you can talk to your physician about getting a prescription for a drug to help you sleep — such as Intermezzo.

An 89 second long television advertisement for Intermezzo contains this spoken, legally required, disclaimer which begins just 24 seconds in and continues for 55 seconds, spanning all but the remaining 10 seconds of the commercial: "Do not take Intermezzo if you have had an allergic reaction to drugs containing Zolpidem such as Ambien. Allergic reactions such as shortness of breath or swelling of your tongue or throat may occur and may be fatal. Intermezzo should not be taken if you have taken another sleep medicine at bedtime or in the middle of the night or drank alcohol that day. Do not drive or operate machinery until at least four hours after taking Intermezzo when you're fully awake. Driving, eating, or engaging in other activities while not fully awake without remembering the event the next day have been reported. Abnormal behaviors may include aggressiveness, agitation, hallucinations or confusion. Alcohol or taking other medicines that make you sleepy may increase these risks. In depressed patients, worsening of depression including risk of suicide may occur. Intermezzo, like most sleep medicines, has some risk of dependency. Common side effects are headache, nausea and fatigue."[157]

Your choice. Change to a healthy diet providing your body all the nutrition it needs to function properly and see if your sleep improves, or opt for a quick fix with a drug like this one and risk experiencing one or more of its side-effects such as forgetting events you engaged in just the day before, hallucinations, aggression, worsening depression, addiction, a fatal swelling of your throat or tongue, or suicide.

Your physician is someone you should be able to trust. To trust that every decision, every bit of advice he or she provides you with is in *your* best interest — your best *health* interest — not their financial self-interest or Big Pharma's.

Diabetes and obesity impair your circulatory system. One of many consequences in men can be erectile dysfunction. To begin to address this, you can shift to a plant-based diet and predominantly nutritious foods and your circulatory system will begin to improve. Or you can talk to your physician about getting a drug prescribed such as Cialis for quick help in this regard.

About 29 seconds into a 60 second Cialis commercial, the narrator says: "Do not take Cialis if you take nitrates for chest pain as this may cause an unsafe drop in blood pressure. Do not drink alcohol in excess with Cialis. Side effects may include headache, upset stomach, delayed back ache, or muscle ache. To avoid long-term injury, seek immediate medical help for an erection lasting more than four hours. If you have any sudden decrease or loss in hearing or vision, or if you have any allergic reactions such as rash, hives, swelling of the lips, tongue or throat, or difficulty breathing or swallowing, stop taking Cialis and get medical help right away."[158] There's only five seconds left in the ad spot at this point.

If I take Cialis and experience the fear of difficulty swallowing or breathing, or the shock of a "sudden" loss of hearing, or vision, I'm dialing 911 if I can still manage to find my phone, four-hour boner notwithstanding.

Try to avoid being a customer of Big Pharma.

Big Pharma does more than spend billions of dollars educating physicians about its newest drugs. In his exposé, *Drug Safety and Media Shaped by Big Pharma*, Dr. Mercola states, "As the drug industry's influence over the U.S. Food and Drug Administration (FDA) increases, dangerous drugs are approved and marketed despite their clear risks to patients."[159] One reason mainstream media news services may fail to report on drug safety risks is because drug companies spend around $5 *billion* each year advertising on these media outlets.[160] Further, as reporter Mike Papantonio is quoted in Gary Bentley's article, *Big Pharma Owns the Corporate Media, but Americans Are Waking Up and Fighting Back*, "According to a 2009 study by Fairness and Accuracy in Reporting, with the exception of CBS, every major media outlet in the United States shares at least one board member with at least one drug company."[161]

Dr. Mercola finds that, "Conflicts of interest are hardly limited to media companies. Government agencies, from the FDA to the Centers for Disease Control and Prevention (CDC) also have disturbing financial conflicts of interest that make a mockery out of objectivity." Big Pharma spent $244 million dollars in 2016 lobbying political leaders in Washington, DC. The industry also spends millions of dollars to enlist professors at top universities in addition to doctors and scientists to write articles endorsing new drugs, articles frequently based on research that, per Dr. Mercola, "has often been ghostwritten by the drug industry with a media professional or professor's name attached for credibility... Thanks to the Bayh-Dole Act of 1980, which enabled lucrative academic/Pharma partnerships and 'technology transfer' (even though most drug development is funded by taxpayers and profits should belong to the public) medical centers are unapologetic arms of the drug industry."[162]

One study found that 40% of U.S. Drug Companies had at least one board member holding a concurrent leadership position at an academic medical center.[163] With regard to new drug testing, a significant and increasing amount of the clinical trial work is now being done by for-profit groups hired by Big Pharma.

Prescription drugs cost more than twice as much in the U.S. as in other developed nations and prices have doubled in the past five years. One reason for this, Annie Waldman notes in her ProPublica article co-published in 2017 with Consumer Reports, is, "The U.S. grants drug makers several years of market exclusivity for their products and remains one of the only industrialized countries that allows them to set their own prices."

She continues, "Pharmaceutical companies have traditionally justified their prices by citing the cost of research and development, but recent research on drug pricing has challenged this argument. Many of the largest drug companies spend more on sales and marketing than on developing their drugs. And notably, one researcher has found that about 75% of new molecular entities, which are considered the most innovative drugs, trace their initial research funding back to the government. 'There is substantial evidence that the sources of transformative drug innovation arise from publicly funded research in government and academic labs,' said Dr. Aaron Kesselheim, an associate professor at Harvard Medical School... Some nations, particularly those with national health care systems, like the U.K., rely on official cost-effectiveness analyses to decide which drugs to pay for. Overpriced drugs are sometimes denied coverage. This powerful negotiating tool has helped keep drug prices down abroad.

spending is now linked to *diet-related* health conditions.[174]

Within that dire statistic lies our solution. It is unavoidable that changes must be made to improve our deeply flawed healthcare system. Chapter 5 will address that.

But for now, beginning at this moment, we don't need to wait.

The vast majority of healthcare costs are under our individual control right now. The solution is at the end of your fork. The solution begins with your next meal.

The solution is healthy eating.

Begin now. With yourself and your loved ones; then sway others.

Start with yourself and your loved ones. Prevent or heal illness or disease with a healthy diet, healthy nutrition and exercise.

The Health Net newsletter article, *Keep Diabetes in Check*, the one with the photo of the protective father helping his young daughter monitor her blood sugar level, provides advice with short lists of things to do and things to have checked when you next visit your physician. The very first paragraph, the very first sentence reads, "We can't yet cure diabetes. But we do know how to treat it."[175] While reassuring, confident, and seemingly well intentioned, this — it seems to me — is exactly what you least want to read. Granted, your doctor has been trained to *manage* diabetes and insurance industry coverage will pay for much of the treatment you will endure while you reside in the city named Type 2 Diabetes, however, the claim written on behalf of medical professionals and the health industry, that "we can't yet cure diabetes" should cause you to wonder.

Apparently, the medical industry doesn't know how to cure diabetes...

But you do.

It starts with the foods you eat. And it starts immediately — with your next bite.

Compassion for self has this almost inescapable ride-along: it fosters and magnifies compassion for others. When you are healthy or once you regain control of your health and wellbeing, and are able to fully realize, and experience and enjoy your life's potential, that's a joyful place to be. You will want others to live healthy, fully realized lives and to join in a compassionate celebration of life with you. It will be hard not to.

There is another bonus ride-along, one that is priceless, fundamental. Joanna Macy describes it wonderfully in *World as Lover, World as Self*:

"We have received an inestimable gift. To be alive in this beautiful, self-organizing universe — to participate in the dance of life with senses to perceive it, lungs that breathe it, organs that draw nourishment from it — is a wonder beyond words. And it is, moreover, an extraordinary privilege to be accorded a human life, with self-reflexive consciousness that brings awareness of our own actions and the ability to make choices. It lets us choose to take part in the healing of our world."[176]

You matter. *You*. You have the power to help create the future you want to see.

Get healthy. Stay healthy. "The body temple" — I love that phrase. Treat your body like a temple; honor yourself. Live and enjoy your full lifespan in this exquisite life you have been born into.

You have been victimized. Big Food, Big Med and Big Pharma are the Cape cobra poised to strike and are focused on you. But you do not need — you never need — to become a victim.

Your voice matters. You must find your voice and use it. Because there are some even bigger problems afoot which we are going to get to. And the planet and the human race need your help.

Find your courage; take a stand. And when you clearly understand who our Arch-Villain is, remember the meerkat's strategy against the Cape cobra and the power of collective action.

Be open-minded. Always be learning.

Heal yourself and maintain your health with the nourishing food you choose to eat. Live fully, compassionately, gratefully and well.

Help others. Heal our planet. You have the power. More than you realize.

You'll see.

· · ·

Brady can't remember ever experiencing this feeling before. Maybe as a child, as a very young boy he may have felt something like this, but not as a young man and not as an adult.

"This was the day — and I wanted to see what I could do." So, he started, and he kept it up. "It felt like I was free. And it was shocking. It felt like I was a new me. It felt really good." Discovering each passing second that he was able to keep going, that he might be able to do it, his excitement grew. "It felt, for lack of a better word, like I was baptized. Go in dirty and come out clean." Brady is at a gym where he is now a member and he is running on a treadmill. Four minutes, four and a half, and he doesn't feel the need to stop. He is running. "It felt so satisfying." He can keep going.

He remembers running for the girls when he was 9, how exciting that was. Not the actual running across to the playground and back, but the fact that two of the cutest girls in his grade had their eyes focused on him the whole way, and they were cheering him on. Five and a half minutes. He's there. He's done it! But he doesn't stop. He runs even faster — to see if he can. Joy swells inside, fills him. At six minutes he stops. Elation rushes, surges, overwhelms him.

As he steps off the machine, he can barely keep it together. Sweat drips down, as do his tears. He is overcome.

"I felt free. I felt good. I felt healthy. It was great."

It is January 2018, about one year since his stomach surgery. Brady weighs 200 pounds. He has lost 138 pounds. He has never run like this on a treadmill before. His body would not let him.

When I last saw him, his body fit on his frame. His goal is to get to an ideal body weight of around 175 pounds. I believe Michelangelo either wrote or said that when he first looks at a block of marble, he can see the statue within that will emerge. There seems to be more Brady because there is less of him, almost as if the essential person that is has been chiseled out of a larger, less feature-defined mass.

The surgery was successful and did not involve complications. Brady healed quickly.

He lost weight in a series of plateaus, 15 pounds in the first month and a half following surgery, then it stabilized for a short while, then another 15 pounds disappeared, more later still. He has to eat smaller portions of food about 5 times a day. While he can eat almost any kind of food, his body tells him what works best and what doesn't. And he listens.

At some point in time, years ago when he was a child, without even consciously realizing it, he *stopped* listening to what his body was telling him when he ate. Over time those signals were overwhelmed by what he was eating — to the point where he no longer even realized he was full. He's back in touch now. His stomach and digestive system are more assertive. He typically begins eating with vegetables and other proteins before shifting to a small amount of a starch. He feels discomfort when he has eaten non-nutritious foods, especially bad carbs like white breads or pasta made from processed flour. He has to be selective.

When I was with him, Brady had to go to the emergency room at the Greenville Memorial Medical Campus. He would remain there seven and a half hours. The ER is busy with a number of sick and injured people getting attended to. Brady is not one of them. He is one of those doing the attending. He works there, logging full time shifts as a medical scribe. He is now in his senior year as a pre-med at North Greenville University.

In the ER, he's on his feet virtually his entire shift. The painful plantar fasciitis he endured for years has disappeared. The persistent soreness in his lower back is gone as well. He sleeps soundly at night. The sleep apnea has vanished like a bad dream.

Brady's BMI is now 29.5%. He is no longer obese.

His recent A1C result — the blood test that measures average blood sugar levels over the preceding three months — is 5.2. Under 5.7 is normal. Brady is no longer pre-diabetic.

While he still doesn't contemplate what life in his late 60's or beyond will be like, the odds are now really high that he'll get there. And that he'll get there with a healthy body and alert active mind ready for new adventures and experiences in this wonderful life.

He enjoys working in the ER because he wants to help make patients well. Nothing gives him greater satisfaction or a larger sense of purpose. He wants to give back.

Brady is now preparing for the MCAT, the super challenging Medical College Admissions Test. A really competitive score is 510; a perfect score is 528. On his most recent practice test he scored a solid 506 which he is pleased with given this stage of his preparation. Studying hard, he knows he can improve even further before taking the official MCAT later this year, "This is the only thing I want to do, so I need to give it my best try."

He also moonlights part time on a national crisis hotline. Once he may have been the one calling for help. Brady now could be the person answering your call. A sensitive boy has become a compassionate man.

Sometimes a day that includes bad news like a dire diagnosis can become your best possible day. Awareness is empowering. Knowledge gives you focus and direction. The day The Kluges learned that the term "pre-diabetic" might soon apply to one of them, The Kluge family became empowered. They avidly sought a solution and their pediatrician started them on a path to one. The journey to health took Brady longer than they thought it would because they didn't fully realize what he was up against. They didn't realize that the shift they were making to healthier food at first included food deceptively designed and packaged that would not be a solution. They didn't realize how addictive processed food, junk food, fast food and sugar-laden beverages were, and how pervasive unhealthy food was throughout their environment. In fact, neither did Brady's peers, his other relatives, school officials, some of his doctors, their community, or their culture, or their country.

It has been seven years since Brady and his parents learned that he was pre-diabetic, that he was on the trail from early onset diabetes, to diabetes, a life path with a vastly increased chance of a heart attack, stroke, cancer, neuropathy, kidney, liver and other organ failure, or some or all of the above. A life path with not only a much shorter lifespan, but a significantly diminished quality of life throughout. They didn't realize the danger — what he was subjecting his young developing body to.

Brady at age 21 is no longer risk-inclined toward any of those conditions.

Tinna proudly regards her son. There are few emotions as sweet as a parent realizing with certainty that their stricken child is going to be fine. Brady, her little "chatterbox," has always done things that made her proud. She smiles looking at his face, a slimmer handsome visage, the double chin gone, throat and neck lean, his back straight as his torso shifts, moving freely in the absence of pain, how he moves deftly and sits with well postured confidence and presence. His clothes fit his slimmed down torso. He has more clothing choices now so he's exploring a sense of style. He carries himself like a man now, a well-proportioned adult, not an overstuffed gawky youth.

He meets her eyes. His eyes are clearer, his gaze more assured. He has the energy, the focus, the clarity, contentment, and a confidence that comes with good health. "When I was younger and I realized I was gaining weight, there were periods when I was self-motivated and where I'd lose weight but then I'd gain it back. As you go on and you keep trying and trying and failing and failing and failing to overcome my appetite and my addiction to food that was not good for me, eventually you give up. The difference now is that I have lost the weight and I can control my weight, and that feeling is what keeps me going. I now have a lot more energy. A month after surgery I started to notice an energy increase. It feels great.

I get out of bed — my feet don't hurt. I go to work all day; my feet don't hurt. My back doesn't hurt. I don't have any health issues. I can go on a run. I can go to the lake. I can do different things. I can go outdoors and play a game of football or basketball — things I couldn't do before."

"I hold valuable my whole experience with the weight problem and the journey. It is a huge motivation for me connected with my physician aspiration, as I want to one day be able to treat not just patients' symptoms but treat the cause."

For Joanna Macy, "Acknowledging the depths and reaches of our own inner experience, we come to... the discovery of what we are. We are experiences of compassion. Buddhism has a term for that kind of being — it is 'bodhisattva.' The bodhisattva, the Buddhist model for heroic behavior, knows there is no such thing as private salvation. She or he does not hold aloof from this suffering world or try to escape from it, but returns again and again to work on behalf of all beings. For the bodhisattva knows that there is no healing without connection."[177]

Brady told me, "Just because someone has had a problem with depression — with anything — that doesn't mean that person doesn't have value and things to add to society. He or she may become a great doctor and can help people who are going through the same thing he or she did."

He wasn't describing himself. He's too modest for that. But he just as well could have been. Based on his life experience and his sensitivity, he feels he can be a really good compassionate doctor and healer.

I do too.

3

Compassion for the Land

I

Lucinda Monarch flies along a winding river bed, then veers into the surrounding meadow amidst its flowers, goldenrod, asters, coneflowers and common milkweed, gliding not deftly with the efficient, seemingly effortless changes of direction as a bird does, instead meandering, slowly, her thin tiny wings fluttering, lifting her along on a curving, wobbling path through the air. If you're familiar with Charles Schultz's *Peanuts* cartoons and Woodstock's flightpath, Lucinda's isn't as convoluted as that — not quite anyway.

Lucinda's name in Spanish means "light." Attracted to many of the flowers in this meadow, she'll feed on their nectar which nourishes and sustains her. She doesn't realize that while seeking out nectar, she's pollinating plants, an essential role she shares with bees, wasps, lacewings

and other insects. Pollinators transport pollen from one plant to another, fertilizing and enabling them to reproduce. These insects are responsible for cross-fertilizing a third of the world's food supply.

And at this moment, Lucinda lands on a milkweed plant.

Her antennae and legs — sensitive to a plant's chemical balance — identify whether or not it is milkweed. Milkweed is the host plant of monarchs; it is an essential stop for them.

Milkweed contains a milky latex sap, which is poisonous to most animals. But not to monarchs. Eating milkweed provides monarchs not only nutrition but protection. They store its toxic compounds — its cardenolides — in their bodies and that gives them their orange coloring, a signal to predators that they are noxious and, therefore, prey to be avoided. Monarchs only place their eggs on milkweed as that is all their larvae will eat, storing its nutrients and its poison. As caterpillars and from the moment they emerge from their chrysalides as butterflies, they will have their protective coloring on full display.

Today, Lucinda is interested in eating and perching — but not in depositing eggs. She can't and there is a special reason why.

On this beautiful autumn day, she's healthy, content, and nourished. She's strong. She needs to be because the time of year is shifting. Temperatures are cooling. The days are getting shorter. The milkweed she eats is aging, and her plant nectar sources are diminishing.

Lucinda and the other monarchs who have been born in August or September are unique, born differently from their parents, their grandparents and their great-grandparents. Her generation realizes this. They were aware they are different even back when they were little

caterpillars.

She is part of a special generation — the migratory generation. Each year, the 4th age group of monarchs is the migratory generation. The three previous generations emerged from their chrysalides sexually mature. They'd mate, the females would find milkweed to eat and to secure their eggs on. The lifespan of Lucinda's parents and the two generations before them was about six weeks. Lucinda and her peers will have a lifespan of up to nine months. They emerged from their chrysalides in a state of reproductive diapause — suspended sexual development — and are unable to mate and reproduce until spring. Until that time, all their life energy is focused toward storing body fats and developing flight muscles for something truly incredible — the upcoming journey.[1]

When the angle of the sun reaches 57° off the horizon, and when the days consecutively shorten, the monarchs of Lucinda's generation realize it's time to go...[2] They get it. They know. A week ago, Lucinda and all of the monarchs in her area left southern Canada. They're now in Minnesota.

This tiny creature, who weighs less than a dime and flies funny pumping paper-thin wings, is beginning a migration along with *all* the other monarchs across the portion of the United States east of the Rocky Mountains. They are traveling from their summer breeding grounds heading south and southwest in search of the overwintering grounds where they can survive the cold.

They are traveling into Central Mexico.

Lucinda's journey will take her 3,000 miles. *Three thousand* miles... to a destination neither she nor any of them has ever been before.

They will fly as many as 50 to 100 miles in a day. With wings thin

and fragile, monarchs will brave gusting winds, rain, whatever weather manifests on their way, over *thousands* of miles...

How do they know the route? They're starting out from different places spread throughout a vast region thousands of miles wide. How do they find a destination not one of them has ever seen and recognize it as *the* destination? Scientists at the University of Kansas discovered in 2009 that monarchs orient themselves using a special internal circadian clock located not in their brain but in their antennae. As they head south following the sun, they orient themselves in a time-compensated manner adjusting their course based on the shifting position of the sun in the sky.[3]

Each day they find refuge in stopover places with nectar sources and shelter from the elements. Heading south toward Texas they will meet other butterflies and merge forming larger groups called kaleidoscopes or swarms. These are big and small groups, but they don't really buddy-up, they just travel and rest together for the evenings in trees and shrubs. If one of them were to be separated from the group, it would know how to complete the journey on its own.

This morning Lucinda got a late start. The evening was cold. Butterflies aren't able to fly if their core body temperature is below 55°, so she had to warm up for awhile in the sunlight. Yesterday she only flew for a half day because it rained. Monarchs can't fly in the rain, and she had to wait in a bush until her wings dried. Monarchs are not only careful travelers but they are also great planners. They exert a great deal of energy on their journey but as long as there are sufficient plants along the way with nectar to sustain them, they will arrive in Mexico weighing a bit more than when they started their migration.[4]

The monarchs that survive the trek will reach their destination in Central Mexico around November 1st, aggregating in the forests of tall oyamel fir trees on twelve south-southwest facing mountain slopes at altitudes between 6,900 and 13,500 feet — the only altitudes where these trees grow. Here they will find water, shelter to protect them from predators, and cool temperatures which will slow down their metabolism enabling them to conserve enough energy to survive the winter.

The monarchs have been migrating annually along this route for the past two million years. As a pollinator, this journey and their place, their role in the ecosystem is a critically important one.

But monarchs are not faring well. Their population is in precipitous decline.[5]

The main factor causing the monarch's demise is the loss of its milkweed, particularly in the Midwest.

Farmers have traditionally tried to eradicate milkweed, which was widely considered a pest-plant, but milkweed survived in agricultural areas as it recovers well to plowing. In recent years, several factors have combined to assure milkweed's decline. The number of small farms has sharply fallen over the past 75 years resulting in cropland consolidation into fewer, vastly larger farms. These larger operations cultivate in the Industrial Agriculture model, which has assumed predominance since World War II and emphasizes monocrop production and maximizing tillable crop acreage. This has resulted in the elimination of hedgerows and other border areas between farms, and the scaling back of divider crops, bordering woodlands and wild areas — all of which contained grasses, nectar plants and milkweed. Urbanization has also consumed millions of acres of former wildlife habitat. On top of that, global warming is increasingly causing droughts and severe weather throughout this region, harming what milkweed remains.

Becca Cudmore writes in *Working Together for Monarchs*, "In 2014, Iowa State University estimated that 98% of the milkweed that once grew where Iowa farmland now exists is gone. 80% of all Midwestern milkweeds have been eradicated as well. According to The Monarch Lab at the University of Minnesota in St. Paul, that percentage closely mirrors the drop in monarch egg production in the Midwest. And in 2014 when University of Guelph researchers in Canada compared the various life threats to the monarch, they found that milkweed loss had the greatest effect on recent declines."[6] The corn belt is a key area for monarch breeding in the summer months as well as an important stopping point for migrating monarchs who rest in the oak and pine trees and feed from flowering plants like the goldenrod and wild bergamot in the meadows below.

Making matters even more dire for monarchs, genetically engineered crops (GMOs, Genetically Modified Organisms) arrived on the scene in 1996. These crop seeds are genetically engineered to be impervious to Roundup, which is an herbicide sprayed on the fields. The active ingredient in Roundup, glyphosate, kills what are deemed unwanted weeds and pests. Farmers embraced this new technology because it promised to make farming easier and increase crop yields. Included in the wide spectrum of plants and soil life that Roundup poisons and kills is milkweed. This has all but wiped out the plant on soybean and corn farms throughout the Midwest thereby reducing monarch butterfly habitat by more than 163 million acres.[7] Other herbicides including dicamba, Enlist Duo, and neonicotinoid pesticides are lethal to monarch caterpillars as well.[8] Jonathan Lundgren, a senior research entomologist working for the USDA, and his research team found neonicotinoid pesticide "in places where it doesn't belong." They discovered that the tissue of "60% of the milkweed in their South Dakota study area was contaminated by the pesticide, which even at low levels causes monarch larvae to grow much more slowly and reach much smaller size."[9]

Lucinda is going for it. She has traveled over 3,000 miles and now flies through the mountains of Central Mexico, upwards, her tiny wings pumping way.

She ascends, reaching an altitude of 7,000 feet.

On November 1st, Lucinda arrives at a forest of oyamel fir trees. There are tens of thousands of monarchs arriving with her — a huge swarm. The humidity in the forest is perfect. Kylee Baumle notes in *The Monarch – Saving Our Most-Loved Butterfly* that this area is not too warm for her to be at risk of drying out and not too wet to foster disease.[10] Lucinda has never seen this place before, but she is certain that this is her intended destination.

Fewer than 5% of monarch eggs survive to become butterflies. Tens of thousands of adult monarchs don't survive their migration. But Lucinda has. This little creature has travelled 3,000 miles.

No matter where they start their migration, monarchs begin to arrive in the oyamel forest around the same day every year. November 1st.

The Mexican national holiday, Día de los Muertos — or Day of the Dead — begins on October 31st. This is when families gather together to honor and remember loved ones who have passed. It has been celebrated by the indigenous peoples of the land that includes today's Mexico since around 1800 B.C.

In her beautiful book, *The Monarch – Saving Our Most-Loved Butterfly*,[11] Kylee Baumle writes, "Because of the arrival of the monarchs during this special time, many people believe that these butterflies are the souls of their loved ones coming back to pay them a visit...

"On Day of the Dead, it is said, the gates of heaven open at midnight on October 31st and the spirits of the children who have died come down to reunite with their families for 24 hours. Then, on November 2nd, the souls of the departed adults join them."

When spring arrives, Lucinda and the other monarchs will return from Mexico and fly north through southern Texas. They will have emerged from reproductive diapause and mated, and they are now in search of healthy milkweed to lay their eggs on — an essential final fervent search before their lives come to a close.

"Populations of the iconic and beloved monarch butterfly (*Danaus plexippus plexippus*) have dropped an astonishing 96.5% over the past few decades, from an estimated 1 billion in 1997 to just 35 million in early 2014" writes John R. Platt in Scientific American.[12] The yearly count of monarchs overwintering in Mexico in March 2018 confirms their continuing rapid decline, occupying just 6.2 forest acres, down from 7.275 acres the year before.[13]

The Monarch Joint Venture program[14] is doing everything it can to help save the monarchs, but a 2016 study determined that there is a "substantial probability" of the quasi-extinction of the monarch population east of the Rockies within the next 20 years.[15] The term "quasi-extinction" means a population decline to a number low enough where the recovery of the species is unlikely.

Lucinda and each one of the monarchs need help from compassionate farmers and compassionate people.

Help from people like Joan and Nick Olson.

*   *   *

Since 2011 Joan and Nick Olson have owned and run Prairie Drifter Farm, a 33-acre organic vegetable farm in Litchfield, Minnesota.[16] They raise a diversity of crops, including greens and root crops in early season, mid-season tomatoes, carrots, peppers and onions, and then fall vegetables. Fruit crops include watermelon and cantaloupes. Nick and Joan operate a Community Supported Agriculture (CSA) program[17] delivering boxes of fresh organic vegetables to pick-up sites for 215 share-member families weekly for 18 weeks, mid-June to mid-October.

While attending an organic farming conference in Wisconsin, Nick and Joan learned about a pollinator conservation program for farmers offered through the Natural Resources and Conservation Service (NRCS). They applied and received a grant in 2013 and were connected with The Xerces Society for Invertebrate Conservation.[18] Sarah Foltz Jordan, a Xerces Pollinator Conservation Specialist, provides habitat restoration support to hundreds of farmers and farm agency professionals across the Upper Midwest. She visited Prairie Drifter Farm and helped Nick and Joan develop a plan to increase pollinator habitat and monarch conservation throughout their homestead.[19]

From common milkweed to prairie blazing star, red osier dogwood to elderberry, big bluestem to blue vervain, The Olsons have now planted dozens of species of forbs and flowering shrubs throughout their farm that the monarchs and other pollinators — bees, moths, wasps and beetles — love to feed on. The planted areas, called pollinator conservation strips, contain a mix of both forms of vegetation that bloom at different times throughout the growing season, providing pollinators with forage for food from spring through fall.

During the summer following one of their pollinator strip plantings, Joan told me, "The perennials came back beautifully and were full of monarchs. So cool. The blazing stars and the wild bergamot were thick with them. It was really beautiful to see them flying around in the mid-summer."

Because Nick and Joan leave portions of their field edges untouched, they have noticed a resurgence of wild milkweed which grows more abundant each season. They regularly see larvae on the milkweed. These are probably third generation monarchs laying eggs in mid-summer, new residents on Prairie Drifter Farm.

Toward the end of melon season, in August, Joan observed that the butterflies love sipping the nectar from melons that have split open in the field. Every fall, The Olsons take their kids out to explore the farm and look for milkweed seed. "Just today we were doing an exploratory hike with our young son Abe and daughter Freya and the milkweed, especially along our waterway, was at peak seed. Much of it had just dried and burst, so we collected milkweed seed and spread it. There is something magical about it."

Joan has a degree in geology. Nick has a master's degree in education with an emphasis in farm-based education and works with Land Stewardship Project. "We like having a CSA farm because it's a really beautiful springboard for educating our members about food, sustainability, healthy eating and monarch and pollinator conservation. Our farm can serve as a palette for people to learn about that because they are more personally connected to our land and our farm." Most of Nick and Joan's customers are seeking out organic food and, year after year, they receive comments from share members that the produce in their CSA boxes tastes so much better than anything they can find in the grocery store.

The Olsons raise bedding plants — vegetable and flower — each spring to sell to two local food co-ops, and each year more and more co-op customers are requesting pollinator friendly flowers to include in their home gardens. Other farmers in the region are installing pollinator conservation strips on their farms as well.

Awareness of the dire plight of the monarchs is spreading.

Iowa farmers — *thousands* of them — living at the center of the monarch's summer breeding grounds have decided to help, including those who farm in the pesticide intensive industrial agricultural manner. Many large-scale row crop farmers have converted portions of their acreage from production into the federal government's Conservation Reserve Program (CRP). President Obama's 2015 National Strategy to Promote the Health of Honey Bees and Other Pollinators established goals to increase the population of monarchs east of the Rocky Mountains to 225 million and to restore 7 million acres of pollinator habitat by 2020.

The government allocated $3.2 million toward restoring the first 200,000 acres in a conservation fund providing grants to landowners who want to conserve habitat.[20] Landowners discovered other benefits as well. Creating buffer strips, pollinator habitats, and planting vegetation around rivers and streams also reduces water runoff and protects against soil erosion. By 2016, 342,000 acres were enrolled in the pollinator program nationwide, about half of them in Iowa.[21]

Joan and Nick Olson are aware of something else too.

From the beginning, their goal on their farm was to improve the soil because that's what feeds the plants.

Cover crops are a big part of that. A cover crop can include a mix of grasses and legumes and is planted on crop-land in the periods in-between the main harvest. The Olsons create a field plan every winter, mapping the whole farm in terms of what gets planted, where and when,[22] including when the cover crops go in: the oats, peas, buckwheat, clover and winter wheat, crops that feed the soil with nitrogen and organic matter, that are a source of forage for pollinators, improve tilth, and prevent erosion. They have learned that stacking certain cover crops together can serve multiple purposes. For example, they plant oats, peas and clover together. The peas and oats take off quickly, the peas adding nitrogen into the soil because they're legumes; the oats add a lot of bulk, serving as a nurse crop for the clover that takes longer to grow. Oats and peas are annuals that will not come back next season, so when the crops are at their peak, they mow them which lets the clover grow up through them. The clover by then is really vigorous and adds a lot of nitrogen into the soil. At that time they'll also graze their small flock of laying hens on the clover. The Olsons raise a few feeder pigs and rotate them in as well. The livestock helps complete the fertility cycle.

Beyond cover crops, Nick and Joan add organic compost to their fields each year and crop residues, materials left after harvest such as stems and leaves, are left to return into to the soil to add organic matter. They have experimented with different types of tillage to improve and maintain soil structure and have recently started using a yeoman plow on their fields at the end of the season to open up the soil, mitigating soil compaction, preserving soil structure and improving drainage. With the yeoman plow, growing cover crops are not turned under at the end of the season but are able to remain and help prevent soil erosion over the winter months.

For pest control, Prairie Drifter Farm primarily relies on preventative strategies including crop rotation and beneficial insects. For example, Joan says, "We have started experimenting with planting bunch grasses within our pollinator strips which are a great habitat for ground nesting beetles. The beetles go out and forage at night as far as 100 feet from their habitat and feed on a lot of the insects we don't want." They also let a portion of their plants, like brassicas, cilantro and dill, bolt and go to flower as they are great sources of forage for bees as well as parasitic wasps which feed on other insect pests. These practices virtually eliminate the need for pesticides on their farm.

Eliminating pesticides is essential to maintaining a thriving healthy habitat for pollinators, and for the well-being and vigor of their vegetables.

They have a beekeeper who keeps 20 honey bee hives on their farm. In addition to benefitting from the bee's role as supreme pollinators, The Olsons are happy to do what they can to help bees recover because they are faring as badly as monarchs.[23] Bees, insects, local and migratory birds, and animals now seem drawn to their farm.

This method is called Regenerative Agriculture and farmers — whether small farms like The Olsons with their 33 acres or large scale like Will Harris' 1,500 acres at White Oak Pastures in Georgia — are applying new scientific understanding with traditional agricultural practices with great success.

Joan Olson believes, "We're only the keepers of the land. It's our duty to do as good by the land as we can and improve it while we're here. We are looking for a diverse rich soil that has good structure, that will feed our plants well and that will feed our families."

Joan and Nick learned the key to their farm's success.

It's all about the soil...

II

Good soil is like chocolate cake.

Robust, fragrant. Easy to penetrate with a shovel or a trowel, simple to sink your fingers and hands into deeply. Separate a palm-full with your fingers and you'll find it dark colored, plant-nutrient and carbon dense, deeply aromatic, rich in microorganisms you can't see, in worms and insects you can, in mystery...

Good soil is fascinating.

Soil is responsible for life on Earth. In the evolution of this planet and of life here, topsoil took hundreds of millions of years to accumulate and for existence to evolve *within* it. All that lives on land originates from our soil. Without soil nothing can grow — it's game over.

"It is extremely rare to have a planet where there is soil," says Dr. Ignacio Chapela, Microbial Ecologist at U.C. Berkeley, in the engaging feature documentary, *Symphony of the Soil*. "This living crust that is smeared over the surface of our planet. Most of the planet is not living. It's mineral. It has never known life. It's just this rock. And yet soil starts forming on it and creates this very thin layer where life is possible."[24]

It is a very important distinction - between living and non-living material. Soil is not dirt. Soil is alive, thriving, teeming with life. Dirt is not. Mineral is not.

Aldo Leopold,[25] a noted conservationist, educator and writer, realized a century ago that "All natural resources, except only subterranean minerals, are soil or derivatives of soil. Farms, ranges, crops and livestock, forests, irrigation water, and even water-power resolve into questions of soil. Soil is therefore the basic natural resource.

"It follows that the destruction of soil is the most fundamental kind of economic loss the human race can suffer. With enough time and money, a neglected farm can be put back on its feet — if the soil is still there. With enough patience and scientific knowledge, an overgrazed range can be restored — if the soil is still there. By expensive replanting and a generation or two of waiting, a ruined forest can again be made productive — if the soil is still there... But if the soil is gone, the loss is absolute and irrevocable."[26]

Over this past century, however, we've managed to lose the majority of our topsoil. Soil degradation has intensified to the point where 20 million acres of cropland are abandoned worldwide each year. 30% of the world's cropland has been abandoned over the last 40 years.[27] This means the world's agricultural lands are losing 26.4 *billion tons* of fertile soil each year, which averages 3.4 tons for each person on the planet.[28] In 2015, the United Nations Food and Agricultural Organization reported that each year an additional .3% of all crop production is lost due to soil degradation.[29]

The soil that remains has lost half the carbon it originally contained. Fertile soil is rich in organic carbon. The organic carbon content on most farms today is 50-80% lower than it was prior to intensive Industrial Agriculture.

David Montgomery in his compelling book, *Growing a Revolution – Bringing Our Soil Back to Life*, places our present situation in a historical perspective: "From the Roman Empire to the Maya and Polynesia's Easter Island, one great civilization after another sank into poverty and eventual demise after destroying their topsoil... The once-Edenic, now-impoverished places that spawned Western civilization illustrate one of history's most underappreciated lessons: societies that don't take care of their soil do not last."[30]

At a time when there are more human beings on this planet than ever before, we are rapidly losing our topsoil. Why, given our knowledge, our technology and our skill sets, is this happening? Why are we *allowing* it to happen?

We tend to think of the earth beneath our feet as inert matter. It's just the ground we walk on, right? The fields, the streets, the solid surfaces we play on and traverse.

Yet, below the surface there is another world, a subterranean realm where there are more living organisms than exist above ground. Half the biomass on earth lives *under* the ground... 90% of species diversity on our planet lives in this underground realm. Just a tablespoon of healthy soil contains billions of microbes. "There's so many microorganisms in one gram of soil that 70 to 80% of them still have never been identified... So, soil is more properly viewed as an ecosystem. It's a living thing," observes Dr. Michael Hansen, Senior Scientist with Consumers Union.[31] James Merryweather, in *Secrets of the Soil*, writes, "Intact soil is the most diverse interactive web of interdependent organisms on Earth."[32]

We are only just beginning to understand the complexity of this biome, of life in the soil. In her beautiful book, *The Soil Will Save Us*, Kristin Ohlson realizes that, "When we stand on the surface of the earth, we're atop a vast underground kingdom of microorganisms without which life as we know it wouldn't exist."[33]

• • •

Healthy soil contains a complex, diversified cast of characters. Pat the Pooper is one of them.

That's Pat, the wider-body in the center of this photo, the one that looks like it's brushing its neighbor with its beard. You can't see Pat with your naked eye. Under a microscope you can.

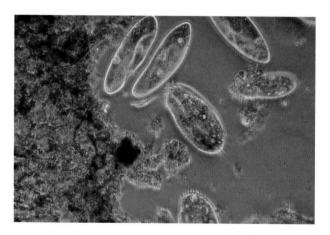

Pat's a single-cell ciliate protozoa. "Ciliate" does not mean Pat tells poor jokes. A ciliate protozoa like Pat has hair-like organelles it uses to move around and gather food.

Pat can live in light but, akin to Hazel, our triplewart sea devil, Pat is a creature of the dark, in this case, the subterranean realm of fertile soil. Pat is a really good eater. Pat eats bacteria and Pat's eating most of the time. And because Pat's a good eater, Pat's also a good pooper.

"It's Times Square on New Year's Eve all the time in the soil," observes Dr. Elaine Ingham, the President and Director of Research at Soil Foodweb, Inc. "When you take that soil and you put it under a microscope, and you start looking, there's a place full of life."

Plants attract bacteria to protect their roots. To do this they put out food through their roots to feed them. Elaine Ingham continues, "Every bit of the surface area of that plant is putting out food to feed the proper sets of microorganisms in the balance that the plant requires — for the purpose of growing bacteria and fungi. And we now have a million-million bacteria and fungi per teaspoon. They grow to really high numbers and are protecting that root system from all the diseases that are trying to come in."[34] This biologically abundant realm — the area around plant roots — is the rhizosphere.

So, what is Pat's role in this neighborhood? Plants want to attract bacteria but Pat eats bacteria, lots of them — one voracious creature. So, why would any plant want Pat around?

The truth is plants love to have Pat and Pat's protozoan pals close by. And this is why: Fungi and bacteria secrete enzymes that free up essential mineral nutrients from the surrounding rock, clay and sand — minerals that the plant needs. However, these minerals are not in a form the plant can use. The process by which these minerals are consumed by bacteria, which are in turn eaten by protozoa or nematodes, converts them into a form that, when excreted near plant roots, the plant can use. The plants want the minerals in Pat's poop.

And it turns out that farmers like Harry MacCormack do too. While scanning his Oregon crop-field, he clues us in: "A really good biological field should have 50,000 protozoa per a unit of soil and each one of those protozoa is eating 10,000 bacteria a day. They poop them out and this becomes a fertilizer, which is your nitrogen reserve in your soil. One hundred-fifty to three hundred pounds of nitrogen reserve per acre is enough to grow anything with no fertilization."[35]

Most of us think that when plants and trees grow, they are taking from the soil. That seems logical. As they grow bigger, their increasing mass must come from somewhere and that somewhere would seem to be the humus, the organic matter in the ground that their roots are expanding into.

The reality is that plants get their carbon, which constitutes most of their mass, *from the air* via photosynthesis. Plants actually *give* to the soil... Through their roots, they exude sugars that feed a flourishing array of microorganisms clustered around them. These microorganisms then protect the plant from disease and free up the remaining nutrients, the minerals and trace elements in the soil, that the plant in turn will need in a form the plant can ingest.

This is fascinating.

It's one of the most fundamental, seminal and consequential interrelationships on this planet. It took hundreds of millions of years for simple life forms to evolve into more complex ones enabling these interrelationships to develop and from which plants could evolve and begin to emerge from the soil. Over hundreds of millions of years, the earth's evolving "table" was beautifully set... for us.

It enabled the rapid ascent of humankind and the Anthropocene epoch.

In keeping the table set for us, Pat also leads a healthy active reproductive life. Protozoa tend to reproduce asexually, a process termed binary fission. Pat, however, can even be a good standard bearer for post-binary thinking as some protozoa can reproduce sexually *and* asexually seven different ways. There's fun to be had under the soil surfaces.

I tell you this so you won't feel badly for Pat. Pat faces a likely fate of being eaten by a nematode. Rampaging nematodes are like the dragons of the depths, bingeing on bacteria and protozoa.

Pat is a good reproducer; a protozoan pillar in the community. When Pat's time comes, Pat will have left the rhizosphere around these field-grass roots a more fertile place for having lived there.

. . .

In forests or jungles, 80 to 90% of the biomass is above ground. On prairies, it is the near opposite — grass plants have about *four times* as much organic matter below ground than they have above ground.

And this is why prairie soils are the most fertile soils on earth.

Here is what the root system of a mature prairie switchgrass looks like. Most of its mass is in its roots which extend 8 to 14 feet into the ground.[36]

Our planet has 12 billion acres of seasonally dried grassland. Prairie soil is the most productive soil in the world. Water infiltrates fertile soil well, and the soil stores it well.

We are very fortunate in the United States because we have more than our share of it. While 7% of the world's landscape is prairie soil, 22.5% of the U.S. landscape is prairie soil.[37]

Aldo Leopold held that "when the soil is gone, whether it be on a farm, range, or forest, the loss is absolute and irrevocable." Can land be farmed in a way that maintains and protects its fertile topsoil? Can degraded topsoil be reinvigorated?

Yes and yes.

In farming, the way to best protect and improve topsoil is **Regenerative Agriculture**.

It is based on these principles, applied in combination:

- cover crops
- compost
- crop rotation
- minimal disturbance of the soil
- protecting the soil's internet
- no pesticides
- animals

and Earl the Worm

Cover Crops

Photosynthesis is the basis of life. It is the process by which plants acquire carbon from the air and transform light energy into biochemical energy in the form of simple carbon sugars. The higher the level of organic carbon in the soil, the higher the nutritional value of the crop and the more valuable the crop.

Gabe Brown[38] is a rancher who is committed to regenerating our natural resources. For the past 35 years he has pioneered regenerative agriculture uniquely suited to the soil and climate on his 5,000-acre Brown's Ranch, located just east of Bismarck, North Dakota. Gabe has been acknowledged as one of the 25 most influential agricultural leaders in the United States and is known nationwide for his soil, his yields and his methods. He told me, "I can tell the profitability of any farming operation by the amount of carbon they have cycling in their system."

Regenerative agriculture farmers have learned that the presence of green plants is the most important factor in soil health. The best way to protect and enrich the soil and its organic carbon content is to keep it covered by either food crops or cover crops year-round. A cover crop consists of plants, usually grown in combination, primarily for this benefit.

Whenever you see exposed soil, that soil is losing carbon and is degrading. Covered soil stays cooler than uncovered cropland exposed to the heat of the sun. This is very important because the denizens of the subterranean realm — the microbes like Pat the Pooper — are more active at cooler temperatures. Cooler soil can also capture and retain many times more water.

Gabe Brown told me he adheres to this rule regarding cover crops: "Along with a cash grain crop, we're going to add a cover crop before it, along with it, or after it. One of the three." In his important book *Dirt to Soil* he writes, "Never, ever pass up the opportunity to convert solar energy into biological energy. As soon as I am done harvesting one crop, be it by combining or grazing, I immediately seed another crop or cover crop. Think of how this ties to the nutrient cycle. If we are not pumping liquid carbon into the soil, we are not feeding soil biology; if we are not feeding soil biology, we are not cycling nutrients... Approximately two-thirds of any increase in organic matter is due to roots. It is critically important to have as many roots in the soil as long as possible throughout the year."[39]

The flow of liquid carbon from plants into the soil is also the main pathway by which new topsoil is formed.[40] The microbes linked to the plant roots via networks of beneficial fungi thrive by feeding on the carbon sugars the plant offers them. This enhances "soil structural stability, aeration, infiltration and water-holding ability," leading Dr. Christine Jones in her essay, *Five Principles for Soil Restoration*, to conclude, "All living things — above and below ground — benefit when the plant-microbe bridge is functioning effectively."[41]

Joan and Nick Olson discovered on their farm that optimal cover crops include a diverse mix of grasses and legumes, often twenty or more plant species interacting. Gabe Brown believes the optimal mix will vary by region and should mimic the diversity of the native system. In his region, what he calls his Diverse Warm Season Mix can include sunflower, sorghum-sudangrass, German millet, soybean, cowpea, kale, radish, turnip, sunn hemp, safflower, buckwheat or fava bean. He told me, "Once you get to eight plant species in a cover crop the plant biomass takes off."

Plants can get all the minerals they need from the soil with just two exceptions: carbon and nitrogen. They take carbon directly from the air via photosynthesis. Plants can't get nitrogen from the air; however, nitrogen-deficient plants are seldom seen in healthy natural ecosystems. They source it from what's in the ground and to do this they need the help of a microbial partner. Legumes, including clover, beans, peas, alfalfa, fava, and vetch are tremendous cover crops because they fix and store nitrogen in nodules on their roots. All green plants to some degree are capable of this.

Iowa farmer Seth Watkins discovered that introducing cover-crop clover naturally increased the nitrogen content in his soil. It decreased his nitrogen fertilizer and herbicide input costs, his climate footprint, and the amount of pollution running off his farm. That in turn led to a resurgence in native birds and grasses, and as he tells Jessica A. Knoblauch in *Happy Cows and Tighty-Whitey Tests: Welcome to the Future of Farming*, "You just give Mother Nature a chance and she will respond kindly."[42]

Dr. Christine Jones, who for decades has helped farmers and ranchers implement regenerative agricultural systems that provide remarkable benefits for biodiversity and yield, concurs and advises maximizing multi-species diversity in both cover crops and cash crops: "Aim for a good mix of broadleaf plants and grass-type plants and include as many different functional types as possible... Every plant exudes its own unique blend of sugars, enzymes... and other biological compounds, many of which act as signals to soil microbes... The greater the diversity of plants, the greater the diversity of microbes and the more robust the soil ecosystem."[43] Pastures consisting of diverse, species-rich mixes of plants offer significantly higher (43% on average) herbage yields for grazing animals.[44]

Compost

Dr. Frederick Kirschenmann, a North Dakota farmer and Distinguished Fellow at the Leopold Center for Sustainable Agriculture, believes that "the most important thing we can do now is to take seriously what Sir Albert Howard called the 'law of return:' The best way to enhance and retain the living capacity of the soil and its capacity for self-renewal, is to return to the soil all of those things that we get from the soil."[45]

Plant residue after food harvest — or a good cover crop — is a precious commodity essential to preserving soil quality. Regenerative farmers do not remove plant residue, instead it is left on the fields before new crop plantings, allowing it to decompose, forming a cover layer, a compost layer on the field. There's no need to bring in mulch and add it to a vast field when the material is right there to begin with.

For farmer Gabe Brown, "One of the worst things we can do is hay a field and remove that biomass."

Retaining crop residues has several essential benefits. Rattan Lal, Ph.D., recipient of the Nobel Peace Prize and Distinguished University Professor of Soil Science at Ohio State University, writes, "In addition to controlling erosion and conserving soil water in the root zone, retaining crop residues on the soil is also necessary for recycling nutrients, improving activity and species diversity of soil micro- and macro-fauna, maintaining soil structure and tilth... and improving / maintaining soil organic matter content."[46]

Soil cover keeps soil temperatures significantly cooler. Living and dead plants provide the food, sugars, carbohydrates and proteins that sustain the microbes in the soil. Increasing the microbial communities that fix nitrogen reduces and eliminates the need to add synthetic fertilizers. Humus is the organic matter digested by microorganisms. Creating humus is creating soil. Humus is porous and can hold between 4 and 20 times its weight in water.

According to Dwayne Beck, the director of Dakota Lakes Research

Farm, composting also aids in weed suppression. "Effective weed management... is not about killing weeds but about taking away their opportunities. Leaving a thick residue from the prior crop makes it hard for weeds to get going, and no-till planting gives the crop a head start, thereby depriving weeds of water, space, and light. Cover crops in crop rotations out-compete weeds."[47] Weeds are restricted 80% better this way when compared to bare soil.

In fact, cover crops and good compost actually till the soil for you. Worms, termites and other creatures feed on the mulch and they aerate and enrich the soil, making it more porous and absorbent. Regenerative farmers are, in effect, letting these creatures plow the soil for them — and they do it in the most natural, optimal manner.[48]

If someone was about to tell you an interesting story about someone they'd heard of, this guy named Earl who was known around town as Earl "the Worm," you might assume the nickname referred to a character flaw, that he's shifty, slippery. Perhaps Earl the Worm plays fast and loose in his relationships with friends and lovers; at best he's undependable, worst, he's untrustworthy, even dishonorable.

Earl the Worm is real. He *is* shifty and slippery but with regard to how he goes about living his life, he's in no way flakey. His character is honorable, tried and true. He hails from a noble clan. Earl, as well as his ancestors, play "an important part in the history of the world." Charles Darwin, *the* Sir Charles Darwin, said so.

Charles Darwin wrote this compliment about Earl's forebears in 1881:

"It may be doubted whether there are many other animals which have played so important a part in the history of the world, as have these lowly organized creatures."[49]

Unlike Pat the Pooper, Earl the Worm is a soil denizen that you can see with your naked eye. He is a little camera shy.

One of the first things a farmer looks for and hopes to see when he or she unearths a section of their soil is whether Earl and of some of his friends are there. It's a good sign if they are.

Worms create holes in the soil and with their movement down these tunnels, they force air in, aerating the soil. Their burrowing loosens the soil, helping moisture penetrate and roots to grow. They significantly increase both soil aeration and water-holding capacity.[50] Micro-organisms flourish in these areas as well. Worms also create worm castings — worm poop — which is very good fertilizer.

How does Earl do it? How does he advance through the soil? With the topsoil in this photograph of Earl, I get it — he just moves it around a bit and bores down through gaps, but how does he get through dense compacted soil? Press your pinky against it and your pinky's going nowhere. And Earl has no teeth. Even if he did and his mouth turned into this wild rototiller, where would all the broken bits of soil go? Under the ground, he can't cast anything aside as there *is* no aside, just the tunnel hole he's making for his body...

And it's just darkness down there. No space, no light... How does he know where he's going? And what for? What's he up to? Do the microbes guide him? Are they his food source as he "processes" the soil?

Charles Darwin wrote that Earl is one of the most important creatures on our planet. What was it about Earl's forebears that brought Mr. Darwin to this conclusion?

Earl feeds on both living and dead organic matter. He's a surprisingly advanced little creature. In the photo, Earl is at least one year old. Earthworms are fully grown at one year and live up to eight years. His digestive system runs the length of his body, he has a circulatory system that circulates blood, and a nervous system that enables him to feel and react to pain. Earthworms don't have lungs, so they respire through their skin. Earl doesn't have eyes but he does have photosensitive cells that enable him to perceive light.

Tonight, Earl travels up to ground level. Night-time is when earthworms are most active. Above ground, their bodies glisten in the moonlight because they are covered in a lubricating mucus they secrete.

They'll eat bits of plants or leaves, or they will search for a mate. Earthworms are hermaphrodites — each one has both male and female sex organs. They have two sex pheromones, Attractin and Temptin, social greeting cards, that facilitate things.[51]

Tonight after Earl eats, he attaches his mouth onto and drags bits of leaves, grass or seeds down into his wormhole and along a tunnel several feet long into his permanent burrow. Earthworms are good crop-field weeders as they like to consume weed seeds. Once home in his burrow, he'll further shred the leaf, eating some of it and storing the rest, creating a future food source because... his burrow contains a cocoon.

After earthworms mate a ring slowly forms around a section of the body of one of them. As it separates away from the worm, the worm inserts its own eggs as well as the sperm from the other worm into it. It will seal and become a cocoon, and after a time, baby worms will emerge. Earl wants his burrow well stocked with food sources awaiting the arrival of the little ones.

So, how does Earl excavate the tunnel down to a burrow and then dig out the burrow itself? It is hard to see but his glistening smooth skin is laced with tiny S-shaped hairs called setae that Earl uses to anchor himself as he moves and burrows. The excavation takes some time, but earthworms expand crevices with force, applying 10 times their body weight.[52] Slowly, steadfastly, diligently, worms create their network of wormholes and their burrows.

When worms poop, the casts they excrete consist of soil along with digested plant material. Compared to the surrounding six inches of soil, worm castings are five times richer in available nitrogen, seven times richer in available phosphates, eleven times richer in available potassium, and contain three times more exchangeable magnesium.[53] Even more importantly, all these digested and excreted nutrients and minerals are now in the exact forms plants can use. In this manner, earthworms break down larger pieces of organic matter and convert it to humus increasing the soil's fertility.

And these guys are busy. Earl rivals Pat the Pooper in output - only he's at *scale*: In *Elements of the Nature and Properties of Soils*, authors Nyle C. Brady and Ray R. Weil observe, "In conditions where humus is plentiful, the weight of casts produced may be greater than *ten pounds per worm* per year."[54] Vandana Shiva notes that earthworm castings "can amount to up to *39.5 tons* per acre per year."[55]...!

Regenerative farmers do not need to add fertilizers. They have Earl and his brethren and a diverse sufficient host of microorganisms doing that for them.

The consistent presence of organic matter on the soil surface provides a food source for earthworms, cools soil temperature and increases soil moisture, building an environment in which they can thrive.

Crop Rotation

As Brady Kluge and his family discovered in Chapter 2 — and modern medicine is beginning to widely realize — a healthy gut microbiome is essential for a healthy human metabolism and for an optimal life. Similarly, a robust vibrant soil microbiome is necessary for fertile cropland and for growing optimally healthful food.

Good soil planted with variable mixed plants and rotating crops nurtures optimal microbial growth and interaction. Regenerative farmers are producing bountiful yields and improving their soil by interplanting crops that cooperate with one another. Each plant species plays a different role. Legumes fix nitrogen. Others specialize in sourcing different nutrients. Some plants feed pollinators. David R. Montgomery writes, "A deep-rooted crop should follow a shallow one. High-biomass-producing crops should follow low-biomass ones. And a nutrient fixer should follow a nutrient scavenger. In other words, there is a pattern and rhythm to crop sequencing."[56]

Vandana Shiva describes the mixed farming of corn, beans, and squash in Mexico: "Nitrogen-fixing beans and pulses provide free nitrogen to cereals, and in return, the stalks of cereals like maize or millets provide support for the bean stalks to climb. In turn, the squash provides cover to the soil, preventing soil erosion, water evaporation, and the emergence of weeds."[57]

For Dr. Laurie Drinkwater of the Department of Horticulture at Cornell University, "One strategy that has a huge impact is to just modify rotations so that you have cover crops alternating with the cash crops. We conducted a study looking at all of the research that has been done on cover crops and we found that on the average, if you introduce cover crops into an annual rotation like corn or soy beans, you reduce nitrate leeching by 70%. So that's a huge reduction."[58]

It gets better. Crop rotation integrated with cover crops and composting reduces or eliminates the need to add any fertilizers at all.

Doug Crabtree and Anna Jones-Crabtree are first generation farmers who farm at scale. They started Vilicus Farms,[59] an organic dryland crop farm, on 1,280 acres in the Northern Great Plains of Montana in 2009. They now grow organic heirloom and specialty grains, pulse, oilseed and broadleaf crops on 7,400 acres. Doug told me, "We were committed from the beginning to crop diversity. However many crops are in our rotation, we want them expressed together across each field. Intimacy at scale. Whether three or four or six Spring-seeded crops, they are in strips all together."

"The other really important piece of our conservation," Anna adds, "is the crop rotation with cover crops as an integral part of that rotation, because inherent in that is how we provide diversity to the soil, how we feed the soil, and how the soil feeds us."

"Looking at nature as our guide," Doug continues, "we were able to design our crop rotation intentionally. It's a work in progress with different combinations. In this ecosystem, the diversity needs to achieve a number of functions, but in general, the more the diversity the better." Doug and Anna's philosophy regarding inputs is that a farm should be self-sustaining. Doug has never bought fertilizer with the single exception of an inoculate for their peas and lentils. "Two macronutrients we need to produce grain crops are nitrogen and phosphorus. The soil has lots of phosphorus but it needs to be converted to a form that is plant available. So, we grow deep-rooted crops and cover crops whose roots will go lower in the soil and bring that nutrient up or make it more available, such as buckwheat. When they are terminated they are left on the soil and the phosphorus in the plant residue remains available for the subsequent crop. To provide nitrogen we grow legume crops, which extract nitrogen from the atmosphere for their own benefit and which remains in the soil for subsequent crops."

Soils worldwide, with the possible exception of volcanic soils, are not lacking in minerals. Unfertile, depleted soil is not lacking in minerals — it is deficient in microbes. 85 to 90% of plant nutrient acquisition is made possible by microbial action.

On Anne Evans and Peter Gegger's Blaencamel Farm in Wales, they increased the organic matter level in their soil from 4% to almost 18%. Farming some of the poorest soil in their region but rotating crops and using cover crops, they produce healthy economic yields year after year and their soil keeps improving. As organic farmers, when they first started, they were buying organically approved inputs, but no longer. Anne said, "We found that compost as well as helping solve disease problems has its own nutrient value and has reactivated the soil biology, so now we are in this rather happy situation of saving money because our only inputs are the seeds and compost."[60]

Minimal Disturbance of the Soil / No Till

Earl the Worm had spent most of the night eating weed seeds and moving others in multiple trips down the wormhole and into his burrow. By dawn, tired, sated, he decided to call it a night. He nestled in on a tiny, rich bed of leaf and grass bits alongside his unbroken cocoon. His unborn young were developing fine, he just knew. The temperature of the soil would remain cool for all of them, thanks to the composting crop residue covering the surface above ground.

Earl was sleeping when it happened.

A noise, a vibration... Not coming from the cocoon — his little ones were not yet ready to emerge. Louder, the earth being struck, shaking. Louder still. Really loud. And all in an instant, darkness was struck through with searing light and his world fell in.

He cried out with a gurgling noise, an earthworm's fearful response, as the plow blade sliced through his burrow obliterating everything. Earl was sliced in two and his blood and life fluids drained quickly as his head and the un-severed section of his body was rocketed up through exploding disintegrating soil, into glaring sunlight and open air. He fell atop a mass of clots of severed overturned ground. Earl died on broken soil in searing sun, while the sound and the fury and the vibration of the plow, its blades, and its engine were still nearby, before the dust finished settling about him.

The plow. Time honored, it remains a venerated symbol of the tradition of farming. The Romans during the centuries of their Empire, as well as the Egyptians along the once fertile banks of the Nile River loved to plow, as did the ascendant peoples throughout The Fertile Crescent, Mesopotamia — the "cradle of civilization." But over relatively short periods of time, they ended up destroying their topsoil. The warning spoken in the *Pirates of the Caribbean* ride at Disneyland, "Dead men tell no tales..." comes to mind as I reread David R. Montgomery's observation: "Societies that don't take care of their soil do not last."

Regenerative farmers understand that plowing is one of the most harmful things you can do to your soil...

When you ask Ray Archuleta about tillage, he doesn't mince words. Ray has over 30 years of experience as a Soil Conservationist, Water Quality Specialist and Conservation Agronomist with the Natural Resources Conservation Service. He operates his own 150-acre farm in Missouri and has a national reputation teaching agroecology principles. Ray told me in no uncertain terms, "Tillage is the most destructive thing we do in modern agriculture. You are destroying the soil and spreading the weeds everywhere."

And Ray is only getting started. Once tilled, "The soil begins to cannibalize itself to heal itself. Tilling destroys the biotic glues and compacts the soil so it no longer can absorb the water. The soils have less water capacity, they become less fungal dominant. The soil balance is thrown off with an excessive growth of bacteria. The soil becomes leaky. It cannot hold on to the calcium or the nutrients." Worse still, tilled soil becomes addicted to synthetic inputs. And Ray doesn't stop there. The final consequence is seismically worse: "Our soil nutrient density has been cut by 50%, so the nutrients in the crops are 50% less because the soil has been destroyed. This connects to our cancers."

Ray even has an apt phrase for this. He calls it "Till-icide."

Earl and his brethren were already plowing this field. Their lattices of wormholes and tunnels, collectively miles in length throughout the field, were aerating and loosening the soil, and enabling it to better trap water. The worms added tens of thousands of pounds of nutrients and fertilizer in the form of their castings while protecting the all-important mitochondria. His death, his murder, was so unnecessary.

Plowing rips apart keystone creatures like Earl. As it breaks up the soil surface, it also breaks up the soil's structure, what Kristin Ohlson describes as, "the internal architecture of sand and silt and clay created over the decades by earthworms and other organisms that allowed air, water, and nutrients to circulate."[61]

No less significantly, plowing tears apart the soil's internet.

Protecting the Soil Internet

We are learning more about "the presence of 'common mycorrhizal networks' (CMNs) in multi-species cover crops, in cash crops grown with companion plants, and in high-diversity pastures." Dr. Christine Jones continues, "It has been found that plants in communities assist each other by *linking together in vast underground super-highways* through which they exchange carbon, water and nutrients."[62] [63] [64]

Hold the phone. *What?*

Mycorrhizal fungi are the plant-dependent, soil-building microbes attached to plant roots that, in exchange for liquid carbon sugars that the plant provides them, transport nutrients including organic nitrogen, phosphorus, sulfur, and essential trace elements into the plant roots.

To best accomplish this, they grow *tube filaments that extend away from plant roots* significant distances out into the soil. Plants communicate their nutrient needs to the mycorrhizal fungi who, through these extended tube networks, seek and procure what is needed and then provide it for the plant in exchange for simple sugars.

Plants send chemical signals through these CMNs, through this vast lattice of filaments, communicating their nutrient shopping list to other mycorrhizal fungi and to colonies of soil bacteria interconnected in this network.

Plants also communicate this way with one another. For example, if one plant is attacked by aphids, it sends a message via this network requesting the nutrients it needs to defend itself. In so doing, it alerts the other plants connected to this network that "The aphids are coming!" and the other plants begin to build their defenses before they arrive onto them.[65]

Plants also communicate with other types of plants via messages sent through these networks.[66] [67] In a diverse plant community, mycorrhizal fungi from different plants link up with one another. From a fungal perspective, they proliferate best when there is greater diversity. Each plant has different chemical signatures, different offerings and varying nutrient needs and the mycorrhizal fungi are the ones directing the traffic.

This system is, in effect, the internet of the soil.

The mycorrhizal fungi distribute this information because they are obligate biotrophs — they can't survive in the soil without their plant hosts. In a system of codependence, they want to protect all the plants in their network — all of their carbon sources.

The extended tubes of mycorrhizal fungi are so small that you can't see

them with the naked eye. This is what they look like under a microscope.

The mycorrhizal fungi are the thin white tubes connecting to the yellow plant root. There are *miles* of these fungal filaments — an estimated *12,000 miles* — beneath every square meter of healthy soil.[68]

Imagine that. Ultra-efficient pathways enabling diverse plant species to communicate with one another and exchange needed nutrients on request. For billions of microorganisms interacting together this is their neighborhood — the rhizosphere.

Things flow in both directions along these micro-thin tubular highways. How does this bi-directional flow happen without head-on collisions between, for example, mineral nutrients heading *in* toward the plant root from the hyphal tips along the frontier regions where the mycorrhizal fungi procured them, and carbon sugar exudates heading *out* of the plant root toward outlying areas?

Mycorrhizal fungi create a hydrostatic barrier in the tubes by transforming the shape and function of water molecules. This means that positively charged water flows in one direction while negatively charged water travels the opposite way *in the same tube* without colliding.

It gets even more interesting.

Using this communication system, millions of bacteria — these *single-celled* organisms — are able to communicate *and work together* as well.[69]

This communication system underground — the internet of the soil — is as mysterious as it is amazing. When we stand on ground, we are standing on the rooftop of another world...

Tilling chops up the soil's structure and destroys these underground networks. The plants become deficient in phosphorus and other mineral nutrients since the Common Mycorrhizal Networks are no longer sufficiently functional. The mycorrhizal fungi, severed from the plants — their essential carbon sources — cannot survive.

Plowing has other detrimental effects as well. Kristin Ohlson, in *The Soil Will Save Us*, notes that it is "the pea-sized soil aggregates that enable soil particles to stick together and moisture to infiltrate more easily preventing both wind and water erosion. After these aggregates break down, the soil particles pack tightly against one another — soil compaction — and the land can't capture and hold the water from either irrigation or rain."[70]

As soil is plowed, its carbon is exposed to oxygen in the air, forming carbon dioxide it releases into the atmosphere. Organic carbon can hold up to 20 times its weight in water, so it follows that carbon depleted soil is also far less able to retain moisture.

Good soil absorbs and retains water. Water infiltrates rapidly and most does not run off. Puddles don't last as the water is absorbed. Kristin Ohlson adds, "Healthy soil that's rich in microorganisms and heavily studded with their aggregates holds water like a sponge, slowly releasing it to plants as well as to rivers and streams. Healthy soil is the best protection for crops during a drought, as well as the best protection against floods anywhere. The soil is the earth's first water purification system, too: The microorganisms will attack and purge water of its pollutants, eventually draining it into a stream or aquifer in a pure form."[71]

Earthworms need water to be present to be active. Activity throughout the entire microbiome is optimal in soil that is cooler because it is covered from the sun and protected from the wind and rain.

I spoke with Gabe Brown about the improvement in the soil on his North Dakota ranch, which in terms of its capacity to absorb and retain moisture, has become legendary. Flooding was an issue in the early 1990s when infiltration tests showed that one of his fields could only absorb a half-inch of rain an hour. The term for water infiltration capacity is "effective rainfall." That same field was tested in 2012 and can absorb 8 inches an hour.

Plowing lays the soil bare. Exposed soil is susceptible to high temperatures and to rapid erosion by wind and rain. David Pimentel's research while Professor of Ecology at Cornell University found that the

United States is losing 3 billion metric tons of soil each year, a rate 10 times faster than the natural replenishment rate; and that soil erosion costs $37.6 billion a year in lost productivity.[72]

Ray Archuleta told me with characteristic bluntness, "We don't have a run off problem. We have a soil infiltration problem."

Topsoil is the most precious resource on our planet since all life comes from it. One goal of regenerative farming is to protect it.

No Synthetic Pesticides

Regular crop rotation is a natural method of reducing pests. It varies with region and weather as everything in nature does, but farmers converting over to regenerative agriculture soon realize a diminishing need to purchase and use pesticides to protect their crops. Experienced regenerative farmers have long since outgrown the need to use any synthetic pesticides at all.

Plants living in untilled fertile soil photosynthesize optimally, and the better they do that, the more resistant they themselves become to insects and other pathogens.

Diverse cover crop plant mixes attract pollinators, as well as providing habitat and food for spiders and other predators of agricultural pests. Plant diversity on the ground means that insect diversity will follow and the damaging role of insect pests declines. I admire Vandana Shiva's perspective on the word "pest" when she states: "The war on pests is neither necessary nor effective... Pests do not emerge in agricultural systems based on diversity, because in an agroecological farming system, no one insect or weed is a 'pest.' Ecological balance through biodiversity is the best pest control mechanism, and friendly insects such as ladybugs, beetles, soldier beetles, spiders, wasps, and the praying mantis all contribute to this process."[73]

Doug Crabtree and Anna Jones-Crabtree at Vilicus Farms in Montana decided to leave 20+ foot wide conservation strips of perennial cover in-between each of the 240 or 360-foot wide crop strips they farm. They originally envisioned them as a way to prevent soil erosion by the wind but have since discovered numerous other benefits. They are now important pollinator habitats as well as wildlife corridors. Birds flourish and many animals live there or use them as migration corridors. Anna told me, "When you think of protecting pollinators you think of the honeybees, but

grazed paddocks than in conventionally grazed ones. And a 2016 analysis found that under regenerative crop and grazing management, cattle could improve soil quality and sequester carbon."[76]

Will Harris at White Oak Pastures, Matt Haute at Cottonwood Creek Farms, Karen and Nate Olson at Prairie View Farm and Lou Preston at Preston Winery are all improving their carbon-rich soil in part with the use of rotationally grazed animals, whether cows, pigs, sheep or chickens. When they have more than one type of animal, larger animals are usually introduced first followed by successively smaller ones.

At Preston Winery, Lou Preston will "mob graze" his sheep (pictured above) paddocked in one area with electric fencing for several days before being herded over to the next section of vineyard. Then in come his chickens as he parks several mobile coops in his vine rows.

The integration of crop and livestock production is the most optimal way to regenerate soil health. As soil improves so do the nutritional, sugar and protein content of the grasses. With animal waste applied directly as fertilizer on the land, input costs go down. Each of these farmers are increasing their crop yields and earning greater profits.

In contrast, on factory farms and in feedlot operations the deluge of manure produced by the excessive numbers of animals crowded together is treated as pollution and waste.

Gabe Brown observes, "The best proven way to transfer massive amounts of carbon dioxide out of the atmosphere and into the soil is by maintaining a landscape that includes grazing animals. It is not the cattle that are the problem, it is our management of them!"[77]

Going forward, if animals are widely reintroduced back into rural American farms, David R. Montgomery envisions a future where "re-integrating animal husbandry with crop production on smaller farms can bring life back to farms — and family farms back to life."[78]

Chapter 1 cited the health benefits of humanely raised grass fed and grass finished beef. Now we complete the circle by revealing, from the rancher and farmer perspective, how beneficial the grazing of ruminants is for the soil and for crop yield — if it is done in a holistic planned grazing manner.

For Wendell Berry, "'Animal science' without husbandry forgets, almost as a requirement, the sympathy by which we recognize ourselves as fellow creatures of the animals. It forgets that animals are so called because we once believed them to be endowed with souls. Animal science has led us away from that belief or any such belief in the sanctity of animals. It has led us instead to the animal factory which, like the concentration camp, is a vision of Hell. Animal husbandry, on the contrary, comes from and again leads to the psalmist's vision of good grass, good water, and the husbandry of God."[79]

There is concern about the methane gas cows emit.

We know that cows, principally by their digestive processes (enteric fermentation) belch out a lot of methane gas. Livestock belching (25.9%) and manure (10.3%) is responsible for 36.2% of global methane emissions.[80] Methane is dangerous as it is 86 times more potent as a heat-trapping greenhouse gas than CO_2 for the first decade or two after it is released.[81] In 2016, methane constituted 10% of the U.S. greenhouse gas emissions making it a significant factor in global warming.[82]

When I learned about the soil's internet, I was amazed.

A short time later, I was walking with Dr. Christine Jones in a pasture at Paicines Ranch in central California when I found out this as well...

There is another lifeform, one we are only just learning about, another resident in a healthy soil microbiome.

We arrived at the pasture's edge where the land gently rises becoming the base of a small hill and stood in the dappled shade cast from the oak trees along the ridgeline. It was a beautiful early winter afternoon. Raptors circling under scattered clouds in the blue sky caught our eye. I crouched down to look closely at the soft compressible soil of this fertile pasture, the diverse mix of the plants and grasses. Looking closely, feeling their textures, it was here that I met Ezra.

Ezra is a Methanotrope. I couldn't see Ezra because, like Pat the Pooper, Ezra is microscopic. So, I didn't start talking to Ezra as that might have caused Dr. Jones concern. But this is exactly where Ezra and Ezra's minions hang out, millions of them...

Methanotrophic bacteria.

I didn't know they were out there. I wasn't even aware they existed. These bacteria are so named because they only ingest one thing — methane. It's their sole energy source. They live in the oceans, and they live amidst prairie grasses and soil. Dr. Jones told me, "If a cow has her head down eating grass, the methane she breathes out is rapidly metabolized by methanotrophs." The molecules of methane methanotrophs metabolize *do not* enter the atmosphere. And Ezra's minions ingest a lot.

There were more ruminants on the planet 200 years ago than there are today, but we've transitioned from huge free-ranging herds like the buffalo to huge concentrations of animals in factory farm and feedlot confinement. That changes everything...

Methanotrophs can only live in aerobic environments in less compacted soil, and they, like most microbes, are killed by synthetic nitrogen fertilizer. Methanotrophs do not survive in factory farm and feedlot environments.[83] The methane cows belch out is considerable, and in factory farms and feedlots all of it, every breath, disperses into the atmosphere. Ezra can't help us there.

The methane belched by pasture grazing cows is largely a meal for earth bound methanotrophs.

. . .

Regenerative farming is a successful business model.

Farmers converting into regenerative agriculture will find that it can take a few years before their soil, degraded by years of industrial agriculture, regains its microbial health and fertility. During this time, even though their crop yield will not outperform their neighbors, their input costs will be significantly reduced. For this reason alone they can become comparatively more profitable.

In *Dirt to Soil* Gabe Brown writes, "my first year of no-till farming was fantastic. Not only did our crop yields go up, but I was also able to move down the path of reducing synthetic fertilizer use by adding nitrogen-fixing field peas to the crop rotation... One of the biggest advancements in the health of the soils on my ranch, not to mention the health of my pocketbook, occurred when I decreased and eventually eliminated the use of synthetic fertilizers."[84]

Planting diversified nitrogen-fixing cover crops and year-round ground cover eliminates the need for nitrogen fertilizer. Going no-till eliminates those operating costs. As the organic-matter, carbon and nitrogen content in their soil improves, regenerative farmers can wean themselves from all synthetic fertilizers. Since healthy soil, crop rotations that include hardy pathogen-resistant plants, and restored insect diversity break up pest and disease cycles, these farmers soon find they don't need to purchase pesticides. Or herbicides. They are soon needing far less water to irrigate their fields. By avoiding GMO Roundup Ready seed and the costly farming equipment of a Big Ag program with its concurrent fuel, maintenance and financing costs, regenerative farmers are operating at far lower cost.

A study in Scientific American found that to produce 100 units of food using crop diversity and farming in the regenerative agriculture method requires 5 units of inputs. To produce the same 100 units of food in the monocrop mode of industrial agriculture requires 300 units of inputs.[85]

Regenerative farmers like Joan and Nick Olson of Prairie Drifter Farm, Lou Preston of Preston Winery and Will Harris at White Oak Pastures are farming with little or no debt and enjoying much better control of their destiny than either factory farmers or industrial agriculture farmers.

Gabe Brown told me the story of a young Canadian farming couple who were borrowing $300,000 a year just for fertilizer. They adopted regenerative practices and, "This last year, after five years, they borrowed just $27,000. And their yields have gone up. That's a huge savings. Add to that their savings on all the *other* inputs they no longer needed — it just goes on and on."

Working with nature, farming becomes easier and less time consuming. I laughed when Gabe confided, "The best thing I can do for my ranch is stay in my house."

Once the soil microbiome is repaired, crop yields increase, and before long they are experiencing higher yields per acre on each type of crop compared to their neighbors who continue to farm in the conventional industrial Big Ag manner.

Degraded soil produces crops of diminished nutritional quality which effects consumer health. Dr. Christine Jones cites studies showing, "Over the last 70 years, the level of every nutrient in almost every kind of food has fallen between 10 and 100%. An individual today would need to consume twice as much meat, three times as much fruit and four to five times as many vegetables to obtain the same amount of minerals and trace elements available in those same foods in 1940."[86] In addition to higher crop yields, regenerative farmers are harvesting crops of superior nutritional quality with no nutrient loss compared to crops of yesteryear. In fact, there is a gain.

Study after study confirms that "organic foods not only have lower pesticide residue but higher phytochemical, antioxidant, and micronutrient density as well."[87] Growing food with higher nutritional value and better taste that is pesticide and toxin residue free, regenerative farmers can command a premium price for superior crops. Regenerative agriculture is a higher standard than organic and is three times more profitable than industrial farm production. This also holds true for pasture-raised meat and dairy products.

Regenerative farmers are able to grow varieties of crops throughout the year. Lou Preston at Preston Winery grows a diverse array of seasonal vegetables, wheat and other grains, chicken eggs, and lamb in addition to his wines and olive oils. His baked breads are renowned. He charges a premium for what he grows, has various crops to market year-round, and has much lower input costs compared to industrial agriculture farmers.

With healthy soil, a healthy insect population follows, pollinators arrive — the monarchs and bees. Farmers soon notice the return of wildlife to their land: Birds of all kinds, weasels, deer. Foxes.

Red foxes like Travis don't migrate. They live their lives in and around the territory where they were born. Their natural habitat is scrub and woodland, but they are very adaptable. They are drawn to healthy land, teeming with life. Red foxes eat a wide variety of things: mice, rats, squirrels, rabbits and birds, as well as eggs, insects, fruit and carrion.

They usually sleep during the day, and hunt at night, but today Travis is out hunting as he needs to bring food back for the young kits in his den. His mate, Amanda is as devoted a mom as he is a dad — she's in the den

protecting and nursing her young. Her kits are nine days old and two of them just opened their eyes for the first time.

Red foxes are not pack animals. Travis and Amanda will devote several months to raising their young, living together as a small family in their underground den. Once the young are grown enough to be independent, Travis and Amanda will hunt and sleep alone.

Alert, wary, red foxes are very smart animals. When Travis is awake, he is always hunting. When he shifts closer to farmland, he may try to catch a chicken, or a lamb or piglet, but if a farmer adds a guard animal, like Stone Barns does with its Maremma sheepdogs, foxes will stay clear.

Most regenerative farmers are pleased when wildlife returns to their land. It's a clear sign of the land's health. Foxes benefit farmers by preying on field mice and rats. This morning, Travis has caught his second one and is bringing it home as well.

For David R. Montgomery, "The degradation of soils and the loss of organic matter are the most underappreciated environmental crisis humanity now faces. But the stage is set for ground-up transformational change, as the short-term interests of farmers increasingly align with preserving long-term soil fertility."[88]

Regarding regenerative farming, Dr. Vandana Shiva notes, "Industrial agriculture only measures what leaves the farm; *we* measure what is returned to the soil. Rejuvenating healthy soils has allowed us to increase productivity."[89]

This kind of farming, this respect for the land, is compassionate farming. Regenerative Agriculture principles — cover crops, compost, crop rotation, minimal disturbance of the soil, protecting the soil's internet, no pesticides, and animals — are more than just principles. They are values.

Given our skillsets and tools, and applying the newest scientific understanding, we now understand:

- that taking good care of all the microorganisms and creatures under the ground is essential for the health of the soil and the quality and value of the crops we harvest from the soil.
- that the denizens of the underground realm are no less important than the plants and animals living above-ground.
- that they need the very same things we do: "Constant high-nutritive-value food sources... a good habitat... and protection from diseases and predators."[90]

Regenerative agriculture is compassionate farming. Regenerative agriculture is the path forward — for the soil, for the health and quality of the harvest, for the land and its wonderful creatures, big, small, miniscule and microscopic.

It is compassionate farming for families, for family businesses, and for each one of us who eats healthy nutritious food and cares a great deal that our families, our children and loved ones, and each one of us, can do so as well.

It is compassionate living, in harmony with the planet we share.

It benefits everyone. And it can heal the planet at this critical time.

The only things regenerative agriculture does not benefit are the bottom lines of the fertilizer, pesticide and other chemical manufacturers, the GMO seed producers, factory farmers, and the fossil fuel industry.

It does not benefit Big Ag.

III

Why is just 1% of U.S. farmland certified organic? And regenerative agriculture acreage covers less than that? This, despite the fact that

American consumer demand for organic food in 2016 soared to $43 billion making this the fastest growing sector of the overall food economy.[91] Why, as of 2013, did the combined acreage of American farmers who practiced cover cropping, composting, or crop rotation account for just 21% of crop land?[92]

The vast majority of American farmland *is not* farmed in a manner that is increasing soil fertility. 94% of soybeans and 72% of corn in the United States are farmed in the industrial agriculture method, using Roundup Ready GMO (Genetically Modified Organism) seed and its attendant suite of synthetic fertilizers, herbicides and pesticides. Worldwide, the land used for Bayer (which acquired Monsanto in 2018) GMO crops has increased from 3 million acres in 1996 to over 282 million acres.[93]

Laura Lengnick, in *Resilient Agriculture*, writes, "The goal of soil quality being a desirable feature on your farm is definitely on the minds of every farmer." But she understands that "we're in a lock-in-trap that's been created. We have sunk massive amounts of resources both public and private into this industrial food system. And so the folks that are the stakeholders that are maintaining the system have a lot to lose if we change."[94]

Vandana Shiva observes, "Where once there was a farming system in which everything was internally recycled and reused, from the soil to the water to the plants, there was now a system that relied on external inputs of seeds, chemicals, and fertilizers that constantly needed to be purchased."[95] This system is **Industrial Agriculture**.

Following World War II, the mechanization and industrialization of agriculture introduced an era of chemical fertilizer-intensive, input intensive farming. It soon required more money to farm. Hundreds of thousands of farm families found they could no longer grow profitably and were forced to stop. They left farming and their rural communities behind, relocating to the cities in search of work. Industrial agriculture is designed to work most efficiently on a larger scale, and surviving farmers, realizing this, acquired their neighbor's "For Sale" or foreclosed land. Between 1930 and 2000 the average size of American farms tripled to 450 acres, and farming shifted from crop diversity to monocrop specialization.

"Biotechnology breakthroughs soon followed that boosted yields and consolidated corporate control of the food system through proprietary seeds, agrochemical products, and commodity crop distribution [became] the foundation of conventional agriculture," notes David R. Montgomery.[96]

Profits for the corporations soared to record highs while, for the farmers that remained, despite these changes, profitability proved elusive. Today, four massive seed and chemical corporations dominate the industrial agriculture food system: Bayer, Syngenta, Dow and DuPont.[97] Five others, Cargill, Archer Daniels Midland, Bunge, Glencore International and Louis Dreyfus control grain supply.[98]

Big Ag crafts a narrative touting increased profitability for farmers. Millions of small farms have failed. Millions. So, what about the survivors — our larger modern-day farmers?

It has now become so expensive to farm in the industrial agriculture manner and monocrop farming so prescribed that these farms are, in effect, operated by financially indentured property managers — farmers so detached from the soil they cultivate, they are "farmers" in the most pejorative sense only; "contract farmers" at best. They ride in the elevated cabs of their combines, which alone are half-a-million-dollar investments they must finance and pay for. They plant Bayer Roundup Ready seeds, fertilize with chemicals manufactured great distances away from their farms, spray with Bayer's pesticides and herbicides, all according to calendar dates predetermined by Big Ag input providers. They must buy these costly inputs at non-competitive prices determined by Bayer and the other dominant corporations in this industry, harvest yields of corn, wheat or soybeans — lower yields per acre than those of established regenerative farmers — and sell these commodity crops at market prices fixed to a large degree by the corporations controlling supply.

David R. Montgomery's observation is profound: "Here is the trap that input-intensive farmers fall into, where they pay high costs at the front end, and focus on yields and gross returns rather than on the spread between expense and income. High input costs and low commodity prices are a recipe for farm failure. This has been the story of the American family farm since the Second World War."[99] The corporations selling these inputs to farmers are profiting handsomely, not the farmers.

Akin to the factory farmers who oversee the pig operations in North Carolina, these contract farmers are mired in debt and fully beholden to the Big Ag industry, which is in near complete control of the crop value the farm generates and any profit margin these farmers cling to. The perception that the monocrop method of farming championed by industrial agriculture is more profitable is not reality. Many of these farms often operate at a loss only to be repeatedly bailed out by federal crop insurance, which eliminates their risk in bad years. Crop insurance is a safety net that the Big Ag industry helped design and lobbied our government to provide in order to prop up the industrial agriculture system. While protecting farmers from loss-harvests, it contains disincentives for farmers to convert over to regenerative farming, which is exactly what the corporations behind industrial agriculture want it to do. The cost to the American taxpayer of this annual bailout of the industrial agriculture system was $4.2 billion in 2016.[100] The federal government provides over *$20 billion dollars* in agricultural subsidies *each year*.

U.S. Congressman Tim Ryan, regarding the Farm Bill formally known as the Agricultural Act of 2014, wrote, "It carried on the gross subsidies (now called crop insurance) to large scale commercial agriculture while offering a paltry sum for sustainable and regional specialty farmers... While 98% of farms are family-owned operations, only a small percentage receive agricultural subsidies. Over the last 10 years, 62% of farms collected no subsidy at all."[101]

Industrial farmers are increasingly aware of the damage they are doing to their land as well as the potential advantages of regenerative farming, but most are reluctant to change over. Bucking convention and peer pressure is not easy. Many are deep in debt and their banks are reluctant to finance what they consider a risky shift in business practices. Big Ag spends millions creating a counter-narrative that all is just fine, that these farmers are "heroically feeding the world," while making sure that crop insurance is available to them as a downside hedge. Sallie Calhoun, who runs Paicines Ranch,[102] informed me that these farmers "are doing exactly what the government, the companies, and the land grant universities are telling them. They are trapped in many cases in very small boxes of debt, devastated communities, degraded soils, and commodity markets... It is not easy to learn the truth about something you and your family have been doing for 50 years, and it is not easy to completely change your way of thinking, growing, and marketing."

In 2015, a study projected that 27% of the crop-land in Iowa would lose more than $100 per acre based on high input costs and low grain prices, leading David R. Montgomery to conclude, "Something is seriously wrong with our agricultural system if hardworking Iowans growing crops on some of the best agricultural soil in the world can't make money farming."[103]

"Time and again, at one farming conference after another," according to David R. Montgomery, "farmers readily acknowledged the possibility that plowing resulted in long-term damage to the soil. A surprising number said they knew this to be true from firsthand experience. Older farmers would share stories about how their soil quality had gone downhill over their lifetimes, too slowly to notice year to year, but plain as day in retrospect. One after another piped up to say that they'd noticed their soil decline under the now-conventional marriage of the plow and intensive fertilizer and agrochemical use."[104]

Midwestern farmers are also very much aware that the fertilizer runoff from their fields enters nearby rivers and is causing the toxic algal blooms in our waterways, the most significant flowing out from the Mississippi River is the 8,500 square mile "dead zone" in the Gulf of Mexico. Dr. Stephanie A. Smith, a biologist developing water monitoring technology with Xylem-YSI, wonders: "I also grew up in a rural community, so I know that farmers, by their nature, are good stewards of the land. It's their livelihood, so to argue that they are just irresponsibly over-fertilizing is not reasonable. Why would they waste their money like that, and why would they willingly hurt the waters that support their livestock and families?"[105]

Why?

"Therein lies the real dilemma at the heart of our modern crisis: the immediate financial interests of corporations that supply farmers do not necessarily align with our collective interest in maintaining the health and fertility of our agricultural soils,"[106] notes David R. Montgomery.

From the perspective of corporate industrial agriculture with its overriding goal of maximizing profit, the economic woes of farmers are not something that is "wrong." It is by design. "The intensification of chemicals and fossil fuels is primarily aimed at substituting the labor of small-scale farmers and concentrating ownership of land in large farms owned by corporations." Vandana Shiva sees the bigger picture, the overarching strategy of the wizard behind the curtain. The reality for Big Ag, for the corporations behind industrial agriculture, is that "high production costs and low commodity prices translate into two-way profits. For the farmer they translate into a negative economy and spiraling debts."[107]

Laura Jackson, an evolutionary biologist at the University of Northern Iowa, describes this agriculture "as a giant open-air factory owned by monopolies and stretching across the Midwest. You can drive for 6 hours and see nothing except for corn and soybeans, and before and after these crops are planted and harvested — a period of about 9 months — the ground is naked and exposed to the elements. This is agriculture but we don't eat what it produces. The corn and soybeans are commodities that feed cattle and other animals in the feedlots."[108]

The concentrated "production" of livestock in factory farms simplified matters for crop farmers because they no longer had to concern themselves with raising livestock as well. Feedlots, the centralized feeding operations where livestock is sent to be brought up to optimal weight over its final couple of months before slaughter, began as a means to utilize excess grain production. This plays nicely into the hands of the corporations underlying industrial agriculture because, once again they profit two ways: the feedlots purchase huge amounts of their commodity crops. 36% of corn crops and 70% of soybeans grown in the U.S. are used for animal feed. And the loss of animal fertilizer on farms creates a fertilizer dependence on the part of the grain growers. [109]

Industrial agriculture further simplifies matters for farmers as it removes what is fundamental about farming from farming — it removes that intimate, sensual, complex interaction between a human being, a farmer, and his or her land.

The French word, terroir, originally used regarding wine regions, refers to that tapestry encompassing all of the conditions in which any food is grown or produced, that intimate geographically unique interrelationship between soil and climate that gives anything grown there its distinctive nutrient characteristics, and distinctive smell and texture and taste. Regenerative farmers are intimately connected to these essences, the terroir of their land and to what they grow. This is their livelihood, what they dedicate their life's time to, their passion and their pride. The concept of terroir is even grander still. More than even the richness and fertility of the soil and its microbiome, and the climate of the region, the word encompasses the history of that land, of its people, the culture, the traditions. Terroir exudes life and alive-ness, and lifestyle. When you buy wine or bread, or a certain vegetable from a region or a specific farm, the discerning can taste qualities unique to it based on its terroir.

In contrast, industrial agriculture is terror on the land.

An industrial agriculture commodity crop farmer today is generally not interested in the biology of the soil. His or her skillsets are ones that have been divorced from the land and its terroir. They include: marketing, in the sense of applying for and taking full advantage of the government programs such as the crop insurance and other handouts that cover the farm's financial losses; management skills in dealing with the banker and land leasing agents to massage the ongoing debt burden necessary to purchase all the requisite industrial agriculture inputs; and the mechanical skills to operate the expensive farming equipment necessary to farm their vast acreage. Gabe Brown writes, "Experience has taught me — and many other farmers will agree — there is no money to be made producing commodities without accepting taxpayer subsidies."[110] He wants no part of that.

Terror on the land is the violence, the lethality of industrial agriculture's methods. Vandana Shiva offers a seminal insight: "Industrial agriculture is not a knowledge system based on the understanding of ecological processes within an agroecosystem; rather, it is a collection of violent tools."[111]

· · ·

Industrial Agriculture's violent tools include:

- monocrop farming
- tilling
- farmer indebtedness
- farmworker exploitation
- synthetic fertilizers
- water
- pesticides and herbicides
- GMO seeds

Monocrop Farming

Industrial agriculture farmers clear their land of all weeds and vegetation as well as crop residues. They then plant and raise a vast single crop, most commonly corn, wheat or soybeans. This cycle leaves the soil bare for up to nine months.

"One of the most unnatural practices of conventional farming is its creation of vast landscapes in which only one plant is grown, usually corn or wheat or soybeans," writes Kristin Ohlson. A natural prairie will contain a wide variety of plant species, each contributing to the complexity and vibrancy of "a correspondingly lush community of microorganisms underground, as the different plants offer different root exudates and attract an array of different microorganisms, making the soil overall more resilient."[112] Monocrops don't exist naturally. Lack of diversity is an open invitation to pests and pathogens and nature will supply them, weakening or killing a monocrop while filling the void.

Dr. Christine Jones has found that "monocultures need to be supported by high and often increasing levels of fertilizer, fungicide, insecticide, and other chemicals that inhibit soil biological activity. The result is even greater expenditure on agrochemicals in an attempt to control the pest, weed, disease and fertility 'problems' that ensue."[113]

Industrial agriculture is causing ecosystem collapse, notes James Merryweather in *Secrets of the Soil*, "not just because wild plants are exterminated, but also because complicated webs of symbiotic partnership are disrupted... In the past, crop rotation and fallowing assisted soils to recover from unsympathetic crops, but nowadays farmers repeatedly plant, for instance, rape or rape/wheat without resting the soil. This effectively deprives mycorrhizal fungi of carbohydrate for a year or more, which is fatal for them. If we want biologically functional soils, we must strive to maintain diverse plant-microbe soil communities, returning biodiversity to agricultural land."[114]

Tilling

Tilling is another violent tool. And not just on account of what happened to Earl.

The primary culprit responsible for soil loss is erosion. Throughout the many months of the year when monocrop farming leaves topsoil unprotected, as well as whenever soil is plowed, the soil is exposed, and wind and rainfall erode it. One storm can strip a century of soil formation off a bare, plowed field.[115]

One third of the world's arable land has been lost to soil erosion. Just since the beginning of industrial agriculture, North America's tilled fields have lost over 40% of their soil organic matter.[116] We lose nearly 2 billion tons of topsoil to erosion each year.[117] Jessica A. Knoblauch in her article, *Farming for the Future* notes that "Iowa's 'black gold,' rich soil built up by thousands of years of natural processes, is also vanishing. Across the state, rivers and streams run muddy brown due to soil erosion caused by tilling and nutrient-depleted soil. A 2007 study found that 10 million

Shiva notes, "As the profits of corporations in food and agriculture systems grow, farmers become poorer by getting deeper in debt and are finally forced off their land."[123]

Children of farmers are acutely aware of this and fewer and fewer of them are willing to invest their lives in taking over the family farm. According to the U.S.D.A. 2012 Census of Agriculture, the average age of American farmers is now 58.3 years old.[124]

Wendell Berry observes, "The farm and all concerns not immediately associated with production have in effect disappeared from sight. The farmer, too, in effect has vanished. He is no longer working as an independent and loyal agent of his place, his family, and his community, but instead as the agent of an economy that is fundamentally averse to him and to all that he ought to stand for."[125]

Factory farming works the same way. Regarding pig factory farms in North Carolina, Smithfield Foods, one of the world's largest hog producers, supplies piglets and feed to its network of factory farmers. Adam Skolnick, in his article *Hog Hell*, reveals that these "contract growers" are "responsible not only for raising the pigs but also for investing the most capital in the operation — where the margins are small — and assuming debts for construction and all of the liabilities for waste disposal." He writes about William Tom Butler, a CAFO contract farmer, who "thought he and his fellow growers would be insulated from the commodities market, but they aren't. 'We found out we were dealing with corporate people and that unfairness is not illegal. I owe about $600,000 on my farm. My payment is $40,000 every 20 weeks, and this bad contract is the only place I can get that. So I have to suck it up.'"[126] Contract farmers are obligated to invest in the construction of their buildings as well as in mandatory upgrades. They must buy their piglets and their feed from Smithfield at prices the corporation sets. And because the system of industrial animal agriculture has reduced factory farmed animals to a commodity, they must sell their market-ready pigs back to Smithfield at low commodity market pricing pre-determined by... Smithfield.

71% of broiler chicken growers whose sole income is chicken raising are living below the poverty line.[127]

These American farmer-owners work long hours living under constant financial pressure and have no control over the economy of their operation. They are in debt bondage from their obligations to industrial agriculture corporations. Just 56% of intermediate-sized farms reported any income at all from farming work in 2014 — not profit mind you, just "any income at all."[128]

In addition to the high input costs industrial agriculture farmers must bear, they are squeezed on the selling end as well. For every $10 the consumer spends on food in a supermarket, only 60 cents winds up with the farmer. The remaining $9.40 is retained to cover the costs and profit of the retailer, distribution, and the Big Ag corporations involved.[129]

Ray Archuleta refers to a farmer who is under contract with Big Ag as a "tenant farmer."

The world over the reality is the same: when crop acreage that was family-farmed in a traditional, regenerative manner is converted over to an industrial agriculture model, it eliminates the hard work and intelligence, the experience, the land-wisdom of these men and women — knowledge which is essential to sustainable food production. It eliminates their ability to continue to provide for and sustain their families. And it eliminates their livelihood, a family livelihood of creating food.

Vandana Shiva's reminder of the distinction between a livelihood and a job is profound: "When we use the term 'livelihood,' we are talking about self-organized work... based on co-creation and coproduction. A livelihood is not a 'job.' The word 'job' was first used during the rise of the Industrial Revolution to describe piecework; a type of work that was measured by the number of items — or 'pieces' — produced... A 'job' is based on the reduction of a creative autonomous human being to 'labor,' and the further reduction of labor to a commodity... Small-scale farmers do not have jobs; they have livelihoods... Reducing human activity to labor, and transforming it from an output to an input, is a prescription for unemployment, displacement, and the destruction of livelihoods of small family farmers and their communities the world over."[130]

Tom Philpott notes that in the United States farmers continue to surrender their land, either because they get too old and their relatives have no interest in taking over the family business, or because they are forced to mortgage it. "According to a USDA report, 40% of the farmland in the United States is rented from banks and investors."[131] In the same report, of the farmers who identified themselves as the principal operators of their farms, just 48% said that was their primary occupation. 52% are part-time farmers having to work a second job as well.

Farmworker Exploitation

This is another violent tool. Regarding labor, Joanna Macy writes, "Meaningful employment is more important than the goods it produces. By linking the person to her fellow beings in reciprocal relationship and enhancing her self-respect, the value of her work is beyond monetary measure. Labor policies and production plans that view work solely in terms of pay or profit degrade it and rob it of meaning."[132]

The labor policies and production plans of industrial agriculture are designed to minimize the input cost of farmworker labor. Big Ag does not benefit from farm labor. Minimizing it as an input cost leaves more of an industrial farm's operating budget available to purchase the inputs that Big Ag corporations do supply and profit from.

What about the farmworkers? Pig factory farms such as those in North Carolina are typical in that they are designed to minimize the people necessary to manage them and, given the scale of their operations, contribute comparatively few jobs to the communities they are located in. Kristin Ohlson observes that, "Thirty years of concentration and consolidation in agribusiness — in meatpacking, seeds and chemicals, grain handling and shipping, farm equipment, fertilizers and food retailing — has allowed these industries to winnow down the opportunities for farmers to just a few."[133]

When farm labor is required, these workers are historically some of the most exploited workers in the United States. Male and female fieldworkers toil long hours to plant, grow, harvest, pick and pack fruits and vegetables for very low wages. Typically, a fieldworker will rise around 5 am each morning to get to the staging area and be transported to the fields, and will return to his or her home that evening around 8 pm. This physical, demanding labor — often performed in extreme heat, and in fields where toxic herbicides and pesticides were recently sprayed — leads to frequent illness and injury. Yet, the vast majority of farm workers are provided no health benefits. Few citizens have interest in doing this work, forcing farm owners to hire itinerant or immigrant labor. Many of these workers are undocumented making them even more vulnerable to exploitation. According to the Food is Power website, "Some of the largest food and beverage companies — including Coca-Cola, Nestlé, PepsiCo and Tyson Foods — are notoriously anti-union and continue to undermine workers' rights."[134]

The film *Food Chains*[135] documents how Walmart's entry into the supermarket industry changed that business model. Wielding its massive purchasing power, it began slashing retail pricing on fruits and vegetables, triggering a nationwide consolidation among supermarket chains. Kroger and Safeway each aggregated over a thousand stores into their folds, gaining the ability to apply competitive volume purchasing leverage. In *Food Chains*, the narrator concludes that this leaves farm owners with "only a handful of supermarkets to sell their product to. These supermarkets have a historically unprecedented amount of power. When a company can dictate pricing structure down its entire supply chain, a free market no longer exists." Dr. Shane Hamilton, an Agribusiness expert, then states how this impacts farmworkers, "It's not the supermarkets telling the workers out in the fields, 'You must do this.' It's the supermarkets having contracts with farm owners or other intermediaries who then have to figure out how to get these demands met." These huge supermarket chains and mass merchants with annual profits in the billions of dollars now control a system where, in Florida in 2014 when *Food Chains* was produced, a fieldworker harvesting tomatoes picks, on average, *4,000 pounds* each day and is paid $40 a day. That works out to one penny per pound. One fieldworker, Lucas Benitez, is acutely aware of the disparity in the life they are living, "You're poor because you're making other people rich."

Synthetic Fertilizers

Synthetic fertilizers do not enhance the soil, yet Big Ag does everything it can to maximize the chemical inputs industrial farmers become increasingly dependent on. Farmers worldwide purchase 100 billion dollars of these increasingly expensive fertilizers every year and frequently react to poor crop yields and poor absorption by purchasing even greater amounts. 187 million tons of chemical fertilizers are applied annually, 115 million tons of nitrogen, 48 million tons of phosphorus, and 24 million tons of potash.[136]

How then can all that fertilizer *not* enhance soil?

David R. Montgomery states, "Growing evidence shows that synthetic fertilizers work like agricultural steroids, propping up short-term crop yields at the expense of long-term fertility and soil health. Consider fertilizers and agrochemicals like antibiotics — a godsend if you really need them, but foolish to rely on for regular use. And this, of course, is exactly what we've been doing for decades."[137]

In fact, these chemical fertilizers disrupt what Kristin Ohlson terms "one of nature's great partnerships."[138] Plants distribute carbon sugars through their roots to microorganisms as their food source in exchange for nutrients. When chemical fertilizers arrive at the plant roots, the plant does not have to surrender carbon to get them, so it stops its flow of carbon sugars which means the microorganisms no longer get enough food. Mycorrhizae bacteria and earthworms do not survive. The more synthetic nitrogen or inorganic phosphorus fertilizer applied to a field, the more the microbial activity is starved and the further that soil deteriorates.

Inorganic chemical fertilizers require enormous amounts of energy. They are very fuel intensive to manufacture and apply. The energy consumed manufacturing synthetic fertilizers worldwide in 2000 was the equivalent of 49 *billion* gallons of diesel fuel.[139] Fertilizer production is one of the most polluting industries on the planet. Plants manufacturing these fertilizers use the century-old Haber-Bosch process, which "catalytically combines atmospheric nitrogen with hydrogen derived from natural gas or gasified coal, to produce ammonia under conditions of high temperature and pressure."[140] These manufacturing plants require so much energy, they are often built directly atop natural gas fields because of the natural gas needed to make this chemical transformation.

Steven Pinker, in his book *Enlightenment Now,* glowingly cites an estimate that Fritz Haber and Carl Bosch, by inventing and perfecting the Haber-Bosch process, have saved 2.7 billion human lives.[141] This estimate appears on a website, ScienceHeroes.com, which considers itself "a community of rambunctious scholars."[142] Clearly not factored in are the catastrophic consequences of this process, something that its inventors were unable to foresee given the boundaries of scientific knowledge in their day, yet something the rambunctious scholars failed to surmise: the immense contribution to global warming from the carbon dioxide and other greenhouse gas emissions of this process, and the extent to which synthetic fertilizers created by this process eviscerate the microbial life and their intricate interrelationships essential to healthy soil. Doing this, in effect, devastates vast tracts of the planet's most valuable and life-essential resource — its topsoil.

Even if you accept the calculation that the Haber-Bosch process has saved 2.7 billion lives, the Haber-Bosch process has put us on a clear path to the near-future annihilation of 7 billion lives and counting.

Just the process of manufacturing this fertilizer, of converting nitrogen to ammonia, requires 1.2% of the world's energy use.[143]

These fertilizers are not only heavily polluting *before and after* being applied to crop land but are very inefficient as well.

In regenerative farming, leguminous cover crops and animal manure add nitrogen to the soil. There is minimal leakage of nitrogen because it is released slowly and most taken up by living organisms.

When synthetic nitrogen fertilizer is added to the soil, 50% of it is lost right away. Only 10 to 40% of synthetic nitrogen fertilizer is absorbed by plants. So, 60 to 90% of synthetic nitrogen fertilizer is lost either by vaporizing into the atmosphere as potent greenhouse gases, ammonia or nitrous oxide, or simply leaches away into the groundwater, polluting rivers and creating toxic algal blooms and dead zones like the one covering thousands of miles in the Gulf of Mexico spreading out from the mouth of the Mississippi river. According to the National Oceanic and Atmospheric Administration, the "dead zone" in the Caribbean in 2017 is the largest ever recorded, over 8,500 square miles — larger than the size of New Jersey.

What is a "dead zone?" How does this happen?

An algal bloom is an absolute explosion of algae that feast on the nitrogen and phosphorus from agricultural fertilizer runoff as well as the wastewater discharge of animal manure and septic leakage from factory farms.[144] As this infinitesimal number of algae die and decompose they suck the oxygen out of the water, creating this vast dead zone, suffocating and ultimately killing all aquatic life.[145] Not just fish travelling the surface waters but *all life* from the surface of the sea down to the ocean floor. This despite ocean currents bringing in fresh waters into the Gulf of Mexico from the Atlantic Ocean...

This is what it takes to create a "dead zone" *the size of New Jersey* in the ocean: In 2017, monitoring equipment determined that in May, 181,500 tons of nitrate and 24,860 tons of phosphorus fertilizer — volume enough to fill 2,800 railroad hopper cars — flowed down the Mississippi River into the Gulf of Mexico.[146] That was just in that single month of May...

The synthetic nitrogen fertilizer that vaporizes into the atmosphere does so in the form of nitrous oxide. Nitrous oxide contributes mightily to global warming. While nitrous oxide constitutes just 6% of all U.S. greenhouse gas emissions, it is one of the most potent greenhouse gases. It is *300 times* more damaging to the atmosphere than carbon dioxide and it has an atmospheric life of 166 years.[147] 77% of U.S. nitrous oxide emissions comes from agricultural soil management practices.[148] "In 2010, nitrogen oxide emissions from agricultural soils caused by the addition of synthetic fertilizers were the equivalent of *683 million tons* of CO_2."[149]

Inorganic phosphorus fertilizer is also remarkably inefficient. Once in the soil, over 80% of it bonds to aluminum and iron oxides or forms calcium or other compounds, *none of which* are plant useful.[150]

The fertilizer industry thrives on nutrient-poor soil. Koch Fertilizer dominates production of nitrogen fertilizers and the Mosaic Company is the biggest producer of phosphate and potash fertilizers.[151] The majority of an industrial farmer's operating costs can be traced to fossil fuels and products requiring intensive fossil fuel use. Farmers caught in this cycle of increasing chemical fertilizer dependency for their degrading cropland find themselves at the mercy of these companies who control the market and can set prices knowing that consumer subsidized crop insurance will bail out insolvent farmers by squaring their bills.

Industrial agriculture farmers, as well as the corporations that supply their fertilizers and other inputs, would like to grow crops that have high nutrient value similar to crops grown a century ago, but they are aware that given the depleted, damaged soil in industrially farmed crop fields, that is not possible.

Fundamentally, it doesn't matter to them. Not when food is treated as a commodity and sold in bulk based on quantity. As a tradable commodity, it can be vitamin and mineral depleted, and laden with toxins and poison residues as well — it will have a market value even though it has lost much of its nutritional value.[152]

Vandana Shiva writes, "Oil-based, fossil-fuel intensive, chemical intensive industrial agriculture unleashes processes that are killing the soil, and hence terminating our future."[153]

In healthy soil, over 85% of plant nutrient acquisition, including organic nitrogen, is microbially mediated. There are thousands of different types of bacteria and archaea living in the soil that "can fix nitrogen simply using light energy from the sun, transformed into biochemical energy during photosynthesis and channeled into the soil by plant roots."[154] Dr. Christine Jones also notes that "The soil's ability to support nutrient dense, high vitality crops, pastures, fruit and vegetables requires the presence of a diverse array of soil microbes from a range of functional groups."[155]

The increase in crop yields when fertilizer is applied to fertile soil is negligible and not worth the cost. Inorganic nitrogenous fertilizers change the soil's pH balance creating acidic conditions that kill earthworms and the soil microbes that organically fix nitrogen. Killing off the soil microbes shifts farmers into a downward spiral of addiction, forcing them to apply increasing amounts of inorganic fertilizer inputs in an attempt to produce passable crop yields from their degrading and dying soil.

Remember that earthworm castings in healthy soil "can amount to up to *39.5 tons* per acre per year." When a farmer surveys his or her field and remarks, "It's going to sh-t," in one way or the other it is. Either Pat the Pooper and Earl's earthworm kin and all the subterranean denizens of a healthy biome and microbiome are busy fertilizing that soil, or that farmer is surveying dying land, having applied another round of synthetic fertilizers or pesticides further eviscerating that soil's biome, its life and its fertility.

We've been there once before. There was another time in our history when misguided agriculture policy destroyed vast swaths of our native prairie grass and our soil: the Dust Bowl years of the Great Depression. President Franklin D. Roosevelt, enacting federal programs to remedy that, observed, "A nation that destroys its soils destroys itself." His words are no less important today.

Synthetic fertilizers *do not* enhance the soil. Maintaining soil health requires that synthetic fertilizers be reduced and phased out in order to allow soil microbes to recover and function.

Water

Industrial agriculture requires exponentially more irrigation per crop acre than regenerative agriculture does. Like every other input, the industrial agriculture system uses it very inefficiently. Since 70% of America's freshwater usage now goes to agriculture, this is a very big deal.[156]

The compacted soil on monocrop fields can only capture small, superficial amounts of water, so rainfall as well as much of the irrigation water seeps out and washes away. Dr. Christine Jones foresees the problem this is creating because "planetary stocks of fresh water are declining alarmingly. More efficient water use is going to be absolutely critical to the survival of our species. Making better use of water requires improved soil structure, which in turn requires actively aggregating soils. If aggregates are breaking down faster than they're forming, the water-holding capacity of the soil can only deteriorate."[157]

Pesticides and Herbicides

Monocrop farming combined with tilling the soil creates the perfect environment for weeds and pests to flourish.

For Bayer and other chemical companies, this was a magnificent opportunity. Farmers embraced products like Roundup with its active ingredient glyphosate, because it did a good job killing weeds. In 1991 over 18 million pounds of glyphosate was used on crops in the United States.[158] Use increased 15-fold since 1995 when GMO crops were introduced. The amount of glyphosate used in 2014 was sufficient to treat between 22 and 30% of globally cultivated cropland.[159] The use of glyphosate worldwide in 2017 exceeds 1.48 million tons. In June 2018, a Newsweek article confirmed: *Glyphosate Now the Most-Used Agricultural Chemical Ever.*[160] In recent years, as more and more targeted insects and plants have evolved to become Roundup resistant, industrial agriculture farmers have been applying even greater amounts of Roundup and at more frequent intervals.[161]

Vandana Shiva writes, "Only 1% of the pesticide sprayed acts on the target, and the rest spreads into the ecosystem, affecting all organisms. Pesticides are highly nonspecific and are toxic to many non-target organisms including humans."[162] In the case of seeds treated with neonicotinoid insecticides, the toxin spreads through the entire plant, so the entire plant becomes poisonous and remains that way for its life. Neonics can also linger in the soil for years.[163] 90% of the corn grown in the U.S. is synthetic pesticide treated and "residues can be found in many of the foods we eat."[164]

A study published in October 2017 analyzing insect-trapping data across Germany, discovered a 76% decrease in the abundance and bio-mass of flying insects over a 27-year period.[165] This is dire news as insect declines adversely impact all species. Entomologist Doug Tallamy explains that nearly 40% of all animal species on earth are herbivorous insects and that "they convert plants into food, in the form of themselves, for all other species. Without insects our food webs would be destroyed." Insect populations in the United States are in freefall and, "There's no doubt that the widespread use of insecticides is a major contributor, both on farms and in suburban yards."[166]

Synthetic pesticides have decimated non-target insects like the pollinators. 90% of all corn seeds in the United States are now coated with Bayer's neonicotinoid pesticide which is devastating bee populations.[167] 57% of bee colonies have collapsed — these essential pollinators who are so vital to our food supply. Roundup eradicates milkweed, the only plant monarchs eat and their caterpillars are raised on. The endangered monarch population has declined 96% over the past two decades. "Endangered" as in, "in danger of" extinction.

Studies indicate that pesticide poisons are having a detrimental effect on bird populations as well. The April-May 2018 issue of National Wildlife reports, "In springtime, U.S. and Canadian farmers plant neonicotinoid-coated seeds on more than 100 million acres, just as birds are stopping in agricultural fields to refuel on their journeys north to breeding grounds."[168]

This is Timothy. He's a white-crowned sparrow from Canada, and like most Canadians, he loves to sing. He has a beautiful voice and, *unlike* most of us, he sings really well.

This photo of him was taken in Canada where he was born. He's been wintering in Tennessee and is now journeying. He's on his spring migration heading back to his home up north. He's spent the night in a small grove of trees in Iowa. He's healthy, he's in his prime — imagine how exhilarating his journey must be, flying over that beautiful countryside, gliding in whenever he likes to eat or drink or rest. He has lots to sing about.

Timothy's flown this path before, but every year the terrain he flies over — the environment itself — changes a little. His flightpath the next few days will prove more dangerous for him than ever before, although he won't realize that. He'll be traveling over seemingly endless farm land — fields of GMO corn and soy. The trees and meadows are fewer and fewer. But Timothy's mobile and he's versatile, so he doesn't worry about that. If he needs to spend the night in a field or near a farmhouse he'll find a spot.

He needs to eat to maintain his traveling weight and energy. He likes to eat insects and seeds, as well as vegetable matter, weeds and grasses. And this is where the principal danger lies and why, while white-crowned sparrows are not yet endangered, their numbers are declining. Timothy will find that there are far fewer insects in this region this year. He won't realize why, but the reason is that their populations have been devastated by two widely used classes of very effective agricultural insecticides: neonicotinoids and organophosphates. But Timothy's mobile and versatile so he doesn't worry about that. Meal of second choice for this traveler will be the tasty seeds he'll scavenge or vegetable matter instead. Problem. These poisons are now present in the seeds, as well as on surviving weeds and grasses far and wide.

A Canadian study reveals that migratory songbirds are particularly susceptible to neonicotinoids and organophosphates: "White-crowned sparrows exposed to realistic concentrations of imidacloprid exhibited rapid and substantial declines in body mass and fat stores within 24 hours of exposure. Other symptoms of acute poisoning observed only in imidacloprid dosed birds include loss of appetite, excess saliva in the crop, and death."[169]

If Timothy has the good fortune to locate some scrub trees, a wild meadow or thicket, perhaps even a winding streambed that although adjacent to industrial cropland, may have been subjected to overspray but not directly doused with these insecticides, he can locate a healthy meal. But Timothy's mobile and versatile so he doesn't worry about that. He will find a meal. He just won't realize whether his next meal is healthy or not until it's in his body's digestive system. For migrating white-crowned sparrows, some will find a healthy meal, others won't. It's a roll of the dice and each year the odds are getting worse.

The Canadian study continues, "Migration is a critical life stage, and birds that use agricultural habitats for refueling during migration may be particularly susceptible to exposure to neurotoxic insecticides. Species associated with grassland and agricultural landscapes are exhibiting severe population declines in North America."[170]

Akin to synthetic fertilizers, these pesticides kill off the soil microbes and reduce the essential plant-carbon flow from the plants that microbes depend on. Dr. Michael Hansen, Senior Scientist with Consumers Union, states, "The trade name was Roundup. The testing they did on the product before it came to market was only on the active ingredient itself (glyphosate), not on the actual formulated product. Not only does glyphosate destroy mycorrhizae in the soil, it can also decrease levels of beneficial soil microorganisms and increase the level of harmful ones."[171] Ironically, limiting the availability of microbe-provided mineral and trace elements to plant roots weakens plants and leaves them more susceptible to pests and disease.

These pesticides, once applied, were thought to degrade rapidly in soil but this is not the case. Once applied on crop fields, glyphosate tends to stick around. Robert J. Kremer in *Soil and Environmental Health after Twenty years of Intensive Use of Glyphosate*, writes, "Researchers have found that, after years of consistent application to agricultural crops, the chemical accumulates and persists in area soil, particularly at the root zone and in the top few millimeters. In part, the accumulation is due to the fact that only 5% of any applied dose tends to reach the weed it is intended to kill, while the rest lands in the soil."[172] Glyphosate is likely also released into the soil from the roots of plants that have absorbed it, as well as from their decomposing mass later on.[173]

Regenerative farmers have no need for any of these synthetic pesticides. They understand that nature strikes a pretty good balance on her own, that there are just as many insects in nature that are detrimental to crops or livestock as there are insects that are beneficial, and many of the beneficial ones are predators of the detrimental ones. They know that diversified, layered crops and cover crops protect their soil and the healthy balance of all of its organisms, as well as optimize the nutritional value of the healthy crops harvested.

The Big Ag industrial agricultural model uses pesticides that eliminate *entire insect communities*. That's why I wanted you to meet Lucinda. When the monarchs, the jaguars or the Mexican red wolf go extinct it will be noticed. As more and more frog and toad species disappear, it is noticed. It's important for you to understand why. But that's also why I wanted you to meet Pat. And Earl. When underground life — the creatures of the dark realm — vanish, those of us above ground may not even realize they're gone until it's too late.

And that is exactly what's happening. A seminal study published in the September 2017 issue of Science Advances "for the first time, links global climate change to the loss of a 'shockingly high' number of critical microbial species essential to ecological systems, biodiversity, and organic land management."[174 175]

They may be unseen but their passing will have profound consequences for us. Whenever something vanishes, it no longer exists to interact with everything it was interacting with, and the entire ecosystem will have to adjust for its absence.

The widespread adoption of GMO corn and soybeans began less than 30 years ago. The heavy spraying of GMO crops with Roundup and other glyphosate-based weed killers is already causing the emergence of mutations with over 200 different varieties of herbicide resistant "superweeds" and "super-pests" appearing on the scene. 2010 U.S. Department of Agriculture data confirmed that "pests" are becoming increasingly resistant to Roundup.[176] These resistant weeds are now present on half of American farmers' fields — on over 100 million acres of cropland.[177] Dr. Christine Jones reminds us, "There's a saying, 'The more you spray weeds, the more weeds there will be to spray.' Reverting to bare ground creates more problems than it solves."[178]

The Big Ag response to this problem has been predictable — develop and introduce new, even more potent pesticides.

In an article, *Bayer-Monsanto Merger Could Be Disastrous for Bees, People*, the Natural Resources Defense Council writes, "Scientific studies have repeatedly linked the devastating losses of bees and monarchs to the skyrocketing use of neonics and glyphosate, yet Bayer and Monsanto appear all too eager to double down on an even more chemical-soaked agricultural future, engineering a new generation of genetically modified crops to withstand increasingly potent pesticide cocktails. Monsanto has predicted that the corn seed of 2025, for example, will have 14 separate genetic modifications to allow farmers to drench it with five different kinds of herbicide."[179]

Danny Hakim, in his article in The New York Times, *Doubts About the Promised Bounty of Genetically Modified Crops*, writes, "Weeds are becoming resistant to Roundup around the world, creating an opening for the industry to sell more seeds and more pesticides. The latest seeds have been engineered for resistance to two weed-killers, but capable of resistance to as many as five is planned. That will also make it easier for farmers battling resistant weeds to spray a widening array of poisons sold by the same companies... One is 2,4-D, an ingredient in Agent Orange, the infamous Vietnam War defoliant... Another is dicamba."[180] One significant problem with dicamba, as noted in Tom Philpott's 2018 article, *This Weed Killer is Wreaking Havoc on America's Crops*, is that, unlike glyphosate in Roundup, "Dicamba is volatile. That is, after it has been applied it's prone to convert into a gas and be carried on the wind to nearby farms. In addition to soybeans, vineyards, home gardens, and oak forests have been hit by dicamba drift." By mid-October 2017, "3.6 million acres had been affected, an unprecedented case of herbicides gone rogue."[181]

The American Cancer Society studied GMO foods and concluded that GMO foods do not cause cancer or any other health problems. The World Health Organization's International Agency for Research on Cancer cast this finding in doubt by unanimously classifying glyphosate as "probably carcinogenic to humans."[182] Recent laboratory research in Australia found that glyphosate interferes with the function and production of hormones in the human body, and that it is an endocrine disruptor,[183] "Notably, the researchers found that Roundup was even more toxic than its active ingredient (glyphosate) alone, suggesting that other ingredients in Roundup work synergistically with glyphosate."[184] Glyphosate has been banned in most of Europe and many other countries around the world.

The number of Americans with cancer increased from one in twenty in 1960 to one in eight by 1995 and is higher still today. Increased pesticide use is linked to this increase.[185] The Centers for Disease Control and Prevention determined that autism in the United States has risen over two years from one in eighty-five children to one in sixty-eight, that the causes are environmental, and occur "where the increasing use of glyphosate and GMOs are the most significant environmental changes."[186]

Charles M. Benbrook in *Trends in Glyphosate Herbicide Use in the United States and Globally*, points out another factor driving the increased use of glyphosate — a newly developed agricultural use pattern called "harvest aid" which is an application, "as a desiccant to accelerate the harvest of small grains, edible beans, and other crops... Harvest-aid uses of glyphosate have become increasingly common since the mid-2000s in U.S. northern-tier states on wheat, barley, edible beans, and a few other crops, as well as in much of northern Europe. Because such applications occur within days of harvest, they result in much higher residues in the harvested foodstuffs. To cover such residues, Bayer and other glyphosate registrants have requested — and generally been granted — substantial increases in glyphosate tolerance levels in several crops."[187]

Glyphosate has now been found in the harvested corn, wheat, soy, and sugar beet crops it is applied to. It is in the food the majority of us eat. Dr. Christine Jones observes, "There is an analogous situation in human health. Not long ago the cancer rate was around one in 100. Now we're pretty close to one in two people being diagnosed with cancer. At the current rate of increase it won't be long until nearly every person will contract cancer during their lifetimes... Isn't that telling us something about toxins in the food chain? We're not only killing everything in the soil, we're also killing ourselves... Cancer is not a transmissible disease. It's simply the inability of our bodies to prevent abnormal cells from replicating... The big breakthrough in cancer prevention will be in changing the way we produce our food."[188]

I was present when Ray Archuleta was speaking to other farmers. He doesn't talk at them nor does he come across as if he's delivering a sermon from the mount. As a fellow farmer, he suggests they just pay attention to their soil, let their soil "speak" to them. "Your soils and your farms reflect you. They reflect your understanding."

Jane Goodall wonders, "Why would anyone spray poison on food you eat?"

Vandana Shiva has a Ph.D. in philosophy and her perspective is encompassing: "Everything we are is made of the soil. The food we eat is a product of the soil. If we have declared a war against the soil itself, if we ensure that the fertility through which the human species can continue is robbed in the soil, then we are literally committing a species level suicide."[189]

Dr. Shiva continues, "What we do to the soil, we do to ourselves: it is not an accident that 'humus' and 'humans' have the same etymological root."[190]

GMO Seeds

A hundred years ago, American agriculture began to realize significant benefits from technological and scientific advances including genetic manipulation. Hybrid plant strains were created through cross breeding and grafting. In the 1930's, farmers embraced a double-cross hybrid strain of corn that increased their crop yields from about 27 bushels per acre in 1937 to about 41 in 1955. Yield today is around 160 bushels per acre.[191] Our toolbox got significantly more sophisticated when scientists began advancing the ability to genetically modify an organism by altering its DNA.

Over the past two decades, however, laboratory attempts to enhance two traits — higher yield and insect resistance — have proven unfruitful. Two extensive analyses, including one by The New York Times using United Nations Food and Agriculture Organization data spanning the last 20 years, corroborated this, finding no evidence that GE (genetically engineered) crops have increased yields in comparison to non-genetically engineered crops.[192 193] The *Failure to Yield* study by the Union of Concerned Scientists concluded, "Despite 20 years of research and 13 years of commercialization, genetic engineering has failed to significantly increase U.S. crop yields."[194]

Throughout history, seeds were never a significant cost for farmers.

Farmers kept seeds from their harvests and stored them for future crops. They maintained their seed reserves and could easily trade for or inexpensively purchase more. Farmers traded or circulated seeds to alter or improve the diversity or quality of their crops, ensuring one another's success and the health of their communities. Nature's essential invaluable diversity of seed strains was a given.

In the United States, biotechnology developed the capability to alter DNA at the cellular level. In 1980, by a one-vote majority, the Supreme Court ruled (*Diamond v. Chakrabarty*) that a genetically altered life-form could be patented. Subsequently, it ruled that seeds could *also* be patented.

Monsanto (now owned by Bayer) engineered its Roundup Ready GMO seeds and patented them. These seeds are designed to work in tandem with Roundup herbicide and a suite of synthetic fertilizers and other Monsanto chemicals.

"The effectiveness of glyphosate gave its manufacturer, Monsanto, a huge advantage in the herbicide market and a monopoly on patented seeds for glyphosate-resistant crops," writes David R. Montgomery. "This, in turn, helped drive widespread adoption of genetically modified corn and soy."[195]

Neil Harl, Emeritus Professor of Agriculture and Economics at Iowa State University told Kristin Ohlson, "Monsanto influences pricing for 90% of the corn and soybean seeds, since they also sell biotech traits to competitors." He concludes, "Given Monsanto's control of the market, it is not surprising that the price of seeds for farmers has skyrocketed. Prices rose 150% between 1999 and 2010."[196]

Farmers are forbidden from using any leftover GMO seeds in the following year. They are obligated to purchase new GMO seeds each year.

Bayer (which acquired Monsanto in 2018) owns 23% of the global proprietary seed market and in the United States 80% of the corn and 93% of soy are grown from GMO Roundup Ready seeds.[197]

Bayer is expanding beyond industrial agricultural GMO wheat, corn and soy farming, developing new GMO seeds of beets and other crops, which it will patent and sell to the world's farmers along with its compulsory suite of synthetic fertilizer, pesticide and other chemical inputs.

Bayer has an even greater objective. Bayer wants to *replace* global ecological diversity with monoculture commodity crops grown only from seeds that it patents and controls. "The rapid erosion of biodiversity has taken place under a food system that sees farms as factories for commodities rather than webs of food production and life," writes Vandana Shiva.[198]

To this end, Bayer is determined to do everything it can to eradicate the diversity of the world's seed supply. Before it was purchased by Bayer, Monsanto bought out local farmers and seed co-ops for years. When it assumed control of these unique seed reserves it prevented anyone else from using them.

For example the only sugar beet seeds now available are patented GMO varieties. No organic or conventional sugar beet seed has been developed for 25 years.

And more than sugar beet seeds have been compromised. According to the State of the World's Plant Genetic Resources for Food and Agriculture report:

- 96% of the 7,098 varieties of apples that once existed in the United States at the beginning of the 20th century have been lost
- Seed sources for 95% of cabbage varieties — lost
- 91% of field maize varieties — lost
- 94% of peas — lost
- 81% of tomato varieties — lost[199]
- 94% of beets — lost
- 94% of cauliflower — lost[200]

"Lost," as in *gone*.

Over the past century *half* of the world's food varieties have been lost.[201]

Bayer wants to sell farmers its patented genetically modified seeds. It wants farmers to have to buy its seeds. Every year. It's a condition for signing up for its industrial agricultural program. And it doesn't hurt to eliminate a farmer's alternative seed choices.

You'd think that because this plot is so diabolical, so ruthless, it must be science-fiction, something worthy of a James Bond villain. It's not. It is our current reality. Bayer wants to gain control of the world's seed supply.

Three corporations, Bayer-Monsanto, ChemChina, and DowDuPont together now control 61% of the world's seed market and, along with a fourth company, BASF, control 70% of the global pesticide market.[202]

Global seed diversity is diminishing rapidly. Natural seed diversity is fundamental to the health of life on this planet.

In her June 4, 2019 article, *The Farms of the Future*, Isabel Marlens writes, "Over all the years that people have been planting seeds, they have been participating in a process of evolutionary adaptation: they've been selecting the seeds that thrived in their particular soil, with their particular weather conditions, their particular light. Seed banks are great — especially those that save only Indigenous, non-corporate patented varieties; but they are not enough. We need living seed banks, seeds planted every year — eased into an uncertain future — if we want a real hope for survival."[203]

Vandana Shiva was born in India and lives there to this day. A renowned international environmental activist and food sovereignty advocate, she has written over 20 books. In 1993, she received the Right Livelihood Award, often referred to as an "Alternative Nobel Prize." In 2003, Time magazine named her an "Environmental Hero."

In *Who Really Feeds the World?* she writes:

"Seed is the first link in the food chain and the repository of life's future evolution: it is the very foundation of our being. Seeds have evolved freely over millennia and given us diversity and richness of life on the planet. For thousands of years, farmers, especially women, have evolved and bred seed freely in partnership with each other and with nature. Farmers' seeds carry within them the knowledge of an agroecological, connected web of food and life."

"In the last half century... GMOs have been introduced with only one purpose: to own seeds and lifeforms through patents. In this way, GMOs become both a source of control and a source of profits... From once being a free resource reproduced on farms, seeds have been transformed into costly inputs that farmers now need to purchase... They are the tool for creating a global system of control over our seed and food."

"In addition to patents, new seed laws are being enforced across the world so that corporations can make farmers' seeds and local diverse varieties illegal. These are laws of uniformity, enforced either through UPOV — the International Union for the Protection of New Varieties of Plants, which allows intellectual property rights on plants in seventy-one member countries — or through seed acts that require seed registration."

"The corporate control over seed is first and foremost a form of violence against farmers. While farmers breed for diversity, corporations breed for uniformity. While farmers breed for resilience, corporations breed for vulnerability. While farmers breed for taste, quality, and nutrition, industries breed for industrial processing and long-distance transportation in a globalized food system. Monocultures of industrial crops and monocultures of industrial junk food reinforce each other, wasting the land, wasting food, and wasting our health."

"We use the term 'seed freedom' to talk about the right of the seed as a living, self-organized system that can evolve freely without the threat of extinction, genetic contamination, or termination through technologies designed to make seeds sterile. Seed freedom is the freedom of the bees to pollinate freely, without fear of extinction due to poisons. Seed freedom is the freedom of the web of life to weave itself in integrity and resilience, fostering interconnectedness and well-being for all. Seed freedom is the right of farmers to save, exchange, breed, and sell farmers' varieties — without interference by the state or by corporations. Seed freedom is the freedom of eaters to have access to food grown from seeds bred for diversity, taste, flavor, quality, and nutrition... Seed freedom is the duty to save and exchange native seeds bred by farmers. This is also seed sovereignty."

"In every country there is a contest between people's movements for seed freedom and the corporate push for seed dictatorship. Food democracy rests on seed freedom... Seed freedom has become an ecological, political, economic, and cultural imperative. If we do not respond, or if we have a fragmented and weak response, species will irreversibly disappear. Agriculture, including the food and cultural spectrum dependent on biodiversity, will disappear. Small-scale farmers will disappear, healthy food diversity will disappear, seed sovereignty will disappear, and food sovereignty will disappear... We have a duty to defend our freedom and protect open source seeds as a commons. We have the duty and the right to defend life on Earth."[204]

IV

Regenerative farmers are restoring soil. They are either not purchasing Big Ag's GMO seeds, synthetic fertilizers, pesticides, and herbicides, or they are in the process of weaning their soil off of them. They are honoring their land according to the Law of Return.

As farmers, these men and women are by definition part of global agriculture and the farming sector. But regenerative farmers are *not* participants in the industrial agriculture practices that Big Ag espouses. Neither are the livestock farmers and ranchers who champion holistic planned grazing and grass-fed grass-finished husbandry.

This is a fundamental distinction.

Industrial agriculture. And factory farming. These are the behemoth dark twins of Big Agriculture. Big Ag.

This is our Arch-Villain.

Animals, insects, the Earth's soil, local and global seed diversity are all jeopardized by Big Agriculture and a corporate insidiousness and viciousness that now threatens our planet.

Big Ag is now, by far, the most polluting industry on our planet – the one contributing most to global warming. Big Ag is the multinational corporate industrial force most responsible for hastening the end of our Anthropocene Epoch.

Exxon and the fossil fuel industry benefits greatly from Big Ag since industrial agriculture and factory farming require and burn a tremendous amount of fossil fuel energy. But the fossil fuel industry, as a stand-alone contributor to global warming, comes in second place – and a distant second by comparison.

Behemoth twin number one – factory farming – has the larger

footprint of the two. The animal agriculture industry by itself is the world's main cause of global warming. A staggering *51%* of all greenhouse gas emissions are created by all of the processes that go into the growing of feed crops for, and the feeding, raising, processing, distribution and consumption of factory farmed animals.[205]

A 2010 ECOFYS World Greenhouse Gas Flow Chart groups greenhouse gas emissions by these global sectors: industry, buildings, transport, agriculture, energy supply, land-use change, and waste. Livestock, which is part of the agriculture sector, accounts for 5.5% of total greenhouse gas emissions.[206] That statistic is cited by Steven Pinker in his book *Enlightenment Now*[207] and others who use it to buttress a defense of and even advocacy for industrial agriculture while acknowledging the severity of the threat of global warming.

However, the total emissions that the animal agriculture industry generates transcend that narrow definition of the agriculture sector. More thorough analyses of Big Ag, which take into account every aspect of this industry's operations, arrive at far more comprehensive, and dire, assessments of the greenhouse gas emissions this industry generates.

In 2017, "using the most comprehensive methodology created to date by the United Nation's Food and Agriculture Organization (FAO)," GRAIN, the Institute for Agriculture & Trade Policy (IATP), and the Heinrich Boll Foundation calculated that, based on greenhouse gas emissions in 2016, if the top 20 meat and dairy corporations were a country, "they would be the world's 7th largest gas emitter. It's now clear that the world cannot avoid climate catastrophe without addressing the staggering emissions from the largest meat and dairy conglomerates... If production continues to grow as projected by the FAO, emissions will escalate to the point where industrial meat and dairy production alone will undercut our ability to keep temperatures from rising to an apocalyptic scenario."[208] 2018 research by GRAIN[209] and the IATP reveals that, if by 2050 the world manages to restrict its global emissions and limits global warming to 1.5° while the animal agriculture industry sector grows as projected, that sector alone can be expected to be creating 80% of the world's total allowable greenhouse gas emissions.[210]

Ben Lilliston, IATP Communications Director, writes, "The top five mega-corporations responsible for factory-farmed meat and dairy are responsible for emitting more combined greenhouse gases (GHGs) than Exxon, Shell, or BP [British Petroleum]." He then makes a key distinction.

"We're not talking about free range beef ranchers, or sustainable poultry farmers, or small and mid-size family dairy farmers, who already do a large part of what they can to minimize GHG emissions. And we're not talking about pastoralists and livestock holders across the world whose production of protein nourishes the producers themselves and the communities surrounding them. It's the corporations who own, run and profit from factory farms and confined animal feeding operations (CAFOs) that are the culprits. These are the landlords of a system so powerful that it is, in large part, determining land-use patterns worldwide... We're talking about some of the biggest and richest corporations in the world... We're talking JBS, Tyson, Cargill, Dairy Farmers of America (the corporation, not the family farmers), and Fronterra group."[211]

In their seminal 2009 analysis of the United Nations' widely cited 2006 FAO report, *Livestock and Climate Change*, Robert Goodland and Jeff Anhang arrived at the 51% figure by identifying uncounted, overlooked, and misallocated categories of livestock-related greenhouse gas emissions:

- Livestock respiration
- Land use
- The effects of worldwide deforestation and the photosynthesis foregone on the vast tracts of land used for grazing animals and growing feed
- Undercounted methane
- The increase in the number of animals since 2006
- Distribution
- Food-related emissions from cooking, packaging and waste
- Carbon-intensive medical treatment of millions of zoonotic illnesses and chronic degenerative illnesses linked to consumption of livestock products[212]

In its 2016 analysis, *How the Industrial Food System Contributes to the Climate Crises*, GRAIN concludes that our Arch Villain contributes as much as 57% of all greenhouse gas emissions. By category: Agricultural production (11-15%), land use change and deforestation (15-18%), processing, transport, packing and retail (15-20%) and waste (2-4%).[213] [214]

In addition, based on what we've learned about the soil microbiome in the past decade, Robert Goodland and Jeff Anhang's estimate with regard to the photosynthesis foregone on the vast tracts of land worldwide used

includes the Farm Bill, its subsidy rules and crop insurance programs that siphon billions of taxpayer dollars into their massive, already extremely profitable industry each year. All of this while simultaneously marginalizing, dis-incentivizing and damaging regenerative farmers and grass-fed, free range ranchers — those who don't subscribe to industrial agriculture or factory farming programs.

The prognosis isn't good. For the industry itself or for our planet.

Based on field tests and data from historic heat waves, the crop yields of major grains can be expected to drop 10% for each degree of global temperature rise.[227] *The Economic Case for Climate Action in the United States* published by the Universal Ecological Fund FEU-US in 2018, conservatively estimated, "The impacts of weather events influenced by human-induced climate change and direct health consequences of pollution from fossil fuel use are currently causing, on average, $240 billion a year in economic losses, damages and health costs — or about 40% of the current growth of the United States economy." The report projects economic losses to escalate to $360 billion per year.[228] This will cripple future American economic growth.

Coauthor Sir Robert Watson writes, "Burning fossil fuels comes at a giant price tag, which the U.S. economy cannot afford and not sustain."[229] The planet is now 1.8 degrees hotter and will be 3.6 degrees hotter by 2050. Stephen Leahy writing *Hidden Costs of Climate Change Running Hundreds of Billions a Year*, concludes, "The impacts of climate change are certainly going to get more than twice as bad."[230]

. . .

So, what can you do? What impact can you possibly have — one human out of seven-plus billion?

It may seem like you're facing down the *Star Wars* Death Star. One person. You.

When you are afraid, of anyone, of anything you hear or see, of anything in this book, do not let your fear paralyze you. Fear means that you get it — you know in your gut, or your heart, in your *being*, that something is really wrong. That your life is threatened.

It is.

Let that inspire you.

You matter. Each one of us is here for a reason.

You have the power to help create the future you want to see. Your voice matters. You must find your voice and use it. Find your courage, take a stand.

Remember the meerkat's strategy against the Cape cobra and the power of collective action.

The Arch-Villain didn't start out as a villain. Companies harnessing new technologies developed products of benefit to the world, and they grew and profited handsomely providing that significant, worthy, and welcome benefit. But as the years passed, animal husbandry devolved into CAFO Hell-on-earth. As industrial agriculture was revealed as a bane for the soil microbiome and, at scale, a death knell for our planet, Big Ag was avariciously expanding, steadfastly and ruthlessly unwilling to acknowledge and own responsibility for, let alone adjust to this, and simply became a villain. Now, Big Ag, comprised of some of the largest wealthiest multinational corporations the world has ever seen, is our *Arch*-Villain. Most of us have been consuming its products, accepting its advertising, its perspective, its rationale, the illusionary self-serving world-view that it espouses. We have been living our lives enabling our Arch-Villain without even realizing it.

Be open-minded. Always be learning.

Like Hazel, shine a light into the darkness. Become fully aware of our predicament. Understand the situation you, as well as each one of us, are in.

You have the power to change and to fix things. More than you realize. You'll see.

V

Here then is the call. Calling out to you. **Our third Compassion** is the **healing of the land**.

The Great Healing will not be possible without this. The healing of the land will stop and reverse global warming and extend the Anthropocene Epoch — and us along with it.

Compassion for the Land is an essential Compassion; one that, once understood, is achievable through our actions.

Without the healing of the land, our Arch-Villain will become our nemesis. If you are a Millennial or a Gen Z, you will experience the ending of the Anthropocene Epoch and the planet's 6th Great Extinction during your lifetime. It's that close.

If we don't correct course quickly there is cruel irony in your label, Gen Z.

If we don't correct course quickly and in a significant way, *all of us* will witness the increasing severity of the weather, species extinctions, disease pandemics and increasing global conflict and social unrest.

There is a solution.

And we have the skills and we have the tools.

The solution is a natural one. It's always been there. However, with our science, we are just beginning to more fully understand it. Great civilizations – the Roman Empire, the Greeks, the Mesopotamians, the Egyptians, the Mayans – didn't understand how to fix their core problem and they went into decline and vanished.

The solution abides in the very thing that gives this planet life. In the vast kingdom that is least understood, the one most taken for granted – the soil.

We come from the soil, we will return to the soil, and in the soil resides our solution.

Before suggesting compassionate actions each of you can take for the land and to help attain the Great Healing, **here are two bits of wonderful news.**

The first is that industrial agriculture is untenable and will fail.

Dr. Frederick Kirschenmann is a North Dakota farmer, author and educator, a Distinguished Fellow at the Leopold Center for Sustainable Agriculture and President of the Board of the Stone Barns Center for Food and Agriculture. In his essay, *It Starts with the Soil and Organic Agriculture Can Help*, Dr. Kirschenmann identifies the three natural resources essential to industrial agriculture, all of which now face steep decline and are reaching the point of collapse.[231]

The first is energy. The energy required by Big Ag chemical manufacturers is immense. Synthetic nitrogen fertilizer manufacturing alone accounts for about 50% of the energy use in agriculture. Just the process of manufacturing this fertilizer, of converting nitrogen to ammonia, requires 1.2% of the world's energy use.[232] "Modern industrial agriculture depends almost entirely on fossil fuels. The nitrogen used for fertilizer is derived from natural gas. Phosphorus and potash are mined, processed and transported to farms with petroleum energy. Pesticides are manufactured from petroleum resources. Farm equipment is manufactured and operated using petroleum-based energy. Irrigation is accomplished with petroleum energy... The era of cheap energy is over and more than any other resource, the lack of cheap energy may force us to rethink how we manage soil."

The solution Dr. Kirschenmann envisions is a transition from "an energy *input* system to an energy *exchange* system. An energy exchange system requires biological diversity, organized so that each organism exchanges energy with other organisms in the land community, forming a web of synchronous relationships, instead of relying on energy-intensive inputs."[233] Regenerative agriculture is an energy exchange system.

Just using cover crops alternating with the cash crops — introducing a cover crop into an annual rotation with corn or soy — reduces nitrate leeching 70% on average. Farmers using multiple species cover crop combinations are discovering that just two seasons of these applications can significantly improve soil health.

The second natural resource essential to industrial agriculture is a stable climate, which Dr. Kirschenmann sees as essential to the highly specialized industrial agriculture production system. For the better part of a century, we have enjoyed this, but going forward, due in large part to the greenhouse gas emissions of this very industry, climate will be increasingly unstable and prone to weather extremes.

The government's *Fourth National Climate Assessment*, released in 2018 by the U.S. Global Research Program, echoes this concern: "Climate change presents numerous challenges to sustaining and enhancing crop productivity, livestock health, and the economic vitality of rural communities... Overall, yields from major U.S. crops are expected to decline as a consequence of increases in temperatures and possibly changes in water availability, soil erosion, and disease and pest outbreaks. Increases in temperatures during the growing season in the Midwest are projected to be the largest contributing factor to declines in the productivity of U.S. agriculture. Projected increases in extreme heat conditions are expected to lead to further heat stress for livestock, which can result in large economic losses for producers."[234]

Dr. Kirschenmann points out that, "Such instability can be especially devastating for the highly specialized, genetically uniform, monoculture systems so characteristic of the industrial agriculture that dominates the landscape today."

The solution mentioned by Sir Albert Howard in 1943 is regenerative agriculture: "Mother earth never attempts to farm without livestock; she always raises mixed crops; great pains are taken to preserve the soil and to prevent erosion; the mixed vegetable and animal wastes are converted into humus; there is no waste; the processes of growth and the processes of decay balance one another; ample provision is made to store the rainfall; both plants and animals are left to protect themselves against disease."[235]

The third natural resource essential to industrial agriculture is water.

Some of the most important things on this planet are underground. The soil microbiome is one. Another is aquifer water.

In addition to drawing a winning hand in the game of Soil Poker and having a disproportionately large share of prairie soil, the United States also has the enormous good fortune to be home to the Ogallala Aquifer. Located underneath an estimated 174,000 square miles of the Central Plains, this vast aquifer is one of the largest underground freshwater sources in the world.[236] This is pure water of ice-age glacial origin. If the aquifer were empty, it would take nature 6,000 years to refill it.

Dr. Kirschenmann notes, "Agricultural irrigation alone consumes more than 70% of our global fresh water resources... We are drawing down our fresh water resources at an unsustainable rate."[237]

Judy Soule and Jon Piper write in *Farming in Nature's Image: An Ecological Approach to Agriculture*, "Water tables in the Ogallala Aquifer, which supplies most of the water for irrigation in the great plains of the United States, are being overdrawn at the rate of 3.1 trillion gallons per year (BBC 2000) and according to some reports this fossil water bank is now half depleted."[238] [239] Bruce Finley notes in, *The Water Under Colorado's Eastern Plains is Running Dry as Farmers Keep Irrigating "Great American Desert,"* that by 2017, as more and more pumps are being drilled into the aquifer, "the drawdown has become so severe that highly resilient fish are disappearing, evidence of ecological collapse. A Denver Post analysis of federal data shows the aquifer shrank twice as fast over the past six years compared with the previous 60."[240]

Regenerative farming significantly reduces the need for irrigation water. Joan and Nick Olson at Prairie Drifter Farms, Gabe Brown at Brown Ranch and Will Harris at White Oak Pastures understand through their own experience how the use of cover crops, composting, multi-cropping and other regenerative practices have enabled them to develop richer topsoil teeming with organic matter, which has a far greater ability to absorb moisture and retain rainfall and weather droughts. Each 1% increase in soil organic matter can enable an acre of soil to hold 20,000 gallons more water.[241] The irrigation water they need is a small fraction of what they once required.

If it's in the cards that industrial agriculture will ultimately fail, how soon? How much irreparable damage will be done to our environment before then?

We can't wait for that day. Given the accelerating effects of global warming, we simply don't have the time. Unchecked, Big Ag will become our nemesis.

Industrial agriculture farmers have been "indoctrinated to believe that yields can be maximized by inserting a few artificial nutrients." But Dr. Kirschenmann concludes that, "rising energy costs, restricted water use and more unstable climates, combined with the growing awareness that the industrial system is rife with its own failures... could well cause farmers to seek alternatives faster than we can currently imagine."[242]

Wendell Berry has arrived at the same conclusion: "From what I see here at home in the watershed of the Kentucky River, and from what I have seen and learned of other places, I know that industrial agriculture is in serious failure, which is to say that it is not sustainable. Projecting from the damages of the comparatively brief American histories of states such as Kentucky and Iowa, one must conclude that the present use of the farmland cannot be sustained for another hundred years. The rates of soil erosion are too high, the runoff is too toxic, the ecological impoverishment is too great, the surviving farmers are too few and too old."[243]

In a recent essay written in 2018, *Renewing Husbandry*, Wendell Berry notes, "The national and global corporate economies... in their understanding and in their accounting, have excluded any concern for the land and the people. Now, in the midst of so much unnecessary human and ecological destruction, we are facing the necessity of a new start in agriculture... We are going to have to return to the old questions about local nature, local carrying capacities, and local needs. And we are going to have to resume the breeding of plants and animals to fit the region and the farm."[244]

I asked Gabe Brown about this. Gabe spends six months of each year traveling the country talking with farmers. Everywhere he goes, people come out to engage him in conversation and listen to what he has to say. Last year he spoke to 25,000 producers.

This is what Gabe told me: "The farm program is based off of the previous year's commodity prices which are in a downward spiral. Revenue insurance is locked into these low prices, so what I'm seeing as I travel around the country is that industrial farmers and ranchers just can't make it anymore. They know they can't continue this way so they are coming to us and adopting regenerative practices quicker.

"Then when you take what's happening with the human health crisis and the nutrient density of our food has declined so much, more and more people are realizing, from a consumer standpoint, that they have to buy more nutrient-dense food. And the only way to get nutrient-dense food is if you have healthy soil."[245]

Gabe continues, "Health care costs are astronomical. And then you have this increasing awareness and concern about climate change. So to me it's becoming a perfect storm. Regenerative and grazing is how we're going to cycle more carbon to mitigate that. We're going to reach that tipping point that you talked about and I really think it's going to happen within the next ten years."

The second welcome bit of wonderful news is *The Solution.*
   The solution is... The Liquid Carbon Pathway
   The soil's ability to sequester carbon.
   In 2015, eighteen scientists and educators who label themselves Ecomodernists, published *An Ecomodernist Manifesto.* In it they fully acknowledge the dire and worsening threat of global warming, yet, while mentioning certain technological advances that can help, they state, "Absent profound technological change there is no credible path to meaningful climate mitigation. While advocates differ in the particular mix of technologies they favor, we are aware of no quantified climate mitigation scenario in which technological change is not responsible for the vast majority of emission cuts."[246]

There is no technological advance which promises a credible path to meaningful climate mitigation.

There *is*, however, a credible path to meaningful climate mitigation. The solution of the necessary magnitude is one we have right now.

The Liquid Carbon Pathway.

"The Liquid Carbon Pathway" is a phrase coined by Dr. Christine Jones. It is the process by which diverse photosynthesizing plants covering healthy soil take carbon dioxide out of the atmosphere, ingest it and drive it into the soil.

Carbon cycles into and out of the atmosphere. Carbon dioxide is taken from the air by plants via photosynthesis. Plants then send chemical substances — all carbon based — to the soil microbes and they use these sugars to create complex, stable forms of carbon, such as humus. 20-60% of the carbon fixed in green leaves is channeled in this manner. This is how carbon is removed from the atmosphere and a significant portion is transferred into stabile humus and *sequestered* in the soil. This is the Liquid Carbon Pathway.

Humus is ideal soil. 60% of its content is carbon. All the nitrogen any plant needs is provided naturally and simultaneously as organic nitrogen travels on this pathway along with the organic carbon. 6 to 8% of humus is nitrogen and phosphorous. 1 to 2% is sulfur and the remaining 30% of humus mass is mineral. This is how plants grow topsoil.

Regenerative farming using cover crops, crop rotation, seed diversity, and other regenerative farming methods, *maximizes* a plant's ability to take carbon out of the atmosphere and creates vibrant rich soil that sequesters carbon for use in the subterranean realm.

Good soil sequesters carbon. *Lots* of carbon. Good soil rejuvenates our atmosphere. Increasing soil carbon sequestration is our best resource in the fight to slow down and reverse global warming.

The Liquid Carbon Pathway has four stages: taking carbon from the atmosphere via photosynthesis, transferring it to plant roots, using it to form aggregates along the roots, and creating humus. This is a nutrient exchange, so in turn, the mycorrhizal fungi send nutrients into the plant, which then increases the plant's rate of photosynthesis significantly. We can impact each of these stages but the last two are microbially driven — they depend on the health of the plant and the soil.

Carbon is also transferred into soil by one other pathway, the Decomposition Pathway, but the preeminent pathway is the Liquid Carbon Pathway. The Liquid Carbon Pathway can carry carbon much deeper into the soil because it travels along all roots including the deeper ones.

When soil is storing more carbon than it is releasing back into the atmosphere, it is termed a "carbon sink." Carbon naturally cycles back into the air via oxidation. When there is more carbon being released into the air than is being soil-sequestered on a given area of land, this soil is termed a "carbon source."

Soil health can be measured by its carbon. If soil carbon levels are decreasing, the levels of organic nitrogen and minerals will be in decline as well. The reverse is also true. The burning of fossil fuels and the laying bare of vast tracts of grassland and forest have released massive quantities of carbon into the atmosphere while severely damaging that soil's ability to act as a carbon sink. The application of synthetic fertilizers and pesticides kills soil microbes, further damaging that soil's ability to act as a carbon sink.

Dr. Paul Hepperly, Research Director of the Rodale Institute between 2002 and 2009 states, "We can sequester over 3 tons of carbon dioxide per acre with organic regenerative methods whereas conventional chemical based agriculture emits carbon dioxide."[247]

The goal must become transforming farms that are losing topsoil and surrendering carbon into the atmosphere into carbon sinks.

The Rodale Institute's research estimated that widespread carbon sequestration could offset up to half of global greenhouse gas emissions. Some believe this estimate is low.

Kristin Ohlson writes, "We have to take care of the billions of microbes and fungi that interact with the plants' roots and turn carbon sugars into carbon-rich humus. And we have to protect that humus from erosion by wind, rain, unwise development, and other disturbances... When good management practices create a ton of carbon in the soil, that represents slightly more than 3 tons of carbon dioxide removed from the atmosphere. Rattan Lal believes that 3 billion tons of carbon can be sequestered annually in the world's soils, reducing the concentration of carbon dioxide in the atmosphere by 3 ppm every year."[248] Rattan Lal, Ph.D., has received the Nobel Peace Prize and is a Distinguished University Professor of Soil Science at Ohio State University.

It all comes down to photosynthesis. There is no other process that can remove as much carbon from our atmosphere. Regenerative farming is all about maximizing photosynthetic capability and photosynthetic rate; and maximizing green plants per acre of land using diversified cover crops, broad leaf plants mixed with grasses, plants growing in all seasons. With good composting, grasses and other cover crops will flourish. Ideally, sunlight should never hit bare ground.

Photosynthesizing green plants covering the soil are constantly storing carbon in the soil through their root exudates. Soil scientist and researcher, Dr. Whendee Silver estimates that "just half of California's 63 million acres of rangeland could absorb 42 million tons of CO_2 — nearly 40% of what California power plants emit in a year — if each acre sequestered an additional 1.5 tons of carbon in its soil."[249]

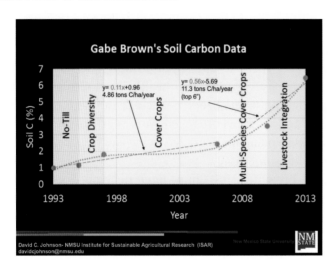

This is the slide plenty of folks are talking about.

It charts the improvement in Gabe Brown's soil on his ranch just outside of Bismarck, North Dakota, over a 20-year span. Gabe's regenerative agriculture techniques improved his soil's ability to sequester carbon and his soil carbon increased from 1% to 6.5%. That's huge. Each percent of carbon in the soil amounts to *8.5 tons* per acre. The chart shows how Gabe discovered and applied regenerative practices one after another, first going no-till in 1993, then diversifying crops, 5 years later adding cover crops, and then 9 years after that discovering the benefits of multi-species cover crops. Once Gabe combined these 4 principals and then added a 5th — livestock integration — his soil carbon skyrocketed from just over 2% to 6.5% *in just six years.*

He told me that based on what he knows now, he could raise his soil carbon from 1% to 6.5% within 5 years and that his soil has even greater potential. He expects to be *over 10%* soon.

In raising his soil carbon level from 1% to 10%, Gabe Brown is sequestering an additional 76.5 tons of carbon *per acre*... This is why plenty of producers are talking about this slide.

So, I asked Gabe for this slide. It turns out it's David C. Johnson's...

David C. Johnson, Ph.D., is a molecular biologist who has spent years focusing his research at New Mexico State University on "unraveling the secrets of soil microbes," the smallest of the small, so that he might find answers to what may be our biggest questions:

What about the 30% of the world's crop-land that has been abandoned as unfertile? What about the vast tracts of farmland with topsoil severely degraded by erosion? What option remains for an American industrial agriculture farmer who has spent years tilling and compacting his soil, killing off its biology, its microbial health, by dousing it over and over with Big Ag's synthetic fertilizers, pesticides and herbicide inputs? If this farmer wanted to switch over to regenerative agriculture, would it even be possible for him to bring his degraded dying soil back to life?

And he's onto something...

David and his wife, Hui-Chun, have developed a fungal dominant compost generated by his bioreactor. They have discovered that inoculating crop soil in their test plots with "barely a dusting" of the compost being generated in their bioreactor has "restored the dynamic of the system and the soil fertility with extraordinary plant biomass growth and regenerated soil microbial diversity." The bioreactor is pictured in this endnote.[250]

David told me, and I am quoting, so forgive me for going a little deep-dish — this is his language: "We've so exhausted the soil of microbes that, based on what I've seen in my research, it helps to inoculate these soils with a broad-spectrum microbial community — not only bacteria but fungi. You have bacteria in these systems that work with the plants and the plants work with the microbes. You have free-living nitrogen fixing bacteria. You have symbiotic nitrogen fixing bacteria. You have phosphorous solubilizing bacteria. You have bacteria that oxidize other metals and pull them out of the soil parent material and make them accessible to the plant. Microbes that are in there specifically for essential carbon cycling. You have to have microbes that can break down almost any kind of molecular structure, break down the zenobiotics and the legacy chemicals that we put into these systems. You need microbes that secrete antibiotics — that can clean up things that are not good for the plant system. You have microbes that promote quorum sensing-"

Wait. Pause button... I asked David what "quorum sensing" in the soil was. "That's when groups of microbes get together in a quorum and do things together that they can't do on their own. For example, enabling the transportation of certain metabolites in this biofilm that they create and in improved soil, this is what comes to the forefront." ...

All of this complexity of lifeform interaction is happening in the healthy soil right under our feet. It is so faceted that even an astute molecular biologist like David, who has spent years studying this, realizes that the more he learns, the more he doesn't yet know. This is the life in the soil, its microbiome, the core life of this planet from which everything else has evolved. It's spectacular in its complexity, its intricacy, its beauty.

Bayer, Dow, Koch and other chemical companies throw the soil microbiome out of balance if not killing it off entirely with virtually every fertilizer, herbicide, and pesticide they manufacture.

David Johnson's static bioreactor, which includes worms like Earl, generates a compost that, over the course of a year, develops a microbial community that becomes four times more species diverse and is now also a fungal dominant compost. The compost is only applied once and as the carbon flows back into the soil through the plants or the root exudates, it enables the soil to heal itself. "It's a very complex interaction and I don't expect we'll ever figure it out. As far as carbon sequestration goes, nature's got the best system. We've just got to allow it to function."

David Johnson points out a common misconception as to what compost is. Compost, like that which his system generates, shouldn't be viewed as a nutrient amendment or a fertilizer. It doesn't have the mass to be considered a fertilizer. It should be categorized as an inoculant because it has so much more power. It is applied just once, with the goal of getting the soil functioning well enough so that it can get its own nutrients from the parent material going forward.

He also points out two common carbon misconceptions. "We have to get away from the perception that carbon is static. Carbon is flowing all the time. We depend on that flow for our life as does every other organism on this planet from the microbes on up." And, "the more carbon you put in the soil, the more efficient the system gets. As you change from a bacteria-dominant to a fungal-dominant soil, you increase net primary productivity."

"Net primary productivity" translated means crop yield.

"We increase carbon use efficiency in the soil so instead of being respired, it's being put into other cellular structures that are stable in the soil."

By "respired" he means it turns back into the air.

"We have to have a healthy soil system that uses carbon very efficiently and the plants and the microbes can do this. I've seen an increase of five times the net primary productivity in soils over 4 and 8 years, and an increase of five times net primary productivity is a significant amount of biomass. Richard Teague is also seeing this same five-times increase in primary productivity in rangeland where adaptive multi-paddock grazing management is being used."

"At the rates that I was storing carbon over the first four and a half years — about 10.7 tons — it would take 50% of arable land to capture all anthropogenic CO_2. Gabe Brown is doing it at twice the rate I was. This is how we are going to solve the problem of climate change."

This is how we are going to solve the problem of global warming.

Carbon sequestration.

This is our singular solution to climate change. We need to do this *at scale* — and quickly. **This is how we are going to solve the problem of global warming.**

Rattan Lal believes that 3 billion tons of carbon can be sequestered annually in the world's soils.[251] David Johnson — based on his results, Gabe Brown's and those of other regenerative farmers and ranchers — believes we can draw down *20 billion tons* a year.

"With the biology, things change. We can do it at least 10 times the rate of carbon capture that anybody else is seeing in their research. So, I see this as hope. I see this as the only mechanism that we can use to capture carbon. Practically. Cost-effectively. And to offer so many co-benefits in the process. But what we're doing to our soils, what we're doing to our rangelands, it will change the whole paradigm of how we grow food on this planet. And implementing the microbes back into this system is the key."[252]

Love this. I see hope as well.

. . .

Farmers raising crops using soil regenerative methods, can take a *very significant* amount of carbon out of the atmosphere and sequester it in the ground. So much so that this is, by far, *the* most effective way we have to sequester carbon.

At scale, this is the essential way to slow, stop, and ultimately reverse global warming. This is our imperative.

We must do everything we can to support regenerative farmers and ranchers.

We have the knowledge, the tools and the skills. Research is now revealing this can be done more rapidly than previously expected. Optimizing conditions enabling soil microbes to thrive improves soil fertility, increasing crop yield as well as the soil's ability to retain carbon. "Even a modest two-or-three species cover crop causes a 90% reduction in sediment runoff, a 50% reduction in fertilizer runoff into the watershed, and sequesters a metric ton of carbon dioxide per acre." Kristin Ohlson continues, "When plants are allowed to work with their partners in the soil, they're givers. They feed carbon exudates to the community of bacteria and fungi to keep them thrumming with life and pulling mineral nutrients from the bedrock as well as from particles of sand, silt and clay because they know — if that word can be applied to organisms without brains — that they will profit from the gift. When the predator soil organisms eat the bacteria and fungi, all those nutrients will be released near the plant. There's always enough... If only 11% of the world's cropland — the land typically not in use — improved its community of soil microorganisms... the amount of carbon sequestered in the soil would offset all our current emissions of carbon dioxide. It's a rather staggering assertion."[253]

In *An Inconvenient Sequel - Truth To Power*, Al Gore's all over this: "Regenerative organic agriculture comprises a range of time-tested practices that contribute to soil's ability to retain carbon. Many of these are easy and relatively inexpensive to adopt. For example, cover cropping, mulching, and composting all keep organic matter (i.e. carbon) in the soil... They also include conservation tillage or no-till farming, which can play a vital role in keeping plant residue in the soil and reducing erosion."[254]

For Dr. Christine Jones, "The potential for reversing the net movement of CO_2 to the atmosphere through improved plant and soil management is immense. Indeed, managing vegetative cover in ways that enhance the capacity of soil to sequester and store large volumes of atmospheric carbon in a stable form offers a practical and almost immediate solution to some of the most challenging issues currently facing humankind."[255]

All across this country, family farmers are discovering:

Mahatma Ghandi said, "Anything that millions can do together becomes charged with unique power."

When you live this way, you are part of a movement, a driver of essential social and environmental change at a critical moment in our destiny.

When Dr. Christine Jones writes, "It is up to us to restore soil integrity, fertility, structure and water-holding capacity... by the way we manage our food production systems,"[258] she is referring not just to farmers as stewards of the land, but to each of us as global citizens who must forge change. "Profitable agriculture, nutrient dense food, clean water and vibrant communities can be ours... if that is what we choose."[259]

Michael Brownlee sees an even more profound shift happening because more and more of us are acting on this awareness. The steady growth of organic sales has been in the double digits each year, *for* years. The local food movement is growing at rates two to three times higher than the organic segment. "Local food is a completely eater-driven industry segment and that's something new. It's revolutionary!"[260]

From 1994 to 2015, the number of farmers' markets across the U.S. increased from 1,755 to over 8,400, and 50,000 farmers are now selling directly to consumers or local retailers.[261]

Using our purchasing power to support these producers, their farms, their businesses, we can help grow their numbers. Organic product sales have increased by 20% every year from 1990 to 2010, exceeding $28 billion in 2010. Al Gore found, "According to the Organic Trade Association, in 2015 Americans spent more than $43 billion on organic products, and nearly 22,000 businesses earned organic certification, up a record 12% from the year before."[262] Natural and organic product sales are projected to reach $107.7 billion in 2019.[263]

Our awareness and our purchasing power are making a difference. For the first time since the Great Depression, the number of small farmers in the United States is growing. In 2016 according to USDA figures, certified organic commodity sales from U.S. farms and ranches increased 23% from 2015, the number of certified organic farms increased 11% to 14,217, and certified acreage increased 15% to 5 million. Kristin Ohlson writes, "As these new, often college-educated farmers practice the kind of agriculture and animal husbandry approved by their customers — reducing or eliminating the use of fertilizers, pesticides, herbicides, hormones, antibiotics, and other chemicals, as well as letting the animals graze on grass instead of stuffing them with soy and corn — foods they didn't evolve to eat — many are surprised to find their soil changing."[264]

Regenerative agriculture is compassionate agriculture. It is being embraced by a new emerging generation of young farmers and put into practice based on the unique climate and geography of their farms. Their soil, compared to that of their neighboring industrial agriculture farmers, requires dramatically less water consumption, is more productive and far better suited to maintain productivity in times of undesirable or unstable weather patterns. More and more farmers trapped in the increasingly unsustainable Big Ag system are also taking a good look at changing over.

At the Quivira Coalition conference in 2011, after championing soil carbon as "the most basic and important life-supporting infrastructure on earth," Abe Collins said, "This is an opportunity for farmers. We know how to build topsoil. We can fix land, not just preserve the degraded landscape that's already in place."[265]

When you drive past the vast monocrop fields of today's industrial agriculture farms with their orderly crop rows, it might create the impression that they are maximizing crop yield per acre. But Peter Rosset finds in *Small is Bountiful*, that the world over, regenerative "family farmers regularly achieve higher and more dependable production from their land than large farms operating in similar environments."[266] A 1992 U.S. agricultural census report confirms this, finding that small farmers are producing more than double the food per acre.

Dr. Tim LaSalle, former CEO of the Rodale Institute which oversees some of the most comprehensive field research spanning decades, says, "What we've watched here at the Rodale Institute over the years is that when we have drought years, our organic fields can produce 30 to 70% more corn or more soybeans — because there's the organic matter in that soil — than a conventional chemical synthetic based farm ever could. So, when they talk about 'What we need is bio-engineered plants for drought resistance,' we're kind of slapping our heads and saying, 'What?' What you need is healthy soil with organic matter in it and you don't have to put a bio-engineered gene into that plant. You can out-produce conventional by a whole bunch by just improving that soil."[267]

The solution according to Dr. Elaine Ingham, President and Director of Research at Soil Foodweb Inc., is simple: "We would solve so many problems if we would just get the biology back into the soil. Stop killing it."[268]

For David R. Montgomery, "The key to maintaining soil health lies in the world of soil life, in the microbial cycling and recycling of nutrients from mineral and organic matter. Herein lies the good news. For the short lifespan of microbial life means that restoring life and fertility to the soil — and increasing the productivity of marginal farms — is not only possible, but can happen faster than we ever imagined."[269]

Regenerative farmers know that by not using synthetic fertilizers and pesticides their soil returns to life, their harvest yield increases, their operating expenses decrease, the amount of pollution running off the farm sharply decreases, and over time, native plants and wildlife return to their land.

Regenerative farming is now nearly three times as profitable as industrial farming. Regenerative farmers avoid the array of costly Big Ag inputs, tend to get higher crop yields, and produce crops of better taste and higher nutritional value that consumers are willing to pay more for.

As more and more farm families practicing regenerative farming and ethical animal husbandry succeed in making a good living, their success could inspire government programs to incentivize a new generation of young American farmers by assisting their acquisition and conversion of, farmland. Producing healthy food in a planet sustaining manner is a path toward creating tens of thousands and then hundreds of thousands of new jobs. That's a path leading to the revitalization of rural communities and small-town America. For those of you thinking about becoming farmers, Matt Kautz (Chapter 1) is a worthwhile example as he and his brother started Cottonwood Creek Farms with very little capital — just two thousand dollars. Joel Salatin's advice for aspiring farmers is well worth listening to in the video *Joel Salatin on Creating Young Farmers*.[270]

Profit in the regenerative farming model remains with the farmers. This is a core reason why Big Ag throws its weight against them. For the farmers working their land utilizing the conventional industrial agriculture model, the lion's share of the profits goes to the corporations that manufacture and deliver the costly inputs — the pesticides and herbicides, the fertilizers and the GMO seeds — to the fuel companies and the heavy farming machinery manufacturers, to the banks that finance farmer's debt, and to the grain companies and meat companies that buy their crop harvests and animals at low commodity-based prices.

What regenerative farmers are achieving is remarkable, prompting Frederick Kirschenmann's optimism, "If we truly honor Sir Albert Howard's 'law of return' and allow microbial life in the hidden half of nature to perform its life restoring work, soil health can be restored in a relatively short period of time!"[271]

Vandana Shiva perceives how the Law of Return applies not only to the farm, but to our society as well. This is the core distinction between Big Ag and its Law of Exploitation and regenerative agriculture based on the Law of Return. "The role of the human community is to act as co-creators and co-producers with Mother Earth. Within this paradigm, knowledge is not owned; rather, knowledge grows through farming where we are all participants in the web of life. In ecological agriculture, the cycles of nature are intensified and diversified so as to produce more and better food, while using fewer resources... the waste of plants becomes foods for farm animals and soil organisms. Adhering to the Law of Return, there is no waste; everything is recycled... The industrial [Big Ag] paradigm is in deep conflict with the ecological [regenerative] paradigm, and the Law of Exploitation is pitted against the Law of Return. They frame the very basis of the food crisis we are facing today."[272]

Worldwide, it is predominantly small-scale farmers and farming families who feed the planet. The United Nations Food and Agriculture Organization (FAO) determined in 2014 that 80% of the planet's food is grown by small family farmers on smaller plots of land. A comprehensive survey of this data by GRAIN determined that these small farmers are growing 80% of the planet's food using just 24% of the world's farmland.[273] "One of the reasons why, despite having so little land, small producers are feeding the planet is that small farms are often more productive than large ones. If the yields achieved by Kenya's small farmers were matched by the country's large-scale operations, the country's agricultural output would double. In Central America, the region's food production would triple. If Russia's big farms were as productive as its small ones, output would increase by a factor of six."[274]

In *Unlike a Globalized Food System, Local Food Won't Destroy the Environment*, Helena Norberg-Hodge notes that measured by output-per-acre, smaller-scale farms "are typically 8 to 20 times more productive. This is partly because monocultures, by definition, produce just one crop on a given plot of land, while smaller, diversified farms allow intercropping — using the spaces between rows of one crop to grow another."[275]

Small-scale farming and livestock production are the livelihoods of well over one billion people. Regenerative "farmers are plant breeders and seed savers, soil conservators and soil builders, water preservers and water keepers," writes Vandana Shiva. While 20% of the food produced comes from large industrial farms, they consume a vastly higher percentage of the world's resources "in spite of all subsidies... and all the governmental policies that promote industrial agriculture... What is growing on large farms is not food; it is commodities. For example, only 10% of the corn and soy taking over world agriculture is eaten. 90% goes to drive cars as biofuel, or to feed animals being tortured in factory farms."[276]

Buy local

Purchase fruit and vegetables that are grown at regenerative farms near you.

Do not support industrial agriculture and Big Ag. Vandana Shiva fully understands who our Arch-Villain is — and our solution: "Every dimension of the food crisis — non-sustainability, injustice, unemployment, hunger, and disease — is linked to the globalized, industrialized food system, and every dimension of the crisis can be addressed through ecological agriculture and local food systems... To grow sustainability, nutrition, and food democracy, we must think small, not big: local, not global... Local means diversity, freshness, safety, and taste. It means support for local farmers and it means rejuvenation of local economies. It means deeper connections between food producers and eaters, and it means cultivating not just food, but community. Localization means taking back our food through food democracy."[277]

In addition to the superior nutrient content and taste of regeneratively or organically grown fruits and vegetables, buying from regenerative farmers, you are:

- protecting and enhancing your health and that of your loved ones, and anyone else you share this food with by consuming vitamin and nutrient robust, healthy food, free of harmful chemical residues and toxins
- supporting and honoring these farmers' livelihoods, their businesses and their workers. A farmer or rancher is paid on average 17¢ per dollar from a big box store. When you purchase that food directly, the farmer or rancher makes 92¢ per dollar[278]
- encouraging seed and crop diversity
- protecting the soil microbiome and its ability to sequester carbon

- supporting ecological farming while safeguarding the atmosphere and our planet. You are no longer supporting Big Ag, industrial farming or factory farming, the most polluting industry on the planet, GMO seed production, or the application of its suite of toxic chemicals
- reducing the pollution from food transportation which Al Gore found, in *An Inconvenient Sequel - Truth To Power,* accounts for 11% of food-related emissions. In addition, locally sourced food requires little or no packaging, processing, or refrigeration, and reduces food waste — all of which contribute greenhouse gas emissions
- increasing the demand for healthy food thereby creating opportunities for new regenerative farms, rural employment, and revitalizing rural communities and small-town economies

For Lou Preston of Preston Winery, the local farmers' markets are a rewarding experience for both the farmers and those in the community. "We are farming for local farmers' markets as well as for our little farm store here so it's all seasonal. We just planted leafy greens for the springtime, lettuces, chards, bok choy, while in the greenhouse we've begun seeding of the summer vegetables, like the tomatoes, peppers and eggplants. We have the olives, olive oils, grapes, the eggs, our own breads from artisanal grains, heirloom fruits from the orchards, apples, peaches and plums. This is something that's very exciting for us. The interaction is a manifestation of community. You've got people that value what we are offering because it's local and it's healthy and it's personal, and we are building a business striving towards sustainability to satisfy those needs."

And this is how Compassion for The Land dovetails in with Compassion for Animals and Compassion for Self to help create The Great Healing.

Reduce your meat consumption

By reducing your meat consumption, you are directly reducing animal suffering on this planet and taking a powerful step toward the goal of eliminating factory farming. Commit to eating better meat only — grass-fed grass-finished. In addition, as revealed in Compassion for Self, you will enjoy the significant benefits to your health, vitality and longevity by ending your over-consumption of meat and dairy products.

And... taking this path has a tremendous bonus ride-along. Since it takes so many resources and energy to create meat and dairy, eating lower on the food chain by consuming more vegetables, fruits, grains and nuts instead is a far more efficient way to gain the protein and nutrition you need while reducing the climate impact of each calorie you consume.

Livestock provide 18% of the calories and 37% of the protein humans consume but require 83% of farmland worldwide.[279] The animal agriculture industry is one of the largest sectors of CO_2 emissions and *the* largest contributor of methane, nitrous oxide and ammonia emissions.[280]

Given the millions of meals Americans eat each day, join millions of us who are eating less meat and dairy. We are getting all the protein we need and eating pleasure we want while helping stem global warming. A research study published in 2017 in *Climatic Change*, determined that if Americans began eating beans instead of beef, just that one change would achieve between 46% to 74% of the U.S. greenhouse gas emission reductions needed to meet our country's 2020 GHG target goals.[281]

Spend time outdoors

Being outdoors, immersed in and experiencing the wilderness, can make you healthier, happier and more productive. Numerous studies confirm this. In her book, *The Nature Fix*, Florence Williams writes that "humans need both wilderness and civilization, and that one makes us all the more poised for the other."[282]

In Japan, where forests cover two-thirds of its landmass yet most people live in cities, there is a practice called forest bathing. Dr. Qing Li advises in his book, *Forest Bathing: How Trees Can Help You Find Health and Happiness*,[283] "The key to unlocking the power of the forest is in the five senses. Let nature enter through your ears, eyes, nose, mouth, hands and feet. Listen to the birds singing and the breeze rustling in the leaves of the trees. Look at the different greens of the trees and the sunlight filtering through the branches. Smell the fragrance of the forest and breathe in the natural aromatherapy of phytoncides. Taste the freshness of the air as you take deep breaths. Place your hands on the trunk of a tree. Dip your fingers or toes in a stream. Lie on the ground. Drink in the flavor of the forest and release your sense of joy and calm. This is your sixth sense, a state of mind. Now you have connected with nature. You have crossed the bridge to happiness."[284] Karin Evans reports in *Why Forest Bathing is Good for Your*

Health, Dr. Qing Li found, "spending time in a forest can reduce stress, anxiety, depression, and anger; strengthen the immune system; improve cardiovascular and metabolic health; and boost overall well-being."[285]

Immersing yourself in wilderness invigorates your spirit as well. The authors of *The Ecomodernist Manifesto* convey a beautiful awareness of this, "By appreciating, exploring, seeking to understand, and cultivating nature, many people get outside themselves. They connect with their deeply evolutionary history. Even when people never experience these wild natures directly, they affirm their existence as important for their psychological and spiritual well-being."[286]

When I am hiking a forested trail in the mountains or breathing the high desert air or swimming in the ocean, life simplifies. The need to take the right action for the planet, to adjust habitual behaviors, to do this or to do that for the greater good, the sense of a moral imperative, disappears. Because, in moments and places like this, my awareness of who I am expands.

In this lifetime, on this day, in this beautiful place, with this breath, alive, one of, one with, one within this exquisite realm. This is your team, this is your world, all of it, and you would no sooner harm it than harm yourself. Add in the dimension of time, the past and the future, your life in the stream of the evolution of life on this planet. This is the "deep ecology" Norwegian philosopher, Arne Naess, wrote about.

In his essay *Conscience and Resistance*, Scott Russell Sanders realizes, "Our ecological crisis is, at root, a spiritual crisis. We abuse and exploit the Earth for the same reason we abuse and exploit one another: because we have lost a sense of kinship with our fellow human beings, with other species, and with our planetary home."[287]

Joanna Macy writes in *World as Lover, World as Self,* that many religions teach this. "We are apt, when we fall in love with our world, to fall into oneness with it as well. We begin to see the world as ourselves. Hunger for this union springs from a deep knowing, which mystics of all traditions give voice to. Breaking open a seed to reveal its life-giving kernel, the sage in the Upanishads tells his student: '*Tat tvam asi* – That art thou.' The tree that will grow from the seed, that art thou; the running water, that art thou; and the sun in the sky, and all that is, that art thou."[288]

Perhaps best not taken for granted, experiencing the exquisite beauty, the wonder of this planet, wherever you are, can foster compassion and a compassionate activism alive on this beautiful journey, to protect everything you sense and see, paying it forward for your children, loved ones and friends — for each one of us, for humanity sharing this special planet at this special time.

. . .

Vandana Shiva writes, "Industrial agriculture and industrial food systems have brought us a triple crisis: a dying planet, diseased citizens, and debt-ridden farmers. Ecological and just alternatives have become an imperative."[289]

As understanding spreads, individual actions aggregate to force change that, in this case and in addition to all other benefits, will slow and reverse global warming, and rescue the health of our planet.

Soil enables life on this planet. Life as we know it.

Ours is a very special planet. Well maintained soil is vital to life on Earth. It is something we need to stop eroding and killing. It is *the* essential resource to protect, and to fight for.

To live or die for.

COMPASSION FOR THE LAND 245

4

Compassion for Community

I

Marlon Foster walks amidst six and seven-foot tall sunflowers, their glowing yellow crowns of petals vivid in morning sun. Flourishing out of raised long beds, green onions, Swiss chard, Traviata eggplant, bell peppers, habaneros, jalapeños, and red tie chilis surround us. Deeply evocative scents — of the plants, of their blossoms and of the fertile soil — rise together on the humid air in this beautiful place. Summer is just arriving, which means that also in-season are three kinds of tomatoes - sun golds, black cherries, and heirloom Cherokee purples.

Marlon is a handsome man, well groomed, dressed sharply today in pressed long sleeve shirt and tie. He regards the raised beds and smiles proudly. These vegetables growing from the dark rich soil, are even more robust than last year's and he anticipates record yields. Ahead of us, several greenhouses are staggered, set amidst more long rectangular raised plant beds on this acre of the farm. We walk down the next row, shifting alongside garlic, cucumbers, Clemson spineless okra, emerald tomatillos, beets and carrots. I do see one hundred shades of green. Herbs make their appearance - sage, thyme, basil, dill, cilantro.

This is Green Leaf Learning Farm, an urban farm in South Memphis, Tennessee.

Today, we are standing amidst some of the most nutritious food on this planet. Nothing on this farm will worsen diabetes, not one plant growing here will harm your heart or your circulation or put you at greater risk of cancer, neuropathy or dementia. Just the opposite. All of the food growing within the waist-high green border fences of Green Leaf Learning Farm will nurture and sustain everyone who eats it, improving their health, vitality, and mental clarity. These vegetables and fruits enrich lives.

Just outside the fence, it changes.

We also happen to be standing in an American food desert: 38126, the poorest urban zip code in the entire United States. The unemployment rate is high, the median household income well below poverty level. There is not one single supermarket or grocery store within the entire community.

"In these neighborhoods," Marlon tells me, "families struggle to find and afford healthy food. Parents have to make trade-offs between basic needs and adequate food." The city of Memphis, Tennessee has the highest child obesity rate *and* the highest child hunger rate in the nation, *at the same time.*

We approach a lean young man as he raises a green onion from the soil. The smell captures us from ten feet away — full, sweet yet slightly astringent, like nothing else. It invigorates your senses. Theo Davies admires it as he rotates it in the sunlight, its texture and its structure. It is perfect. His eyes smile meeting ours. He wears a well-worn leather farm belt strapped around his waist, his work knife, multi-tool and shears at the ready. He is the Farm Manager. He casts the green onion into a harvest basket, bends down to harvest others. Theo is 29. He has undergraduate and graduate degrees in Anthropology from the University of Memphis.

We've arrived, having just crossed the street from the office of Christ Quest Community Church, where Marlon is pastor. Beside it is a house with a narrow and deep profile, a design called a "shotgun house" by locals, well suited for the lot sizes in this neighborhood. A colorful, freshly painted mural adorns one entire side of the building facing a children's playground with a swing set and play apparatus. This building is called the Pack House. Farm produce is being washed and assorted into boxes for the KQ-90 program, Green Leaf's version of a community CSA program. This afternoon, 20 families will arrive to collect their KQ-90 food boxes and there will be a cooking recipe demonstration for those who have a few minutes to hang around. The green onions Theo is gathering will be included in those boxes.

This is Marlon Foster's neighborhood. He was born here and raised in a house just a few blocks east of us. He and his family live now in a house four blocks to the west. He is 46.

Marlon's seen the population and economics of the neighborhood shift over the years. People have moved out, businesses closed, buildings became dilapidated. Blight bloomed. Residents no longer have access to fresh, healthy food.

Green Leaf Learning Farm is redressing this.

"Our goal at this farm is to provide the highest quality service to one of the most under-resourced and underserved neighborhoods. We don't just grow vegetables. We're committed to growing the *healthiest* vegetables. We're passionate about vegetables with high amounts of nutrients, like leafy greens — hence our name." In 2012, Green Leaf Learning Farm was certified as a USDA organic farm.

Over the past ten years, Marlon has acquired forty-five blighted lots. He cleared thirty of them and set to work rebuilding the soil planting sunflowers and starting Green Leaf Learning Farm.

"More than just the beauty of the sunflowers and this farm, is that all the neighbors love it, and we're drawing the bees, the beneficials." Marlon gives Theo a nod, "And for our farmer here, it's his science."

Theo adds, "The main purpose of the sunflowers is to attract the bees, the pollinators we need to bring into the crop to make sure we are producing fruit. Another good thing about black oil sunflowers is that the root ball is huge, and the taproot is wide and goes deep down. When you plant them on soil that hasn't been worked on, they will draw out the heavy metals so you are taking toxins out of the soil, and they will pull out a lot of clay. They do a cleansing of the ground before you plant."

Today, we are standing on some of the richest soil in all of Memphis.

At Green Leaf they do their own composting using produce waste and clippings. They use shredded leaves and straw, running it through a chipper and putting it down on the beds. When he needs it, Theo gets additional straw and leaf compost free of charge from the city's supply. "We cover the ground with plant residues, so the sun doesn't dry it out. It keeps the moisture in the soil and also acts like a mulch for us." Theo plants a month later.

He uses clover as cover crop. "The clover, beans, peas, peanuts, soy, they all fixate nitrogen from the air and put it back in the soil. By the time we plant greens in the fall in these hoop houses we're not going to have to add anything in there to the soil. We're eventually going to turn all the clover under, and it will put even more nutrients back into the soil. The root systems from the clover are keeping moisture in the soil, and at the same time are keeping the soil in place. We're on a slight grade and so every time it rains it can wash soil away."

They now use much less water to irrigate. During hot summer days like today, they have to irrigate twice a day. Water was on nine-minute cycles — now five-minute cycles suffice. The eggplant is now twice as big as last year, its flowers twice the size, and the zucchini and the squash are doing just as well. Each year, as the soil continues to improve and yields increase significantly, they are able to further reduce their irrigation. As the farm expands from one acre to two, the two acres combined will need less irrigation water than the first one originally did.

I ask Theo about the effect industrial agriculture is having on the soil in this region and he shakes his head, "They're turning all the delta silt into sand. And there is no nutrient value in sand."

The only fertilizer inputs the farm still needs are small amounts of fish emulsion and chicken manure. Before long they'll no longer need to purchase those because, just this morning, the farm's first layer hens arrived and are now in coops that were built and awaiting them. In addition to the eggs the hens will provide, Theo's looking forward to composting their droppings and degraded straw according to USDA specifications.

Green Leaf sells its produce at two weekly outdoor farmer's markets. Demand is especially robust at Cooper-Young where, in season, they'll take 35-40 pounds of okra, 200 pounds of cucumbers and 1,000 pounds of carrots each week. Their wholesale business is brisk, especially for their flowers. Memphis restaurants like Café Eclectic, which were importing flowers, now have the blooms of Green Leaf's zinnias adorning their tables. The KQ-90 food program is fully subscribed, neighborhood food sales are increasing, yet they always have fresh produce for the Benevolence, free meals provided to all church goers before Sunday services.

Something else is very important for Marlon. "We are also trying to bring dignity back around agriculture to African Americans throughout the south. We'd have black kids helping out and their grandparents would come by and see them with a hoe in their hand and it brings back memories of the challenges around agriculture for them, of sharecropping, slavery, and cotton. I've got three or four personal horror stories around agriculture in my family and I'm just one guy. We would even have kids saying 'I'm not a slave. I'm not going out there on that farm.'"

Marlon was adamant that Green Leaf Learning Farm *be* a learning farm. As the seasons pass, compassionate action and benevolence are healing even this stigmatized wound. Increasing numbers of neighborhood youths are helping out at the farm, either volunteering or coming in groups as part of student programs. They learn about agriculture, about farming, where food comes from, and how to plant and grow it and nurture it. Marlon appreciates this to no end. "Our goal is to have a child experience all the elements of the food cycle. If they want to go into an agribusiness career or be an urban farmer or a chef one day, they'll have the experience to do that."

Marlon continues, "What's really valuable about Theo is not just his understanding of anthropology and the science of agriculture but his heartfelt understanding of this community, and of people in general. That's the real asset, that's the distinguishing factor of him as our farm manager over and above the science of agriculture."

Hearing that Theo responds, "I just say I plant things." Marlon interjects, "That's a loaded word. He plants a lot of things."

Marlon Foster plants a lot of things as well. He originated Knowledge Quest which includes not only Green Leaf Farm but a community and counseling center and the Extended Learning Academy (ELA) which provides reading and enrichment classes for students from preschool through 12th grade.

Yolanda Manning is the Programs Manager at both Green Leaf and their Jay Uiberall Culinary Academy. She oversees the student education curriculum and leads classes in good health and nutrition. An accomplished and innovative cook, this afternoon she will be hosting the cooking demo for the families arriving to pick up their KQ-90 boxes. Her recipe will feature one of the vegetables in this week's box. Today it will be eggplant pescatta.

KQ-90 stands for Knowledge Quest 90. Marlon believes that it takes someone 21 days to form a habit and 90 days for a habit to become a lifestyle. Building on the Community Supported Agriculture (CSA) share concept, Green Leaf's food boxes not only contain an array of USDA certified organic produce from their farm but added value and surprise bonus features. These include contributions of olive oil and other ingredients from companies like Whole Foods, recipe cards, durable shopping bags, certificates for free Zumba or yoga classes, and Explore-Bike-Share (EBS) program free memberships enabling them to access any of 600 bikes at 60 bike-share stations throughout Memphis. For a cost of $20 bi-monthly, Green Leaf Learning Farm's KQ-90 boxes provide community members healthy nutrition and exercise access. They elevate lives.

The idea of growing food — of a community garden — was Miss Ernestine Ward's. She was a school teacher who, in 1999, simply wanted children to know where their food came from. Marlon was 26 years old then and just starting Knowledge Quest. It became his livelihood. Teaching was hers. Miss Ernestine Ward became Knowledge Quest's first full-time teacher and soon after, she proclaimed, "We're going to do this," and so began the first community garden on a small plot in the Fowler Homes Public Housing project.

One day nine years later, Miss Ernestine Ward stood right here when they broke ground at Green Leaf Learning Farm. She was standing in the poorest urban zip code in the country, on barren ground, on underutilized, underappreciated soil. And she smiled. She was pleased. She knew the importance of an urban farm, she surmised its potential. She knew the feeling, the importance of what it's like to discover one's livelihood, one's calling. And she had an idea of what this community could become.

. . .

Wendell Berry distinguishes livelihood as a vocation, as one's calling. "For all persons there are specific kinds of work to which they are summoned by God or by their natural gifts or talents. The kind of work may be cabinet-making or music-making, cooking or forestry, medicine or mechanics, science or law or philosophy or farming... People who are doing the work they are called to do are happy doing it. For them there is no distinction between work and pleasure. A 'job,' by contrast, is understood as any work whatever that one can earn money by doing."[1]

Job income may be all that many of us need and aspire to. A job can be broad or narrow in its responsibilities and involvement. It can be the perfect platform for employees to utilize their talents to accomplish tasks at hand. Working as an employee, as part of a business, does not mean that your valued labor cannot include aspects of self-organization, co-creation and coproduction, which Vandana Shiva sees as qualities of livelihood.[2] Creative and innovative endeavor, which can be characterized as entrepreneurial, is commonly encouraged and utilized within the framework of a larger company.

A job's income can also enable a separate livelihood. For a musician, an artist or an actor, performing, creating or auditioning at every opportunity is their livelihood even though a job may be paying the bills.

Livelihoods — the life blood of entrepreneurs and inventers exploring the novel and new — can create businesses and jobs, often many jobs. Livelihoods can also link us to our cultural identity, our traditions, and our history; adapting them and carrying their relevance and value into the future. Craftmanship is one example, regenerative farming is certainly another.

In *Renewing Husbandry*, an essay published in 2018, Wendell Berry observes that husbandry resides at the core of livelihood. "The word 'husbandry' is the name of a connection… To husband is to use with care, to keep, to save, to make last, to conserve." While husbandry is a connection to a household, "Old usage tells us that there is a husbandry also of the land, of the soil, of the domestic plants and animals — obviously because of the importance of these things to the household… Husbandry is the name of all the practices that sustain life by connecting us conservingly to our places and our world; it is the art of keeping tied all the strands in the living network that sustains us."

Big Ag with its twin systems of industrial agriculture and factory farming, severs those strands.

Livestock is cleft from pastures, small farmers are forced away from their land, community small business owners are divorced from solvency. In American agriculture alone, over the past four generations the livelihood of farming has been extinguished for six million American families. Wendell Berry continues, "Most and perhaps all of industrial agriculture's manifest failures appear to be the result of an attempt to make the land produce without husbandry. The attempt to remake agriculture as a science and an industry has excluded from it the age-old husbandry which was central and essential to it."[3]

Big Ag operates as an extractive process, one that has succeeded in doing far more than removing the farmers from the land. It purchases the raw materials out of a local economy or region, while over time, gaining economic control over their origin, the farms and farming practices, to secure this flow while lowering cost as much as possible. Industrial agriculture forces remaining farmers to incur high input costs, money that is paid to corporations far removed from the farmer's community. Reducing the number of farms and farmers extinguishes any possible collective bargaining power they might have discovered they had and solidifies this economic control over the minority who remain. The loss of farming families strangles the commerce in that community, creating corresponding job losses in the towns. Because farming families no longer produce food for themselves and their community, food must now be brought in from afar to supply any grocery stores that remain as well as the budget-priced fast food outlets and restaurant chains in this struggling and increasingly impoverished community. The money from the sale of this food is also largely destined for distant corporations — it no longer circulates in the local economy. Remaining residents in the towns and surrounding countryside will now find a Walmart or other super-center nearby that aggregates the things they need. These goods are also not made locally but brought into the area from elsewhere, their purchase siphoning more revenue from the region. Cash-strapped denizens are offered cheaper and cheaper goods, a path descending to the cheapest possible items from the cheapest provider, the dollar store. This process has been described as a colonization of rural America.

Joanna Macy believes in the importance of recognizing the value to an individual of worthwhile work, "The work a person performs not only expresses his character but modifies it in turn. High value, therefore, must be placed on the nature of this work. Instead of being considered as a necessary evil to which one is condemned, or 'disutility' as in classical economics, work is a vehicle for the creation and expression of our deepest values."[4]

There is a profound, soul-fulfilling essential to livelihood. It is in part subconscious: discovering the calling that feeds and nourishes your soul, the reason why you are on this path, the inner certainty that this is the endeavor, the work, the life-labor that you are here, in this life, to engage in and do.

For Wendell Berry, husbandry is so fundamental that it *encompasses* science. "Husbandry, which is not replaceable by science, nevertheless uses science, and corrects it too. It is the more comprehensive discipline. To reduce husbandry to science, in practice, is to transform agricultural 'wastes' into pollutants, and to subtract perennials and grazing animals from the rotation of crops. Without husbandry, the agriculture of science and industry has served too well the purpose of the industrial economy in reducing the number of landowners and the self-employed. It has transformed the United States from a country of many owners to a country of many employees."[5]

•　•　•

One day, as Theo Davies was harvesting from one of the raised beds at Green Leaf Learning Farm, a boy approached him. He stood watching as this magician made long, orange round things appear as if from nothing, out of the ground. "What are those?" the boy wondered.

Theo regarded him. This 10-year-old had never fathomed where carrots on his plate come from. Theo told him what they were, cleaned the dirt off one, and offered it to him. "He bit into it and it was like a firecracker went off in his eyes, 'This is so good!' And I told him, 'This is what they're supposed to taste like.' He said he wanted to eat more things like that, and I knew he was going to go home to his mom or dad or grandmother and ask for that. That really spoke to me."

When Theo was studying for his graduate anthropology degree at the University of Memphis, his area of focus was urban food systems with an emphasis on how people cope, living in a food desert. "These corner food stores used to be full-service grocery stores selling produce and eggs, deli meats and cheeses, but as the middle class moved out of the neighborhood, so too did the tax base. The stores could no longer afford to stock food that would spoil so they shifted to non-perishable items — the chips and candy, cigarettes, soda and beer. The neighborhood food became unhealthy and the people became unhealthy. The infrastructure began to crumble and the people began to crumble.

"To me food is culture. The easiest way to pass on culture is through food. Not just the food itself, but the ritual that goes into making, presenting and serving food. There is a lot of history in the South that is undiscovered, particularly in neighborhoods like this. This neighborhood has two of the best soul food restaurants in the city but nobody outside the neighborhood knows about them.

"I'm here doing this because I like interacting with culture. I like interacting with *this* culture. That's a dream come true for me. And I'm helping people who don't have a lot of options when it comes to good, healthy food."

Big Ag doesn't think in these terms. Livelihood. Enriching the land. Making the soil better, not just so you can grow something to take away from it but improving it by making it better today than tomorrow, better after harvest for your next harvest, better for future stewards who will arrive to care for it and whose livelihoods will one day depend on it. Big Ag pays lip service to that as part of its advertising and public relations pushes, creating a sense of nostalgia, the illusion that time-honored ways of farming and land stewardship continue, and that, as agents of modern agriculture, they are just enhancing or modernizing them. That's a deceitful illusion. Protecting livelihoods and enriching communities doesn't enter into the Big Ag equation. That's not factored into their ruthlessly profit-driven soulless bottom line.

. . .

Because livelihood is intimately tied to home and sense of place, your culture, and your terroir, it is about community.

Small family farming — regenerative farming — involves a livelihood, or livelihoods, almost without exception. For Matt and Alyssa Kautz at Cottonwood Creek Farms, for Joan and Nick Olson at Prairie Drifter Farm, for Gabe Brown and his family at Brown Ranch, and for Lou Preston and his family at Preston Vineyards, this is their livelihood. And their families and their successful businesses enrich and enliven their communities.

According to 2014 USDA census data, between 2007 and 2012, while the total number of American farmers decreased by 3.1%, the number of farmers between ages 25 to 34 *grew* by 2.2%.[6] While there remain tremendous challenges to making a living from agriculture, Caitlin Dewey reported in *The Washington Post* that this is just the second time in the last century that the number of farmers age 35 or younger is increasing. In California, Nebraska, and South Dakota since 2007, the number of new farmers has grown by 20% or more.[7]

69% of these farmers have college degrees. 14% have master's degrees. 60% are female. 75% are first generation farmers. 75% describe their farms as "sustainable," 63% as "organic."[8] Caitlin Dewey notes that they are "already contributing to the growth of the local-food movement and could help preserve the place of midsize farms in the rural landscape."[9] In the same report, Kathleen Merrigan, the head of the Food Institute at George Washington University and a deputy secretary at the Department of Agriculture under President Barack Obama, is quoted: "We're going to see a sea change in American agriculture as the next generation gets on the land. The only question is whether they'll get on the land, given the challenges."

Doug Crabtree and Anna Jones-Crabtree are first generation farmers. Doug has a degree in Agriculture Economics with a specialty in Farm

Management from Purdue University and a master's degree from South Dakota State in Plant Science focusing on organic crop rotations. Anna has undergraduate and master's degrees from Purdue University in Construction Engineering and Management, Civil Engineering, and her Ph.D. from Georgia Institute of Technology in Civil and Environmental Engineering with a minor in sustainable systems. Their 7,400-acre Montana farm, Vilicus Farms, enriches their community. Their property and income taxes contribute to the local economy. Their family living and farming expenses such as machinery, parts and repair are purchased locally. Some of their farm workers are local hires, their apprentices and interns are paid. The *way* they run their organic farm, however, contributes even more significantly.

Doug and Anna don't buy a single ounce of fertilizer, pesticides, herbicides, GMO seed or other industrial agriculture inputs, so the vast majority of their spending stays within, and supports, their community. The inputs required by nearby non-organic farms are bought from a local supplier who in turn purchases them from distant corporations and has them transported in over long distances.

Doug sees opportunity in their region. "We need to get more people out here managing farms at scale. It's not uncommon out here to have 20 and 30 thousand-acre farm units." Passionate advocacy resonates in Anna's voice, "This is one of the most entrepreneurial, awesome things that you could be doing with your life. It's got all of the great pieces of growing your own food, being outside, working with spreadsheets and taking care of the land, and doing something that's bigger than just yourself. That's the narrative we're trying to build with our apprentice program." Doug adds, "We need to bring educated people back to the land. The goal of our apprentice program[10] is to create more stewards, more thoughtful practicing professional farmers who will raise the level of stewardship across the landscape. With the success and growth of the organic market, there is an opportunity, whether for the second or third son or daughter of a farming family that doesn't have the opportunity or the desire to farm in the industrial agriculture system, or for someone who didn't grow up in agriculture. We are looking for those who want to avail themselves to such an opportunity."

Vocation is tied to community, local ecosystem, local economy.

On average, when two small farms close down, one local small business disappears with them. The reverse will prove to be the case as well.

At White Oak Pastures, Will Harris's 3,200-acre farm in Bluffton, Georgia, his concern for animal welfare and raising free-range humanely treated animals, led directly to regenerative land management that dramatically improved the health and fecundity of his soil. This then led to a focus on revitalizing his rural community in recent years.

Will told me that he now has 155 employees, making his farm the largest private employer in his or any of the surrounding counties. "Bluffton is an incorporated city east of the Mississippi River. It was a thriving place until the industrialization, commoditization and centralization of agriculture. When that occurred that simply made Bluffton irrelevant. So, it did what everything does when it becomes irrelevant — it atrophied. For the past 50 years nothing has been going on in Bluffton except that poorer and poorer people have been living in the old houses using up the equity. Anybody that could leave Bluffton did, and the people who stayed were the ones who had ownership in an old house and couldn't afford to move so they lived there until they died. Then the house sold to someone who was even poorer — because it was devalued — until they died, and so on until the house fell down and no one lived there anymore."

Will pauses, reflecting. "This is not a Southern phenomenon. This is a rural phenomenon. And it happened because industrialized agriculture made these places, these economies irrelevant, which is a shame because this is a gem. It's this lifestyle here that caused us to have the democracy that we have. But it became irrelevant. So, everyone went away. So, what's that going to do to the democracy they created? It's not healthy for it."

There wasn't a single new house constructed in Bluffton from 1972 to 2016. In 2016, Will had two nice homes built for two of his managers and their families. He renovated 10 units for other employees to live and built a general store and a restaurant. It used to be that the only thing you could buy in the town, or within a 12-mile radius, was a postage stamp at the post office. No longer. He also leases buildings in Bluffton like the church where his administrative offices are.

"John Muir has told us that in nature when you pull a string you see that everything is connected. There is no reason to believe that the health of the soil is not connected to the health of the community. In rebuilding the soil, we are rebuilding a farmer middle class."[11]

One of the most important ways a business can support its community is to keep as much of its spending as possible within the local economy. "What we do is very closed-loop at the farm and in terms of the community.

Industrial agriculture farmers must spend incredible amounts of money for inputs, and all of that money goes outside of their territory. And out of the country in many cases. The nitrogen component is a byproduct of distant petroleum distillation. Chemical fertilizers, the phosphate and the potassium are mined all over the world. Pesticides are bought from international companies. The same is true for genetically modified seeds."

By shifting to regenerative agriculture, Will no longer buys fertilizers, pesticides, GMO-seeds or any other industrial agriculture inputs. None. Will's significant expenses are the land tax paid by White Oak Pastures, which helps support the county in a big way, and his labor costs. "Almost every bit of my labor costs, $90,000 each week, is spent locally. Our employees and their families eat at my restaurant for half price and they can buy at the general store for a 20% discount. They're incentivized to keep the money here."

The farm's business model has three components. "There's production in the pasture, processing to make it marketable, and then distribution to get it to a consumer who will pay the higher price to cover the production of the product. You've got to have all three of them, they've got to work, and you can't let any one of them get too far ahead or far behind the other two." Will takes advantage of his improved soil by farming four acres as well. He grows organic seasonal vegetables. Beans and peas in the summer, swiss chard, bok choy and collard greens in the winter, tomatoes and squash. His farm is USDA Certified Organic. He grows these healthy vegetables for the restaurant, the general store, and sells them online. Will would like to sell at farmer's markets except that the nearest one is three hours away. Bluffton, Georgia was a food desert for decades. No longer.

Will Harris enjoys his livelihood. "The expression is 'I get paid for what I was made for.' Technically, I work 16 hours a day because 16 hours a day I'm on this farm, but I don't feel like I work at all. I would do for free what I do for a living."[12]

Will now oversees a $20 million a year business, and he told me with the conviction born from experience, "What we're doing here in Bluffton is highly replicable."

Livelihoods flourish within healthy communities. Healthy communities have vibrant economies.

"Regionalism," as Robert Wolf terms it, fosters not only a local food system, but local production so money can recirculate within the region, development banks prioritizing investment in the local economy to create housing and businesses, the evolution of local culture, the arts and a sense of belonging, and develops the employment base enabling rural areas to stabilize their populations and retain their high school graduates.[13] The economies of communities are central.

This can be the economy of the counties, of bio-regions; the economy of districts, of parishes, of neighborhoods.

This is the economy of the shires.

Marlon Foster, Wendell Berry, Doug Crabtree, Anna Jones-Crabtree, and Will Harris each know a secret.

It's all about livelihood.

II

It was her green smoothies.

When Marlon brought Yolanda Manning on as Programs Manager at both Green Leaf and at the Jay Uiberall Culinary Academy, he told her, "I want your passion and your personal experience with health and nutrition to permeate the whole organization. Our staff of forty is your first audience. I want us living as whole, complete and healthy individuals who are trying to steward that in the lives of those that we serve."

Yolanda told me, "I would prepare plant-based foods so everyone could try them. For smoothies, I was using the kale and the spinach from the farm with apples and some frozen fruit. Over time I came to realize that people, before they come to work, now have morning regimens which include green smoothies."

Yolanda has a master's degree from the University of Memphis in Public Administration with a focus on Policy. Originally from Nashville, "When I learned about the community of South Memphis and how historic it is, and the people of South Memphis are so passionate about their community, and for Mr. Foster to be a product of the community and to invest back into it, I just think it's a wonderful thing." She leads classes in health and nutrition, culinary arts, hospitality and management. Students who have taken enrichment courses at the culinary academy have graduated high school and gone on to train in a cooking school in New York or into internships in the Memphis food industry. "It's an opportunity for them not only to learn how to cook, but to discover what they are passionate about as well."

Yolanda is 29. She is a beautiful woman, tall, graceful, articulate with a gentle soft-spoken voice. Her journey, it turns out, has a similarity with Brady Kluge's. Growing up, she was 90 pounds overweight. "I've always been the heavier child, I always struggled with my weight. I struggled with physical ailments like eczema."

When she was 21, she committed to exercising three to five days a week, and to changing her diet. She was living at the time with an uncle who did not allow her to eat pork for religious reasons, and three months went by and she noticed she felt better. She transitioned away from meat entirely and felt even better. Yolanda began cutting back on dairy as well. "My skin improved - the eczema went away." Today, her skin is beautiful. Over three years she lost 90 pounds and is now at her ideal weight.

"The best way to lose weight throughout your journey is being self-aware of how your body is reacting to foods. I used to think that every time I ate ice cream my stomach was *supposed* to hurt. I didn't realize that that was my body saying, 'No. I don't want that.'"

"I also started cooking more. Restaurant food and processed foods have a lot of salt, fat, and a lot of sugar most times." Preparing her own foods, she knows what is going in. "Once you get on this journey of health and wellness, you want to know where your food is coming from. So, I started going to farmer's markets and learning.

"My family history — my mom and my dad — is one of diabetes, high blood pressure, and heart disease." Her grandfather transitioned from heart disease, her grandmother from cancer. She uses the word "transitioned" because "died" is difficult for her. "My cousin and I, we'd watch all the documentaries — *Food, Inc.* was one of them — and we'd realize it just had to be the food. I don't need the health care system to heal me when I have the tools and the knowledge and the resources to do it myself.

"I think about my generation and the generation to come. Of my children one day. Do I want to continue the legacy of disease?

"So, how can we do small things in our diets to reach the goals we have in mind? It can be overwhelming if you are new to the journey, if you don't know where to start. So, I would say plan out your meals. What does your meal prepping look like? What are some things you enjoy? What are some fruits and vegetables you really like, and how can we incorporate more of these into the food that you are used to?"

In 2015, Marlon acquired the lot west of the church. The boarded-up house on it will be renovated to become a café-bistro with a modern kitchen. The brick two story building across the street will be resident apartments for the students of the cooking school. The two biggest restaurant costs are staff and food. The produce for this café will be grown across the street and the staff will include culinary students who will be learning from professional chefs.

Yolanda has a lot on her plate. But this is her livelihood. There's little else she'd rather be doing.

• • •

Alan Lewis champions livelihoods. He navigates food and agriculture policy for Natural Grocers at the federal, state and local level. Alan helps agricultural producers grow food that meets both consumer demand and the company's high standards. As a member of several standards organizations and advocacy groups, he is an advocate of regenerative agriculture and organic farming, protecting small family farms and revitalizing rural communities.

Natural Grocers' net sales for the first fiscal quarter of 2018 were $202.5 million, a net increase of 10.3% over the previous year. Clearly, more and more people are focusing on healthy, sustainable, and humanely produced food. Natural Grocers' purchasing commitments support hundreds of small organic farmers and ranchers who pasture their livestock. Matt Kautz of Cottonwood Creek Farms is one of them. Alan told Matt that Natural Grocers would commit to buying every egg Matt could produce from his pastured hens, and for the most part they have done just that.

Natural Grocers understands how the quality of the food they sell effects consumer health, farmer's livelihoods, small community survival, and the environment of the planet we all share. They believe food "is the foundation upon which we build health and vitality; it should taste good and entice our senses; it should contribute to our wellbeing. The way it is grown should be sustainable; supporting the health of farmers, farm workers, farm communities, farm animals and the overall environment. Animals should be raised humanely and in accordance with their natural biology. We believe that farmers should be provided with markets that allow them to choose pasture-based and biodynamic practices... Our goal is to impact how the food in this nation is raised and produced by supporting and promoting pasture-based products and the farmers and ranchers who raise them."[14]

Akin to Steve Ells and Chipotle's mandate to source locally grown wherever possible — to buy from farms "that plant a variety of crops and rotate the fields where they're planted, keeping the soil nutrient-rich and the land healthier year after year" — many family farmers and ranchers celebrate their livelihood due in no small part to Alan Lewis and his role at Natural Grocers.

Natural Grocers has sales of over $800 million each year. Chipotle operates over 2,000 restaurants. By 2019, the annual demand for meat, dairy, grain, vegetable and other organic products has increased dramatically to over $50 billion.

However...

Just 1% of the farmland in the United States is certified organic. The remaining 99% is farmed in the industrial agriculture manner.[15]

In 2011, only 4.3 million acres — including the two at Green Leaf Learning Farm — of the 277 million acres of the Mississippi River Basin were planted in cover crops.

The percentage of farmed animals that are pastured, and humanely and ethically raised is also very small.

The number of American farms has decreased by 6 million, a loss in less than four generations of 75% of American small farms. Behind that number is the lost livelihood for each one of these farmers - many, *many* farmers. And the loss of property ownership by these millions of families. And for most, the loss of community and a way of life.

Why?

It was Ezra Taft Benson, President Dwight D. Eisenhower's Secretary of Agriculture, who first decreed in the 1950's that the choice for the American farmer was to either "Get big or get out."[16] His assertion was based on the advent of mechanization and new science and technology. But something else was going on as well, a hidden undercurrent... Before the 1950's, well before even the beginning of the twentieth century, American farmers and rural communities have not been treated well. They haven't been treated well since the years immediately following the American Revolution.

Why?

There are darker forces at play...

Alan Lewis proves an able guide on this journey.

COMING FULL CIRCLE
RECLAIMING DEMOCRACY WITH LOCAL FOOD

by Alan Lewis

In residential subdivisions along the Front Range of Colorado, there is often one house that doesn't fit in. It's the house at the top of the hill, with dying cottonwoods along the north side and remnants of a barbed wire fence that once marked the property line. It's the house that used to be a family farm, sitting on a 160-acre square of good soil along a single-track road leading in from the eastern horizon.

These farmsteads were once part of a vibrant agricultural community, linked together by feed and seed supply stores, grain elevators, food markets, equipment and implement dealers, and all the other businesses that comprise a rural economy. Citizens contributed to the vitality of schools, churches, hospitals, grocery stores, diners, town halls, courts, granges, and post offices, where the day-to-day business of life played out in face-to-face conversations and robust public debate.

The story of our vanishing family farms is a familiar one. Expanding cities encroach on fertile land while cheap food grown elsewhere undermines local farm profits. A developer buys the land to relieve the farmer of his or her growing debt. The farmer's name is remembered only by the sign over the gated entry to the community of tract homes that surrounds what's left of the family homestead. Miller Crossing. Johnson's Corner. Pittz Hollow. The number of American farms has dropped from nearly 8 million to just over 2 million in the last 50 years. As farm families left the countryside, rural communities lost their citizens, their tax base and their economic vitality. In many cases they lost their reason for existing at all. For most Americans, the loss of a farm or a farming community merits at most a shrug. Businesses fail and people move all the time. Food shows up in the supermarket anyway. So why would it matter if unseen rural towns are fading away?

Since our first years as a nation, our democratic ideals have been most fully realized in rural agricultural communities. While the founding fathers wrote high-mindedly about the equal rights of men to seek liberty and happiness, in practice these rights took root most deeply where all citizens owned property — especially productive farmland. With enough land to live independently, but not enough to dominate his neighbor, each farmer could advocate confidently for himself in the local political forum. Keenly aware of his equality of means as well as his dependence on others, he kept the best interests of the whole community in mind. Having enough meant making sure others did, too. He based social status and personal honor on what was contributed over a lifetime, not how much he took for himself.

Yet, long before the American Revolution, a British-American aristocracy had established itself in the new merchant cities, rural estates and plantations of America. Disproportionate accumulation of wealth and property led to unequal levels of political power. Most people were not allowed to vote; even fewer could run for office. Only members of the wealthy families were elected or appointed to rule the lives of commoners. The needs of the many were often overlooked in favor of the wealth of a few. The aristocracy controlled the markets for land, money, manufacturing and trade. Court judges and militias defended their interests.

Thomas Jefferson's ideal of dispersed democratic rural townships morphed into a national ethic of extraction and control. Under this system, the yeoman American farmer has been used as a pawn in a game of wealth accumulation and political domination. British sovereigns used farmers to break new ground on the western frontier and suppress indigenous people. Colonial landholders extracted rents and taxes, then conscripted fathers and sons for war. Merchants lent farmers money against the next harvest but demanded land as collateral; they set the cost of goods high and the price of crops low to slowly steal full title to the land. Railroads and landmen lured settlers to largely fictional western townships with tales of lush land and lavish precipitation. They charged burdensome tariffs to haul equipment and supplies westward, and again to carry farm produce back to urban markets. Speculators circled farmsteads with foreclosure warrants in one hand and new loan money in the other.

To get a clearer understanding of what happened to our farmers, our food system, and our democratic ideals, it helps to revisit a story from the beginning of the industrial revolution, when much of the modern economic, political and social structure of Europe and America was molded. The early transformation of ownership, production and markets among farmers, artisans, tradesmen, factory owners, and financial elites is still recognizable in today's economy.

For centuries before the Industrial Revolution, three longstanding traditions had kept villages and families economically stable. A man learned his father's trade, as did his son. A skill such as metalworking, weaving, farming, shoe making, or baking provided income from barter and currency. Ubiquitous production of food for the household supplemented the income from cottage industry and trades. Every home had a vegetable garden and kept chickens, goats or pigs for meat, milk, and eggs. Extensive public commons — shared open areas, which were accessible to the entire community — allowed for foraging, farming, livestock rearing, fishing and hunting. Income from the family's trade, augmented by cottage food production at home and food sourced from the commons, generally supported families through seasons both bountiful and lean.

Then came the machines.

The Luddites are often said to have feared new technology and fought to stop it out of simpleminded ignorance. In this view, steam-powered machinery increased productivity and freed human and animal workers from inefficient manual labor. Machines required only unskilled labor, and much less of it. A deeper look reveals that the longstanding conventions and social structures of village life were rendered irrelevant by the consequences of industrial technology. Factory owners could hire women and children for a tenth the cost of a skilled tradesman. They amassed fortunes and lived lavishly while the typical working man saw his traditional skills become obsolete, his earning power decimated, and his ability to feed his family disrupted — all within the span of a few years. Heads of families had no work, no trade, no pay, and no station in the social hierarchy. The quality of life of entire populations was sacrificed for the benefit of those who owned the new machines. To make matters worse, wage-earners themselves were taxed to support the unemployed poor whose livelihoods were destroyed.

Thousands of farmers and tradesmen assessed this new order and found it intolerable. Why should one man get fabulously rich by refusing to pay his countrymen a fair wage? How had the shared commons been fenced in to become the property of a few? What was to be done about the air heavy with soot and the river running black with factory waste?

In desperation, families banded together, swore each other to a secret brotherhood, and smashed hundreds of mechanized looms. Luddite uprisings occurred nearly simultaneously across dozens of English towns. No single Luddite leader's call to action spread from town to town. Self-awareness and self-respect arose spontaneously in every settlement where families faced off against the malignant methods of mechanized production and the factory owners who profited from them. We will fight for what matters to our families. *Give us back the things we value.* Human beings should not contort themselves to serve the needs of technology and its owner's greed. The fictitious King Ludd was a shared idea — a legend, a figurehead, a talisman, a hope. He embodied the belief that machines and technology must first serve people, families and communities.

The response to the populist threat to factory owners' profits was brutal and swift. Government assembled the largest police presence ever mustered outside of wartime. Protesters were rounded up, interrogated and some were hanged. The displaced and unemployed poor lived in horrid welfare houses, did penance in debtor prisons or were transported to overseas colonies. Thus began the use of government authority to protect industrial production and profit — at the expense of the dispossessed. The intractable poverty of sick, depressed, hopeless, and begging families has prevailed, in one form or another, since then.

The destruction of civic life and the pollution of the environment still describe America today, 200 years after the Luddites in England made their desperate last stand. The concentration of ownership and control of production and markets is stronger than ever. One need only look at the beef, pork and poultry industries to see how these patterns continue. With control of markets, agriculture conglomerates can dictate to farmers how to raise animals at the very lowest possible cost. With control of government, they can ignore the stench and contamination of manure lagoons. With gag orders that make free speech a criminal offense, they can keep prying eyes away from the horrors of concentrated livestock feeding operations. With control of an industry and its profits, they can disregard the decline in human health around hog and chicken factories and claim not to notice the widespread poverty their system creates. By hiring minimal staff at substandard wages, they can force surrounding communities to pay the cost of hunger, health care, and education. A Luddite mother in 1812 would be all too familiar with our current plight. *Give us back the things we value.*

We don't often think of American farmers as unruly rebels, but history shows we should. In the late 1700's, Shays' Rebellion pitched a thousand poorly armed farmers, most of whom were veterans of the colonial wars, against 4,000 members of the Massachusetts militia in a dispute over crop prices, taxes and rents. In the early 1800's, tenant farmers in New York state waged an armed guerrilla war against wealthy absentee landlords who, based on suspect land deeds, sought to evict them over unpaid rents. In the 1880's, over two million plainsmen joined the National Farmers Alliance to gain access to affordable credit and cooperative buying at fair prices. After World War I and through the depression, farmers protested foreclosures caused by low prices by burning crops, dumping milk, blockading highways, protesting auctions, and taking judges hostage in their courtrooms. In Springfield, Colorado, the American Agricultural Movement organized a nationwide shutdown of crop shipments in an attempt to bolster prices and force the federal government to intervene on behalf of failing farms. In 1978, soaring interest rates on farm debt emboldened a small army of AMA farmers to drive their tractors across country, right up onto the lawn of the US Capitol. When the farmers demanded meetings, the Secretary of Agriculture escaped through his office window into a waiting limousine. Farmers were ridiculed, beaten and arrested.

In every case, our farmers rose up in protest because the prices offered for their production was less than the cost to produce it. They demanded fair access to land, fair access to credit, and fair access to transport and markets. Land rents made landlords richer. Whenever the global agricultural market generated too much supply, shifting demand drove market prices down in regular cyclical corrections. Improved technology and larger machines increased efficiency and yields, but only the farmer with access to capital to buy the most land first could take advantage of it. The result, as plain as the farmer's day is long, was the systematic loss of wealth and opportunity across the American Heartland. Owners became renters. Renters became laborers. Laborers moved on.

Especially in the United States, technological escalation in agriculture has reached extremes. 10,000-acre farms planted with a single crop are common. The specialized equipment built to service these farms can plant and fertilize a sixty-foot wide swath in a single pass and can cost a million dollars. Commodity production and the vast land, equipment and chemical investments it requires is now so expensive that only the wealthy, and wealthy corporations, can afford to farm. Now as then, renters and sharecroppers are simply starved off. Small farms without access to markets and capital fail and are absorbed into larger farms. Unemployed farmers and their hired hands migrate, heading to cities hoping for work.

The ideology of innovation is the belief that the complexity, standardization, and centralized control enabled by technology is *always* better than what was before. It is deeply embedded in our national way of thinking. It informs all our laws and policies. As if our country's land is just a dirt factory that makes food, we measure only the cost of inputs and the quantity of outputs. If a community, a family, or a farm is destroyed in the process, so be it. If a watershed, a river, or an ocean is polluted in the process, that's the price of cheap food. If an animal suffers its whole life until the day of its death, it's just an animal. This is the norm of our technology-driven American economy: increase shareholder value.

Lobbyists and fixers for the agrochemical industry protect its domination and profits. Whether it's GMO contaminated pollen, pesticide drift, stench from manure lagoons, antibiotic resistance, or the patenting of God-given genetic traits, industry has always found a way to manipulate courts and lawmakers to gain power and profit from new technologies without concern for common sense precaution or basic human values. Apologists for global agricultural conglomerates — including legislators and academics — are fully aware that overproduction of commodities on vast mono-culture farms is a risky economic venture. No worries: when overproduction drives down commodity prices, their friends in Congress have already authorized the U.S. taxpayers to subsidize crop prices to keep the system working. No such luck for small family farms. From 1995 to 2012, more than 75% of USDA farm subsidy payments were received by fewer than 10% of farms — all at taxpayer expense.

The unquestioned acceptance of technological innovation is so ingrained in our culture that the belief in hard work, robust rural communities, humane treatment of animals, resource conservation, and alternative fuel use are now considered "ideological impediments" to proper farm management. Agricultural industry think-tanks and their public relations teams openly mock smallholders, organic farmers and grassland ranchers — even at times, without irony, disparaging them as Luddites. Nowhere is this broken logic more apparent than in the biotech industry's efforts to promote genetically engineered (now awkwardly re-named "bio engineered") crop varieties and the destructive chemical-intensive cropping systems that are required to support them. Bayer alone claims to spend hundreds of millions of dollars to find viable varieties of artificially mutated crops. But Bayer's agricultural system is not designed to grow more food or make farming more profitable for farmers. It is designed to force farmers to buy more patented seeds, synthetic fertilizers, and toxic herbicides — from Bayer, of course. The numbers are in: fewer farmers are making less money because the expensive system diverts profits into the overflowing pockets of company stockholders. The ideology of innovation works well for those who propound it.

Mechanization and concentrated ownership sparked the great labor migrations of our nation's history. Out of the agrarian south, a mass exodus by freemen and dispossessed poor white farmers led families both to northern industrial cities and homesteads in newly opened western territories. During the Dust Bowl, starving farmers fled the ravaged plains, a tragedy caused by vast steam-powered tilling that left millions of square miles of open earth defenseless before the wind. Over time, these migrations manifested as permanent relocation from farm areas to regional industrial centers, where factories, construction, commercial services, and other economic activity were concentrated.

Not everyone left the heartland, at least not all at once. Families and communities sought to protect their agrarian way of life by borrowing heavily to purchase new machinery, fertilizers, pesticides, and seeds that industry salesmen and agricultural extension agents offered. But the result was the same after every economic crisis or natural catastrophe. Instead of receiving help and relief, struggling farmers were hustled toward foreclosure so they could be rolled up into bigger, more efficient operations to grow commodity crops at lower and lower cost.

In almost every segment of the American industrial food system, only a handful of companies control what is grown, how it is processed, and where it is sold. In the pork and poultry industry, growers are often indentured to the corporate contract. They must buy animals, feed, and medicine from the company. If the animals stay alive and grow, the company will buy them back at a barely profitable "market" price. If animals die or wither, the risk of financial loss falls entirely on the farmer. Like Luddite village workers facing life in the factory mills, farmers have never fared well when they depend on inputs and markets controlled by others.

But don't blame the farmer. To access reliable markets for their hogs, farmers must agree to raise them the way corporate buyers tell them to. If a pork producer wants a ready market for 1,000 fats, he or she must accept the price the aggregator offers. Industrial pork is a mainstay in supermarkets, restaurants, schools and institutions. But they won't buy live animals from the grower or carcasses from the slaughterhouse. They only buy processed cuts and ground meat encased in plastic and packed into clean cardboard cases. Industrial hog factories and large-scale high-speed processing plants are required by big brands and big retailers to deliver an inexpensive and uniform product. They'll pay the lowest possible price to growers and sell for the highest possible margin to consumers. And they are often the only game in town. Protest is mostly futile. They created a loophole that allows cheap foreign meat to be labeled as Product of USA; that's the price American farmers are told they have to beat.

It's impossible to criticize the farm families that have chosen to scale up and compete within a global system, because, by design, that is often the only choice they have left. The lowest risk crops are those with ready markets that can be stored for long periods: corn, wheat, and soy. But the bet only works if the farm's costs are low relative to its size: get big sell them to eager metropolitan buyers. These direct sales provide more profit for the farmer. More importantly, they provide a market for products that would otherwise go unproduced or unsold.

Farming and democracy work best on a human scale.

Food safety, nutrient density, carbon capture, economic security, and rural sovereignty have become core principles of the local food movement. Fixing the food system means fixing farmers' connection to markets for their goods. If farmers can sell to consumers who understand agriculture, farmers can again choose to grow better food in better ways and make more money doing it. Food production, processing, storage, marketing and distribution must be reestablished at the regional and county level. Renewed commitment to food issues in urban areas creates a natural connection to the remaining small producers in the countryside. In a classic free market scenario, small specialty producers are meeting urban demand for quality food produced by a compassionate, resilient, safe and fair agricultural system. One group links to the other in an exchange of ideas, support, learning, and, yes, money.

How can these producers rebuild the heartland? The success of smaller farms and ranches depends on many factors. On-farm income is almost always subsidized by a day job because farm income is now too erratic and seasonal to depend on. Small operations avoid competing with industrial crop producers by growing specialized crops and raising meat and dairy animals using methods that appeal to particular consumer needs. Small farms also tend to operate using mixed crops and animals. By using the waste from one to nourish the other, and rotating crops and animals through the fields, biologically diverse farms reduce the cost of inputs while producing superior products. For consumers buying an expensive pork chop, the taste and texture of the meat is as important as the farm's regenerative practices, her economic resilience, and the muddy pig's happy squeal.

Many longtime conventional farmers can see that commodity cropping has become a losing proposition. Unreliable profits, blowing topsoil, and long days in the cab of a tractor spraying pesticides is not what they envisioned for themselves and not what their children feel is an attractive future. It's not wholesome farm life on a human scale. It's a boring corporate life sitting in a tiny glass cubicle on top of a big diesel engine powering a fully automated tractor. Farmers know nature, and nature adapts. Naturally, farmers are trying new ways to grow and sell new kinds of crops. That's their only hope of enticing their kids back when it comes time to retire.

A satisfying characteristic of urban-rural grassroots connections is how they can be insulated from corporate meddling. Membership depends on local citizenship and participation. Cargill would have a hard time convincing my neighbors that it holds the best interests of the community above its own goals. Unlike corporate marketing online, into which companies can insert artificial influence and authority through public relations efforts, paid bloggers, and advertising, the town hall meeting is hard for Big Ag to manipulate. Living *here* is often the first requirement for participation. (Even so, food groups are reporting offers of corporate sponsorship, advice and product samples as companies seek to influence and profit from the democratic food movement. It seems to them that fearful, misled, uninformed and ideologically misguided consumers need a paternalistic corporate shill to set them straight.)

Beyond the better taste of fresher food and building strong relationships, the new food movement is supporting something even more important: democratic participation. However hypocritical they appear in hindsight, Thomas Jefferson's democratic ideals were based on observations of small communities. Each citizen was entitled to use the community's resources, but only to a certain extent. None would extract so much that she destroyed the commons or wielded inordinate power, and none would have so little use of the commons as to be dependent on another. This idealized democracy depended on both private property and shared community resources. Today, this ideal exists in tentative form in many towns and neighborhoods that are building infrastructure and logistics to allow everyone to build wealth.

Collectively, food activists are responding to the conglomerate food crisis and the lack of democratic participation in governing our communities. These individuals and groups intend to bring back food production, preservation, and sharing to their neighborhoods and towns. They provide a direct link between consumers and regional producers of meat, grains, and vegetables so farmers can exchange their goods at a fair price. A struggling community can get a sense of individual and collective empowerment from participating in a movement to build its own food security.

The movement's aims are powerfully simple: provide healthy food, grown with safe regenerative methods, bring neighbors together to create community trust through growing and sharing food and to provide a method for small rural producers to sell their goods to urban customers at a fair price. Everyone in the community is included, and everyone has equal access to safe, nutritious food. It took two hundred years to come full circle, but our 19th century Luddite forebears would certainly understand the motivation behind these efforts: *Give us back the things we value.*

Over the past few years we have rediscovered the *soil biome.* Now we are rediscovering the *rural economic biome.* Agricultural communities create wealth from soil, sun, water and seed. They increase the value of raw materials by cleaning, processing and preserving them. Excess is aggregated for transport to larger markets. Wealth is captured and accumulated by families for food, education, housing and medical care. Wealth is deployed by communities for water, energy, education, roads, sanitation and safety.-

The rural biome of our agricultural communities provides the food for America. To come full circle, what nourishment are we providing them in return?

III

Imagine you are a farmer from a multi-generational farming family — and you are the one who loses the farm. How do you live with that loss? And which loss? Which loss cuts the deepest? The loss of your legacy, the pride of a family heritage passed down through generations and entrusted to you? The loss of your livelihood, your passion, and the sense of purpose it endows? The loss of home and property ownership? The loss of a respected and dignifying role within your community, of being severed from your community, from where you're from? Of having to take your children away from their familiar schools and friends to an unfamiliar place, a distant city, and to have to search there for work and a way to survive? To have to apply qualities of your character as a farmer — your perseverance, determination, independence, a willingness to labor, and to work long hours — to new employment, to a job where your strength and steadfastness of character may be deemed of merit, yet one that has little use for your actual expertise. One divorced from the soil, from your terroir. Odds are you won't farm crops on the shop floor, in the sales or administrative office, or out on sales meetings.

Rural America, writes Wendell Berry, is "damaged and suffering now because the policy since the middle of the twentieth century has been to abandon the actual country and its actual people to the determinism of 'market forces' and Ezra Taft Benson's decree, 'Get big or get out.' The consequence, as you know as well as I do, and as anybody who looks can see, is that Rural America is a colony belonging to the corporations, and its economy is a colonial economy. If you compute the difference between what a thousand pounds of beef pays into Rural County when it is sold and what Rural Countians pay to buy it back as hamburger or steak, you will have described the action of a siphon that takes everything — the produce of the land, the work of the people, the young people — and gives back as near as possible to nothing. And this computation leaves out the 'side effects' of land loss, soil erosion, forest degradation, toxic contamination of soil and water, bad health, etc."[17]

"The people of Rural America became obsolete as small farmers, small merchants, and trades-people in the country towns, and then became obsolete again as 'blue-collar workers.'"[18]

Vandana Shiva notes that over the 15 year span beginning when industrial agriculture was introduced in India, "284,000 farmers have committed suicide because of the non-sustainability of capital- and chemical-intensive farming based on nonrenewable seeds."[19] In America, 6,000,000 farming livelihoods have been lost — a huge number of people to assimilate, every one of whom has a unique, distinctive family story. Through that lens, this diaspora can seem unbearable.

How does it feel if you are a first-generation farmer? Someone who has discovered their livelihood, one committed to regenerative agriculture, to growing the healthiest possible food and nurturing the environment, to the ethical treatment of pastured animals? Someone who can't make a go of it because he or she is gamed out of government subsidies simply because they elected to farm in a non-industrial agriculture, non-factory farming way? Or is unable to get a start on land they can own because farmland is so overpriced; overpriced not because the industrial agriculture farmers of their region are flourishing — most of them aren't even making a profit — but because the massive Farm Bill crop insurance agricultural subsidies salvage their solvency year after year. And because land speculators backed by consortiums of exceedingly wealthy investors, are buying up distress-sale cropland as investment property to be operated by tenant farmers.

As Will Harris observed, "This is not a Southern phenomenon. This is a rural phenomenon. And it happened because industrialized agriculture made these places, these economies irrelevant."

In 2018, Feeding America reported that 2.7 million rural households now face hunger, 75% of the counties with the highest rates of food insecurity are rural, and 86% of counties with the highest rates of *child* food insecurity are rural.[20] Key indicators of socioeconomic lack of well-being such as unemployment rates, disability, divorce, teen pregnancy, crime, and death rates from heart disease, cancer, suicide, and drug abuse, are now higher in rural America than in America's inner cities.[21]

John Ikerd writes in *The Economic Colonization of Rural America*, "When the sense of community is lost, the sense of common commitment and shared hope for the future is lost."[22]

This is more than a rural phenomenon. Ask the residents of South Memphis or other blighted urban or suburban neighborhoods across this nation. 55% of American zip codes are now food deserts — the remaining denizens of these communities, urban and rural, do not have the economic means to support a single supermarket or grocery store.

The largest portion of the 2018 Farm Bill, comprising nearly 77% of total spending — $663.8 *billion* over 10 years — is allocated to nutrition programs like the Supplemental Nutrition Assistance Program (SNAP) that help ensure Americans don't go hungry.[23] There are tens of millions of Americans who need this assistance.

Farm subsidies provided by our federal government were originally intended to help farmers in times of market uncertainty. The Environmental Working Group's analysis of the $369.7 billion in subsidies American farmers received from 1995 to 2017 concluded, "Despite the rhetoric of 'preserving the family farm,' the vast majority of farmers do not benefit from federal farm subsidy programs and most of the subsidies go to the largest and most financially secure farm operations. Small commodity farmers qualify for a mere pittance, while producers of meat, fruits, and vegetables are almost completely left out of the subsidy game."[24] The vast majority of this money is corralled by the top 10% of those who receive subsidies, primarily Big Ag farms — the ones who least need it. Around 62% of American farmers receive no subsidies at all.[25]

"Corporate agriculture has used its political power and the hard-won reputation for integrity of farmers to transform the 'right to farm' into a 'right to harm,'" notes John Ikerd. "A corporate strategy to turn rural areas into 'agricultural sacrifice zones' is revealed in a progression of laws protecting factory farms from public scrutiny and exempting industrial agriculture from environmental and public health regulations. In vast rural areas zoned for 'agriculture,' corporate agriculture will be free to pollute and plunder as it pleases."[26]

The large industrial farms, and the industry itself, use that aid to keep prices of their products unnaturally low and maintain this competitive market advantage over smaller farmers who don't receive similar benefit. It is also used to aid in marketing and advertising to promote their products in a desirable light to the American consumer, and to further increase its lobbying of the government to protect and expand future subsidy programs.

Crop insurance is another example of a federal program, ostensibly designed to support farmers, that has been largely commandeered by industrial agriculture. Kristin Ohlson writes, "Farmers pay a reduced rate for crop insurance when they plant seeds that are Roundup-ready or have some other genetic modification, because these crops are seen as being less risky than non-GMO crops. On the other hand, they pay a premium on their crop insurance if they farm organically. And farmers who plant cover crops — cover crops! — can actually be denied crop insurance in some situations. Farmers like Gabe Brown who plant companion crops — clover along with his oats, for instance — are booted from the program entirely. 'I'm saving fossil fuels and fertilizer and improving soil health, but I'm penalized for it,' Brown told me. 'The government knows nothing about how nature works. You'd probably see a lot of changes in the system if we stopped crop insurance.'"[27]

The majority of the agricultural research undertaken at the country's 105 land-grant universities has also been co-opted by Big Ag money. Junk science is developed which masks the harmful effects of industrial agriculture's synthetic fertilizers, GMO seeds, pesticides, and herbicides on the environment and in human consumption. Food and Water Watch reports, "In 2009, corporations, trade associations, and foundations invested $822 million in agricultural research at land-grant schools, compared with only $645 million from the USDA... Industry-sponsored research effectively converts land-grant universities into corporate contractors, diverting their research capacity away from projects that serve the public good."[28] The Department of Agriculture itself is also significantly coerced by Big Agribusiness money.

John Ikerd discerns historic echoes, "Much like colonial empires of the past, transnational corporations have been extending their economic power to dominate people in rural places all around the globe. Rural people are losing their sovereignty, as corporations use their economic power over local economies to gain control of local governments. Irreplaceable precious rural resources, including rural people and cultures, are being exploited — not to benefit rural people but to increase the wealth of corporate investors. These corporations are purely economic entities with no capacity for caring or commitment to the future of rural communities. Their only interest is in extracting the economic wealth from rural areas. This is classic economic colonialism."[29]

Isabel Marlens, in her June 4, 2019 article *The Farms of the Future*, sees another historic parallel: "Colonizers have long removed Indigenous people from their land knowing this in turn will deprive them of their food culture, and so make them dependent on the colonizer's economy — creating widening ripples of destruction."[30]

Wendell Berry yearns for a return "from the global economy — which for five hundred years has plundered the land and exploited, enslaved, or murdered the people of the 'foreign' or 'rural' world — to a local economy that would care for and conserve all the goods of a place, including the membership of its living creatures... If a place — a family farm, a country town and its neighboring countryside, a city and its tributary region — does not keep and care for and use enough of its natural and human goods for its own maintenance and its people's thriving, the result is destruction, *permanent* damage... So far as I can see, and I have been looking hard for a long time, the only defense of land and people against a predatory or colonial economy, which has been global, really, for as long as humans have traveled the globe, is a reasonably coherent, reasonably self-sufficient and self-determining local economy... We seem to have forgotten that there might be, or that there ever were, mutually sustaining relationships between resident humans and their home places in the world of Nature. We seem to have no idea that the absence of such relationships, almost everywhere in our country and the world, might be the cause of our trouble."[31]

Families trying to run small farms profitably can't possibly compete with all this stacked against them. Or can they?

Urban and suburban families living in economically drained and blighted shires where job opportunities are scarce, who are finding it more difficult each day just to get by, can't possibly thrive financially, let alone help reinvigorate their local economies. Or can they?

You and I can't avoid supporting industrial agriculture and factory farming given the vast array of food products containing their ingredients that dominate supermarket aisles and restaurant menus? Or can we?

Michael Brownlee, editor of *Local Food Shift*, writes, "Altogether, the industrial food system — now by far the largest and most destructive industry in the world — burns about 23% of global oil and gas supplies, and is already responsible for more than half of global greenhouse gas emissions and 80% of fresh-water resource use." He states that this food system "is now an overwhelming contributor to the sixth mass extinction of species in planetary history, producing what Paul Ehrlich and his fellow researchers are now calling 'a global spasm of biodiversity loss,' the worst planetary crisis in 65 million years."[32]

There's not much chance that we can change this in time to save humankind's presence on our rapidly warming planet. Or is there?

· · ·

In 1947, when Marlon's parents moved into this neighborhood it was predominantly white middle class. They were the 1st black family on their block. A second family moved in that same week. Marlon's father, K.C. Foster, worked in production and manufacturing, spending several decades at Kimberly Clarke. He was a good, well respected employee, but the company wasn't named after him. They moved into the house where Marlon was born in 1955.

Upwardly mobile black families had been moving into this and adjacent neighborhoods in small numbers for decades. In 1885, ten black families lived among whites on three blocks in this neighborhood. In 1910, it was still ten families. Not many but as Preston Lauterbach writes in *Memphis Burning*, "The decennial census is a small sample, but it shows a stable, racially mixed neighborhood in the heart of the South during what were bleak decades for African Americans. And these weren't Negro servants living in backhouse quarters, but a professional class of homeowners. A child growing up on this street would have absorbed a certain sense of equality. These white families tolerated black neighbors, and these black families kept pace with white elites."[33]

Marlon remembers that dinner often included aunts, uncles, grandparents, first cousins... "My grandmother and my mother were awesome cooks, so you can imagine healthy Southern cuisine in the home every day. We ate good with plenty of vegetables, sweet potatoes, peas, corn, greens, probably about six vegetables at a dinner."

The neighborhood changed rapidly following the federal government's decision to integrate schools. White flight began in the late 1950s with working class whites moving into the suburbs. Smaller Evangelical schools, such as Briar Crest and The Woodlands, opened up in the neighborhood, admitting white children only. In the 1960s, as the African-American population within the community grew, segregation patterns developed based on streets. Over time, many of these Evangelical schools faded away amidst public school integration nationwide. Memphis is the only city in the country where these schools are still standing. Today, 80 – 90% of the students in the Memphis city schools are African-American while they number only around 6 - 7% in the suburban Shelby County public school system. "A little while ago we asked our mid-city schools to give up their charter and force Shelby County to be the educator for all students thinking that that would bring us all together," recounts Marlon. Preston Lauterbach notes what happened next: "In 2011, that sparked a new segregationist revolt. Within two years, six suburban municipalities withdrew from the consolidated system and established their own schools, with a huge assist from the Tennessee state legislature, which changed a law that had prohibited new school districts. Now, those suburban districts no longer need to share their resources with the city."[34]

While he was in school, Marlon witnessed his neighborhood become increasingly impoverished. Everywhere: disrepair, decay, and blight. As an aspiring entrepreneur, his teenage goal was to own his own liquor store because the corner liquor store was the best example he had of a successful business in his area.

Marlon especially respected his biology teacher, Mr. Harris. "He was just a cool guy. He came into class one day and he played Bobby Womack's *Hairy Hippy* and I knew all the words, and I was singing it, and he and I began to connect. One day, senior year, I was out in the hallway cutting class, and Mr. Harris, well, he made me go into the class where they were taking the A.C.T. test, no study, no practice, no nothing, just made me go in there and take the test. Thank goodness he did because I got a 19. So, then I went and applied to Lemoyne-Owen College, and with that score they accepted me. That put me on the path to a business degree."

Other classmates were less fortunate. "All the things I'd seen around me, the urban core street life, the drug culture of location, location, location, wholesale, retail, supply and demand. This is what the kids see on the streets." It prepared him for business school. "These are the kids that could be running businesses. A friend of mine, he was making honor roll, he was naturally smart, he was brilliant — and he got killed. That's what can happen when you are ignored, when you fall through the cracks."

When the work opportunities disappear and the neighborhood's tax base drains, budgets are cut, which means less money for the schools. Segregation of schools leads to unequal funding of school districts. Inadequately funded schools compromise teacher's ability to educate their students, to develop the potential for academic competence and excellence in their young minds. Entire student bodies are cast adrift in a poverty of knowledge.

Marlon understands the essential importance of a good education, that a person's sense of self-worth and the self-esteem that accompanies that are related to his or her depth of knowledge and understanding. A good education enabled him to become conversant in the business world, to be gainfully and creatively employed, and to discover his livelihood. He was unable to sleep at night witnessing kids trapped, unable to move from doubt or despair to hope — from stagnancy to growth. So, he opened the Knowledge Quest Extended Learning Academy (ELA) knowing that, so often, it's just a matter of finding a trajectory or an inspiration.

Nestled beside the church and across the street from Green Leaf farm is the ELA's early literacy program for pre-K through 1st graders. Two other Extended Learning Centers each offer afterschool enrichment for 2nd through 12th graders. The Gaston Community Center, adjacent to a library and an indoor basketball court, is home to the ELA's theater stage, rehearsal area, art room, and well-maintained classrooms.

All of the enrichment classes are designed to introduce the students to hands-on experience out in the world. If a student is envisioning a career as a chef or in the food industry, Marlon has them in the Jay Uiberall Culinary

Seek and purchase locally sourced food.

By doing so you are supporting stewardship of the land. Your spending has a significant benefit for the farming communities closest to you in your greater community or region. Whole food, healthy food, is your best choice for your health and contributes to the livelihoods of regenerative farmers and humane ranchers: and by increasing the demand for their products, will enable these farms to thrive and for more of them to get their start. If you live in a rural community, farmland is probably nearby. If you live in a city, the food available to you may travel 15 miles or 3,000. Its source is unseen. Buy local whenever possible. Buy organic, buy regeneratively grown. Buy grass fed and pastured meat and dairy.

"Since food is what catalyzed human civilization in the first place, it is only appropriate that the effort towards healing and regeneration should also begin with food. There is no issue or human activity more fundamental than the way we feed ourselves," writes Michael Brownlee. "We have an opportunity to help build localized regional food sheds that are economically robust, environmentally sustainable, resilient, and self-reliant; that ensure food security, food sovereignty, and food justice for all citizens; that contribute to the health and well-being of our communities."[36]

Support your community economy.

Keep money circulating within your community by spending on what is locally made whenever possible.

Support local restaurants by eating there. Your reach can extend further by selecting eateries that source their food locally, from regenerative farms and providers of humanely raised and ethically treated animals. The food will taste better, be more nutritious and healthier for you — and you keep your spend within the greater community.

In contrast, for most fast food restaurants, virtually their entire food spend is trucked in from distant processing facilities. Very little of the money you spend there will stay within your community. When characterizing a cluster of fast food chain restaurants as "Death Row" in Chapter 2, the reference was to the increased risk of adverse health consequences to you from eating fast food. They can be considered "Death Row" in an even greater sense as well. In sourcing their food ingredients, these corporations are and have historically been, large customers of both of our dark villainous twins: industrial agriculture and factory farms. They are paying for, complicit with, and enabling the expanding scope of horrendous animal cruelty and suffering in factory farms. They are contributing to and expanding the killing of our topsoil and its microbiome by industrial agriculture through their large purchases of acre after acre of commodity crops. They are sustaining and further empowering our Arch Villain's acceleration of global warming, hastening all of us toward oven-on-Earth and the end of our Anthropocene Epoch. For all of us, whether we are their customers or not, they are Death Row.

Keeping money in a community feeds the economy of the shire. In food deserts, as the local economy rebounds and its residents express the demand for healthy wholesome groceries, they will discover that supermarket chains are attuned. The moment food providers feel they can operate profitably again there, one or more will accept the risk and decide to do so.

Local economies grow as businesses support one another, the interplay building the revitalization, indeed rebirth, of rural and urban communities across the land.

Support local craftsmen. Support livelihoods. Even in a big city where virtually anything in the world can be available to you and delivered to your door, be aware of your local culture, farmer's markets, local businesses, groups, and events.

Embrace a present-day version of the community commons.

Stewardship of a just, vibrant local economy means embracing a present-day version of the community commons.

"The commons is an idea that generates meaning and hope." For John Thackara, "In *The Commons: A New Narrative for Our Times*, Silke Helfrich and Jorg Haas talk about the commons as 'all the things that we inherit from past generations that enable our livelihoods.' Seen through that lens, the commons can include land, watersheds, biodiversity, common knowledge, software, skills, or public buildings and spaces. The maintenance, health, and sustainability of these resources are in our shared interest, as they have always been. No individual, company, or government created these common goods; therefore, none has a right to claim them as private property. On the contrary: we inherited them from previous generations and have a moral obligation to look after them for future generations."[37]

An increasing number of people, businesses and organizations have been developing and promoting local food systems, local businesses, local energy production and community development banks as a means of revitalizing local economies.

Maintaining and expanding public lands, parks and beaches, for the community to enjoy can also incentivize outsiders to visit. Honoring and invigorating public libraries, institutions and facilities increases an area's attraction and value. Properly financing public schools is the single greatest gift a community can give its young — providing them with a solid education — while also an essential enabler of neighborhood revitalization, both urban and rural, because parents do not want to relocate into an area with underperforming schools.

Patronize financial institutions focused on economic revitalization.

Economic revitalization improves livability, desirability, and the shift of young families to home ownership on less expensive land. Economic revitalization can utilize these underutilized tools:

Land trusts are a viable strategy to enable young farmers long-term access to property. One of the main obstacles to land access is that so much farm acreage is controlled by larger operations farming commodity crops. Because they are the recipients of lavish federal subsidies that inflate their operation's profitability, the price of farmland is artificially inflated.

Robert Wolf writes, "To increase the locally grown food supply and revitalize small towns... A land trust is a non-profit organization whose purpose is to acquire land within a specific region for the purpose of preserving it from unwanted development. A trust may acquire the land either through purchase or donation, or it may protect the land by arranging for a donation of an easement with the owner."[38]

The Agrarian Trust[39] is one example, helping young and beginning farmers in their struggles with land access, affordability, and tenure.

A huge and growing obstacle are financial trusts and hedge funds that purchase tens of thousands of acres of farmland and aggregate it into investment packages for global speculators. The syndicate then hires tenant farmers to raise the crops, charging them rent to work what is now corporate land, and then commanding a solid share of the crop sales while the tenant farmers do the sweaty work of plowing, planting, and nurturing the crops.[40]

This is a new, huge barrier to young farmers getting access to their own land to begin farming.

According to The Oakland Institute, "The first years of the twenty-first century will be remembered for a global land rush of nearly unprecedented scale. An estimated 500 million acres, an area eight times the size of Britain, was reported bought or leased across the developing world between 2000 and 2011, often at the expense of local food security and land rights... Today, enthusiasm for agriculture borders on speculative mania. Driven by everything from rising food prices to growing demand for biofuel, the financial sector is taking an interest in farmland as never before. As the Oakland Institute reported in 2012, a new generation of institutional investors — including hedge funds, private equity, pension funds, and university endowments — is eager to capitalize on global farmland as a new and highly desirable asset class."[41]

In *For a New Generation of Farmers, Accessing Land is the First Step Toward Tackling Consolidation*, Tom Perkins notes, "Over the next 20 years, 400 million acres, or nearly half of all U.S. farmland, is set to change hands as the current generation retires. With an estimated $10 billion in capital already looking for access to U.S. farmland, institutional investors openly hope to expand their holdings as this retirement bulge takes place."[42]

The Oakland Institute finds that a rising generation of young farmers, "Is fighting for food justice in a variety of ways through a variety of movements. The idea that healthy, sustainable food is a basic human right runs through many of today's most contentious struggles... As part of the burgeoning food justice movement, there is undeniably a generation of prospective farmers eager to return to the land and work it responsibly. The problem is access, not enthusiasm. In order to translate this enthusiasm into action, new institutional structures must be built — and older ones updated — to help foster intergenerational links between farmers and ensure reliable access to farmland."[43]

In a middle ground, between land trusts and speculators, Iroquois Valley Farms is an investment firm whose objective is to increase the percentage of organic crop and rangeland in America. Lela Nargi reports, "Farmers approach Iroquois Valley having identified the land they need to get started or to scale up. The firm buys it then leases it back to them for five years, after which the lease renews every two years until either the firm or the farmer wants to make a change. This gives farmers who need to convert to organic a low fixed rent until they're making more lucrative sales. The firm also makes it somewhat easier for farmers to buy the land directly when the lease is up."[44] Iroquois Valley Farms also offers mortgages that farmers can pay off at any time.

Community development banks, as a necessary alternative to large urban banks, can be an important way to keep more money circulating within local economies. They can be powerful financial tools to rebuild the economies of the shires. Community development banks are committed to the underserved, to their communities, and will often provide financing for business projects that the larger commercial banks deem too risky. Robert Wolf writes about ShoreBank, which was started by 4 friends in 1973 with $800,000 in capital and a $2.4 million loan, who "believed that a commercial bank, flanked by complimentary development organizations, could effectively restore neighborhood economies."[45] Over 30 years, it took investment risks that the larger commercial banks would not, lending to 13,000 businesses and individuals. It discovered that "its repayment rate was well within industry standards... By 2010, ShoreBank had invested $4.1 billion in Chicago, Detroit, Cleveland and elsewhere, and financed 59,000 affordable housing units. By 2008, ShoreBank had assets of over $2.4 billion and $4.2 million in net income."[46]

The simple act of choosing to do your personal or business banking at a community bank rather than a national one, enables that bank, while protecting your money, to prioritize putting it to work on projects in your community. Many of us prefer that over the national banks whose assets are heavily vested in and working on behalf of the fossil fuel industry and Big Ag.

Public banks are another solution. While commonplace around the world, in the United States there is currently just *one*, the Bank of North Dakota, which was established in 1919 by progressive farmers seeking independence from big banks.[47] This is the concept: The local sales tax you pay as well as any parking tickets, business licenses and other city fees, go into the city or county treasury. Typically, this money is deposited in an account with a national bank to generate interest income. What if this money is kept instead at a local public bank to finance local improvements in housing, infrastructure, small businesses and community development? David Dayen reports in *What if Banks Were Publicly Owned? In L.A., this may Soon be a Reality*, "Because a public bank is not a for-profit business, it can offer lower interest rates than private options, saving billions of dollars over time. And because the city owns the bank, any interest income would flow back into its coffers. That reduces financing costs and facilitates more lending. Plus, the money stays at home, circulating in the local economy." [48]

The Bank of North Dakota has evolved into a *$7.4 billion* bank and, as noted author, attorney and chairman of the Public Banking Institute, Ellen Brown writes in her April 17, 2019 article, *The Public Banking Revolution Is Upon Us*, "is reported to be even more profitable than JP Morgan Chase and Goldman Sachs, although its mandate is not actually to make a profit but simply to serve the interests of local North Dakota communities. Along with hundreds of public banks worldwide, it has demonstrated what can be done by cutting out private shareholders and middlemen and mobilizing public revenues to serve the public interest."

Ellen Brown observes that, "Over 25 public bank bills are currently active, and dozens of groups are promoting the idea. Advocates include a highly motivated generation of young millennials, who are only too aware that the old system is not working for them and a new direction is needed."[49]

. . .

Compassion has this bonus ride-along: Once you are living with compassionate regard for your health and your self, for animals, for the land, and as a member of your community, your shire, you will find yourself living less apprehensively, less fearfully. And your compassion for others expands.

"Our sorrow is the other face of love, for we only mourn what we deeply care for," writes Joanna Macy. "The courage to speak our fear is evidence of our trust; our anger reveals our passion for justice; and the emptiness creates space for the new to arise... When we face the darkness of our time, openly and together, we tap deep reserves of strength within us. Many of us fear that confrontation with despair will bring loneliness and isolation, but — on the contrary — in the letting go of old defenses, truer community is found. In the synergy of sharing comes power. In community, we learn to trust our inner responses to our world — and find our power."[50]

A sense of livelihood and community can be inspiring.

Compassion with a purpose is compassionate activism.

V

Marlon Foster is laying on his back in the grass, staring up at the clouds. He is unable to rise. This hurts as much as any loss he has ever suffered. More. This...

"There was a moment for me, I was eighteen, nineteen, just a kid really. My best friend had just been shot to death."

Marlon regards the passing clouds. "We'd do everything together. Pierre and I sang together in the church choir. On the football team he was the quarterback, I was the wide receiver. In track running the 4 by 400, I'd run the first leg and he was always the one I'd hand the baton to. I was this entrepreneurial kid. I was the kid with the lemonade stand. I had an uncle who worked at a make-up distributor so in junior high they called me the 'Avon lady' because I was selling make-up to the girls. But he was the really smart, really savvy one.

"I see so many kids now who are quick on their feet, smart, sharp witted and it's all about taking those natural gifts and directing them in the right way. My best friend was that to the nth degree. No telling how successful in business he could have been.

"The middle school we went to, Bellevue, had a mix of kids, middle class and poor. Kids would check one another. One of my first days I sat down at a table and the kids started checking each other over who stayed in a one story versus a two-story house. So, I got up and kinda slipped away before they asked me. So, we figured a way. We had this Izod shirt. Every day we would take the emblem off that shirt and sew it on another shirt for another one of us to wear. It was Pierre's idea to *also* sew the Izod collar tag in the back. And just when people would call you on your Izod shirt — you know kids'll grab your collar and see if you got this fake thing going on by looking in the back. Just taking that much time and attention, trying to be ingenious just to fit in with these preppy kids.

"For our prom, kids have these limousines going on. Pierre's mom worked at a funeral home, so we got their limousine to use that night. I remember, my best friend and I doing senior prom with our dates in the limo from the funeral home...

"Laying in the grass, on my back, looking up at the clouds. My best friend was gone... I was having thoughts like 'I don't even want to be here any longer myself,' I was so distraught. And I turned my head to the side and there was a little blade of grass, right by my eye, just blowing in the wind. And there was something in that moment, this little thin blade of grass... It has life in it. I just began to value life on a whole different level."

And Marlon rose. He stood up with a resolve, "I want my life to honor his."

A compassionate activism became a vision and he built all of this. "I look at our farm and our community center, its value set, my compassion that developed despite all this death of humans around me — I can trace it all back to that blade of grass."

Forty people now work with Marlon. Green Leaf Learning Farm's produce is in high demand. They sell out most of what they take to the farmer's markets. His KQ-90 boxes nourish neighborhood families and contain other incentives to healthy lifestyle choices, and the interest in home-cooked meals, plant strong meals and healthy eating is slowly returning to this community, this food desert. Knowledge Quest counselors are saving lives and instilling hope. Theo Davies, Yolanda Manning, Michelle Miller have found their livelihoods, fulfilling a calling, a passion unique to each of them.

For Marlon, it's a natural progression. It's just the way to do things.

He took me to the house where he grew up. His grandparents lived with them "so you had their wisdom and presence while parents worked. A three generational family." Near the intersection of Phillips Place and Whitford Place, Marlon pointed to the houses of his neighbors. "These two streets, I can still take you to most of these houses now, not only to visit and sit down but to have something to eat and drink. You could even lay down on the couch. It's that kind of close-knit community."

Marlon's old house appears narrow facing the street, but it goes back a-ways. It has five bedrooms and two bathrooms. "At church they'd call our home 'hotel happiness' because of the spirit of hospitality. I'd come home and there would be one of the musicians from the church. 'Oh, you living with us now?' 'Yeah.' 'Ok.' And it was just a thing. People would be having a hard time and need someplace to stay, and my grandmother would have them over. My Aunt and her boyfriend who owned a business came and lived with us when their business did bad – and one of their workers did too.

"People would stay with us a month, three months, six months, and the hospitality was such that that person would get their own room. I'd come home and my bedroom would be occupied by somebody. We'd have to double up, make adjustments in other parts of the house. They'd be having a hard time and needed someplace to stay. They'd come with nothin' but their clothes and a television, and now they'd have a bed and a room.

"As a kid you'd come home and that would be a norm. It was all communal and love and respect. In-laws in my family, in African-American families, are held in highest regard. They are called sons and daughters. Always valued. Loyalty, service, and family hospitality. We had food so we'd share food, we'd feed neighbors who were going through a tough time out of our refrigerator.

"When we had enough stuff, we'd always share. And it was anything. My Grandmother Doris had this thing about 'You better not give away anything that you did not like or was not nice.' You didn't give away a sock with a hole in it or a raggedy shirt with bleach stains. You had to give away nice stuff. She used to say about charity that you always give away good stuff, the stuff that if you saw it, you'd want to have."

Marlon operates the community centers, the farm, and the classrooms in the same manner. "I like having premium experiences in food and technology, and engaging people in one of the most under-resourced communities with that. I like bringing those two extremes together. We are not just a farm, but a USDA certified Organic farm. We grow the healthiest possible food. When you visit our classrooms, you'll see kids learning in an iMac environment; when you visit our theater and our performance stage, you'll see it's the same stage like the premium one over in the Memphis arts district. We will draw top chefs to our bistro and cooking school. The reality is that the people here are exceptional, they are worth the investment.

"What I do a direct confront to is the idea, 'What's good enough for those folks.' You know what my grandmother would say about that. Because we get all the hand-me-down computers that are 10 years old and faded. So, when people come and see these new iMacs they say 'Wow. I wish I had one of those.' I want our kids inspired working on modern, high-speed, beautiful computers. When I go to the local private schools and speak, I visit their computer labs with all the iMacs and nobody ever thinks they're strange."

"I love the thrill of building something new and creating something from nothing and challenging traditional structures like 'What's good enough for those in poverty?' We don't do poverty programs. People who are under-resourced want the same things resourced people want. The best way to eradicate poverty is to not treat it like poverty. The compassionate aspect of this is, why would I identify a person with the most challenging aspect of their life?; a person who is experiencing a temporary lack of resources as a poor person? If I don't know you and I'm going to assume, I'm going to assume the best-case scenario. If I'm going to answer some doubt, I'm going to give someone the benefit of the doubt.

"In South Memphis you see these children. If you see a poor African-American child whose family is struggling in a lot of areas, through that lens it can elicit a certain response — but what if I can get you to see *your* kid in that kid? That's a whole different response when that's my child in that child."

When Marlon and I were talking at a table in Martin Luther King Jr. Park, his 14-year-old daughter, Alexandria, was over by the lakeside. Their black-haired dog, Champ, was swimming and came back on shore. It bolted up our way, stopped beside us and shook its whole body vigorously, casting a spray of a thousand drops of water over both of us. Marlon laughed, "That's his way of saying hello." After Alexandria collected Champ, Marlon told me, "In elementary school all Alexandria wanted to do was read. She would never stop reading. And she's quiet and introverted so she got into trouble with her teachers, she was on the verge of not passing 4th grade and went through this whole bullying thing. They were all set to medicate her and put her in Special Ed. I said to my wife, 'She needs a social adjustment, a Montessori program. The way she's operating, that's Montessori.' So, through the help of a juiced friend, I got her in Montessori. It was the right place for her, and she was there for the rest of elementary school. Now we have her back in the public school with a thousand some kids and she's performing honor roll.

"I thought to myself, 'What about all the other children in the neighborhood just like my baby — smart, that have good potential, and they have the limitations of their learning style not being honored?'"

As a father, when Marlon helps out one of his children, he is incapable of not extending that feeling to the other children in his community. It's as if it's in his DNA. Marlon and the counselors at Knowledge Quest cultivate self-worth and instill hope that has been diminished or lost. They help people discover their path. They build and empower community.

. . .

You and I. We've both been knocked down. We've *all* been knocked down.

And each one of us has gotten up.

Today, one of those closest to us has been knocked down. And brutally beaten. And it's up to each of us to help. We owe our lives to this someone — without that someone we wouldn't even be here. And their torment is ongoing — they are being beaten again and again and will continue to be. Every single day. That "someone" is our planet. Her ability to provide for us, and to enable us to continue living is being taken away from her.

We need to engage our compassion for Mother Earth, to turn compassion into compassionate activism. We need to get into gear.

For each one of us, our actions, like Marlon's, can collectively have an immense impact. We can save mountains. Every dollar, every spending choice and decision you make, your attitude, your voice, your complacency — or lack thereof — it all matters.

Heal yourself. Thrive. Find your balance, your strength, your truth. Enlist your voice, and your resolve. Let's get on this.

Marlon and I are walking through Green Leaf Learning Farm's orchard. We are walking in-between pomegranate trees, persimmons, figs, muscadines, pawpaw trees, "the only native fruit tree in Tennessee," pear and apple trees, and blueberry and blackberry bushes. For years, the woman who owns these deep lots that we are traversing has been asking for Marlon's help to keep her grass trimmed. Marlon agreed if she would grant him permission to plant an orchard. The fruit trees are a year or two away from producing, but Theo will soon be overseeing the picking of the first blueberries and blackberries.

"If you're going to build a community, the most essential asset is the human capital, the people, and amongst the people is the children. So, youth development was the practical starting point for me. Human development is the starting point for community development."

For three years Marlon was a professional volunteer. He then applied for and got a United Way grant and started Knowledge Quest. Over a five year span he built out Knowledge Quest from a single room in public housing to the community center where it is now, married Sheila, had three children, and bought and renovated his two-story house, which is beautiful to look at now, but was on the demolition list when he purchased it. He also entered seminary, graduated with an Ecumenical Master of Divinity Degree, founded a church and began thinking about an urban farm.

Memphis is like Marlon. The community of South Memphis will turn a new leaf. More and more people are realizing opportunity there. You can buy land for next to nothing. In the coming years, as more and more people are drawn into the neighborhood and rediscover it thanks in part perhaps to Marlon's farm, bistro and community center, they may discover the opportunity there. Young people living in Midtown or Cooper-Young, where rents are high and the dream of buying property deferred, perhaps they'll look south. This was once a prosperous neighborhood where black families lived side by side with white families as early as 1900 and for the following 60 years. Marlon is developing educational programs for the schools. He understands the essential value to a community of having good education available. As more and more residents of this community are empowered and leading healthier lives, hope blooms like the sunflowers on Marlon's farm.

It's about livelihood. And community.

Martin Luther King, Jr., had a dream. And his dream did not end in Memphis. Marlon Foster has one, too.

And they're not the only ones.

VI

Our Arch Villain, Big Ag, is led by several of the richest and most powerful corporations the world has ever seen, multinational corporations with global reach. They are more powerful than many countries. They may prove to be even more powerful than our democracy. They are dedicated to playing hardball to prevent change, to staying the course, protecting their business interests and maximizing their profits. Yet Big Ag's dark twins, industrial agriculture and factory farming, are killing our planet.

Fifteen or twenty years from now, with the committed effort of 5% of us, then 7%, then 10%, we will approach the essential mass, the 13 to 17% where the tipping point Malcolm Gladwell writes about will arrive and change will occur. It will happen swiftly and broadly and the system of industrial agriculture as well as the absolute concentration-camp horror of factory farming will be eradicated from our planet. The abolition of slavery. Worker's rights. Women's right to vote. Every bit as seminal as each of these social movements, ours will become one of the most important, if not the most essential, in the history of civilization.

For those of us taking action to bring it about, when we prevail, it will be an immensely satisfying moment.

At least it would be.

In the past, when they succeeded, advocates of social change could celebrate their triumph. Having prevailed, having achieved the change they had strived valiantly for, taken risks on behalf of, struggled mightily, endured, and suffered for — they were jubilant when change was realized, immensely gratified witnessing change enacted.

Our situation is unique. It doesn't allow us the luxury of fifteen years' time.

We are hurtling toward apocalyptic global warming. We are accelerating the end of our Anthropocene Epoch. "Winter is coming," is the phrase foretelling the end of the known world of *Game of Thrones*. Here on earth, it will feel more like being in an oven.

Should we lose hope? Should we not even try?

Don't give it a thought. We are, each one of us, alive at a very special time.

We were born for this challenge.

Joanna Macy believes, "We may have endured for eons of lifetimes as other life forms, under the heavy hand of fate and the blind play of instinct, but now at last we are granted the ability to consider and judge and make decisions... That our world is in crisis — to the point where survival of conscious life on Earth is in question — in no way diminishes the value of this gift; on the contrary. To us is granted the privilege of being on hand to take part, if we choose, in the Great Turning to a just and sustainable society. We can let life work through us, enlisting all our strength, wisdom, and courage, so that life itself can continue. There is so much to be done, and the time is so short."[51]

How can we accelerate change? How can we possibly avoid a 4° (7.2 degrees Fahrenheit) or 5° (9 degrees Fahrenheit) climate increase and along with it, the ending of our Anthropocene Epoch?

In our toolkit, there is one more essential Compassion.

5

Compassion for Democracy

I

If every human alive today regardless of age — your friend's newborn, children, Gen Z, millennials, mom and dad, grandpa, great grandma — can be considered a member of a generation, our generation — like Lucinda Monarch's — is a special generation. Each one of us has been born at a time of historical reckoning.

Lucinda's generation, the migratory generation, had a long, arduous task and the stakes were high — the survival of their species. For our generation, the stakes are significantly higher: Our survival as well as that of virtually every multicellular species and living organism — plant and animal — on Earth.

Our task, our challenge, is that we have to make the changes necessary to stop and reverse global warming. We must implement change on a massive scale, in the face of dominant, allied, entrenched corporations — the wealthiest and most powerful business entities ever created.

A very unwelcome guest, Mr. Heat, has warmed up our front yard and is now at our doorstep. He has two unsavory companions with him: Ms. Misery, Mother Earth's pestilent cousin, who creates a rapidly deteriorating environment wherever she sets foot, unconcerned by the attendant suffering of its living creatures; and Mr. Grim, who is already reaching out and extinguishing — reaping if you will — an increasing number of species. These unwanted guests will enter our house, the Anthropocene, turn up the furnace and accelerate its end. This will happen *during our children's lifetimes.*

When I was writing the introduction to this book, I cited Ashley Strickland's July 2017 CNN report, *Earth to Warm 2 Degrees Celsius by the End of this Century, Studies Say.* Different research studies concurred that even with best efforts at immediately combating climate change, an additional global temperature rise of a minimum of 1.5 degrees Celsius (2.7

degrees Fahrenheit) by 2100 may already be "baked in."[1]

In October 2018, just 15 months later, scientists on the world's leading scientific group studying global warming, the Nobel-prize winning Intergovernmental Panel on Climate Change (IPCC), announced they now anticipate temperatures to rise 1.5° between 2030 and 2052. The final draft of this report dated three months prior on June 4, 2018, states, "If emissions continue at their present rate, human-induced warming will exceed 1.5°C by around 2040."[2] This report takes into consideration 25,000 comments from experts and a wide pool of scientific literature. This is a definitive undebatable conclusion.

This IPCC report shaves 60 to 70 years off estimates made *just a year earlier*. A temperature increase of 1.5° to our Earth is no longer projected for year 2100, but for 2030 and, at the latest, around *2040*.

This reveals how rapidly the adverse effects of global warming are reinforcing and accelerating one another. We do not want Mr. Heat in our neighborhood but there he is. We certainly don't want him in our front yard, but we've stood idly, watching as he passed through our gate.

His accomplice, Ms. Misery, is wreaking havoc in every corner of our world. Megafires are each ravaging hundreds of thousands of acres of forests not just throughout the Western United States, but burning across the colder northern regions, Canada, Alaska, Siberia, as well as the Arctic forests even further north. "500-year storms," "cyclone bombs," "polar vortexes," tornados, typhoons and hurricanes of record size and force are increasingly common. The 2019 flooding throughout much of the Midwest has kept parts of the Mississippi River above flood stage for over three months – flooding not seen since the Great Flood of 1927.[3] The injury and suffering to living creatures, human and non-human, from these events is unimaginable. The cost of recovery from this devastation is commanding a growing share of our nation's economic resources.

When you think of Mr. Grim, an image might come to mind of a hooded figure with a large scythe, a slow-moving cloaked sack of bones shifting along down the street. Mr. Grim actually moves at lightning speed — he's everywhere it seems — and these days he's increasingly busy. The report released on May 6, 2019 by the United Nations Intergovernmental Science-Policy Platform on Biodiversity and Ecosystem Services (IPBES) confirms that *one million* plant and animal species are now vanishing or threatened with extinction due to human activities.[4]

In December 2018, a report by Climate Action Tracker analyzed the lack of overall progress by the majority of nations that signed the Paris Agreement in 2016 and determined that, even if each country now suddenly mobilized and got fully on board and, "If all governments achieved their Paris Agreement commitments the world will likely warm 3° — twice the 1.5° limit they agreed in Paris." Each passing year is critical. The absence of effective remedy implementation in just the years since the Paris Agreement has already caused irreparable damage to our planet. Of our world community of nations, five countries were singled out as making "critically insufficient progress," the worst designation, steering us toward a 4° increase: Russia, Saudi Arabia, Turkey, Ukraine and the United States.[5]

Mr. Heat is now on our front porch and he's reaching to open our door. Ms. Misery is pleased with herself. And Mr. Grim is looking at you.

The IPCC report concluded that to avoid racing past warming of 1.5°(2.7°F) over preindustrial levels would require a "rapid and far-reaching" transformation of human civilization at a magnitude that has never before happened.

· · ·

We must have a plan. Our plan must be inspiring, broadly accepted, and set in motion our singular solution — regenerative agriculture — at scale and quickly.

Each one of us, through our purchasing decisions and our compassionate activism, must do all that we can. Realize the power you have in your choices, in your day-to-day actions, informing others and setting an example by using your voice and speaking up for what you believe. Your choices, one person's actions aligned with millions of others — our collective action — can set significant change in motion.

Naomi Klein raises the ante in *No Is Not Enough*, "We know that the time for this great transition is short. Climate scientists have told us that this is the decade to take decisive action to prevent catastrophic global warming. That means small steps will no longer get us where we need to go."[6]

Fortunately...

There is another powerful tool we have in our toolboxes. And we must put it to use to achieve The Great Healing.

It is the essential tool enabling us to take big steps, to fully harness the power of collective action to make change happen quickly. We have this tool because we are citizens in a democracy.

Realize your power as a citizen in our democracy.

Governmental leadership, in terms of decisive policy and action, is essential. Our history has several examples of our government taking decisive action, demonstrating clearly the power we can harness and what that can achieve. Our government enabled the World War II generation to do what it was called upon to do. It took the initiative and succeeded in transforming our entire economy into a wartime economy in a matter of months. Government is a very powerful and necessary tool.

It is upon us to best ensure it is governing intelligently, insightfully and when the situation calls for it, boldly. We can accomplish that through our involvement as citizens in our democracy.

The essential starting point is our compassionate activism. We have to raise our voices to inspire and force change. Increasing everyone's awareness by petitioning, demonstrating, revealing and reveling in our growing numbers.

The key imperative then becomes presenting a solution and flying its flag.

When our government lacks a plan, it is up to us to provide them one. Taking a lead role in shaping and defining the policy solution enables us to use our voices and our numbers not just to raise awareness about the problem, but to advocate for a solution.

We have to focus our government's attention on this solution. As we approach a new election cycle, this puts every candidate running for public office in the position of having to declare clearly and unambiguously their support or opposition.

We will then vote for or against them based on their promise.

We have to get our government to fundamentally repurpose its most important piece of legislation: The Farm Bill.

And...

The solution is nonpartisan.

Wait. Time out... Given the level of divisiveness in American politics, how can *any* issue, let alone one that involves the entirety of agriculture and massive corporate interests, one that is going to be decided by our elected officials — our politicians — possibly be nonpartisan?

Because there is such a pervasive, fundamental lack of understanding about the immediacy and the severity — the *catastrophic* environmental consequences of global warming in store for us — among members of both dominant political parties, it is nonpartisan.

Because there is such an incomplete understanding of the human *cause* of global warming, and the magnitude of Big Ag's role as our Arch Villain — the industry responsible for creating the lion's share of greenhouse gas emissions — it is nonpartisan.

Because American farmers and rural communities have as much or even more to gain economically as any other region of the country, it is nonpartisan.

Because economic growth and prosperity is a goal of both parties, it is nonpartisan.

Because the values residing at the core of our democracy and abiding in the hearts of Americans — our compassion, our decency, our love for our environment and this planet, *our very humanity* — are aligned with the imperative that this dire problem must be remedied, it is nonpartisan.

Because global warming is destroying our environment — our biome — and will soon be jeopardizing our very survival, this is nonpartisan.

Our essential singular solution is regenerative agriculture implemented rapidly onto the vast majority of American cropland, combined with the end of factory farming and the return of pastured livestock. Once this plan of action is advocated and fought for, manifest and put in practice across the land, and its benefits realized, agriculture will become one of the key sectors transitioning — *and growing* — our economy into a robust, sustainable, thriving New Economy. That, as well as healing our planet, and *saving* us on it.

Democracy itself keeps a secret. Lady Liberty, like Hazel, silently holds out a light. Hazel's just trying to see where's she's going, navigating dark water while attracting a meal and a mate along the way. Lady Liberty's flame offers an invitation and a destination. An invitation: For everyone. To a destination: Democracy in its purest form.

We need to make the "Democracy" Lady Liberty represents *our* democracy. She's set on our soil — a precious gift positioned on our most invaluable resource. "I lift my lamp beside the golden door."[7] Let's make American democracy approach this Ideal.

Democracy in its purest form is one-person-one-vote. That is its ideal manifestation.

Our Founding Fathers, when they crafted our constitution and our democracy, while brilliantly constructed for its time, didn't quite get that. Today, most of us do.

Historically, the powerful, to better secure their interests, have often sought to limit the ability of the public to actually have one-person-one-vote by usurping it. They often succeeded, even to the point of undermining democracy itself. It is not in the long-term best interests of a country, of a democracy, to allow that to happen.

By taking the lead and turning Mr. Heat away from our door, we can set an example and America can be a beacon to the world once again.

One citizen, one vote.

It's all about majority rule...

II

The Farm Bill addresses almost the entirety of U.S. agricultural and food policy. It is one of the largest and most far reaching pieces of legislation our federal government produces. The government releases a new Farm Bill every five years. The financial outlay calculated and allocated by the Congressional Budget Office in the Farm Act of 2014 (titled the Agricultural Act of 2014), totaled just under *half a trillion* dollars ($489 billion). The 2018 Farm Bill (titled the Agriculture Improvement Act of 2018) allocates spending of $428 billion from 2019 - 2023. In both bills, 99% of the funding is distributed across four program categories: Commodity Crops, Crop Insurance, Nutrition, and Conservation.

Political debate spanning months leading up to the vote on the final version of the 2018 Farm Bill centered around Nutrition programs, primarily SNAP and food assistance to Americans in financial need, and Conservation programs. While important, these two categories do not constitute the heart of the bill; its agricultural core.

The two other program categories — Commodities, and Crop Insurance — effectively determine how American agriculture is done. For the last 50 years, these categories have emphasized and subsidized the rise to dominance of Industrial Agriculture.

349 of our senators and representatives, the vast majority of both Republicans and Democrats, voted for the 2018 Farm Bill. Only 49 opposed it.

This is another reason why the solution for the core problem with the Farm Bill is nonpartisan.

Of the $428 billion cost of the 2018 Farm Bill, 7.3% was allocated to Commodities and 8.9% to Crop Insurance. Combined, these two categories command $69 billion in federal assistance. While constituting just 16.2% of the bill's total spending, this is taxpayer money that enables industrial agriculture to continue.

The 2018 Farm Bill is *the* most important piece of legislation this country has *ever* produced. This is why:

With regard to the category of **Commodity Crop programs**, billions of dollars are allocated prop up commodity crop prices, in effect guaranteeing commodity crop farmers a minimum purchase price for their crops protecting them from severe losses.

This enables industrial agriculture commodity crop farmers to continue to survive despite their enormous and growing input costs — the costs of buying the GMO seeds, synthetic fertilizers, pesticides, herbicides, machinery, irrigation water, fuel and all other operating expenses necessary to farm on this scale in this manner. It allows them to spend all this money because no matter how low the commodity market prices sink — something they have no control over — they are guaranteed the market will be artificially propped up by billions of taxpayer dollars ensuring them a certain minimum return. And no matter how high their input costs get they can continue to get bank loans and incur increasing debt to purchase these inputs for the next crop season because the bank operates on the certainty that farmers have this government guarantee.

Commodity prices have been dropping, which means more and more federal money is necessary to prop them up. The National Sustainable Agriculture Coalition, analyzing the Congressional Budget Office's Spring 2018 forecasts that became the official baseline for the 2018 Farm Bill, found that the cost of farm bill commodity program subsidies has been steadily climbing. "The estimated cost of the major commodity program benefits has increased a staggering 121% — nearly $15 billion for the coming five years relative to the 2014 estimate; this increase includes a 172% increase projected for Price Loss Coverage payments."[8]

It is more and more common that even when depressed commodity crop prices are artificially inflated by commodity crop programs, farmers are still not making a profit. This is when the second category, **Crop Insurance**, comes into play.

Crop Insurance is considered an additional safeguard for farmers. When farmers have no alternative but to sell their crops at a loss, this insurance kicks in to make up for much of that shortfall. Farmers growing in the industrial agriculture manner are virtually pre-qualified for crop insurance. Crop insurance is more of our tax dollars allocated by the government via the Farm Bill enabling farmers to survive. But as Gabe Brown explained in Chapter 3, "The farm program is based off of the previous year's commodity prices which are in a downward spiral. Revenue insurance is locked into these low prices, so what I'm seeing as I travel around the country is that industrial farmers and ranchers just can't make it anymore." The crop insurance is paying them less and less based on the declining market value of their commodity crops. Most American small and midsize farmers are operating at a loss. A majority of them now have second jobs just to make ends meet.

When you buy food, you are actually paying for it three times:

- you are paying its purchase price at retail
- you are paying with a significant portion of your tax dollars to prop up and subsidize the food production of commodity farmers
- you are paying through your medical bills and your health insurance to cope with the health consequences, either directly (your medical bills) or collectively (America's health care costs), of eating nutrient depleted, toxin laden food[9]

The Farm Bill is a blanket endorsement of industrial agriculture and factory farming. As John Ikerd, Professor Emeritus at the University of Missouri, writes in *Farm Policy at a Crossroads; A Time to Choose*, "The farm policies of the Nixon-Butz era were designed specifically to support, subsidize, and promote specialization, standardization, and consolidation of agricultural production into ever larger farming operations. Every major farm policy since the 1970s — price supports, farm credit, crop insurance, disaster payments, farm tax credits and depreciation allowances, etc. — in one way or another has supported the industrial paradigm."[10]

To an overriding extent, the components of the Farm Bill are conceived, drafted, lobbied for, and paid for by Big Ag.

The Farm Bill increases global warming more than any other bill. The Farm Bill enables the continued killing of the soil microbiome on 231 million crop acres, eliminating that soil's life and its ability to sequester atmospheric carbon.

The 2018 Farm Bill unlocks our front door just as Mr. Heat's hand is reaching for the doorknob and the way in.

This is a path to disaster.

· · ·

The Farm Bill's agricultural core is devoid of compassion for animals. While several of the Conservation programs make an effort to protect pollinators and other wildlife, the bill's agricultural core subsidizes factory farming. The concept and design of a factory farm is to treat animals as production units and market them as commodities. Regenerative farmers and ranchers raising pastured livestock, as well as family dairy farms that produce healthy organic milk of superior nutritional value from pastured animals, are sidelined, spectators looking on as lavish federal subsidies are commandeered by the larger factory farming operations enabling them to sell their "products" and flood the market at unrealistically low prices. In 2018, as a consequential example, several thousand small organic dairy farms couldn't compete and went out of business, despite producing healthier, better tasting milk.

As we do everything we can with our compassionate activism and our purchasing choices to help end factory farming, the Farm Bill provides billions of dollars in subsidies to Big Ag's greedy cruel behemoth twin.

Despite the fact that Nutrition is the largest category of assistance in the Farm Bill, subsidizing programs like SNAP whose aim is to ensure millions of Americans of limited means are able to eat when otherwise they wouldn't be able to afford to, the Farm Bill puts American's health at risk.

Because the Farm Bill subsidizes industrial agriculture, it promotes the continued mass production of nutrient deficient GMO commodity crops —

crops containing glyphosate and other toxin residues. In just one example of many, huge government subsidies lower the production cost of highly refined carbohydrates making this unhealthy food inexpensive compared to healthier unprocessed carbohydrates.[11] This is food that we consume directly or will be used as ingredients in the processed foods on our grocery store shelves or in restaurants. The Farm Bill, as presently conceived, is contributing significantly to the expanding American epidemic of poor health and disease, obesity, diabetes, cardiovascular disease, stroke, cancer, loss of brain function, liver disease, kidney and renal failure, and on and on.

80% of our health care spending goes toward chronic diseases that are not only reversible but preventable.[12] 18% of our Gross National Product currently goes to cover health care costs, yet we have the highest rates of obesity, hypertension and chronic illness in the world. And our health care spending continues to rise at an average exceeding 4% per year.[13] Without a course correction, American health costs will reach the point when they alone will undermine our economy.

The Federal government, it may be argued, is appropriating our tax dollars unwisely twice over. By subsidizing our Arch Villain and its dark twins, industrial agriculture and factory farming, it is encouraging and enabling the production of nutritionally diminished, toxin laden food while destroying our soil and our environment. Then, as a direct consequence, our government is footing the bill for our immense and increasing costs of healthcare and lost worker productivity.

By propping up the system of industrial agriculture on 231 million acres of American cropland,[14] the Farm Bill is a death sentence for our most precious resource, American topsoil. It ensures that the soil acres currently growing industrial agriculture commodity crops will continue to be farmed in the industrial agriculture manner. It guarantees that this vast living soil microbiome will continue to be poisoned with additional seasonal onslaughts of synthetic fertilizers, herbicides and pesticides — in increasing amounts — decreasing its life, vitality, nutrient value, and ultimately transforming it into lifeless dirt. Moreover, these inputs kill countless numbers of insects, birds and animals, and poison every plant that grows out of the ground unless it is a GMO Roundup Ready seed.

The Farm Bill, as presently conceived, ensures the increasing wealth of our Arch Villain. Billions and billions of taxpayer dollars each year, allocated via the Farm Bill, will be disseminated to farmers to enable them to continue to farm by purchasing another crop-year's worth of Big Ag chemical inputs and GMO seed. This soil warfare is also corporate welfare.

Despite its original purpose and contrary to the worthy intentions of our elected officials, the Farm Bill limits American livelihoods and continues to undermine and devastate rural and urban communities. The largest industrial agriculture farming operations and factory farms require very little labor. They are designed that way. They offer exponentially fewer job opportunities than the many smaller family farms they have eviscerated, and they do not enable livelihoods. The Farm Bill, as currently conceived, ensures that massive amounts of government funding — on the order of nearly half a trillion dollars, the biggest government bailout on the books — goes to the biggest growers, the industrial growers. As of 1995, of federal farm subsidies totaling over $322 billion, 75% of that was allocated to just 10% of farmers, primarily the larger operations — the ones who need it the least. This is federally subsidized industrial agriculture. 62% of smaller family farmers receive no aid at all and the percentage is even higher for regenerative farmers. These programs are rigged to continue the crop dominance of GMO industrial agriculture crops — not only guaranteeing that farmers farming in this manner can remain in business, but by gaming smaller farmers — the regenerative and organic farmers — out of these commodity and crop insurance programs. In this way, the Farm Bill profoundly limits the expansion of regenerative and organic farmers and acts as disincentive for new and aspiring young farmers to get their start.

Crop insurance, while originally a program intended to minimize risk, as Gabe Brown sees it, "has become a monster that now dictates most of the cropping decisions made in the United States... I contend that over 95% of planting decisions farmers make today are based on how much money they can guarantee themselves by insuring through crop insurance programs. Farmers know exactly the minimum amount of gross dollars per acre they will receive that year from crop insurance. Keep your expenses below that amount and you will make a profit. What other business is offered those guarantees? Certainly not Ma and Pa's restaurant on Main Street!"[15]

By subsidizing the input costs of industrial and factory farmers, the Farm Bill continues to ensure that these massive spends by these farming

This Farm Bill is at war with animals, with our health, with our land, with our communities, and with our democracy.

Hard as it is to conceive that the 2018 Farm Bill could make matters even worse, it manages to.

The Farm Bill is a gift to our Arch-Villain, industrial agriculture and factory farming, enabling this industry that is one of the most polluting industries on the planet by itself, to produce massive and increasing amounts of these pestilent products. Just the manufacturing of synthetic nitrogen fertilizer alone accounts for about 50% of the energy use in agriculture. The process of manufacturing this fertilizer, of converting nitrogen to ammonia, requires 1.2% of the *world's* energy use.[19] Big Ag's collective greenhouse gas emissions make it, by far, the greatest contributor to global warming.

If this is allowed to continue as business as usual for the next five years, it is very likely the United States will be unable to dial back its collective greenhouse gas emissions to meet the reduction thresholds of the Paris agreement. Even more dire for our planet and our future is that this action may prove America is unable to limit global warming to a 2° increase by 2035.

Kevin Anderson, professor of energy and climate change at the University of Manchester in the U.K., one of the world's leading climate scientists and an authority on carbon budgets, reminds us, "Realistically, unless emissions start coming down very rapidly in the next three or four years — I mean very rapidly indeed — then I think we will fail on 2°C of warming. We have a handful of years to make some very rapid and radical changes. We know what we need to do. We know it's all our responsibility to engage with this. We have everything at our fingertips to solve this problem. We have chosen to fail so far but we could choose to succeed."[20] Professor Anderson also reminds us that a 2° temperature increase is, "Incompatible with any reasonable characterization of an organized, equitable and civilized global community."[21] He was saying this *in 2013*.

Unchecked, if global temperatures rise 1.5° by 2030 it is increasingly likely the planet will experience that 2° temperature rise by 2035... For you, your friends and loved ones, your children born and yet to come, the world at that time will be, "incompatible with any reasonable characterization of an organized, equitable and civilized global community."

If you are middle-aged or older in 2035 and you are fortunate enough to still be surviving amidst the chaos of a world in shambles — in a society lacking "any reasonable characterization of an organized, equitable and civilized global community" — you may not survive the ire of your children who will be in your face demanding an answer, "How did you let this happen?!"

The 2018 Farm Bill takes us *one step further* along this dire path. By keeping us locked on our present course, the Farm Bill prevents soil carbon sequestration at scale, which is our singular solution to global warming.

By allowing the 2018 Farm Bill to stand, we ourselves, are now opening the front door for Mr. Heat and his companions and welcoming them into our living room. It won't be a "living" room much longer.

The dying topsoil covering this vast acreage of industrial agriculture crop land is a carbon source, releasing additional amounts of CO_2 into the atmosphere. This is *in addition to* the greenhouse gases rising up from the millions and millions of tons of synthetic nitrogen fertilizer, phosphate fertilizer and other chemical inputs this soil is repeatedly being doused with. For carbon sequestration to be realized at scale, the first step is that this soil must be made available for conversion to regenerative farming. Application of the industrial inputs eviscerating topsoil needs to stop. Once it does, it will then take several years to repair and heal the life of the soil, its microbiome, to the point where it can become a truly fertile carbon sink and begin to sequester carbon again.

Too many farmers are amenable, however reluctantly, to continue farming in the industrial agriculture manner knowing that as their soil continues to die and their yields wane, their economic losses will be largely covered by the federal corporate welfare of the Farm Bill. Other farmers interested in transitioning to regenerative are trapped in debt, locked in and beholden to a banking system that, in lock-step with Big Ag, is intolerant of and inflexible to change.

The process of either conversion to regenerative farming or back to native prairie, which could and must begin, on 231 million acres of industrial agriculture crop land to become our global warming remedy, will not happen in a significant way for the five years that the 2018 Farm Bill enables these practices to continue.

This is why Farm Bills are the most important pieces of legislation our federal government produces, and why the 2018 Farm Bill may be the most important piece of legislation our federal government will *ever* produce. In its current form, it prevents the entire world from collectively succeeding in making the necessary progress on slowing the increase in global warming.

• • •

Each farm bill is a five-year plan. We cannot let the 2018 Farm Bill stand for five years or anywhere close. It is crippling our ability to slow global warming. This Farm Bill must be jettisoned and replaced with a New Food and Farm Bill that will become *the* most important piece of legislation our federal government will produce.

Steven Pinker, in *Enlightenment Now*, writes, "In *The Big Ratchet: How Humanity Thrives in the Face of Natural Crisis*, the geographer Ruth DeFries describes the sequence as 'ratchet-hatchet-pivot.' People discover a way of growing more food, and the population ratchets upward. The method fails to keep up with the demand or develops unpleasant side-effects, and the hatchet falls. People then pivot to a new method."[22] We can't afford to wait until Mr. Heat drops his hatchet on us. That's one big Epoch ending hatchet. *We* have to drop our hatchet and force the pivot to a new farming method. Now.

The funding for a transition from industrial to regenerative agriculture is already allocated in existing subsidies — it's just being commandeered into a failing system instead of the planet saving solution.

The cost to the American taxpayer of this annual bailout of the industrial agriculture system was $4.2 billion in 2016.[23] The federal government provides over *$20 billion dollars* in agricultural subsidies *each year*. It's a matter of redirecting these existing appropriations, incentivizing the transition of the majority of our cropland from industrial agriculture to regenerative, ending factory farming, and modernizing crop insurance to incentivize new farmers and cover industrial agriculture farmers' risks in transitioning to regenerative — while eliminating all subsidies for industrial agriculture commodity crops and factory farming. Thus, the historic protection that a Farm Bill provides farmers as a buffer against the vicissitudes of nature, market swings, and the unexpected, will remain but as an aid in transition.

Esteemed climate scientist and soil microbiologist Walter Jehne, in *Regenerate Earth*, understands precisely where humanity stands in the climate crisis: "After over 50 years of warnings and 30 years of global policy denial and delay, it is now too late for reductions in future CO_2 emissions to adequately slow down its rise or its greenhouse effects. It is now too late even for the drawdown of carbon to zero or negative net emissions, by itself, to prevent accelerating the dangerous hydrological feedbacks and climate extremes... Our imperative, responsibility and 'response-ability' is clear: We know what we must and can do and we know how to do it, practically and beneficially. The only issue left is to *do it*, now, before climate extremes limit our last chance to do so."[24]

Saving and healing our soil accompanied by ending the factory farming of animals and returning to the ethical and humane rearing of pastured livestock will enable American agriculture once again produce bountiful robust harvests of healthy nutrient dense toxin-less food. *The* bonus ride-along is that this fully harnesses our sole solution to global warming and we will begin, at the eleventh hour, to turn the tide on Mr. Heat — and prevail in humanity's pivotal battle.

Other bonus ride-alongs abound:

- a reallocation of government incentives will balance out the cost of organic and regenerative produce and healthy whole foods for consumers. Consumer demand will be beyond measure because most every truthfully informed and aware person wants to eat healthy food. Having farming operations pay for the cost of the environmental pollution they create will further balance these costs and speed the transformation.
- Shifting health care emphasis to disease and illness prevention and healthy living, and incentivizing people to eat plant-based diets, will dramatically lower health care costs. 80% of American health care costs are for illnesses and diseases that are preventable and avoidable.
- The food industry will have access to an abundant supply of healthy food ingredients so it can begin to create healthy processed foods. Corporations in this sector can be further incentivized by having to pay for any adverse health costs attributable to the food products they create.

"We do not need to protect ourselves from change, for our very nature is change," notes Joanna Macy. "Defensive self-protection, restricting vision and movement like a suit of armor, makes it harder to adapt. It not only reduces flexibility but blocks the flow of information we need to survive."[25]

More than compassion for other animals, more than taking good care of our health, our "selves" and one another, protecting and preserving the land, of discovering new livelihoods, reinvigorating communities, and more than protecting our democracy, a new agrarian revolution is essential. This is about protecting our planet. This is about our survival.

Imagine for a moment you are a meerkat in the middle of your morning mob scene.

I don't mean metaphorically. That's you: Shifting around amidst field grasses, seeking a bit of something, a scent of something, something to eat. And you freeze; full-stop. You sense it before you even see it. Danger. Ahead. Somewhere. You peer that way with your eyeballs, keeping your body still, not moving in the slightest... Your keen eyesight locks on a slight movement; a hint of something. Ahead. And you see it, camouflaged amidst the dry grass: A Cape cobra. Just five feet away. It's staring — dark viscous eyes staring — at you. You don't move; you barely breathe. If you flinch or turn to flee it will strike before you can even set a paw down and it will kill you. It's too fast, it's in position, and it's hungry just as you are. You've stepped in range. You are its target. You've stopped moving closer to it, so it's going to strike. All you can do, your slim chance of surviving this, is to time its strike, which will be lightening quick, shifting to one side, hoping that it's just enough so that its venomous fangs miss, giving you an instant as it recovers to bolt away.

In your peripheral vision there's movement ahead to one side. Then the other. You are not alone. We are there.

Your mob buddies, a couple of them shift silently to either side of the Cape cobra. Others a bit further away, carefully, quietly nearing as well. You are not alone. They anticipate, as you do, the instant the snake will strike.

Suddenly, split second, a meerkat lunges at it, its long sharp claws cutting into the earth an inch away from the cobra's side. The cobra hisses and adjusts quickly to face that threat. That meerkat retreats, facing the cobra the whole time, then another strikes from the other side — and the cobra shifts its attention defensively in that direction.

You could run now — you aren't targeted any longer. But the only thought in your mind is to stay with your group and vanquish this foe. It's your mob. It's your turn. You lunge at the cobra's exposed flank, stopping just short, then recoil as its eyes and the long fangs to each side of its open mouth reorient... on you.

Its neck sets, it's ready again to strike you. But you feel differently now. You're staring death in the eye just as you did seconds before, but now you have the upper hand. If the snake chooses to strike at you, it will likely bite you and kill you, but it will never devour you because your meerkat companions will be tearing its sides open. And it knows that. And in the wild, there are no snake doctors — it can't risk that kind of injury. You and your companions have command.

We are in the throes of Earth's 6th Great Extinction. It has already started. It has you in its sights. Me too. And we are staring it down. "Not on my watch." You and me. Others. Many others. Many more every day. Each one of us, on behalf of everyone, every animal and life form on the planet today or yet to come, "Not on my watch."

You stare down the Cape cobra. It's set to strike at you, but you trust that another meerkat will lunge at it — and you watch that happen. The meerkats shift allowing the snake an opening to retreat through.

"Not on my watch."

* * * *

The Economic Case for Climate Action in the United States published by the Universal Ecological Fund FEU-US in 2018, conservatively estimated that "The impacts of weather events influenced by human-induced climate change and direct health consequences of pollution from fossil fuel use are currently causing, on average, $240 billion a year in economic losses, damages and health costs — or about 40% of the current growth of the United States economy." The report projects economic losses to escalate to $360 billion per year.[26] This will cripple future American economic growth.

For the prosperity of our country going forward, we have to take a different path. The New Economy depends on regenerative agricultural production; on profitable, environmentally-friendly family farming. The economic costs involved in making and incentivizing the transformation away from industrial agriculture and factory farming will be small in comparison to the economic benefits. And the rewards — saving our health, our economy, our society, and our planet — will be immeasurable.

The United Nations Conference on Trade and Development, in its Trade and Environment Review of 2013, *Wake Up Now Before It Is Too Late: Make Agriculture Truly Sustainable Now for Food Security In A Changing Climate*, states, "Developing and developed countries alike need a paradigm shift in agricultural development: from a 'green revolution' to a 'truly ecological intensification' approach. This implies a rapid and significant shift from conventional, monoculture-based and high external-input-dependent industrial production towards mosaics of sustainable, regenerative production systems that also considerably improve the productivity of small-scale farmers. We need to see a move from a linear to a holistic approach in agricultural management, which recognizes that a farmer is not only a producer of agricultural goods, but also a manager of an agro-ecological system that provides quite a number of public goods and services (e.g. water, soil, landscape, energy, biodiversity, and recreation)."[27]

Americans know in their gut that something is fundamentally wrong. As of December 2018, 73% of Americans believe global warming is happening — a majority in every state and congressional district — 72% say it is personally important to them, and 69% of us are worried about it.[28] A majority of us want our government to take action to stop global warming. The question on many people's minds is, "Why isn't government acting?"

This is a mystery that Frances Moore Lappé and Adam Eichen investigate in *Daring Democracy*: "A strong clue lies in one fact: between 1990 and 2016, fossil-fuel industry political contributions leaped eight-fold... Americans are losing trust that their democracy is really theirs. By 2014, only 11% of Democrats and 15% of Republicans reported trusting that members of Congress are 'significantly' influenced by their constituents."[29] The fossil fuel industry has spent nearly $2 billion in lobbying since year 2000 and legislation to address climate change has repeatedly died in Congress.[30]

There are a number of things we can do to reclaim our democracy as representative of our interests. And this endeavor is nonpartisan.

I believe that awareness and understanding matter more than the persuasiveness of money in politics. I don't believe our representatives, or even many of us, have a solid understanding of the causes underlying global warming, the reasons why Mr. Heat is at our door, let alone how dangerous he is. The solution then is to increase awareness and understanding. This is something each one of us can do; in every one of our actions and our conversations. This is compassionate activism.

Compassionate activism is nonpartisan in a larger sense as well. Compassion for humanity means compassion towards *all* humans, each one of us. The belief that if our citizens are provided a clear understanding, an awareness based on clear scientific rationale of the imperative to make significant changes, they will get it.

An informed majority will decide correctly. That goes for our citizens and our elected officials. This is compassion for our democracy, for majority rule.

The Farm Bill isn't really for farmers anymore. It benefits Big Ag and the multinationals immensely by incentivizing and enabling five more years of industrial agriculture.

The 2018 Farm Bill:

- condemns billions of animals to lifetimes of misery and suffering in factory farms, propping up the most virulent and environmentally damaging industry on Earth
- produces nutrient-depleted commodity crops from GMO seeds, food that is a significant contributor to our health crisis
- accelerates the evisceration of our soil microbiome on hundreds of millions of crop acres
- perpetuates the economic strangulation and impoverishment of rural and urban communities across the land
- undermines our democracy itself, rewarding Big Ag with tens of billions of dollars in business as a return for the billions of dollars Big Ag has spent and will continue to spend corrupting our elected officials and co-opting our political process

Our Arch Villain remains defiantly steadfast in an increasingly desperate attempt to fake climate and crop science, to misdirect and mask the truth in order to maximize profits until the day that is no longer possible, the day when the Earth just tells us, "You're done."

. . .

Food sovereignty is your right as a human being.

Food sovereignty, a term which originated in 1996 by Via Campesina, an alliance of 148 international organizations, is defined as, "The right of peoples to healthy and culturally appropriate food produced through ecologically sound and sustainable methods, and their right to define their own food and agriculture systems."[31]

For Professor John Ikerd, "Food sovereignty is grounded in the proposition that food is a basic human right... A reaffirmation of a God-given, self-evident, unalienable right that is stated in the American Declaration of Independence: the rights of life, liberty, and the pursuit of happiness. Nothing is more fundamental to the right to life than the right to clean air and water and safe, healthful food. The rights of liberty include the right to choose culturally appropriate foods and the right to define our own food systems. Ecologically sound and sustainable farming methods simply extend those basic human rights to those of future generations. The Declaration of Independence also states that 'to ensure these rights, governments are instituted among men.' I fail to see how anything could be more fundamentally American than government policies designed to ensure the right of all people to healthy, culturally appropriate food produced by ecologically and socially sustainable methods."[32]

Protecting food sovereignty is one role of a properly focused and functioning American government.

In 2017, Earl Blumenauer, a U.S. Congressional Representative from Oregon, introduced the Food and Farm Act, which he drafted after years of research and conversations throughout his community and his state. It was a beautifully thought through, viable alternative farm bill that would be a big step forward.

As summarized in a press release, it, "Advances Farm Bill reforms based on four principles: (1) focusing resources on those who need it most; (2) fostering innovation; (3) encouraging investments in people and the planet; and (4) ensuring access to healthy foods."[33]

It "cuts, caps, and clarifies the farm subsidy programs available in the commodity, conservation and crop insurance titles of the Farm Bill."[34] It eliminates excessive subsidy programs limiting "the aggregate payment a farmer or agribusiness can receive from the commodity, conservation, and crop insurance programs to $125,000 per year," making payments more equitably distributed while expanding subsidies for non-industrial agriculture, non-commodity crop farms. Funds will be made available to organic and regenerative farmers and to support those who are transitioning to organic or regenerative. Farmers can only receive subsidies if they comply with conservation requirements such as improving water quality, reducing soil erosion or adding vegetation buffers. It adds incentives for improving the environment such as planting erosion-reducing cover crops or creating pollinator habitats. Crop insurance will be made more available to farmers with diversified crops.

It, "Establishes the first Animal Welfare Title in the Farm Bill to ensure that the treatment of animals is a central part of the country's food and agriculture policy."[35] There will be no payments to factory farms. None. Funds will be allocated to pasture-based livestock producers. Programs would support farmers or ranchers who lower or eliminate routine use of antibiotics on animals, factory farms will be forced to report accurate greenhouse gas emissions, and funding will be made available to develop local meat and poultry processing infrastructure.

A key focus will be that the bill "invests in existing programs and creates new ones to support vibrant local and regional food systems... By supporting the growth and advancement of local and regional food systems, the U.S. invests in an environmentally and economically resilient food and agriculture system"[36] The bill will provide support for beginning farmers and ranchers to enter and stay in agriculture, including tax credits on the purchase of land and equipment. It increases funding for specialty crops to incentivize crop and seed diversity. It opens loan funding to agricultural cooperatives, which is a business forum commonly utilized by farmers just starting out. It invests in research and education programs that improve sustainable agriculture practices including climate change adaptation and mitigation.

Leah Douglas writes that, "Congressman Blumenauer wants everyone to understand that when the Farm Bill can be changed to become more effective, we all benefit. The legislation effects commodity crop farmers as well as those 'engaged in value-added agriculture. There are people who care about animal welfare, people who are fighting against hunger, who are concerned about obesity, who want to protect wildlife habitat. So, this is potentially a very significant coalition.'"[37]

Every aspect of the Food and Farm Act is a significant shift in the right direction. Congressman Blumenauer is an example of an elected official advocating for essential, common sense change.

Government leaders worldwide are stepping up. For example, realizing that reduced meat consumption is essential if their countries are to meet the Paris climate goals, many political leaders acknowledge it is their government's necessary role to develop policy to legislate and incentivize this shift. Despite its burgeoning middle-class and sustained economic prosperity, China has announced plans to reduce per capita meat consumption by 50% by 2030. In the Netherlands, the Dutch government is acting on a September 2018 report from its primary strategic advisory board that concluded, "Livestock numbers will need to be cut and a plant-based diet promoted in order for the Netherlands to meet its climate change targets." Similar legislation is now under consideration in the Great Britain and Scotland as well.[38]

Ryan Alexander, President of Taxpayers for Common Sense, applauds Mr. Blumenauer for, "Spearheading this critical conversation on the federal farm bill. By many measures, Washington is broken. The complex, convoluted, and increasingly costly farm bill is a shining example of what today's broken legislative process will produce. Mr. Blumenauer's efforts to engage everyone from farmers, to environmentalists, to fiscal conservatives in developing a farm bill that works for Oregon, is a process we need repeated in Ohio, in Oklahoma, and ultimately in our nation's capital."

Bill Wenzel, Food and Farm Program Director for the U.S. Public Interest Research Group (PIRG), notes, "Existing farm policy largely ignores consumer interests in sustainably produced foods to prop up and support farming practices and systems that have real downsides for the environment and the public health. By eliminating the preferential treatment of commodity producers and factory farm livestock and poultry producers in farm support programs, reforming conservation programs to ensure that the taxpayer gets environmental bang for the buck and investing in sustainable food production businesses and infrastructure, the *Food and Farm Act* provides new opportunities for farmers and farming systems that are good for the environment and the public health."

Jessica A. Knoblauch quotes Peter Lehner in *Farming for the Future*, "The biggest challenge to making farms more sustainable is getting laws and policies in place that incentivize farmers to consider agriculture's full environmental impact, including its climate impact."[39]

Here is Congressman Earl Blumenauer, in his own words:

"The farm bill has flown under the radar for too long, with large agribusinesses and their lobbyists exercising an outsized influence on our nation's food and farm policy while the rest of the country is left fighting for crumbs. That is — unless more people raise their voices.

"It's time for *everyone* to wake up and get involved. Sadly, our current food and farm policies fail to meet the needs of the American people. We pay too much to the wrong people to grow the wrong food in the wrong places. The federal government spends an exorbitant amount of taxpayer dollars to help the wealthiest and most powerful agriculture operations get bigger and more profitable. Recent data shows that the bill's high dollar farm subsidy programs paid the same 28,000 farmers $19 billion for 32 straight years. Meanwhile, small and medium-sized farmers and ranchers, the environment, and American families receive too little attention, too little concern, and too little help. This is unacceptable.

"Rather than investing in family farmers who grow real and healthy foods, the legislation helps large operations grow six commodity crops — many of which we already have in excess and are made into unhealthy processed foods. The bill also shortchanges farmers' markets and local food promotion programs. All of this together puts Americans at greater risk of health problems, such as diabetes and obesity. We are subsidizing a diet that is literally making Americans sick.

"The policies outlined in my Food and Farm Act would force the federal government to reset its priorities. It focuses resources on those who need it most, helping beginning and socially disadvantaged farmers get the support they need. It promotes access to healthy foods, expanding assistance for farmers' markets and strengthening regional food infrastructure. It encourages investments in the planet, doubling resources for key conservation programs and reforms them to better help the environment. All the while, it cuts and reforms wasteful subsidy programs for commodity crops."

None of the provisions in Congressman Blumenauer's Food and Farm Act were accepted into the 2018 Farm Act.

On December 11, 2018, with the Farm Bill vote pending and its passage a foregone conclusion, Congressman Blumenauer issued a press release confirming his opposition, stating, "Congress is bringing up yet another bad Farm Bill that pays too much to the wrong people to grow the wrong foods in the wrong places... While the agriculture committees have been drafting this disappointing proposal behind closed doors, I spent three years listening to the needs of farmers around the country and this bill does not address those needs. This bill cuts an important conservation program and expands subsidies paid to non-farming cousins, nieces and nephews. My Food and Farm Act is an example of how it could be done right. We can and must do better."[40]

III

According to the Center for Responsive Politics, over the past two decades the agriculture sector has contributed almost *half a billion* dollars to national political campaigns. Leading up to the passage of the 2014 Farm Bill, 350 organizations including the American Farm Bureau and the International Dairy Foods Association lobbied heavily to shape it and for its passage. Robbie Feinberg noted in his article, *Special Interests Heavily Involved in Farm Bill Maneuvering*, "In 2013 alone, the industries combined to spend more than $57.5 million on lobbying. Leading the charge among those groups were chemical giant Monsanto and the American Farm Bureau, which over the past five years have spent $36 million and $27.9 million, respectively."[41]

The United Republic analyzed the 467 congressional races in 2012 and found that the better-financed candidate won 91% of the time.[42] During the 2017-18 election cycle, Agribusiness donations to Congress totaled $50,608,312 as of November 13, 2018. Of that, 430 members of the House of Representatives received $31,863,560, which is an average of $74,101 per Representative. Senators received $9,943,961, averaging $96,543 per Senator.[43]

Democracy is an evolving dynamic system of government, one that is never static, and in our case, one that has been co-opted. Citizen's voices have been marginalized by the immense power of corporations and the vast amounts of money they spend to control the media message, manipulate the marketplace, craft our government policy and, by extension, our laws by influencing the votes of our elected representatives. For Big Ag, the billions of dollars spent are an investment, and one that continues to produce very handsome returns with every Farm Bill.

Voting is a choice between alternatives. However, our members of Congress are voting in the absence of a real choice. There are two fundamental reasons why.

First, they are voting in an absence of complete knowledge and awareness. They lack an understanding of who our Arch-Villain is; of how significantly industrial agriculture and factory farming contribute to greenhouse gas emissions; how dire our situation is with regard to global warming; and how the action plan legislated in the current Farm Bill will prohibit the United States from taking the necessary steps to reduce climate emissions and keep temperature rise below the 1.5° necessary to protect life on this planet.

In Chapter 3, *Compassion for The Land*, David R. Montgomery placed our present situation with regard to soil loss in a historical perspective: "From the Roman Empire to the Maya and Polynesia's Easter Island, one great civilization after another sank into poverty and eventual demise after destroying their topsoil... The once-Edenic, now-impoverished places that spawned Western civilization illustrate one of history's most underappreciated lessons: societies that don't take care of their soil do not last."[44] Those civilizations faced a critical problem and failed to find a solution.

Our planet's temperature has not been this high for 15 million years. Global warming's impact on humankind is therefore unique to our age.

What is also unique, is that this is a life-endangering problem we have a solution for.

Awareness of this problem has not sufficiently spread to enable us to arrive at an understanding, a consensus, and the resolve giving us the ability to act on it. Robert Wolf notes, "A healthy society is defined in part by its ability to take self-corrective measures." And he warns, "Like a belief system before it dies, a civilization rigidifies as it atrophies: dominant beliefs become dogma, and the civilization becomes incapable of adapting to change, incapable of self-corrective, rectifying measures."[45] He references American historian Brooks Adams who in 1896 cited historical examples reinforcing his conclusion that "when past civilizations grew excessively centralized, they exhausted themselves. The result was collapse."[46] The centralization of immensely wealthy industry-dominant multinational corporations, more powerful than many governments — perhaps even including our own — has never been more apparent.

The second fundamental reason our members of Congress are voting in the absence of a real choice is they lack an alternative vision and policy to consider. They have no developed, vetted, viable option to vote for. Earl Blumenauer's Food and Farm Act attempted to start that discussion.

The imperative to change course was not clear: change direction or perish.

And facing the most powerful Arch-Villain the world has ever seen, a new plan containing the answer to the question, "How can we possibly change course?" was not on the table.

So.

How can we possibly change course?

You'll see.

IV

Here then is the call. Calling out to you. An essential component of **The Great Healing** is **compassion for our democracy**.

The Great Healing will not be possible without rescuing and reclaiming our democracy.

In *An Inconvenient Sequel - Truth to Power*, former Vice President Al Gore knows from experience, "Political will is a renewable resource, but it can only be renewed with the passionate involvement of individuals around the world who are willing to put time and energy toward learning the best ways to encourage political and business leaders at every level of society to make these changes a priority — and then take action."[47]

Joanna Macy senses a seismic shift is underway, "a revolution that is comparable in magnitude to the agricultural revolution of the late Neolithic era ten thousand years ago and the industrial revolution of the past two-and-a-half centuries. The first one took centuries to unfold. The second only took generations. Right on its heels, as the industrial growth society spins out of control comes this third revolution, which thinkers have referred to as the environmental or ecological or sustainability revolution. As they point out, this transition must happen not in centuries or generations, but within a matter of years."[48]

Realize the value of your opinion and your power sharing your vision.
With your understanding comes conviction.

- By living your life with compassion for animals, by demonstrating the courage to look at and realize the horror and immensity of animal suffering on factory farms, and choosing to contribute to zero part of that with your consumer dollars, you lead by setting a moral, virtuous example.
- By taking compassionate care of yourself, of your health and your body temple by choosing to eat mostly whole, plant-based foods rich in the G-Bombs Dr. Fuhrman espouses, you can best protect your vitality, mental sharpness, your quality of life, and your lifespan. Realizing the predominance of unhealthy foods in our environment, you can now protect yourself and your loved ones. Knowing that many physicians, as representatives of a profit-obsessed medical industry that would rather sell you a new drug and/or a procedure than provide you with sound fundamental nutritional advice to heal your illness at cause, you can ask the right questions and find an enlightened doctor to trust.
- By loving the land, the soil and all the exquisite lifeforms on it and in it, you may realize there is no difference based on size or appearance — that a tiger is just as magnificent and essential as Earl "the Worm" or Pat the Pooper. And that Pat and Earl's home, our Earth's soil — from which all life comes and returns — must be valued and protected above all to enable life as we know it on this planet to continue. And you may begin to understand the extent to which the opposite is happening, how industrial agriculture, in addition to contributing to global warming more than any other industry, is killing the microbiome of billions of crop acres worldwide, turning our most essential resource into lifeless dirt. Regenerative agriculture is ideal agriculture — and always has been.
- Feeling compassion for our livelihoods and our shires, you might now understand how this gargantuan, seemingly intractable system, Big Ag, is extinguishing not only life on our land and life underground, but American livelihoods along with the life and

vitality of our communities and local economies. After World War II, scientific advances, new inventions and technology enabled industrial agriculture to take hold, and over several decades to fulfill its agricultural promise. While its benefits might once have been accepted as a tradeoff for the loss of small family farms and livelihoods, of community, of local economies, of the comfort and security for millions of Americans living a middle-class life, this is no longer the case. Big Ag's system of industrial agriculture and factory farming sucks billions of dollars out of communities nationwide, bleeding these emaciated local economies dry. It now threatens our very survival.

- By conceiving of our democracy as a living, evolving creature, one that has been infected, sickened, and subverted by wealthy corporate interests, and by realizing how our future is dependent on a New Farm Bill, you may discover a feeling of compassion for our democracy itself, the beauty of our democratic government, its necessity, how exquisite and invaluable it is. And how you can help heal it by harnessing the tools of citizenship and compassionate activism to achieve The Great Healing.

Realize and step into your power. And the power of compassionate activism. And like the Meerkats, our little earth men, the power of collective action.

Al Gore advises, "In order to bring about the changes we need, activists need to focus not only on communicating the truth about the climate crisis and the readily available solutions, but they need to also focus on learning how to wield political power — the healthy and liberating form of power that democracy puts in the hands and hearts of every citizen who wants to exercise it."[49]

Empowered, aware, you can begin to ask yourself, "What can I do?"

Marco Lambertini, the Director General of World Wildlife Fund, in its seminal *Living Planet Report 2016*, writes about the Anthropocene Epoch as, "An era in which humans rather than natural forces are the primary drivers of planetary change. But we can also redefine our relationship with our planet from a wasteful, unsustainable and predatory one, to one where people and nature can coexist in harmony. We need to transition to an approach that decouples human and economic development from environmental degradation — perhaps the deepest cultural and behavioral shifts ever experienced by any civilization. The speed and scale of this transition is essential."[50]

We are the rock stars of the Anthropocene — this is our era, our geological epoch. The Earth has become our stage. Our performance started out really well, our set was mercurial, exhilarating, but if our next song or two play really poorly and disrespectfully, we will be facing End Time. Exit stage left. And a speedy, involuntary, ugly exit it will be.

Create the vision for our leaders.

In his Time Magazine article, *The Thing About Millennials*, Trevor Noah writes, "Not only are young people growing into the world of politics, but they're engaged in a way where they understand that they can actually change the course of history, as opposed to just being part of it... Standing up and saying we don't accept the status quo, we can change our destiny, we can change the future, we can be a part of this world. You feel it."[51]

- Vote in every election at every level from school board on up. Vote for compassionate, open-minded politicians who have intellectual clarity and courage.
- Vote for politicians who retain their voting integrity by not accepting campaign contributions from corporations or from the PACs that represent them. In October 2018, prior to the November midterm elections, 1257 elected officials and candidates for office at national, state and local levels took the *No Fossil Fuel Money Pledge.*[52]
- If you are social media savvy, you have tools that give you unprecedented range and access with your messaging. Use them. As an e-activist, make your voice and your opinion heard. Sign petitions, share content, join like-minded groups.

Wait. That's it? "Vote?" ... No. There's more. But voting is essential. Never underestimate the power of your vote.

In the 2018 midterm elections, 36% of young voters, ages 18 to 29, voted, a *180% increase*, almost double the turnout from the 2014 midterm when only 20% voted.[53] This turnout shifted party control of the House of Representatives decisively.

In 2017 in the United Kingdom when Prime Minister Theresa May called for a "snap" general election to consolidate her power and push through Brexit, 64% of registered voters aged 18-24 nationwide *voted* — a 60% increase from the previous election and the highest turnout in 25 years.[54] Voting 18-24-year-olds handed Theresa May and her fellow Brexiteers a stinging repudiation across the entire country. Her party lost of control of Parliament and she had to scramble, barely forming a coalition enabling her to survive as Prime Minister.

In the May 2019 European Union Parliament elections, a "Green Wave" rolled across the continent as politicians and environmental activists from a Green alliance of over 30 parties scored resounding victories. Greenpeace spokesperson Laura Ullmann noted that voters across Europe "have turned out in the largest numbers in over 20 years, and millions of people — young and old — have been taking to the streets to demand a socially just Europe that takes drastic action to prevent climate breakdown. The EU must act now. There's no time to waste."[55] In Germany the Green party finished second, but voters aged 18 to 24 turned out in huge numbers and out-voted the first-place party by over 3 to 1. Ska Keller, a German Green MEP and co-convenor of the Green group in the European Parliament stated, "The three key principles unifying these parties are: climate action, civil liberties, and social justice."[56]

Your vote, your activism, your advocacy. Your voice is needed.

But...

We can't wait for our elected leaders when they lack a full understanding of the problem at hand, when they don't realize the imperative of significant fundamental change. What happens when the vision for a policy solution does not exist?

"Movements are dreams with feet and hands, hearts and voices."[57] Paul Hawken wrote that. He is a beautiful writer.

We can dream with our minds. We can use our brains to problem solve as well.

We have to supply the vision and a plan. The solution. It's time. We have to frame the issue, create awareness of our solution and a groundswell forcing politicians to take note, and to state their definitive position regarding it.

To help enable us to attain The Great Healing, here are two bits of wonderful news.

The first is the Green New Deal.

The Green New Deal is a comprehensive plan to transform the U.S. economy off fossil fuels in the next decade by eliminating warming emissions from all major industries and creating millions of green jobs in the process. The policy report by Data for Progress titled *A Green New Deal* was released in September 2018. Lead author Greg Carlock and contributing author Emily Mangan envision the Green New Deal as, "An equitable transition to a 21st century economy and clean energy revolution that guarantees clean air and water, modernizes national infrastructure, and creates high-quality jobs." It is, "designed to mitigate the causes of global warming while building resilience to its effects in ways that prioritize justice and equity."[58]

Its ambitious goals include the transformation to a low-carbon economy (100% zero emission passenger vehicles by 2030, 100% clean and renewable energy by 2035, etc.), fulfilling American's *right* to clean air and water, reforesting 40 million acres of Public and Private Land, restoring 5 million acres of wetlands, and expanding sustainable farming and soil practices to 70% of agricultural land by 2050. The Green New Deal will create 10 million new jobs over 10 years to facilitate this transition.

The Green New Deal is based on the principles of freedom and justice, "that public policy is based on mutual respect for all people, free from all forms of discrimination or bias, particularly low-income, indigenous peoples, and minority groups. That Americans demand an ethical, responsible, and sustainable use of lands, waters, and renewable resources with future generations in mind. That all Americans have the right to participate in the decision-making of environmental action, including planning, implementation, enforcement, and evaluation."[59]

Alexandria Ocasio-Cortez, seeking election to the U.S. House of Representatives, fearlessly made this bold proposal a central campaign issue. It's as if it's part of her DNA. She won her race with 93% of the vote. Other progressive candidates advocating the Green New Deal prevailed as well. "At first, establishment Democrats scoffed at the Green New Deal as some ultraleft policy demand, but the more the idea of job creation through building renewable energy and climate-adapted infrastructure were floated with the American public, the more support they gained. Not to mention, the notion of slowing rampant income inequality and leaving no American behind sits favorably with working people throughout the nation," wrote Monica Medina and Miro Korenha in the Huffington Post.

"The Green New Deal is a unifying political message that gets back to the basics of creating an economy that works for all people and protects the planet as a result."[60]

Just one week after the midterm election, having helped her party win control of the House of Representatives, Alexandria Ocasio-Cortez joined a sit-in in House Majority Leader-to-be, Nancy Pelosi's, office to insist she form a Select Committee for a Green New Deal. Over 1,000 people, organized by the Sunrise Movement,[61] participated. 143 were arrested. Varshini Prakash, Sunrise co-founder, said as the sit-in began, "The U.N. says we have 12 years to transform our economy and avert catastrophe... Over 1,000 young people took over Capitol Hill today because we all deserve good jobs and a livable future."[62]

In her December 2018 article, *At Bernie Sander's Big Climate Town Hall, Alexandria Ocasio-Cortez Steals the Show*, Rebecca Leber reported, "Newly elected New York representative Alexandria Ocasio-Cortez has elevated the Green New Deal, a rallying cry for a complete realignment of the US economy for a carbon-free future to top billing in the Democratic party."[63]

As of May 2019, the Green New Deal's growing list of Co-Sponsors includes 12 Senators and 91 Congressional Representatives.[64]

Naomi Klein writes, "For the first time, I see a clear and credible political pathway that could get us to safety, a place in which the worst climate outcomes are avoided and a new social compact is forged that is radically more humane than anything currently on offer... The draft text calls for the committee, which would be fully funded and empowered to draft legislation, to spend the next year consulting with a range of experts."[65]

The Green New Deal at this stage is a resolution, a well thought out set of policy goals. The details of the policies to be enacted to achieve them, as Tom Philpott notes in *Why the Green New Deal is so Vague About Food and Farming*, will emerge, "through transparent and inclusive consultation, collaboration, and partnership with frontline and vulnerable communities, labor unions, worker cooperatives, civil society groups, academia, and businesses... Rather than consult and gain permission from Big Ag and dirty energy before enacting climate legislation, they're going straight to the public."[66]

The Green New Deal. A New Farm Bill. These are goals.

We must advance them rapidly. After the election, once their legislation is finalized and passed into law, only then, will the essential transition we need to make at scale for our survival begin. At that time, it will still take severely damaged topsoil several years to recover, to grow healthy food, and to begin functioning as a carbon sink.

We have a headwind. 67% of millennials believe environmental protection should be a top priority of the government.[67]

Support is even broader than that. The report, *Politics & Global Warming, December 2018*, surveyed a nationally representative sampling of Democratic, Independent, and Republican registered voters. When the Green New Deal was described as, "Producing jobs and strengthening America's economy by accelerating the transition from fossil fuels to clean, renewable energy... generating 100% of the nation's electricity from clean, renewable sources within the next 10 years; upgrading the nation's energy grid, buildings, and transportation infrastructure; increasing energy efficiency; investing in green technology research and development; and providing training for jobs in the new green economy," it was supported by "81% of registered voters, 92% of Democrats, 88% of Independents, and 64% of Republicans."[68]

On January 10, 2019 a letter signed by 626 environmental groups representing millions of members, was sent to congressional representatives urging them to draft ambitious climate legislation and advocating for the Green New Deal.[69] [70]

On April 10, 2019 a letter signed by over 300 food, farming, fishing, worker, environmental and public health organizations representing millions of members, was sent to congressional representatives advocating the Green New Deal as the way to "transform our food system and revitalize rural America."[71]

April 28, 2019 was national election day in Spain. One party's core campaign platform promise was a New Green Deal for Spain, an "El Green Deal de España." Turnout was massive: Three out of every four registered voters, 75.8% of the electorate, voted.[72] [73] That party won.

We have a plan. And as we approach the 2020 election, every candidate for every level of office is going to have to answer the question: Do they support it or not? Vote. And vote accordingly.

The second welcome bit of wonderful news is Compassionate Activism is spreading rapidly.

In the United States, the Women's March on January 21st, 2017, the day after the Presidential inauguration, was likely the largest single-day national protest in American history.[74] Over 4 million Americans marched that day. The Climate March later that year had millions in the streets as well. **Like voting, demonstrating is an essential tool of a democracy.**

If you have never attended a protest, please realize this: Being visible, showing up and standing out is exhilarating. It is a joyful, celebratory experience to be amidst hundreds, thousands of like-minded people, to feel the power in unity. People of all ages are there. Families with children, babies in strollers or body harnesses. Festive signs and banners adorn wide city streets you may have driven on or walked curbside, but never had a chance to *own* like you do on this day, walking center lanes, enjoying good food along the route, the music of marching musicians, the chants and banter, good conversation with friends and the kindred spirits you meet. On stage at the march's end there will be impassioned speeches and you can behold the vastness of your numbers. Imagine all those watching the news coverage of your event who did not or could not attend, getting your message, witnessing your masses.

In *Daring Democracy*, Francis Moore Lappé and Adam Eichen describe emotionally transformative shifts that can happen when you engage in this kind of compassionate activism, ones that enable you to experience the "thrill of democracy": "First is *civil courage, or the power of choosing to walk with fear...* Our body's sensations are reminding us that, yes, we're stepping out beyond our comfort zones, and it is exciting and enlivening... Second is *the power of discovering deep connections with strangers sharing a higher value...* Being shoulder to shoulder with complete strangers on behalf of deeply held principles can present such possibilities... Third is an inner shift from feeling like a protesting outsider to a powerful *'owner'* of our democracy."[75] Experiencing the "thrill of democracy" for Francis Moore Lappé and Adam Eichen satisfies three needs they identify as essential to human thriving — power, meaning, and connection. Further, "Gaining a voice is so essential for human dignity that the experience can trigger deep emotion."[76] During and after participating use your social media: post your photos, write about your experience. Let everyone know.

Francis Moore Lappé and Adam Eichen want to remind you that activism can be joyful, protesting can be celebratory. "Let's have a better time than they are."

In England in November 2018, the British government delivered its national budget. It was a plan woefully lacking in addressing global warming at this critical moment in human history. The group Extinction Rebellion protested immediately, blocking Parliament Square in London, its activists declaring their refusal "to bequeath a dying planet to future generations by failing to act now."

Later that week and 6,000 strong, Extinction Rebellion protests shut down five main London bridges gaining attention worldwide. Their declaration states, "The ecological crises that are impacting upon this nation, and indeed this planet and its wildlife can no longer be ignored, denied, nor go unanswered by any beings of sound rational thought, ethical conscience, moral concern, or spiritual belief." As such, we "declare ourselves in rebellion against our government and the corrupted, inept institutions that threaten our future." Extinction Rebellion accuses the British government of "willful complicity" that "has shattered meaningful democracy and cast aside the common interest in favor of short-term gain and private profits... This is our darkest hour... The science is clear — we are in the sixth mass extinction event and we will face catastrophe if we do not act swiftly and robustly."[77]

Extinction Rebellion is now a global movement with participants in 35 countries including the United States.

On April 15, 2019 Extinction Rebellion protesters in Sweden occupied the country's Parliament and staged a die-in. In Berlin, protesters shut down a main traffic artery, the Oberbaum bridge. But the biggest events happened in London...

In her article, *Thank These Climate Activists for Resisting Our Extinction*, Sonali Kolhatkar reported, "Nothing matters anymore except for action. That is what thousands of people, young and old, have expressed in London over the past several days. On April 15, members of Extinction Rebellion occupied key landmarks across the city: Parliament Square, Marble Arch, Oxford Circus, Waterloo Bridge and Piccadilly Circus. They articulated a simple set of three demands to the government: declare a climate and ecological emergency, enact policies to become carbon-neutral by 2025, and declare a citizens assembly to deepen democracy, given how spectacularly our existing governments have failed us. Over eight days of actions, more than 1,000 people were arrested in London as they engaged in nonviolent civil disobedience in the form of sit-ins, road blockages and die-ins — the largest number of arrests resulting from any coordinated set of actions in the city. Activists super-glued themselves to the front of Labour Party leader Jeremy Corbyn's home, to the top of a train carriage, and also to a train window. They brought London to a standstill and made clear that climate action is a nonnegotiable demand."[78]

Then something remarkable happened.

On May 1, 2019 Great Britain's Labour Party put forth a motion to declare an environment and climate emergency. Party Leader Jeremy Corbyn made this appeal to the Prime Ministers: "We have no time to waste. We are living in a climate crisis that will spiral dangerously out of control unless we take rapid and dramatic action now. This is no longer about the distant future. We are talking about nothing less than the irreversible destruction of our environment within our lifetimes. Young people know this. They have the most to lose. I was deeply moved a few weeks ago to see the streets outside this parliament filled with color and noise by children on strike from school chanting 'our planet, our future.' For someone of my generation it was inspiring but also humbling that children felt they had to leave school to teach the adults a lesson. The truth is they are ahead of the politicians on this — the most important issue of our times. We are witnessing an unprecedented upsurge of climate activism with groups like Extinction Rebellion forcing the politicians in this building to listen... Today we have the opportunity to say: 'We hear you.'"[79]

After debate the Parliament voted and the motion passed.

Jeremy Corbyn said after Great Britain's historic vote, "Today we have seen something incredible. The UK parliament has passed Labour's motion and become the first in the world to declare an environment and climate emergency. This can set off a wave of action from parliaments and governments around the globe... Protesters and school-strikers told us to act. Governments never act without pressure and we must keep the pressure up. I'm proud that the Labour Party brought this motion to the House, and now we will carry on this work by developing our plans to deliver a Green Industrial Revolution."[80]

Eight days later on May 9, Ireland became the second country to declare a climate emergency.[81]

On June 11, 2019, the British government announced a new policy — a commitment enshrined into law — to become an entirely "net zero" carbon emissions economy by 2050, making them the world's first major economy to make this commitment.[82]

. . .

She was 15 years old, a student attending school in her native Sweden. The more she learned about the threat of global warming, the increasingly alarmed she became. The issue haunted her for several years.

Greta Thunberg decided the inaction of her government's leaders as well as those of other countries in the face of this dire threat was intolerable. So, in September 2018, by herself, she went on strike — she ditched school and demonstrated outside Swedish Parliament in Stockholm. Her sign read *School Strike for Climate*. And she was active on social media. Over several weeks her protest caught on. The #ClimateStrike movement grew out of that direct action — and spread with lightning speed.

On October 20, she spoke before 10,000 people in Helsinki. It became Finland's largest ever climate demonstration. She "urged marchers to fight for the major systemic changes that experts have said are necessary to limit greenhouse gas emissions and avert a looming climate catastrophe. 'The politics that's needed to prevent the climate catastrophe — it doesn't exist today. We need to change the system.'"[83]

In December, Greta Thunberg, this 15-year-old student who just three months earlier decided to stop going to school and begin a protest against her government, addressed COP24, the United Nations Climate Change Conference in Katowice, Poland. In January, she spoke to the world's most powerful and wealthy political and business leaders convening at Davos, Switzerland, "harshly criticizing them for amassing huge wealth with the help of pollution-causing industries, to the detriment of future generations." In February, Greta was in Brussels joining a 7th week of protests by Belgian children skipping school. While there, she spoke before the European Commission. Jean-Claude Juncker, President of the European Union, standing beside her, then announced for the budget period of 2021-2027, 25% of the European Union budget — over $250 *billion* — will be allocated to mitigating global warming.[84]

In an open letter on March 1, 2019, two weeks before their "Global Day of Action,", #ClimateStrike activists wrote, "We, the young, are deeply concerned about our future. Humanity is currently causing the sixth mass extinction of species and the global climate system is at the brink of catastrophic crisis... We will no longer accept this injustice... We finally need to treat the climate crisis as a crisis. It is the biggest threat in human history and we will not accept the world's decision-makers' inaction that threatens our entire civilization. We will not accept life in fear and devastation... You have failed us in the past. If you continue failing us in the future, we, the young people, will make change happen by ourselves. The youth of this world has started to move and we will not rest again."[85]

On March 15, 2019 over 1.6 million students in over 2,000 locations in 133 countries participated in Climate Strike protests.[86] On May 24, over 1.8 million people in 125 countries took part in a global climate strike.[87]

Greta Thunberg had turned 16 years old, when, on March 14th she learned that she was nominated for the Nobel Peace Prize.

. . .

You matter. You. There is a reason you were born here in human form at this very special time. You have the power to help create the future you want to see. Your voice matters. You must find your voice and use it. This is a call out to you — to act. Find your courage, take a stand.

Join with us in what will become the most important cause of all of humanity's endeavors to date. Most of us have been enabling the Arch-Villain without even realizing it. Like Greta, like Hazel, shine your light into the darkness.

Help others, heal our planet.

You have the power. More than you realize. You'll see.

When the vision of our leaders is clouded, when they are coerced and corrupted by contributions from the corporations who are creating the problem, compassionate activists must act. We must show them the solution, and we must show them the door.

There must be a plan that candidates running for office *at every level*, must state their position on, for or against. That declaration lets you know whether or not they deserve your vote. It must become *the* campaign issue in 2020.

The Green New Deal is this kind of a plan. A New Farm Bill must be another. They may even evolve together.

When Earl Blumenauer presented his plan, the *Food and Farm Act* in 2017, it made an impression but had little impact on the negotiations leading up to the 2018 Farm Bill. We must get a resolution for a New Farm Bill centerstage as a campaign issue in the build-up to the 2020 elections. Earl Blumenauer's *Food and Farm Act* can be a starting point. It needs to be expanded much further to include the conversion of 100% of industrial agriculture cropland to regenerative agriculture.

And any candidate for office at any level must be asked repeatedly what their position is with regard to this plan. They will have to have a position or they won't be considered credible as a candidate — they can't duck the issue because there is no plan.

They must make a commitment and promise that if elected or re-elected, they will act on it accordingly — or they do not deserve your vote. If you can attend your candidate's rally, ask the candidate directly. If you have children and take your child to a rally, have the candidate express their position on this issue to you and your child. Have them make eye contact. Have them promise you — and promise your children.

For Glen Peters, Research Director of the Center for International Climate Research in Oslo, "Even if it is technically possible, without aligning the technical, political and social aspects of feasibility, it is not going to happen. To limit warming below 1.5°, — or 2° for that matter — requires all countries and all sectors to act."[88]

Vice President Al Gore observes, "Short-term decision-making is now commonplace in politics, culture, business, and industry. And it is now abundantly clear that if we continue to ignore the long-range consequences of our present actions and behaviors, we will put our future at dire risk."[89]

This is nonpartisan at its core because if global warming is not addressed, none of us will be voting in 20 years. By definition, two or more strong political parties are an essential component of a vital vigorous democracy. This vote isn't for party. Step outside of your clubhouse and vote for the candidate who commits to supporting the Green New Deal and a New Farm Bill, and to acting on this to pass this legislation into law.

This vote is for survival.

We need a New Farm Bill.

In his remarkable analysis, *Drawdown*, Paul Hawken presents the most promising solutions to combating global warming, ranking them based on the total amount of greenhouse gases they can either avoid the generation of, or remove from the atmosphere. Out of 100 solutions, regenerative agriculture ranks eleventh. "From an estimated 108 million acres of current adoption, we estimate regenerative agriculture to increase to a total of 1 billion acres by 2050. This rapid adoption is based in part on the historic growth rate of organic agriculture, as well as on the projected conversion of conservation agriculture to regenerative agriculture over time. This increase could result in a total reduction of 23.2 gigatons of carbon dioxide, from both sequestration and reduced emissions."[90]

He notes, "Formal schemes to finance regeneration will be a necessary stimulus to action, helping landowners to make changes without (sometimes literally) having to bet the farm."[91]

A New Farm Bill must be one of these "formal schemes." Paul Hawken calculates, "Regenerative agriculture could provide a $1.9 trillion financial return on an investment of $57 billion."[92] A *33-fold return* on your investment? — that's a pretty remarkable return.

This benefit will be exponentially more if regenerative agriculture, combined with pastured livestock, and the halting of land clearing and deforestation, is incentivized and implemented *at scale rapidly.* Beyond the economic benefit, the sequestering of atmospheric carbon in the soil is our most important solution for global warming.

Right now, regenerative agriculture is being stymied at every turn by Big Ag, and most significantly by the 2018 Farm Bill, which at its core is designed to secure the perpetuation of the industrial agriculture system.

GRAIN states in *Food Sovereignty: Five Steps to Cool the Planet and Feed its People,* "25% to 40% of the current excess of CO_2 in the atmosphere comes from the destruction of soil and its organic matter... If the right policies and incentives were in place worldwide, soil organic matter contents could be restored to pre-industrial agriculture levels... This would offset between 24% and 30% of all current global greenhouse gas emissions."[93]

A rapid conversion to regenerative agriculture must be accelerated. That can only happen with the powerful tool of government incentive and direction — with a decisive New Farm Bill replacing the existing one — inciting change on the scale of a modern-day Marshall Plan for America. A new "New Deal" is required. Right now.

America has experienced the imperative to change things up in a big way before. In the 1930's, the Great Depression combined with an environmental crisis, the Dust Bowl (interestingly, an environmental crisis similarly caused by vast agricultural mismanagement), to devastate our economy. President Franklin D. Roosevelt acted decisively, and the government stepped in with the New Deal. This is one of the most important benefits of a democratic government. In our nation's history, this was one of America's stellar examples of the power of our government in action.

The time to act is upon us again.

"Because small farms grow most of the world's food, it makes no sense that industrial agriculture should hog 80% of subsidies and 90% of research funds," John Thackara writes in *How to Thrive in the Next Economy*.[94]

Peter Lehner is convinced that "if we took those billions of dollars currently spent on subsidies for industrial corn and soy and applied them to healthy food, we would have a healthier food system and we'd save hundreds of billions of dollars — perhaps even trillions of dollars — in terms of better healthcare outcomes."[95]

Repeal of the Farm Bill and replacement with a New Farm Bill that incentivizes a comprehensive shift to regenerative agriculture and pastured animals will create hundreds of thousands of new jobs, new family farms, livelihoods, a rebirth of a modern-day Grange movement, and the revitalization nationwide of local small town and regional economies and rural communities. It will broadly accelerate the scope and impact of carbon sequestration far exceeding Paul Hawken's *Drawdown* estimates.

As *the* band on the Anthropocene stage, we have a new song. There is some debate as to whether or not we should play it, but we *will* be playing it. We have to — and if we perform it well, our new song will be a huge hit. It will rocket to #1 at the top of the *Drawdown* charts. It is our soul solution, our soil solution, *the* essential solution to global warming. And we will certainly be invited by our planet to remain on stage for an encore.

Every candidate running for election or re-election at every level of government needs to make an unambiguous public statement of support for this New Farm Bill so they are on record. No caveats. No equivocating. No vacillation. They support it — or not. That is how they will merit your vote — or not.

A New Farm Bill will save trillions of dollars.

Beyond a 100% conversion from industrial agriculture to regenerative and a return to pastured livestock...

- What if farmers were rewarded for increasing carbon sequestration, for reducing their irrigation needs by improving their soil's ability to retain water, and for increasing wildlife habitat preservation?

  At present the primary benefit a business receives from operating in an environmentally responsible manner tends to be the savings it realizes from its cost reductions. For example, a regenerative farmer's bottom line benefits from significantly reduced input costs. It is much less expensive for that farmer to farm. The fact that their farms generate far less environmental pollution and greenhouse gas emissions benefits our planet but offers them no additional financial reward.

  Nobel Peace Prize recipient Rattan Lal has studied the hypothetical dollar value of carbon sequestration, so that it might no longer remain a hypothetical. "Carbon farming is rapidly becoming the new agriculture where carbon sequestered in soil/trees/wetlands could be traded just as any other farm produce. Alternatively, farmers would be compensated for provisioning of ecosystem services through carbon sequestration in soil/biomass." His research enabled him to calculate this value and to recommend in 2014, "Through adoption of best management practices, farmers should be compensated for provisioning of ecosystem services (climate change mitigation, water quality, biodiversity, etc.) at the rate of $16 per acre per year."[96] This compensation, can be allocated in a New Farm Bill from repurposed existing funding.

- What if farmers, as well as *all* agri-businesses are not just rewarded for the environmental benefit their operations create, but incur an offset cost for environmental damage they cause?

  When corporations in polluting industries are not held responsible for the environmental damage they are causing, either we or the planet are the ones saddled with the burden and responsibility of dealing with it. Consequential health problems are our responsibility. As are the tax dollars our government, federal, state or local, will have to allocate to clean up the mess. Superfund sites are an example. Or the damage is simply cast off into nature, like greenhouse gases into the atmosphere, for the planet to "clean up" as best it can.

  A "pay as you go" system requiring corporations to incur the cost of the environmental damage they cause will elicit corporate accountability and responsibility. And in any given industry, the corporations that act aggressively to implement ways to curb their pollution will begin to operate at a competitive advantage to those who don't. The shift to heal the planet and improve quality of life for everyone will happen quickly.

Regarding the food industry, Paul Hawken writes in *Drawdown*, "Just as you can manufacture fake food cheaply using fillers, fats, sugars, and starches, conventional industrial agriculture produces food cheaply by not paying the cost of the damage it causes."[97] Once a "pay as you go" cost applies to food industry corporations, healthy regeneratively grown and organic food as well as meat and dairy products from pastured, humanely raised animals will become comparatively less expensive and rapidly gain market share replacing the unhealthy foods currently pervasive throughout our food system.

- What if policymakers, in designing a New Farm Bill, calculate in and advocate for its health benefits and immense health cost savings? Regenerative farms will be growing healthy, nutrient dense food and lots of it. Healthy food will become affordable for everyone. Unhealthy food, due to the environmental pollution inherent to industrial agriculture and factory farming that will become a production cost, will become increasingly more expensive — reflecting at last the damages it does to our environment, our health and wellbeing. Right now, millions of Americans shy away from regenerative or organic foods, or pastured or free-range meat and dairy products, because they cost more.

Current government subsidy programs enable meat prices to remain artificially low because they are not aligned with the real costs of production. Vaclav Smil, in *Eating Meat: Constants and Changes*, concludes from his extensive research that "consumers in the rich countries should be willing to pay more for food in order to lower the environmental impacts of its production, especially when that higher cost and the resulting lower consumption would also improve agriculture's long-term prospects and benefit the health of the affected population. Analogically, without higher prices and gradually reduced consumption there is no realistic possibility of limiting the combustion of fossil fuels and moderating the rate of global climate change."[98]

The United Nations Committee on Livestock, Environmental and Agricultural Development believes, "Reaching a sustainable balance of demand for livestock and the capacity of ecosystems to provide goods and services in the future will require adequate pricing of natural resources." Should our government expand "health taxes" like cigarette or soda taxes to foods determined to contribute to unhealthy diets and our epidemic of disease and ill-health, to reflect their "social and environmental externalities?"[99]

With access to much healthier and affordable food, Americans will become a much fitter and even more productive population.

- What if carbon pricing was established involving a "cap and trade" program? According to the World Bank, as of January 2019, cap and trade, carbon taxes, and other measures are proven tools for successfully curbing carbon emissions. They are already in place or scheduled to launch in the European Union and 30 nations worldwide.[100]

For Walter Jehne, "Firms and nations must fully account for their carbon dynamics. This must and can be readily verified globally via satellites. We must value such carbon accounting so that verified negative emissions have a value as drawdown credits that can be traded as offsets against positive net emissions obligations in a global carbon trading system. This system could readily set a commercial price on verified carbon emissions and offsets.

"Only when verified carbon credits have a value in such a global carbon market will farmers, industry, and nations have the commercial incentive and policy certainty they currently lack to invest in the urgent drawdown of carbon... By putting a valid price on verified carbon credits, carbon will be recognized not as a pollutant but as a valuable resource when sequestered in soils rather than a costly liability when emitted."[101]

Elliott Negin, in his article, *The California Green Rush: How UCS Helped Point the Way*, notes that California's state government passed "a landmark bill in 2006 calling for a reduction in carbon emissions to 1990 levels by 2020." California is not only the largest economy of any state in the United States by far, but if it were a country, would be the world's 6th largest economy. Negin writes in

2018, "This July, the state announced it had accomplished that goal in 2016, four years ahead of schedule. Emissions were down 13 percent from their 2004 peak — equivalent to taking 12 million cars off the road. Equally impressive, over that same 12-year span the state's economy grew 26 percent."[102]

Imagine that.

The California economy grew 26% and this larger economy in total now emits 13% less carbon emissions than the *smaller* state economy did 12 years before. That 12-year span includes the years of the Great Recession, yet California during this time, while significantly reducing its carbon emissions, expanded its economy immensely.

- What if product labeling truthfully, simply, and accurately communicated food nutrient information? Chapter 2 described the sugar industry's efforts to avoid sugar labelling on food packaging. Another example is: Bayer and other huge corporations are fighting hard and sparing little expense to resist mandatory GMO labeling on food products in this country. Why? Given the synthetic fertilizers, the pesticides, the herbicides, all the toxins and poisons unleashed on the environment that are part of the process of growing GMO crops, and research revealing increasing concentrations of glyphosate in the GMO food we eat, the corporations don't want consumers to be able to identify food products on retail shelves as containing GMO ingredients.

In 2014, Vermont voters passed a bill by a wide margin that required the labeling of genetically modified foods. Signing the bill into law, Governor Peter Shumlin said, "Vermonters take our food seriously and we believe we have a right to know what's in the food we buy. More than 60 countries have already restricted or labeled these foods, and now one state — Vermont — will also ensure that we know what's in the food we buy and serve our families."[103] The new law went into effect on July 1, 2016. A federal bill "with solid support from both Democrats and Republicans," was signed into law in July 2016, which overrode and nullified Vermont's law, and mandatory GMO labeling did not happen. Governor Peter Shumlin stated, "Vermont was overpowered by the food industry's lobbying power and financial resources in the fight over labeling of genetically modified food."[104]

If for the time being, Big Ag's control over our government thwarts mandatory, clear GMO product labeling and American consumer's "right to know," then manufacturers and providers of non-GMO foods need to exercise their right to label their products as GMO-free. More and more consumers are seeking "non-GMO" labelled products. We have a right to know.

Do we break them up?

Have corporations gotten too powerful, too influential? Our Arch-Villain right now can lead us almost singlehandedly to the brink, the end of the Anthropocene...

Our government has broken up corporations before.

Just over a century ago, when several companies grew large enough to dominate an industry they were called trusts. There are numerous ways in which they can then collude to manipulate the marketplace to their gain to the detriment of smaller competitors and consumers. A common tactic is to fix prices low enough to drive smaller competitors out of business. Once market domination is achieved, a common tactic is to then fix prices high enough to maximize profit from consumers who have no alternative but to pay that price for essential items. The Sherman Anti-Trust Act was enacted by Congress in 1890 to prevent corporations with significant market share from using their power to gain these kinds of advantages that were deemed unfair and exploitative.

Big Ag, including some of the largest multinational corporations the world has ever seen, has a pervasive history of this kind of behavior.

In 1902, President Theodore Roosevelt took on the Beef Trust, which was a group of the largest meatpackers who controlled half of the national market. *Swift & Co. v. United States* on Wikipedia provides this succinct history, "The evidence at trial demonstrated that the 'Big Six' leading meatpackers were engaged in a conspiracy to fix prices and divide the market for livestock and meat in their quest for higher prices and higher profits. They blacklisted competitors who failed to go along, used false bids, and accepted rebates from the railroads... When they were hit with federal injunctions in 1902, the Big Six agreed to merge into one National Packing Company in 1903, so they could continue to control the trade internally. The case was heard by the Supreme Court in 1905... Speaking for the court, Oliver Wendell Holmes, Jr. broadened the meaning of 'interstate' commerce by including actions that were part of the chain where the chain was clearly interstate in character. In this case, the chain ran from farm to retail store and crossed many state lines. The federal government's victory in the case encouraged it to pursue other antitrust actions."[105]

Today, after decades of industry consolidation, just four companies — Tyson, Cargill, JBS, and National Beef — process 80% of animals in the United States.[106] Tyson Foods exerts control over the entirety of both pork and poultry operations throughout the entire lifespan of the animals. Farmers are under contracts that dictate what inputs they must purchase, improvements they must make, and how their farms are operated. Tyson also controls the processing and distribution of the end product. Industrial agriculture works the same way from providing crop seed, exerting control over the inputs farmers are required to purchase and use, the commodity prices they will sell their crop for, and the distribution and processing of those harvests. The *Living Planet Report 2016* notes, "A few transnational corporations such as big food traders, producers and retailers increasingly direct what and how food is produced across the globe... In the farming sector, 1% of farms now control 65% of agricultural land (FAO, 2014). These large farms dominate production methods in the market (FAO, 2014). Large-scale farmers and landowners often have a dominant political and economic role and are able to maintain their positions of power and privilege, leaving small farmers at a disadvantage (Piketty, 2014). Similarly, powerful groups of crop breeders, pesticide and fertilizer manufacturers, grain traders and supermarket retailers encourage food systems in which uniform crop commodities can be produced and traded on a massive scale (IPES-Food, 2016)."

Big Ag has learned one lesson from the historic federal antitrust break-up of the Beef Trust. It now goes one step further by directing a significant portion of its billion dollar lobbying efforts toward the government and our elected officials to gain their complicity and their "trust."

Will Harris was at White Oak Pastures, his farm in Bluffton, Georgia, when we last spoke. "The first step toward a solution is realizing that the whole system based on short term profit. The public corporation's mandate to profit for their shareholders, is the direct reason for these problems we have. Most of the sweeping powerful decisions made by corporate businesses come from a short-term perspective. My family has been on this farm 152 years and my grandchildren here will be the 6th generation.

We make decisions generationally. I'm planting trees right now that won't benefit me, they won't benefit my children much, but they'll benefit my grandchildren. When publicly traded companies are driven by their quarterly and annual reports, the CEO does not have the right to think generationally. When they make a decision, they are beholden to the earnings of the shareholder. That's their obligation.

"The industrialization and commoditization and centralization of agriculture was done to make food abundant and cheap and safe. And it made it wastefully abundant and obscenely cheap and safe probably in the acute sense of the word. It was wildly successful in achieving what it set out to achieve but it had horrible unintended consequences that were, until now, unnoticed. Consequences that were terribly destructive for animal welfare, the land and water and air and the rural economy. Agriculture was kinder and gentler for the animals, environment and community before we reinvented it. The question now is can we reinvent it again to go back?

"I don't think that the trap we're in was designed by anybody. It evolved. And it evolved in a horrible way. The corporate executives are not evil, but they are greedy. And if government ever was the solution, by now I believe it's too late because it's now owned by these powerful corporations."

Is a new and necessary era of antitrust in our near future?

Historically, it takes a significant event or crisis to galvanize public opinion and force government to act.

Upton Sinclair's 1904 novel, *The Jungle*, which depicted the horror for workers and animals in Chicago's meatpacking plants, galvanized public opinion in support of President Theodore Roosevelt's successful antitrust initiatives breaking up the Beef Trust.

In 2008, the government brandished the sword of antitrust recourse amidst the precipitous economic downturn of the Great Recession. Should we have broken up the banks? Not to spite them for causing the crisis, but to remedy it and to best insure it couldn't happen in a similar way again. Were they really "too big to fail?"

In pushing for the New Deal in the 1930s, President Franklin D. Roosevelt said, "We had to struggle with the old enemies of peace – business and financial monopoly, speculation, reckless banking, class antagonism, sectionalism, war profiteering. They had begun to consider the government of the United States as a mere appendage to their own affairs. We know now that government by organized money is just as dangerous as government by organized mob."

90 years later, in pushing for a New Farm Bill and a Green New Deal, the resistance is coming from the very same enemies.

There will come a moment in time in the near future, if Big Ag continues to succeed in both destroying our environment and our health, when Mr. Heat is in our living room. Global warming will reach a point where smiles vacate human faces, when a wariness permeates expressions, tension becomes fear, and it will become clear to more and more and then most of us: that we are in deep trouble. We will then understand who exactly is responsible and that something game-changing must be done. At that point, Big Ag's billion dollar spends on product advertising and PR, on political lobbying and currying political favor will become worthless. At that point, at the precipice of crisis as nature's systems begin to collapse and our economic system begins to falter and each of us realizes how truly vulnerable we are, realizes that day to day we are just six meals away from the breakdown of social order and we're beginning to stock up on food, the government will have to act and antitrust will be one of their tools. But if the year is 2035, our global temperatures will have increased 2°. We will try to put on the brakes with increasing resolve and desperation — only to realize that it will be too late.

We cannot wait until then. Or anywhere close.

Historically, it takes a significant event or crisis to galvanize public opinion and force government to act. For our special generation the time is now. The looming catastrophe of global warming is that event.

We have to rise up with our compassionate activism to broaden awareness and urgency, to present the government with a plan and to force government to take action implementing it.

The World Wildlife Fund's *Living Planet Report 2016* asks the question on many people's minds today. "What is keeping the unsustainable food system in place? Many of the patterns, systemic structures and mental models that shape the current food system will prevent us from enjoying a viable food system in the future. This system has already helped usher the Earth into the Anthropocene. Continuing without significant change will lead to further, untenable transgressions of Planetary Boundaries and diminish the very resources on which the food system is based. New models of both production and consumption are needed to form a sustainable, resilient food system that can absorb and recover quickly from shocks, while continuously providing food to many more people (Macfadyen et al., 2015)."[107]

Corporations will get on board.

Why?

The Arch-Villain has proven stalwartly intractable to date. Brutal Capitalism is in full global bloom.

Because we, the consumers, are a corporation's life blood: we create and sustain their market share. Our informed individual actions about what to purchase and what to avoid are collectively very powerful. Our word-of-mouth is even more consequential.

Wayne Pacelle writes in *The Humane Economy*, "When a company's greatest fear is a knowledgeable, ethically alert customer, that company has problems that won't go away. Any economist will tell you that when new, relevant information is acquired on the supply side, then people will adjust their expectations on the demand side. This is happening throughout our economy, as more and more of us ask questions and act on the answers. And one by one, cruel industries find themselves on the wrong side of a market that is changing, fundamentally, forever, and for the better."[108]

A brand is a corporation's identity, its currency, its value. They spend billions of dollars promoting their brands. Undermining and preventing essential change makes them pariahs on the wrong side of history and will irrevocably tarnish their brands. A 2018 research study by the Shelton Group found that, "86% of consumers believe that companies should take a stand for social issues," and that, "64% of those who said it's 'extremely important' for a company to take a stand on a social issue said they were 'very likely' to purchase a product based on that commitment."[109] With our social media tools and skillsets, consumers have more power than ever to broadcast their opinions, to elevate or to attack and stigmatize a brand.

Perhaps even more importantly, corporations are run by human beings. Executives who are frequently exceptionally smart, skillful employees who have risen through the ranks based on their singular dedication to the success and profitability of that corporation want, as we all want, the same thing: a healthy planet for ourselves, for our families and loved ones, and for future generations to experience and enjoy. We all want to return home at night into our communities, proud of what we are accomplishing and who we are working for, successful, well regarded, heads held high.

Corporations will get on board when they realize the global economic system can and will break down due to the consequences of global warming — that no-one is too big to fail if we all fail.

And this is why the corporations destined to be the most successful going forward will get on board sooner rather than an hour and a half before doomsday:

A New Farm Bill, if enacted soon, very soon, will become *the* essential step that will enable, shape and lead to *the* solution: The New Economy.

The $26 *trillion* dollar New Economy.

That New Economy.

There is a vast marketplace and tremendous business opportunity in the New Economy. The corporations who realize this opportunity soonest and take the lead utilizing their vast wealth to get ahead of the change, to have an active role in accelerating and shaping it, will have a lucrative future. The money to be made in the future will be made by the businesses embracing the New Economy, by retooling and reconfiguring to embrace *its values*, not the fading corporations clinging intractably in decline and increasing despair to the values of the old economy.

Ones that refuse, as our Arch Villain has steadfastly and stridently done to date, will become pariahs. Pariahs will not be participants in any meaningful way in the New Economy. Nobody wants to work for a pariah; fewer and fewer will want to purchase a pariah's products.

Corporations with their vast wealth and large-scale operations have a unique ability to leverage change. *Living Planet Report 2016* notes, "Concentration of power, when wielded responsibly, can also bring positive change (Stephan et al., 2016): companies with significant market share are able to single-handedly create new standards and put pressure on their supply chains to innovate toward, for example, emissions reductions."[110]

Corporations deciding to make this shift can discover a government willing to assist them. In World War II, American industry retooled itself in just a matter of months, mobilizing for the war effort. The government was there to catalyze this transition. Why wait for the day when Mr. Heat is seated on our sofa and has it smoldering? Why wait for the government to strike with antitrust? Align and partner with the government in this transition.

This is the government's essential role in a democracy in times of necessary change: forging the new policy, stalwartly implementing the new direction while enforcing it so it isn't diluted, corrupted, or subverted.

Imagine our government as if it were a race car, or a rocket ship, or an athlete. This is what it's designed and built for, the big race, the launch, the championship game. For the players on our team, our democratically elected representatives, this is what they've come on board for, to be a part of crafting and drafting visionary historic legislation bold enough and intelligent enough to take on *the* challenge of our time. Heroes can step forward. Game on.

The asset, the measuring stick, is soil carbon content and optimized carbon sequestration. Regenerative agriculture is impassioned farmers, their livelihoods in full bloom, animals back on the land, exposed soil covered, erosion ended. It's the soil microbiome rebounding and after just a short time, nutrient-dense robust crops yielding unprecedented farmer profitability. It's healthy real food returning to our shelves and into our bodies, decreasing risk of superbug pandemics, decreasing obesity, diabetes, cancer, heart attacks, strokes, other dis-eases, and health care costs. It's all of this as scientists around the world begin to measure, with smiles returning to their faces... the decreasing acceleration of global warming.

A New Farm Bill is huge. It will take tremendous effort to draft it, pass it into law and set in motion with the necessary speed to lock our front door and keep Mr. Heat at bay.

But it will enable The Great Healing.

And... I love things designed with bonus features and "added value." While ensuring our survival, what will be the biggest ride-along, the huge bonus value from achieving The Great Healing?

The New Economy.

What is the New Economy? Come see.

V

The New Economy

We have the skills and the toolset. We have the singular solution and with it, the ability to meet the challenge of global warming. Awareness leads to widespread understanding and a resolve, a determination. One by one, many of us, many more every day, soon a majority of us will take the bold essential action necessary to succeed and prevail.

Mr. Heat has entered our living room. As we make it clear to him that he is unwanted, and take action to restrain him, he and his intemperate companions will doddle and loiter, reluctant to leave even as their threat is diminished, lingering as the uninvited can tend to do. When they finally turn away and leave us, which our compassionate activism and our government resolve leave them no choice but to do, and we rise and walk them to the door, we will discover a surprising alchemy.

The shift to regenerative agriculture and pastured animals, and every other change we implemented to reduce our greenhouse gas emissions while forcing Mr. Heat and his accomplices outside and away, has changed the composition of our door. It is now a *golden* door.

As we step through it, we will behold beauty and health and riches as the prosperity of the economy we have created to combat Mr. Heat and protect our Anthropocene home is now manifest — realized beyond our imaginings — the New Economy.

The New Economy is sustainable, earth friendly, and just.

Our golden door is also Lady Liberty's golden door because we will have more fully realized our democracy.

The 2018 report, *Unlocking the Inclusive Growth Story of the 21ˢᵗ Century*, from the Global Commission on the Economy and Climate that includes former heads of government, business leaders and economists, reveals that strong action to fight global warming can create 65 million new low-carbon jobs and add $26 *trillion* to the global economy *between now and 2030*. It strongly advocates that all governments incentivize economies to move rapidly in this direction: "This is the only growth story of the 21ˢᵗ century. It will result in efficient, livable cities; low-carbon, smart and resilient infrastructure; and the restoration of degraded lands while protecting valuable forests. We can have growth that is strong, sustainable, balanced, and inclusive."[111]

The New Farm Bill will enable a new generation of young American farmers to begin regenerative farming and humane animal husbandry and succeed in making a good living. Carbon sequestration in reinvigorating soil will increase exponentially — and that soil will be growing healthier food for all of us. Tens of thousands of livelihoods, given a chance to be discovered, will be realized. Hundreds of thousands of new agriculture jobs will lead to the revitalization of rural communities, small-towns, and regional economies across America.

The New Economy is also a humane economy. Wayne Pacelle writes, "We can produce high-quality goods, services, or creative content and also honor animal protection values in the process. We can feed the world's surging population without resorting to extreme confinement of animals... Factory farming, for example, is the creation of human resourcefulness detached from conscience. What innovations in agriculture might come about by human resourcefulness guided by conscience?" [112]

Millions more new jobs are created in the lucrative, burgeoning renewables and clean energy sector. As of 2018, over 3.2 million Americans work in solar, wind, energy efficiency, clean vehicles, and other clean energy jobs outnumbering fossil fuel jobs 3 to 1. [113] [114] That number will increase dramatically.

Millions of workers will find employment retrofitting existing buildings to be GHG neutral. More and more property owners will discover how energy efficient climate-neutral structures are — and how much cheaper they are to run.

This is a new Marshall Plan, a *New* New Deal. This is what we have a government for. To lead. To lead our nation intelligently into the future, keeping our economy thriving and by extension positioning our nation as a global leader in technology, industry, innovation; and as an example of not only a highly functioning democracy, but a fair, equitable, moral, and honorable one.

The Global Commission on the Economy and Climate also noted, "Ambitious climate action does not need to cost much more than business-as-usual growth... We are not making progress anywhere near fast enough. While many private sector players are stepping-up, policy-makers in most countries still have the hand-brake on." [115] Helen Mountford, the lead author, told Reuters that, "There's still a perception that moving toward a low-carbon path would be costly. What we are trying to do with this report is once and for all put the nails in the coffin on that idea." [116]

In 2015, Naomi Klein and the group drafting the Leap Manifesto worked with a team of economists and determined that the money to pay for this global transformation is available from these areas: "An end to fossil fuel subsidies (will generate $775 billion globally annually), financial transaction taxes ($650 billion, according to the European Parliament), increased resource royalties, higher income taxes on corporations and wealthy people (for example, a 1% increase on billionaire's alone would raise $45 billion according to the United Nations), a progressive carbon tax ($450 billion), 25% cuts to the top 10 military defense budgets ($325 billion)." In addition, the closing of international tax havens could constitute the largest potential revenue source of all of these.[117]

Stephanie Kelton, Andres Bernal and Greg Carlock, in their article *We Can Pay for a Green New Deal*, suggest that a better question to ask than "How are we going to pay for it?" is, "'What's the best use of public money?' Giving it away to the top 1 percent who don't spend it, widening already dangerous wealth and income gaps? Or investing it in a 21st century, low-carbon economy by rebuilding America's infrastructure, bolstering resilience, and promoting good-paying jobs across rural and urban communities?"[118]

They add this important insight: "The federal government can spend money on public priorities without raising revenue, and it won't wreck the nation's economy to do so... It's how the U.S. economy has been functioning for nearly half a century. That's the power of the public purse... Anything that is technically feasible is financially affordable. And it won't be a drag on the economy unlike the climate crisis itself, which will cause tens of billions of dollars worth of damage to American homes, communities and infrastructure each year. A Green New Deal will actually help the economy by stimulating productivity, job growth and consumer spending, as government spending has often done."[119]

The Green New Deal resolution states, "using a combination of the Federal Reserve, a new public bank or system of regional and specialized public banks, public venture funds and such other vehicles or structures that the select committee deems appropriate, to ensure that interest and other investment returns generated from public investments made in connection with the plan will be returned to the treasury, reduce taxpayer burden and allow for more investment."[120]

Author and Founder of the Public Banking Institute, Ellen Brown, points out, "A network of public banks could fund the Green New Deal in the same way President Franklin Roosevelt funded the original New Deal... Infrastructure projects of the sort proposed in the Green New Deal are 'self-funding,' generating resources and fees that can repay the loans. For these loans, advancing funds through a network of publicly owned banks will not require taxpayer money and can actually generate a profit for the government. That was how the original New Deal rebuilt the country in the 1930s when the economy was desperately short of money."[121]

Public Banks can be an invaluable resource in rebuilding community economies as mentioned in Chapter 4. Ellen Brown offers this seminal insight, "This annual injection of new money not only can be done without creating price inflation; it actually needs to be done to reverse the massive debt bubble now threatening to propel the economy into another Great Recession. Moreover, the money can be added in such a way that the net effect will not be to increase the money supply. Virtually our entire money supply is created by banks as loans, and any money used to pay down those loans will be extinguished along with the debt."[122]

The New Economy: earth-friendly and just, regionally acclimated. The shift, the mindset, can be applied to all industries including our food industry (healthy food), our medical industry (single payer, Medicare for All), and the fossil fuel industry (conversion to 100% clean energy).

. . .

Big Ag and the food and fossil fuel industries are spending billions of dollars to try and prevent or delay the rise of a New Farm Bill. Multinational and domestic corporations with entrenched, and in their mind, intractable modes of operations will continue to try and thwart significant change — although the incentives for them to shift and participate meaningfully in the New Economy are increasingly clear.

What we might not all be aware of is there is *another* very powerful villain, a separate sinister force steadfastly opposed to change. This villain thrives in darkness, in anonymity, its leaders much prefer to avoid public scrutiny. They direct and impose their agenda from behind a curtain.

As with Hazel, our photogenic triplewart sea devil, it is essential for our survival that we illuminate our path. Our light is one of awareness, the understanding that awareness leads to, and the compassionate activism that understanding in turn inspires.

Our light enables us to peer behind the curtain, to illuminate this villain and to reveal its darkness.

This villain is a cabal, a group of individuals that have made their fortunes in our current economy, most in industries that, because of the damage they do to our environment, will not be able to participate in this New Economy. Viability in the New Economy will not be the path for corporations that refuse to adapt their operations to the principals of the New Economy: sustainable, earth friendly, humane, and just.

This cabal has chosen a specific battleground and is allocating its financial riches to dangerously effective use through its organizations, think-tanks and political action committees (PACs), to further its interests. That battleground is our social order. What's at stake is democracy itself.

If we look at this conflict in its purest form, which is in the following arena, the villain reveals itself.

The Commons vs. Privatization

Seen through this lens, the majority of our politicized issues, virtually any issue you can think of, however disparate, become interrelated — and the battle line becomes clear.

A New Economy, sustainable, earth-friendly, humane, and just, in essence has an overriding focus on protecting the greater commons, the planet, for the greater good, for all of us to share.

Part of a just economy and an invigorated democracy is a robust national commons: Well-maintained, efficiently operating public institutions, infrastructure and assets. Public schools, libraries, post offices, national museums, local and national parks, public roads, and public lands.

Public utilities including water, power, and gas, should be affordable and publicly owned. 63% of the 3,175 electric utilities in the U.S. are publicly owned. Their rates are 6.9% lower than the rates charged by investor-owned utilities.[123] The Clean Power Plan can be expanded to the point where our electricity is free. The internet, even though a modern invention, is a natural resource and a public utility. Net neutrality should be protected so the internet remains easily affordable and uniformly accessible, this powerful high-speed tool available to everyone.

Social security, national healthcare, quality modern education, childcare and other safety net social services are part of the commons. Every one of the world's leading economies has its own version of a national health care system in place. Except us. Citizens of these countries are receiving better and far more cost-effective health care than what is available to Americans. Their governments shoulder the responsibility of keeping health costs and their medical industries in check. The average life expectancy in many countries today, such as in the Scandinavian countries, is now five years longer than ours.

Naomi Klein asks, "How do we build the public sector so we, the *public*, feel part of it? We should all feel ownership over public housing, public resources."[124]

The privatization of virtually anything that is or can be privatize-able is the objective of this villain behind the curtain. Because there can be money made by doing so. And because there is an authoritarian (and anti-democratic) element of social control inherent in gaining control of these resources — a power which this villain finds immensely desirable.

The Threat to the Commons

The threat to the commons is the ideology of neoliberalism. The name "neoliberalism" can be confusing because it contains "liberal" and implies "new liberalism" — however, this ideology is anything but. Naomi Klein characterizes neoliberalism as "an extreme form of capitalism that started to become dominant in the 1980s under Ronald Reagan and Margaret Thatcher, but since the 1990s has been the reigning ideology of the world's elites, regardless of partisan affiliation... The primary tools of this project are all too familiar: privatization of the public sphere, deregulation of the corporate sphere, and low taxes paid for by cuts to public services, and all of this locked in under corporate-friendly trade deals. It's the same recipe everywhere, regardless of context, history, or the hopes and dreams of the people who live there."[125]

One label for this doctrine is "brutal capitalism." Brutal capitalism, characterized by myopic self-interest, shameless greed, and ruthless competition lacking in concern for human and environmental well-being, has now created a huge wealth disparity in America. The richest families, the top 1% of Americans, possess over 40% of the nation's wealth while 78% of American workers — nearly four out of every five of us — now live paycheck to paycheck. Almost as many say they are in living in debt.[126] One out of five Americans now has more credit-card debt than savings for an emergency. Nearly 40% of United States citizens, living in what for decades was perceived worldwide as one of the most prosperous nations, do not have enough money saved to cover a $1,000 emergency room visit or a car repair.[127]

In their book, *Daring Democracy*, Francis Moore Lappé and Adam Eichen posit that from the neoliberalist perspective, "Human beings coming together, deliberating, setting standards, and choosing the rules governing the market — in other words, democracy — is increasingly viewed as downright dangerous. Yet it is, of course, the only safeguard of basic fairness, healthy communities, and our irreplaceable commons."[128] They summarize the rise in the 1970s of American Neoliberalism — which they term the Anti-Democracy Movement — with its leadership centering around a small group of billionaire families including the Koch, DeVos, and Mercer clans. Their well-funded think-tanks include the American Enterprise Institute, the Heritage Foundation and the Cato Institute.

One neoliberalist strategy is to delegitimize democracy's norms and institutions, reducing our trust and faith in our democracy itself. Francis Moore Lappé and Adam Eichen observe this "has helped turn Americans against the key institution that could have been used to help them — their government."[129]

One citizen, one vote is superseded by "We know what's best for you." Suppressing the vote by gerrymandering districts, making it difficult to vote by limiting access to polling places, corrupting politicians with financial contributions to create a bastion of defense when votes don't go their way — all these political tools get a useful assist from neoliberal efforts to create an overriding sense of individual powerlessness, malaise, disenchantment, and hopelessness as a means of fomenting political disinterest. Jane Mayer's acclaimed 2016 book, *Dark Money*, investigates and expands on this.

Another strategy is to divide us. Into this cauldron of anxiety and discontent, billions of dollars have been invested in the politics of division. The goal is to make us feel divided — by race, by religion, by gender, by social class. It is achieved by instilling fear and keeping us fearful: of change, of the unknown, of the "other."

Neoliberalism seeks, as in the time of the Luddites, to restrict the commons, to diminish our access, in effect to keep most of us, the "commoners," out of the commons. The more privatized our world is, the more it becomes controllable, exploitable, and less democratic.

Increasing numbers of us wonder, despite the overwhelming, irrefutable scientific evidence, what is the reason behind the ongoing steadfast denial of global warming? Chris D'Angelo reported in the HuffPost in 2019: "The Mercers divvied out a total of $15,222,302 to 37 nonprofits in

2017, according to the foundation's most recently available 990 tax form... Roughly one-third of all the foundation's 2017 contributions — just shy of $5 million — went to nonprofits that oppose federal regulations targeting greenhouse gas emissions, challenge the scientific consensus that human-caused climate change is an immediate crisis, or promote or funnel cash to denial proponents. Kent Davies, director of the Climate Investigations Center, told HuffPost, 'It appears that climate denial is a priority of the Mercer family.'"[130]

For Naomi Klein in *No Is Not Enough*, the answer is clear: "Climate change, especially at this late date, can only be dealt with through collective action that sharply curtails the behavior of corporations such as ExxonMobil and Goldman Sachs. It demands investment in the public sphere... Climate change detonates the ideological scaffolding on which contemporary conservatism rests. To admit that climate change is real is to admit the end of the neoliberal project... There is a reason why science has become such a battle zone - because it is revealing again and again that neoliberal business as usual leads to a species-threatening catastrophe."[131]

Naomi Klein understands, "So many of the crises we are facing are symptoms of the same underlying sickness: a dominance-based logic that treats so many people, and the earth itself, as disposable... We all know that our historical moment demands transformative change... The hesitancy to identify the *systems* we are up against are robbing us of our full potential... If we want a shot at avoiding catastrophic warming, we need to start a grand economic and political transition *right now*."[132]

American Democracy

In an ideal Democracy, governance truly reflects the will of the people, the mandate determined by the majority, not corporate interests or private interests. One person, one vote.

Realize the power of your compassionate activism. Being engaged in the issues of our time and in the process of shaping our democracy is emboldening. It is enlivening. It can be exciting, even thrilling.

To toss your hat in the ring and get involved, as Frances Moore Lappé and Adam Eichen recognize, is to experience your freedom as a citizen to participate in power. "It is not democracy that is failing. It is the lack of democracy that's taking us down — primarily, the growing crisis of concentrated wealth controlling our political system. So, the big threat we can take on is citizens' lost hope for real democracy."[133]

Cure this with your compassionate activism. Inspire others. Rather than fighting against something, fight *for* something. There has been no more important time — ever — than now.

Widespread awareness of exactly what neoliberalism is will hasten its retreat, behind smaller and smaller curtains. Neoliberalists want us to be polarized, to believe that we are divided. But a majority of Americans, 70% and growing, are increasingly concerned about global warming and want our government to take action to limit greenhouse gases.

On issue after issue regarding the environment, fairness and justice, on protecting the commons, we, at our core are not a divided people, so the solutions are nonpartisan.

Neoliberals do not have numbers and the authoritarian darkness of their doctrine underlying their corrupt message will not stand in the light of a just and sustainable world. Francis Moore Lappé and Adam Eichen write, "So in this moment of extreme threat, we may come to see that the opposite of evil is no longer goodness. It is courage. Goodness without action isn't good enough."[134]

We have to move rapidly.

Providing our elected leaders with a vision and a plan, insisting they state their unequivocal support of or opposition to it, and demanding legislation to mobilize change, we are harnessing ourselves to a very important tool. Advocate for the Green New Deal. Insist on a New Farm Bill — not one to replace the existing one in 2023, but one to supersede it in 2020. This cannot happen soon enough. We must slow down Mr. Heat and his companions, then stop them in their tracks and force them away.

Our democracy, our government is there for us. Let's put it to use to achieve The Great Healing.

We, A Special Generation

Like Hazel, shine your light into the darkness, be aware, ever more aware. Shine your light at the darkness. Always be learning, smarter, wiser, open to new ideas. Increase your understanding, and with it, your compassion.

Imagine how powerful you can be. Realize how powerful you are.

Robert Wolf, in *Building the Agricultural City*, writes, "A new world, now in embryo, is struggling to be born. Human scale communities and human scale sustainable institutions are arising around the planet, and they are arising in reaction to the inhumanity and self-destructive tendencies of the present system."[135]

Like the "little earth men," the meerkats, do not fear a fight.

Each one of us is facing the Cape cobra. Right now. Feel the power as part of your community, your power in ever increasing numbers. Discover what your role as part of the solution will be.

"The interplay between lofty dreams and earthly victories has always been at the heart of moments of deep transformation. The breakthroughs won for workers and their families after the Civil War and during the Great Depression, as well as for civil rights and the environment in the sixties and early seventies, were not just responses to crisis. They were responses to crises *that unfolded in times when people dared to dream big,* out loud, in public."[136] That is Naomi Klein's exquisite observation in *No Is Not Enough.*

Like Lucinda Monarch, we are a special generation.

As the plant nectars in the meadows were waning and the degree of the sun's light was changing each day in the sky, the moment arrived when she felt it was time — she knew it was time — to begin her journey. Neither she, nor any of the monarchs she would meet on the way, had ever seen their destination — but each one of them knew the direction they were going and that they'd recognize it when they got there.

For us, the temperature of the globe is rising, natural disasters are increasingly commonplace and of increasing severity. More and more events, from the global to the intimately personal, are signaling us. We sense it — that something is really wrong — and getting worse. In our gut we are feeling an upwelling, a growing resolve. And we know this: It is time for each of us to rise in awareness of our task at hand.

Lucinda had no second thoughts. If she didn't migrate, she would die. It was time.

We are facing a similar choice — but within our complex society and our busy mob scenes, we have many preoccupations, lots on our minds. There are many reasons, many rationales, and many opportunities to resist change, to resist getting involved and taking action, to resist risk.

For the monarchs scattered across a thousand miles of fields and forests, each one understood nature's signal — that it was time to fly. Some of us, like Greta Thunberg, already know what we are facing and are taking action. Others are wary, watching; still others unaware or in denial. We are a special generation and we will rally. The question is how soon to get to critical mass? It can't be too soon to ensure our survival.

The Five Compassions are powerful tools. A powerful way of living. Do everything you can to hasten us toward the essential tipping points when significant change will happen and manifest quickly.

Naomi Klein describes the meeting she attended in 2015 in Toronto with leaders of movements representing a broad spectrum of issues, the meeting that ultimately produced the Leap Manifesto, "As we talked, that became a frame within which everything seemed to fit: the need for a shift from a system based on endless taking — from the earth and from one another — to a culture based on caretaking, the principle that when we take, we also take care and give back. A system in which everyone is valued, and we don't treat people or the natural world as if they were disposable... Though many of us (including me) had originally thought we were convening to draft a list of policy goals, we realized that this shift in values, and indeed in morality, was at the core of what we were trying to map."[137] Care and caretaking. This is compassion.

Jean-Jacques Rousseau, a Swiss philosopher who influenced the progress of the Enlightenment throughout Europe in the 1700s, asks, "What wisdom can you find that is greater than kindness?"

Compassionate activism will bring about The Great Healing.

CONCLUSION

I hope I was a good lookout on my watch.

I wanted to introduce you to exquisite creatures and their stories. Immersed in our daily mob scenes, utilizing tools, skillsets, and talents uniquely our own, each one of us is an exquisite creature. I hope you fully realize that.

I spotted a snake and I've alerted you. A Cape cobra directly ahead of us is set to strike. Each of you are now aware of the threat and its severity. We have to face our Cape cobra. Right now.

Imagine how potent our collective power can be — resolute, rising and taking action together. Realize how much you can contribute to it, and will benefit from it.

Now is the time.

You could choose to ignore the threat and dive down your bolt hole, but the Cape cobra will follow you down there. You could choose to flee and perhaps survive another day, but your community will be thinned out and lost without your help. And your day to day wandering will be in a world increasingly more precarious, scavenging by yourself, for yourself, without the help of your mob, of each one of us protecting one another.

I'm not suggesting Big Ag is the equivalent of a lethally venomous snake. Snakes are fascinating essential creatures. They hunt to eat but they do not consume more than what they need to survive. They are not willfully malicious, greedy, or environmentally toxic.

Joanna Macy writes in *World as Lover, World as Self,* that the task of "restoring our ravaged Earth... not only puts us in league with the stones and the beasts, but also in league with the beings of the future. All that we do to mend our planet is for their sake, too. Their chance to live and love our world depends in large measure on us and our uncertain efforts."[1]

As lookout, I can report one other thing with certainty:

It's all about compassion...

●　●　●

Thomas Q. Piglet is now Thomas Q. Pig. As you can see, he still has the pointy ears and an even bigger-than-big nose. He backs away from us, retreats as far as he can — although there's not too much space in this crowded transport truck.

Every interaction Thomas has had with humans has been unfriendly, if not painful, so he remains fearful. Once it was different, just for a moment — just that one time. The day when he was a piglet on another transport truck and he looked over at Jemarion and the other young human faces on the school bus, how they regarded him, their wide eyes and their smiles.

Thomas has never once in his whole life been allowed to be outside and bask in the warming sunshine, to eat field grass and frolic in it, to wander into some muddy soil to root around and snoggle in. He was unaware a date had been calendared for him — and that today that date has arrived. When his pen doors opened, Thomas Quicksilver seized the opportunity to dash out and find freedom. He was steered onto and crowded into this

animal transport truck.

He found the space to stand beside an opening in the metal side wall and he gazes out on the passing countryside, the green grass waving in the fields in a sunny breeze, tree leaves fluttering. Maybe, at long last, he's going to be allowed to wander out there. He hasn't lost hope.

Pigs are among the most intelligent animals, on a level with chimpanzees and dolphins.[2] He would recognize his mother if they crossed paths. Maybe she will be wherever it is he is going.

All of us, we animals, want the same things: to be able to avoid pain and suffering, to eat and live in places where we can relax and feel safe.

At what point will Thomas lose hope? As the transport drives within a mile of the slaughterhouse, smells began to reach him. The wafting scent of pigs. Thousands of them are delivered to this final destination each day. But there is another smell as well. Pigs have an acute sense of smell. They smell better than we do, and they smell more.[3] Thomas's nose is bigger than most, but each of them takes it in: The smell of the smoke billowing out of the processing plant's towering chimneys. Of pig body parts. It grows stronger — they realize that this place is getting closer. Thomas senses that this is not a safe place, it is not a good place.

That concern is what you see in Thomas's eyes now as the transport has stopped outside its destination.

The transport pulls into the yard; journey's end. As Thomas is forced out of the truck and herded toward an entry, he hears high pitched shrieks of terror — of panicked pigs within.

At what point will hope leave him? Thomas has lived so much of his life in fear. Does fear ebb as hope drains away? He is forced into the building, shoulder to shoulder with his companions. He has grown to maturity with them yet never had any opportunity to form social groups with any of them. As the sunlight leaves him and he advances into shadow, the screams are more acute, bone-chilling. Nothing is worse than the sound of the terror ahead, indoors, reverberating off machine metal and cement walls. The dominant smell now is fresh blood and entrails — and it's the smell of his kind.

Thomas Quicksilver, fleet of foot, glances around. He's done it before, he's spotted that door ajar, that escape path, that opportunity to dash to a safer better place, a kinder place, a sunlit place, to freedom. He's seen children's smiles, their adoring faces, he's just seen sunlit fields. Unlike his mother, he's still able of body. His heart beats rapidly but is heavy in this horrific place, a Hell on Earth. His soul is wounded — but he can still scurry. He hasn't lost hope. He'll find an open door, a sliver of a crack, a way out. He will find it. Here and now or here and hereafter.

Thomas Quicksilver, we cannot save you, we cannot comfort you in the slightest, we cannot improve your life. We cannot even communicate to you one thing that we really wish we could: That many of us, and many more of us with each new day, are aware of what factory farming is, and we are acting with our purchasing power, deciding that whatever we choose to eat, it will no longer include the products of factory farms. We will no longer sustain and enable this cruelty. We will no longer be complicit in allowing this shameful abomination to continue.

In the early Latin translations of the Bible, the word "dominion" was used declaring that God gave humans "dominion" over animals. Given Christianity's message of love and mercy, theologians are now interpreting that verse using the word "stewardship" instead, finding that more harmonious with passages appearing elsewhere in the Bible. Teachings like, "Blessed are the merciful," and "Whatever you do unto the least of these, you do unto Me."

We take responsibility. We own this and we are raising our voices and taking action to end the horror of factory farms so that future generations of animals will not suffer as you have.

· · ·

On the day I took this photo, Sherneka told me it was Sky's choice which colors to wear that day: pink and white.

A few months later, in September 2018, Hurricane Florence rolled into North Carolina bringing with it four days of damage, destruction, and unrelenting, record setting rain — up to 35 inches in some areas.

"The winds were very, very strong. It rained a lot. We knew the storm was coming so we had prepared food for a few days. We had extra batteries and water." The storm's intensity forced Jennifer Dudley, along with husband Corey and sons J'vion and Jemarion to leave their trailer home, "My family, along with my mom and two brothers, my sister and aunt, we all went to stay in a church nearby.

"That night the power went out, so we weren't able to cook. We had a generator so we could power up the TV to check the news and charge our phones." The tight-knit extended family played cards and told stories passing the time. However, the unrelenting rain merged with the flood waters now flowing down from inland elevations. "After one or two days, the bridge overflowed just down the road and the water started coming up to where we was and started coming in there." They had to leave the church while they still could. "When we left there, the water was so high there was no road, and if you didn't know there was a bridge there you would've never known."

They decided to drive back to their trailer home, which is at a small elevation in the pines, perhaps 30 feet above road grade. They advanced carefully along a road they could no longer see, as if they were driving on the surface of a lake. It was like driving down the middle of the Mississippi river — the fields to either side just one big wide river of water along with the road they were on. On either side of the road the now invisible embankment dropped off several feet. They had to stay on the road... At one point that was no longer certain. "The water was gushing up out from under one of the ditches and pouring across the road so if you wasn't careful going through there, water would push you on over into the ditch on the other side." They made it back to the unpaved path rising out of the water winding around pine trees up toward their home. They stopped midway up to look back: "The road and fields looked like a big ole' wide river, the water just flowing past." They learned later that further down, the road had washed away. If they lived beyond that they would have driven off an underwater cliff.

"Power was out for a week. The kids were out of school for a month. I was able to get to work. I work in a doctor's office. We opened up. If it was an emergency and you had to be seen, we'd see you, but we couldn't see anyone else because there was only one doctor who could get in. The other ones were stranded and couldn't get to us."

Just as we have a new name, "mega-fires," to describe the fires of increasing intensity and severity that are now routinely devastating western states, there are two new terms now in common use throughout the eastern United States to describe recent storms of record setting size and magnitude: one is "superstorms." The other is "500-year storms."

In the aftermath of Hurricane Florence, Mitch Colvin, the mayor of Fayetteville, observed, "Something has happened. You know, this is our second 500-year storm in two years."[4] It's actually their third in 19 years.

In September 1999, Hurricane Floyd, one of the most powerful Atlantic hurricanes ever recorded, threatened landfall along a five-state area, triggering one of the largest evacuations in U.S. history. It slammed into North Carolina with 105 mph winds and became the deadliest hurricane in 25 years, causing $6.5 billion in damage and killing 51 people. 46 factory farm waste lagoons were damaged spilling millions of gallons of hog waste into tributaries of the Cape Fear, Neuse and Tar rivers. More than 2 *million* turkeys and chickens, trapped in factory farm enclosures, died.

In 2016, a new "500-year storm," Hurricane Matthew, caused similar damage.[5] 26 North Carolinians died, 680,000 were without power, and rivers were cresting as much as a foot higher than flood levels during Hurricane Floyd. Nearly 2 million factory farmed animals died. Factory farm lagoons were breached and overflowed spilling hundreds of millions of gallons of hog waste along with E. coli and fecal coliform bacteria across flooded highways, rural roads and low-lying lands.

In 2018, once again, this time with Hurricane Florence, factory farm-enclosed animals were abandoned. 3.4 *million* chickens and thousands of pigs drowned. Julie Cappiello with Mercy For Animals writes, "Unlike companion animals, who by law must be included in government evacuation plans during natural disasters, farmed animals are afforded no legal protections. So, while floodwaters rush into factory farms, animals drown in cages and crates with absolutely no chance of survival. Meanwhile farmers flee with companion animals for safety. Drowning is one of the worst things imaginable. Submerged underwater, fully conscious, you panic, unable to call for help... It's easily one of the most terrifying ways to die."[6]

Devon Hall told me, "I knew, because of the work that I do, that there was going to be lagoons flooded, that there was going to be dead animals in the creeks, and in the river, but when you are going through something like that, your concern isn't for those animals. I was checking on family and friends. My truck is four-wheel drive, I have a generator, a spare generator, extra gas cans, and things like that, so I'm driving as far as I could in the nearby area to see what I could do to help people, but even at that I couldn't do much physically because I'm recovering, four days out from a back surgery. I'm not even driving. My wife, Alice is driving. I'm sitting on the passenger side. But we had to get out and do what we can to help people. That's what you do."

The call came in and he was asked if his REACH community center office could be used as a distribution center. Immediate "Yes." And once the flood waters subsided enough for the roads to reappear, relief supplies started arriving.

Global warming is turning California wildfires into megafires and making hurricanes like Florence more common and more severe. As temperatures rise, hurricanes tend to advance more slowly, their heavy rainfall a creeping deluge far greater than storms of years past, their fury prolonged creating wide swaths of brutal damage and destruction. With warming temperatures, the paths of North Atlantic hurricanes are also changing, migrating further and further north.

Faced with un-evolving and intractable local government leaders, bought and paid for by Big Ag and the multinational corporations behind factory farming, the residents of Duplin and Sampson counties are doing everything they can to try and change things for the better.

The word "nuisance" suggests something causing an annoyance, like a mosquito buzzing around your head — a bother, an irritation. In legal parlance, the phrase "nuisance lawsuit" actually has some teeth. It is a type of lawsuit utilized when something invades or interferes with another person's rights or their ability to enjoy their property. In July 2018, a verdict was reached in a nuisance lawsuit filed against Murphy Brown, LLC, a contractor subsidiary of the world's largest pork producer, Smithfield Foods, by two North Carolina residents whose property and living conditions had been impacted by the proximity of pig factory farms. They were awarded $26 million in damages. Can you imagine how badly impacted their living conditions were to motivate a jury to arrive at this amount for two people?

North Carolina legislators quickly drafted and put in place a new state law limiting punitive damages. The award was reduced to the new legally allowable maximum of $250,000.

In April 2018, a federal jury in a separate case, awarded 10 plaintiffs, who live near the Kinlaw hog farm, a 14,000-animal facility in Bladen County, and who endured the stench from pig waste lagoons and dead animals, were pestered by flies and had their homes covered with pig feces, $750,000 in compensation plus another $50 million in damages.[7]

Moving quickly to protect the factory farms and Big Ag corporate parent Smithfield Foods from further "nuisances," in June, 2018 the North Carolina General Assembly passed a bill, House Bill 467, which eliminates "the ability of the 270,000 who own property within a mile of a factory farm in North Carolina of their right to use the court system to seek compensation for negative health impacts, pain and suffering, diminished quality of life or lost income." Krissy Kasserman, in her article *Nobody Should Have Hog Poop on the Walls of Their Home*, continues, "You can only sue for lost property value, but let's be real — if your property is next door to a hog farm, it's likely worth very little... Corporate influence in our political system is one of the biggest threats to our health, environment, food and water."[8] Smithfield Foods has given $3,759,628 to state and federal candidates and political committees like the ones drafting and passing these laws.

Residents have also filed a class action lawsuit with help from Waterkeeper Alliance who stated, "Using the Civil Rights Act as a tool to stem industrial pollution may seem unorthodox to some, but it is not a new concept... Access to clean water — and air — are rights that are fundamental for citizens of a nation that is governed by the people. Ultimately, the residents of eastern North Carolina have been deprived of the rights to life, liberty and the pursuit of happiness promised to Americans by the Founding Fathers, and Waterkeepers have a responsibility to speak for them when their voices are not heard."[9]

In the aftermath of Hurricane Florence, residents found themselves faced with a new kind of disregard. "A lot of people around us lost their houses, lost everything they had, and they still aren't placed in a home," Jennifer told me. This was in 2019, four months after landfall. "FEMA came down, but FEMA denied the claims of a lot of people — a lot of people — which is why those people aren't back." Many residents who showed their storm damaged homes to the insurance company claim adjusters, and were then relocated to temporary housing or trailers because their dwellings were declared unlivable, subsequently found out that they were not approved for emergency assistance to repair or rebuild. Many were not in a financial position to take out a loan. "One of the girls I work with, when she walked back to her house the water was up to her neck. FEMA told her that her house was not livable, it was totally damaged. They got her in a trailer and they still denied her claim for money to repair her home. She lost everything. Even her clothes, everything."

Months later, people are still living in FEMA trailers or with friends and relatives. Devon acknowledges, "These things can contribute to a sense of hopelessness with some in our community. That is what we are fighting."

Neither Sherneka's wish, nor Sky's, nor Jemarion's, J'vion's or their parents, Jennifer and Corey's, have come true. The pig factory farms have not gone away. In fact, the number of pigs have increased and efforts are underway to further expand factory farmed chicken operations.

We will do everything we can to make your wish come true. Many of us, and many more of us each day, are making compassionate choices for animals. We are acting with our purchasing power, deciding that whatever we choose to eat, it will no longer include the products of factory farms. With our compassionate activism, we will do everything possible to end factory farming in North Carolina, and everywhere else.

As factory farms become increasingly unviable, smaller family farms will begin to reappear. Livestock will no longer cause a problem as there will be fewer animals and they will be pastured so their waste will be enhancing the soil. There will be no cesspool lagoons and pig-waste will no longer be distributed to over-saturation in fields through high-pressure sprayers or center pivot reel field irrigation systems. Unpleasant odors will no longer foul the air you breathe, and fecal particulate drift will no longer poison it. Far fewer children will develop asthma, and those that have asthma will find their episodes lessening in duration and intensity. Fewer infants and children will struggle to breathe, let alone lose their lives in the night, unable to do so. There will still be pigs transported for processing, but less of them, and they will be healthy pigs humanely and ethically raised on smaller family farms, like they once were. Dead man's trucks will be seldom seen. There will be no dead bins. The fecal-contaminated, bacteria laden waterways will heal and clear. Clean drinking water will return, not just in your counties, but for each of the 45% of North Carolinians whose water is no longer healthy.

Getting the animals back on pasture, especially with holistic planned grazing methods, will create healthy, fertile, microbially rich grasses and soil. It will enhance the soil's ability to sequester carbon. Your fields once again will be growing healthy foods, they will be major carbon sinks, contributing a beneficial effect on global warming for you, and for each one of us. You will once again, and at long last, be living amidst the natural beauty of your area, enjoying clean air, clean fields, healthy animals, healthy everything.

There will be more North Carolinian's employed on small family farms and more small family farmers. More farming jobs means the residents of Yellow Cut, of all of Duplin and Sampson counties, will have money to spend and a revitalized local economy will create new service and sales job opportunities. Grocery stores and supermarkets will reopen as residents' food budgets increase.

At long last, new home construction will begin along the roadway Sky continues to take to school. New mobile homes will arrive and be set in place — set to stay. People will be able to afford to make home improvements and more money will stay in your local economy.

We will fight alongside you — as your local and state government no longer does. This is in their interest although they do not yet realize it. We know that your state is heavily gerrymandered, that multinational factory farming operations have contributed immense amounts of money to undermine your democracy, that laws are in place to suppress your voices, your community, your vote, and your rights to a safe, clean and healthy environment to live in.

Your beloved area will once again become a really nice place to live. One where you can open your windows to the day and the evening, and hang laundry in the clean fragrant breeze and cook food and eat outdoors under clear skies with friends and family.

We're on this.

"How wonderful it is that nobody need wait a single moment before starting to improve the world."
-Anne Frank

Anne Frank wrote *The Diary of a Young Girl*, while she and her family, who were Jewish, were in hiding from the Nazis from 1942 into 1944 during the World War II German occupation of the Netherlands. In 1944, they were found out and Anne was sent to the Bergen-Belsen concentration camp in Germany. In February 1945, at age 15, her life ended there. But her compassion, and her life's ability to touch us, have never died. Over 70,000,000 copies of her diary have been read.

Thomas Quicksilver spent the entirety of his life in a CAFO, a concentrated animal feeding operation, a concentration camp for animals. He was sent to slaughter in November 2018. He never once was given the chance to run around in sun light, to spend time foraging in the wet fields amidst grass and bugs and all kinds of scents and mysteries, or to root around and play in muddy wet soil. Only once did he ever see a human being smile.

Sherneka Johnson and Sky Smith along with other residents of Duplin and Sampson counties, have lived their lives side by side with factory farms, with all the pestilence, degradation, and horror that goes with it, treated with disrespect and disdain by an industry interested in relentless profit — profit regardless of the environmental consequences, the illness and disease, the loss of quality of life, the "nuisance" their factory farms are creating. Residents are trapped economically, with increasingly limited rights or recourse, without empathy or compassion.

Devalued as human beings, they have not lost their dignity or their determination.

His Holiness the Dalai Lama has said, "Kindness and compassion are not luxuries; they are necessities for our human species to survive."

Joan Halifax, in *Principled Compassion*, writes, "We must recognize that we have no alternative but to cultivate radical compassion at this time... Our survival depends on us cultivating the courageous and wise qualities of mind and heart that will deliver us into a future that is characterized by relational well-being with and for all species. We have to take responsibility for nourishing a future that is not only sustainable but is characterized by the flourishing of all beings."[10]

Sherneka and Sky, J'vion, Jemarion, Jennifer, Corey, and Devon, we are working for this. We want the Farm Bill replaced by a New Food and Farm Act. We all want to more fully realize Democracy in America. That is a start to rebuilding and reinvigorating places like Duplin county, your beloved Yellow Cut, your shire.

Your strength of character, your perseverance, and your dignity are an inspiration. Whether nearby, or far away, we care, and in increasing numbers, we are on this.

•   •   •

Brady was at work recently. He was assisting at an internal medicine clinic, and in-between patients, when the call came on his cellphone. He didn't recognize the number. But his heart started racing, he sensed it was important — something was going on. He went off by himself into an unoccupied patient room and closed the door. The caller said she was from a med school Brady had applied to. She was calling on behalf of the admissions committee. She congratulated him. "You have been accepted into medical school."

"I was jumping up and down in there. It was a pretty proud moment for myself. I was excited. I was 'whooping!' I was relieved. I was so happy. It was like, 'I can do it. I can get in!' It was humbling too. They had had probably thousands of other applications and they chose me."

He emerged and he told his co-workers. "They were screaming and shouting and hugging me. That was the biggest moment. You can finally actually verbally say to someone you got into medical school."

In college, Brady weighed 338 pounds and was morbidly obese. His life expectancy was 14 years lower compared to non-overweight men his age. Graver still, the death rate from heart disease and diabetes for him was "especially elevated." He was at higher risk, *right then and there at age 20*, of premature death from *all* causes, including injury and chronic respiratory infections.[11] He survived. His weight is now under 200 pounds. All of his physical ailments have disappeared, he is no longer pre-diabetic, he is no longer obese. He has recovered his health, regained his vitality, sharpened his intelligence, and now he has acceptance into medical school.

As a doctor, he will be invaluable to his patients and to us.

Each one of us has a vital role to play in human form at this critical time.

The solutions for Brady's health and well-being, and ours, are the same — it's the food we eat.

We take responsibility, we own this, and we are taking action. Many of us, many more of us each day, are aware of what unhealthy food is: junk food, processed foods, foods high in sugars, some of our favorite foods, meat and dairy from factory farms, GMO commodity crops, or food that includes ingredients of GMO seed origin. We are choosing to eat a mostly plant-based diet of whole, organic, healthy foods.

Honor your body temple, your life and its potential. For yourself, for those who love you, who depend on and need you — those you matter to.

The enormity of the pain, suffering, and premature death millions of Americans are experiencing is avoidable. The vast ocean of lost human potential is preventable. We are raising our voices and taking action to minimize the number of lives cut short from diabetes, heart attack, stroke, cancer, and diseases of the circulatory system or of the brain. And to minimize the grief of so many of us who have needlessly lost loved ones or friends. We all know people who are overweight and infirm, whose day to day is much less productive and fulfilling than it could be, who are harming themselves, unknowingly in part or in whole, with the food they are eating.

Brady's mother was overjoyed when he gave her the news. "I was thoroughly excited — excited for him and for myself because he was going to be okay. I no longer had to worry about his future."

"Seeing how happy he is now, how far he has come, how much confidence he has compared to before, I would never wish him any different." Tinna realizes that for Brady, losing the weight made all the difference in the world. "When he started losing the weight is when he started caring more about what he ate. Now he can go to the gym, he is able to do whatever he wants. He's been taking the dog on these long walks. He wants to be out by himself. I think he's working on his meditative or spiritual self-awareness. He's connected with his inner self a bit more, with who he is. It's wonderful."

Let's strive to change our medical care system back into a health care system. If your doctor isn't educated in healthy nutrition and addressing illness at cause, find a new doctor who is. As citizens in this democracy, we will push back against a medical industry whose paramount interest and overriding incentive is profit — not your health — by advocating health *care*, national health care like universal Medicare or another version of a national healthcare system like those of other leading nations the world over that guarantee and provide better health care for their citizens and at far lower cost than ours.

We will take the food industry to task by proposing surcharges on unhealthy foods, like a cigarette or soda-tax, commensurate with the health damage they cause.

The rising health care costs of our increasingly unhealthy and diseased population will cripple our country's economy. It doesn't have to. Let's not walk that path. Money saved from reducing the cost of healthcare, can be repurposed on education, on infrastructure, on research and new technologies, on the public commons and national wellbeing.

Human suffering due to poor health, illness and disease, is on a magnitude of the animal suffering on factory farms. The solution for both is the same.

Brady is going to thrive in med school. He will be a doctor with a purpose. Healthy eating, healthy living. I have a feeling his impact won't wait until the day he meets his first patient. He will influence his peers. He may even influence the nutrition education curriculum at his school.

I have a feeling.

. . .

Her thin tiny wings fluttering, lifting her along on a curving, wobbly path in the warming spring air, Lucinda descended from the forest of oyamel fir trees in the mountains of Central Mexico returning north. She found milkweed in southern Texas, and she laid her eggs there before dying.

While the number of farm families planting pesticide free milkweed corridors is growing, industrial agriculture farmers are using more Roundup than ever before as well as newer and even more lethal pesticides and herbicides. In 2018, the population of eastern monarchs, which range from the Rocky Mountains all the way across to the east coast and from the central U.S. up into Canada, has diminished further. Once numbering in the hundreds of millions, today, massed together, monarchs would only cover an area the size of 16 football fields. In the forest of oyamel fir trees they occupied 14.7% less acreage than they did just a year before.[12]

In late Spring, Joan and Nick Olson are pleased to see monarchs arriving back on Prairie Drifter farm.

Lucinda's offspring have an ability to perceive things we can't begin to understand. They're returning to Canadian meadows they've never seen — and they'll realize when they arrive that's their home. Their next migratory generation will know that their destination is thousands of miles to the south, at 7,000-foot altitude in mountains forested by trees that don't exist anywhere else, on a November 1st. If monarchs are capable of perceiving all of that, then perhaps, somehow, in some way, they can sense this:

Tens of thousands of us are aware of your plight, we are taking action to try and save you. Farmers are creating butterfly corridors, homeowners are creating butterfly friendly gardens, planting forage plants and milkweed in their yards. Scientists and townspeople in the mountains of Central Mexico are planting a new forest of oyamel fir trees at a 1,000 foot higher altitude so when the planet warms you can overwinter at the temperature you need to survive.[13]

We're taking on Big Ag as well — and they're going to pay, and pay handsomely, for what they've done to you and yours, and for a few other reasons as well. They are going to stop killing virtually every plant, animal, and microbe that lives in or above ground in fields far and wide, poisoning your milkweed, wiping out millions upon millions of you, and turning your migratory pathways into evermore perilous passages.

Lucinda, like you and your migratory generation, we too are a special generation.

"We are now at a point unlike any other in our story," observes philosopher Joanna Macy. "Perhaps we have, in some way, chosen to be here at this culminating chapter or turning point. We have opted to be alive when the stakes are high to test everything we have ever learned about interconnectedness and courage — to test it now when it could be the end of conscious life on this beautiful water planet hanging like a jewel in space.

"In primal societies rites of passage are held for adolescents, because it is then that the fact of personal death or mortality is integrated into the personality. The individual goes through the prescribed ordeal of the initiation rite in order to integrate that knowledge, so that he or she can assume the rights and responsibilities of adulthood. That is what we are doing right now on the collective level in this planet-time. We are confronting and integrating into our awareness our mortality as a species. We must do that so that we can wake up and assume the rights and responsibilities of planetary adulthood."[14]

Regenerative agriculture with the soil's ability to drawdown and sequester carbon from our atmosphere is our single solution for global warming. Soil health can ensure our survival and the monarch's as well.

Gabe Brown, North Dakota farmer and rancher, told me, "I used to farm in the conventional manner. When I woke up in the morning, I'd think about what I was going to kill that day... Weeds. Insects. Et cetera. Now I wake up thinking 'How can I bring more life to my farm?'"

Compassion is about getting away from killing.

The full rapid transition of American industrial agriculture to regenerative agriculture will stop all this killing while providing us our greatest savings. It will shift us away from Big Ag, the most polluting and Earth damaging industry on the planet. It will end the evisceration of the denizens of the soil, the living organisms that compose 90% of the living biomass on this planet. Industrial agriculture's chemical fertilizers, pesticides and herbicides will cease killing off the Earth's insects, Lucinda Monarch and her brethren, migratory birds and animals, and us.

Regenerative agriculture will enable our soil to begin to repair itself, soil that is the basis for all life on this planet — and it will enable the soil to exponentially increase its ability to sequester carbon which is, by itself, our singular solution to global warming.

Monarch companions, exquisite creatures, you are an inspiration.

Our solution is your solution. It is a time-honored solution. We owe our existence to the soil and we must entrust our survival to its health.

More and more of us are purchasing healthy, nutritious foods, food grown by regenerative farmers and ranchers. Our purchasing decisions support their livelihoods. We will set an example through our actions, and we will use our voices and our social media — our compassionate activism — making others aware, so that we can end the war on our soil, the war on our environment, on the planet itself, and on our very survival.

. . .

Marlon and I were sitting at a table in Martin Luther King, Jr., Park in South Memphis, Tennessee. The lake was before us, lush green lawns extended in every direction up to a beautiful forest of trees bordering us on all sides. We had just finished setting up a volleyball net. Church members are setting up picnic games and a barbeque area. They are expecting about 70 people by lunch time.

A woman approached us, smiling broadly. The second he saw her, Marlon stood up in surprise and embraced her. He wasn't expecting to see Otha Mae Mosley. Miss Otha is a deaf mute. She articulates words in a cropped way with a high-pitched inflection that I couldn't decipher. Marlon understood her perfectly. She spoke with us, and as he told me her story, she smiled acknowledging it, glancing back and forth between us. She reads lips.

"Miss Otha's house is right across from the church. Her kids are in

Knowledge Quest. She is the hardest working woman I've known in my life. Period. She will wake up every day and just start making the neighborhood better. On her property, she'd take a steak knife and start cutting the grass, clearing fence lines, the sidewalks — not just on her property but on other people's property, on vacant lots, anywhere in the neighborhood. Neighbors gave her proper yard tools. She keeps going. She'd cut and sweep those streets, and on a curb you'd think was clean, she'd have seven bags. I said, 'Every time I get a paycheck, you get a paycheck.' I put her on the payroll. The attention she paid to detail, her excellence. Her work ethic. These are the people I come into contact with all day long.''

It isn't just Miss Otha. Marlon knows we are all exquisite creatures.

He was born in a neighborhood that was beautiful and had a vibrant economy at the time, one that many people soon chose to move away from. As he grew up amidst deteriorating streets and schools and blighted buildings, and the loss of friends and loved ones, he never stopped dreaming, aspiring to run a business, to find a way to thrive. Other places offered greater opportunity, but Marlon decided not to leave this neighborhood to pursue his dream. He chose to make this place better, to turn it around. He discovered his livelihood, in turn enabling Theo, Yolanda, Michelle, and many others to find theirs. In extending a compassionate hand to his neighbors, he is restoring hope, value, and a sense of community to an underappreciated, undervalued shire. His optimism is contagious. He grows USDA certified organic produce from the soil on Green Leaf Learning Farm. The Extended Learning Academy has created educational opportunities and inspired young minds at every grade level. His Knowledge Quest counseling centers have saved or turned the lives around for residents throughout South Memphis. He is lifting lives in the poorest urban zip code in the United States out of scarcity and lack; and what he is achieving in South Memphis, Tennessee, is a replicable example and can be an inspiration everywhere.

We get it. We see the essential need for a shift in our paradigm from industry and an economy that exploits the planet to one focused on stewardship of the earth: sustainable, earth friendly, and just. The reinvigoration of smaller regional economies, the economy of the shires — one fostering livelihoods and enriching community.

We are working for this. We will set an example through our actions, and our compassionate activism, making others aware that a shift to restorative regenerative agriculture and a return of livestock back onto pasture, will lead thousands of people to discover livelihoods in agriculture, and many thousands more to land job opportunities there. Just as the shift to clean energy has already created 500,000 new jobs in California and millions across America, far exceeding job decline in the dirty energy sector (which includes not just the fossil fuel industry but the chemical industry as well), the shift from industrial to regenerative agriculture will be a job creation engine. The shift to the New Economy will begin an era of unprecedented job creation.

We all want vibrant communities that we can afford to live in, work in, and improve. We want to have money and discover ways to spend it so that it can remain recirculating within our local economies. We want to have our savings and our mortgages in financial institutions who's primary focus is supporting our local economy. We all want a safe, non-toxic, healthy environment to live in.

The economic reinvigoration of local economies and communities, rural and urban, will coincide with a migration back into these areas, as people choose to take advantage of their beauty, seizing an opportunity given their depressed value, to help build community and equity along with it.

We will lead lives of compassion and compassionate activism in support of all people's livelihoods, the national commons and the public good until the war on livelihoods, vocations, craftsmanship, education and callings — the war on the economies and the residents of rural and urban American shires, is over.

● ● ●

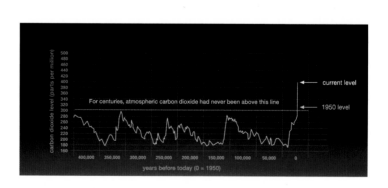

We are in a time crunch. If you look at this NASA chart as if it were an electrocardiogram (EKG) monitoring the planet's heartbeat, our Earth is suffering a massive heart attack. Right now.

The carbon dioxide concentration in our atmosphere is the highest it's been in 15 million years. Each year forest fires are devastating wide swaths of our warming forests from Alaska, the Arctic, Sweden, all the way down through Europe, North America, and Asia. The warming oceans are more acidic, coral reefs are dying. The Arctic Ocean has now lost 95% of its oldest, thickest ice.[15] Hurricanes, typhoons and other "500 year" superstorms are increasing in frequency and severity.

Our CO_2 emissions in the United States rose 3.4% in 2018, the second largest *gain* in over two decades.[16] What are we doing?

The United States Government's *Fourth National Climate Assessment*, compiled by 13 federal agencies released in November, 2018, states, "Global climate is projected to continue to change over this century and beyond. The magnitude of climate change beyond the next few decades will depend primarily on the amount of greenhouse (heat-trapping) gases emitted globally and on the remaining uncertainty in the sensitivity of Earth's climate to those emissions (very high confidence). With significant reductions in the emissions of greenhouse gases, the global annually averaged temperature rise could be limited to 3.6°F (2°C) or less. Without major reductions in these emissions, the increase in annual average global temperatures relative to preindustrial times could reach 9°F (5°C) or more by the end of this century."[17]

What this, **our government's** *Climate Science Special Report*, doesn't say is what this *means*.

A rise of 5° is a mass extinction level event. Our civilization will break down as our environment does and the end of our Anthropocene Epoch will soon follow.

Volume 2 of this report is 1515 pages long. A dryly worded assessment of long-term global warming continues: "The climate change resulting from human-caused emissions of carbon dioxide will persist for decades to millennia. Self-reinforcing cycles within the climate system have the potential to accelerate human-induced change and even shift Earth's climate system into new states that are very different from those experienced in the recent past. Future changes outside the range projected by climate models cannot be ruled out, and due to their systematic tendency to underestimate temperature change during past warm periods, models may be more likely to underestimate than to overestimate long-term future change."[18]

Hold the phone. Full stop. "Future changes *outside the range* projected by climate models *cannot be ruled out.*" ...

What is *happening* is, as our planet warms, things that are warming are interacting in unanticipated ways to further accelerate and increase global warming — to the point where the results are blowing the lid off existing climate model projections.

We thought, just a year ago, we had until 2100. Today we realize we only have until 2030 until bad things begin to get very bad, and natural disasters become environmental catastrophes.

Arctic ice may already be a goner. A United Nations climate report released March 14, 2019 revealed that no matter how effectively the international community succeeds in cutting greenhouse gas emissions, a 3-5° rise in winter temperatures in the Arctic by 2050 is already "locked in."[19]

Mr. Heat has opened our front door and is entering our living room. Ms. Misery and Mr. Grim are right there with him.

What this *is*, is... scary. This is very scary.

In a November 2018 article in the Guardian, *Climate-heating Greenhouse Gases at Record Levels, Says UN*, the secretary general of the World Meteorological Organization (WMO), Petteri Tallas stated, "The science is clear. Without rapid cuts in CO_2 and other greenhouse gases, climate change will have increasingly destructive and irreversible impacts on life on Earth. The window of opportunity for action is almost closed."[20] The United Nations estimates that our greenhouse gas emissions must be reduced by 40% over the next 11 years.

Global warming will continue — and will worsen — there's no way we can stop that. What we can do is take action to reign it in. Countries need to take action, a massive mobilization towards zero-emission economies to slow the increase of carbon into our atmosphere and over time stop it. What can play a significant role in that regard *and* draw atmospheric carbon back down?

In that same article, the deputy secretary general of the WMO, Elena Manaenkova, said, "There is currently no magic wand to remove all the excess CO_2 from the atmosphere."

There is.

There is one.

And you know what it is. Regenerative agriculture — at scale — quickly. To accomplish this, we need to reclaim our American democracy.

We are working for this. We want a new Food and Farm Act to replace the 2018 Farm Bill. We realize that our Arch-Villain, Big Ag, factory farming and industrial agriculture, has contributed and will continue to contribute immense amounts of money to delay meaningful essential change.

We realize there is a separate cabal of dangerous villains actively striving to undermine our democracy, and our constitution if need be, to spread fear, to divide us, and to suppress our voices, our public commons — and our rights to a safe, clean and healthy environment to live in.

We are on this. And in increasing numbers. Each of us has a light, just like Hazel's. And we re shining our awareness into the dark places. We will strengthen our democracy, one person one vote.

We seek a new generation of politicians, some already in office, to be joined by new faces, all of whom understand this reality and have not been coerced by accepting contributions from our Arch-Villain or other industries contributing to global warming, unhealthy food, unnecessary drugs and medical care. If a candidate accepts financial contributions from corporations or PACs in or associated with Big Ag, Big Food, Big Pharma or Big Med, or the Chemical or Fossil Fuel industries, they do not deserve your vote. They are corrupted. They are standing in the way of essential change.

Candidates for office must prioritize a commitment to ending global warming. They must endorse the Green New Deal. They must endorse a New Farm Bill.

When President Franklin D. Roosevelt announced the New Deal, the U.S. economy was mired in the Great Depression. Our government didn't have the necessary money to spend, but they figured it out and they got it done.

Today, the money to realize the Green New Deal and a New Farm Bill is there — it's a question of shifting subsidies and priorities. This can be done rapidly and well, and the economy can transition without significant contraction. We will emerge from this shift stepping into an unprecedented economic expansion, the New Economy.

We must find and elect incorruptible leaders of courage and integrity to get this done. These are the leaders who deserve your vote regardless of political party.

We will no longer be complicit with the weakening and perverting of our democratic principles. We will lead lives of compassion and compassionate activism, protecting majority rule, and strengthening and growing the collective commons — until the war on our democracy is over.

. . .

So...

That is how the seemingly diverse challenges faced by each one of these exquisite creatures, Sherneka Johnson and Sky Smith, Thomas Quicksilver, Brady Kluge, Lucinda Monarch, Earl 'the Worm,' and Marlon Foster are interrelated. The severity of what is confronting each of them reveals the immensity of the threat facing each one of us. Our Arch-Villain's impact is all pervasive. It's brought all of us together.

Earth's last mass extinction ended the Mesozoic era 65 million years ago. It was caused by a large asteroid striking into the Yucatan peninsula in Mexico. Each one of Earth's five previous mass extinctions was the result of an uncontrollable event.

The sixth mass extinction event, which is now underway, is the direct result of what, for a very short period of time, is a controllable and therefore, for most of the species that remain, a survivable, event.

Naomi Klein relates what Brave Bull Allard, the official historian of the Standing Rock Sioux tribe, told her regarding the showdown in 2016 when the scattered Indian tribes banded together, and were joined by concerned citizens and veterans of the U.S. military. They all stood side by side several thousand strong to stop the construction of the Dakota Access Pipeline in North Dakota: "We knew this day was coming — the unification of all the tribes... We are here to protect the earth and the water. This is why we are still alive. To do this very thing we are doing. To help humanity answer its most pressing question: how do we live with the earth again, not against it?"[21]

On the subject of our humanity, Steven Pinker writes about each of us accepting our citizenship in the world. "Given that we are equipped with the capacity to sympathize with others, nothing can prevent the circle of sympathy from expanding from the family and tribe to embrace all of humankind, particularly as reason goads us into realizing that there can be nothing uniquely deserving about ourselves or any of the groups to which we belong."[22]

Sympathy becomes compassionate understanding. Realizing "world as lover, world as self" extends to animals and their humane treatment, to everything in nature, the entirety of life, seen and unseen, discovered and undiscovered.

When things start to come undone, how bad can that get? Do we wind up walking side by side with the last human survivors, the father and son in Cormac McCarthy's *The Road*?

Enough of Doomsday. Things are under tremendous strain. And there are a lot of us. We get it.

We are equipped. We've got the tools and our skillsets. Our knowledge, our science and human understanding increases every day. If we can raise awareness and unite behind policy to begin to achieve our singular existing solution, regenerative agriculture and soil carbon sequestration at scale, we can slow and stop greenhouse gas emissions. That can set the stage for a future time when draw down technologies that do not currently exist can be implemented to further reduce atmospheric CO_2. If we engage our compassionate activism for the animals, for our health, for the soil, for community and for our democracy, we are on our way.

It's all about the soil.

Civilizations have flourished, usually because they had a new invention, a superior technology, method, or insight, that gave them an advantage. Frederick Kirschenmann and WC Lowdermilk remind us that, "Soil erosion due to human activity has, for centuries, been a major contributing factor to humankind's failure to sustain civilized societies."[23] [24]

Egyptian farmers plowed the fertile soil of the Nile River Valley, producing bountiful harvests of grains, vegetables, figs and melons, and the people flourished. Over time, the low-lying soil began to lose its fertility. Farmers began to plow the hillsides. But due to erosion, over time that fertile topsoil washed away. Scant and scanter harvests led to famine, desperation, and their civilization's decline. They created desert out of what once was some of the planet's most fertile land.

Charles Kellogg, in the 1938 Yearbook of Agriculture, asked a fascinating and important question: "Does a civilization fall when the soil fails to produce, or does a soil fail only when the people living on it no longer know how to manage their civilization?"[25]

We are in a very similar situation right now. We have the knowledge to change course. But powerful forces, the very forces responsible for our tremendous growth and prosperity over two centuries, are the ones resistant to change, locked on maintaining their profit, their power, and the status quo.

It has been prophesied for centuries in numerous religions and forecast in the spiritual and theological writings of many cultures, that humankind will be entering a New Age. The word "apocalypse" in Biblical terms, connotes the total destruction of the world. However, the word "apocalypse" is of ancient Greek origin and means a disclosure of something hidden, a revelation.

What if the "end of days" or "end time" foretold in several religions, turns out not to be the end of recorded history, not to be the end of the Anthropocene Epoch, not to be humankind exiting the stage? What if the overriding transformation at the "end of days," contains the seed of redemption?

Perhaps the "end of days" will be the end of the Old Economy, our current economy, of humankind treating the planet as a resource subject to unsustainable exploitation. Perhaps the "end of days" is the heralding of a shift into a New Economy, a humane economy, one prioritizing stewardship over dominion, a regenerative era based on coexistence with, and the renewal of nature, an era that sustains us.

Jesus the Christ, when he walked the Earth, brought a message of love. What if the foretold second coming is not a singular individual but communities of the heart? For Reverend Michael Bernard Beckwith, our generation is a special generation. "We came to this planet to be the next stage in the evolution of humanity. Jesus and the Buddha were examples to humanity of the next stage of evolution. We're living in a time now where the global mind has already been established. We can communicate with someone anywhere on the planet on the internet right now. You've come to establish the global heart. That's why you're here. To make those connections. The global mind without the global heart is disastrous. You have come to change the narrative and allow the global heart to emerge. You are the ones that are going to make that difference."

The coming millennium of the Aquarian age is envisioned as an age of enlightened compassion. Our path forward, I believe, must be one of enlightened, emboldened, compassionate activism.

"Every great moral cause in human history was initially launched at a time when the overwhelming majority of men and women believed that the change called for was not only impractical but completely implausible," notes former Vice President Al Gore."[26]

Nelson Mandela said, "It is always impossible until it is done."

The Vice President continues, "The pattern is always the same: once the underbrush of obfuscation, straw men, and distractions are cleared away and the underlying issue is resolved into a binary choice between what is clearly right and what is clearly wrong, then the outcome becomes preordained — because of who we are as human beings. And then the change comes quickly."[27]

Philosopher Joanna Macy is tuned in: "A revolution is under way because people are realizing that our needs can be met without destroying our world. We have the technical knowledge, the communication tools, and material resources to grow enough food, ensure clean air and water, and meet rational energy needs. Future generations, if there is a livable world for them, will look back at the epochal transition we are making to a life-sustaining society. And they may well call this the time of the Great Turning. It is happening now... Although we cannot know yet if it will take hold in time for humans and other complex life forms to survive, we can know that it is under way. And it is gaining momentum, through the actions of countless individuals and groups around the world. To see this as the larger context of our lives clears our vision and summons our courage."[28]

Joanna Macy also writes, "The insights and experiences that enable us to make this shift are accelerating, and they take many forms. They arise as grief for our world, giving the lie to old paradigm notions of rugged individualism, the essential separateness of self. They arise as glad response to breakthroughs in scientific thought, as reductionism and materialism give way to evidence of a living universe. And they arise in the resurgence of wisdom traditions, reminding us again that our world is a sacred whole, worthy of adoration and service."[29]

In *How to Thrive in the Next Economy*, John Thackara writes, "A variety of changes, interventions, and disruptions accumulate across time until the system reaches a tipping point: then, at a moment that cannot be predicted, a small release of energy triggers a much larger release or phase shift, and the system as a whole transforms."[30] This is the same tipping point that Malcolm Gladwell refers to.

French philosopher Edgar Morin, in *Homeland Earth: A Manifesto for the New Millennium - Advances in Systems Theory, Complexity and the Human Sciences*, echoes Nelson Mandela: "All great transformations have been unthinkable until they actually came to pass."[31]

This is the coming evolution, the necessary change at a critical time. To avoid the earth's sixth global extinction, this is the path forward — what the future MUST look like.

The fight is on. Everything you purchase, everything you consume, every action you take is a choice. Live well, make the healthy choices, the right choices, compassionate choices. Inform others, enable them. Rise up and be heard. From this day forward.

Let's fix this. Together, let's save the planet.

Let's win this.

* * *

Wendell Berry was born in 1934 in Henry County, Kentucky into a 5th generation farming family. His father taught him how to farm. He has always been deeply connected to the soil and the land; its harmonies, its ways. The challenge he faces has increased in severity over five decades. He has witnessed the rise of industrial agriculture, its takeover of the countryside, and its environmental destruction. He has seen topsoil eroded. He has seen soil poisoned. He has seen nature defiled. He has witnessed farming livelihoods ended, families, neighbors — husbands, wives and children — forced to vacate land passed down to them through generations, honest, moral, steadfast, frugal folk bankrupted and shamed. He and his father worked for years to find ways to protect their agricultural community, its wages, and livelihoods, succeeding over several decades only to have it all undermined and undone. He has remained steadfast, this gentle spirit, while witnessing the consequences to human lives, to his family and relatives, to his friends, neighbors, and colleagues. He has watched communities decimated. He has written and advocated to stop the scourge of industrial agriculture, to change it, to bargain with it, even to ameliorate it. And to that end, he has not succeeded.

Wendell Berry's voluminous writings — books, poems, and essays — have been praised for 60 years. They are archived at the Berry Center, available to all of us. He is recipient of the Jefferson Lecture in the Humanities award, the highest award our government bestows for intellectual achievement in the humanities.

He writes nobly and with an artistry grounded in the land, the seasons, the light on the trees, the wind in the valleys, the plants and the creatures. Writing imbued with the virtues of husbandry, justice, integrity, caring, kindliness, neighborliness, honor, and compassion. I believe his vision, the influence of his intellect and his humanity will grow over time. Especially at this time.

At this point some of you may be wondering...

"Wait a minute... Hold on... You've referenced Mr. Berry. You've quoted him in a few places in this text. But you've quoted lots of folks. Here you are talking about him again!? You listed him as one of the exquisite creatures. Well, where is he? His name's on this book cover as a *contributor*. What gives?! Time to grab my laptop and key it in. How do you spell 'Refund?'"

Well...

I'm a writer. Wendell Berry is a craftsman. He is a national treasure.

Wendell Berry has allowed me to include this. And he gets the final word.

A VISION
by Wendell Berry

A VISION
by Wendell Berry

If we will have the wisdom to survive,
to stand like slow-growing trees
on a ruined place, renewing, enriching it,
if we will make our seasons welcome here,
asking not too much of earth or heaven,
then a long time after we are dead
the lives our lives prepare will live
here, their houses strongly placed
upon the valley sides, fields and gardens
rich in the windows. The river will run
clear, as we will never know it,
and over it, birdsong like a canopy.
On the levels of the hills will be
green meadows, stock bells in noon shade.
On the steeps where greed and ignorance cut down
the old forest, an old forest will stand,
its rich leaf-fall drifting on its roots.
The veins of forgotten springs will have opened.
Families will be singing in the fields.
In their voices they will hear a music
risen out of the ground. They will take
nothing from the ground they will not return,
whatever the grief at parting. Memory,
native to this valley, will spread over it
like a grove, and memory will grow
into legend, legend into song, song
into sacrament. The abundance of this place,
the songs of its people and its birds,
will be health and wisdom and indwelling
light. This is no paradisal dream.
Its hardship is its possibility.

ACKNOWLEDGEMENTS

I want to acknowledge *you* for reading this. Thank you. I tried to engage your interest, even entertain, but I realize parts of this book may not have been pleasant. It had to begin with Compassion for Animals, which meant introducing you to human and non-human beings in North Carolina whose situations are less than stellar. I can imagine what you may have been thinking: "Okay, tough ride to school, but maybe... Ugh-oh. Now he's taking me *inside* to visit Thomas Q. Piglet... And *now* 'poop — yogurt' comparisons? What the heck?!" And after a short respite at Cottonwood Creek, this author, yours truly, chooses to show you *more* mistreated animals! ...? "My son got this for me as a *gift*, he said it was important. What's he trying to do to me?!" I can envision readers closing the book — for good!

Thank you for staying with me. For journeying with these exquisite creatures and their stories, for traveling across these pages.

We are, each one of us, more than exquisite creatures — we are a special generation. If the path is to be one of widespread compassionate awareness and action, and this book was of assistance to you on your journey, wonderful. The Great Healing cannot manifest without you, without impactful numbers of inspired compassionate activists. The term "critical mass" is the exact amount or number necessary to make change happen. Your compassionate activism will help all of us reach the critical mass necessary to achieve significant, essential, rapid change. The word "critical" is no overstatement with regard to the urgency of our endeavor.

There are two people without whom this book wouldn't come anywhere close to its final finished form.

My wife, Melanie Paykos, has been a comrade-in-arms since our relationship began, a superlative sounding board, not only vetting but developing and enriching my thoughts and ideas, an enabler and an inspiration. Researching this book, it was not easy for me to journey into places that are Hells on Earth, where the ugliest and cruelest manifestations of the human spirit are unabashedly on display, where the torture and suffering of living creatures is routine and the scale vast, where living souls, human and non-human, are eviscerated without just or humane regard. Places where people's rights are assailed, where our biosphere — our living planet — is being harmed beyond our ability to repair it or recover exquisite creatures on the brink of extinction, where powerful people in charge are turning blind eyes, oblivious to or in denial of the fact that the suicide watch they are placing each of us on is theirs as well.

When I return from my journeys to reflect on this and write, in the dark hours, she is there, Melanie, my love. Her strength and compassion reinforce me and inspires mine. Like the "blue-eyed son" in Bob Dylan's *A Hard Rain's Gonna Fall*, I will have to go back out there. It means a great deal, our love, and that she is here for me.

The other person essential to this book and to whom I am exceedingly grateful, is Alan Lewis. I had interviewed Alan for a series of blog posts on my Farm Animal Compassionate Engagement (FACE) site, farmanimalce. com. When he invited me to attend the American Grassfed Association conference at Stone Barns in Pocantico Hills, New York, in January 2017, this book was little more than a vision that came to me in a dream, a title, a core idea, and a sketch of five chapters on compassion. Mary Berry, Wendell Berry's daughter, was at that AGA event, as were Will Harris whom you've read about, and Kari Hammerschlag of Friends of the Earth who became very helpful. After a sunny day followed by one where we were deep in snow, my resolve to write this book became an imperative — a certainty — and the approach through the lens of compassion validated.

Throughout this endeavor Alan has read chapters and provided notes. He continued to make masterfully timed introductions to people who would make significant contributions. While acutely aware of the reach, power and insidiousness of Big Ag, Alan, with his soft-spoken charm and self-depreciating sense of humor, soldiers on, doing everything he can — including writing an essay as a Thought Leader for this book — to support regenerative producers, and humane livestock farmers and ranchers.

The generosity of those I interviewed, their patience, hospitality, and time, is something I am very thankful for. Beyond my visits and interviews, they made themselves available and amenable to follow-up conversations, and to read and comment on what I had written about them, often reviewing revised pages.

Maia Raposo and Lindsey Muzzio of Waterkeeper Alliance provided information and contacts regarding factory farming in North Carolina. It was Naeema Muhammad of the North Carolina Environmental Justice Network who personally introduced me to Devon Hall, in effect handing me the key to the door — and the pathway into Duplin and Sampson counties.

Devon Hall is a hero, truly a bodhisattva, given his steadfast commitment to the wellbeing of those in his community. He generously toured me, and over several visits introduced me to Sherneka Johnson and Sky Smith, to the Dudley's — Jennifer, Corey, J'vion, and Jemarion — and to others who invited me into their homes and shared stories no less compelling than those included in this book.

Cody Carlson is a hero, a bodhisattva walking among us, one who is no stranger to dark places. I needed to visit and to know Thomas Quicksilver and through Cody, I did.

Thank you, Brady Kluge, for agreeing to become part of this, and for your honesty, openness and candor. Tinna Kluge, your participation and perspective proved valuable. Thanks to Mark Hyman, M.D., for introducing me to Brady and for championing this book with your quote-use permissions.

To all of the farmers, ranchers and soil scientists who were so insightful and generous with their time, I am grateful beyond words: Dr. Christine Jones, Frederick Kirschenmann, Gabe Brown, Ray Archuleta, David C. Johnson, Tim LaSalle, Will Harris, Lou Preston, Joan and Nick Olson, Matt Kautz, Anna Jones-Crabtree and Doug Crabtree.

Thank you Danielle Nierenberg and your staff at Food Tank for expanding my lists of resources.

Thank you to Lucinda Monarch's crew for your help with this book and for everything you are doing to save the Monarch butterfly: Wendy Caldwell at Monarch Joint Venture, Sarah Foltz Jordan at the Xerces Society for Invertebrate Conservation, and author Kylee Baumle.

In addition to those whom I spent time with, there are other voices appearing in this manuscript. Deborah Koons Garcia wrote and directed the documentary feature, *Symphony of the Soil*. John McMahon was the central subject and an Executive Producer of the 9-part documentary series, *iThrive! Rising from the Depths of Diabetes & Obesity*. I am grateful to both of you for sharing several of your interviews.

Diane Terell, Co-founder and President of The 275 Food Project, also presented me with a key for which I am indebted. This was a key to Memphis, Tennessee, to Marlon Foster, and to Green Leaf Learning Farm.

Thought Leaders. I label the following individuals my "Thought Leaders" because they are. Each one is making a vast contribution to their field, and their insight and perspective is ahead of the curve. Each one writes beautifully, so there is a bonus ride-along for me as I get to surround my writing with beautiful prose.

Wendell Berry's books, poems, and essays have been praised for 60 years. He is a national treasure, a recipient of the Jefferson Lecture in the Humanities award, the highest award our government bestows for intellectual achievement in the humanities. Five books written by Joel Fuhrman, M.D., which are leading thousands upon thousands of people to live healthier lives, are New York Times bestsellers. In addition to supporting livelihoods and invigorating communities across the country in his role at Natural Grocers, Alan Lewis writes insightfully and well. If I had to bet, I'd wager that photojournalist Jo-Anne McArthur is out there right now. And by "out there" I mean *out there* – at risk on a clandestine investigation, capturing images of some atrocity humans are perpetrating on animals. She is a bodhisattva with a lens, a preeminent photographer on our Earth.

I am immensely grateful that these Thought Leaders responded to the concept – the idea of this book – strongly enough, and decisively enough, to risk contributing material to the endeavor of an unknown author. It is an honor to share the cover of this book with them.

Despite the fact that I spend a lot of time traveling to do the necessary research for my writing, or parked at my computer writing, I have friends. I do.

Thanks to friend John Fischer, aka "Pescador," whom I've known since middle school, for reading (and re-reading) every section of this book and providing insightful notes, props when warranted, and both a legal perspective as well as that of a corporate executive. Thank you, Andrea Hein, aka "Andrea," for your notes, savvy, and support from conception to publication. Sophia Bilinsky, a seminal insight regarding Chapter 3 was very welcome.

Thank you to the other friends and colleagues, including my

screenwriting group, who read chapters and shared their thoughts.

I am more than fortunate to have Linda Morris as editor. Far more than keeping my grammar in line — no easy task — her broad grounded knowledge guarded against emotion-fueled overstatement, and her story suggestions were welcome.

Melanie Paykos, one of the most gifted designers around, put together an outstanding production team: Gregg Nakawatase created the exquisite book cover design from a concept by Caroline Placensia based on my idea, Sara Vadgama and Caroline Placensia developed the style guide. Trish Church Podlasek diligently executed the layout. Pam Koehler was our production manager and printer liaison. When she's on press all is well.

For me family is core. In addition to my wife, Melanie, I want to thank my 26-year-old daughter, Kira, for reading chapter drafts and revisions, for her notes and encouragement. This book is written for all of us, but particularly for your millennial generation and for Generation Z — because *you* need to mobilize in a big way immediately, so that one day you can raise your family in a stable society and an environment fairly similar to the one we now enjoy, as opposed to being trapped along with the rest of humanity in a sweltering, ugly, calamity — an increasingly chaotic and dangerous exit from the global stage. Thank you, Sven Walderich for your help with Chapter 2. And thanks to my son Theo, who didn't really help much at all, but by doing remarkably well in an exceedingly difficult college major, Computer Science - Game Design, at one of the top engineering schools in the country, saved me time to get this done.

NOTES

Introduction

[1] Ocean Pressure Calculator http://www.wolframalpha.com/widgets/gallery/view. jsp?id=f5c3dd7514bf620a1b85450d2ae374b1

[2] Allowing photosynthesis.

[3] Solvin Zankl and Biographic, *See the Weird and Fascinating Deep-Sea Creatures That Live in Constant Darkness*, Biographic, Nov. 7, 2016 https://www.atlasobscura.com/articles/see-the-weird-and-fascinating-deepsea-creatures-that-live-in-constant-darkness

[4] Harold Johnson, *Plastics in the Ocean: How Dense Are We?* Scientific American, Aug. 16, 2012 https://blogs.scientificamerican.com/guest-blog/plastics-in-the-ocean-how-dense-are-we/

[5] Sarah Zielinski, *Your Garbage is Polluting Even the Deep, Remote Reaches of the Ocean* Smithsonian. com Apr. 30, 2014 https://www.smithsonianmag.com/science-nature/garbage-polluting-deep-remote-ocean-180951271/

[6] Fiona Harvey, *Fish Mistaking Plastic Debris in Ocean for Food*, Study Finds, The Guardian, Marine Life, Aug. 16, 2017 https://www.theguardian.com/environment/2017/aug/16/fish-confusing-plastic-debris-in-ocean-for-food-study-finds#comments

"Matthew Savoca, of the National Oceanic and Atmospheric Administration and lead author of the study, told the Guardian: 'When plastic floats at sea its surface gets colonised by algae within days or weeks, a process known as biofouling. Previous research has shown that this algae produces and emits DMS, an algal based compound that certain marine animals use to find food. [The research shows] plastic may be more deceptive to fish than previously thought. If plastic both looks and smells like food, it is more difficult for animals like fish to distinguish it as not food.'"

[7] Alina M. Wieczorek, Liam Morrison, Peter L. Croot, et al. *Frequency of Microplastics in Mesopelagic Fishes from the Northwest Atlantic*, Frontiers in Marine Science, Feb. 19, 2018 https://www.frontiersin.org/articles/10.3389/fmars.2018.00039/full

[8] Matthew Robinson, *Dead Whale Found with 40 Kilograms of Plastic Bags in Its Stomach*, CNN, Mar. 18, 2019, https://edition.cnn.com/2019/03/18/asia/dead-whale-philippines-40kg-plastic-stomach-intl-scli/

[9] Lee Moran. *This Sperm Whale was Found Dead with 64 Pounds of Trash in its Digestive System*, Huffington Post, Apr. 7, 2018, https://www.huffingtonpost.com/entry/dead-sperm-whale-plastic-spain_us_5ac8b736e4b09d0a11942cd4

[10] Please watch *Midway*, a 4-minute documentary film by Chris Jordan. Chris asks each of us, "Do we have the courage to face the realities of our time? And allow ourselves to feel deeply enough that it transforms us and our future?" https://www.youtube.com/watch?v=ozBE-ZPwi8c

[11] World Wildlife Fund, *Living Planet Report 2018*, https://www.worldwildlife.org/pages/living-planet-report-2018

[12] *The State of Obesity 2017*, Trust For America's Health, Reports, August 2017 http://healthyamericans. org/reports/stateofobesity2017/

[13] Dr. John Reganold, Regents Professor of Soil Science, Washington State University. Quoted from his appearance in the documentary film *Symphony of the Soil*, Directed, Written and Produced by Deborah Koons Garcia, Lily Films, 2012

[14] David Pimental, Michael Burgess, *Soil Erosion Threatens Food Production*, Agriculture 2013, 3, 443-463; doi:10.3390 Aug. 8, 2013 https://www.bmbf.de/files/agriculture-03-00443.pdf

[15] Chris Arsenault, *Only 60 Years of Farming Left if Soil Degradation Continues*, Reuters, as reported in Scientific American, Dec. 9, 2017 https://www.scientificamerican.com/article/only-60-years-of-farming-left-if-soil-degradation-continues/#

[16] *Farming and Farm Income*, USDA, Economic Research Service using data from USDA, National Agriculture Statistics Service, Censuses of Agriculture (through 2012) and Farms and Land in farms:

2016 Summary. 2016 https://www.ers.usda.gov/data-products/ag-and-food-statistics-charting-the-essentials/farming-and-farm-income/

[17] Richard Florida, *It's Not the Food Deserts: It's the Inequality*, CityLab, Jan. 18, 2018, https://www.citylab.com/equity/2018/01/its-not-the-food-deserts-its-the-inequality/550793/

[18] John Donne, *Devotions Upon Emergent Occasions*, "Meditation XVII" 1624. "No man is an island, entire of itself; every man is a piece of the continent, a part of the main. If a clod be washed away by the sea, Europe is the less, as well as if a promontory were, as well as if a manor of thy friend's or of thine own were: any man's death diminishes me, because I am involved in mankind, and therefore never send to know for whom the bell tolls; it tolls for thee." Popularized by the title of Ernest Hemingway's novel *For Whom the Bell Tolls*.

[19] Edward O. Wilson, *Fifty Fifty, A Biologist's Manifesto For Preserving Life on Earth*, article appearing in Sierra Magazine, Jan./Feb. 2017, pg. 28

[20] *Global warming* is a more specific term than *climate change*, which implies movement in either direction. Global temperatures overall are going in one direction only: things are heating up. https://climate.nasa.gov/evidence/

[21] Steven Pinker, *Enlightenment Now*, New York, New York: Viking, 2018. Pgs. 137-8

[22] John Cook, Dana Nuccitelli, Sarah A Green, et al. *Quantifying the Consensus on Anthropogenic Global Warming in the Scientific Literature*, IOP Science, Environmental Research Letters, Vol. 8, Num. 2, May 15, 2013, http://iopscience.iop.org/article/10.1088/1748-9326/8/2/024024/meta

[23] Al Gore. *An Inconvenient Sequel - Truth to Power*. New York, New York: Rodale, 2017. pg. 44

[24] Jeff Tollefson, *Humans Are Driving One Million Species to Extinction*, Nature, May 6, 2019, https://www.nature.com/articles/d41586-019-01448-4

[25] Matt McGrath, *Nature Crisis: Humans 'Threaten 1m Species with Extinction,'* BBC News, May 6, 2019, https://www.bbc.com/news/science-environment-48169783

[26] Gerardo Ceballos, Paul R. Ehrlich, Rodolfo Dirzo, *Biological Annihilation Via the Ongoing Sixth Mass Extinction Signaled by Vertebrate Population Losses and Declines*, Proceedings of the National Academy of Sciences of the U.S.A. Vol. 114 No. 30 E6089-E6096 May 23, 2017 http://www.pnas.org/content/114/30/E6089.abstract

[27] Rodolfo Dirzo, Hillary S. Young, Mauro Galetti, et al. *Defaunation in the Anthropocene*, Sciencemag.org, Jul. 25, 2014, http://science.sciencemag.org/content/345/6195/401/tab-figures-data

[28] Claire Regnier et all, *Mass Extinction in Poorly Known Taxa*, Proceedings of the National Academy of Sciences of the U.S.A. Vol. 112 No. 25 7761-7766 May 5, 2015 http://www.pnas.org/content/112/25/7761.abstract

[29] Francisco Sánchez-Bayo, Kris A.G. Wyckhuys, *Worldwide Decline of the Entomofauna: A Review of its Drivers*, Science Direct, Jan. 1, 2019, https://doi.org/10.1016/j.biocon.2019.01.020

[30] *State of the World's Birds*, BirdLife International 2018 Report, https://www.birdlife.org/sites/default/files/attachments/BL_ReportENG_V11_spreads.pdf

[31] Laura Parker, *How Megafires Are Remaking American Forests*, National Geographic Aug. 9, 2015 http://news.nationalgeographic.com/2015/08/150809-wildfires-forest-fires-climate-change-science/

[32] Heyck-Williams, S., L. Anderson, B.A. Stein. *Megafires: The Growing Risk to America's Forests, Communities, and Wildlife*. Washington, DC: National Wildlife Federation. 2017 https://www.nwf.org/-/media/Documents/PDFs/NWF-Reports/NWF-Report_Megafires_FINAL_LOW-RES_101717.ashx

[33] Jonathan Watts, *Wildfires Rage in Arctic Circle as Sweden Calls for Help*, The Guardian, Jul. 18, 2018, https://www.theguardian.com/world/2018/jul/18/sweden-calls-for-help-as-arctic-circle-hit-by-wildfires

[34] Bob Berwyn, *Thawing Alaska Permafrost Sends Autumn CO2 Emissions Surging*, Inside Climate News, May 8, 2017 https://insideclimatenews.org/news/08052017/arctic-permafrost-thawing-alaska-temperatures-co2-emissions

[35] Katrin Kohnert, Andrei Serafimovich, Stefan Metzger, et al. *Strong Geologic Methane Emissions From Discontinuous Terrestrial Permafrost in the Mackenzie Delta, Canada*, Scientific Reports 7, Article 5828, Jul. 19, 2017. doi:10.1038/s41598-017-05783-2 https://www.nature.com/articles/s41598-017-05783-2

[36] David Wallace-Wells, *The Uninhabitable Earth*, New York Magazine, Jul. 9, 2017 http://nymag.com/

daily/intelligencer/2017/07/climate-change-earth-too-hot-for-humans.html

[37] Jessica Corbett, *Thawing Permafrost Emitting Higher Levels of Potent Greenhouse Gas than Previously Thought*, Common Dreams, Apr. 16, 2019 https://www.commondreams.org/news/2019/04/16/thawing-permafrost-emitting-higher-levels-potent-greenhouse-gas-previously-thought

[38] Jordan Wilkerson, Ronald Dobosy, David S. Sayres, et al. *Permafrost Nitrous Oxide Emissions Observed on a Landscape Scale Using the Airborne Eddy-covariance Method*, Atmospheric Chemistry and Physics, Atmos. Chem. Phys., 19, 4257-4268, 2019 https://doi.org/10.5194/acp-19-4257-2019 Apr. 3, 2019, https://www.atmos-chem-phys.net/19/4257/2019/

[39] Patrick Brown, Ken Caldeira, *More-severe Climate Model Predictions Could be the Most Accurate*, Carnegie Institution For Science, Dec. 6, 2017 https://carnegiescience.edu/news/more-severe-climate-model-predictions-could-be-most-accurate

[40] Paul Nicklen photograph, Artic meltwater gushes from an ice cap, Nordaustlandet, Norway Aug. 7, 2014 http://paulnicklen.com

[41] David Wallace-Wells, *The Uninhabitable Earth*, New York Magazine, Jul. 9, 2017, Richard Alley, a leading climatologist, quoted in the parenthetical, http://nymag.com/daily/intelligencer/2017/07/climate-change-earth-too-hot-for-humans-annotated.html

[42] Jelor Gallego, *NASA Satellite Data Sets Record on How Much Ice the Arctic is Losing*, Futurism.com. Nov. 7, 2016, https://futurism.com/nasa-data-shows-just-how-much-ice-the-arctic-is-losing/

[43] Seth Borenstein, *Antarctica's Ice Sheet is Melting 3 Times faster than Before*, AP News, Jun. 13, 2018, https://www.apnews.com/547d9ca2c5524b558356d5b2a75449cc

[44] Andrew Shepherd, Erik Ivins, Eric Rignot, et al. *Mass Balance of the Antarctic Ice Sheet from 1992 to 2017*, Nature 558, 219-222, Jun. 13, 2018 https://www.nature.com/articles/s41586-018-0179-y

[45] Lijing Cheng, Jiang Zhu, John Abraham, et al. *2018 Continues Record Global Ocean Warming*, Advances In Atmospheric Sciences, Vol. 36, Mar. 2019, 249-252, https://link.springer.com/article/10.1007%2Fs00376-019-8276-x

[46] Laurie J. Schmidt, NASA's Jet Propulsion Laboratory, *Satellite Data Confirm Annual Carbon Dioxide Minimum Above 400ppm*, NASA Global Climate Change, Jan. 30, 2017 https://climate.nasa.gov/news/2535/satellite-data-confirm-annual-carbon-dioxide-minimum-above-400-ppm/

[47] NASA https://climate.nasa.gov/evidence/

[48] Naomi Klein, *No Is Not Enough*, Chicago, Illinois: Haymarket Books, 2017, pg. 71.

[49] World Meteorological Organization, *Greenhouse Gas Concentrations Surge to New Record*, Oct. 30, 2017 https://public.wmo.int/en/media/press-release/greenhouse-gas-concentrations-surge-new-record

[50] Global Carbon Project, *Global Carbon Budget 2017*, Nov. 13, 2017, http://www.globalcarbonproject.org/carbonbudget/18/files/GCP_CarbonBudget_2018.pdf

[51] Doyle Rice, *Global Carbon Dioxide Emissions Reach Record High*, USA Today, Nov. 13, 2017, https://www.usatoday.com/story/news/world/2017/11/13/global-carbon-dioxide-emissions-reach-record-high/859659001/

[52] Brad Plumer, Nadja Popovich, *CO_2 Emissions Were Flat for Three Years. Now They're Rising Again*, The New York Times, Nov. 13, 2017, https://www.nytimes.com/interactive/2017/11/13/climate/co2-emissions-rising-again.html

[53] CO_2 Earth, https://www.co2.earth/daily-co2#

[54] Ralph Keeling, The Keeling Curve, Scripps Institute of Oceanography, University of California San Diego, scripps.ucsd.edu, Apr. 19, 2017, https://twitter.com/Keeling_curve/status/854882582877491200

[55] The Keeling Curve, Scripps Institution of Oceanography, May 12, 2019, https://scripps.ucsd.edu/programs/keelingcurve/

[56] Paul Rauber, *All the Environmental News in Case You Missed it*, Sierra Magazine, Jun. 28, 2018, https://www.sierraclub.org/sierra/2018-4-july-august/speed/all-the-environmental-news-in-case-you-missed-it

[57] Kate Lunau, *Mathematical Formula Predicts Global Mass Extinction Event in 2100*, Motherboard Sep. 20, 2017 https://motherboard.vice.com/en_us/article/ne7zyw/mathematical-formula-predicts-

global-mass-extinction-event-in-2100

[58] Ashley Strickland, *Earth to Warm 2 Degrees Celsius by the End of this Century*, Studies Say, CNN Jul. 31, 2017 http://www.cnn.com/2017/07/31/health/climate-change-two-degrees-studies/index.html

[59] William J. Ripple, Christopher Wolf, Thomas M. Newsome, et al. *World Scientists' Warning to Humanity: A Second Notice*, BioScience, Vol. 67, Issue 12, 1 Dec. 2017, Pgs. 1026–1028, https://doi.org/10.1093/biosci/bix125
Pub: Nov. 13, 2017 https://academic.oup.com/bioscience/article/67/12/1026/4605229

[60] Alliance of World Scientists, *World Scientists' Warning to Humanity: A Second Notice, 2019*, view the 20,000 scientists signing the article at publication or subsequently endorsing it. http://scientistswarning.forestry.oregonstate.edu/?cid=em_mdr-

[61] Charlotta Lomas, *2˚ C: 'We Have a 5 Percent Chance of Success'*, DW Akademie, Nov. 16, 2017, https://p.dw.com/p/2njXd , https://www.dw.com/en/2c-we-have-a-5-percent-chance-of-success/a-41405809

[62] Chris Mooney, *We Only Have a 5 Percent Chance of Avoiding 'Dangerous' Global Warming, a Study Finds*, The Washington Post, Jul. 31, 2017, https://www.washingtonpost.com/news/energy-environment/wp/2017/07/31/we-only-have-a-5-percent-chance-of-avoiding-dangerous-global-warming-a-study-finds/?utm_term=.8687765f43db

Chapter 1

[1] Adam Skolnick, *Hog Hell – The CAFO Industry's Impact on the Environment and Public Health*, Sierra Magazine, Feb. 23, 2017 https://www.sierraclub.org/sierra/2017-2-march-april/feature/cafo-industrys-impact-environment-and-public-health

[2] Rob Percival, *Why Animal Sentience Matters – and Why We Need a Charter for Animal Compassion*, AlterNet, Aug. 11, 2017 https://www.alternet.org/animal-rights/why-animal-sentience-matters-and-why-we-need-charter-animal-compassion

[3] Dr. Meg Cattell and Dr. Arden Nelson told me that "Pigs are made to live half underground. They need all those microbes and dirt stuff in their gut. When we take pigs into a sterile environment it messes them up. Most pigs that die prematurely die from ingestive disorders."

Drs. Meg Cattell and Arden Nelson are board certified dairy veterinarians and proponents of grass feeding and keeping animals healthy through nutrition and management. Their farm, Windsor Dairy, was certified organic in 2002 and switched to grass feeding in 2007. As consulting veterinarians and educators they have worked with many sizes and types of dairies throughout the United States and have lectured around the world. As a researcher, Dr. Cattell has tested many treatments including natural remedies on farms as a contract research organization and for her own education. http://windsordairy.com/learning-center.html

[4] Castration is handled more humanely on smaller family farms. They have far fewer pigs to manage so more time is taken. A scalpel is used, organs are not "torn out" of animals. On factory farms pig tails are cut off ("docked") because, pigs forced to live in these crowded conditions can become frustrated and aggressive, biting the tails of other pigs.

[5] ASPCA American Society for the Prevention of Cruelty to Animals website https://www.aspca.org/animal-cruelty/farm-animal-welfare/animals-factory-farms

[6] Farm Sanctuary, *Factory Farming's Effect on Rural Communities*, Farm Sanctuary website, https://www.farmsanctuary.org/learn/factory-farming/factory-farmings-effect-on-rural-communities/

[7] Shylo E. Wardyn, Brett M. Forhey, Sarah A. Farina, et al. *Swine Farming is a Risk Factor for Infection With and High Prevalence of Carriage of Multidrug-Resistant Staphylococcus Aureus*, Center For Emerging Infectious Diseases, Jul. 2015, CID 2015:61 (1 July), https://pdfs.semanticscholar.org/838e/424b2ded981288fd6e7e28e1633cfa1b3cab.pdf

[8] Adam Skolnick, *Hog Hell – The CAFO Industry's Impact on the Environment and Public Health*, Sierra Magazine, Feb. 23, 2017 https://www.sierraclub.org/sierra/2017-2-march-april/feature/cafo-industrys-impact-environment-and-public-health

[9] Statista, The Statistics Portal, 2018, https://www.statista.com/statistics/194371/top-10-us-states-by-number-of-hogs-and-pigs/

[10] *Table 19. Hogs and Pigs – Inventory: 2012 and* 2007, Ag Census USDA, 2012, https://www.agcensus. usda.gov/Publications/2012/Full_Report/Volume_1,_Chapter_1_State_Level/North_Carolina/ st37_1_017_019.pdf

[11] Christina Cooke, *In North Carolina, New Pollution Allegations Add to Resident's Woes Over Factory Farms*, Civil Eats, Jun. 26, 2018 https://civileats.com/2018/06/26/in-north-carolina-new-pollution- allegations-add-to-residents-woes-over-factory-farms/

[12] Lindsey Muzzio, Waterkeeper Alliance, *Combating CAFOs* Mission: Water Magazine Issue 3, Summer 2017, "Airborne threats include asthma and other respiratory disorders, which are common especially in the young and elderly, as well as exposure to antibiotic resistant bacteria such as methicillin-resistant staphylococcus aureus (MRSA). Emissions of hazardous gasses from CAFOs are linked to coughing, nausea, headaches, burning eyes, and psychological impairments."

[13] Olga Naidenko Ph.D and Sydney Evans, *Duke University Study: N.C. Residents Living Near Large Hog Farms Have Elevated Disease, Death Risks*, Environmental Working Group, Sep. 19, 2018, https:// www.ewg.org/news-and-analysis/2018/09/duke-university-study-nc-residents-living-near-large- hog-farms-have

[14] Julia Kravchenko, Sung Han Rhew, Igor Akushevich, et al, *Mortality and Health Outcomes in North Carolina Communities Located in Close Proximity to Hog Concentrated Animal Feeding Operations*, North Carolina Medical Journal, Sep. - Oct. 2018, vol .79 no. 5, 278-288, http://www.ncmedicaljournal. com/content/79/5/278.full#app-7

[15] Christina Cooke, *North Carolina's Factory Farms Produce 15,000 Olympic Pools Worth of Waste Each Year*, Civil Eats, Jun. 28, 2016 http://civileats.com/2016/06/28/north-carolinas-cafos-produce-15000- olympic-size-pools-worth-of-waste/

[16] *How Much is Iowa Getting Pooped On?*, Raygun, Oct. 4, 2017 https://www.raygunsite.com/blogs/ news/how-much-is-iowa-getting-pooped-on

[17] Adam Skolnick, *Hog Hell – The CAFO Industry's Impact on the Environment and Public Health*, Sierra Magazine, Feb. 23, 2017 https://www.sierraclub.org/sierra/2017-2-march-april/feature/cafo- industrys-impact-environment-and-public-health

[18] ibid Lindsey Muzzio, Waterkeeper Alliance, *Combating CAFOs* Mission: Water Magazine Issue 3, Summer 2017

[19] "Iowa has more than 10,000 factory farms — more than any other state. These facilities come under fire from animal rights groups, environmentalists and the Centers for Disease Control and Prevention. They are breeding grounds for diseases and generate 22 billion gallons of manure annually, which contaminates our rivers, streams and wells with E. coli bacteria. Today, Iowa has a record-breaking 750 polluted waterbodies. The burden of clean-up falls upon everyday Iowans." - Jan McGinnis, Contributing Writer, *We Can't Wait Any Longer*, published in the Times-Republican, Oct. 9, 2017 http://www. timesrepublican.com/opinion/your-view/2017/08/we-cant-wait-any-longer/

[20] Melinda Wenner Moyer, *How Drug-Resistant Bacteria Travel from the Farm to Your Table*, Scientific American, Dec. 1, 2016 https://www.scientificamerican.com/article/how-drug-resistant-bacteria- travel-from-the-farm-to-your-table/

[21] Melinda Wenner Moyer, *How Drug-Resistant Bacteria Travel from the Farm to Your Table*, Scientific American, Dec. 1, 2016 https://www.scientificamerican.com/article/how-drug-resistant-bacteria- travel-from-the-farm-to-your-table/

[22] Gray Jernigan, Waterkeeper Alliance Staff Attorney, *North Carolina's Waterkeepers Are Using the Civil Rights Act to Clean Up Minority Communities.* Waterkeeper Magazine Vol. 31 Issue 2, pg. 32

[23] Joseph Mercola, D.O., *Polluting Pigs Part IV*, Mercola.com, Jul. 17, 2018, https://articles.mercola.com/ sites/articles/archive/2018/07/17/factory-farming-air-pollution-lawsuits.aspx?utm_source=dnl&utm_ medium=email&utm_content=art3&utm_campaign=20180717Z1_UCM&et_cid=DM222157&et_ rid=368155790

[24] Bill Walker, Soren Rundquist, *N.C. Bill to Shield CAFO's Liability Would Curb Legal Rights For Hundreds of Thousands*, Environmental Working Group, Apr. 17, 2017 https://www.ewg.org/research/ north-carolina-bill-shield-cafos-liability-would-curb-residents-legal-rights#.WnJC5pM-dhF

[25] Adam Skolnick, *Hog Hell – The CAFO Industry's Impact on the Environment and Public Health*, Sierra Magazine, Feb. 23, 2017 https://www.sierraclub.org/sierra/2017-2-march-april/feature/cafo-

industrys-impact-environment-and-public-health

[26] Bill Walker, Soren Rundquist, *N.C. Bill to Shield CAFO's Liability Would Curb Legal Rights for Hundreds of Thousands*, Environmental Working Group, Apr. 17, 2017 https://www.ewg.org/research/north-carolina-bill-shield-cafos-liability-would-curb-residents-legal-rights#.WoXFq5PwZhE

[27] Cottonwood Creek Farms, http://www.cottonwoodcreekfarms.com

[28] The quality of life for pigs on Cottonwood Creek Farms qualifies Matt for Level 3 of the GAP Standards, the Global Animal Partnership standards in connection with the USDA focused on animal welfare. Matt believes his farm is actually at Level 4, even though they are certified as Level 3. For example, GAP standards want 40 square feet of space allocated per sow, which can include the interior space. Matt allows 250 to 300 square feet per sow in his farrowing areas.
Here is an infographic summarizing what the standards mean for farm animal welfare: https://globalanimalpartnership.org/5-step-animal-welfare-rating-program/pig-standards-application/
Here is a link to a summary of the 5-Step Animal Welfare Program: https://globalanimalpartnership.org/5-step-animal-welfare-rating-program/

[29] In June 2017, California lists a key ingredient in Monsanto's Roundup as cancer-causing. https://www.ecowatch.com/california-list-glyphosate-cancer-2449079385.html

[30] As of October 2015, 19 European countries opted out of growing GMO crops in all or part of their territories. https://www.ecowatch.com/its-official-19-european-countries-say-no-to-gmos-1882106434.html

[31] Vaccinations are for erysipelas and for mycoplasmal pneumonia because these are found in the soil. Matt believes, "Factory farmed animals get their immunity from vaccines. Ours we get it from the environment, but we do need vaccination for just these two."

[32] Matt has tremendous insight into starting and operating a small family farm. He advises that, "The hurdles that everybody is worried about getting in aren't really hurdles." But he stresses that you have to be able to communicate your story and find an emotional connection with people who will support you.

For Matt, the goal is that you need to get to the size where your inertia gets you through the ups and downs, and where you become a player in the market. "I want to be at that point where if I'm out of the market it makes a difference." He considers Joel Salatin's advice about the million dollar farm.

Matt began with free-range layer hens. He packaged his eggs in distinctive pink dozen-cartons that retail for $5.99 in grocery chains like Natural Grocers. He then diversified into pigs but advises, "Stay with your main enterprise, the partner you brought to the dance. Keeping a goal in mind, you need to know when to stop growing your core item and diversify."

[33] Chipotle website: https://www.chipotle.com/food-with-integrity

[34] Rob Percival, *Why Animal Sentience Matters - and Why We Need a Charter for Animal Compassion*, Alternet, Aug. 11, 2017 https://www.alternet.org/animal-rights/why-animal-sentience-matters-and-why-we-need-charter-animal-compassion

[35] Barry Yeoman, *When Animals grieve*, National Wildlife Magazine, National Wildlife Federation, Jan. 18, 2018 issue, pg. 30, https://www.nwf.org/Home/Magazines/National-Wildlife/2018/Feb-Mar/Animals/When-Animals-Grieve

[36] Rhea Parsons, *10 Things To Love About Cows*, One Green Planet, Jun. 3, 2017 http://www.onegreenplanet.org/animalsandnature/things-to-love-about-cows/

[37] Kristin Hagen. Donald M. Broom, *Emotional Reactions to Learning in Cattle*, Applied Animal Behaviour Science, Vol. 85, Issues 3-4, pages 203-213, Mar. 25, 2004, https://www.appliedanimalbehaviour.com/article/S0168-1591%2803%2900294-6/abstract

[38] Amy Hatkoff, *The Inner World of Farm Animals*, New York, NY: Stewart, Tabori & Chang, 2009

[39] Rhea Parsons, *10 Things To Love About Cows*, One Green Planet, Jun. 3, 2017 http://www.onegreenplanet.org/animalsandnature/things-to-love-about-cows/

[40] Matthew Kadey, R.D., *4 Things You Need to Know About Grass-Fed Milk*, Good Housekeeping, Aug. 3, 2017 http://www.goodhousekeeping.com/health/diet-nutrition/g4569/grass-fed-milk/

[41] Joel Fuhrman, M.D., *Fast Food Genocide*, New York, New York: Harper Collins, 2017 pg. 51.

[42] Bulletproof Staff, *The Bulletproof Guide to Omega 3 Vs. Omega 6 Fats*, https://blog.bulletproof.com/omega-3-vs-omega-6-fat-supplements/

[43] Marina A.G. von Keyserlingk, Andressa Amorim Cestari, Becca Franks, et al. *Dairy Cows Value Access*

to Pasture as Highly as Fresh Feed, Scientific Reports 7, Article number: 44943, Mar. 23, 2017, https://www.nature.com/articles/srep44953

[44] Mercy For Animals, *What Cody Saw Will Change Your Life*, Aug. 17, 2015 Video, You Tube https://www.youtube.com/watch?v=7FhHgYjymNU

Mercy For Animals is an outstanding organization working tirelessly to end factory farming and animals suffering on factory farms. Please check out their site, https://www.mercyforanimals.org/

I cannot recommend their work highly enough. The site has great information on healthy eating, meat and dairy free. MFA's undercover investigations have been instrumental in raising awareness of the institutional horror animals endure on factory farms, as evidence resulting in animal cruelty convictions, and effective in forcing humane change in factory farm operation, changes in laws, and changes in public opinion.

One of the most courageous things a compassionate animal lover can do is to work undercover at a factory farm, and to witness and videotape the animal suffering. Imagine the courage it takes. You are a compassionate person, an animal lover, and you volunteer to go into a workplace where you will witness unconscionable acts of animal cruelty. That will become part of your job. And you are wearing a recording device — you could be outed at any time.

The footage these investigators emerge with is heartbreaking, but it is legal evidence and moral evidence in the court of public opinion.

One such investigator is Cody Carlson. His extensive experience working undercover at pig factory farms and his help with this section is immensely and very gratefully appreciated. Thomas Quicksilver and his mother lived and suffered. Their lives are not fiction. Their world is what Cody saw. Watch the video, *What Cody Saw Will Change Your Life*. It just might.

[45] Corn and soy feed are each harder on cow's ruminant digestive tracks which are designed to graze on field grasses.

[46] USDA, *Dairy 2014 - Milk Quality, Milking Procedures, and Mastitis on U.S. Dairies, 2014*, U.S. Department of Agriculture, Sep. 2016, https://www.aphis.usda.gov/animal_health/nahms/dairy/downloads/dairy14/Dairy14_dr_Mastitis.pdf

[47] An HSUS Report, *The Welfare of Cows in the Dairy Industry*, The Humane Society of the United States, http://www.humanesociety.org/assets/pdfs/farm/hsus-the-welfare-of-cows-in-the-dairy-industry.pdf

[48] Rhea Parsons, *10 Things To Love About Cows*, One Green Planet, Jun. 3, 2017 http://www.onegreenplanet.org/animalsandnature/things-to-love-about-cows/

[49] ASPCA Meat, Eggs and Dairy Label Guide https://www.aspca.org/take-action/help-farm-animals/meat-eggs-dairy-label-guide

[50] Carolyn L. Stull, Michael A. Payne, Steven L. Berry, et al. *A Review of the Causes, Prevention, and Welfare of Nonambulatory Cattle*, Journal of the American Veterinary Medical Association 231(2):227-34. Jul. 15, 2007 https://avmajournals.avma.org/doi/full/10.2460/javma.231.2.227

[51] An HSUS Report, *The Welfare of Cows in the Dairy Industry*, The Humane Society of the United States, http://www.humanesociety.org/assets/pdfs/farm/hsus-the-welfare-of-cows-in-the-dairy-industry.pdf

[52] Watch this very well done 5-minute video about the dairy industry, *Dairy is Scary*. https://www.youtube.com/watch?v=wB72wd819Ck

[53] White Oak Pastures website: https://www.whiteoakpastures.com/

[54] Will Harris quoted from the 15-minute video, *One Hundred Thousand Beating Hearts*, Peter Byck, Producer, Director, Jun., 2016 https://vimeo.com/170413226

[55] Joseph Mercola, D.O., *Soil Regeneration at White Oak Pastures*, Mercola.com, Jul. 6, 2016, Will Harris quoted from the video, 30:57. https://www.youtube.com/watch?v=L8ZOO_pRvp4

[56] Emilene Ostlind, *The Big Four Meatpackers*, High Country News, Mar. 21, 2011, https://www.hcn.org/issues/43.5/cattlemen-struggle-against-giant-meatpackers-and-economic-squeezes/the-big-four-meatpackers-1

[57] FoodPrint.org, *The FoodPrint of Beef*, GRACE Communications Foundation, 2018, https://foodprint.org/wp-content/uploads/2018/10/FoodPrintofBeef.pdf

[58] Barry Estabrook, *This Man Wants You to Eat More Meat*, EatingWell, Jan./Feb. 2018, http://www.

eatingwell.com/article/290723/this-man-wants-you-to-eat-more-meat/

[59] Joel Fuhrman, M.D., *Fast Food Genocide*, New York, New York: Harper Collins, 2017 pg. 120.

[60] Scott David, *America's Horrifying New Plan for Animals: Highspeed Slaughterhouses*, The Guardian, Mar. 6, 2018, https://www.theguardian.com/commentisfree/2018/mar/06/ive-seen-the-hidden-horrors-of-high-speed-slaughterhouses

[61] Amélie Rouger, Odile Tresse, Monique Zagorec, *Bacterial Contaminants of Poultry Meat: Sources, Species, and Dynamics*, Microorganisms, Aug. 25, 2017, Sep; 5(3); 50. 10.3390/microorganisms5030050, https://www.ncbi.nlm.nih.gov/pmc/articles/PMC5620641/

[62] Melinda Wenner Moyer, *How Drug-Resistant Bacteria Travel from the Farm to Your Table*, Scientific American, Dec. 1, 2016 https://www.scientificamerican.com/article/how-drug-resistant-bacteria-travel-from-the-farm-to-your-table/

[63] American Grassfed Association website, https://www.americangrassfed.org/about-us/our-standards/

[64] ASPCA Meat, Eggs and Dairy Label Guide https://www.aspca.org/take-action/help-farm-animals/meat-eggs-dairy-label-guide

[65] Pasture raised animals have less fat, saturated fat, and calories than feedlot meat. Their Omega-3 content, the "good fats" is 2 to 4 times higher. Having an ample amount of Omega3 fatty acids in your body decreases your risk of high blood pressure or heart attack. They are good for your entire body including your brain making you less likely to experience depression, schizophrenia or attention deficit disorder (ADD). They reduce your cancer risk. Grass-fed meat and dairy contains much higher vitamin levels, especially E. Grass-fed grass-finished meat is not treated with hormones, growth-promoting additives or antibiotics so there is none of this residue in the meat passed on for human consumption. http://eatwild.com   http://eatwild.com/healthbenefits.htm

[66] Lori Marino, *Thinking Chickens: A Review of Cognition, Emotion, and Behavior in the Domestic Chicken*, Animal Cognition, 2017; DOI: 10.1007/s10071-016-1064-4 reviewed in Science Daily, Jan. 2017 https://www.sciencedaily.com/releases/2017/01/170103091955.htm

[67] 99% of broiler chickens in U.S. factory farmed. http://www.huffingtonpost.com/nil-zacharias/its-time-to-end-factory-f_b_1018840.html

[68] *U.S. Broiler Performance*, National Chicken Council, 2017 http://www.nationalchickencouncil.org/about-the-industry/statistics/u-s-broiler-performance/

[69] Karen Lange, *Super-size Problem*, The Humane Society of the United States, Feb. 16, 2017 http://www.humanesociety.org/news/magazines/2017/03-04/super-size-problem-broiler-chickens.html

[70] ASPCA American Society for the Prevention of Cruelty to Animals website https://www.aspca.org/animal-cruelty/farm-animal-welfare/animals-factory-farms

[71] Nathan Runkle, *Big Food Is Worried About Millennials Avoiding Animal Products*, Ecowatch, Oct. 23, 2017 https://www.ecowatch.com/meat-marketing-millennials-2497594994.html

[72] Karen Lange, *Super-size Problem*, The Humane Society of the United States, Feb. 16, 2017 http://www.humanesociety.org/news/magazines/2017/03-04/super-size-problem-broiler-chickens.html

[73] Eileen Guo, *No 'Dirty' American Chickens, Say British Food Safety Experts*, Inverse Science, Dec. 17, 2017 https://www.inverse.com/article/39489-brexit-american-chickens

[74] Preston Vineyards, farm and winery. http://prestonfarmandwinery.com

[75] Tamara Pearson, *Investigative Report: How Common is Male Chick Grinding in America? (Warning: Graphic Video)*, The Alternative Daily, Sep. 15, 2017 https://www.thealternativedaily.com/how-common-is-male-chick-grinding-in-america

[76] Nil Zacharias, *It's Time to End Factory Farming*, Huffington Post, The Blog, Oct. 19, 2011 https://www.huffingtonpost.com/nil-zacharias/its-time-to-end-factory-f_b_1018840.html

[77] Christel Marie-Etancelin, Herve Chapuis, Jean-Michel Brun, et al. *Genetics and Selection of Ducks in France*, ResearchGate, Sep. 2007, DOI: 10.13140/2.1.2679.8087 https://www.researchgate.net/publication/267324850_GENETICS_AND_SELECTION_OF_DUCKS_IN_FRANCE

[78] Wikipedia, *Foie Gras*, https://en.m.wikipedia.org/wiki/Foie_gras

[79] Christel Marie-Etancelin, Herve Chapuis, Jean-Michel Brun, et al. *Genetics and Selection of Ducks in France*, ResearchGate, Sep. 2007, DOI: 10.13140/2.1.2679.8087 https://www.researchgate.net/publication/267324850_GENETICS_AND_SELECTION_OF_DUCKS_IN_FRANCE

[80] *We Animals* Jo-Anne McArthur, 2017, Brooklyn, NY, Lantern Books https://lanternbooks.

presswarehouse.com/Home/home.aspx

[81] Rhiann Moore, *Animal Cruelty and the Importance of Ending the Commercial Fur Trade*, The Plaid Zebra, Aug. 29, 2017 http://theplaidzebra.com/animal-cruelty-and-the-importance-of-ending-the-commercial-fur-trade/

[82] Tom Knudson, *More than 100 Countries ban this Cruel Trap. The U.S. Isn't one of Them*, Reveal – The Center for Investigative Reporting, Sep. 14, 2016 https://www.revealnews.org/blog/more-than-100-countries-ban-this-cruel-trap-the-us-isnt-one-of-them/

[83] Veal Calves

Newborn calves need their mothers to suckle and to learn from, to be cared for and protected by. As they grow more confident in their young lives, they'll seek the companionship of other calves to pal around and bond with. Veal calves will experience none of this. Within hours of being born, they are separated from their mothers and will never see them again.

Veal meat is promoted as more tender. It is. This is accomplished by isolating veal calves by themselves in narrow enclosures. They are fed a liquid milk substitute that is deliberately deficient in iron and fiber. Confined in these tiny spaces, veal calves are unable to exercise, so their bodies become soft and swollen — their flesh remains tender.

They will spend their days separated from other calves, by themselves, barely able to turn around in the tiny spaces they are allotted, standing or lying in their own waste. They will not be allowed to spend time in pasture.

In 1986, 3.4 million veal calves were raised annually in the United States and the market was increasing. The Humane Farming Association, http://www.hfa.org began an active campaign informing Americans of the suffering of veal calves and called for a national veal boycott. It was a tremendous success. The demand for veal began a steady decline as compassionate informed consumers increasingly avoided it. Today, factory farms produce about 450,000 veal calves in the United States every year.*

*About Calves Reared For Veal, Compassion In World Farming, https://www.ciwf.com/farm-animals/cows/veal-calves/

[84] Farm-raised fish

Wild salmon journey thousands of miles, swimming downriver from the stream where they are born, into the ocean. They live in the ocean until the moment in time arrives in their life cycle when they return to that river mouth and labor, swimming back upstream to reach their birthplace where they will lay and fertilize their eggs before dying.

Factory-farmed salmon and other farmed fish spend their entire lives in vastly overcrowded tanks, ponds or sea cages. Many fish are injured from collisions with the walls and collisions and conflict with one another. "Water quality is usually poor, and disease is common. Many fish die from parasitic infections. According to a recent study, farmed salmon suffer from severe depression, and some simply give up and float lifelessly."*

Farm raised salmon do not have the rich orange-pink coloring of wild salmon because their muscles have never been allowed to put in the kind of exercise living in the wild requires. Wild salmon eat plankton which contains an antioxidant that gives them their color. Farmed salmon would appear comparatively like a white-fish so they are fed a "knockoff version that's created from petrochemicals like coal"** which turns their muscle a pale pink approximation of what their natural hue would be.

Mary Squillace reports in the Bulletproof Blog, "Farmed salmon is more likely to be affected by pollution, parasites and disease."** Farm-raised fish are far likelier to contain more dangerous contaminants than wild fish, including dioxins linked to diabetes and heart disease, and PCBs, the chemicals used in paint and plastics, which have been linked to stroke and cancer. The important ratio of omega-3 fats to omega-6s is far better in wild caught fish which are more robust in terms of vitamin and mineral content per calorie as well.

We vastly underappreciate fish, perhaps because they're quiet, their faces seemingly less expressive. Yet recent scientific research reveals that fish have a level of intelligence rivaling chimpanzees.* Wild fish have been living complex wonderful lives as intended until the day they were caught. The entire life of a factory-farm raised fish is one of misery, vastly overcrowded captivity, pestilence, and silent suffering.*** Don't purchase farm-raised fish.

*Mercy For Animals http://www.mercyforanimals.org/home2
And
Heather Murphy, *Fish Depression Is Not a Joke*, New York Times,
Oct. 16, 2017 https://www.nytimes.com/2017/10/16/science/depressed-fish.html
**Mary Squillace, *5 Reasons to Avoid Farm-Raised Salmon – and Why Wild Salmon is Better*, Bulletproof Blog, https://blog.bulletproof.com/farm-raised-salmon-vs-wild-salmon/
***Brendan Montague, *Horrific Cruelty of Underwater Factory Farms*, TheEcoligist.org, Dec. 7, 2018, https://theecologist.org/2018/dec/07/horrific-cruelty-underwater-factory-farms

85 Reprinted from *World As Lover, World As Self* (1991, 2007) by Joanna Macy with permission of Parallax Press, Berkeley, California, www.parallax.org pg. 86
86 P.J. Huffstutter, Reuters *Everything Seems to be Going Wrong for America's Hog Farmers*, Business Insider, Feb. 8, 2015 http://www.businessinsider.com/r-growing-us-hog-herd-flat-chinese-demand-slams-pork-prices-2015-2
87 *Animal Welfare: Issues and Opportunities in the Meat, Poultry and Egg Markets in the U.S.*, Research and Markets, ID: 4229100, Apr. 2017 https://www.researchandmarkets.com/reports/4229100/animal-welfare-issues-and-opportunities-in-the
88 Maria Chiorando, *Poll Shows 47% of Americans 'Agree With Ban on Slaughterhouses'*, Plant Based News, Nov. 20, 2017 https://www.plantbasednews.org/post/poll-shows-47-of-americans-agree-with-ban-on-slaughterhouses
89 Katie O'Reilly, *Yes, Animals Have Personalities – and They're Altering Wildlife Biology*, Sierra Club, Feb. 6, 2018, https://www.sierraclub.org/sierra/yes-animals-have-personalities-and-they-re-altering-wildlife-biology?utm_source=insider&utm_medium=email&utm_campaign=newsletter
90 Melinda Wenner Moyer, *How Drug-Resistant Bacteria Travel from the Farm to Your Table*, Scientific American, Dec. 1, 2016 https://www.scientificamerican.com/article/how-drug-resistant-bacteria-travel-from-the-farm-to-your-table/
91 Joseph Stromberg, *Factory Farms May be Ground-Zero for Drug Resistant Staph Bacteria*, Smithsonian.com, Jul. 2, 2013, https://www.smithsonianmag.com/science-nature/factory-farms-may-be-ground-zero-for-drug-resistant-staph-bacteria-6055013/
92 Dawn Undurraga, *Supermarket Meat Still Superbugged, Federal Data Show*, Environmental Working Group, Jun. 28, 2018 https://www.ewg.org/research/superbugs/
93 U.S. Food & Drug Administration, *2015 NARMS Integrated Report*, https://www.fda.gov/AnimalVeterinary/SafetyHealth/AntimicrobialResistance/NationalAntimicrobialResistanceMonitoringSystem/ucm059103.htm
94 National Antimicrobial Resistance Monitoring System (NARMS), *2012 Retail Meat Report*, U.S. Food and Drug Administration, Department of Health and Human Services, https://www.fda.gov/downloads/animalveterinary/safetyhealth/antimicrobialresistance/nationalantimicrobialresistancemonitoringsystem/ucm442212.pdf
95 *Antibiotic / Antimicrobial Resistance*, Centers for Disease Control and Prevention, https://www.cdc.gov/drugresistance/index.html
96 Joseph Mercola, D.O., *CAFO Meat is Even More Dangerous*, Mercola.com, Dec. 20, 2016 https://

articles.mercola.com/sites/articles/archive/2016/12/20/dangerous-cafo-meat.aspx

[97] FoodPrint.org, *A Tale Of Two Cows*, Infographic, https://foodprint.org/wp-content/uploads/2018/10/Beef_Infographic_AllSectionsTogether_1500pxWide_R.png

[98] Joseph Mercola, D.O., *What Is Organic Pasture-Raised Chicken Good For?*, 2017 https://foodfacts.mercola.com/organic-pasture-raised-chicken.html

[99] Local Harvest   https://www.localharvest.org

[100] The Cornucopia Institute. The scorecards tab on their home page rates and ranks organic brands of eggs, dairy and a variety of products and brands.   https://www.cornucopia.org/

[101] The Environmental Working Group's (EWG) Food Scores site: http://www.ewg.org/foodscores

[102] A Greener World   https://agreenerworld.org/

[103] *The Center For Food Safety has a free phone app, the True Food Shoppers Guide:* https://www.centerforfoodsafety.org/issues/311/ge-foods/non-gmo-shoppers-guide-325/1847/get-the-app-for-iphone-or-android

[104] *Meat, Eggs and Dairy Label Guide*, American Society for the Prevention of Cruelty to Animals, https://www.aspca.org/sites/default/files/frm_wlfr_food_lbl_guide_013117.png

[105] Contact list of other groups and organizations to help you identify and locate healthy food. Great sources of information as well:

- This is the USDA's National Farmers' Markets Directory. A national listing lets you easily find the farmers' markets closest to you. Once you locate a market, it provides additional information on market hours and what products are typically available there. https://www.ams.usda.gov/local-food-directories/farmersmarkets

- This Natural Grocers webpage clarifies what product standards you should be looking for when purchasing body care, dairy, dietary supplements, meat, grocery, and pet products. https://www.naturalgrocers.com/our-standards

- Eat Wild has a "state-by-state plus Canada" directory to help you locate 100% grass-fed animals, as well as eggs and dairy products from animals fed natural diets. http://www.eatwild.com/

- The Organic Authority website is a source for recipes, nutrition and wellness advice. Organic Authority https://www.organicauthority.com/

- The Happy Cow site lets you find nearby restaurants. While the box says "Vegan restaurants nearby," the search includes vegan and vegetarian restaurants along with restaurants that offer veg-options. Also included are juice bars, health stores, ice cream shops, food trucks, etc. The site has recipes as well. https://www.happycow.net/

- Seafood Watch has a free phone app that provides up-to-date recommendations on sustainable seafood as well as local restaurants serving ocean-friendly seafood. https://www.seafoodwatch.org/seafood-recommendations/our-app

- The Eat Well Guide site has a Guides navigation tab that is handy when traveling. Select a city and discover hand-picked restaurants, farms, and markets presenting local, sustainable, delicious food. https://www.eatwellguide.org/

- The Good Guide rates 75,000 different foods and products based on whether they are safe, ethical, or healthy. Click on the Categories Index at the bottom of the home page and 45 product categories will appear. The site also has a free phone app that lets you scan the bar code of items while shopping to check their rating. https://www.goodguide.com/#/

- Nosh Planet has a free phone app which connects you to sustainable and ethical food at local restaurants. Their list continues to expand with more restaurants added. http://www.noshplanet.com/yoursustainablefoodapp.html#APP

[106] Food Label Guide, Foodprint.org, https://foodprint.org/eating-sustainably/food-label-guide/

[107] Natural Grocers website, https://www.naturalgrocers.com/standards/meat-standards

[108] Natural Grocers website, https://www.naturalgrocers.com/about/the-natural-grocers-story/#finder-box

[109] Independent Natural Food Retailers Association   http://www.naturalfoodretailers.net/

[110] USDA, *Food Access Research Atlas*, United States Department of Agriculture Economic Research Service, https://www.ers.usda.gov/data/fooddesert

[111] The State of Obesity. *Food Insecure Children*, https://stateofobesity.org/food-insecurity/

[112] Joel Fuhrman, M.D., *Fast Food Genocide*, New York, New York: Harper Collins, 2017 pgs. 154-6.

[113] *Humane Farm Animal Care Announces Big Advance in Farm Animal Welfare* Certifiedhumane.org http://certifiedhumane.org/humane-farm-animal-care-announces-big-advance-in-farm-animal-welfare/

[114] Chipotle website http://www.chipotle.com/food-with-integrity

[115] blitzresults.com *The Meat-Calculator: How Many Animals Could Continue Living if you Switched to Vegetarian Diet? How Does the Environment Benefit?* https://www.blitzresults.com/en/meat/

[116] Meatless Monday site: https://www.meatlessmonday.com/

[117] AVaaz – The World in Action, *Help End the Unbearable Cruelty of Meat* Pledge, 2018, https://secure.avaaz.org/campaign/en/meatless_day_loc/

[118] Claire Wotherspoon, *Is 2018 the Year Brits go Vegan?*, Kantar Worldpanel, Kantar UK Insights, Jan. 31, 2018, https://uk.kantar.com/consumer/shoppers/2018/is-2018-the-year-brits-go-vegan/

[119] Melanie Zanoza Bartelme, *2018 Summer Food and Drink Trends*, Mintel, 2018, https://downloads.mintel.com/private/zgXKu/files/688043/

[120] Gustavo Guadagnini, *New GFI Research Indicates 60 Million Brazilians Are Choosing Plant-Based Foods*, GFI Research, Oct. 31, 2018, https://www.gfi.org/kroger-walmart-increase-plant-based-offerings

[121] Melissa Healy, *Hot Dogs, Bacon and Other Processed Meats Increase Risk of Cancer, Scientists Say*, Los Angeles Times, Oct. 26, 2015, https://www.latimes.com/science/la-sci-meat-dangers-20151027-story.html

[122] Dr. Neal Barnard, *Meat Consumption and Cancer Risk*, Physicians Committee for Responsible Medicine blog, https://www.pcrm.org/health/cancer-resources/diet-cancer/facts/meat-consumption-and-cancer-risk

[123] Michael J. Orlich, MD, Pramil N Singh, DrPH, Joan Sabate, MD, DrPH, et al, *Vegetarian Dietary Patterns and Mortality in Adventist Health Study 2*, JAMA Intern Med. 2013;173(13):1230-1238. doi:10.1001/jamainternmed.2013.6473
Jul. 8, 2013, https://jamanetwork.com/journals/jamainternalmedicine/fullarticle/1710093

[124] The Green Plate website: http://thegreenplate.com/

[125] Sites with delicious vegetarian and plant-based recipes:

- Meatless Monday Recipes: https://www.meatlessmonday.com/favorite-recipes/
- Chowhound 11 Vegetarian Blogs to Inspire Healthy Eating All Year Long https://www.chowhound.com/food-news/159772/best-vegetarian-blogs-inspire-healthy-eating-habits/
- The Kitchn, The 5 Vegetarian Blogs I Read Every Day https://www.thekitchn.com/5-vegetarian-blogs-i-read-every-day-245208
- Cookie + Kate, fresh vegetarian recipes: https://cookieandkate.com/
- Organic Authority (primarily plant-based recipes, a few fish dishes): https://www.organicauthority.com/
- New York Times - Cooking: 30 Vegetarian Dishes https://cooking.nytimes.com/68861692-nyt-cooking/2274598-30-vegetarian-dishes-you-can-cook-30-minutes-or-fewer
- Forks Over Knives - All Recipes https://www.forksoverknives.com/recipes/#gs.2rl11s
- Vegetarian Times https://www.vegetariantimes.com/
- Cooking Light Our Best Show-Stopping Vegetarian Recipes https://www.cookinglight.com/food/top-rated-recipes/best-vegetarian-recipes#best-vegetarian-recipes

[126] For meat eaters, here are some sites to explore with healthy recipes that can include meat:

- Well Plated https://www.wellplated.com/
- Cooking Light https://www.cookinglight.com/food

- The Kitchn https://www.thekitchn.com/

[127] *U.S. Plant Based Foods Industry Tops $5 Billion in Annual Sales*, Prweb.com, Mar. 6, 2017 http://www.prweb.com/releases/2017/03/prweb14121969.htm

[128] Sarrie Collins, *America's Largest Grocer Predicts Vegan Food Will be Top Trend in 2019*, Mercy For Animals, Oct. 29, 2018, https://mercyforanimals.org/americas-largest-grocer-predicts-vegan-food

[129] Baum + Whiteman, *Consultants Predict 11 Hottest Food & Beverage Trends in Restaurant & Hotel Dining for 2018*, baumwhiteman.com https://docs.wixstatic.com/ugd/0c5d00_90935d6fda344991a8fc2452eb112c83.pdf

[130] StreetAuthority, *How The 'Death Of Meat' Could Impact Your Portfolio*, Nasdaq.com, Jan. 22, 2015 http://www.nasdaq.com/article/how-the-death-of-meat-could-impact-your-portfolio-cm435607

[131] Tony Dokoupil, *The decline of Red Meat in America*, MSNBC, Oct. 26, 2015 http://www.msnbc.com/msnbc/the-decline-red-meat-america

[132] Sam Tanenhaus, *Generation* Nice, The New York Times, Aug. 15, 2014 http://www.nytimes.com/2014/08/17/fashion/the-millennials-are-generation-nice.html

[133] *How Reduced Meat Consumption Could Save $31 Trillion - and the Planet,* The Food Revolution Network, Mar. 29, 2016 https://foodrevolution.org/blog/benefits-of-reduced-meat-consumption/

[134] Learn more about the nutrition provided by a plant-based diet:

- Katherine D. McManus, *What is a Plant-based Diet and Why Should You Try It?*, Harvard health Publishing, Harvard Medical School, Sep. 26, 2018, https://www.health.harvard.edu/blog/what-is-a-plant-based-diet-and-why-should-you-try-it-2018092614760
- Naomi Imatome-Yun, *Plant-Based Primer: The Beginner's Guide to Starting a Plant-Based Diet*, Forks Over Knives, Jan. 3, 2019, https://www.forksoverknives.com/plant-based-primer-beginners-guide-starting-plant-based-diet/#gs.lwmshYIL
- *Becoming a Vegetarian*, Harvard health Publishing, Harvard Medical School, Updated: Oct. 23, 2018, https://www.health.harvard.edu/staying-healthy/becoming-a-vegetarian
- Vera Churilov, *Plant-Based Diet for Beginners: How to Get Started*, Mind Body Green Health, https://www.mindbodygreen.com/0-952/PlantBased-Diet-for-Beginners-How-to-Get-Started.html

[135] Jeanine Bentley, *Trends in U.S. Per Capita Consumption of Dairy Products, 1970-2012*, USDA Economic Research Service, Jun. 2, 2014 https://www.ers.usda.gov/amber-waves/2014/june/trends-in-us-per-capita-consumption-of-dairy-products-1970-2012/

[136] Michelle Neff, *America's Largest Dairy Processor Just Shut Down Another Plant Because Sales Are So Bad*, One Green Planet, Aug. 16, 2017 http://www.onegreenplanet.org/news/dean-foods-shuts-down-plant/?utm_source=Green+Monster+Mailing+List&utm_campaign=8734a801e4-NEWSLETTER_EMAIL_CAMPAIGN&utm_medium=email&utm_term=0_bbf62ddf34-8734a801e4-106096333

[137] Dr. Richard A. Oppenlander, *Comfortably Unaware*, New York, New York: Beaufort Books, 2012 pg. 61

[138] David S. Ludwig, Walter C. Willett, *Three Daily Servings of Reduced-Fat Milk. An Evidence-Based Recommendation?*, JAMA Pediatrics, Sep. 2013, 167(9):788-789. doi:10.1001/jamapediatrics.2013.240 http://jamanetwork.com/journals/jamapediatrics/article-abstract/1704826

[139] Feskanich D, Willett WC, Colditz GA. *Calcium, Vitamin D, Milk Consumption, and Hip Fractures: a Prospective Study Among Postmenopausal Women*, NCBI PubMed, Feb. 2003, 77(2):504-11. https://www.ncbi.nlm.nih.gov/pubmed/12540414

[140] Twyla Francois, *Ditching in Droves: Why Canadians Are Dropping Milk*, Twyla Francois, Huffington Post blog article, Dec. 15, 2014 http://www.huffingtonpost.ca/twyla-francois/canadians-dairy-industry_b_6280934.html

[141] Elizabeth Crawford, *Almond Milk Sales Continue to Surge, as Dairy Milk Contracts, Neilsen Data Shows*, Food Navigator-USA.com Apr. 14, 2016 https://www.foodnavigator-usa.com/Article/2016/04/15/Almond-milk-sales-continue-to-surge-as-dairy-milk-contracts-Nielsen

[142] Packaged Facts, *Dairy and Dairy Alternative Beverage Trends in the U.S., 4th Edition*, Pub ID:

LA15417200, Oct. 25, 2017, https://www.packagedfacts.com/Dairy-Alternative-Beverage-Trends-Edition-11000293/

[143] Michael Robbins. *Plant-Based Food Sales Grow 20 Percent*, Plant Based Food Association, Jul. 30, 2018, https://plantbasedfoods.org/wp-content/uploads/2018/07/PBFA-Release-on-Nielsen-Data-7.30.18.pdf

[144] Maria Chiorando, *US Vegan Milk Sales Up 9% as Cow Milk Sales Drop 6% in Just 12 Months*, Plant Based news, Jul. 31, 2018, https://www.plantbasednews.org/post/us-vegan-milk-sales-up-9-cow-milk-sales-drop-6-12-months

[145] Innova Market Insights, *Global Plant Milk Market to Top US $16 Billion in 2018: Dairy Alternative Drinks Are Booming, Says Innova Market Insights.* Cision PR Newswire, Jun. 13, 2017 https://www.prnewswire.com/news-releases/global-plant-milk-market-to-top-us-16-billion-in-2018--dairy-alternative-drinks-are-booming-says-innova-market-insights-300472693.html

[146] Renub Research, *Dairy Alternatives Market is Expected to Exceed USD 34 Billion by 2024*, MyNewsDesk.com Jan. 15, 2018, http://www.mynewsdesk.com/us/pressreleases/dairy-alternatives-market-is-expected-to-exceed-usd-34-billion-by-2024-2373780?utm_campaign=Alert&utm_source=alert&utm_medium=email

[147] Catherine Greene, William McBride *Consumer Demand for Organic Milk Continues to Expand – Can the U.S. Diary Sector catch Up?* Choices Magazine, 1st. Qtr., 2015 – 30(1) https://ageconsearch.umn.edu/bitstream/197653/2/cmsarticle_406.pdf

[148] The Cornucopia Institute's Organic Dairy Scorecard, https://www.cornucopia.org/scorecard/dairy/

[149] Sarah Fecht, *Want to Save the World? Start by Eating Less Beef*, Phys.org, Earth Institute, Columbia University, Dec. 5, 2017. https://phys.org/news/2017-12-world-beef.html

[150] Vaclav Smil, *Eating Meat: Constants and Changes*, Global Food Security, Jun. 19, 2014, *https://doi.org/10.1016/j.gfs.2014.06.001*

[151] Vaclav Smil, *Eating Meat: Constants and Changes*, Global Food Security, Jun. 19, 2014, *https://doi.org/10.1016/j.gfs.2014.06.001*

[152] Joel Fuhrman, M.D., *Fast Food Genocide*, New York, New York: Harper Collins, 2017 pg. 193.

[153] Katy Askew, *Go Flexitarian to 'Eat Better' Cut CO2 Footprint and Save Money, French Consumer Urged*, Food Navigator.com Nov. 8, 2017 https://www.foodnavigator.com/Article/2017/11/08/Go-flexitarian-to-eat-better-cut-CO2-footprint-and-save-money-French-consumer-urged

[154] Janet Renee, MS, RD, *The Average Calorie Intake by a Human Per Day Versus the Recommendation*, SFGate, Mar. 15, 2018, http://healthyeating.sfgate.com/average-calorie-intake-human-per-day-versus-recommendation-1867.html

[155] Ocean Robbins, *10 Secrets for Eating Healthy On a Budget (Yes, It Is Possible!)*, Food Revolution, Jun. 15, 2018, https://foodrevolution.org/blog/how-to-eat-healthy-on-a-budget/

[156] Deloitte *Capitalizing on the Shifting Consumer Food Value Equation*, Deloitte Development, LLC, 2016, https://www2.deloitte.com/content/dam/Deloitte/us/Documents/consumer-business/us-fmi-gma-report.pdf

[157] https://en.wikipedia.org/wiki/Foie_gras_controversy
+ Los Angeles Times article regarding California reinstating ban: http://www.latimes.com/local/lanow/la-me-ln-foie-gras-9th-circuit-20170915-story.html

[158] Lawrence Hurley, Reuters, *U.S. Supreme Court Rejects Challenge to California Foie Gras Ban*, The New York Times, Jan. 7, 2019, https://www.reuters.com/article/us-usa-court-foiegras/u-s-supreme-court-rejects-challenge-to-california-foie-gras-ban-idUSKCN1P11LD

[159] Khaleda Rahman for Mailonline and Reuters, *Norway Announces Total Ban on Fur Farming, which sees a Million Foxes and Mink Killed in the Country Each Year for the Fashion Industry*, Daily Mail UK, Jan. 15, 2018, http://www.dailymail.co.uk/news/article-5271483/Norway-announces-total-ban-fur-farming.html

[160] Jill Ettinger, *Germany Just Shut Down its Last Fur Farm*, Live Kindly, Apr. 5, 2019, https://www.livekindly.co/germany-fur-farm-ban/

[161] Ephrat Livni, *The New Science of Animal Cognition is Forcing Countries to Overhaul Their Laws*, Quartz, Jan. 24, 2018, https://qz.com/1181881/proof-of-animal-cognition-is-recognized-by-new-laws-in-europe/

162 Jill Ettinger, *Germany Just Shut Down its Last Fur Farm*, Live Kindly, Apr. 5, 2019, https://www.livekindly.co/germany-fur-farm-ban/

163 A Humane World - Kitty Block's Blog, *Wildlife Gains for 2018 Range from Bans on Wild Animal Circus Acts to Major Fur-free Announcements*, Humane Society, Dec. 26, 2018, https://blog.humanesociety.org/2018/12/wildlife-gains-for-2018-range-from-bans-on-wild-animal-circus-acts-to-major-fur-free-announcements.html

164 A Humane World - Kitty Block's Blog, *Luxury Fashion Brand St. John Says No to Fur, Exotic Skins*, Humane Society, Jan. 18, 2019, https://blog.humanesociety.org/2019/01/luxury-fashion-brand-st-john-says-no-to-fur-exotic-skins

165 Kitty Block's Blog, *Breaking News: San Francisco Says a Resounding 'No' to Fur*, A Humane Nation, Mar. 20, 2018, https://blog.humanesociety.org/2018/03/breaking-news-san-francisco-says-resounding-no-fur.html

166 Kitty Block, *Breaking News: Los Angeles Votes to Ban Fur; Largest U.S. City to Do So*, A Humane Nation, Kitty Block's Blog, Sept. 18, 2018 https://blog.humanesociety.org/2018/09/breaking-news-los-angeles-votes-to-ban-fur-largest-u-s-city-to-do-so.html

167 Compassion Over Killing, *Compassion Over Killing Meatless Mondays Program*, 2013, http://cok.net/camp/meatless-mondays/

168 The Humane Society of the United States: http://www.humanesociety.org/

169 Emily Monaco, *Vegan School Lunches Could Become the Norm in Nation's 2nd Largest School District Next Year*, Organic Authority, Dec. 6, 2017 http://www.organicauthority.com/vegan-school-lunches-could-become-the-norm-in-californias-largest-school-district-next-year/

170 Hannah Freedberg, *Victory! The Nation's Second-largest School District Ends McTeacher's Nights*, Corporate Accountability, Apr. 26, 2017 https://www.corporateaccountability.org/blog/victory-the-nations-second-largest-school-district-end-mcteachers-nights/

171 Corporate Accountability, *About Our Food Campaign*, 2018, https://www.corporateaccountability.org/food/about-our-food-campaign/

172 Julia Gabbert, *Victory! National Teachers Union Takes Historic Stand to Reject McTeacher's Nights*, Corporate Accountability Spotlight, 2019 Issue 1, https://www.corporateaccountability.org/wp-content/uploads/2019/03/CA_Newsletter_2019_Issue2.pdf

173 Alexa Kaczmarski, *No More Predatory Marketing in Our Schools*, Corporate Accountability, Oct. 10, 2018, https://www.corporateaccountability.org/blog/no-more-predatory-marketing-in-our-schools/

174 Mercy For Animals, Compassionate Living, Spring, 2018 http://www.mercyforanimals.org/home2

175 Joel Fuhrman, M.D., *Fast Food Genocide*, New York, New York: Harper Collins, 2017 pg. 39.

176 Joel Fuhrman, M.D., *Fast Food Genocide*, New York, New York: Harper Collins, 2017 pgs. 60-62.

177 Anna Starostinetskaya, *California School District Bans Processed Meat*, VegNews, Sep. 25, 2018 https://vegnews.com/2018/9/california-school-district-bans-processed-meat

178 Doug Criss, *New York Public Schools to Have 'Meatless Mondays' Starting this Fall*, CNN, Mar. 12, 2019, https://www.cnn.com/2019/03/12/us/new-york-meatless-mondays-trnd/index.html

179 Food Revolution, *10 Revolutionary Ways School Lunch in America is Improving (Plus Healthy School Lunch Ideas)*, Food Revolution, Aug. 31, 2018, https://foodrevolution.org/blog/healthy-school-lunch-ideas/

180 The Humane Farming Association, *HFS's National Veal Boycott - Campaign Decimating Sales*, 2018, https://www.hfa.org/vealBoycott.html

181 The Voiceless Animal Cruelty Index, Voiceless.org.au, https://vaci.voiceless.org.au/

182 Susan Sontag, *Regarding the Pain of Others*, New York, New York: Picador, 2003

183 Cynthia Millburn, *How Showing Compassion for Animals Can Improve Your Health*, One Green Planet, May 6, 2017 http://www.onegreenplanet.org/animalsandnature/how-showing-compassion-for-animals-can-improve-your-health/

184 Reprinted from *World As Lover, World As Self* (1991, 2007) by Joanna Macy with permission of Parallax Press, Berkeley, California, www.parallax.org pg. 41

Chapter 2

[1] Emelia J. Benjamin, Paul Muntner, Alvaro Alonso, et al. *Heart Disease and Stroke Statistics — 2019 Update: A report from the American Heart Association.* AHA Journals Circulation. Vol. 139, No. 10, Jan. 31, 2019, https://www.ahajournals.org/doi/10.1161/CIR.0000000000000659

National Center for Health Statistics, *Health, United States, 2016 – Individual Charts and Tables, Keyword: Overweight/obesity,* Centers for Disease Control and Prevention, https://www.cdc.gov/nchs/hus/contents2016.htm

[2] There is a more accurate calculation of Body Fat based on Body Mass Index, which has been validated and shown to be precise. The relationship between BMI and Body Fat percentage is curvilinear, and the conversion depends on sex and age.

In adults the prediction formula is:

BF% = 1.20 x BMI + 0.23 x age – 10.8 x sex – 5.4

In children the BF% could be predicted by the formula:

BF% = 1.51 x BMI – 0.70 x age – 3.6 x sex + 1.4

Where the variable for sex is: males = 1, females = 0

Deurenberg P, Weststrate JA, Seidell JC. *Body Mass Index as a Measure of Body Fatness: Age- and Sex-specific Prediction Formulas.* Br J Nutr. 1991 Mar;65(2):105-14. https://www.ncbi.nlm.nih.gov/pubmed/2043597

Thank you Sven Walderich.

[3] Emelia J. Benjamin, Paul Muntner, Alvaro Alonso, et al. *Heart Disease and Stroke Statistics — 2019 Update: A report from the American Heart Association.* AHA Journals Circulation. Vol. 139, No. 10, Jan. 31, 2019, https://www.ahajournals.org/doi/10.1161/CIR.0000000000000659

[4] Emelia J. Benjamin, Paul Muntner, Alvaro Alonso, et al. *Heart Disease and Stroke Statistics — 2019 Update: A report from the American Heart Association.* AHA Journals Circulation. Vol. 139, No. 10, Jan. 31, 2019, https://www.ahajournals.org/doi/10.1161/CIR.0000000000000659

[5] Maria I. Constantino, L Molyneaux, F Limacher-Gisler, et al. *Long-term Complications and Mortality in Young-onset Diabetes: Type 2 Diabetes is More Hazardous and Lethal than Type 1 Diabetes*, Diabetes Care, Dec. 2013, 36(12):3863-9. doi: 10.2337/dc12-2455. Epub 2013 Jul 11. https://www.ncbi.nlm.nih.gov/pubmed/23846814

[6] Emelia J. Benjamin, Paul Muntner, Alvaro Alonso, et al. *Heart Disease and Stroke Statistics — 2019 Update: A report from the American Heart Association.* AHA Journals Circulation. Vol. 139, No. 10, Jan. 31, 2019, https://www.ahajournals.org/doi/10.1161/CIR.0000000000000659

[7] Emelia J. Benjamin, Paul Muntner, Alvaro Alonso, et al. *Heart Disease and Stroke Statistics — 2019 Update: A report from the American Heart Association.* AHA Journals Circulation. Vol. 139, No. 10, Jan. 31, 2019, https://www.ahajournals.org/doi/10.1161/CIR.0000000000000659

[8] American Diabetes Association, *Statistics About Diabetes*, Mar. 22, 2018, http://www.diabetes.org/diabetes-basics/statistics/

[9] Emelia J. Benjamin, Paul Muntner, Alvaro Alonso, et al. *Heart Disease and Stroke Statistics — 2019 Update: A report from the American Heart Association.* AHA Journals Circulation. Vol. 139, No. 10, Jan. 31, 2019, https://www.ahajournals.org/doi/10.1161/CIR.0000000000000659

[10] Emelia J. Benjamin, Paul Muntner, Alvaro Alonso, et al. *Heart Disease and Stroke Statistics — 2019 Update: A report from the American Heart Association.* AHA Journals Circulation. Vol. 139, No. 10, Jan. 31, 2019, https://www.ahajournals.org/doi/10.1161/CIR.0000000000000659

The State of Childhood Obesity, Childhood Obesity Trends, The State of Obesity, a collaborative project of the Trust for America's Health and the Robert Wood Johnson Foundation, Oct., 2017 https://stateofobesity.org/childhood/

[11] The NS, Suchindran C, North KE, et al. *Association of Adolescent Obesity with Risk of Severe Obesity in Adulthood*, JAMA, Nov. 10, 2010, 304(18):2042-7. doi: 10.1001/jama.2010.1635. https://www.ncbi.nlm.nih.gov/pubmed/21063014

[12] Emelia J. Benjamin, Paul Muntner, Alvaro Alonso, et al. *Heart Disease and Stroke Statistics — 2019 Update: A report from the American Heart Association.* AHA Journals Circulation. Vol. 139, No. 10, Jan. 31, 2019, https://www.ahajournals.org/doi/10.1161/CIR.0000000000000659

[13] *Overweight & Obesity Statistics*, National Institute of Diabetes and Digestive and Kidney Diseases, Aug. 2017 https://www.niddk.nih.gov/health-information/health-statistics/overweight-obesity

[14] Pencina, Michael J., Navar AM, Wojdyla D, et al., *Quantifying Importance of Major Risk Factors for Coronary Heart Disease*. Circulation, Mar. 26, 2019, 139.13 (2019): 1603-1611.) doi: 10.1161/CIRCULATIONAHA.117.031855. https://www.ncbi.nlm.nih.gov/pubmed/30586759

[15] American Heart Association, *Cardiovascular Disease and Diabetes*, Heart.org, https://www.heart.org/en/health-topics/diabetes/why-diabetes-matters/cardiovascular-disease--diabetes

[16] Emelia J. Benjamin, Paul Muntner, Alvaro Alonso, et al. *Heart Disease and Stroke Statistics — 2019 Update: A report from the American Heart Association.* AHA Journals Circulation. Vol. 139, No. 10, Jan. 31, 2019, https://www.ahajournals.org/doi/10.1161/CIR.0000000000000659

[17] National Center for Chronic Disease Prevention and Health Promotion, Division for Heart Disease and Stroke Prevention, *Heart Disease Facts*, Centers for Disease Control and Prevention, Nov. 28, 2017 https://www.cdc.gov/heartdisease/facts.htm

[18] Emelia J. Benjamin, Paul Muntner, Alvaro Alonso, et al. *Heart Disease and Stroke Statistics — 2019 Update: A report from the American Heart Association.* AHA Journals Circulation. Vol. 139, No. 10, Jan. 31, 2019, https://www.ahajournals.org/doi/10.1161/CIR.0000000000000659

[19] Benjamin EJ, Blaha MJ, Chiuve SE, et al. *Heart Disease and Stroke Statistics 2017 At-a-Glance*, A report from the American Heart Association. Jan. 25, 2017 Circulation. doi: 10.1161/CIR.0000000000000485 https://healthmetrics.heart.org/wp-content/uploads/2017/06/Heart-Disease-and-Stroke-Statistics-2017-ucm_491265.pdf

[20] Joel Fuhrman, M.D. *Fast Food Genocide*, New York, New York: Harper Collins, 2017 pg. 32.

[21] *Cancer Facts & Figures 2019*, The American Cancer Society, 2019 https://www.cancer.org/research/cancer-facts-statistics/all-cancer-facts-figures/cancer-facts-figures-2019.html

[22] C. Brooke Steele, Cheryll C. Thomas, S. Jane Henley, et al. *Vital Signs: Trends in Incidence of Cancers Associated with Overweight and Obesity - United States, 2005 - 2014*, MMWR Morb Mortal Wkly Rep 2017;66:1052-1058 Centers for Disease Control and Prevention, Oct. 3, 2017 https://www.cdc.gov/mmwr/volumes/66/wr/mm6639e1.htm

[23] Mark Hyman, M.D. *Eat Fat, Get Thin*, New York, New York: Little, Brown and Co., Hachette Book Group, 2016 pg. 167

[24] Emily J. Gallagher, Derek LeRoith, *Minireview: IGF, Insulin, and Cancer, Endocrinology*, Vol 152, Issue 7, Jul. 1, 2011, Pgs. 2546-2551, https://doi.org/10.1210/en.2011-0231 https://academic.oup.com/endo/article/152/7/2546/2457127

Thank you Sven Walderich.

[25] American Cancer Society. *Cancer Facts & Figures 2019*. Atlanta: American Cancer Society; 2019. https://www.cancer.org/content/dam/cancer-org/research/cancer-facts-and-statistics/annual-cancer-facts-and-figures/2019/cancer-facts-and-figures-2019.pdf

[26] Liesi E. Hebert, Jennife Weuve, Paul A. Scherr, Denis A. Evans, *Alzheimer Disease in the United States (2010-2050) Estimated Using the 2010 Census*, American Academy of Neurology, US National Library of Medicine, May 7, 2013 Neurology. 2013 May 7; 80(19): 1778-1783. https://www.ncbi.nlm.nih.gov/pmc/articles/PMC3719424/

[27] Yi-Fang Chuang, Yang An, Murat Bilgel, et al. *Midlife Adiposity Predicts Earlier Onset of Alzheimer's Dementia, Neuropathology and Presymptomatic Cerebral Amyloid Accumulation*, Mol Psychiatry. Jul, 2016 21(7): 910-915. https://www.ncbi.nlm.nih.gov/pmc/articles/PMC5811225/

[28] Samantha Budd Haeberlein, *Why This Scientist is Hopeful a Cure to Alzheimer's Disease Isn't Far Off*, Time Magazine, Jan. 4, 2018, http://time.com/5087364/scientist-hopeful-cure-to-alzheimers-disease-isnt-far-off/

[29] Joel Fuhrman, M.D. as stated in *iThrive! Rising From the Depths of Diabetes & Obesity*, 9 part documentary series, Executive Producers: Jonathan Hunsaker, Jonathan McMahon, Michael Skye, 2017, iThrive Publishing LLC, https://go.ithriveseries.com/

[30] Mike Stobbe, *U.S. Life Expectancy Will Likely Decline for Third Straight Year*, Associated Press, May 23, 2018 https://www.bloomberg.com/news/articles/2018-05-23/with-death-rate-up-us-life-expectancy-is-likely-down-again

[31] Mark Hyman, M.D. *Eat Fat, Get Thin*, New York, New York: Little, Brown and Co., Hachette Book

Group, 2016 pg. 20

[32] Jason Fung, M.D. *The Obesity Code*, British Columbia, Vancouver: Greystone Books, 2016 pg. 78

[33] Joseph Mercola, D.O., as stated in *iThrive! Rising From the Depths of Diabetes & Obesity*, 9 part documentary series, Executive Producers: Jonathan Hunsaker, Jonathan McMahon, Michael Skye, 2017, iThrive Publishing LLC, https://go.ithriveseries.com/

[34] Mark Hyman, M.D. *Food – What the Heck Should I Eat?*, New York, New York: Little, Brown and Company, 2018

[35] Adams KM, Kohlmeier M, Zeisel SH, *Nutrition Education in U.S. Medical Schools: Latest Update of a National Survey*, Academic Medicine – Journal of the Association of American Medical Colleges, Sep., 2010 Acad Med. 2010 Sep;85(9):1537–42. doi: 10.1097/ACM.0b013e3181eab71b. https://www.ncbi.nlm.nih.gov/pubmed/20736683

[36] Mark Hyman, M.D. *Eat Fat, Get Thin*, New York, New York: Little, Brown and Co., Hachette Book Group, 2016 pg. 111

[37] Joel Fuhrman, M.D. *Fast Food Genocide*, New York, New York: Harper Collins, 2017 pg. 77.

[38] For more information about Dr. Fuhrman and the Nutritarian Eating Plan go to https://www.drfuhrman.com/

[39] For more information about Dr. Fuhrman and the Nutritarian Eating Plan go to https://www.drfuhrman.com/

[40] Health Net News, *Keep Diabetes in Check*, Spring, 2018

[41] Xiaohui Zhuo, Ping Zhang, Lawrence barker, et all, *The Lifetime Cost of Diabetes and Its Implications for Diabetes Prevention*, Diabetes Care, American Diabetes Association, 2014 Sep; 37(9): 2557–2564. http://care.diabetesjournals.org/content/37/9/2557

[42] Elisabeth Rosenthal, *An American Sickness*, New York, New York: Penguin Books, 2017, pg. 186

[43] Joel Fuhrman, M.D. *Fast Food Genocide*, New York, New York: Harper Collins, 2017 pg. 78.

[44] Joel Fuhrman, M.D. *Fast Food Genocide*, New York, New York: Harper Collins, 2017 pg. 97.

[45] Jason Fung, M.D. *The Obesity Code*, British Columbia, Vancouver: Greystone Books, 2016 pgs. 31 and 69

[46] Benjamin EJ, Blaha MJ, Chiuve SE, et al. *Heart Disease and Stroke Statistics 2017 At-a-Glance*, A report from the American Heart Association. Jan. 25, 2017 Circulation. doi: 10.1161/CIR.0000000000000485 https://healthmetrics.heart.org/wp-content/uploads/2017/06/Heart-Disease-and-Stroke-Statistics-2017-ucm_491265.pdf

[47] Jamie Ducharme, *There's No Such Thing as a Single 'Best' Diet*, Time Magazine, Time Health, Mar. 15, 2018, http://time.com/5183371/which-diet-is-best/

[48] Joel Fuhrman, M.D. *Fast Food Genocide*, New York, New York: Harper Collins, 2017 pg. 75.

[49] Wenpeng You and Maciej Henneberg, *Meat in Modern Diet, Just as Bad as Sugar, Correlates with Worldwide Obesity: An Ecological Analysis*, Journal of Nutrition & Food Sciences 6:517, Jun. 8, 2016, doi:10.4172/2155-9600.1000517, https://www.omicsonline.org/peer-reviewed/meat-in-modern-diet-just-as-bad-as-sugar-correlates-with-worldwideobesity-an-ecological-analysis-74168.html

[50] Reuters, *Red Meat Linked to Increased Stroke Risk*, Fox news Health, Nov. 27, 2015, http://www.foxnews.com/health/2015/11/27/red-meat-linked-to-increased-stroke-risk.html

[51] An Pan, Qi Sun, Adam M Bernstein, et al. *Red Meat Consumption and Risk of Type 2 Diabetes: 3 Cohorts of U.S. Adults and an Updated Meta-Analysis*, The American Journal of Clinical Nutrition, Vol. 94, Issue 4, Oct. 1, 2011, Pages 1088–1096, https://doi.org/10.3945/ajcn.111.018978, https://academic.oup.com/ajcn/article/94/4/1088/4598110

[52] Mark Reynolds, *REVEALED: A 'Western' Diet Increases Risk of Alzheimer's Disease*, Express, Aug. 28, 2016, https://www.express.co.uk/life-style/health/704723/western-diet-increases-risk-Alzheimer-disease-red-meat-dairy

[53] Maryam S. Farvid, Eunyoung Cho, Wendy Y Chen, et al. *Dietary Protein Sources in Early Adulthood and Breast Cancer Incidence: Prospective Cohort Study*, British Medical Journal, Jun. 10, 2014, BMJ 2014;348:g3437 https://www.bmj.com/content/348/bmj.g3437#aff-2

[54] Harvard T.H. Chan School of Public Health, *Red Meat May Raise Young Women's Breast Cancer Risk*, https://www.hsph.harvard.edu/news/hsph-in-the-news/red-meat-may-raise-breast-cancer-risk/

55 Yale University, *Animal-Based Nutrients Linked With Higher Risk of Stomach and Esophageal Cancers*, YaleNews, Oct. 15, 2001, https://news.yale.edu/2001/10/15/animal-based-nutrients-linked-higher-risk-stomach-and-esophageal-cancers

56 Thibault Fiolet, Laury Sellem, Benjamin Alles, et al. *Consumption of Ultra-processed Foods and Cancer Risk: Results from NutriNet-Sante Prospective Cohort*, The BMJ, BMJ 2018; 360 Feb. 14, 2018, https://www.bmj.com/content/360/bmj.k322

57 Neal Barnard, M.D., TEDxBismarck, *Power Foods for the Brain with Dr. Neal Barnard*, TEDx Talks, Sep. 20, 2016, https://www.youtube.com/watch?v=v_ONFix_e4k

58 Lassale C, Batty GD, Baghdadli A, et al. *Healthy Dietary Indices and Risk of Depressive Outcomes: a Systematic Review and Meta-analysis of Observational Studies*, Molecular Psychiatry, Sep. 26, 2018, doi: 10.1038/s41380-018-0237-8 https://www.ncbi.nlm.nih.gov/pubmed/30254236

59 Good Medicine, *Healthful Diet Helps Prevent Depression*, The Physicians Committee For Responsible Medicine, Winter, 2019, Vol. 28, No. 1, pg. 5 https://p.widencdn.net/ayfskf/2019-No.-1-Winter-Good-Medicine

60 Laurie David and Katie Couric's *Fed Up*, 2014 https://www.amazon.com/Fed-Up-Katie-Couric/dp/B00MRHF9LE/ref=sr_1_1?s=movies-tv&ie=UTF8&qid=1520694651&sr=1-1&keywords=fed+up

61 C. Ayyad and T. Andersen, *Long-term Efficacy of Dietary Treatment of Obesity: a Systematic Review of Studies Published Between 1931 and 1999*, US National Library of Medicine, National Institutes of Health, Obes Rev. 2000 Oct: 1(2):113-9 https://www.ncbi.nlm.nih.gov/pubmed/12119984

62 Mark Hyman, M.D. *Eat Fat, Get Thin*, New York, New York: Little, Brown and Co., Hachette Book Group, 2016 pg. 33

63 Joel Fuhrman, M.D. *Fast Food Genocide*, New York, New York: Harper Collins, 2017 pg. 24.

64 Adrian Meule and Ashley N. Gearhardt, *Food Addiction in the Light of DSM-5*, Nutrients 2014 Sep; 6(9): 3653-3671. US National Library of Medicine, National Institutes of Health, Sep. 16, 2014 https://www.ncbi.nlm.nih.gov/pmc/articles/PMC4179181/

65 Almudena Sanchez-Villegas, Estefania Toledo, Jokin de Irala, et al. *Fast-food and Commercial Baked Goods Consumption and the Risk of Depression*, Public Health Nutrition: 15(3), 424-432 Aug. 11, 2011 https://pdfs.semanticscholar.org/529c/d930e5662b3aabcf9b3b9f26a6982fdfbcbb.pdf

66 Anika Knuppel, Martin J. Shipley, Clare H. Llewellyn, Eric J. Brunner, *Sugar Intake from Sweet Food and Beverages, Common Mental Disorder and Depression: Prospective Findings from the Whitehall II Study*, Scientific Reports 7, Article # 6286, Jul. 27, 2017, https://www.nature.com/articles/s41598-017-05649-7

67 Robert L. Reece, *Fighting Fat Stigma With Science*, Teaching Tolerance, a publication of the Southern Poverty Law Center, Fall, 2017

68 Mark Hyman, M.D. *Eat Fat, Get Thin*, New York, New York: Little, Brown and Co., Hachette Book Group, 2016 pg. 58

69 Caitlin Bove. MD, Vivek Jain, MD, Naji Younes, PhD, et al. *What You Eat Could Affect Your Sleep: Dietary Findings in Patients With Newly Diagnosed Obstructive Sleep Apnea*, American Journal of Lifestyle Medicine, Apr. 27, 2018 http://journals.sagepub.com/doi/abs/10.1177/1559827618765097

70 Dean Ornish, M.D., as stated in *iThrive! Rising From the Depths of Diabetes & Obesity*, 9 part documentary series, Executive Producers: Jonathan Hunsaker, Jonathan McMahon, Michael Skye, 2017, iThrive Publishing LLC, https://go.ithriveseries.com/

71 Julia Boehm, LD Kubansky *The Heart's Content: the Association between Positive Psychological Well-being and Cardiovascular Health*, Psychological Bulletin, Jul. 2012, 138(4):655-91. doi: 10.1037/a0027448. Epub 2012 Apr 16. https://www.ncbi.nlm.nih.gov/pubmed/22506752

72 "Compelling evidence shows your net carbohydrate intake is a primary factor that determines your body's fat ratio, and processed grains and sugars (particularly fructose) are the primary culprits behind skyrocketing obesity, diabetes and chronic disease rates." Joseph Mercola, D.O., *Obesity Takes Greater Than Ever Toll on Global Health*, Mercola.com, Jun. 28, 2017, https://articles.mercola.com/sites/articles/archive/2017/06/28/obesity-global-epidemic.aspx

73 Jason Fung, M.D. *The Obesity Code*, British Columbia, Vancouver: Greystone Books, 2016 pg. 163

74 George A. Bray, et all, *Consumption of High-Fructose Corn Syrup in Beverages May Play a Role in the Epidemic of Obesity*, American Journal of Clinical Nutrition 79, no 4 (2004): 537-543

[75] Department of Biology, University of Indiana, *Obesity, Type 2 Diabetes and Fructose*, Aug. 24, 2010, http://www.indiana.edu/~oso/Fructose/Fructose.html (access via Safari)

[76] Mark Hyman, M.D. *Eat Fat, Get Thin*, New York, New York: Little, Brown and Co., Hachette Book Group, 2016 pg. 49

[77] Mark Hyman, M.D. *Eat Fat, Get Thin*, New York, New York: Little, Brown and Co., Hachette Book Group, 2016 pg. 48

[78] Robert H. Lustig, M.D., *Current Controversies in Nutrition: Letting Science Be the Guide — Sugar: The Bitter Truth*, University of California Television , Jul. 30, 2009, https://www.youtube.com/watch?v=dBnniua6-oM

[79] Hilary Parker, *A Sweet Problem: Princeton Researchers Find that High-fructose Corn Syrup Prompts Considerably More Weight Gain*, Princeton University, Mar. 22, 2010, https://www.princeton.edu/news/2010/03/22/sweet-problem-princeton-researchers-find-high-fructose-corn-syrup-prompts

[80] Kristin Wartman, *What's Really Making Us Fat?*, The Atlantic, Mar. 8, 2012 https://www.theatlantic.com/health/archive/2012/03/whats-really-making-us-fat/254087/

[81] Tim Ryan, *The Real Food Revolution*, Carlsbad, California: Hay House, 2014

[82] Tim Ryan, *The Real Food Revolution*, Carlsbad, California: Hay House 2014, pgs. 39-40

[83] Lisa LaPoint, *FDA Added Sugar Label Could be a Cost-effective Way to Improve Health, Generate Savings*, Tufts Now, Apr. 15, 2019, https://now.tufts.edu/news-releases/fda-added-sugar-label-could-be-cost-effective-way-improve-health-generate-savings

[84] Yue Huang, Chris Kypridemos, Junxiu Liu, et al. *Cost-Effectiveness of the US Food and Drug Administration Added Sugar Labeling Policy for Improving Diet and Health*, AHA Journals - Circulation, doi.org/10.1161/CIRCULATIONAHA.118.036751 Apr. 15, 2019, https://www.ahajournals.org/doi/10.1161/CIRCULATIONAHA.118.036751

[85] Cristin E. Kearns, DDS, MBA, Laura A. Schmidt, PhD, MSW, MPH, Stanton A. Glantz, PhD, *Sugar Industry and Coronary Heart Disease Research - A Historical Analysis of Internal Industry Documents*, American Medical Association, 2016, JAMA Intern Med. 2016;176(11):1680-1685. doi:10.1001/jamainternmed.2016.5394 https://jamanetwork.com/journals/jamainternalmedicine/article-abstract/2548255?redirect=true

[86] Kevin D. Hall, Alexis Ayuketah, Robert Brychta, et al. *Ultra-Processed Diets Cause Excess Calorie Intake and Weight Gain:* An Inpatient Randomized Controlled Trial of Ad Libitum Food Intake, Cell Metabolism, May 16, 2019, DOI: https://doi.org/10.1016/j.cmet.2019.05.008 https://www.cell.com/cell-metabolism/fulltext/S1550-4131(19)30248-7

[87] Maria Godoy, *It's Not Just Salt, Sugar, Fat: Study Finds Ultra-Processed Foods Drive Weight Gain*, NPR, May 16, 2019, https://www.npr.org/sections/thesalt/2019/05/16/723693839/its-not-just-salt-sugar-fat-study-finds-ultra-processed-foods-drive-weight-gain

[88] Jason Fung, M.D. *The Obesity Code*, British Columbia, Vancouver: Greystone Books, 2016 pg. 175

[89] Kyro C, Tjonneland A, Overvad K, et al. *Higher Whole-Grain Intake is Associated with Lower Risk of Type 2 Diabetes among Middle-Aged Men and Women:* The Danish Diet, Cancer, and Health Cohort, Journal of Nutrition, Sep. 1, 2018, 148(9):1434-1444. Doi: 10. 1093/jn/nxy112. https://www.ncbi.nlm.nih.gov/pubmed/30016529

[90] Good Medicine, *Whole Grains Help Protect Against Type 2 Diabetes*, The Physicians Committee For Responsible Medicine, Winter, 2019, Vol. 28, No. 1, pg. 5 https://p.widencdn.net/ayfskf/2019-No.-1-Winter-Good-Medicine

[91] Mark Hyman, M.D. *Eat Fat, Get Thin*, New York, New York: Little, Brown and Co., Hachette Book Group, 2016 pg. 48

[92] *The Mineral Depletion of Foods Available to Us as a Nation (1940 - 2002) - A Review of the 6th Edition of McCance and Widdowson*, research article by David Thomas, July 2007 http://journals.sagepub.com/doi/abs/10.1177/026010600701900205

[93] Helena Bottemiller Evich, *The Great Nutrient Collapse*, The Agenda - Politico, Sep. 13, 2017 https://www.politico.com/agenda/story/2017/09/13/food-nutrients-carbon-dioxide-000511

[94] *The Mineral Depletion of Foods Available to Us as a Nation (1940 - 2002) - A Review of the 6th Edition of McCance and Widdowson*, research article by David Thomas, July 2007 http://journals.sagepub.com/doi/abs/10.1177/026010600701900205

[95] Joel Fuhrman, M.D. *Fast Food Genocide*, New York, New York: Harper Collins, 2017

[96] Joel Fuhrman, M.D. *Fast Food Genocide*, New York, New York: Harper Collins, 2017

[97] *IARC Monographs Volume 112: Evaluation of Five Organophosphate Insecticides and Herbicides*, World Health Organization, International Agency for Research on Cancer, Mar. 20, 2015, http://www.iarc.fr/en/media-centre/iarcnews/pdf/MonographVolume112.pdf

[98] Guyton K.Z., Loomis D, Grosse Y, et al. International Agency for Research on Cancer Monograph Working group, IARC, Lyon, France. *Carcinogenicity of Tetrachlorvinphos*, Parathion, Malathion, Diazinon, and Glyphosate, Lancet Oncol. 2015 May;16(5):490-91

[99] *California Defeats Monsanto in Court to List Glyphosate as Carcinogen*, Sustainable Pulsa, Apr. 20, 2018 https://sustainablepulse.com/2018/04/20/california-defeats-monsanto-in-court-to-list-glyphosate-as-probable-carcinogen/#.WvtpUxMvxhE

[100] Luoping Zhang, Iemaan Rana, Rachel M. Shaffer, et al. *Exposure to Glyphosate-Based Herbicides and Risk for Non-Hodgkin Lymphoma: A Meta-Analysis and Supporting Evidence*, Science Direct, doi.org/10.1016/j.mrrev.2019.02.001 Feb. 10, 2019, https://www.sciencedirect.com/science/article/pii/S1383574218300887

[101] Emily Dixon, *Common Weed Killer Glyphosate Increases Cancer Risk by 41%*, Study Says, CNN, Feb 14, 2019. https://www.cnn.com/2019/02/14/health/us-glyphosate-cancer-study-scli-intl/index.html

[102] Yelena Sukhoterina, *Sorry, Monsanto: GMO Crops Now banned in Nearly 40 Countries, Grown in Just 28*, AltHealth Works, Apr. 21, 2016 https://althealthworks.com/9778/list-of-38-countries-that-banned-gmos-and-28-that-grow-themyelena/

[103] *Labeling Around the World*, Just Label It!, http://www.justlabelit.org/right-to-know-center/labeling-around-the-world/

[104] David Montgomery, Anne Biklé, *The Hidden Half of Nature*, New York, New York: W.W. Norton & Company, 2016, pg.255

[105] Alexis Temkin, Ph.D, Toxicologist, *Breakfast With a Dose of Roundup?* Environmental Working Group Children's health Initiative, Aug. 15, 2018 https://www.ewg.org/childrenshealth/glyphosateincereal/#.W5c2VJNKhhG

[106] Center for Environmental Health, *Glyphosate in School Cereals*, ceh.org Dec. 2018, https://www.ceh.org/glyphosate-school-cereals/

[107] Caroline Cox, *There's a Toxic Weedkiller on the Menu in K-12 Schools Across the U.S.*, Common Dreams, Jan. 9, 2019, https://www.commondreams.org/views/2019/01/09/theres-toxic-weedkiller-menu-k-12-schools-across-us

[108] Kara Cook, *Glyphosate Pesticide in Beer and Wine*, U.S. PIRG Education Fund, Feb. 2019, https://uspirg.org/feature/usp/glyphosate-pesticide-beer-and-wine

[109] Carey Gillam. *Whitewash*. Washington, DC: Island Press, 2017. Pg.237

[110] Kara Cook, *Glyphosate Pesticide in Beer and Wine*, U.S. PIRG Education Fund, Feb. 2019, https://uspirg.org/feature/usp/glyphosate-pesticide-beer-and-wine

[111] Monica Amarelo, *Jury Slams Monsanto for Corporate Malfeasance in Roundup Cancer Trial, Awards $80 Million in Damages*, Environmental Working Group, Mar. 27, 2019, https://www.ewg.org/release/second-time-8-months-bayer-monsanto-s-roundup-liable-cancer-lawsuit

[112] Joel Rosenblatt and Tim Loh, *Bayer's $2 Billion Roundup Damages Boost Pressure to Settle*, Bloomberg, May 13, 2019, https://www.bloomberg.com/news/articles/2019-05-13/bayer-loses-its-third-trial-over-claims-roundup-causes-cancer

[113] Andreas Becker, *Bayer Investors Angry Over Plummeting Share Price*, DW, Apr. 26, 2019, https://www.dw.com/en/bayer-investors-angry-over-plummeting-share-price/a-48495269

[114] Kara Cook, *Glyphosate Pesticide in Beer and Wine*, U.S. PIRG Education Fund, Feb. 2019, https://uspirg.org/feature/usp/glyphosate-pesticide-beer-and-wine

[115] Center For Food Safety, *Get the App for iPhone or Android*, https://www.centerforfoodsafety.org/issues/311/ge-foods/non-gmo-shoppers-guide-325/1847/get-the-app-for-iphone-or-android

[116] Jeffrey M. Smith MBA, *Survey Reports Improved Health After Avoiding Genetically Modified Foods*, International Journal of Human Nutrition and Functional Medicine, 2017 https://pdfs.semanticscholar.org/49b2/91e5fcfbf0efbfc1eea34a74e99c8cf6fb6e.pdf

[117] Vandana Shiva. *Who Really Feeds The World?*. Berkeley, California: North Atlantic Books, 2016. pg.

i Vandana Shiva cites: Marie-Monique Robin, *Our Daily Poison: From Pesticides to packaging, How Chemicals Have contaminated the Food Chain and Are Making Us Sick* (New York: New Press, 2014)

[118] Joseph Mercola, D.O., *Top 22 Intermittent Fasting Benefits*, Fitness.mercola.com, Jan. 18, 2019, https://fitness.mercola.com/sites/fitness/archive/2019/01/18/incorporate-intermittent-fasting-daily-routine.aspx

[119] Jason Fung, M.D., Medical Director and co-founder of the Intensive Dietary Management Program, as stated in *iThrive! Rising From the Depths of Diabetes & Obesity*, 9 part documentary series, Executive Producers: Jonathan Hunsaker, Jonathan McMahon, Michael Skye, 2017, iThrive Publishing LLC, https://go.ithriveseries.com/

[120] Max Roser, *Life Expectancy*. Published online at OurWorldInData.org. 2018, Retrieved from: https://ourworldindata.org/life-expectancy

[121] Max Roser, *Life Expectancy*. Published online at OurWorldInData.org. 2018, Retrieved from: https://ourworldindata.org/life-expectancy

[122] Karen Bluth, *How to Help Teens Become More Self-Compassionate*, Greater Good Magazine, Oct. 19, 2017 https://greatergood.berkeley.edu/article/item/how_to_help_teens_become_more_self_compassionate

[123] Mark Hyman, M.D. *Eat Fat, Get Thin*, New York, New York: Little, Brown and Co., Hachette Book Group, 2016 pg. 7

[124] Ford ES, Bergmann MM, Kroger J, et al. *Healthy Living is the Best Revenge: Findings From the European Prospective Investigation into Cancer and Nutrition-Potsdam Study*, Arch Intern Med. 2009 Aug 10;169(15):1355-62. doi: 10.1001/archinternmed.2009.237. https://www.ncbi.nlm.nih.gov/pubmed/19667296

[125] *Best Diets U.S. News & World Report Rankings*, U.S. News & World Report, 2019 https://health.usnews.com/best-diet/best-diets-overall

[126] Jamie Ducharme, *These Are the 5 Best Diets for 2019*, According to Experts, Time Magazine, Jan 2, 2019 http://time.com/5486616/best-diet-mediterranean-diet/

[127] Marco Springman, H. Charles, J. Godfray, et al, *Analysis and Valuation of the Health and Climate Change Co-benefits of Dietary Change*, Proceedings of the National Academy of Sciences of the U.S.A. PNAS Apr 12, 2016. 113 (15) 4146-4151; http://www.pnas.org/content/113/15/4146.full

[128] Sinha R, Cross AJ, Graubard BI, et al. *Meat Intake and Mortality: a Prospective Study of Over Half a Million People*, Arch Intern Med. 2009 Mar 23;169(6):562-71. doi: https://www.ncbi.nlm.nih.gov/pubmed/19307518

[129] Institute for Health Metrics and Evaluation, *Americans Make Progress Against Some Health Risks, but Obesity and Smoking Cause More Deaths*, 2015 http://www.healthdata.org/news-release/americans-make-progress-against-some-health-risks-obesity-and-smoking-cause-more-deaths

[130] Kathryn Doyle, *Too Much Animal Protein Tied to Higher Diabetes Risk*, Reuters Health News, Apr. 14, 2014, https://www.reuters.com/article/us-animal-protein-diabetes/too-much-animal-protein-tied-to-higher-diabetes-risk-idUSBREA3D1HV20140414

[131] Najjar RS, Moore CE, Montgomery BD. *A Defined, Plant-based Diet Utilized in an Outpatient Cardiovascular Clinic Effectively Treats Hypercholesterolemia and Hypertension and Reduces Medications*, Clin Cardiol. 2018 Mar;41(3):307-313. doi: 10.1002/clc.22863, Mar. 25, 2018 https://www.ncbi.nlm.nih.gov/pubmed/29575002

[132] Nicole Peranick, *How to Veg Out for Plant-powered Customers*, New Hope Network, May 30, 2017, http://www.newhope.com/retail-and-distribution/how-veg-out-plant-powered-customers

[133] *Recommendations for Cancer Prevention*, American Institute for Cancer Research, 2018, http://www.aicr.org/reduce-your-cancer-risk/recommendations-for-cancer-prevention/

[134] Kathryn E Bradbury, Neil Murphy, Timothy J Key, *Diet and Colorectal Cancer in UK Biobank: A Prospective Study*, Oxford Academic - International Journal of Epidemiology, dyz064, https://doi.org/10.1093/ije/dyz064 Apr. 17, 2019, https://academic.oup.com/ije/advance-article/doi/10.1093/ije/dyz064/5470096

[135] Heather Fields, MD; Denise Millstine, MD; Neera Agrwal, MD; et all, *Is Meat Killing Us?*, Mayo Clinic Arizona in Scottsdale, The Journal of the American Osteopathic Association, May, 2016 Vo. 116, No. 5 296-300. doi:10.7556/jaoa.2016.059

http://jaoa.org/article.aspx?articleid=2517494

[136] Julia Baudry, PhD, Karen E. Assmann, PhD, Mathilde Touvier, PhD, et al. *Association of Frequency of Organic Food Consumption With Cancer Risk*, Dec. 2018, JAMA Intern Med. 2018;178(12):1597-1606. doi:10.1001/jamainternmed.2018.4357
https://jamanetwork.com/journals/jamainternalmedicine/article-abstract/2707948

[137] Alex Formuzis, Environmental Working Group, *Massive Study Finds Eating Organic Slashes Cancer Risks*, Oct. 22, 2018, https://www.ewg.org/release/massive-study-finds-eating-organic-slashes-cancer-risks

[138] Chris Wark, *The Top 10 Vegetables You Can Eat to Prevent and Reverse Cancer*, Food Revolution Network, July 5, 2018, https://foodrevolution.org/blog/cancer-fighting-foods/

[139] Dale Bredesen, M.D, *The End of Alzheimer's: The First Program to Prevent and Reverse Cognitive Decline*, New York, New York: Avery, an inprint of Penguim Random House, 2017

[140] Bryan D. James, Sue E. Leurgans, Liesi E. Hebert, et al. *Contribution of Alzheimer Disease to Mortality in the United States*, Neurology, Mar. 15, 2014, DOI: https://doi.org/10.1212/WNL.0000000000000240
http://n.neurology.org/content/early/2014/03/05/WNL.0000000000000240

[141] Fanfan Zheng, Li Yan, Zhenchun Yang, et al. HbA1c, *Diabetes and Cognitive Decline: the English Longitudinal Study of Ageing*, Diabetologia, Apr. 2018, Vol. 61, Issue 4, pp839-848, Jan. 25, 2018, https://link.springer.com/article/10.1007/s00125-017-4541-7

[142] Dale Bredesen, M.D., *The End of Alzheimer's: The First Program to Prevent and Reverse Cognitive Decline*, New York, New York: Avery, Penguin Random House, 2017 https://www.amazon.com/End-Alzheimers-Program-Prevent-Cognitive/dp/0735216207/ref=sr_1_1?ie=UTF8&qid=1501612928&sr=8-1&keywords=recode+bredesen

[143] Susan Levin, *How Eating Beans Instead of Beef Will Save You and the Planet*, AlterNet, Jun. 18, 2017 https://www.ecowatch.com/diet-climate-change-2435942459.html

[144] Neal Barnard, M.D., *Dr. Neal Barnard's Cookbook for Reversing Diabetes*, Rodale Books, 2018, https://www.amazon.com/Neal-Barnards-Cookbook-Reversing-Diabetes/dp/1623369290/

[145] Jason Fung, M.D., Medical Director and co-founder of the Intensive Dietary Management Program, as stated in *iThrive! Rising From the Depths of Diabetes & Obesity*, 9 part documentary series, Executive Producers: Jonathan Hunsaker, Jonathan McMahon, Michael Skye, 2017, iThrive Publishing LLC, https://go.ithriveseries.com/

[146] Joel Fuhrman, M.D. *Fast Food Genocide*, New York, New York: Harper Collins, 2017 pg. 7.

[147] Bradley Sawyer, Cynthia Cox. *How Does Health Spending in the U.S. Compare to Other Countries?* Kaiser Family Foundation, Feb. 13, 2018, Analysis from data from OECD (2017), *OECD Health Data: Health Expenditure and Financing: Health Expenditure Indicators*, OECD Health Statistics (database). DOI: 10.1787/health-data-en https://www.healthsystemtracker.org/chart-collection/health-spending-u-s-compare-countries/?_sf_s=health+spending#item-start

[148] Mark Hyman, M.D. Food - *What the Heck Should I Eat?*, New York, New York: Little, Brown and Company, 2018, pg.11

[149] Philip J. Tuso, Mohamed H Ismail, Benjamin P Ha, Carole Bartolotto, *Nutritional Update for Physicians: Plant-Based Diets*, The Permanente Journal, 2013 Spring; 17(2): 61-66. doi: 10.7812/TPP/12-085 https://www.ncbi.nlm.nih.gov/pmc/articles/PMC3662288/

[150] The Physicians Committee for Responsible Medicine, *Changing Lives Through Clinical Research*, Good Medicine, Sum., 2018 Vol 27, No.3

[151] Elisabeth Rosenthal, *An American Sickness*, New York, New York: Penguin Books, 2017, pg. 195

[152] Elisabeth Rosenthal, *An American Sickness*, New York, New York: Penguin Books, 2017, pg. 195-6

[153] Elisabeth Rosenthal, *An American Sickness*, New York, New York: Penguin Books, 2017, pg. 23

[154] Joseph Mercola, D.O., *Ghost in the Machine, Part 1 - Drug Safety and Media Shaped by Big Pharma*, mercola.com, Dec. 27, 2017, https://articles.mercola.com/sites/articles/archive/2017/12/27/drug-safety-media-shaped-by-big-pharma.aspx

[155] Beth Snyder Bulik, *The Top 10 Most-advertised Prescription Drug Brands*, FiercePharma, https://www.fiercepharma.com/special-report/top-10-most-advertised-prescription-drug-brands

[156] Elisabeth Rosenthal, *An American Sickness*, New York, New York: Penguin Books, 2017, pg. 100

[157] Paul Crozier, *Prescription Drug Commercials*, 17/51 Intermezzo Commercial, You Tube, https://www.

youtube.com/watch?v=cD8nlUHyVak&list=PLQZTk4BbrTExLq1L.mdj1HqEOZRxv0zbN2&index=4

[158] Paul Crozier, *Prescription Drug Commercials*, 39/51 Cialis Commercial, You Tube, https://www.youtube.com/watch?v=mRoG-HyKcqA&index=39&list=PLQZTk4BbrTExLq1Lmdj1HqEOZRxv0zbN2

[159] Joseph Mercola, D.O., *Ghost in the Machine, Part 1 - Drug Safety and Media Shaped by Big Pharma*, mercola.com, Dec. 27, 2017, https://articles.mercola.com/sites/articles/archive/2017/12/27/drug-safety-media-shaped-by-big-pharma.aspx

[160] Gary Bentley, *Big Pharma Owns the Corporate Media, but Americans Are Waking Up and Fighting Back*, The Ring of Fire Network, story: Big Pharma's Influence, reported by Mike Papantonio, Apr. 11, 2017 https://trofire.com/2017/04/11/big-pharma-owns-corporate-media-americans-waking-fighting-back/

[161] Gary Bentley, *Big Pharma Owns the Corporate Media, but Americans Are Waking Up and Fighting Back*, The Ring of Fire Network, story: Big Pharma's Influence, reported by Mike Papantonio, Apr. 11, 2017 https://trofire.com/2017/04/11/big-pharma-owns-corporate-media-americans-waking-fighting-back/

[162] Joseph Mercola, D.O., *Ghost in the Machine, Part 1 - Drug Safety and Media Shaped by Big Pharma*, mercola.com, Dec. 27, 2017, https://articles.mercola.com/sites/articles/archive/2017/12/27/drug-safety-media-shaped-by-big-pharma.aspx

[163] Timothy S. Anderson, M.D., Shravan Dave, BS, Chester B. Good, Md, MPH, et al. *Academic Medical Center Leadership on Pharmaceutical Company Boards of Directors*, JAMA. 2014;311(13):1353-1355. doi:10.1001/jama.2013.284925 Apr. 2, 2014 https://jamanetwork.com/journals/jama/fullarticle/1853147

[164] Annie Waldman, *Big Pharma Quietly Enlists Leading Professors to Justify $1,000 Per Day Drugs*, ProPublica co-published with Consumer Reports, Feb. 23, 2017, https://www.propublica.org/article/big-pharma-quietly-enlists-leading-professors-to-justify-1000-per-day-drugs

[165] Marshall Allen, *Why Your Insurer Doesn't Care About Your Big Bills*, ProPublica co-published with NPR, May 25, 2018, https://www.propublica.org/article/why-your-health-insurer-does-not-care-about-your-big-bills

[166] Elisabeth Rosenthal, *An American Sickness*, New York, New York: Penguin Books, 2017, pgs. 241-2

[167] Marshall Allen, *Why Your Insurer Doesn't Care About Your Big Bills*, ProPublica co-published with NPR, May 25, 2018, https://www.propublica.org/article/why-your-health-insurer-does-not-care-about-your-big-bills

[168] Elisabeth Rosenthal, *An American Sickness*, New York, New York: Penguin Books, 2017, pg. 19

[169] Elisabeth Rosenthal, *An American Sickness*, New York, New York: Penguin Books, 2017, pg. 300

[170] Federal Spending: *Where Does the Money Go?*, National Priorities Project https://www.nationalpriorities.org/budget-basics/federal-budget-101/spending/

[171] Centers for Medicare & Medicaid Services, *National Health Expenditure Data*, CMS.gov, Jan. 8, 2018 https://www.cms.gov/Research-Statistics-Data-and-Systems/Statistics-Trends-and-Reports/NationalHealthExpendData/NationalHealthAccountsHistorical.html

[172] Elisabeth Rosenthal, *An American Sickness*, New York, New York: Penguin Books, 2017, pg. 3

[173] Milken Institute, Lynda and Stewart Resnick Center for Public Health, *Weighing Down America - The Health and Economic Impact of Obesity*, Nov., 2016, https://assets1b.milkeninstitute.org/assets/Publication/ResearchReport/PDF/Weighing-Down-America-WEB.pdf

[174] The Physicians Committee for Responsible Medicine, *Changing Lives Through Clinical Research*, Good Medicine, Sum., 2018 Vol 27, No.3

[175] Health Net News, *Keep Diabetes in Check*, Spring, 2018

[176] Reprinted from *World As Lover, World As Self* (1991, 2007) by Joanna Macy with permission of Parallax Press, Berkeley, California, www.parallax.org pg. 75

[177] Reprinted from *World As Lover, World As Self* (1991, 2007) by Joanna Macy with permission of Parallax Press, Berkeley, California, www.parallax.org pg. 107

Chapter 3

[1] Kylee Baumle, *The Monarch*, Pittsburgh, Pennsylvania: St. Lynn's Press, 2017 pg. 36

[2] Kylee Baumle, *The Monarch*, Pittsburgh, Pennsylvania: St. Lynn's Press, 2017 pg. 37

[3] The Annenberg Learner, *Which Way to Mexico? Exploring the Mysteries of Monarch Navigation*
http://www.learner.org/jnorth/tm/monarch/sl/38/0.html

[4] Kylee Baumle, *The Monarch*, Pittsburgh, Pennsylvania: St. Lynn's Press, 2017 pg. 38

[5] The Environmental Defense Fund *A Future for Monarchs - Bringing the Iconic Butterfly Back From the Brink* https://www.edf.org/card/future-monarchs

[6] Becca Cudmore, *Working Together for Monarchs*, World Wildlife Magazine, Sum. 2017 https://www.worldwildlife.org/magazine/issues/summer-2017/articles/working-together-for-monarchs

[7] John R. Platt, *Monarch Butterflies Could Gain Endangered Species Protection*, Scientific American, Extinction Countdown, Jan. 5, 2015 https://blogs.scientificamerican.com/extinction-countdown/monarch-butterflies-could-gain-endangered-species-protection/

[8] Center For Food Safety, *Annual Monarch Count Shows Butterfly Still Threatened*, Mar. 5, 2018 https://www.centerforfoodsafety.org/press-releases/5283/annual-monarch-count-shows-butterfly-still-threatened

[9] Maria L La Ganga, *Government Rejects Scientist's Claim it Tried to Cover Up his Pesticide Research*, The Guardian, Feb. 29, 2016 https://www.theguardian.com/environment/2016/feb/29/scientist-usda-negative-pesticide-research-neonicotinoids-environment

[10] Kylee Baumle, *The Monarch*, Pittsburgh, Pennsylvania: St. Lynn's Press, 2017 pg. 42

[11] Kylee Baumle, *The Monarch*, Pittsburgh, Pennsylvania: St. Lynn's Press, 2017 pg. 44 This is a beautiful book, with wonderful color photos and information, well worth buying: https://www.amazon.com/Monarch-Saving-Our-Most-Loved-Butterfly/dp/1943366179/

[12] John R. Platt, *Monarch Butterflies Could Gain Endangered Species Protection*, Scientific American, Extinction Countdown, Jan. 5, 2015 https://blogs.scientificamerican.com/extinction-countdown/monarch-butterflies-could-gain-endangered-species-protection/

[13] Center For Food Safety, *Monarch Butterfly Migration Could Collapse, Scientists Warn*, Mar. 6, 2018 https://www.ecowatch.com/monarch-butterfly-population-migration-2543505935.html

[14] Monarch Joint Venture https://monarchjointventure.org/

[15] Brice X. Semmens et all, *Quasi-extinction Risk and Population Targets for the Eastern, Migratory Population of Monarch Butterflies (Danaus Plexippus)*, Scientific Reports 6, Article 23265 (March 21, 2016) https://www.nature.com/articles/srep23265

[16] Prairie Drifter Farm in Litchfield, Minnesota http://prairiedrifterfarm.com

[17] Community Supported Agriculture (CSA) farm program https://www.nal.usda.gov/afsic/community-supported-agriculture#top

[18] The Xerces Society for Invertebrate Conservation. In 2016, their monarch project, a joint venture between Xerces, Monarch Joint Venture, the University of Minnesota Monarch Lab and (Paligraph) Prairie Institute.

[19] Joan Olson: Since their initial work with Sarah, Nick and Joan have been part of several research grants surrounding pollinator and monarch conservation. Their farm is one of several farms doing demonstration plots of a variety of conservation practices related to monarchs and other pollinators.

[20] Kylee Baumle, The Monarch, Pittsburgh, Pennsylvania: St. Lynn's Press, 2017, pg. 54

[21] "That's why farmers like Kerry Meyer and landowners like Spin and Mindy Williams — among thousands of other stewardship-minded farmers —are so important. By doing the right thing and sharing their stories, they are demonstrating not only a public commitment to monarchs and other pollinators, but also that it's possible to make the future success of American farming and American wildlife one and the same."
Becca Cudmore, *Working Together for Monarchs*, World Wildlife Magazine, Sum., 2017 https://www.worldwildlife.org/magazine/issues/summer-2017/articles/working-together-for-monarchs

[22] Their farm contains a six-acre area of wetter land along the river that winds through their property. They initially installed field borders and buffer strips to buffer this land from the river running through their property so they weren't losing soil.

They don't farm that area because, as Joan told me, "Vegetables don't like wet feet, you need to have well drained soil for vegetables to grow. Water-logged soil doesn't have the good anaerobic environment with the free flowing oxygen the roots need."

[23] Bees are natures supreme pollinators. Sarah Foltz Jordan explained this to me. Butterflies, wasps, lacewings and other insects feed themselves on flower nectar. While doing so they incidentally pick up pollen and move it around on their travels, flower to flower. Bees, however, intentionally collect large amount of pollen to bring back to their hives. They've evolved hairy bodies and other adaptations to help them do this.

"One out of every three bites of food eaten worldwide depends on pollinators, especially bees, for a successful harvest."[1]

Huge numbers of bees are dying, entire hives or colonies — a phenomenon termed colony collapse disorder. Over the last decade, over 30% of bee hives have been "collapsing" in Europe and the United States, a level of loss that is not sustainable.

Historically bees have been killed by diseases and parasitic mites, but entomologists say that no single pathogen or parasite explains the current rate of hive collapse.[2]

Something else is happening.

Studies suggest that neonicotinoids in pesticides may be the culprit. Neonicotinoids attack a bee's central nervous system. They are also toxic to earthworms and other terrestrial invertebrates. Neonicotinoids are used on 75% of food crop acreage in the United States, including corn, cotton, soybeans, fruits and vegetables, as well as grains and nuts. They are also ingredients in urban use and in home pest-control products like Round-Up. Jim Doan, a director of the American Beekeeping Foundation says, "In the U.S., neonicotinoids are currently used on about 95% of corn and canola crops; the majority of cotton, sorghum, and sugar beets; and about half of all soybeans. They're also used on the vast majority of fruit and vegetable crops, including apples, cherries, peaches, oranges, berries, leafy greens, tomatoes, and potatoes. Neonicotinoids are also applied to cereal grains, rice, nuts, and wine grapes... There is no place to go hide. The outlook is not good."[3]

Many farmers don't realize the pesticides and other chemicals they are using have this effect. A 76-page report from the Center For Food Safety, based on peer-reviewed science, concluded that "the large majority of neonic corn seed coating is not needed to protect corn productivity," and that there are viable alternatives "which allow farmers to avoid these pests without the use of insecticides in the vast majority of cases."[4]

The report notes that the EPA, when first allowing neonic clothianidin on the market in 2003, only granted it a 'conditional registration,' admitting that its potential adverse effects were not fully described or known. Neonics including imidacloprid, clothianidin, thiamethoxam and dinotefuran, kill bees and were a significant factor in the massive 23% decline in bee populations from 2008 to 2013.

On March 20, 2015, the world's leading cancer authority, the World Health Organization's International Agency for Research on Cancer, classified glyphosate, the key ingredient in Monsanto's Roundup herbicide, as a "probable carcinogen."[5]

In 2017, California's regulatory agency, the Office of Environmental Health Hazard Assessment (OEHHA), listed glyphosate as a known cancer-causing chemical.[6]

Footnotes in this section:

[1] Elizabeth Grossman, *Declining Bee Populations Pose a Threat to Global Agriculture*, Yale. Edu, Apr. 30, 2013 http://e360.yale.edu/features/declining_bee_populations_pose_a_threat_to_global_agriculture

[2] Elizabeth Grossman, *Declining Bee Populations Pose a Threat to Global Agriculture*, Yale. Edu, Apr. 30, 2013 http://e360.yale.edu/features/declining_bee_populations_pose_a_threat_to_global_agriculture

[3] Elizabeth Grossman, *Declining Bee Populations Pose a Threat to Global Agriculture*, Yale. Edu, Apr. 30, 2013 http://e360.yale.edu/features/declining_bee_populations_pose_a_threat_to_global_agriculture

[4] *Alternatives to Neonicotinoid Insecticide-Coated Corn Seed: Agroecological Methods Are Better For Farmers and the Environment*, May 22, 2017 http://www.centerforfoodsafety.org/reports/4954/alternatives-to-neonicotinoid-insecticide-coated-

corn-seed-agroecological-methods-are-better-for-farmers-and-the-environment#

[5] World Health Organization, *Evaluation of Five Organophosphate Insecticides and Herbicides*, IARC Monographs Volume 112, International Agency for Research on Cancer, Mar. 20,2015 http://www.iarc.fr/en/media-centre/iarcnews/pdf/MonographVolume112.pdf

[6] *It's Official: California Lists Key Ingredient in Monsanto's Roundup as Cancer-Causing*, Jul. 7, 2017 https://www.ecowatch.com/glyphosate-cancer-2454487516.html

[24] Dr. Ignacio Chapela, Microbial Ecologist, UC Berkeley as spoken in the feature documentary film *Symphony of the Soil*, directed, written and produced by Deborah Koons Garcia, Lily Films, 2012 https://www.amazon.com/dp/B00KZ2FIXC/_encoding=UTF8?coliid=IM7GTBPUT0P7A&colid=2481PBY7CN9C9

[25] "Considered by many to be the father of wildlife ecology and the United States' wilderness system, Aldo Leopold was a conservationist, forester, philosopher, educator, writer, and outdoor enthusiast. Among his best known ideas is the 'land ethic,' which calls for an ethical, caring relationship between people and nature." The Aldo Leopold Foundation https://www.aldoleopold.org/about/aldo-leopold/

[26] Aldo Leopold, *Erosion and Prosperity*, The Essential Aldo Leopold Quotations and Commentaries, Edited by Curt Meine, Richard Knight., Pgs. 76-7 http://lib.dr.iastate.edu/leopold_letter/77/

[27] David Pimental, Michael Burgess, *Soil Erosion Threatens Food Production*, Agriculture 2013, 3, 443-463; doi:10.3390 Aug. 8, 2013 https://www.bmbf.de/files/agriculture-03-00443.pdf

[28] Deborah Bossio, *A Month On Land: Restoring Soils and Landscapes*, CGIAR Research Program on Water, Land and Ecosystems, Oct. 18, 2013, http://ciatblogs.cgiar.org/soils/a-month-on-land-restoring-soils-and-landscapes/

[29] *Status of the World's Soil Resources: Technical Summary*, Intergovernmental Technical Panel on Soils, L. Montanarella, chair. Food and Agricultural Organization of the United Nations (FAO), 2015

[30] David R. Montgomery. *Growing A Revolution*. New York, New York: W. W. Norton & Company, 2017. pg. 18

[31] Dr. Michael Hansen, Senior Scientist with Consumers Union, and Publisher of Consumer Reports as spoken in the feature documentary film *Symphony of the Soil*, directed, written and produced by Deborah Koons Garcia, Lily Films, 2012 https://www.amazon.com/dp/B00KZ2FIXC/_encoding=UTF8?coliid=IM7GTBPUT0P7A&colid=2481PBY7CN9C9

[32] James Merryweather, *Secrets of the Soil*, Resurgence No. 235 26-8, Mar/Apr, 2006, http://www.slef.org.uk/userfiles/file/slef-pdfs/secrets-soil.pdf

[33] Kristin Ohlson. *The Soil Will Save Us*. New York, New York: Rodale, 2014. pg. xii

[34] Dr. Elaine Ingham, President and Director of Research at Soil Foodweb Inc. as spoken in the documentary film *Symphony of the Soil*, directed, written and produced by Deborah Koons Garcia, Lily Films, 2012, https://www.amazon.com/dp/B00KZ2FIXC/_encoding=UTF8?coliid=IM7GTBPUT0P7A&colid=2481PBY7CN9C9

[35] Harry MacCormack, Farmer, Sunbow Farm, Oregon as spoken in the documentary film Symphony of the Soil, directed, written and produced by Deborah Koons Garcia, Lily Films, 2012, https://www.amazon.com/dp/B00KZ2FIXC/_encoding=UTF8?coliid=IM7GTBPUT0P7A&colid=2481PBY7CN9C9

[36] Becky Harlan, *Digging Deep Reveals the Intricate World of Roots*, National Geographic Proof, Oct. 15, 2015 https://www.nationalgeographic.com/photography/proof/2015/10/15/digging-deep-reveals-the-intricate-world-of-roots/

[37] Dr. John Reganold, Regents Professor of Soil Science, Washington State University as stated in the feature documentary film *Symphony of the Soil*, directed, written and produced by Deborah Koons Garcia, Lily Films, 2012 https://www.amazon.com/dp/B00KZ2FIXC/_encoding=UTF8?coliid=IM7GTBPUT0P7A&colid=2481PBY7CN9C9

[38] Gabe Brown is one of our foremost experts on regenerative agriculture. His book, Dirt to Soil, is a must read. He along with Ray Archuleta, Dr. Allen Williams and David Brandt run http://soilhealthconsulting.com and provide consulting services for farmers wishing to begin or convert their land to regenerative farming. Their advice is invaluable.

[39] Gabe Brown. *Dirt to Soil*. White River Junction, Vermont: Chelsea Green Publishing, 2018 pg. 118

[40] Dr. Christine Jones, *SOS: Save Our Soils*, interviewed by Tracy Frisch, ACRES, Mar. 2013 http://www.amazingcarbon.com/PDF/Jones_ACRES_USA%20(March2015).pdf

[41] Dr. Christine Jones, *Five Principles for Soil Restoration*, 2017, pg. 1, https://www.ecofarmingdaily.com/build-soil/soil-restoration-5-core-principles/

[42] Jessica A. Knoblauch, *Farming For the Future*, Earthjustice Magazine, Fall, 2017, https://earthjustice.org/blog/2017-october/farming-for-the-future

[43] Dr. Christine Jones, *SOS: Save Our Soils*, interviewed by Tracy Frisch, ACRES, Mar. 2013, https://www.ecofarmingdaily.com/build-soil/soil-restoration-5-core-principles/
And
Dr. Christine Jones, *Five Principles for Soil Restoration*, 2017, pg. 6, https://www.ecofarmingdaily.com/build-soil/soil-restoration-5-core-principles/

[44] James M. Bullock, Richard F. Pywell, Kevin J. Walker, *Long-term Enhancement of Agricultural Production by Restoration of Biodiversity*, Journal of Applied Ecology, 2007, http://onlinelibrary.wiley.com/doi/10.1111/j.1365-2664.2006.01252.x/abstract

[45] Dr. Fred Kirschenmann, Farmer, Distinguished Fellow at the Leopold Center for Sustainable Agriculture, President of the Board of the Stone Barns Center for Food and Agriculture as stated in the feature documentary film *Symphony of the Soil*, directed, written and produced by Deborah Koons Garcia, Lily Films, 2012 https://www.amazon.com/dp/B00KZ2FIXC/_encoding=UTF8?coliid=IM7GTBPUT0P7A&colid=2481PBY7CN9C9.

[46] Rattan Lal, *There Is No Such Thing As A Free Biofuel From Crop Residues*, Argonomy News, 2007, May 52:5 12 "Crop residue is not a waste. It is a precious commodity and essential to preserving soil quality. In addition to controlling erosion and conserving soil water in the root zone, retaining crop residues on the soil is also necessary for recycling nutrients, improving activity and species diversity of soil micro- and macro-fauna, maintaining soil structure and tilth, reducing nonpoint source pollution and decreasing the risks of hypoxia in the coastal regions, increasing use efficiency of fertilizers and other inputs, sustaining biomass/agronomic yield, and improving/maintaining soil organic matter content."

[47] Dwayne Beck, director of Dakota Lakes Research Farm commentary as transcribed in *Growing a Revolution*, David Montgomery, 2017, pgs. 99 and 100

[48] Kristin Ohlson. *The Soil Will Save Us*. New York, New York: Rodale, 2014. pgs. xii and 3.

[49] Presented in the Wikipedia page on Earthworm, this Charles Darwin quote is from *The Formation of Vegetable Mould Through the Action of Worms*, Charles Darwin, 1881 http://www.gutenberg.org/ebooks/2355

[50] Vandana Shiva. *Who Really Feeds The World?*. Berkeley, California: North Atlantic Books, 2016. pg. 19

[51] Novo M, Riesgo A, Fernández-Guerra A, Giribet G (2013). "Pheromone evolution, reproductive genes, and comparative transcriptomics in mediterranean earthworms (annelida, oligochaeta, hormogastridae)". *Mol. Biol. Evol.* 30 (7): 1614–29. doi:10.1093/molbev/mst074. PMID 23596327.

[52] Earthworm description sourced in part from Wikipedia, Earthworm section, https://en.wikipedia.org/wiki/Earthworm

[53] Nyle C. Brady, Ray R. Weil, *Elements of the Nature and Properties of Soils (3rd Edition)*. Pearson ISBN 978-0-13-501433-2

[54] Nyle C. Brady, Ray R. Weil, *Elements of the Nature and Properties of Soils (3rd Edition)*. Pearson ISBN 978-0-13-501433-2

[55] Vandana Shiva. *Who Really Feeds The World?*. Berkeley, California: North Atlantic Books, 2016. pgs. 21–22

[56] David R. Montgomery. *Growing A Revolution*. New York, New York: W. W. Norton & Company, 2017. pg. 126

[57] Vandana Shiva. *Who Really Feeds The World?*. Berkeley, California: North Atlantic Books, 2016. pg. 6

[58] Dr. Laurie Drinkwater of the Department of Horticulture at Cornell University as spoken in the documentary film *Symphony of the Soil*, directed, written and produced by Deborah Koons Garcia, Lily Films, 2012, https://www.amazon.com/dp/B00KZ2FIXC/_encoding=UTF8?coliid=IM7GTBPUT0P7A&colid=2481PBY7CN9C9

[59] Vilicus Farms website, https://www.vilicusfarms.com/

[60] Anne Evans and Peter Gegger, Farmers, Blaencamel Farm, Wales as spoken in the documentary film *Symphony of the Soil*, directed, written and produced by Deborah Koons Garcia, Lily Films, 2012, https://www.amazon.com/dp/B00KZ2FIXC/_

encoding=UTF8?coliid=IM7GTBPUT0P7A&colid=2481PBY7CN9C9

[61] Kristin Ohlson. *The Soil Will Save Us*. New York, New York: Rodale, 2014. pg. 9

[62] Dr. Christine Jones, *Farming Profitably Within Environmental Limits*, 2017, http://pureadvantage. org/news/2017/05/18/farming-profitably-within-environmental-limits/

[63] *Plant "Social Networks" – Is this why Companion Planting & Inter-cropping Work?*, The Plant Guy, 2012 https://www.howplantswork.com/2012/06/13/plant-social-networks-is-this-why-companion-planting-inter-cropping-work/

[64] Walder, F. et al, *Mycorrhizal Networks: Common Goods of Plants Shared Under Unequal Terms of Trade*, 2012 http://www.plantphysiol.org/content/159/2/789

[65] Plants also communicate with other plants altruistically by releasing chemical signals through the air. When mustard plant leaves are damaged by insects, the plant sends emergency signals from its leaves via airborne chemicals alerting neighboring mustard plants, which then build up defenses to ward off the insects.
Connor Sweeney, Venkatachalam Lakshmanan, Harsh P. Bais, *Interplant Aboveground Signaling Prompts Upregulation of Auxin Promoter and Malate Transporter as Part of Defensive Response in the Neighboring Plants*, Frontiers in Plant Science, Apr. 19, 2017, https://doi.org/10.3389/fpls.2017.00595 and https://www.frontiersin.org/articles/10.3389/fpls.2017.00595/full

[66] *SOS: Save Our Soils*, Dr. Christine Jones interviewed by Tracy Frisch, ACRES, March 2013 http://www. amazingcarbon.com/PDF/Jones_ACRES_USA%20(March2015).pdf

[67] Dr. Christine Jones, *Five Principles for Soil Restoration*, 2017, pg. 6, https://www.ecofarmingdaily. com/build-soil/soil-restoration-5-core-principles/

[68] Moises Velasquez-Manoff, *Can Dirt Save the Earth?*, The New York Times Magazine, Apr. 18, 2018, https://www.nytimes.com/2018/04/18/magazine/dirt-save-earth-carbon-farming-climate-change. html

[69] Giles Oldroyd, *Plant Interaction With Friendly Bacteria Gives Pathogens Their Break*, Prof. Giles Oldroyd of the John Innes Center explains how plant roots form beneficial interactions with microbes in the soil. YouTube Video, 4min.55sec, Nov. 1, 2012. https://www.youtube.com/watch?v=owdhvAJ-nE8

[70] Kristin Ohlson. *The Soil Will Save Us*. New York, New York: Rodale, 2014. pg. 80

[71] Kristin Ohlson. *The Soil Will Save Us*. New York, New York: Rodale, 2014. pg. 42

[72] David Pimentel, *Soil Erosion: A Food and Environmental Threat*, Environment, Development, and Sustainability 8, 2006: 119-137

[73] Vandana Shiva. *Who Really Feeds The World?*. Berkeley, California: North Atlantic Books, 2016. pg. 37

[74] Kathy Voss, *Great "Grass Farmers" Grow Roots*, National grazing Lands Coalition, 2015, https:// onpasture.com/2015/11/09/great-grass-farmers-grow-roots/

[75] Dr. Christine Jones, *Carbon That Counts*, New England and Northwest 'Landcare Adventure', Mar. 2011 http://www.amazingcarbon.com/PDF/JONES%27CarbonThatCounts%27.pdf

[76] David R. Montgomery. *Growing A Revolution*. New York, New York: W. W. Norton & Company, 2017. pg. 193

[77] Gabe Brown. *Dirt to Soil*. White River Junction, Vermont: Chelsea Green Publishing, 2018 pg. 120

[78] David R. Montgomery. *Growing A Revolution*. New York, New York: W. W. Norton & Company, 2017. pg. 194

[79] Wendell Berry, *Renewing Husbandry*, Orion Magazine, June 2018, https://orionmagazine.org/ article/renewing-husbandry/

[80] EPA Greenhouse Gas Emissions, *Inventory of U.S. Greenhouse Gas Emissions and Sinks: 1990-2016*, Pub: 2018 https://www.epa.gov/sites/production/files/2018-01/documents/2018_chapter_5_ agriculture.pdf

[81] Gayathri Vaidyanathan, *How Bad of a Greenhouse Gas is Methane?*, Scientific American, Dec. 22, 2015 https://www.scientificamerican.com/article/how-bad-of-a-greenhouse-gas-is-methane/

[82] EPA Greenhouse Gas Emissions, *Overview of Greenhouse Gases*, https://www.epa.gov/ghgemissions/ overview-greenhouse-gases

[83] Dr. Christine Jones, *SOS: Save Our Soils*, interviewed by Tracy Frisch, ACRES, March 2013 http:// www.amazingcarbon.com/PDF/Jones_ACRES_USA%20(March2015).pdf

[84] Gabe Brown. *Dirt to Soil*. White River Junction, Vermont: Chelsea Green Publishing, 2018 pgs. 12 & 141

85 Francesca Bray, *Agriculture for Developing Nations*, Scientific American, July 1994: 33-35

86 Dr. Christine Jones, *Five Principles for Soil Restoration*, 2017, pg. 2, https://www.ecofarmingdaily. com/build-soil/soil-restoration-5-core-principles/

87 David R. Montgomery. *Growing A Revolution.* New York, New York: W. W. Norton & Company, 2017. pg. 268

88 David R. Montgomery. *Growing A Revolution.* New York, New York: W. W. Norton & Company, 2017. pg. 30

89 Vandana Shiva. *Who Really Feeds The World?.* Berkeley, California: North Atlantic Books, 2016. pg. 134

90 Kristin Ohlson. *The Soil Will Save Us.* New York, New York: Rodale, 2014. Kris Nichols as quoted by Kristin Ohlson, pg. 97

91 Joe Fassler, *While Demand Soars, Less Than 1 Percent of U.S. Farmland is Certified Organic. So Why Don't Farmers Switch?*, New Food Economy, Feb. 28, 2017 https://newfoodeconomy.org/kashi-certified-transitional-organic/

92 David R. Montgomery. *Growing A Revolution.* New York, New York: W. W. Norton & Company, 2017. pg. 83

93 Food and Water Watch, *Monsanto: A Corporate Profile*, Food and Water Watch, Apr. 8, 2013 https://www.foodandwaterwatch.org/insight/monsanto-corporate-profile

94 Laura Lengnick quote, *Resilient Agriculture* http://www.gracelinks.org/blog/8074/building-a-more-resilient-food-system-requires-a-paradigm-s?platform=hootsuite

95 Vandana Shiva. *Who Really Feeds The World?.* Berkeley, California: North Atlantic Books, 2016. pg. 8

96 David R. Montgomery. *Growing A Revolution.* New York, New York: W. W. Norton & Company, 2017. pg. 27

97 Ethan A. Huff, *Consolidation of Seed Companies Leading to Corporate Domination of World Food Supply*, Natural news, Jul. 27, 2011 https://www.naturalnews.com/033148_seed_companies_Monsanto. html

98 Nigel Morris, *The Big Five Companies That Control the World's Grain Trade*, The Independent, Jan. 23, 2013 http://www.independent.co.uk/news/uk/home-news/the-big-five-companies-that-control-the-worlds-grain-trade-8462266.html

99 David R. Montgomery. *Growing A Revolution.* New York, New York: W. W. Norton & Company, 2017. pg. 234

100 *Crop Year Government Cost of Federal Crop Insurance Program*, RMA, USDA. 2017, https://www.rma.usda.gov/aboutrma/budget/16cygovcost.pdf

101 Tim Ryan, *The Real Food Revolution*, Carlsbad, California: Hay House 2014

102 Paicines Ranch, California https://paicinesranch.com/index.php

103 David R. Montgomery. *Growing A Revolution.* New York, New York: W. W. Norton & Company, 2017. pg.274

104 David R. Montgomery. *Growing A Revolution.* New York, New York: W. W. Norton & Company, 2017. pg.23

105 *Under the Microscope - Q&A with Dr. Stephanie A. Smith*, Mission: Water, Issue 3, Sum. 2017, pg. 17

106 David R. Montgomery. *Growing A Revolution.* New York, New York: W. W. Norton & Company, 2017. pg. 40

107 Vandana Shiva. *Who Really Feeds The World?.* Berkeley, California: North Atlantic Books, 2016. pgs. 57 & 58

108 Laura Jackson as quoted in *The Soil Will Save Us*, Kristin Ohlson, 2014, pg. 172

109 USDA Factsheet. *USDA Coexistence Fact Sheets - Soybeans*, Feb. 2015 https://www.usda.gov/sites/default/files/documents/coexistence-soybeans-factsheet.pdf

110 Gabe Brown. *Dirt to Soil.* White River Junction, Vermont: Chelsea Green Publishing, 2018 pg. 95

111 Vandana Shiva. *Who Really Feeds The World?.* Berkeley, California: North Atlantic Books, 2016. pg. 3

112 Kristin Ohlson. *The Soil Will Save Us.* New York, New York: Rodale, 2014. pg. 94

113 Dr. Christine Jones, *Five Principles for Soil Restoration*, 2017, pg. 2, https://www.ecofarmingdaily.com/build-soil/soil-restoration-5-core-principles/

114 James Merryweather, *Secrets of the Soil*, Resurgence No. 235 26-8, Mar/Apr 2006, http://www.slef.org.uk/userfiles/file/slef-pdfs/secrets-soil.pdf

[115] David R. Montgomery. *Growing A Revolution*. New York, New York: W. W. Norton & Company, 2017. pg. 63

[116] David R. Montgomery. *Growing A Revolution*. New York, New York: W. W. Norton & Company, 2017. pg. 224

[117] American Farmland Trust, https://www.farmland.org

[118] Jessica A. Knoblauch, *Farming For the Future*, Earthjustice Magazine, Fall, 2017, https://earthjustice.org/blog/2017-october/farming-for-the-future

[119] David R. Montgomery. *Growing A Revolution*. New York, New York: W. W. Norton & Company, 2017. pgs. 56-57

[120] Intergovernmental Technical Panel on Soils, L. Montanarella, chair. *Status of the World's Soil Resources: Technical Summary*, Food and Agricultural Organization of the United Nations (FAO), 2015

[121] Al Gore. *An Inconvenient Sequel - Truth To Power*. New York, New York: Rodale, 2017. pg. 269

[122] Kristin Ohlson. *The Soil Will Save Us*. New York, New York: Rodale, 2014. pg. 82

[123] Vandana Shiva. *Who Really Feeds The World?*. Berkeley, California: North Atlantic Books, 2016. pg. xv

[124] *USDA 2012 Census of Agriculture*, United States Department of Agriculture, https://www.nass.usda.gov/Publications/AgCensus/2012/Full_Report/Volume_1,_Chapter_1_US/

[125] Wendell Berry, *Renewing Husbandry*, Orion Magazine, June 2018, https://orionmagazine.org/article/renewing-husbandry/

[126] Adam Skolnick, *Hog Hell - The CAFO Industry's Impact on the Environment and Public Health*, Sierra Magazine, Feb. 23, 2017 https://www.sierraclub.org/sierra/2017-2-march-april/feature/cafo-industrys-impact-environment-and-public-health

[127] Pew Trusts, *The Business of Broilers: Hidden Costs of Putting a Chicken on Every Grill*, Dec. 20, 2013, https://www.pewtrusts.org/en/research-and-analysis/reports/2013/12/20/the-business-of-broilers-hidden-costs-of-putting-a-chicken-on-every-grill

[128] Melinda Wenner Moyer, *How Drug-Resistant Bacteria Travel from the Farm to Your Table*, Scientific American, Dec. 1, 2016 https://www.scientificamerican.com/article/how-drug-resistant-bacteria-travel-from-the-farm-to-your-table/

[129] John Thackara, *How to Thrive in the Next Economy*, New York, New York: Thames & Hudson, 2015 pg. 70

[130] Vandana Shiva. *Who Really Feeds The World?*. Berkeley, California: North Atlantic Books, 2016. pgs. 57-58

[131] Tom Philpott, *Wall Street Investors Take Aim at Farmland*, Mother Jones, Mar. 14, 2014 http://www.motherjones.com/food/2014/03/land-grabs-not-just-africa-anymore/

[132] Reprinted from *World As Lover, World As Self* (1991, 2007) by Joanna Macy with permission of Parallax Press, Berkeley, California, www.parallax.org pgs. 50-1

[133] Kristin Ohlson. *The Soil Will Save Us*. New York, New York: Rodale, 2014. pg. 173

[134] Food Is Power website, Food Empowerment Project http://foodispower.org/water-usage-privatization/

[135] *Food Chains*, a compelling documentary film directed by Sanjay Rawal, produced by Smriti Keshari, Illumine Group and Two Moons, 2014 Illumine Opportunity Group LLC Please watch this feature length documentary. Available on Netflix, Amazon, other platforms. https://www.amazon.com/Food-Chains-Eva-Longoria/dp/B00PJX75TW/

[136] *Of Soils, Subsidies and Survival: A Report on Living Soils*, Greenpeace India Society, 2011, 12.

[137] David R. Montgomery. *Growing A Revolution*. New York, New York: W. W. Norton & Company, 2017. pg.49

[138] Kristin Ohlson. *The Soil Will Save Us*. New York, New York: Rodale, 2014. pg. 83

[139] Vandana Shiva, *Soil Not Oil*, pg. 101

[140] Dr. Christine Jones, *Farming Profitably Within Environmental Limits*, 2017, pg. 1, http://pureadvantage.org/news/2017/05/18/farming-profitably-within-environmental-limits/

[141] Steven Pinker. *Enlightenment Now*, New York, New York: Viking, 2018 pg. 75.

[142] ScienceHeroes.com, *Who saved the Most Lives in History?!*, http://scienceheroes.com/

[143] Paul Hawken, *Drawdown*, New York, New York: Penguin Books, 2017 pg. 201

[144] Dr. Stephanie A. Smith, *Under the Microscope Q & A with Dr. Stephanie A. Smith* and *A System Out of*

Balance, Mission Water Issue 3, Sum. 2017 Waterkeepers, pgs. 17-18

She notes the clear connection with global warming and nutrients like phosphorus and nitrogen causing algal blooms in waterways. "Algal blooms used to be a rare thing. Now, over 70% of surface waters in the U.S. have experienced an algae bloom."

[145] Lorraine Chow, *Mexico's Dead Zone Could be Largest Ever, Thanks to the Meat Industry*, Ecowatch, Aug. 1, 2017 https://www.ecowatch.com/gulf-of-mexico-dead-zone-2467931985.html

[146] Bill Wenzel, *Shrinking the dead Zone, Reducing fertilizer Use*, U.S.PIRG The Federation of State PIRGs, Jun. 23, 2017 https://uspirg.org/blogs/blog/usp/shrinking-dead-zone-reducing-fertilizer-use

[147] Jessica A. Knoblauch, *Farming For the Future*, Earthjustice Quarterly Magazine, Fall, 2017

[148] EPA Greenhouse Gas Emissions, *Overview of Greenhouse Gases*, https://www.epa.gov/ghgemissions/overview-greenhouse-gases#nitrous-oxide

[149] Intergovernmental Technical Panel on Soils, L. Montanarella, chair. *Status of the World's Soil Resources: Technical Summary*, Food and Agricultural Organization of the United Nations (FAO), 2015

[150] Olaf Czarnecki, et al. *A Dual Role of Strigolactones in Phosphate Acquisition and Utilization in Plants*, International Journal of Molecular Sciences, 2013, pg. 14 https://www.ncbi.nlm.nih.gov/pmc/articles/PMC3645710/

[151] Charles M. Benbrook, *Trends in Glyphosate Herbicide Use in the United States and Globally*, Environmental Sciences Europe, Feb. 2, 2016 28:3, https://enveurope.springeropen.com/articles/10.1186/s12302-016-0070-0

[152] Vandana Shiva. *Who Really Feeds The World?*. Berkeley, California: North Atlantic Books, 2016. pg. 129

[153] Vandana Shiva. *Who Really Feeds The World?*. Berkeley, California: North Atlantic Books, 2016. pg. 24

[154] Dr. Christine Jones, *SOS: Save Our Soils*, interviewed by Tracy Frisch, ACRES, March, 2013 http://www.amazingcarbon.com/PDF/Jones_ACRES_USA%20(March2015).pdf

[155] Dr. Christine Jones, *Five Principles for Soil Restoration*, 2017, pg. 3, https://www.ecofarmingdaily.com/build-soil/soil-restoration-5-core-principles/

[156] *Water Uses*, AQUASTAT, Food and Agriculture Organization of the United Nations, 2014, http://www.fao.org/nr/water/aquastat/water_use/index.stm

[157] Dr. Christine Jones, *SOS: Save Our Soils*, interviewed by Tracy Frisch, ACRES, March, 2013 http://www.amazingcarbon.com/PDF/Jones_ACRES_USA%20(March2015).pdf

[158] Carey Gillam. *Whitewash*. Washington, DC: Island Press, 2017. Pg.50

[159] Charles M. Benbrook, *Trends in Glyphosate Herbicide Use in the United States and Globally*, Environmental Sciences Europe, Feb. 2, 2016 28:3, https://enveurope.springeropen.com/articles/10.1186/s12302-016-0070-0

[160] Douglas Main, *Glyphosate Now the Most-Used Agricultural Chemical Ever*, Newsweek, Tech & Science, Jun. 25, 2018, http://www.newsweek.com/glyphosate-now-most-used-agricultural-chemical-ever-422419

[161] *Sustained Glyphosate Use Reveals Risks to Soil and Environmental Health*, Beyond Pesticides , July 21, 2017 https://beyondpesticides.org/dailynewsblog/2017/07/sustained-glyphosate-use-reveals-risks-soil-environmental-health/

[162] Vandana Shiva. *Who Really Feeds The World?*. Berkeley, California: North Atlantic Books, 2016. pg. 30

[163] *Fighting Pesticides That Harm Pollinators*, Nature's Voice, Natural Resources Defense Council, Spring 2018, pg. 3, https://issuu.com/nrdc/docs/naturesvoice-spring-2018

[164] Nichelle Harriott, *Bees, Birds and Beneficials - How Fields of Poison Adversely Affect Non-target Organisms*, Pesticides and You, Beyond Pesticides, Vol. 33, No.4, Winter 2013-14 https://www.beyondpesticides.org/assets/media/documents/infoservices/pesticidesandyou/documents/BeesBirdsBeneficials.pdf

[165] Caspar A. Hallmann, Martin Sorg, Eelke Jongejans, et al. *More Than 75 Percent Decline Over 27 Years in Total Flying Insect Biomass in Protected Areas*, PLOS One, Oct. 18, 2017, http://journals.plos.org/plosone/article?id=10.1371/journal.pone.0185809

[166] Doreen Cubie, *Make Your Yard a Spray-Free Zone*, National Wildlife, Apr.-May 2018 pgs. 36-39 https://www.nwf.org/Magazines/National-Wildlife/2018/April-May/Gardening/Pest-Control

[167] Tom Philpott, *90 Percent of Corn Seeds Are Coated with Bayer's Bee-Decimating Pesticide*, Mother jones, May 16, 2014 http://www.motherjones.com/food/2012/05/catching-my-reading-ahead-

pesticide-industry-confab/

[168] National Wildlife, *Songbirds Making Serious Headlines,* Apr.-May 2018. National Wildlife Federation, pg. 8 https://www.nwf.org/Home/Magazines/National-Wildlife/2018/April-May/Animals/News-of-the-Wild

[169] Margaret L. Eng, Bridget J. M. Stutchbury, Christy A. Morrissey, *Imidacloprid and Chlorpyrifos Insecticides Impair Migratory Ability in a Seed-eating Songbird,* Scientific Reports 7, Article # 15176, 2017, doi:10.1038/s41598-017-15466-x https://www.nature.com/articles/s41598-017-15446-x#Abs1

[170] Margaret L. Eng, Bridget J. M. Stutchbury, Christy A. Morrissey, *Imidacloprid and Chlorpyrifos Insecticides Impair Migratory Ability in a Seed-eating Songbird,* Scientific Reports 7, Article # 15176, 2017, doi:10.1038/s41598-017-15466-x https://www.nature.com/articles/s41598-017-15446-x#Abs1

[171] Dr. Michael Hansen, Senior Scientist with Consumers Union, and Publisher of Consumer Reports as spoken in the feature documentary film *Symphony of the Soil,* directed, written and produced by Deborah Koons Garcia, Lily Films, 2012 https://www.amazon.com/dp/B00KZ2FIXC/_encoding=UTF8?coliid=IM7GTBPUT0P7A&colid=2481PBY7CN9C9

[172] Robert J. Kremer, *Soil and Environmental Health after Twenty years of Intensive Use of Glyphosate,* MedCrave Vol. 6 Issue 5, 2017 https://medcraveonline.com/APAR/APAR-06-00224.pdf

[173] *Sustained Glyphosate Use Reveals Risks to Soil and Environmental Health,* Beyond Pesticides , Jul. 21, 2017 https://beyondpesticides.org/dailynewsblog/2017/07/sustained-glyphosate-use-reveals-risks-soil-environmental-health/

[174] *Study Shows Climate Change Threatens Soil Organisms Essential to Life,* Beyond Pesticides, Sept. 29, 2017 https://beyondpesticides.org/dailynewsblog/2017/09/study-shows-climate-change-threatens-soil-organisms-essential-life/

[175] Colin J. Carlson, et al, *Parasite Biodiversity Faces Extinction and Redistribution in a Changing Climate,* Science Advances, Vol.3, No.9, e1602422 Sep. 6, 2017 http://advances.sciencemag.org/content/3/9/e1602422

[176] Jorge Fernandez-Cornejo and Craig Osteen, *Managing Glyphosate Resistance May Sustain its Efficacy and Increase Long-Term Returns to Corn and Soybean Production,* Amber Waves, May 4, 2015

[177] Charles M. Benbrook, *Trends in Glyphosate Herbicide Use in the United States and Globally,* Environmental Sciences Europe, Feb. 2, 2016 28:3, https://enveurope.springeropen.com/articles/10.1186/s12302-016-0070-0

[178] Dr. Christine Jones, *SOS: Save Our Soils,* interviewed by Tracy Frisch, ACRES, March, 2013 http://www.amazingcarbon.com/PDF/Jones_ACRES_USA%20(March2015).pdf

[179] Nature's Voice, *Bayer-Monsanto Merger Could Be Disastrous for Bees, People,* Natural Resources Defense Council, Spring 2017, pg. 4, https://issuu.com/nrdc/docs/naturesvoice-spring17

[180] Danny Hakim, *Doubts About the Promised Bounty of Genetically Modified Crops,* The New York Times, Oct. 29, 2016 https://www.nytimes.com/2016/10/30/business/gmo-promise-falls-short.html

[181] Tom Philpott, *This Weed Killer is Wreaking Havoc on America's Crops,* Mother Jones, Jan.-Feb. 2018 Issue, https://www.motherjones.com/environment/2018/01/dicamba-monsanto-herbicide-neighbor-farms-soybeans/

[182] International Agency for Research on Cancer, *IARC Monographs Volume 112: Evaluation of Five Organophosphate Insecticides and Herbicides,* World Health Organization, Mar. 20, 2015, https://www.iarc.fr/en/media-centre/iarcnews/pdf/MonographVolume112.pdf

[183] Douglas Main, *Glyphosate Now the Most-Used Agricultural Chemical Ever,* Newsweek, Tech & Science, Jun. 25, 2018, http://www.newsweek.com/glyphosate-now-most-used-agricultural-chemical-ever-422419

[184] J. D. Heyes, *Monsanto Roundup Harms Human Endocrine System at Levels Allowed in Drinking Water, Study Shows,* Natural News, Apr. 5, 2015, Global Research, https://www.globalresearch.ca/monsanto-roundup-harms-human-endocrine-system-at-levels-allowed-in-drinking-water-study-shows/5441051

[185] David Pimentel, *Environmental and Economic Costs of the Application of Pesticides in the U.S.* Environment, Development and Sustainability 7 (2005), 229-252

[186] *Why Are Autism Spectrum Disorders Increasing?,* Centers for Disease Control and Prevention, Jun. 18, 2014, cdc.gov/features/autismprevalence

[187] Charles M. Benbrook, *Trends in Glyphosate Herbicide Use in the United States and Globally*, Environmental Sciences Europe, Feb. 2, 2016 28:3, https://enveurope.springeropen.com/articles/10.1186/s12302-016-0070-0

[188] Dr. Christine Jones, *SOS: Save Our Soils*, interviewed by Tracy Frisch, ACRES, March, 2013 http://www.amazingcarbon.com/PDF/Jones_ACRES_USA%20(March2015).pdf

[189] Vandana Shiva, as spoken in the documentary film *Symphony of the Soil*, directed, written and produced by Deborah Koons Garcia, Lily Films, 2012, https://www.amazon.com/dp/B00KZ2FIXC/_encoding=UTF8?coliid=IM7GTBPUT0P7A&colid=2481PBY7CN9C9

[190] Vandana Shiva. *Who Really Feeds The World?*. Berkeley, California: North Atlantic Books, 2016. pgs. 22-23

[191] R.L. (Bob) Nielsen, *Historical Corn Grain Yields for the U.S.*, Agronomy Dept., Purdue University, Corny News Network, May 2017 https://www.agry.purdue.edu/ext/corn/news/timeless/yieldtrends.html

[192] Danny Hakim, *Doubts About the Promised Bounty of Genetically Modified Crops*, The New York Times, Oct. 29, 2016 https://www.nytimes.com/2016/10/30/business/gmo-promise-falls-short.html

[193] The National Academies of Sciences, Engineering, and Medicine, *Distinction Between Genetic Engineering and Conventional Plant Breeding Becoming Less Clear, Says New Report on GE Crops*, Committee on Genetically Engineered Crops: Past Experience and Future Prospects, May 17, 2016 http://www8.nationalacademies.org/onpinews/newsitem.aspx?RecordID=23395

[194] Doug Gurian-Sherman, *Failure to Yield: Evaluating the Performance of Genetically Engineered Crops (2009)*, Union of Concerned Scientists, 2009, https://www.ucsusa.org/food_and_agriculture/our-failing-food-system/genetic-engineering/failure-to-yield.html

[195] David R. Montgomery. *Growing A Revolution*. New York, New York: W. W. Norton & Company, 2017. pg. 143

[196] Kristin Ohlson. *The Soil Will Save Us*. New York, New York: Rodale, 2014. pgs. 173-174

[197] *Who Owns Nature? Corporate Power and the Final Frontier in the Commodification of Life*, ETC Group, Nov. 12, 2008, http://etcgroup.org/content/who-owns-nature

[198] Vandana Shiva. *Who Really Feeds The World?*. Berkeley, California: North Atlantic Books, 2016. pg. 42

[199] ADB Institute, *Usefulness of and Threats to Plant Genetic Resources*, State of the World's Plant Genetic Resources for Food and Agriculture report, Jun. 5, 2014.

[200] Gabe Brown. *Dirt to Soil*. White River Junction, Vermont: Chelsea Green Publishing, 2018 pg. 175

[201] Charles Siebert, *Food Ark*, National Geographic Magazine, Jul 2011, https://www.nationalgeographic.com/magazine/2011/07/food-ark/

[202] Leonid Bershidsky, *Why the EU Approved Bayer-Monsanto*, Bloomberg, Mar. 22, 2018, https://www.bloomberg.com/opinion/articles/2018-03-23/bayer-monsanto-analysis-eu-approval-is-about-competition

[203] Isabel Marlens, *The Farms of the Future*, Local Futures, Jun. 4, 2019, https://www.localfutures.org/the-farms-of-the-future/

[204] Vandana Shiva. *Who Really Feeds The World?*. Berkeley, California: North Atlantic Books, 2016. pgs. 67-83

[205] Robert Goodland, Jeff Anhang, *Livestock and Climate Change - What if the Key Actors in Climate Change are... Cows, Pigs and Chickens?* World Watch, Nov./Dec. 2009 http://www.worldwatch.org/files/pdf/Livestock%20and%20Climate%20Change.pdf

[206] Ecofys, *World GHG Emissions Flow Chart 2010*, Ecofys.com, https://ingmarschumacher.files.wordpress.com/2013/05/asn.ecofys-2013-world-ghg-emissions-flow-chart-2010.pdf

[207] Steven Pinker, *Enlightenment Now*, New York, New York: Viking, 2018. pg. 140

[208] GRAIN, IATP, Heinrich Boll Foundation, *Big Meat and Dairy's Supersized Climate Footprint*, GRAIN.org, Nov. 7, 2017, https://www.grain.org/article/entries/5825-big-meat-and-dairy-s-supersized-climate-footprint

[209] GRAIN.org https://www.grain.org/en/pages/organisation

[210] GRAIN, ITAP, *Emissions Impossible: How Big Meat and Dairy are Heating Up the Planet*, GRAIN.org, Jul. 18, 2018, https://www.grain.org/article/entries/5976-emissions-impossible-how-big-meat-and-dairy-are-heating-up-the-planet

[211] Ben Lilliston, *New Research Shows the Industrial Livestock Industry is Creating a Climate Crisis*, Institute for Agriculture and Trade Policy, Common Dreams, Nov. 7, 2017 https://www.commondreams. org/newswire/2017/11/07/new-research-shows-industrial-livestock-industry-creating-climate-crisis

[212] Robert Goodland, Jeff Anhang, *Livestock and Climate Change - What if the Key Actors in Climate Change are... Cows, Pigs and Chickens?* World Watch, Nov./Dec. 2009 http://www.worldwatch.org/files/pdf/Livestock%20and%20Climate%20Change.pdf

[213] GRAIN, Henk Hobbelink, *The Great Climate Robbery*. Oxford, UK: New Internationalist Publications, 2016. Pgs. 1-7

[214] GRAIN, *Commentary IV: Food, Climate Change and Healthy Soils: The Forgotten Link*, Trade and Environment Review, 2013, https://www.grain.org/media/ W1siZiIsIjIwMTUvMTEvMDUvMDhfNDZfMDZfNTIyX0dSQUlOX1VOQ1RBRF8yMDEzLnBkZiJdXQ

[215] *Wake Up Now Before It Is Too Late: Make Agriculture Truly Sustainable Now For Food Security In A Changing Climate*, Trade and Environment Review 2013, United Nations Conference on Trade and Development, http://unctad.org/en/pages/PublicationWebflyer.aspx?publicationid=666

[216] World Wildlife Fund, *Living Planet Report 2016*, Pg. 95, http://awsassets.panda.org/downloads/ lpr_living_planet_report_2016.pdf

[217] World Wildlife Fund, *Appetite For Destruction Summary Report*, Oct. 2017, https://www.wwf.org. uk/sites/default/files/2017-10/WWF_AppetiteForDestruction_Summary_Report_SignOff.pdf

[218] Rebecca Smithers, *Vast Animal-Feed Crops to Satisfy Our Meat Needs are Destroying Planet*, The Guardian, Oct. 5, 2017, https://www.theguardian.com/environment/2017/oct/05/vast-animal-feed-crops-meat-needs-destroying-planet

[219] Worldwatch Institute, *Peak Meat Production Strains Land and Water Resources*, Aug. 26, 2014, http://www.worldwatch.org/peak-meat-production-strains-land-and-water-resources-1

[220] Vandana Shiva. *Who Really Feeds The World?*. Berkeley, California: North Atlantic Books, 2016. pg. 8

[221] Kristin Ohlson. *The Soil Will Save Us*. New York, New York: Rodale, 2014. pg. 15

[222] *Wake Up Now Before It Is Too Late: Make Agriculture Truly Sustainable Now For Food Security In A Changing Climate*, Trade and Environment Review 2013, United Nations Conference on Trade and Development, http://unctad.org/en/pages/PublicationWebflyer.aspx?publicationid=666

[223] Kristin Ohlson. *The Soil Will Save Us*. New York, New York: Rodale, 2014. pg. 19

[224] John R. Teasdale, Charles B. Coffman, CB, Ruth, W. Mangum, *Potential Long-Term Benefits of No-Tillage and Organic Cropping Systems for Grain Production and Soil Improvement*, Agronomy Journal, American Society of Argronomy, Sept./Oct. 99: 5 1304 https://pubag.nal.usda.gov/download/13149/ PDF

[225] David R. Montgomery. *Growing A Revolution*. New York, New York: W. W. Norton & Company, 2017. pg. 12

[226] Other trade groups include the National Dairy Council, National Livestock and Meat Board, National Pork Producer's Council, United Egg Producers, American Meat Institute.

[227] David R. Montgomery. *Growing A Revolution*. New York, New York: W. W. Norton & Company, 2017. pg. 33

[228] The Universal Ecological Fund (Fundacion Ecologica Universal FEU-US), *The Economic Case for Climate Action in the United States*, 2018, https://feu-us.org/case-for-climate-action-us3/

[229] Sir Robert Watson, Dr. James J. McCarthy, Liliana Hisas, *The Economic Case for Climate Action in the United States, Universal Ecological Fund*, Sep. 2017, https://feu-us.org/case-for-climate-action-us/

[230] Stephen Leahy, *Hidden Costs of Climate Change Running Hundreds of Billions a Year*, National Geographic, Sep. 27, 2017 https://news.nationalgeographic.com/2017/09/climate-change-costs-us-economy-billions-report/

[231] Dr. Frederick Kirschenmann, *It Starts with the Soil and Organic Agriculture Can Help*, Soil and Culture, Springer Press. 2008. Presented at the 16th International Federation of Agriculture Movements (IFOAM) Organic World congress, Jun., 2008 in Modena, Italy

[232] Paul Hawken, *Drawdown*, New York, New York: Penguin Books, 2017 pg.201

[233] Dr. Frederick Kirschenmann, *It Starts with the Soil and Organic Agriculture Can Help*, Soil and Culture, Springer Press. 2008. Presented at the 16th International Federation of Agriculture Movements (IFOAM) Organic World congress, Jun. 2008 in Modena, Italy

[234] U.S. Global Change Research Program, USGCRP, 2018: *Impacts, Risks, and Adaptation in the United States: Fourth National Climate Assessment, Volume II* [Reidmiller, D.R., C.W. Avery, D.R. Easterling, K.E. Kunkel, K.L.M. Lewis, T.K. Maycock, and B.C. Stewart (eds.)]. U.S. Global Change Research Program, Washington, DC, USA, 1515 pp. doi: 10.7930/NCA4.2018 pg. 29 https://nca2018.globalchange.gov/downloads/NCA4_2018_FullReport.pdf

[235] Sir Albert Howard, *An Agricultural Testament*, New York, New York: Oxford University Press, 1943 pg. 4

[236] Char Miller, *One of the Largest Aquifers in the World is Disappearing Because of Farmers*, The Conversation, Inverse.com, Aug. 17, 2018 https://www.inverse.com/article/48142-ogallala-aquifer-conservation-measures-us-drought-farm-irrigation

[237] Dr. Frederick Kirschenmann, *It Starts with the Soil and Organic Agriculture Can Help*, Soil and Culture, Springer Press. 2008. Presented at the 16th International Federation of Agriculture Movements (IFOAM) Organic World congress, Jun. 2008 in Modena, Italy

[238] Judy Soule and Jon Piper, *Farming in Nature's Image: An Ecological Approach to Agriculture*, Island Press, Washington, D.C., 1992

[239] Dr. Frederick Kirschenmann, *It Starts with the Soil and Organic Agriculture Can Help*, Soil and Culture, Springer Press. 2008. Presented at the 16th International Federation of Agriculture Movements (IFOAM) Organic World congress, Jun. 2008 in Modena, Italy

[240] Bruce Finley, *The Water Under Colorado's Eastern Plains is Running Dry as Farmers Keep Irrigating "Great American Desert"*, The Denver Post, Oct. 8, 2017 https://www.denverpost.com/2017/10/08/colorado-eastern-plains-groundwater-running-dry/

[241] Lara Bryant, *Organic Matter Can Improve Your Soil's Water Holding Capacity*, Natural Resources Defense Council, May 27, 2015, https://www.nrdc.org/experts/lara-bryant/organic-matter-can-improve-your-soils-water-holding-capacity

[242] Dr. Frederick Kirschenmann, *It Starts with the Soil and Organic Agriculture Can Help*, Soil and Culture, Springer Press. 2008. Presented at the 16th International Federation of Agriculture Movements (IFOAM) Organic World congress, Jun. 2008 in Modena, Italy

[243] Wendell Berry. *The Art of Loading Brush*, Berkeley, California: Counterpoint, 2017 pg. 20

[244] Wendell Berry. *Renewing Husbandry*, Orion Magazine, June, 2018, https://orionmagazine.org/article/renewing-husbandry/

[245] Gabe Brown cautions that, "Just because it's organic does not mean it's nutrient dense because many organic producers have degraded the soil too."

[246] John Asafu-Adjaye, Linus Blomqvist, Stewart Brand, et al. *An Ecomodernist Manifesto*, Apr., 2015, pgs. 21-22, http://www.ecomodernism.org/

[247] Dr. Paul Hepperly, Research Director 2002-9 Rodale Institute, Kutztown, PA as stated in the feature documentary film *Symphony of the Soil*, directed, written and produced by Deborah Koons Garcia, Lily Films, 2012 https://www.amazon.com/dp/B00KZ2FIXC/_encoding=UTF8?coliid=IM7GTBPUT0P7A&colid=2481PBY7CN9C9

[248] Kristin Ohlson. *The Soil Will Save Us*. New York, New York: Rodale, 2014. pg. 17

[249] Kristin Ohlson. *The Soil Will Save Us*. New York, New York: Rodale, 2014. pg. 207

[250]

David C. Johnson, Ph.D., is a molecular biologist at New Mexico State University unraveling the "secrets of soil microbes." He and his wife, Hui-Chun, are pictured with the Composting Bioreactor they developed in their research. It pumps out a uniquely biodiverse and fungal-dominant compost product that, when used in their experimental plots by inoculating with just a few hundred pounds per acre and using regenerative management to support that life, demonstrated restored soil fertility with extraordinary plant biomass growth and regenerated soil microbial diversity. The regeneration of soil microbial communities and their functionality in agroecosystems can improve farm productivity, soil fertility, and system water-use efficiency. Learn how to build these low-cost minimal-labor bioreactors on your farm, ranch, or at your home.

[251] Rattan Lal, Pete Smith, Hermann F. Jungkunst, et al. *The Carbon Sequestration Potential of Terrestrial Ecosystems*, Soil and Water Conservation Society - Journal of Soil and Water Conservation, Nov/Dec 2018 - Vol. 73, No. 6, 73(6): 145A-152A www.swcs.org   http://www.css.cornell.edu/faculty/lehmann/publ/JSoilWaterConservation%2073,%20145A-152A,%202018%20Lal.pdf

[252] This final David C. Johnson quote: Center For Food Safety, *David C. Johnson, Ph.D*, on Rapid Carbon Sequestration, Interview on Vimeo, Nov. 2017, https://vimeo.com/237134837

[253] Kristin Ohlson. *The Soil Will Save Us*. New York, New York: Rodale, 2014. pgs. 108, 232 and 233

[254] Al Gore. *An Inconvenient Sequel - Truth to Power*. New York, New York: Rodale, 2017. pg. 269

[255] Dr. Christine Jones, *Five Principles for Soil Restoration*, 2017, pg. 4, https://www.ecofarmingdaily.com/build-soil/soil-restoration-5-core-principles/

[256] Walter Jehne, *Regenerate Earth*, Healthy Soils Australia, Global Cooling Earth, 2017, http://www.globalcoolingearth.org/wp-content/uploads/2017/09/Regenerate-Earth-Paper-Walter-Jehne.pdf

[257] Vandana Shiva. *Who Really Feeds The World?*. Berkeley, California: North Atlantic Books, 2016. pg. 65

[258] Dr. Christine Jones, *Five Principles for Soil Restoration*, 2017, pg. 3, https://www.ecofarmingdaily.com/build-soil/soil-restoration-5-core-principles/

[259] Dr. Christine Jones, *Five Principles for Soil Restoration*, 2017, pg. 10, https://www.ecofarmingdaily.com/build-soil/soil-restoration-5-core-principles/

[260] Michael Brownlee, *Towards A Local Food Revolution*, Local Food Shift Colorado, Fall, 2015, pg. 49

[261] USDA Agricultural Marketing Service, *Number of U.S. Farmers Markets has Nearly Tripled Over Last 15 Years* https://www.ers.usda.gov/data-products/chart-gallery/chart-detail/?chartId=78388

[262] Al Gore. *An Inconvenient Sequel - Truth to Power*. New York, New York: Rodale, 2017. pg. 269

[263] Joseph Mercola, D.O., *Regenerative Agriculture - The Next Big Thing*, Mercola.com, Mar. 27, 2018, https://articles.mercola.com/sites/articles/archive/2018/03/27/regenerative-agriculture-the-next-big-thing.aspx

[264] Kristin Ohlson. *The Soil Will Save Us*. New York, New York: Rodale, 2014. pg. 19

[265] Kristin Ohlson. *The Soil Will Save Us*. New York, New York: Rodale, 2014. pg. 126

[266] Peter Rosset, *Small Is Bountiful*, The Ecologist, vol. 29 issue 8, Dec. 1999. http://naturefirstusa.org/Special%20Reports/family%20farms/Small%20Is%20Bountiful.htm

[267] Dr. Tim LaSalle, CEO from 2007-2010 of the Rodale Institute in Kutztown, PA as stated in the feature documentary film *Symphony of the Soil*, directed, written and produced by Deborah Koons Garcia, Lily Films, 2012 https://www.amazon.com/dp/B00KZ2FIXC/_encoding=UTF8?coliid=IM7GTBPUT0P7A&colid=2481PBY7CN9C9

[268] Dr. Elaine Ingham, President and Director of Research at Soil Foodweb Inc. as stated in the feature documentary film *Symphony of the Soil*, directed, written and produced by Deborah Koons Garcia, Lily Films, 2012 https://www.amazon.com/dp/B00KZ2FIXC/_encoding=UTF8?coliid=IM7GTBPUT0P7A&colid=2481PBY7CN9C9

[269] David R. Montgomery. *Growing A Revolution*. New York, New York: W. W. Norton & Company, 2017. pg. 50

[270] *Joel Salatin on Creating Young Farmers Video*, Center For Food Safety, 2017 "Joel Salatin of Polyface Farms explains his vision for the farm of the future: one that is mobile, modular, and management intensive. This changes the economic profile of the farm, providing an opportunity for young farmers to get in and old folks to get out so that we can have a transition between generations." https://vimeo.com/164349616

[271] Dr. Frederick Kirschenmann, *Rethinking Soil, Economics and Health*, Leopold Letter, Leopold Center

for Sustainable Agriculture, Winter, 2015

272 Vandana Shiva. *Who Really Feeds The World?*. Berkeley, California: North Atlantic Books, 2016. pg. xi

273 *Hungry for Land: Small Farmers Feed the World with Less Than a Quarter of All Farmland, Grain*, May 28, 2014 https://www.grain.org/article/entries/4929-hungry-for-land-small-farmers-feed-the-world-with-less-than-a-quarter-of-all-farmland

274 GRAIN, *Telling Family Farming Fairy Tales*, GRAIN, Nov. 7, 2014, https://www.grain.org/article/entries/5072-telling-family-farming-fairy-tales

275 Helena Norberg-Hodge, *Unlike a Globalized Food System, Local Food Won't Destroy the Environment*, Truthout, Dec. 1, 2018, https://truthout.org/articles/unlike-a-globalized-food-system-local-food-wont-destroy-the-environment/

276 Vandana Shiva. *Who Really Feeds The World?*. Berkeley, California: North Atlantic Books, 2016. pgs. xix & 60

277 Vandana Shiva. *Who Really Feeds The World?*. Berkeley, California: North Atlantic Books, 2016. pgs. 88 & 131

278 Holistic Management International, *Our Role in the Food Ecosystem*, 2019, https://holisticmanagement.org/the-regenerative-solution/role-food-ecosystem/

279 J. Poore, T Nemecek, *Reducing Food's Environmental Impacts Through Producers and Consumers*, Science, Jun. 1, 2018, Vol. 360, Issue 6392, pp. 987–992 DOI: 10.1126/science.aaq0216 https://science.sciencemag.org/content/360/6392/987 and https://josephpoore.com/Science%20360%206392%20987%20-%20Accepted%20Manuscript.pdf

280 Dr. Richard A. Oppenlander, *Comfortably Unaware*, New York, New York: Beaufort Books, 2012 pg. 18

281 Helen Harwatt, Joan Sabaté, Gidon Eshel, et al. *Substituting Beans for Beef as a Contribution Toward US Climate Change Targets*, Climatic Change, (2017) 143: 261. https://doi.org/10.1007/s10584-017-1969-1

282 Florence Williams, *The Nature Fix*, as reviewed in The Nature Conservancy, Winter, 2017 https://www.amazon.com/Nature-Fix-Happier-Healthier-Creative/dp/0393242714/ref=sr_1_1?ie=UTF8&qid=1515806025&sr=8-1&keywords=the+nature+fix

283 Dr. Qing Li, *Forest Bathing: How Trees Can Help You Find Health and Happiness*, Amazon Link: https://www.amazon.com/Forest-Bathing-Trees-Health-Happiness-ebook/dp/B077CQKQRR/

284 Dr. Qing Li, *"Forest Bathing" Is Great for Your Health. Here's How to Do It*, Time Magazine, May 1, 2018, http://time.com/5259602/japanese-forest-bathing/

285 Karin Evans, *Why Forest Bathing is Good for Your Health*, Greater Good Magazine, Aug. 20, 2018, https://greatergood.berkeley.edu/article/item/why_forest_bathing_is_good_for_your_health?

286 John Asafu-Adjaye, Linus Blomqvist, Stewart Brand, et al. *An Ecomodernist Manifesto*, Apr., 2015, pg. 25, http://www.ecomodernism.org/

287 Scott Russell Sanders, *Conscience and Resistance*, Orion Magazine, Spring 2018, https://orionmagazine.org/article/conscience-and-resistance/

288 Reprinted from *World As Lover, World As Self* (1991, 2007) by Joanna Macy with permission of Parallax Press, Berkeley, California, www.parallax.org pg. 27

289 Vandana Shiva. *Who Really Feeds The World?*. Berkeley, California: North Atlantic Books, 2016. pg. 138

Chapter 4

1 Wendell Berry, *The Art of Loading Brush*, Berkeley, California: Counterpoint, 2017 pgs. 78–79

2 Vandana Shiva, *Who Really Feeds the World?* Berkeley, California: North Atlantic Books, 2016. pgs. 57–58

3 Wendell Berry, *Renewing Husbandry*, Orion Magazine, June, 2018, https://orionmagazine.org/article/renewing-husbandry/

4 Reprinted from *World As Lover, World As Self* (1991, 2007) by Joanna Macy with permission of Parallax Press, Berkeley, California, www.parallax.org pg. 50

5 Wendell Berry, *Renewing Husbandry*, Orion Magazine, June 2018, https://orionmagazine.org/article/renewing-husbandry/

6 USDA - NASS, Census of Agriculture - Farm Demographics, ACH12-3 May 2014, https://www.

agcensus.usda.gov/Publications/2012/Online_Resources/Highlights/Farm_Demographics/#fewer_new

[7] Leanna Garfield, *Kimbal Musk – Elon's Brother – Predicts a Movement of Millennial Workers Fleeing Desk Jobs for Farms*, Business Insider, Jan. 22, 2018, https://www.businessinsider.nl/food-trend-young-people-leaving-desk-jobs-become-farmers-kimbal-musk-2018-1/?international=true&r=US

[8] Brian Frederick, "*The Time is Now for Our Country to Help Young Farmers,* Food Tank – Farmers, Nov. 2017, https://foodtank.com/news/2017/11/2017-national-young-farmer-survey/

[9] Caitlin Dewey, *A Growing Number of Young Americans are Leaving Desk Jobs to Farm*, The Washington Post, Nov. 23, 2017, https://www.washingtonpost.com/business/economy/a-growing-number-of-young-americans-are-leaving-desk-jobs-to-farm/2017/11/23/e3c018ae-c64e-11e7-afe9-4f60b5a6c4a0_story.html?utm_term=.0f01c62d1c18

[10] Vilicus Farms Apprenticeship Program https://www.vilicusfarms.com/apprenticeship.php

[11] Will Harris quoted from the 15-minute video, *One Hundred Thousand Beating Hearts*, Peter Byck, Producer, Director, Jun. 2016 https://vimeo.com/170413226

[12] Will Harris quoted from the 15-minute video, *One Hundred Thousand Beating Hearts*, Peter Byck, Producer, Director, Jun. 2016 https://vimeo.com/170413226

[13] Robert Wolf, *Building the Agricultural City*, Decorah, Iowa: Ruskin Press, 2016

[14] Natural Grocers website, https://www.naturalgrocers.com/products/our-product-standards/dairy-standard/

[15] Joe Fassler, *Only 1 Percent of US Farmland is Certified Organic*, New food Economy, Mar. 2, 2017 https://geneticliteracyproject.org/2017/03/02/1-percent-us-farmland-certified-organic-arent-american-farmers-making-switch/

[16] James E. Sherow, *The Grasslands of the United States: An Environmental History* 2007, 139

[17] Wendell Berry, *The Art of Loading Brush*, Berkeley, California: Counterpoint, 2017 pgs. 77-8

[18] Wendell Berry, *The Art of Loading Brush*, Berkeley, California: Counterpoint, 2017 pg. 72

[19] Vandana Shiva, *Who Really Feeds The World?*. Berkeley, California: North Atlantic Books, 2016. pg. 60

[20] Feeding America, *Millions of Rural Children Struggle With Hunger*, FeedingAmerica.org, https://www.feedingamerica.org/hunger-in-america/rural-hunger-facts

[21] Janet Adamy and Paul Overberg, *Rural America is the New 'Inner City'*, The Wall Street Journal, May 26, 2017, https://www.wsj.com/articles/rural-america-is-the-new-inner-city-1495817008

[22] John Ikerd, *The Economic Colonization of Rural America*, Daily Yonder, Feb. 28, 2018, https://www.dailyyonder.com/economic-colonization-rural-america/2018/02/28/24068/

[23] National Sustainable Agriculture Coalition Blog, *2018 Farm Bill by the Numbers*, Dec. 21, 2018, http://sustainableagriculture.net/blog/2018-farm-bill-by-the-numbers/

[24] Environmental Working Group, *Farm Subsidy Primer*, Environmental Working Group, 2018, https://farm.ewg.org/subsidyprimer.php

[25] Kristin Ohlson, *The Soil Will Save Us*, New York, New York: Rodale, 2014, pg. 177

[26] John Ikerd, *The Economic Colonization of Rural America*, Daily Yonder, Feb. 28, 2018, https://www.dailyyonder.com/economic-colonization-rural-america/2018/02/28/24068/

[27] Kristin Ohlson, *The Soil Will Save Us*, New York, New York: Rodale, 2014, pg. 178

[28] Kristin Ohlson, *The Soil Will Save Us*, New York, New York: Rodale, 2014, pg. 180

[29] John Ikerd, *The Economic Colonization of Rural America*, Daily Yonder, Feb. 28, 2018, https://www.dailyyonder.com/economic-colonization-rural-america/2018/02/28/24068/

[30] Isabel Marlens, *The Farms of the Future*, Local Futures, Jun. 4, 2019, https://www.localfutures.org/the-farms-of-the-future/

[31] Wendell Berry, *The Art of Loading Brush*, Berkeley, California: Counterpoint, 2017 pgs. 6, 83-4, 103

[32] Michael Brownlee, *Towards A Local Food Revolution*, originally published in Local Food Shift Colorado, Fall 2015, pg. 52

[33] Preston Lauterbach, *Memphis Burning*, Places Journal, Mar. 2016, https://placesjournal.org/article/memphis-burning/

[34] Preston Lauterbach, *Memphis Burning*, Places Journal, Mar. 2016, https://placesjournal.org/article/memphis-burning/

[35] John Thackara, *How to Thrive in the Next Economy*, New York, New York: Thames & Hudson, 2015 pg. 31

[36] Michael Brownlee, *Towards A Local Food Revolution*, originally published in Local Food Shift Colorado, Fall 2015, pg. 54

[37] John Thackara, *How to Thrive in the Next Economy*, New York, New York: Thames & Hudson, 2015 pg. 146

[38] Robert Wolf, *Building the Agricultural City*, Decorah, Iowa: Ruskin Press, 2016 pg. 59

[39] Agrarian Trust website: https://agrariantrust.org/

[40] Jim Hightower, *Big-Money Speculators are Buying up and Renting Out Farms, and Pricing Real Farmers Out of the Market*, AlterNet, Feb. 22, 2017 https://www.alternet.org/2017/02/big-money-speculators-are-buying-and-renting-out-farms-and-pricing-real-farmers-out-market/

[41] The Oakland Institute, *Down On the Farm - Wall Street: America's New Farmer*, OaklandInstitute. org, 2014, Publisher: The Oakland Institute (OI) is an independent policy think tank bringing fresh ideas and bold action to the most pressing social, economic, and environmental issues. https://www.oaklandinstitute.org/sites/oaklandinstitute.org/files/OI_Report_Down_on_the_Farm.pdf

[42] Tom Perkins, *For a New Generation of Farmers, Accessing Land is the First Step Toward Tackling Consolidation*, Civil Eats, Nov. 20, 2018, https://civileats.com/2018/11/20/for-a-new-generation-of-farmers-accessing-land-is-the-first-step-toward-trackling-consolidation/

[43] The Oakland Institute, *Down On the Farm - Wall Street: America's New Farmer*, OaklandInstitute. org, 2014, Publisher: The Oakland Institute (OI) is an independent policy think tank bringing fresh ideas and bold action to the most pressing social, economic, and environmental issues. https://www.oaklandinstitute.org/sites/oaklandinstitute.org/files/OI_Report_Down_on_the_Farm.pdf

[44] Lela Nargi, *Can an Investment Firm Help Increase U.S. Organic Farmland?*, Civil Eats, Sep.18, 2018, https://civileats.com/2018/09/18/can-an-investment-firm-help-increase-u-s-organic-farmland/

[45] Robert Wolf, *Building the Agricultural City*, Decorah, Iowa: Ruskin Press, 2016 pg. 74

[46] Robert Wolf, *Building the Agricultural City*, Decorah, Iowa: Ruskin Press, 2016 pg. 75

[47] David Dayen, *What if Banks Were Publicly Owned? In L.A., this may Soon be a Reality*, Huffington Post, Aug. 10, 2018 https://www.huffingtonpost.com/entry/public-bank-los-angeles_us_5b6bef33e4b0ae32af954495

[48] David Dayen, *What if Banks Were Publicly Owned? In L.A., this may Soon be a Reality*, Huffington Post, Aug. 10, 2018 https://www.huffingtonpost.com/entry/public-bank-los-angeles_us_5b6bef33e4b0ae32af954495

[49] Ellen Brown, *The Public Banking Revolution Is Upon Us*, Truthdig, Apr. 17, 2019, https://www.truthdig.com/articles/the-public-banking-revolution-is-upon-us/

[50] Reprinted from *World As Lover, World As Self* (1991, 2007) by Joanna Macy with permission of Parallax Press, Berkeley, California, www.parallax.org pg. 100

[51] Reprinted from *World As Lover, World As Self* (1991, 2007) by Joanna Macy with permission of Parallax Press, Berkeley, California, www.parallax.org pg. 76

Chapter 5

[1] Ashley Strickland, *Earth to Warm 2 Degrees Celsius by the End of this Century, Studies Say*, CNN Jul. 31, 2017 http://www.cnn.com/2017/07/31/health/climate-change-two-degrees-studies/index.html

[2] Alister Doyle, *Exclusive: Global Warming Set to Exceed 1.5°, Slow Growth - U.N. Draft*, Reuters, Jun. 14, 2018, https://www.reuters.com/article/us-climatechange-report-exclusive/exclusive-global-warming-set-to-exceed-15c-slow-growth-un-draft-idUSKBN1JA1HD

[3] Brian Donegan, *2019 Mississippi River Flood the Longest-Lasting Since the Great Flood of 1927*, The Weather Channel, May 13, 2019, https://weather.com/news/weather/news/2019-05-14-one-of-longest-lived-mississippi-river-floods-since-great-flood-1927?cm_ven=wu_videos?cm_ven=hp-slot-1

[4] Matt McGrath, *Nature Crisis: Humans 'Threaten 1m Species with Extinction,'* BBC News, May 6, 2019, https://www.bbc.com/news/science-environment-48169783?fbclid=IwAR0phQ37H8CcCstLIEPuGuxA0i2xmC3AV112S5eg5LImq_kerQ-FWlvhzHo

[5] CAT Briefing - Warming Projections Global Update, *Some Progress Since Paris, but not Enough as Governments Amble Towards 3° of Warming*, Climate Action Tracker, Dec. 11, 2018, https://climateactiontracker.org/publications/warming-projections-global-update-dec-2018/

[6] Naomi Klein, *No Is Not Enough*, Chicago, Illinois: Haymarket Books, 2017, pg. 268

[7] Emma Lazarus, *The New Colossus* Poem, mounted on a plaque at the base of the Statue of Liberty, https://www.poetryfoundation.org/poems/46550/the-new-colossus

[8] National Sustainable Agriculture Coalition Blog, *Understanding the Billions Behind the CBO Farm Bill Baseline*, Apr. 11, 2018 http://sustainableagriculture.net/blog/cbo-baseline-breakdown-2018/

[9] A variation on: Dan Imhoff, *Despite Small Wins, the New Farm Bill is a Failure of Imagination*, Civil Eats, Dec. 13, 2018, https://civileats.com/2018/12/13/despite-small-wins-the-new-farm-bill-is-a-failure-of-imagination/

[10] John Ikerd, *Farm Policy at a Crossroads; A Time to Choose*, 2016, http://web.missouri.edu/ikerdj/papers/TexasFRFAFarmPolicyBastrop.pdf

[11] Jason Fung, M.D. *The Obesity Code*, British Columbia, Vancouver: Greystone Books, 2016 pg. 140

[12] Mark Hyman, M.D. *Food – What the Heck Should I Eat?*, New York, New York: Little, Brown and Company, 2018

[13] Bradley Sawyer, Cynthia Cox. *How Does Health Spending in the U.S. Compare to Other Countries?* Kaiser Family Foundation, Feb. 13, 2018, Analysis from data from OECD (2017), *OECD Health Data: Health Expenditure and Financing: Health Expenditure Indicators*, OECD Health Statistics (database). DOI: 10.1787/health-data-en https://www.healthsystemtracker.org/chart-collection/health-spending-u-s-compare-countries/?_sf_s=health+spending#item-start

[14] Bayer - Monsanto, *Crop Map: Who Grows What in the U.S.*, Monsanto.com https://monsanto.com/innovations/modern-agriculture/articles/crop-map/

[15] Gabe Brown. *Dirt to Soil*. White River Junction, Vermont: Chelsea Green Publishing, 2018 pg. 179

[16] Union of Concerned Scientists, *Poll Showcases Farmers' Strong Support for Sustainable Agriculture*, Catalyst, Sum. 2018, pg.5 https://www.ucsusa.org

[17] Robbie Feinberg, *Special Interests Heavily Involved in Farm Bill Maneuvering*, OpenSecrets News, Center for Responsive Politics, Jan. 30, 2014 https://www.opensecrets.org/news/2014/01/special-interests-heavily-involved/

[18] Kari Hamerschlag, Anna Lappé, Stacy Malkan, *Spinning Food - How Food Industry Front Groups and Covert Communications are Shaping the Story of Food*, Friends of the Earth. Aug. 2015, https://1bps6437gg8c169i0y1drtgz-wpengine.netdna-ssl.com/wp-content/uploads/2017/legacy/FOE_SpinningFoodReport_8-15.pdf

[19] Paul Hawken, *Drawdown*, New York, New York: Penguin Books, 2017 pg.201

[20] Charlotta Lomas, *2˚ C: 'We Have a 5 Percent Chance of Success'*, DW Akademie, Nov. 16, 2017, https://p.dw.com/p/2njXd , https://www.dw.com/en/2c-we-have-a-5-percent-chance-of-success/a-41405809

[21] Naomi Klein, *No Is Not Enough*, Chicago, Illinois: Haymarket Books, 2017, pg. 71.

[22] Steven Pinker, *Enlightenment Now*, New York, New York: Viking, 2018. Pg. 128

[23] *Crop Year Government Cost of Federal Crop Insurance Program*, RMA, USDA. 2017, https://www.rma.usda.gov/-/media/RMAweb/AboutRMA/Program-Budget/18cygovcost.ashx?la=en

[24] Walter Jehne, *Regenerate Earth*, Healthy Soils Australia, Global Cooling Earth, 2017, http://www.globalcoolingearth.org/wp-content/uploads/2017/09/Regenerate-Earth-Paper-Walter-Jehne.pdf

[25] Reprinted from *World As Lover, World As Self* (1991, 2007) by Joanna Macy with permission of Parallax Press, Berkeley, California, www.parallax.org pg. 96

[26] The Universal Ecological Fund (Fundacion Ecologica Universal FEU-US), *The Economic Case for Climate Action in the United States*, 2018, https://feu-us.org/case-for-climate-action-us3/

[27] United Nations Conference on Trade and Development, *Wake Up Now Before It Is Too Late: Make Agriculture Truly Sustainable Now For Food Security In A Changing Climate*, Trade and Environment Review 2013, https://unctad.org/en/PublicationsLibrary/ditcted2012d3_en.pdf

[28] Leiserowitz, A., Maibach, E., Rosenthal, S., Kotcher, J., Ballew, M., Goldberg, M., & Gustafson, A. (2018). Climate change in the American mind: December 2018. Yale University http://climatecommunication.yale.edu/wp-content/uploads/2019/01/Climate-Change-American-Mind-December-2018.pdf

[29] Frances Moore Lappé and Adam Eichen, *Daring Democracy*, Boston, Massachusetts: Beacon Press, 2017, pg. 76

30 Joe Romm, *Fossil Fuel Industry Spent Nearly $2 Billion to Kill U.S. Climate Action, New Study Finds*, Think Progress, Jul. 19, 2018, https://thinkprogress.org/fossil-fuel-industry-outspends-environment-groups-on-climate-new-study-231325b4a7e6/

31 Nyelini Forum on Food Sovereignty, *Declaration of Nyéléni*, Feb. 27, 2007, https://nyeleni.org/spip.php?article290

32 John Ikerd, *Farm Policy at a Crossroads; A Time to Choose*, 2016, http://web.missouri.edu/ikerdj/papers/TexasFRFAFarmPolicyBastrop.pdf

33 Press Release, Congressman Earl Blumenauer 3rd District of Oregon, *Blumenauer Convenes Fiscal hawks, Food and Agriculture Policy Experts, Environmentalists, Animal Welfare Advocates, Others to Call for Farm Bill Reform, Nov. 16, 2017*, https://blumenauer.house.gov/media-center/press-releases/blumenauer-convenes-fiscal-hawks-food-and-agriculture-policy-experts

34 Congressman Earl Blumenauer, *The Food and Farm Act Highlights*, 2017, https://blumenauer.house.gov/sites/blumenauer.house.gov/files/2017-11-15%20Food%20and%20Farm%20Act%20Highlights.pdf

35 Congressman Earl Blumenauer, *Blumenauer Convenes Fiscal Hawks, Food and Agriculture Policy Experts, Environmentalists, Animal Welfare Advocates, Others to Call for Farm Bill Reform, Press Release, Nov. 16, 2017* https://blumenauer.house.gov/media-center/press-releases/blumenauer-convenes-fiscal-hawks-food-and-agriculture-policy-experts

36 Congressman Earl Blumenauer, *The Food and Farm Act Highlights*, 2017, https://blumenauer.house.gov/sites/blumenauer.house.gov/files/2017-11-15%20Food%20and%20Farm%20Act%20Highlights.pdf

37 Leah Douglas, *A Radical Farm Bill is Born*, Civil Eats, Nov. 16, 2017 https://civileats.com/2017/11/16/a-radical-farm-bill-is-born/

38 Abi Kay, *Livestock Numbers Must be Cut to Meet Climate Targets, Dutch Government Told*, Farmers Guardian, Sep. 3, 2018, https://www.fginsight.com/news/news/livestock-numbers-must-be-cut-to-meet-climate-targets-dutch-government-told-69033

39 Jessica A. Knoblauch, *Farming For the Future*, Earthjustice Magazine, Fall, 2017, https://earthjustice.org/blog/2017-october/farming-for-the-future

40 Congressman Earl Blumenauer, *Congressman Blumenauer Statement on Latest Farm Bill Agreement*, Press Release, Dec. 11, 2018, https://blumenauer.house.gov/media-center/press-releases/congressman-blumenauer-statement-latest-farm-bill-agreement

41 Robbie Feinberg, *Special Interests Heavily Involved in Farm Bill Maneuvering*, Center For Responsive Politics, Jan. 30, 2014 https://www.opensecrets.org/news/2014/01/special-interests-heavily-involved/

42 Wesley Lowery, *91% of the Time the Better-financed Candidate Wins. Don't Act Surprised.*, The Washington Post, Apr. 4, 2014 https://www.washingtonpost.com/news/the-fix/wp/2014/04/04/think-money-doesnt-matter-in-elections-this-chart-says-youre-wrong/?utm_term=.ded3c04b9b24

43 Center For Responsive Politics, *Agribusiness: Money to Congress*, OpenSecrets.org, Nov. 13, 2018, https://www.opensecrets.org/industries/summary.php?ind=A&recipdetail=A&sortorder=U&mem=Y&cycle=2018

44 David R. Montgomery, *Growing A Revolution.* New York, New York: W. W. Norton & Company, 2017. pg. 18

45 Robert Wolf, *Building the Agricultural City*, Decorah, Iowa: Ruskin Press, 2016 pg. 5

46 Brooks Adams, *The Law of Civilization and Decay*, published: 1896, and referenced by Robert Wolf, Building the Agricultural City, Decorah, Iowa: Ruskin Press, 2016 pg. 23

47 Al Gore. *An Inconvenient Sequel - Truth to Power.* New York, New York: Rodale, 2017. pg. 178

48 Reprinted from *World As Lover, World As Self* (1991, 2007) by Joanna Macy with permission of Parallax Press, Berkeley, California, www.parallax.org pgs. 141-2

49 Al Gore. *An Inconvenient Sequel - Truth to Power.* New York, New York: Rodale, 2017. pg. 180

50 World Wildlife Fund, *Living Planet Report 2016*, https://c402277.ssl.cf1.rackcdn.com/publications/964/files/original/lpr_living_planet_report_2016.pdf?1477582118&_ga=1.148678772.2122160181.1464121326

51 Trevor Noah, *The Thing About Millennials*, Time Magazine, Jan. 15, 2018

52 *Tell Our Leaders: Take the No Fossil Fuel Money Pledge*, http://nofossilfuelmoney.org/

53 Tara Golshan, *Young People, Women, Voters in Cities: How Democrats Won in 2018*, by the Numbers, Vox, Apr. 26, 2019, https://www.vox.com/2019/4/26/18516645/2018-midterms-voter-turnout-census

[54] Zack Beauchamp, *The Shocking UK Election Results, Explained*, Vox, Jun. 9, 2017, https://www.vox.com/world/2017/6/9/15767522/uk-election-results-hung-parliament

[55] Imogen Calderwood, *Young Voters Across Europe Led to a 'Green Wave' to Fight for Climate Action*, Global Citizen, May 28, 2019, https://www.globalcitizen.org/en/content/european-elections-green-surge-young-vote-activist/?utm_source=Iterable&utm_medium=email&utm_campaign=US_May_30_2019_content_digest

[56] Imogen Calderwood, *Young Voters Across Europe Led to a 'Green Wave' to Fight for Climate Action*, Global Citizen, May 28, 2019, https://www.globalcitizen.org/en/content/european-elections-green-surge-young-vote-activist/?utm_source=Iterable&utm_medium=email&utm_campaign=US_May_30_2019_content_digest

[57] Paul Hawken, *Drawdown*, New York, New York: Penguin Books, 2017 pg.216

[58] Greg Carlock, Emily Mangan, *A Green New Deal*, Policy Report by Data For Progress, Sep. 2018, https://static1.squarespace.com/static/5aa9be92f8370a24714de593/t/5ba14811032be48b8772d37e/1537296413290/GreenNewDeal_Final_v2_12MB.pdf

[59] Greg Carlock, Emily Mangan, *A Green New Deal*, Policy Report by Data For Progress, Sep. 2018, https://static1.squarespace.com/static/5aa9be92f8370a24714de593/t/5ba14811032be48b8772d37e/1537296413290/GreenNewDeal_Final_v2_12MB.pdf

[60] Monica Medina, Miro Korenha, *The Green New Deal's Sudden Popularity is a Reason for Climate Change Optimism*, Huffington Post, Jan. 11, 2019, https://www.huffingtonpost.com/entry/opinion-2020-democrats-climate-change_us_5c378db0e4b0c469d76c3538

[61] Sunrise Movement https://www.sunrisemovement.org/

[62] Stephen O'Hanlon, *1000+ Youth Sit-in, 143 Arrested Demanding Dem Leadership Back Green New Deal*, Sunrise Movement Press Release, Dec. 10, 2018, https://www.commondreams.org/newswire/2018/12/10/1000-youth-sit-143-arrested-demanding-dem-leadership-back-green-new-deal

[63] Rebecca Leber, *At Bernie Sanders' Big Climate Town Hall, Alexandria Ocasio-Cortez Steal the Show*, Mother jones, Dec. 4, 2018, https://www.motherjones.com/environment/2018/12/sanders-ocasio-cortez-climate-town-hall-2020/

[64] Sunrise Movement https://www.sunrisemovement.org/gnd

[65] Naomi Klein, *The Game-Changing Promise of a Green New Deal*, The Intercept, Nov. 27, 2018, https://theintercept.com/2018/11/27/green-new-deal-congress-climate-change/

[66] Tom Philpott, *Why the Green New Deal is so Vague About Food and Farming*, Mother Jones, Feb. 13, 2019, https://www.motherjones.com/food/2019/02/why-the-green-new-deal-is-so-vague-about-food-and-farming/

[67] Pew Research Center, *Economic Issues Decline Among Public's Policy Priorities*, People Press, Jan. 25, 2018, http://www.people-press.org/2018/01/25/economic-issues-decline-among-publics-policy-priorities/012518_8/

[68] Anthony Leiserowitz, Edward Maibach, Seth Rosenthal, et al. *Politics & Global Waring, December 2018*, Yale Program on Climate Cgange Communication, Feb. 5, 2019, http://climatecommunication.yale.edu/publications/politics-global-warming-december-2018/2/

[69] Jessica Corbett, *'As World Teeters on Brink of Climate Catastrophe,' 600+ Groups Demand Congress Back Visionary Green New Deal, Common Dreams*, Jan. 10, 2019, https://www.commondreams.org/news/2019/01/10/world-teeters-brink-climate-catastrophe-600-groups-demand-congress-back-visionary?

[70] Biological Diversity, Letter to Congressional Representatives: *Legislation to Address the Urgent Threat of Climate Change*, Jan. 10, 2019, https://www.biologicaldiversity.org/programs/climate_law_institute/legislating_for_a_new_climate/pdfs/Letter-to-Congress-%20Legislation-to-Address-the-Urgent-Threat-of-Climate-Change.pdf

[71] Friends of the Earth, Letter to Congressional Representatives: *To Address the Climate Crisis, the Green New Deal Must Transform Our Food System and Revitalize Rural America*, Apr. 10, 2019, http://foe.org/wp-content/uploads/2019/04/Green-New-Deal-Food-and-Agriculture-sign-on-letter_Final.pdf

[72] Kate Aronoff, *Spanish Socialists Running for Re-election Sunday on a "Green New Deal de España"*, The Intercept, Apr. 27, 2019, https://theintercept.com/2019/04/27/spain-elections-green-new-deal/

73 Olivia Rosane, *Winning Party in Spain's Election Campaigned on a Green New Deal*, Ecowatch, Apr. 29, 2019, https://www.ecowatch.com/spain-green-new-deal-2635822115.html

74 Erica Chenoweth and Jeremy Pressman, *This is What we Learned by Counting the Women's Marches*, The Washington Post, Feb. 7, 2017, https://www.washingtonpost.com/news/monkey-cage/wp/2017/02/07/this-is-what-we-learned-by-counting-the-womens-marches/?utm_term=.f374b9b9a051

75 Frances Moore Lappé and Adam Eichen, *Daring Democracy*, Boston, Massachusetts: Beacon Press, 2017, pgs. 142-145

76 Frances Moore Lappé and Adam Eichen, *Daring Democracy*, Boston, Massachusetts: Beacon Press, 2017, pg. 146

77 Andrea Germanos, *'This Is Our Darkest Hour': With Declaration of Rebellion, New Group Vows Mass Civil Disobedience to Save Planet*, Common Dreams, Oct. 31, 2018 https://www.commondreams.org/news/2018/10/31/our-darkest-hour-declaration-rebellion-new-group-vows-mass-civil-disobedience-save

78 Sonali Kolhatkar, *Thank These Climate Activists for Resisting Our Extinction*, Truthdig, Apr. 25, 2019, https://www.truthdig.com/articles/thank-these-climate-activists-for-resisting-our-extinction/

79 Labour Party Leader Jeremy Corbyn, *Jeremy Corbyn Declares Environment and Climate Emergency*, Labour.org, May 1, 2019, https://labour.org.uk/press/jeremy-corbyn-declares-environment-climate-emergency/

80 Labour, *Labour's Successful Climate Emergency Motion Can Set Off Wave of Action Around Globe*, Labour.org, May 1, 2019, https://labour.org.uk/press/labours-successful-climate-emergency-motion-can-set-off-wave-action-around-globe/

81 Michelle Devane, *Ireland Declares Climate Emergency: 'Things Will Deteriorate Rapidly Unless We Move Very Swiftly'*, Independent, May 10, 2019, https://www.independent.ie/irish-news/politics/ireland-declares-climate-emergency-things-will-deteriorate-rapidly-unless-we-move-very-swiftly-38098129.html

82 James Hitchings-Hales, *Britain Becomes First Major Country to Commit to Legally Binding Zero Emissions Target*, Global Citizen, Jun. 12, 2019, https://www.globalcitizen.org/en/content/britain-net-zero-emissions-target-theresa-may/

83 Jessica Corbett, *Teen Climate Activist to Crowd of Thousands: 'We Can't Save the World by Playing by the Rules Because the Rules have to Change'*, Common Dreams, Oct. 20, 2018, https://www.commondreams.org/news/2018/10/20/teen-climate-activist-crowd-thousands-we-cant-save-world-playing-rules-because-rules

84 Clare Roth, *Swedish Student Leader Wins EU Pledge to Spend Billions on Climate*, Reuters, Feb. 21, 2019, https://www.reuters.com/article/us-climatechange-teen-activist-idUSKCN1QA1RF

85 #ClimateStrike, *Climate Crisis and a Betrayed Generation*, The Guardian, Mar. 1, 2019, https://www.theguardian.com/environment/2019/mar/01/youth-climate-change-strikers-open-letter-to-world-leaders

86 Louise Hazan, *Massive School Strikes Worldwide*, The 350.org Team, Mar. 16, 2019, https://350.org/page/3/

87 Julia Conley, *As Millions March to Demand Climate Action, Research Reveals Protests Make People More Optimistic About Effecting Change*, Common Dreams, May 24, 2019, https://www.commondreams.org/news/2019/05/24/millions-march-demand-climate-action-research-reveals-protests-make-people-more?

88 Chris Mooney, Brady Dennis, *The World has Just Over a Decade to Get Climate Change Under Control, U.N. Scientists Say*, The Washington Post, Oct. 7, 2018 https://www.washingtonpost.com/energy-environment/2018/10/08/world-has-only-years-get-climate-change-under-control-un-scientists-say/?utm_term=.060d42497759

89 Al Gore. *An Inconvenient Sequel - Truth to Power*. New York, New York: Rodale, 2017. pg. 308

90 Paul Hawken, *Drawdown*, New York, New York: Penguin Books, 2017 Pg. 55

91 Paul Hawken, *Drawdown*, New York, New York: Penguin Books, 2017 Pg. 41

92 Paul Hawken, *Drawdown*, New York, New York: Penguin Books, 2017 Pg. 55

93 GRAIN, Henk Hobbelink, *The Great Climate Robbery*, Oxford, UK: New Internationalist Publications,

2016. Pgs. 8-12

[94] John Thackara, *How to Thrive in the Next Economy*, New York, New York: Thames & Hudson, 2015 pg. 82

[95] Peter Lehner, *Earthjustice Magazine*, Sum, 2016.

[96] Rattan Lal, *Societal Value of Soil Carbon*, Journal of Soil and Water Conservation, vol. 69 no. 6 186A-192A doi: 10.2489/jswc.69.6.186A Nov./Dec. 2014 http://www.jswconline.org/content/69/6/186A.full.pdf+html

[97] Paul Hawken, *Drawdown*, New York, New York: Penguin Books, 2017 pg.54

[98] Vaclav Smil, *Eating Meat: Constants and Changes*, Global Food Security, Jun. 19, 2014, https://doi.org/10.1016/j.gfs.2014.06.001

[99] Paul Hawken, *Drawdown*, New York, New York: Penguin Books, 2017 pg.40

[100] Environmental Defense Fund, *Who's Putting a Price on Carbon?*. Solutions, Vol. 50. No.1 / Winter 2019, pg. 4 https://www.edf.org/sites/default/files/documents/Solutions-Winter-2019.pdf

[101] Walter Jehne, *Regenerate Earth*, Healthy Soils Australia, Global Cooling Earth, 2017, http://www.globalcoolingearth.org/wp-content/uploads/2017/09/Regenerate-Earth-Paper-Walter-Jehne.pdf

[102] Elliott Negin, *The California Green Rush: How UCS Helped Point the Way*, Union of Concerned Scientists, Fall 2018, https://www.ucsusa.org/sites/default/files/attach/2018/11/Catalyst-Fall-2018.pdf

[103] Dana Ford and Lorenzo Ferrigno, *Vermont Governor Signs GMO Food Labeling Into Law*, CNN, May 8, 2014 https://www.cnn.com/2014/05/08/health/vermont-gmo-labeling/index.html

[104] Kathleen Masterson, *Congress Passes a GMO Labeling Law that Nullifies Vermont's Law*, Vermont Public Radio, Jul. 15, 2016, http://digital.vpr.net/post/congress-passes-gmo-labeling-bill-nullifies-vermonts-law#stream/0

[105] Wikipedia, *Swift & Co. v. United States*, https://en.wikipedia.org/wiki/Swift_%26_Co._v._United_States

[106] Emilene Ostlind, *The Big Four Meatpackers*, High Country News, Mar. 21, 2011, https://www.hcn.org/issues/43.5/cattlemen-struggle-against-giant-meatpackers-and-economic-squeezes/the-big-four-meatpackers-1

[107] World Wildlife Fund, *Living Planet Report 2016*, https://c402277.ssl.cf1.rackcdn.com/publications/964/files/original/lpr_living_planet_report_2016.pdf?1477582118&_ga=1.148678772.2122160181.1464121326

[108] Wayne Pacelle. *The Humane Economy*. New York, New York: HarperCollins, 2016, pg. xv

[109] Shelton Group, *Brands & Stands - Social Purpose is the New Black*, Shelton Communications Group, Inc., 2018, https://storage.googleapis.com/shelton-group/Pulse%20Reports/Brands%20%26%20Stands%20-%20Final%20Report%202018.pdf

[110] World Wildlife Fund, *Living Planet Report 2016*, Pg. 102 https://c402277.ssl.cf1.rackcdn.com/publications/964/files/original/lpr_living_planet_report_2016.pdf?1477582118&_ga=1.148678772.2122160181.1464121326

[111] The New Climate Economy 2018 Report, *Unlocking the Inclusive Growth Story of the 21st Century*, Global Commission on the Economy and Climate, 2018, https://newclimateeconomy.report/2018/key-findings/

[112] Wayne Pacelle. *The Humane Economy*. New York, New York: HarperCollins, 2016, pgs. xi & xii

[113] E2.org *Clean Jobs America*, 2018, https://www.e2.org/cleanjobsamerica/

[114] Frances Moore Lappé, *The green New Deal is Not a Choice*, Common Dreams, Mar. 12, 2019, https://www.commondreams.org/views/2019/03/12/green-new-deal-not-choice

[115] The New Climate Economy 2018 Report, *Unlocking the Inclusive Growth Story of the 21st Century*, Global Commission on the Economy and Climate, 2018, https://newclimateeconomy.report/2018/key-findings/

[116] Alister Doyle and Nina Chestney, *Greener Growth Could Add $26 Trillion to World Economy by 2030: Study*, Reuters, Sep. 4, 2018, https://www.reuters.com/article/us-climatechange-economy/greener-growth-could-add-26-trillion-to-world-economy-by-2030-study-idUSKCN1LL09J

[117] Naomi Klein, *No Is Not Enough*, Chicago, Illinois: Haymarket Books, 2017, pgs. 247 & 270

[118] Stephanie Kelton, Andres Bernal, Greg Carlock, *We Can Pay for a Green New Deal*, Huffington Post, Nov. 30, 2008 https://www.huffingtonpost.com/entry/opinion-green-new-deal-cost_

us_5c0042b2e4b027f1097bda5b

[119] Stephanie Kelton, Andres Bernal, Greg Carlock, *We Can Pay for a Green New Deal*, Huffington Post, Nov. 30, 2008 https://www.huffingtonpost.com/entry/opinion-green-new-deal-cost_us_5c0042b2e4b027f1097bda5b

[120] David Roberts, *Alexandria Ocasio-Cortez is Already Pressuring Nancy Pelosi on Climate Change*, Vox, Nov. 15, 2018, https://www.vox.com/energy-and-environment/2018/11/14/18094452/alexandria-ocasio-cortez-nancy-pelosi-protest-climate-change-2020

[121] Ellen Brown, *This Radical Plan to Fund the Green New Deal Just Might Work*, Yes Magazine, Dec. 26, 2018, https://www.yesmagazine.org/new-economy/this-radical-plan-to-fund-the-green-new-deal-just-might-work-20181226

[122] Ellen Brown, *This Radical Plan to Fund the Green New Deal Just Might Work*, EllenBrown.com, Dec. 17, 2018, https://ellenbrown.com/2018/12/17/this-radical-plan-to-fund-the-green-new-deal-just-might-work/

[123] Frances Moore Lappé, *"I'm a Capitalist," Says Warren... But Why?*, Common Dreams, Apr. 26, 2019, https://www.commondreams.org/views/2019/04/26/im-capitalist-says-warrenbut-why?

[124] Naomi Klein, *No Is Not Enough*, Chicago, Illinois: Haymarket Books, 2017, pg. 239

[125] Naomi Klein, *No Is Not Enough*, Chicago, Illinois: Haymarket Books, 2017, pgs. 79-80

[126] Career Builder Survey, *Living Paycheck to Paycheck is a Way of Life for Majority of U.S. Workers, According to CareerBuilder Survey*, Career Builder, Aug. 24, 2017, http://press.careerbuilder.com/2017-08-24-Living-Paycheck-to-Paycheck-is-a-Way-of-Life-for-Majority-of-U-S-Workers-According-to-New-CareerBuilder-Survey

[127] Kari Paul, *America's 1% Hasn't Controlled This Much Wealth Since Before the Great Depression*, Market Watch, Aug.5, 2018, https://www.marketwatch.com/story/wealth-inequality-in-the-us-is-almost-as-bad-as-it-was-right-before-the-great-depression-2018-07-19

[128] Frances Moore Lappé and Adam Eichen, *Daring Democracy*, Boston, Massachusetts: Beacon Press, 2017, pg. 17

[129] Frances Moore Lappé and Adam Eichen, *Daring Democracy*, Boston, Massachusetts: Beacon Press, 2017, pg. 52

[130] Chris D'Angelo, *Pro-Trump Billionaires Continue to Bankroll Climate Denial*, Huff Post, Feb. 28, 2019, https://www.huffpost.com/entry/mercers-trump-climate-denial_n_5c76b643e4b0031d9564572e

[131] Naomi Klein, *No Is Not Enough*, Chicago, Illinois: Haymarket Books, 2017, pgs. 81-82

[132] Naomi Klein, *No Is Not Enough*, Chicago, Illinois: Haymarket Books, 2017, pg. 233-5

[133] Frances Moore Lappé and Adam Eichen, *Daring Democracy*, Boston, Massachusetts: Beacon Press, 2017, pg. 23

[134] Frances Moore Lappé and Adam Eichen, *Daring Democracy*, Boston, Massachusetts: Beacon Press, 2017, pg. 163

[135] Robert Wolf, *Building the Agricultural City*, Decorah, Iowa: Ruskin Press, 2016 pg. 23

[136] Naomi Klein, *No Is Not Enough*, Chicago, Illinois: Haymarket Books, 2017, pg. 217

[137] Naomi Klein, *No Is Not Enough*, Chicago, Illinois: Haymarket Books, 2017, pg. 241

Conclusion

[1] Reprinted from *World As Lover, World As Self* (1991, 2007) by Joanna Macy with permission of Parallax Press, Berkeley, California, www.parallax.org pg. 191

[2] Reynard Loki, *How Can You Talk to Kids About Factory Farming? These Books Can Help.*, Truthout, Oct. 28, 2018, https://truthout.org/articles/how-can-you-talk-to-kids-about-factory-farming-these-books-can-help/

[3] Reynard Loki, *How Can You Talk to Kids About Factory Farming? These Books Can Help.*, Truthout, Oct. 28, 2018, https://truthout.org/articles/how-can-you-talk-to-kids-about-factory-farming-these-books-can-help/

[4] Hayley Miller, Chris D'Angelo, *Climate Change Comes Home to Roost in North Carolina*, Huffington Post, Sep. 22, 2018 https://www.huffingtonpost.com/entry/hurricane-florence-climate-change_

us_5ba53abae4b069d5f9d2a909

[5] James Bruggers, *In Florence's Floodwater: Sewage, Coal Ash and Hog Waste Lagoon Spills*, Inside Climate News, Sep. 18, 2018, https://insideclimatenews.org/news/18092018/hurricane-florence-flood-sewage-hazardous-coal-ash-hog-waste-lagoons

[6] Julie Cappiello, *Farmers Leave 3.4 Million Chickens, 5,500 Pigs to Drown or Starve During Hurricane Florence*, Mercy For Animals, Sep 19, 2018, https://mercyforanimals.org/farmers-leave-34-million-chickens-5500-pigs

[7] Joseph Mercola, D.O., *Polluting Pigs Part IV*, Mercola.com, Jul. 17, 2018, https://articles.mercola.com/sites/articles/archive/2018/07/17/factory-farming-air-pollution-lawsuits.aspx

[8] Krissy Kasserman, *Nobody Should Have Hog Poop on the Walls of Their Home*, Food and Water Watch, Apr. 18, 2018, https://www.foodandwaterwatch.org/news/nobody-should-have-hog-poop-walls-their-home

[9] Gray Jernigan, Waterkeeper Alliance Staff Attorney, *North Carolina's Waterkeepers Are Using the Civil Rights Act to Clean Up Minority Communities*. Waterkeeper Magazine Vol. 31 Issue 2, pg. 35

[10] Joan Halifax, Principled Compassion, Center For EcoLiteracy, May 10, 2012, https://www.ecoliteracy.org/article/principled-compassion

[11] Melissa Healy, *Extreme Obesity Cuts Average Life Span Extremely*, Los Angeles Times, Jul. 8, 2014, https://www.latimes.com/science/la-sci-sn-extreme-obesity-cuts-lifespan-20140708-story.html

[12] Environmental Action, *Working to Save Monarch Butterflies*, Environmental Action Blog, Jun 12, 2018, https://environmental-action.org/blog/working-to-save-monarch-butterflies/

[13] Kate Linthicum, *To Save the Monarch Butterfly*, Mexican Scientists are Moving a Forest 1,000 Feet up a Mountain, Los Angeles Times, Apr. 9, 2019, https://www.latimes.com/world/mexico-americas/la-fg-col1-mexico-monarch-butterfly-20190409-htmlstory.html

[14] Reprinted from *World As Lover, World As Self* (1991, 2007) by Joanna Macy with permission of Parallax Press, Berkeley, California, www.parallax.org pg. 18

[15] Chris Mooney, *The Arctic Ocean has Lost 95 Percent of its Oldest Ice — a Startling Sign of What's to Come*, The Washington Post, Dec. 11, 2018, https://www.washingtonpost.com/energy-environment/2018/12/11/arctic-is-even-worse-shape-than-you-realize/?utm_term=.5371fb18061e

[16] Energy and Climate Staff, *Preliminary US Emissions Estimates for 2018*, Rhodium Group, Jan. 8, 2019, https://rhg.com/research/preliminary-us-emissions-estimates-for-2018/

[17] U.S. Global Change Research Program, USGCRP, 2017: *Climate Science Special Report: Fourth National Climate Assessment, Volume I* [Wuebbles, D.J., D.W. Fahey, K.A. Hibbard, D.J. Dokken, B.C. Stewart, and T.K. Maycock (eds.)]. U.S. Global Change Research Program, Washington, DC, USA, 470 pp., doi: 10.7930/J0J964J6. https://science2017.globalchange.gov/downloads/CSSR2017_FullReport.pdf

[18] U.S. Global Change Research Program, USGCRP, 2018: *Impacts, Risks, and Adaptation in the United States: Fourth National Climate Assessment, Volume II* [Reidmiller, D.R., C.W. Avery, D.R. Easterling, K.E. Kunkel, K.L.M. Lewis, T.K. Maycock, and B.C. Stewart (eds.)]. U.S. Global Change Research Program, Washington, DC, USA, 1515 pp. doi: 10.7930/NCA4.2018 pg. 100 https://nca2018.globalchange.gov/downloads/NCA4_2018_FullReport.pdf

[19] UN Environment, GEO6, GRID Arendal, *Global Linkages: A Graphic Look at the Changing Arctic*, Mar. 14, 2019, https://wedocs.unep.org/bitstream/handle/20.500.11822/27687/Arctic_Graphics.pdf?sequence=1&isAllowed=y

[20] Damian Carrington, *Climate-heating Greenhouse Gases at Record Levels*, Says UN, The Guardian, Nov. 22, 2018, https://www.theguardian.com/environment/2018/nov/22/climate-heating-greenhouse-gases-at-record-levels-says-un

[21] Naomi Klein, *No Is Not Enough*, Chicago, Illinois: Haymarket Books, 2017, pgs. 225

[22] Steven Pinker, Enlightenment Now, New York, New York: Viking, 2018. Pg. 11

[23] WC Lowdermilk, *Conquest of the Land Through 7,000 Years*, U.S. Department of Agriculture, Soil Conservation Service, Agriculture Information Bulletin 99, GPO, Washington D.C., 1953, https://www.ncat.org/wp-content/uploads/2015/08/Lowdermilk-Conquest-of-the-Land.pdf

[24] Dr. Frederick Kirschenmann, *It Starts with the Soil and Organic Agriculture Can Help*, Soil and Culture, Springer Press. 2008. Presented at the 16th International Federation of Agriculture Movements (IFOAM) Organic World congress, Jun. 2008 in Modena, Italy

[25] Peter Donovan, *A Field Guide to the Most Powerful and Creative Planetary Force*, Soil Carbon Coalition. Oct. 2017, https://soilcarboncoalition.org/files/guide.pdf

[26] Al Gore. *An Inconvenient Sequel - Truth to Power*. New York, New York: Rodale, 2017. pg. 309

[27] Al Gore. *An Inconvenient Sequel - Truth to Power*. New York, New York: Rodale, 2017. pg. 310

[28] Joanna Macy, *The Great Turning*, Center For EcoLiteracy, Jun. 29, 2009, https://www.ecoliteracy.org/article/great-turning

[29] Joanna Macy, *The Great Turning*, Center For EcoLiteracy, Jun. 29, 2009, https://www.ecoliteracy.org/article/great-turning

[30] John Thackara, *How to Thrive in the Next Economy*, New York, New York: Thames & Hudson, 2015 pg. 9

[31] Edgar Morin, *Homeland Earth: A Manifesto for the New Millenium - Advances in Systems Theory, Complexity and the Human Sciences*, New York, New York: Hampton Press, 1999

PHOTO CREDITS

Cover
Pexels - Pixabay

Introduction
p. X   Tratong/Shutterstock
p. XI   Simon Eeman/Shutterstock
p. XII   © Solvin Zankl
p. XIII   © Solvin Zankl
p. XX   © Paul Nicklen
p. XXI   Vostok ice core data/J.R. Petit et
            al.; NOAA Mauna Loa CO2 record
            climate.nasa.gov

Chapter 1
p. 6   Waterkeeper Alliance
p. 7   Jo-Anne McArthur/Essere
            Animali
p. 11   Jo-Anne McArthur/Essere
            Animali
p. 24   talseN/Shutterstock
p. 29   symbiot/Shutterstock
p. 31   © Mercy for Animals
p. 35   Dieter Hawlan/Shutterstock
p. 36   © Farm Sanctuary
p. 39   © Stephen Erickson
p. 39   © Stephen Erickson
p. 40   Jo-Anne McArthur/Animal
            Equality
p. 40   © Mercy for Animals
p. 41   Martin Harvey/Shutterstock
p. 42   © Stephen Erickson
p. 43   © Stephen Erickson
p. 44   franz12/Shutterstock
p. 45   Jo-Anne McArthur/We Animals
p. 46   hecke61/Shutterstock
p. 47   L214 - Éthique & Animaux/L214 -
            Ethics & Animals https://
            creativecommons.org/licenses/
            by/3.0/legalcode.fr
p. 50   Jo-Anne McArthur/
            Djurrattsalliansen
p. 50   Jo-Anne McArthur/
            Djurrattsalliansen

p. 51   Jo-Anne McArthur/
            Djurrattsalliansen
p. 52   Jo-Anne McArthur/
            Djurrattsalliansen
p. 54   Jo-Anne McArthur/
            Djurrattsalliansen

Chapter 3
p. 147   Dave/Adobe Stock
p. 148   withthesehands/
            Shutterstock
p. 149   Glass and Nature/Shutterstock
p. 153   © Kylee Baumle
p. 158   TanaCh/Shutterstock
p. 160   © Deborah Koons Garcia, Lily
            Films LLC
p. 163   © Jim Richardson
p. 167   Maryna Pleshkun/Shutterstock
p. 175   © Iowa State University Extension
p. 180   © Stephen Erickson
p. 185   Sandy Hedgepeth/Shutterstock
p. 205   rbrown10/Shutterstock
p. 229   © David C. Johnson, NMSU
            Institute for Sustainable
            Agricultural Research (ISAR)

Conclusion
p. 369   Simon Eeman/Shutterstock
p. 371   Jo-Anne McArthur/We Animals
p. 373   © Stephen Erickson
p. 379   Krumanop/Adobe Stock
p. 381   © Brady Kluge
p. 383   Ira_Kalinicheva/Adobe Stock
p. 386   © Marlon Foster
p. 388   Vostok ice core data/J.R. Petit et
            al.; NOAA Mauna Loa CO2 record
            climate.nasa.gov
p. 396   © Mercy for Animals

Notes
p. 414   Jo-Anne McArthur/Animal
            Equality
p. 441   © David C. Johnson